# MANAGING RISK IN REINSURANCE

# MANAGING RISK IN REINSURANCE

## *From City Fires to Global Warming*

*Edited by*
NIELS VIGGO HAUETER
*and*
GEOFFREY JONES

OXFORD
UNIVERSITY PRESS

OXFORD
UNIVERSITY PRESS

Great Clarendon Street, Oxford, OX2 6DP,
United Kingdom

Oxford University Press is a department of the University of Oxford.
It furthers the University's objective of excellence in research, scholarship,
and education by publishing worldwide. Oxford is a registered trade mark of
Oxford University Press in the UK and in certain other countries



First Edition published in 2017



Published in the United States of America by Oxford University Press
198 Madison Avenue, New York, NY 10016, United States of America

British Library Cataloguing in Publication Data
Data available

Library of Congress Control Number: 2016939409

ISBN 978–0–19–875491–6

# CONTENTS

# List of Figures

# List of Tables

# List of Contributors

**Hans Bühlmann** is Professor Emeritus of the Swiss Federal Institute of Technology (ETH) Zurich, where he taught mathematics for more than thirty years. He has held visiting appointments at UC Berkeley, University of Michigan, Université Libre de Bruxelles, University of Tokyo, University of Manitoba, Sapienza—Università di Roma, Scuola Normale Superiore di Pisa. His interest in actuarial sciences dates back to his first employment, when he worked in the insurance industry. His book *Mathematical Methods in Risk Theory* is a classic in the actuarial literature. Hans Bühlmann is Honorary Chairman of ASTIN, Honorary President of the Swiss Actuaries (SAV), and Honorary Member of DAV (German Actuaries). He served Swiss Re as a member of their board of directors for more than thirty years.

**Forrest Capie** is Professor Emeritus of Economic History at the Cass Business School, City University, London. He has taught at the London School of Economics, the University of Warwick, and the University of Leeds. He has been a British Academy Overseas Fellow at the National Bureau, New York, a Visiting Professor at the University of Aix-Marseille and at the London School of Economics, and a Visiting Scholar at the International Monetary Fund. He has written widely on money, banking, and trade and commercial policy. He was Head of Department of Banking and Finance at City University from 1989 to 1992 and Editor of the *Economic History Review* from 1993 to 1999. He recently completed the commissioned history of the Bank of England (2010). His latest book (with G. E. Wood) is *Money over Two Centuries* (2012).

**Geoffrey Clark** is Professor of History and Director of the National Endowment for the Humanities Faculty Development Program at the State University of New York at Potsdam. He is the author of *Betting on Lives: The Culture of Life Insurance in England, 1695–1775* (1999) and editor of *The Appeal of Insurance* (2010), among other articles and essays on the history of insurance in relation to warfare, slavery, religious thought, and urban life.

**Lorraine Daston** is Director at the Max Planck Institute for the History of Science, Berlin, and Visiting Professor in the Committee on Social Thought at the University of Chicago. Her recent publications include (co-edited with Elizabeth Lunbeck), *Histories of Scientific Observation* (2011), and (with Paul Erikson et al.) *How Reason Almost Lost Its Mind: The Strange Career of Cold War Rationality* (2014), as well as essays on the history of scientific facts, objectivity, curiosity, probability, attention, and the moral authority of nature, which have appeared in various journals and collections.

**Niels Viggo Haueter** is Head of Swiss Re's Corporate History unit and the company's historical archives. He is a Guest Lecturer at Hitotsubashi University in Tokyo and serves as Deputy Chairman of the Academic Council of the European Association for Banking and Financial History in Frankfurt. Together with Peter Borscheid, he edited *World Insurance: The Evolution of a Global Risk Network* (2012).

**Geoffrey Jones** is the Isidor Straus Professor of Business History at the Harvard Business School. He has written extensively on the history of global business, and its social and environmental impact. He holds MA and PhD degrees from Cambridge University in Britain, and has honorary PhDs from Copenhagen Business School, Denmark, and from the University of Helsinki, Finland. Professor Jones's books include *British Multinational Banking 1830–1990* (1993), *Merchants to Multinationals* (2000), *Multinationals and Global Capitalism: From the Nineteenth to Twenty First Century* (2005), *Renewing Unilever* (2005), and *Beauty Imagined* (2010). He is currently researching the history of sustainable entrepreneurship. Professor Jones is co-editor of the journal *Business History Review* and a Fellow of the Academic of International Business.

**Lawrence Kenny** is an independent writer on emerging risk and reinsurance issues. He was previously a Director of Communications at Swiss Re, responsible for publications, and a Senior Manager at the Management Consulting arm of Coopers & Lybrand, where he worked across the media, telecoms, and finance industries.

**Alexandros-Andreas Kyrtsis** is Professor of Sociology in the Department of Political Science and Public Administration at the National and Kapodistrian University of Athens. His main fields of research are the sociological and historical analysis of the techno-organizational backstage of financial markets and the dynamics of complex projects. He has also done research and published on the social history of ideas, and the social theory of urban and geographical space. He has been Academic Visitor at the Massachusetts Institute of Technology, the London School of Economics and Political Science, the University of Edinburgh, the Institute of Advanced Studies on Science, Technology and Society in Graz, and at the ETH Zurich. His publications in English include, in addition to several research articles, two edited volumes: *Financial Markets and Organizational Technologies: System Architectures, Practices and Risks in the Era of Deregulation* (2010) and the *Routledge Handbook of European Sociology* (co-edited with S. Koniordos, 2014).

**Roman Lechner** is Senior Economist and Deputy Head of Swiss Re's Economic Research & Consulting department. Since 1992, he has regularly authored and co-authored *sigma* studies covering a broad spectrum of non-life insurance topics, including reinsurance and the London market. His publications also include (with T. Holzheu) 'The Global Reinsurance Market', in *Handbook of International Insurance: Between Global Dynamics and Local Contingencies* (2007).

**Martin Lengwiler** is Professor for Modern History at the University of Basle (Department of History) and associated member of the Research Group 'Science Policy Studies' at the Social Science Research Center Berlin (Wissenschaftszentrum Berlin für Sozialforschung (WZB)). He works and publishes in the fields of history of knowledge, modern European history, welfare history, and historical methodology. He has been member of the interdisciplinary research group Historical and Interpretive Approaches to Standards, Quantification and Formal Representations at the Historical Research Institute, University of California, Irvine (in 2001) and Invited Professor at the École des Hautes Études en Sciences Sociales, Paris (in 2009).

**Robin Pearson** is Professor of Economic History at the University of Hull. He has published widely on British and international economic and business history, with a particular focus on the insurance industry. His article on moral hazard and insurance in eighteenth-century London won the 2002 Harvard-Newcomen Best Article Prize. His books include *Insuring the Industrial Revolution: Fire Insurance and the British Economy, 1700–1850*, which won the 2004 Wadsworth Prize for Business History; *The Development of International Insurance* (2010); and *Shareholder Democracies? Corporate Governance in Britain and Ireland before 1850* (2012), co-authored with Mark Freeman and James Taylor, which was awarded the 2013 Ralph Gomory Prize for Business History by the US Business History Conference. His latest book, co-edited with Takau Yoneyama, is *Corporate Forms and Organizational Choice in International Insurance* (2015).

**Tilmann J. Röder** is a Managing Director of the Max Planck Foundation for International Peace and the Rule of Law (Heidelberg). He holds two state exams in law and a doctor's degree from Frankfurt University (2005). He publishes in the areas of constitution building, legal pluralism, rule of law promotion in post-conflict societies, and legal history, and is co-editor of the *Max Planck Yearbook of United Nations Law*. His recent works include *Constitutionalism in Islamic Countries: Between Upheaval and Continuity* (co-edited with R. Grote; 2012), *From Industrial to Legal Standardisation, 1871–1914: Transnational Insurance Law and the Great San Francisco Earthquake* (2012), and *Non-state Justice Institutions and the Law: Decision-Making at the Interface of Tradition, Religion and the State* (co-edited with M. Kötter et al.; 2015).

**Miloš Vec** is Professor of European Legal and Constitutional History at Vienna University and a Permanent Fellow at the Institute for Human Sciences (IWM). He received his Habilitation in legal history, philosophy of law, theory of law, and civil law from Goethe University, Frankfurt am Main. Until 2012 he worked at the Max Planck Institute for European Legal History, and taught at the Universities of Bonn, Frankfurt, Hamburg, Konstanz, Lyon, Tübingen, and Vilnius. His awards include: Studienstiftung des Deutschen Volkes, 1989–91; Otto Hahn Medal of the Max Planck Society, 1997; appointment as Founding Member of the Young Academy at the Berlin-Brandenburg Academy of Sciences and Humanities and the German Academy of Natural Scientists

Leopoldina, 2000; Walter Kalkhof-Rose Memorial Award of the Academy of Sciences and Literature, Mainz, 2006; Academy Award of the Berlin-Brandenburg Academy of Sciences and Humanities, 2008; Fellow to the Wissenschaftskolleg, Berlin, 2011/12; Teaching Award 2015 of Vienna University. His main research interests are the history of international law and multi-normativity.

**Welf Werner** is Professor of International Economics at Jacobs University, Germany. He works in the fields of international trade and finance, economic policy, and economic history. He has published widely on international trade in services, trade policy on financial services, and the development of international insurance markets. In recent years Werner advised the Federal Ministry of Economics and Labor in Berlin and the Ministry of Industry and Trade in Amman, Jordan, on the General Agreement on Trade in Services (GATS) negotiations at the World Trade Organization (WTO). Before joining Jacobs University in 2004 he worked at the Freie Universität Berlin, the School of Advanced International Studies, Johns Hopkins University, and, as a John F. Kennedy Memorial Fellow, at Harvard University.

# CHAPTER 1

# RISK AND REINSURANCE

NIELS VIGGO HAUETER AND GEOFFREY JONES

## 1.1 Introduction

This book is about the historical evolution of reinsurance, and how it changed dealing with risk. Reinsurance is based on a simple idea. The broader you spread the risks, the cheaper they are to insure. So, rather than insuring risks directly, reinsurers help insurers spread their risks over time, across geographical locations, and through different lines of business. Placing their risks in a bigger pool of diversified risks gives insurers more financial security and thus more room to manoeuvre. Insurance protects against losses of goods, health, or lives. Reinsurance protects insurance companies against abnormal financial losses.

While the financial services offered by reinsurers are straightforward, the process behind managing the entire risk exposure of both clients and the reinsurance companies themselves is complex. The reinsurance industry deals with virtually all insurable risks and manages, by definition, global enterprises in different legal environments and risk landscapes, and often in volatile economies. The most unusual characteristic of the industry is that it appears largely disconnected from the world of global business, or, rather, how that world of business has been written by historians and others. For much of its history, reinsurance has been silent. But behind this apparent silence, the industry has had a major impact on global social, political, financial, scientific, and even natural history. This present book seeks to make this apparently silent world more vocal. It cannot be comprehensive, but it is intended as at least a starting point for new research agendas. The editors have sought to focus on key issues in the industry, including the business model of reinsurance and the development of markets, risk management techniques, financial issues, and legal as well as political aspects.

Each of the following chapters examines the evolution of these key issues over time. In Chapter 2, Geoffrey Clark examines the culture of insurance, describing the changes that came about with the advent of modern insurance, especially in Britain in the seventeenth and eighteenth centuries, and how modern insurance prepared the grounds for reinsurance. The chapter describes insurance and related forms of probabilistic reasoning and practice as a comparatively late stage in the quest for material security and psychological relief from the hazards of life. Robin Pearson in Chapter 3 provides a high-level historical overview of the reinsurance market and business development. In Chapter 4, Forrest Capie describes the changing monetary, financial, and macroeconomic conditions across the period within which Swiss Re operated. It discusses the principal macro variables that insurers need to consider.

In Chapter 5, Hans Bühlmann and Martin Lengwiler detail how, since the late nineteenth century, reinsurance played a special role in the history of actuarial science, in particular by acting as a platform for the formation and development of innovative actuarial knowledge. Alexandros-Andreas Kyrtsis, in Chapter 6, uses Swiss Re's vast collection of reinsurance contracts to describe the fundamentals of doing reinsurance and how the financial function of reinsurance eventually gave rise to new forms of doing business. In Chapter 7, Tilmann J. Röder looks at the gradual change from seeing reinsurance contracts broadly as 'gentlemen's agreements' to them being used as a legal instrument. He uses German sociologist Niklas Luhmann's theory on legal evolution to describe major historic events which shaped reinsurance contracts and also compares Western-style approaches to alternatives such as Islamic *takaful* law.

In Chapter 8, Miloš Vec looks at the regulatory environment of reinsurance. The law of the global reinsurance industry is a unique, normative order, formed, above all, by the relationships between reinsurers and the reinsured. Characteristic of this normative order in the twentieth century was the interest of parties engaged in international activities in, first, keeping contracts as free as possible from legal requirements and, second, keeping disputes resulting from breaches of contract out of the courts. In Chapter 9, Lorraine Daston studies the case of Swiss Re dealing with atomic reactors during the 1950s and 1960s, and demonstrates how a risk at first considered uninsurable was eventually made insurable and served as a model to tame other emerging risks. Welf Werner, in Chapter 10, looks at the growing attention that natural catastrophes (widely known in the reinsurance industry as natcats) attract in recent times. He compares the increase in scientific interest in the matter to the still modest financial and economic perspective given to the effects of natural catastrophes and the role of the insurance and reinsurance industry. Finally, Roman Lechner, Niels Viggo Haueter, and Lawrence Kenny in Chapter 11 provide a detailed look at the main market changes which came about during the 1990s, and how the reinsurance industry shaped its current image.

## 1.2 The Concept of Risk

The modern reinsurance industry emerged in the nineteenth century, but the phenomenon of risk did not. In the broadest sense, the planet Earth is a dangerous and ever-changing place, from which there currently remains no means of escape. There have been five mass extinction events in Earth's history. In the worst one, the Permian–Triassic mass extinction of 250 million years ago, it seems 95 per cent of species were killed off. We appear to be currently living in the sixth great extinction event, with vertebrate species disappearing in large numbers, probably because of human actions. The brief span of human history itself can be interpreted as the story of individuals buffeted by, overcoming, or succumbing to risks of many sorts. Natural catastrophes, climate changes, crop failures, revolutions, wars, business cycles, disease, and epidemics were constant disrupters of people's dreams to have normal lives.

It is sometimes argued that the scale of risk has grown with the technological complexities of modern societies, but this is almost certainly an illusion. The historian Geoffrey Parker has described the multiple crises in the seventeenth century throughout the world—revolutions, droughts, famines, and wars—and related to them to a dramatic cooling in the climate. One-third of the world's population may have died from the toxic mixture of natural and human catastrophes.[1] The climate eventually warmed up again, but the risks of living on the Earth did not go away. Natural and man-made catastrophes have remained staples of human history.

It is the understanding of risk which has evolved. Information about risks and their consequences has globalized and become instant over the last two centuries. The spread of railways and the invention of the electric telegraph in the middle of the nineteenth century began a process whereby the speed and cost of communicating information across distances fell sharply. News of the Great Lisbon Earthquake in 1755, one of the most catastrophic earthquakes in European history, spread around the world at the speed of the fastest horse or sailing ship. News of the San Francisco Earthquake of 1906 was spread instantly to cities connected by the electric telegraph, primarily at that time located in the West and its colonies. News of the Fukushima Daiichi nuclear disaster in 2011 reached much of the world's urban population soon after it happened.

Co-existing with this diffusion of information has been a long-term decline in tolerance of risk. As societies became richer, people had more to lose if things went wrong. During the nineteenth century, Western Europe and its settler offspring, including the USA, began to undergo spectacular increases in wealth as well as individual longevity in the wake of the Industrial Revolution. As Western societies got rich, they worried more about risks. This was the age when the reinsurance industry emerged.

As Geoffrey Clark writes in Chapter 2 of this book, the advent of modern insurance and, later, reinsurance, can be seen as a continuation of a long evolutionary process of societies sharing and mitigating risks. The underlying urge to protect against misfortune, Clark argues, has remained the same throughout human history. What has changed are the means to do so. Affluent developed societies today not only use insurance, but all manner of other means to externalize or mitigate even the smallest risks. There are even toasters equipped with algorithms that prevent daily slices of toast from getting burnt. This is an astonishing evolution from when people used prayers as a risk management tool to secure their daily bread. Mathematics and, with it, probabilistic thinking and statistical methods—important prerequisites for insurance and reinsurance—were, however, comparatively late additions to dealing with risk. During

[1] Geoffrey Parker (2013) *Global Crisis: War, Climate Change and Catastrophe in the Seventeenth Century*. New Haven, CT: Yale University Press.

the Age of Enlightenment, the world began to be measured and more and more things were expressed in quantitative and later monetary equivalents. This became the basis for ex ante calculations of losses in insurance and to a more positive risk understanding. Today, 'probabilistic practices' (as Clark terms them) have infiltrated modern societies and permeated virtually all aspects of life.

The Industrial Revolution significantly accelerated this process. Before the eighteenth century, most risks came from nature and could thus readily be interpreted as divine punishments. Interfering with such risks was seen as futile and, in several religions, sinful tampering with divine providence. For centuries, the market for indulgences and pilgrimages in Catholic Christianity outperformed insurance markets. So, rather than perceiving what is today seen as risk, most hazards were interpreted as fate, with all the connotations of impuissance. The Industrial Revolution not only brought new wealth but also a wide variety of new risks on hitherto unseen scales. As these were clearly man-made, they caused a gradual change in perceiving risks as being constructed by mankind and not exclusively God-given, thus allowing the abstract concept of insurance to spread.[2] Moral objections to calculating risk and mitigating it through insurance soon diminished, not least because the clergy adopted a view that statistical evidence ultimately served to prove divine power. Also, economic reason helped establish insurance as an almost moral duty by the later eighteenth century when Adam Smith argued in the *Wealth of Nations* that it was foolish not to protect oneself against risks.[3] The emergence of big business in the second half of the nineteenth century, and the professionalization of management, further increased this shift. Significantly, this period marked the coming of age of modern reinsurance, although it should be noted that imaginative interpretations of natural disasters can be found even today.[4]

Business helped interpret risk as something which included positive aspects. Business logic may always have had to rely on positive aspects of risk. Without risk, there was no business. Mitigating risk via insurance and the first instances of reinsurance-like transactions consequently developed in shipping and its thriving business communities. Early marine insurance may have been the first to distinguish man-made from natural and God-given risks.[5] In fact, it may be responsible not only

[2] Borscheid (2013, 31).

[3] 'Many sail, however, at all seasons, and even in time of war, without any insurance. This may sometimes, perhaps, be done without any imprudence. When a great company, or even a great merchant, has twenty or thirty ships at sea, they may, as it were, insure one another. The premium saved up on them all may more than compensate such losses as they are likely to meet with in the common course of chances. The neglect of insurance upon shipping, however, in the same manner as upon houses, is, in most cases, the effect of no such nice calculation, but of mere thoughtless rashness, and presumptuous contempt of the risk.' <https://en.wikisource.org/wiki/The_Wealth_of_Nations/Book_I/Chapter_10> (accessed 18 May 2016).

[4] Hurricane Katrina in 2005 was interpreted by some as God's punishment for allowing abortions in the USA, and by others as a response for tolerating gay parades in New Orleans. Steinberg (2006, xi).

[5] As in *ad risicum et fortunam Dei maris et gentium*, see H. Kahane and R. Kahane (1968) 'Risk', in H. Stimm and J. Wilhelm (eds), *Verba et Vocabula. Ernst Gamillscheg zum 80. Geburtstag*. Munich: Wilhelm Fink Verlag, 275–83.

for the introduction of the term 'risk' into many European languages via insurance and marine legal parlance, but also for broadening the concept of risk to include positive aspects of good fortune. In other words, this meant a shift from fate to at least partly manageable risk, or, in the terms of Frank Knight, a shift from uncertainties to risk. German sociologist Max Weber and others demonstrated that risk-conscious behaviour, which took into account a potentially positive outcome of risk, was atypical of pre-modern times, but that trade which developed around the Mediterranean and early forms of marine insurance showed hallmarks of modern, positive risk understanding.[6] This would, by definition, be true for any business activity. Such positive aspects of risk seem to be more prevalent in entrepreneurial contexts, especially insurance, while today's everyday usage of the word is usually negatively biased.

Mitigating risk via insurance was also linked to externalizing guilt and responsibility. For most of history it was considered people's own fault if something happened to them. But as religious resignation to fate gave way to accepting more responsibility, risk became increasingly abstract. This abstraction made it possible to cede risk on to other parties. Paradoxically, it was the acceptance of risk and responsibility by individuals that made their externalization possible, as someone other than a divine force was able to assume people's risks. Large-scale industrialization in particular helped shift responsibility for accidents from workers to factory owners who neglected safety measures. Later, responsibility was further shifted to manufactures who delivered dangerous machines, eventually leading to modern concepts of liability.[7]

Changing perceptions of risk were often linked to technological shifts. The Industrial Revolution had started a tendency to hold technology responsible for what was perceived as an increasingly risky environment. Such views were corroborated by an abundance of technical failures and catastrophes, such as the sinking of the *Titanic* liner in the Atlantic Ocean in 1912 or the 1986 nuclear accident in Chernobyl in Ukraine. The latter event coincided with the publication of a widely discussed book called *Risk Society: Towards a New Modernity* by the German sociologist Ulrich Beck. The book explicitly blamed an increase in risks on modernization. Along with other authors, Beck's views restricted risk to mainly technological issues, but neglected a wider spread of risk awareness and aversion.[8] Still, Beck was perceptive in identifying a collective unease with technological progress. As various tables in the Appendix of this

[6] Bonβ (1995, 49f.).

[7] Changing views on liability and who was ultimately responsible for creating risk affected the insurance industry considerably. The changes involved a shift from interpreting negligence as contributory, to seeing it as comparative. This was manifested with the gradual erosion of the privity doctrine. Benjamin Cardozo started his 'assault on the citadel of privity' as early as 1916 (with a case against car manufacturer Buick for a lost wheel: *MacPherson* v. *Buick Motor Co.* (1916), Judge Benjamin Cardozo; see W. L. Prosser (1960) 'The Assault upon the Citadel. Strict Liability to the Consumer', *Yale Law Journal* 69: 7, 1099–148) but strict liability only came about in the 1960s. This eventually brought about liability crisis of 1984–7 in the USA, one of the biggest crises of the insurance industry, characterized by large price increases, reduction of coverage, and even unavailability of coverage at any price for some sectors.

[8] Bonβ (1995, 13–14, 18).

book show, natural catastrophes have, though, caused far more damages than man-made disasters. In addition, man-made disasters in a majority of the cases can be traced back to human rather than technological failure. Still, damage to modern infrastructures enabled by technological progress is causing the majority of insured losses. As Lorraine Daston suggests in Chapter 9, the lines between man-made and natural disasters is blurred. She joins a long discussion that started with the publication of Barry A. Turner's seminal work *Man-Made Disasters* in 1978.[9] There is a long way from biblical plagues to modern perception of natural catastrophes, but some of the biblical interpretation lingers on in this view of natural catastrophe effects being man-made or self-inflicted. This line of thought has received fresh arguments from the global warming debate.[10] Today, natural catastrophes, whether caused by human action or not, have become the most severe risks for the insurance and reinsurance industry.

With the exception of the San Francisco Earthquake, the first half of the twentieth century saw few natural catastrophes that made international headlines. Natural catastrophes made a reappearance in 1965 with Hurricane Betsy, the first such disaster to cost more than a billion dollars (nicknamed 'Billion Dollar Betsy'). Natural catastrophes made it quite explicit that risk was not directly linked with technological progress. In fact, developing countries suffered more from natural catastrophes, and were far less insured against them. Over the last fifty years, there is some empirical evidence suggesting a rise in the numbers and severity of natural catastrophes.[11] The main problem with natural catastrophes, however, was the concentration of values in geographical regions prone to them. The US state of Florida showed that natural catastrophes were not confined to the developing world: Florida was home to more and more retired and wealthy Americans, as well as the wealthy elites of Latin America.

In recent decades mega-risks have become global phenomena. Few people, even within the industry, could have predicted the huge losses from floods in Thailand in 2011, a natural catastrophe exacerbated by high levels of governmental incompetence. Floods are among the worst natural catastrophes in terms of damage to lives and property. In Thailand, like many Asian countries except Japan, the cultural preference was for people to insure themselves by building up savings rather than paying fees to an institution which insured them.[12] Only about 1 per cent of home owners and small businesses in Thailand had flood insurance at the time of the flood. However, a large part of the losses were covered not by reinsurance from Thailand, but places such as Japan, which has outsourced manufacturing production to that country. In other words, risks had become global. Emerging markets were more at risk because they are often growing fast, highly polluted, and lacking safety infrastructure such as

[9] Turner (1978).

[10] S. R. Weart (2003) *The Discovery of Global Warming*. Cambridge, MA: Harvard University Press.

[11] See Figure A.6 in Appendix.

[12] 'Insurance in Asia: Astounding Claims' (*The Economist*, 13 June 2015).

building codes. Many such urban manufacturing sites were, for transport reasons, located close to water and at additional risk of flooding. While newer buildings were more resilient to various risks, they were also more vulnerable to water damage due to the sophisticated electricity systems placed underground.[13] For individual insurance companies it was difficult to keep up with such increase in exposure.

The global warming and climate change debates have served to make natural catastrophes a political issue and hence a high-profile subject. Yet governments as a whole have remained chronically slow to respond and to coordinate their responses.[14] In the USA, the home of many devastating natural catastrophes, governmental responses were, historically, reactive rather than preventive. The US Army was the only federal institution involved for a long time. Natural catastrophes only started being considered a matter of national security with the US House of Representatives' Committee on Flood Control in 1916, and it took until 1979 before the Administration of President Jimmy Carter created the Federal Emergency Management Agency (FEMA) to bring all aspects of disaster relief under the responsibility of one federal organization.[15] Four decades later, most disaster relief worldwide remains ex post. Much still remains to be done to lessen the impacts of disasters. The same observation applies to many insurance companies. The effects of global warming appear relatively slow, and this has allowed insurers to react by gradually adapting premium levels. In the long run, however, this is unlikely to be a viable solution. Reinsurers, by definition, have to take a long-term view; consequently, they were among the first to consider the effects of global warming a long-term threat to the industry, and presented policy papers at the First Conference of the Parties to the Framework Convention on Climate Change in Berlin in 1995.[16]

The American political scientist Virginia Haufler posits that there has been a big difference in European and North American responses to climate change. She argues that European insurers, led by reinsurers, have been more proactive in addressing climate change.[17] She attributes this to a European public leadership in such issues, a European tradition of businesses accepting 'a larger role in social issues [ . . . ] because of a history of corporatism, social welfare, and high expectations from society', and the fact that European rather than North American reinsurers often bear the brunt of North American natural catastrophe losses. Also, she argues that European insurers are better at perceiving the financial opportunities from climate change actions, such as insuring carbon footprints, than their North American counterparts.[18] However, the

[13] *Financial Times Special Report*, 26 April 2015.

[14] Haufler (2009, 241).

[15] See Rivera and Miller (2006) or Mener (2007).

[16] SRCA Accession 000029. See also Haufler (2009, 247–8).

[17] This is confirmed by a report published by Ceres (2014) *Insurer Climate Risk Disclosure Survey Report & Scorecard: 2014 Findings & Recommendations*: <http://www.ceres.org/resources/reports/insurer-climate-risk-disclosure-survey-report-scorecard-2014-findings-recommendations/view> (accessed 8 July 2015).

[18] Haufler (2009, 254).

European reinsurance industry has not been unanimous about climate change and its direct effects on natural catastrophes.[19]

The new millennium brought about a plethora of new and renewed risks, from asset price collapses to an increase in natural catastrophes and armed conflicts. One risk, the threat of terrorism, suddenly loomed larger than any other both in the reinsurance world and in public perception. The 9/11 terrorist attack on New York City was by far the largest man-made catastrophe in history. But, oddly, the turn of the millennium was marked by one of the largest risks that never materialized, the so-called Y2K or millennium bug, which was thought to upset computer systems as the years 1900 or 2000 could not be distinguished anymore when abbreviated to 00. The risk was far overrated and goes to show that public and even professional risk perception may at times be far from reality. What society considers the greatest risks may not always be the ones which are at the top of reinsurers' watch lists. Climate change and natural catastrophes appear to be a constant in risk perception in recent decades. Perceptions of other risks appear to be shorter lived. Since 2006, the World Economic Forum (WEF) at Davos has monitored how risks are rated in terms of impact and likelihood and what risk trends can be identified.[20] Within less than ten years, the perception of certain likelihoods of risks has changed considerably, while the perception of how severe their impacts are has changed less. The first report, published in 2006, reflected on the risks which had made headlines in the course of 2005: Hurricane Katrina, the terrorist attack on the London Underground during the G8 talks, the oil price spike with the price of a barrel of oil going over USD 70, as well as a United Nations (UN) warning that a virus such as H5N1 could kill up to 150 million people. All of these risks were perceived to be high in terms of likelihood. Ten years later, some of these risks appeared to be less threatening. Despite Ebola and Zika, pandemics were not perceived as very likely (albeit having a potentially large impact). Oil prices spent much of 2015 below USD 50 a barrel. Fracking of natural shale gas and oil shale reserves in the USA had completely shifted the cost basis and political economy of world petroleum. Next to extreme weather events and interstate conflict, there has been another constant. Threats to the economy have been on top of the impact scale throughout all but the most recent of the ten reports, which listed a water crisis and the spread of an infectious disease as having the potentially highest impacts. A collapse of asset price was considered the top risk in terms of impact from 2007 to 2010. In 2011 and 2014, a fiscal crisis ranked highest, and in 2012 and 2013, it was a major systemic financial failure. In 2015, however, it was interstate conflict which was seen as the most likely global threat.

These reports appear to show a global society which has become worried mainly about televised risks and their financial impact. Traffic accidents in almost all countries, however, continue to kill more people than armed conflicts, and while the latter do have many more repercussions, traffic, with millions of injuries per year, poses a more

[19] Johnson (2011, 38).

[20] WEF (World Economic Forum) (ed.) (2006–) *Global Risks*. Geneva: World Economic Forum.

real and direct threat to most people in advanced societies.[21] But despite a long list of threats, most people in today's societies live a safer life than their predecessors. One reason why people do not perceive driving a car or even smoking a major threat is that there seems to be a much higher acceptance of self-inflicted risks. This is in line with a historically increasing tendency to accept risk taking as a basis for modern societies,[22] while acceptance of risks inflicted by others or by external circumstances has declined.

Insurance plays an important role in this worldview. People who are insured against something perceive it to be less threatening. In some cases, insurance clients may take this security to extremes. The direct insurance industry in particular has been blamed for encouraging people to take on too much risk, inducing them to so-called moral hazard. But where does moral hazard start? Some people want to live in San Francisco, on the slopes of Mount Vesuvius, or below sea level in the Netherlands. People lived in areas exposed to natural catastrophes long before the advent of insurance and reinsurance. They relied on alternative risk hedging within their communities or charity from the church or charitable organizations. If insurance is morally hazardous are the village community and the church also? In theory, insurance and reinsurance per se are morally hazardous. The very reason to take out insurance is to become able to assume risks beyond what we can or want to carry ourselves. The industry tries to tackle the problem by requiring that an insurable interest can be identified. As soon as people with insurance start wishing for a loss which will be compensated, moral hazard is felt. But moral hazard does not necessarily involve morality. Insurance in general builds on some of the main causes for market failure, such as information asymmetries, principal–agent problems, and externalities. These exist independently of insurance. Decision-making often happens with a basic acceptance of such possible failures. This means that moral hazard can also be seen as a purely economic function.[23]

The German sociologist Niklas Luhmann sought to differentiate between risk and danger. He suggested that risk can only come about if there is a human, conscious decision involved. In primitive societies natural catastrophes are pure danger, while a human decision to begin farming turns them into risks. The invention of risk management, according to Luhmann, makes risk-free life impossible. He illustrated this in his famous umbrella analogy: before the invention of umbrellas rain was just a danger. The umbrella turned rain into a risk which could be protected against but brought about another risk, that of forgetting the umbrella. The implication is that civilized societies are increasingly risk exposed while constantly getting more sophisticated at managing risks. Insurance and, with it, reinsurance can be seen as the cost of civilization.

[21] 'Nearly 3,400 People Die on the World's Roads Every Day' according to WHO: <http://www.who.int/violence_injury_prevention/road_traffic/en/> (accessed 7 September 2015). The overall death toll of the twenty deadliest conflicts in 2014 was *c.*160,000.

[22] See Bonβ (1995, 19). [23] E.g. Pauly (1968).

## 1.3 The Business Response to Risk

Apart from company portraits, insurance history has not produced an abundance of literature, much less has the history of reinsurance.[24] This is not surprising given that reinsurance has, in the best sense of the word, been an invisible trade for most of its existence.[25] It was only towards the end of the twentieth century that the public profile of reinsurers began to rise after investor relations had become important and the public started taking more interest in risk issues such as natural catastrophes. The function of reinsurance was historic, however, though it has been remarkably slow in changing.[26] With few exceptions it has always been an adaptive rather than an innovative industry. Early forms of sharing insured risks were known already in medieval Genoa. But there is disagreement over whether this qualified as reinsurance rather than co-insurance.[27] As the British economic historian Clive Trebilcock noted in his pioneering work on the history of Phoenix Assurance, the 'line between allocated co-insurance and facultative reinsurance may be rather fine'.[28]

Reinsurance co-existed along co-insurance and subscription insurance in European marine insurance during the seventeenth and eighteenth centuries, as Pearson describes in Chapter 3, but was probably not widely used, especially after the ban in England in 1746. These early forms were based on reinsuring individual larger risks, so-called facultative reinsurance. There was, however, no apparent need to found marine reinsurance companies as this sector had developed an efficient co-insurance system. Also, facultative reinsurance was a comparatively simple affair in shipping,

[24] Pioneering works in insurance history include Arps (1965a, 1965b, 1970, 1976); Trebilcock (1985, 1998); and Feldman (2001). The first history of reinsurance was written by Golding (1927); Hollitscher (1931) was the first to collect historical data from several countries and to apply economic analysis to the industry (our thanks to Robin Pearson for this reference); van der Haegen (1956) was the first to give a condensed overview of the historical development of reinsurance practices, markets, and economies—albeit short it may still be regarded as the best-informed historical essay on reinsurance so far—; and Gerathewohl et al. (1979) dedicated a long chapter to the subject. The history of Munich Re by Bähr and Kopper was published in 2015.

In this series of three volumes on the history of insurance and reinsurance Borscheid and Haueter (2012) provided the first global history of insurance markets; James (2013a) (together with Borscheid, Gugerli, and Straumann) gave an overview of the history of reinsurance and the history of Swiss Re; while the third in this series looks at the history of risk from the perspective of reinsurance.

[25] This means that public sources are scarce. Also corporate sources are not easily accessible. In addition, corporate reporting in reinsurance on an annual basis distorted respective yearly results as the business had to be assessed over much longer periods. What makes a quantitative history of overall reinsurance virtually impossible is the fact that many alternative forms existed in the secondary risk market, such as co-insurance, reciprocal insurance, or risk pools. Much of such data was never recorded.

[26] For an overview of reinsurance before the foundation of independent reinsurance companies see Mossner (1959).

[27] The oldest reinsurance-like contract dates from 1370. Mossner (1959, 28–31).

[28] Trebilcock (1985, 268).

where each voyage required individual insurance and a closed network of actors had access to relevant risk intelligence.

So, why were reinsurance companies needed and why was this need most felt in the German-speaking part of the world?[29] As Kyrtsis argues in Chapter 6, the Industrial Revolution not only brought about larger risks, but also increased the number of smaller and mid-size insured risks, especially in fire insurance. Individually reinsuring these made no sense and insurers were looking for efficient ways of ceding entire portfolios.[30] Reinsuring these portfolios with their competitors implied unwanted disclosure of business, while reinsuring with non-competing foreign insurers meant that premium capital left the country. This was the business opportunity which the first dedicated reinsurers seized.

The main reason to found reinsurance companies was of a financial nature. Both the Kölnische Rückversicherungsgesellschaft (Cologne Re), the first ever independent reinsurer,[31] and the Schweizerische Rückversicherungsgesellschaft (Swiss Re), in their foundation proposals, stressed the importance of keeping premium capital and reserves within their national economies.[32] Promoting the financial argument may have mainly served the purpose of convincing local investors. But the importance of reinsurance for national economies was also considered a major factor by others, including the modernizing Russian finance minister Count Sergei Witte. During the 1890s, Witte initiated the foundation of the country's first reinsurance company with the main purpose of bolstering the country's entry into the gold standard. As Kyrtsis suggests, the Prussian government also was well aware of the importance of reinsurance to support the local fire insurance industry against British dominance. A wave of nationalizations and state foundations of reinsurance, which started in the early twentieth century, further suggests that modernizing national states had a vital interest in the reinsurance business.

Professional reinsurance was to become the main financial service that was never to be dominated by the English-speaking world, even though it hosted its largest markets. The fact that Germany became the birthplace of the first dedicated reinsurance companies can possibly best be explained by the failures of Great Britain and the USA, the two largest insurance markets at the time, to take the market lead.

[29] See Tables A.1 and A.2 in Appendix for early foundations by country.

[30] Reinsuring entire portfolios came up in the 1820s, see Chapters 3 and 6, this volume, and became known as treaty reinsurance as it was binding the parties over a longer time. It also took the name of obligatory reinsurance as each risk in the portfolio was binding. See Mossner (1959, 88–94) for a discussion of the first treaties.

[31] Cologne Re's foundation date usually refers to the licence given in 1846. The articles of association had been set up already in 1842 but, due to political and economic instabilities, the company only started doing business in 1852.

[32] Neither mentioned the need to reinsure against devastating catastrophes such as the 1842 Hamburg Fire and the 1861 Glarus Fire, which are often quoted as the reasons for the two companies being founded. For a discussion see Gugerli (2013, 157).

Reinsurance appears to have been used by British companies mainly outside of Britain.[33] Piggybacking on other insurers' ventures in new markets was also an efficient way to collect intelligence about foreign markets.[34] But the success of large British fire insurers, the thriving co-insurance practices, as well as the ban on marine reinsurance between 1746 and 1864, which had made Lloyd's the main market for business that would otherwise have gone to reinsurers, all help to explain why there was scarcely any perceived need for an independent British reinsurance industry. As Pearson shows in Chapter 3, the British market also had little positive experience with reinsurance after a wave of unsuccessful foundations in the 1870s and a series of heavy losses in foreign markets. Similar to Britain, the USA had developed a co-insurance market, and many states entertained close ties with the London market and Lloyd's. But founding dedicated reinsurers was also complicated by the legal fragmentation of the states and the requirement for mono-line companies, which prevented spreading risks by category. The bulk of pure reinsurance business was being serviced from continental Europe, as became evident with the San Francisco Earthquake in 1906.

While the success of British fire insurers may have been one of the detriments for expanding British reinsurance, German fire insurance provided a better basis for developing a reinsurance industry. The German fire market was more heterogeneous than Britain's, with smaller companies and a slow shift from state-owned fire societies, which did not need reinsurance, to private enterprises, which were more dependent on finding reinsurance than their British counterparts.

The German-speaking world soon came to dominate the world reinsurance markets. Firms based in either Germany or Switzerland have held this position ever since. As of 2013, the two countries accounted for over 40 per cent of global gross premium written.[35] The supply of reinsurance today still appears oddly distributed. Switzerland alone writes about the same amount of premiums as the entire Americas. Europe, including London, writes over 60 per cent. Except for the addition of Bermuda and Asia Pacific (AP) not that much has changed in over 170 years of reinsurance supply.[36] This concentration is even more astonishing in that, for most of the almost 170 years of professional reinsurance history, the largest part of the world markets were served by only two leading companies—Munich Re and Swiss Re. In 1913, Alfred Manes, a pioneer in modern insurance studies, wrote that 'German reinsurers [ . . . ] control the reinsurance markets of the world.'[37] This started changing dramatically only one year

[33] 'Most obviously, reinsurance was a means of diluting and spreading risk, foreign risk, lying under strange suns and ruled by unfamiliar customs, often needed diluting and spreading more than their homespun counterparts.' Trebilcock (1985, 269).

[34] Trebilcock (1985, 271–2).

[35] The numbers here refer to what is often called 'professional reinsurance'.

[36] AP and Bermuda each write about 11 per cent of global business today. See Figure A.1 in Appendix.

[37] Manes (1913, 106), quoted in Arps (1970, 21). Domination of German reinsurance started provoking politically influenced reactions with the outbreak of war, especially in London, which was heavily dependent on German reinsurance. Germany at the time tried to get less dependent on London market and London in return tried to get less dependent on German reinsurance. Manes later even went

later. Global supply and demand of reinsurance were severely disrupted with the world wars. Supply shifted to hard currency countries and demand to soft currency markets. A country as (apparently) unlikely as Denmark briefly rose to become number two in reinsurance export surplus in the world next to Switzerland, also thanks to two major Russian reinsurers having defected there.[38]

The two world wars also seriously challenged the business model of reinsurers, as the absence of German reinsurers from major markets such as the USA caused severe capacity problems. This was, to a large degree, absorbed by Swiss Re, which almost singlehandedly conducted the bulk of professional global business during the world wars and the decade following the Second World War, while Munich Re expanded its home market. Britain had managed to build a significant reinsurance industry, especially after the return to the gold standard in 1924, albeit predominantly with composite companies.[39] The leading British reinsurance company at the time, Mercantile & General, was owned by Swiss Re. Another resort to deal with the capacity shortage was reciprocity, which became known as 'exchanging one's dirty washing'. Exchanging rather than co-insuring risks between insurers was also a convenient and popular way to circumvent capital transfers, as shown in Chapter 4 by Capie. From the 1920s until well after the Second World War, reciprocity was considered the main threat to global reinsurance by professional reinsurers. As the leading reinsurance journal noted: 'Professional reinsurance has [ . . . ] had to move up to the second floor.'[40] But, as was later stated: '[reinsurers] *mirabili* [sic] *dictu* manage to survive'.[41] The main threats from the war were thus indirect, but nevertheless resulted in questioning the business model of reinsurance. The poor business logic of reciprocity started giving way to professional reinsurance again once capacity had been re-established with the German market re-entry.

Britain and the USA again failed to take the market lead, while the German reinsurance industry was isolated during the world wars. Equally, during the first half of the 1940s, a rival organization of mainly German and Italian reinsurers, joined by Swiss Re, failed to take over the business of Lloyd's in fascist-dominated markets.[42]

as far as seeing the First World War as also being a war against German reinsurance. Manes (1924, 337), quoted in Arps (1970, 21).

[38] The companies Rossiya and Salamandra also left behind what Mira Wilkins has termed orphan companies in the USA, but the headquarters were run from Copenhagen. See Haegen (1956, 42–6).

[39] *The Review*, 22 November 1946, 670. As reinsurance business was not always reported separately, and reciprocity agreements in particular did not appear in reports at all, the overall size of reinsurance business done by non-professional and composite insurers is impossible to assess.

[40] *The Review*, 1946, 671.

[41] *The Review*, 1953, 1562. *The Review* also commented: 'The different functions of professional and non-professional reinsurers might be defined as thus: The professional reinsurer has to look for and identify chance fluctuations in international economics which it is his task to even-out by international spread. On the other hand, the task of the non-professional reinsurer is to get compensation for an exaggerated outflow of financial strength by exchanging the uncertainties of his own portfolio for other uncertainties deemed of lesser magnitude.' *The Review*, 1953, 66.

[42] Borscheid (2012c, 110). Bähr and Kopper (2015, 221–5). Swiss Re's membership was probably designed not to jeopardize its significant German business during the war.

**Table 1.1 Total net premiums in reinsurance by country, 1950 (GBP m)**

| Countries | No. of companies | Premium |
|---|---|---|
| United States | 23 | 61.6 |
| Switzerland | 5 | 42.9 |
| West Germany* | 6 | 19.0 |
| Britain | 4 | 11.6 |
| France | 6 | 10.2 |
| Denmark | 5 | 7.2 |
| Algeria (French) | 1 | 5.0 |
| Brazil | 1 | 2.6 |
| Italy | 3 | 2.6 |
| Norway | 1 | 2.5 |
| Sweden | 3 | 2.1 |
| Czechoslovakia | 1 | 1.9 |
| Chile | 1 | 1.5 |
| Japan | 1 | 1.4 |
| Tangiers (International Zone) | 1 | 1.1 |
| Turkey | 1 | 0.9 |
| Netherlands | 1 | 0.7 |
| Argentina | 1 | 0.6 |
| Total | 61 | 163.80 |

* German reinsurers only starting reporting reliable results from 1953 on.
List not complete, and possibly the focus on premium and not number of companies led to omissions, such as Israel.
*Source*: *The Review, Annual Reinsurance Number*, 7 December 1951, 1143.

The USA were hesitant to do without German insurance and reinsurance services at the start of the First World War.[43] Only after the Second World War did US insurers slowly start extending their local reinsurance industry as they took over reinsurance business from German companies.[44] Helped also by the requirements for mono-line business being eroded in the 1950s, the USA, as Table 1.1 shows, did manage to become the largest reinsurance hub by premium written and number of reinsurance companies in the world, although the industry was not home-grown.

The American reinsurance industry found it difficult to internationalize. A large home market made global efforts less of a requirement, while the devaluation of the US dollar in the 1970s attracted more European reinsurers, pushing the country into the demand side again, as Capie shows in Chapter 4. Urgent attempts during the 1980s at creating an US reinsurance market modelled on Lloyd's failed rather miserably, mainly

[43] A day after US entry into war, Washington declared that German reinsurers should be allowed to carry on their US business 'as if we were not at war with Germany' (Arps 1970, 38). Some months later this was revoked by fear of reinsurance bordereaux being used for espionage.

[44] *The Review*, 1953, 130. Most earlier reinsurance foundations were by European parent companies.

due to poor financing.[45] As Lechner, Haueter, and Kenny point out in Chapter 11, also the liability crisis of the 1980s was a severe blow to the US insurance and reinsurance industry, and much business relocated offshore to the British colony of Bermuda, which began to grow its reinsurance industry at the expense of US reinsurers.[46] In 2016, the USA remained the largest reinsurance market in the world, generating over half of worldwide reinsurance premiums.[47] But the country also remains a net importer of reinsurance, with over 60 per cent being ceded to foreign-owned reinsurers. If the parent companies of US-based reinsurers are taken into account, this figure reached over 90 per cent in 2013.[48] Until this day, Continental European and Bermudan reinsurers continue to bear the brunt of US natural catastrophes.

It took until the 1990s to create a third international hub for reinsurance, when offshore locations such as Bermuda joined the Continental reinsurers and the London market. In contrast to most other supply and demand shifts, which were a consequence of changing monetary environments, booming economies, or legislative changes to create common markets, offshore locations grew in the wake of a changing disaster landscape and subsequent capacity shortages. First, the 1980s liability crisis in the USA made insurers look for attractive unbureaucratic alternatives and then, as the late 1980s and early 1990s provided unusually severe and frequent natural catastrophes, such as Hurricane Andrew in 1992, Bermuda saw several reinsurers founded. They were dubbed the 'class of 1992–1993', as reinsurance foundations tended to happen in the wake of large disasters.[49] Providing cover mainly for natural catastrophes, they paved the grounds for Bermuda becoming the home for new alternative risk transfer (ART) products such as insurance-linked securities (ILS). As the Internet made remoteness less of a problem in this particular line of business, which required less face-to-face interaction, Bermuda provided an ideal home.[50] Bermuda's importance in world markets expanded after Hurricane Katrina in 2005.

[45] 'Insurance Exchanges Climb' (*New York Times*, 1 February 1983); 'Tumultuous History of the New York Insurance Exchange' (*Financial Times*, 5 March 2010).

[46] Today Bermuda is the largest supplier of reinsurance to the USA. Federal Insurance Office, US Department of the Treasury (2014) *The Breadth and Scope of the Global Reinsurance Market and the Critical Role Such Markets Play in Supporting Insurance in the United States*, 36: <http://www.treasury.gov/initiatives/fio/reports-and-notices/Documents/FIO%20-%20Reinsurance%20Report.pdf> (accessed 12 June 2015).

[47] See Figures A.3.1 to A.3.3 in Appendix.

[48] Federal Insurance Office, US Department of the Treasury (2014) *The Breadth and Scope of the Global Reinsurance Market and the Critical Role Such Markets Play in Supporting Insurance in the United States*, 35: <http://www.treasury.gov/initiatives/fio/reports-and-notices/Documents/FIO%20-%20Reinsurance%20Report.pdf>.

[49] Such as the 'class of 2001–2002' in the wake of 9/11 and 'the class of 2005–2006' after Hurricane Katrina. See Federal Insurance Office, US Department of the Treasury (2014, 5).

[50] For the importance of face-to-face interaction in reinsurance and the according differences between the London and the Bermuda market see Jarzabkowski, Smets, and Spee, 'Trading risk: The value of relationships, models and face-to-face interaction in a global reinsurance market' (n.d.): <http://www.cassknowledge.com/sites/default/files/article-attachments/trading-risk-cass-knowledge.pdf> (accessed 16 May 2016).

It is striking that most twentieth-century foundations of reinsurance companies happened in financially favourable environments and much less in markets with a direct need for reinsurance. International reinsurers have usually proved better equipped to serve developing economies than newly founded local reinsurers. A case in point was the era of the oil price rises in the 1970s when oil-producing countries went from almost zero insurance companies to multiple local and foreign insurers by the 1980s. But the local market absorbed as little as 5 per cent of the risks, ceding the rest to global reinsurers.[51] Reinsurance not only made it possible to immediately distribute risks globally but it also provided locals access to risk expertise.

In Asia, only Japan has a long reinsurance history serving one of the worldwide largest domestic insurance markets. In other Asian countries, locally owned reinsurance companies only started appearing with the maturing of fast-growth economies such as Singapore, and a subsequent excess of market capital during the 1990s. Few of them were felt on the world markets.[52] By 2014, Bermuda's reinsurance market was still about 20 times the size of Singapore's, despite increasing business opportunities in the AP.

A handful of German and Swiss companies dominated the entire global reinsurance market throughout most of this industry's history. Cologne Re, the pioneer, and follower Swiss Re, were initially confronted with all the problems of early movers and suffered from the early immaturity of the fire market. They lost ground to Munich Re, which was founded in 1880 when market conditions had improved significantly. Unencumbered by other reinsurers' earlier difficulties Munich Re was able to show a healthier risk appetite, enabling it to gain large market shares soon after its foundation.[53] Part of Munich Re's strategy relied on expanding the business as much and fast as possible, to reach a sufficiently high proportion of risks, including some particularly riskier ones, which would then balance themselves according to the law of large numbers.

Munich Re and Swiss Re came to dominate the industry. Why did these two companies succeed in retaining such a dominating hold over the global market? The entry barriers to reinsurance are surprisingly low. With cycles of excess capital, capacity shortages causing premium rates to rise, often favourable regulatory environments, lean organization structures providing high flexibility, and reinsurance business cycles showing little relation to other macroeconomic developments, reinsurance was and continues to be an often coveted niche for investors.[54]

However, sustainable business models are hard to develop for new entrants. This partly has to do with the fact that reinsurance was a very international business from the start. Foundations catering to local markets rarely made sense, as global supply was usually available more readily. Also, risk expertise was not easily acquired. Staffing problems were evident from the very start of the fledgling business in the

[51] *The Review*, 9 July 1984, 2–5.

[52] With the exception, again, of Japanese reinsurers, which started globalizing recently.

[53] Bähr and Kopper (2015, 38).

[54] See Swiss Re, *sigma* 3, 2015, for an analysis of the current merger and acquisition (M&A) activities and the role of alternative capital being invested in reinsurance.

mid-nineteenth century, to the rise of Bermuda which caused a brain drain from the London market. Another important factor that may have prevented major shifts among market players was that trust was an essential factor in doing reinsurance. As Pearson describes in Chapter 3, business relations had to be built up over years. Also, treaty business was an affair that could last several decades or even up to over a century based on one initial single agreement amended over time. Another factor was size. A large capital base is the main value proposition of a reinsurance company, with large size attracting more business. Once established in the market, the dominance of leading reinsurers was hard to break. Munich Re proved this repeatedly as it almost seamlessly re-entered foreign markets after years of absence during the wars.[55]

Only a few new foundations reached considerable market shares from the second half of the twentieth century on, typically through acquiring pre-existing firms. Hannover Re was founded in 1966 as a marine company, at a time when reinsurance demand of the by then again internationalizing insurers grew exponentially. By 2000 it had entered the global top five through a series of acquisitions. Newcomers in this business needed strong financial standing. As explained in Chapter 11, the primary example was Warren Buffett's Berkshire Hathaway, which took over US-based General Re in 1998, and with it Cologne Re, which had entered a strategic alliance with General Re four years previously.

Corporate survival depended on adaptation to changing risk landscapes. A shift towards increasingly covering peak risks, for example, started with the economic miracle in Europe and Japan after the Second World War. While the increase in numbers of risks during the Industrial Revolution in particular had given rise to treaty reinsurance, Kyrtsis, in Chapter 6, shows that it was the size of risks which changed the nature of reinsurance in the second half of the twentieth century. But risks tended to change slowly, giving the industry enough time to adapt. As Röder suggests in Chapter 7, with the exception of ART products, all basic forms of reinsurance had been developed in the nineteenth century; thus, the basic business model of reinsurance has changed little since the beginnings.

## 1.4 Managing Risk

Frank H. Knight, in 1921, contributed the possibly most pellucid definition of risk so far. According to Knight, risk differs from uncertainty in that some known factors or, in actuarial terms, quantifiable probabilities, apply. Knight wrote about entrepreneurial risk and uncertainty, not primarily about insured risk, which, in his view, differed from

[55] In at least the case of Munich Re this also had to do with the fact that the practice of depositing premium payments with clients, so-called deposits or *fonds de roulement* (see Kyrtsis, Chapter 6), allowed Munich Re to fulfil all their financial obligations throughout the war despite restrictions on doing business and transferring capital. See Bähr and Kopper (2015, 254).

the former. Still, his distinction can to some degree serve to define insurance risks: risks, broadly speaking, are insurable but uncertainties less so.[56]

Managing risk certainly became one of the insurance and reinsurance industries' competitive advantages. It was the known factors of risks which allowed them to be analysed and managed. But risk management is a rather heterogeneous field. Today, the term seems ubiquitous. Risk management has evolved from a choice to an imperative. Since the 1990s, it increasingly encompasses virtually all aspects of enterprise steering.[57]As a term, risk management only came about in the middle of the last century. As a practice, it has existed for much longer than that. Three main fields emerged in insurance history: actuarial measuring, technical engineering, and scenario modelling.

Life insurance was the pioneer in measuring risk. It relied on two things. As discussed in Chapter 5 by Bühlmann and Lengwiler, it thrived on probability calculations which had developed around problems in gambling in the seventeenth century. Meanwhile, as Clark shows in Chapter 2, the Age of Enlightenment changed attitudes from accepting fate towards more responsibility of the individual. As opposed to the more unpredictable material risks, death was a certainty. But, also, the uncertainty of when it would happen proved to be a calculable factor, at least statistically. This led to mortality tables being used to calculate average life expectancies, and eventually to sophisticated rating and accounting models first applied by the Equitable Life Assurance Society in the 1760s. By the advent of modern reinsurance in the mid-nineteenth century, life actuarial methods had become fairly advanced and reliable. Partly thanks to such practices, but also due to the relative stability of life business, life insurance was less in need of reinsurance. For fire, however, reinsurance became essential.

There were no statistics available in fire insurance, and reinsurance was to become an essential tool for insurers to manage fire risks. The other important measure was to analyse and engineer risks and to avoid accumulating them. This was done in several ways. Cadastral plans with risk indicators were used to avoid accumulations and identify the need for safety measures. Building codes for fire protection were introduced, large-risk buildings were inspected in detail, and, before they could be insured, security and safety measures had to be applied. Risk management, for a long time, meant culling so-called bad risks from good risks and went by the name of quality control. Reinsurers often relied on their clients to monitor non-life risks. These provided so-called bordereaux to their reinsurers, which listed each reinsured risk for

[56] 'The word "uncertainty" seemed best for distinguishing the defects of managerial knowledge from the ordinary "risks" of business activity, which can feasibly be reduced if not eliminated by applying the insurance principle through some organization for grouping cases' (Knight 1957, lix).

[57] Michael Power describes this as a 're-organization and reconceptualization of management activity in the name of risk [which] marks a distinctive form of administrative innovation' (Power 2007, 28).

inspection.[58] Reinsurers in turn mainly monitored external factors, as becomes evident in the many travel reports written up until the 1970s. One Swiss Re report on India from 1952 described religious aspects with references to Shiva and Indian attitudes towards creation and destruction. It dwells on demographic aspects such as birth rates and mortality trends, dietary habits and famines, caste systems and associated fatalism. It goes on to sacred animals and people's refusal to eat them, as well as observing that such animals take away food from human beings. Life conditions in rural and urban environments, problems with economic prosperity after independence, working conditions and salaries, credit and loan systems, as well as moral hazard in repaying loans, finally lead to contemplating national politics and the threat of communism.[59] Such Euro-centric knowledge did not always lend itself to sound risk evaluation.[60] The main source of risk intelligence for reinsurers appears to have been the loss history and integrity of their clients. Travel reports usually added detailed accounts of individual companies, their business success, strategies, and staffing, all with a view to assessing the reliability of such business partners.

Risk management as a term, and the profession of the risk manager, were only propagated in insurance in the 1960s.[61] It remained a specialist concern as late as the 1980s.[62] It had taken until the 1950s for non-life actuarial methods to start developing after so-called collective risk theories had opened up new fields for mathematicians (see Bühlmann and Lengwiler, Chapter 5). The Second World War also helped in that a large number of former military mathematicians and statisticians were now seeking new work in insurance. And technical expertise in loss assessment had also advanced considerably during the war, for example by analysing air crashes.

Risk management gradually came to encompass both risk engineering and risk measurement. The two areas, however, led separate lives. Throughout a century of professional reinsurance, the non-life sector had managed to do quite well without mathematicians. Underwriting decisions were still based on acquired instinct and trusting the client rather than on statistical evidence. Even life insurance had been hesitant to rely purely on statistics. Medical officers for a long time had more influence in accepting new clients than actuaries did. In essence, of course, the non-life sector did rely on a mathematical basis. The advantages of risk sharing had been recognized long before Jacob Bernoulli discovered the law of large numbers. Reinsurance functioned on

[58] The importance of such risk lists is evident in an industry joke still virulent in the 1970s about reinsurers only showing up for work twice a month, once to collect their pay and the other time to have a look at the bordereaux.

[59] SRCA 10.169 410.10.

[60] There was a striking irony in British life insurers refusing to do business with Indians on account of their perceived moral inferiority while British subjects in India turned out to be much riskier life clients, with high proportions of early mortality due to the tropical conditions. Balachandran (2012, 445).

[61] Mehr and Hedges (1963).

[62] Writing about an upcoming conference of the US-based Risk and Insurance Management Society (RIMS, founded in the 1950s) *The Review* published an article about the 'relatively unfamiliar' term risk management, seeing it as an integral part of financial management. *The Review*, 3 April 1981, 27.

this very basis, allowing smaller insurers to place their portfolios among a sufficiently large number of risks. But old hands were reluctant to accept actuarial methods. They saw reinsurance as a 'human' business where mathematics had no place. One comment in *The Review* read: '[there are] many imponderables which make reinsurance a far from exact science, thus putting it beyond the bounds of underwriting on a formula basis'.[63]

Actuarial approaches based on collective risk theory were ideally suited to calculate mass or portfolio businesses such as accident or motor businesses. Their use for large individual risks was less obvious. This meant that technical risk engineering developed at an at least equal pace. Also, the increasing size of facultative risks after the Second World War and the scarcity of loss histories called for more engineering expertise to assess large risks. Such expertise was essential in making new risks such as atomic reactors insurable, as shown by Daston in Chapter 9. Engineering risks had developed out of a wish to reduce insurance expenses. In the wake of large fire catastrophes, cities were sometimes rebuilt in stone rather than wood, not only to make them safer but also to reduce insurance premiums.[64] For corporations, risk management basically meant taking out insurance. Insurance turned business contingencies into a fixed cost,[65] and there were repeated attempts at cutting such costs. When the US insurance market turned from a sellers' into a buyers' market after the Second World War, large enterprises started looking for ways to cut insurance expenses without reducing cover.[66] This was only possible by analysing risks in detail.[67] Such activities were often perceived to run counter to insurers' and reinsurers' interests. Up until the late 1980s, the adage prevailed that losses were good for business as they created more need for insurance.

This view gradually changed. Actuarial insight helped demonstrate that, in fact, both risk engineering and actuarial intelligence could render thus far uninsurable risks insurable. The development of coverage for so-called substandard risks in life insurance is a case in point.[68] A good illustration of this principle can be found in the South African introduction of policies providing cover for critical illness, including AIDS, from the late 1980s on.[69] The introduction of such covers was not a humanitarian act but a necessity for the life insurance industry, which feared that their market was bound to collapse due to the high rates of HIV infections. This excluded a large percentage of the population from buying insurance and eventually could result in the available risk pool becoming too small for the law of large numbers to work. Insuring possibly HIV-infected people allowed the industry to considerably expand the

[63] *The Review*, 2 December 1955, 1165.

[64] Such as the Swedish town Sundsvall after the 1888 fire. Rohland (2011a, 105).

[65] Knight (1921, 213).

[66] Swiss Re, *sigma*, 1981, 2.

[67] Some companies combined risk management consulting with insurance specializing in so-called HPRs (highly protected risks).

[68] See Chapter 5, this volume.

[69] Verhoef (2012, 337–8).

life market. Ironically, such products were difficult to sell due to the stigma associated with AIDS.[70]

Risk management started maturing when risk became a public concern in the wake of several catastrophes during the 1970s and 1980s, all of which were covered extensively by mass media.[71] A causality between broadly communicated catastrophes and an increase in risk management has not been proved but, as Röder argues in Chapter 7, the US liability crisis in the 1980s greatly increased insurers' sensitivity towards unexpected risks. This crisis brought about some of the historically greatest financial losses. Neither actuarial methods or risk engineering nor utmost good faith or trained instinct had been able to prevent the massive insured losses. But these 'unknown unknowns' or 'black swans' were different from earlier risks in that the main financial threat to insurers came from a legal system. US tort law in the 1980s challenged the traditional trust between insurers and reinsurers, as shown by Röder, and forced the industry to rethink their rating methods.

The contemporary perception of the reinsurance industry as leading risk expertise is surprisingly recent. The hallmarks of engineering experts, actuaries, and other scientists were only starting to be felt in the business from the 1960s on.[72] From the 1980s on, reinsurance companies increasingly marketed their risk expertise.[73] Advertising technical expertise replaced traditional ads which simply listed capitalization. While risk management grew out of a necessity, it was felt to have repercussions on the business of reinsurers. Progress of risk prevention measures meant that the need to insure gravitated towards larger and more severe risks, while companies retained smaller calculable risks themselves. Even some larger risks were increasingly dealt with by companies big enough to insure themselves via captives, some of them better capitalized than reinsurers. Still, reinsurers were better equipped to spread such risks globally and technically asses these risks. On the other hand, growing risk awareness was also starting to be seen as being good for business as it motivated clients to take out more insurance.[74]

The 1980s and 1990s also saw an increase in natural catastrophes that were now being televised. There had been a long period of relatively few severe weather catastrophes, with the exception of Hurricane Betsy in 1965. Betsy drastically demonstrated the difficulty of a large part of the reinsurance sector to deal with natural catastrophes, as such risks had been reinsured without detailed knowledge (as Werner describes in Chapter 10). But the situation got worse. The 1980s saw over three times more economic losses from natural catastrophes than the 1960s.[75] The problem was not just the increase in catastrophes but, possibly more importantly, an increased density and accumulation of insured risks in weather-exposed areas. In addition, weather

[70] Interview with Douglas Keir in 2010, formerly with Swiss Re Life & Health.

[71] Flixborough (1974), Seveso (1976), Amoco Cadiz (1978), Mount St. Helens (1980), El Niño (1982–3), Bhopal (1984), Chernobyl (1986), Exxon Valdez (1989).

[72] Gugerli (2013, 206–9).

[73] Haueter (2012, 12).

[74] Swiss Re, *sigma*, 1981, 8.

[75] Haufler (2009, 246).

events are erratic, and accumulated risks make reinsurers' balance sheets fluctuate much more than predictable mass business and thus require additional risk capital to absorb fluctuations. Actuarial research discovered this in the 1980s and argued that natural catastrophes needed to be rated separately as they required far higher premiums than normal business. The message, however, had not arrived when Hurricane Andrew, in 1992, created the, by then, greatest ever loss from a natural disaster. Despite improved calculations, natural catastrophe cover was difficult to price adequately in competitive environments.

Reinsuring natural catastrophes was put on a sounder basis by another risk management tool: computer-aided scenario modelling. Earthquake risks were among the first to be modelled in the early 1980s.[76] The models combined four elements which could be quantified separately to estimate a loss event: frequency and intensity of events, extent of damage according to intensity, value distribution of insured risks, and insurance conditions of risks. Sophisticated risk modelling complemented actuarial methods, which were based on past statistical evidence, and risk engineering, which aimed at making present constructions safer with a third, forward-looking component.

One element, however, in reinsurers' risk management strategies was, for a long time, somewhat neglected: the interdependency of insured liabilities and invested assets. The new developments in the management of financial risks in the banking sector went somewhat unnoticed in reinsurance for a long time. Measuring, engineering, and modelling so-called technical risks had been sophisticated within the insurance industry, but managing financial risks had happened on a relatively primitive, albeit not necessarily unsuccessful, level. Reinsurers' asset management was traditionally risk averse. As the focus had traditionally been on underwriting risks, reinsurers traditionally held conservative low-risk asset portfolios which did not require the new tools developed in the broader financial world. Investment risks were avoided by preferring bonds over equities, as shown in Chapter 4 by Capie, while equities were somewhat reluctantly acquired to a degree that guaranteed reasonable liquidity.

There had been early attempts at determining the optimal relation of insurance and investment portfolios,[77] but, overall, modern finance was not highly thought of by traditional asset managers in reinsurance. As Bühlmann and Lengwiler point out in Chapter 5, even the International Actuarial Association (IAA) struggled to accept the foundation of a section in 1988 dedicated to the actuarial approach to financial risks (Actuarial Approach for Financial Risks, AFIR). Only by the late 1980s did reinsurers start discovering analogies between financial and insurance risk management on the non-life side, and embark on insurance-specific asset-liability-management (ALM), while life reinsurance had, for a long time, balanced technical risks and interest rates.[78] The balance sheet of the reinsurers has two sides. As a result it is affected by two types of risks stemming from the underwriting portfolio and the investment portfolio. The

[76] Interview with Peter Hausmann, Swiss Re Cat Perils team, May 2015.

[77] Such as Kahane (1977), who used Sharpe's single-index technique to do so.

[78] Such as Marbacher (1989).

impact of these on each other had to be managed to guarantee optimal return. On the underwriting side, as Capie notes in Chapter 4, different portfolios showed varying degrees of dependency on the overall economy.[79] These, together with investment risks, had to be combined to be put in a relation to solvability and liquidity requirements, to thus allow for a comprehensive risk-steering process at a top level. From the mid-1990s on, considerations of both modern portfolio theories for optimizing insurance portfolios and also the interdependency between insurance and investment portfolios paved the grounds for economic value management (EVM) models. Such tasks now fell to newly appointed chief risk officers or chief financial officers, who soon started incorporating broader aspects of risk exposure. Managing economic value on such a scale eventually resulted in what Michael Power sees as a general shift towards risk as a ubiquitous governing framework.[80]

The progress in managing and monitoring risk allowed a continuous expansion of the range of insurable risks. Some risks deemed uninsurable earlier on show how much progress has been achieved. As Bühlmann and Lengwiler describe in Chapter 5, mathematician James Dodson was refused life insurance in the mid-eighteenth century due to his advanced age of over forty-five; he set out to found his own insurance company, the Equitable Life Assurance Society, the first life insurer to be successful on actuarial grounds.[81] Over two centuries later, in 1982, when fears were running high about large risks pushing the limits of insurers, Baruch Berliner published a classic text about the limits of insurability. It listed thirteen examples of risks which, according to sound actuarial thinking, should not, or only restrictively, be insured. This included natural catastrophes, political risks, crimes such as kidnapping or tax evasion, civil commotion, punitive damages, or awards for mental suffering.[82] The reasons given ranged from difficulties in avoiding accumulation and calculating maximum possible losses, so-called MPLs, (for example, for natural catastrophes), to uncontrollable degrees of randomness (political risks and nationalization), moral hazard (crime and punitive damages),[83] and public policy (for mental suffering),[84] to legal restrictions (tax evasion).

In theory, though, everything can be insured provided someone is willing to take the risk and someone else is willing to pay the premium. Many of the above risks were insured and reinsured, some of them involuntarily, such as punitive damages. Medical

[79] Credit reinsurance, for example, correlates highly with the macroeconomy, while weather events show little or no relation to the economy.

[80] Power (2007, 6, 19–20).

[81] De Morgan (1868, 346). History repeated itself with Hugh C. Baker, who, in 1845, was asked for a higher life insurance premium in the USA due to the health hazards of living in Canada and went on to found Canada Life. Darroch and Kipping (2012, 254).

[82] Berliner (1982, 109–17).

[83] Moral objections to insuring not only applied in a criminal context. Some religions, such as Islam, objected to insurance on much broader grounds, as Röder explains. In the wake of Islam-conforming finance principles being introduced across the Islamic world, *takaful* solutions were developed for the insurance and reinsurance industry.

[84] Defined as 'community common sense and common conscience', Berliner (1982, 78).

malpractice, which Berliner lists under mental sufferings, was an example which was to bring part of the US insurance industry to the verge of collapsing during the 1980s liability crisis. *Time* magazine's famous headline in 1986 read: 'Sorry, America, Your Insurance has been Cancelled.' Lloyd's particularly suffered from unlimited liability in the 1980s, as Lechner, Haueter, and Kenny point out in Chapter 11. While many insurers went out of business during the liability crisis of the 1980s or relocated parts of their business to offshore locations, reinsurers worked on making large risks insurable. As Daston describes in Chapter 9, atomic insurance had provided an example of how an apparently uninsurable risk could, at least to some degree, become insurable. The critical question was not only the MPL but also the legal handling of liability issues by different governments. Eventually, atomic risks were dealt with in pools made up of insurers and reinsurers with wide-ranging responsibilities for governments.

Natural catastrophes posed more problems than just difficult-to-estimate MPLs. As natural catastrophes in most areas tend to happen relatively rarely, the risk is underestimated by many people who take out insurance. In many cases, especially flood, the risk community can become too small to make insurance effective. In order to distribute flood risks, these have to be packaged with other risks to increase the community. But why should people who do not live in flood-prone areas take out flood insurance and subsidize people who have chosen to live in such areas? This led to widespread thinking that floods are not insurable. It was easy for insurers to avoid covering flood-prone areas. In 1929, US insurers stopped providing cover for floods, and it took until 1968 before the National Flood Insurance Act made the creation of the National Flood Insurance Program possible. Subsidized state insurance premiums for weather catastrophes had an adverse effect, though, in that they encouraged construction work in dangerous areas, such as much of Florida.

Floods were seen as acts of God and were traditionally excluded in insurance contracts. But many acts of God gradually turned into insurable natural catastrophes. As Röder shows in Chapter 7, exclusions often led evolutionary steps, with new specific products covering such formerly uninsurable events. Insuring natural catastrophes on larger scales was made possible from the 1980s onwards by applying excess-loss (XL) covers rather than proportional contracts to reduce administrative efforts. It was also aided by developing risk modelling techniques in the 1980s. The need for additional risk capital was later solved by creating natural catastrophe-specialized reinsurers in offshore locations, which were less bureaucratic and were tax friendly towards large capital accumulations. From the late 1980s on, risk capital was starting to be found in the capital markets via ILS.

A surprisingly difficult-to-insure risk that made Berliner's list deserves special attention. He deemed small or trivial risks as 'in general not suitable for insurance' (Berliner 1982, 113), for being contrary to public policy. The main problem with small risks was that they created excessive administrative work, which had to be compensated via premium payments, thus upsetting any economic sense. This, Berliner argues, was conducive to moral hazard. This may not be a serious problem in developed economies where people can afford to carry such risks themselves. It did, however, become problematic in underdeveloped economies where individual losses may, at least by international insurance companies' standards, be relatively trivial economically but very severe for those affected. In many areas of the world, alternative methods for collectively carrying risk are still more effective than insurance. Poverty and the high administrative costs of insurance combined make professional risk protection almost impossible in low-income countries. Chapter 10 provides examples of uninsured events. Tackling this problem has proved one of the main challenges to the insurance industry as a whole. Recently, micro-insurance developed in the wake of micro-banking activities, which originated in the mid-1970s. Problems with administrative efforts for loss settlements were later solved by applying so-called parametric triggers, which prompt payment not according to actual losses but relative to the severity of a weather event. Interestingly, parametric insurance had developed in the highly capital-intense ILS market.

## 1.5 Risk and Finance

Compensating losses in monetary equivalents is an essential and distinctive feature of modern insurance. Putting a price tag on people's lives was a rather courageous and, to religious proponents, provocative concept in the eighteenth century. But money is a convenient means to alleviate losses. It tends to be less complicated than products as it does not carry the inherent risks of goods.[85] It also requires a far less diversified organization than replacing losses in kind. In many cases, replacement in kind is impossible. Life insurance policies cannot make up for the loss of loved ones. But they are an efficient way to hedge against the loss of income when the breadwinner dies. Indeed, early life insurance was often taken out to meet funeral costs that were expected to exceed means and to protect widows against financially bleak futures.

As the loss of goods entails financial consequences, it can be said that insurance is essentially a hedge against potential financial difficulties. This is even truer for reinsurance, as it directly and exclusively hedges against financial liabilities.[86] Recipients of insurance indemnities are free to choose to what use they put the money but insurance companies receiving claims payments from reinsurers are bound by their financial obligations. This means that the element of risk transfer in reinsurance, while still being an essential part of the business transaction, is less directly connected to the underlying

[85] For a discussion of the difference of risks associated with money versus goods see Luhmann (2003, 188).

[86] Alfred Manes distinguished three main categories which can be insured: people (*Personenversicherung*), property (*Sachversicherung*), and capital (*Vermögenswertversicherung*). Reinsurance, in his view, belongs to the last category, along with credit, mortgage, and liability insurance. Manes (1930, 1706). For a discussion see Hollitscher (1931, 5).

risk than in direct insurance. But it is very directly linked with the financial liabilities of the insurance company. Indeed, transferring insured risks could, in theory, be ignored in reinsurance in favour of insuring irregular financial liabilities. Reinsurance was created as a secondary market for risks shortly before Chicago saw the first modern commodity exchange. Further trading beyond reinsurers was, though, relatively limited, with the exception of the Lloyd's and London brokerage market.[87] Securing that material risk is transferred has also been the job of regulators ever since marine insurers abused reinsurance to such purposes and provoked a ban on marine reinsurance in England in 1746.

Reinsurance is an arranged but nonetheless predominantly happy marriage of absorbing insured risks and helping manage clients' finances. Surprisingly, though, matching reinsurers' assets and liabilities often proved to be a more strenuous affair. Managing capital in a sound relation to risk exposure lacked a systematic approach throughout most of reinsurers' history up until the advent of modern finance. As noted in Section 1.4, reinsurance benefited from various risk management strategies developed in the financial world before proprietary ALM models and eventually models of EVM to measure asset risks versus liability risks were created.

The relationship between the reinsurance industry growth and the macroeconomic environment appears to be only general. As Capie describes in Chapter 4, the formative years of professional reinsurance companies happened during a largely calm economic period of the later nineteenth century, which was supported by the exchange-rate stability offered by the gold standard. This proved to be of vital importance to the international nature of the business, as it greatly simplified bookkeeping and capital transfers. The mostly safe investment climate allowed reinsurers to minimize investment risks with bonds and real estate in order to countervail the risk exposure on the underwriting side. On the surface, Capie shows that the macroeconomic environment appears to have little direct influence on reinsurance. This is largely because reinsured risks and catastrophes do not correlate with investment risks. On the other hand, large catastrophes do have enormous financial consequences which can impact the macroeconomy. The San Francisco Earthquake in 1906, for example, provoked a 'monetary aftershock', which, according to some authors, resulted in the 1907 recession, which in turn led to the creation of the Federal Reserve System.[88] The magnitude of the shock may have been due to the huge amounts of insurance payments from Britain, where most of the San Francisco losses had been insured. These insurance payments caused a massive outflow of gold which the Bank of England had to counteract by limiting

[87] Retrocession, i.e. ceding reinsured risks on to third parties (insurers or reinsurers) was common from the start and used as a tool to temporarily expand capacity. However, trading risks several times was to become a feature of the London market only during the twentieth century, reaching a peak during the so-called LMX (London market excess of loss) spiral in the second half of the 1980s. For LMX spiral see e.g. Bain (1998).

[88] K. A. Odell and M. D. Weidenmier (2002) *Real Shock, Monetary Aftershock: The San Francisco Earthquake and the Panic of 1907*. NBER Working Paper: <http://www.nber.org/papers/w9176>.

capital flows to the US in order to maintain the Britain gold standard.[89] The impact of 9/11 on the macroeconomy has been the subject of much research, which has sought to assess the direct role of the attack in the early 2000s recession. But while overall costs of the catastrophe were massive,[90] albeit in terms of GDP percentage not as big as San Francisco,[91] there has not, so far, been any attempt to link the economic downturn of that period to insurance and reinsurance payments.[92]

The economic impact of large catastrophes remains surprisingly under-researched. Single shocks, such as the earthquakes in New Zealand and Chile in 2011, caused damages that amounted to over 20 per cent of the national GDPs.[93] This impacts national budgets and often leads to tax increases and rising debt levels. However, research aimed at capturing aggregate impact of natural catastrophes was belated and remains patchy.[94] A policy paper published by the World Bank in 2009 suggested that, globally, since the 1960s, the economic impact had increased in absolute value but that, once normalized in relation to GDP, the trend of impacts became insignificant.[95] The authors also found that, based on UN data, during the period from 1970 to 2007, disasters had caused at least USD 2 trillion in damages and killed over 2.5 million people. However, while the economic impact of disasters was shown to be rising, the number of fatalities per catastrophe was shown to be decreasing. As the authors noted, 'these observations lead to the fact that disasters have become more menacing to the well-being of societies, while they have become less life-threatening'.[96] The increase of economic impact was largely due to a concentration of values in densely populated or industrialized areas. But it was also due to an increasingly globally interlinked economy. Large catastrophes often cause repercussions far beyond their immediate impact area or national boundaries. The 2011 floods in Thailand, for example, severely disrupted supply chains in computer hard disks, as the world output was temporarily decreased by some 30 per cent.[97] This particular catastrophe also highlighted additional risks of a globalized economy and production outsourcing. As most of the risks had been underwritten in Japan, no adequate risk accumulation control was applied for this particular site lying outside Japan, resulting in heavy losses for the reinsurance industry.

[89] Odell and Weidenmier (2002).

[90] Estimates range from *c.*USD 27 billion immediate losses from the collapse of the towers (Organisation for Economic Co-operation and Development (OECD)) to several trillion (including US military costs in Afghanistan). Insured losses were around USD 40 billion.

[91] Compare 9/11 with 1 per cent of GDP and San Francisco with between 1.3 and 1.8 per cent of GDP. Odell and Weidenmier (2002, 2).

[92] Economic consequences today would differ from those at the time of the San Francisco Earthquake as there is now no need to maintain a gold standard. Also, after 9/11, the US government provided liquidity to banks to restore confidence, while, in 1906, there was no institution in the US to do this.

[93] OECD (2014, 3).

[94] Okuyama (2008, 2). Pioneering work in this field done by Dacy and Kunreuther (1969).

[95] Okuyama and Sahin (2009). [96] Okuyama and Sahin (2009, 5).

[97] A particularly hard-hit area was the manufacturing cluster of computer hard disks responsible for about 45 per cent of the world production.

Reinsurance from the start was designed to absorb such disruptive shocks from catastrophes for the insurance industry. A main function of reinsurance was and continues to be 'to protect [clients'] balance sheets, reduce earnings volatility and make better use of capital'.[98] As Kyrtsis describes in Chapter 6, the financial support function of reinsurance contracts and treaties was refined over time. This could happen through the choice of contracts, which either specified a proportional sharing in the risk or agreed upon a threshold above which reinsurers became liable, as well as a mixture of both. This allowed for reduced volatility and hence provided additional risk capital. In the long run, treaty reinsurance, which was more suited to extending the capacity of clients, experienced a certain decline in importance in favour of products which focused more on peak losses. The latter became essential in protecting against large-scale fluctuations in insurers' results. This became crucial after the Second World War when larger risks not only increased volatility but also required more risk capital. In addition, the relatively rare occurrence of large losses demanded extra capital, which again required additional loading in the premiums. With large amounts of capital already blocked by increasing mass business, especially in the automobiles, such capital requirements were not easy to deal with.

Reinsurers had, in the meantime, become more accustomed to dealing with financial and monetary risks. As Capie points out in Chapter 4, the monetary shocks and the inflation that followed the demise of the gold standard in 1914, and the outbreak of the Great Depression in 1929, which hit globally active reinsurers in several of their markets, were lessons that put financial and monetary risks at least on a par with aggregate underwritten risks. Inflation was not necessarily a bad thing, as it helped some reinsurers create a large volume of business. But the ones who profited most from inflation were reinsurers located in hard currency markets. Strategies to deal with foreign exchange risks mainly consisted of currency congruent matching of assets and liabilities within respective markets. This proved largely successful, but in essence amounted to a balance sheet hedging only. But the large teams of monetary and financial specialists recruited from the 1920s on changed the nature of the business and the companies. After the Second World War, the large increase in mass business, especially the motor business, created a situation which technically produced large losses. The increase in accidents was mainly responsible for turning the combined ratio of insurers and reinsurers negative. Income had to be generated from assets and reinsurance companies were forced to employ more financially skilled personnel. To some degree, reinsurance companies gravitated towards investment companies. This was also translated into business offerings. As Kyrtsis explains, reinsurers in many cases chose to or, more often, were asked or required to leave the financial management of reserves with their clients in so-called deposits or *fonds de roulement*. This pushed reinsurers into reluctantly accepting the role of asset portfolio advisers for their clients.

[98] Swiss Re (2010, 9).

Reinsurance for financial sectors such as credit and surety had begun to develop from the 1920s to form a new line of business which, unlike more traditional lines, was heavily dependent on macroeconomic factors. Credit insurance had been invented by Cuthbert Heath of Lloyd's in late nineteenth-century Britain, but was initially used only for domestic trade. The changing monetary situation in and especially after the First World War provided a massive fillip to this particular branch.[99] The success was mixed. In the 1930s it created the by then largest proportional losses in one line of business for Swiss Re and was discontinued for some years. However, the US market in particular, in later years, proved hugely profitable. But surety reinsurance was to be responsible for the first global reinsurance crisis caused by financial products. During the 1950s, Venezuela saw a huge spread of *avales*: a particular form of surety bonds which were heavily reinsured and eventually lead to a sobering crisis on the London market. Total insured (and mostly reinsured) losses were close to USD 200 million in 1958.[100] Many reinsurers refused to pay as there was plenty evidence of fraudulent behaviour. Sudden changes in the real estate sector proved equally devastating in the mid-1980s when mortgage protection reinsurance suffered from the Texas Savings and Loans Crisis.[101] This created one of Swiss Re's largest losses ever. Problems with mortgage-backed securities (MBS) reoccurred in 2008, along with asset-backed securities (ABS) and credit default swaps.[102]

The need for technical advice with large financial implications, however, came from another front. A large unknown in the results of clients were large losses which had happened but had not yet been reported. So-called 'incurred but not reported' claims (IBNR) upset the balance sheets of insurers, in that possibly heavy losses had occurred but positive results had to be published, which were accordingly taxed. Settling such losses can take a long time, and insurers as well as reinsurers were looking for efficient ways to deal with the irregularities this caused in the balance sheets. During the 1980s, new products were developed to take such fluctuations into better account. Eventually these evolved into pure instruments to manage capital surplus. Such financial reinsurance, or finite re,[103] remained a niche product, especially after it caught the attention of regulators, as some companies were deemed to exclude any kind of material risk transfer.[104] Still, this marked the beginnings of a more conscious financial product

[99] Borscheid (2012e, 51).

[100] SRCA 10.108 185, Guggenbühl, 30; L. M. Avila Merino (2002) *La fianza mercantil*. Caracas: Universidad Católica Andrés Bello, 114–15. As a comparison: Super Typhoon Vera in 1959, still the largest typhoon damage in Japan's history, caused overall losses of *c*.USD 260 million, only a small part of which was insured.

[101] Straumann (2013, 335). See also Chapter 4, this volume.

[102] Straumann (2013, 345).

[103] As a technical term, financial reinsurance is sometimes restricted to pure surplus management products and, by some authors, to describe a much broader financial function of reinsurance products.

[104] Record of Society of Actuaries (1985) *Reinsurance: Current Financial Reporting Topics*, vol. 11, no. 2: <https://www.google.ch/#safe=strict&q=reinsurance+current+financial+reporting+topics+SOA> (accessed 15 September 2015).

offering from reinsurers. As Kyrtsis demonstrates in Chapter 6, it helped tailor contracts more specifically to the respective financial requirements of clients.

Such developments led many in the industry to hail the advent of a new era where reinsurance and financial services were merging,[105] as gradual regulatory changes in the USA during the 1980s had opened new possibilities and paved the way for financial reinsurance. Yet the convergence of the insurance and banking sector was, in the long run, mainly successful in so-called bancassurance, where distribution channels could be shared.[106] For reinsurers this convergence was less pronounced except for one particular area, the so-called ART.

As noted in Section 1.4. and explained in Chapter 11, Hurricane Andrew in 1992 highlighted and aggravated capacity shortage at the time in a drastic way.[107] The catastrophe caused insured losses of around USD 17 billion, more than twice the amount insurance risk managers had anticipated.[108] Several insurers went bankrupt and reinsurers withdrew from the market.[109] Natural catastrophe risks tended to, proportionally, be more reinsured than other risks due to their irregularity and the accumulation of insured risks. In some markets this could reach over 90 per cent. When Hurricane Gilbert struck Jamaica in 1988 it caused *c.*USD 700 million in insured losses, almost 99 per cent of which were reinsured.[110] This explains why the reinsurance industry took a particular interest in finding new capital resources for natural catastrophe cover. As rates increased significantly after Andrew, the business started not only attracting new players and capital but hurricane also triggered the development of new ART products.

The obligation of reinsurers to pay out for losses is conditional and hence reinsurance has, occasionally, been compared to secondary financial markets products. Insurance and reinsurance contracts, especially XL treaties, have, for example, been likened to (call) options, where the option can be exercised at the time of an insured or reinsured loss.[111] Reinsurance was interpreted as conditional money by Richard L. Sandor during his time as chief economist at the Chicago Board of Trade (CBOT), and, shortly after inventing financial futures, he published a paper on the possibility of reinsurance futures. Sandor and his co-author Robert C. Goshay, an insurance academic, saw 'striking parallels in [the] purpose and function' of financial futures and reinsurance but significant differences in their institutional frameworks.[112] The parallels were seen mainly in the future obligation to assume a liability or a right (call) as well as in reinsurance being a risk market that was supposed to establish a fair market value of risk. The long-term business relation between reinsurers and their clients, and the elaborate process of individually tailoring products and finding prices, led the

[105] Marbacher (1989); Swiss Re, *sigma*, 1992; Swiss Re (2004, 13ff.).

[106] See Gugerli (2013).

[107] Chilchinsky and Heal (1998, n.p.): worldwide reinsurance capacity dropped by 30 per cent between 1989 and 1993, over 20 per cent of which the authors attribute to Andrew.

[108] Swiss Re (2011, 7).

[109] Chilchinsky and Heal (1998, n.p.).

[110] Group of Thirty (2006, 11).

[111] Marbacher (1989, 284).

[112] Goshay and Sandor (1973, 56).

authors to argue that market forces did not play well in reinsurance. In their view, real price competition was absent.[113] Reinsurance futures then, as conceived by the two, were mainly supposed to help establish a fair price for risk. Enhancing the secondary market would facilitate a move from negotiated to competitive markets. Still, according to the authors, a standardized secondary market for risks could arrange risks into larger classifications and thus create a more homogenous actuarial basis. All this, however, would be at the expense of personal interaction, tailored products, and selective price finding. Turning reinsurance into homogenous products in order to create a cash market for risk required standardized classes of risk. These might be possible in, for example, windstorms, which differed according to region, if a major market such as the USA were separated into geographically varying risk regions. This, combined with a set of indices, ultimately would allow individuals with cash to buy and sell reinsurance.

The industry was not alarmed. Possibly because it took a long time before it noticed what was going on in Chicago. But the matter also proved somewhat more complicated. Understanding the underlying risk required both expertise and resources. This meant that informed buyers were hard to come by. Those in the know shunned the expenses and efforts of assessing the traded risks. In the 1980s, when Swiss Re received a call from Chicago for help building a natural catastrophe index the enquiry was turned down, not for fear of losing business to the capital markets but out of scepticism towards reinsurance futures and possibly modern finance in general.[114] Increases in underwriting capacity had been mentioned by Goshay and Sandor but were only briefly treated as a welcome side effect of reinsurance futures. But it was this additional capacity that sparked the trade in alternative products after Hurricane Andrew. More than any other product it turned ILS into one of the reinsurance industry's greatest recent innovations.

That reinsurers should excel in this field was also due to the fact that the informed market was relatively small. This meant that exchange markets for such products soon ran into difficulties. Insurers who wanted to obtain cover on the financial markets rather than through reinsurance were forced to realize that there were few informed buyers and that the cost of acquiring relevant risk information was disproportional to the cost of the transactions. The CBOT started trading in 1992 but met with low interest and eventually gave up trading in 2000 after trying out several products such as futures and options. Other exchanges experienced similar problems.[115] Over-the-counter (OTC) trading, on the other hand, where reinsurers could offer their products, were more successful. Some authors attribute this to the information exchange which Goshay and Sandor thought could be eliminated by larger aggregates. But, for an insurance company, the decisive factor for placing their risks was ultimately a financial one. It turned out that reinsurers were offering risk expertise at a more competitive price and in a more efficient way than other financial institutions.[116]

[113] Some competition was acknowledged for the Lloyd's market and the role of brokers. Goshay and Sandor (1973, 59).

[114] Interview with Josef Marbacher, former chief economist at Swiss Re, 15 February 2013.

[115] Gibson, Habib, and Ziegler (2007).

[116] Gibson, Habib, and Ziegler (2007, 3).

Transaction cost and risk services proved to be decisive factors in making or breaking it in the early reinsurance futures and options market.

Although the rise of ILS was slow, it continued steadily receiving some boosts, with subsequent catastrophes such as 9/11, Hurricane Katrina, and several earthquakes in the late twentieth and early twenty-first centuries. In the meantime, it expanded into life products as well.[117] Katrina, however, differed from earlier large catastrophes in one peculiar aspect. The market was very quick at establishing sufficient new capacity within a short time, as Lechner, Haueter, and Kenny describe in Chapter 11. Some believe that too much capacity was made available as alternative players wanted to profit from the surge in prices.[118] Catastrophe models had delivered a poor performance in New Orleans but, once they had been recalibrated, alternative investors such as hedge funds and pension funds started being more confident. This started an inflow of capital of a size that the industry had never seen before. By 2016, capacity shortage, the very reason why ILS became important, had virtually disappeared. But this did not spell the end for alternative products. Help came from somewhat unexpected quarters—the recent financial crisis. During and in the wake of the 2008 crunch, ILS made a stunning performance as they were not correlated with the overall economy.[119] ILS compared very favourably with corporate bonds of similar credit quality and other financial benchmarks. In addition, ILS provided a source of diversification, as they are largely uncorrelated with other asset classes. This fuelled the demand from investors, leading to the strong growth of the ILS market. On the other hand, risk, oddly enough, has become a relative scarcity, at least in relation to the capital available to hedge it. As Capie points out in Chapter 4, all this keeps providing sufficient appeal to alternative capital holders. While reinsurers welcomed additional capacity for a long time, there are now signs that this may turn against them. Rather than investing via reinsurers' products, the competition for risk is leading players to seek direct access to marketable risk. Additionally, this particular function of alternative capital has been described as increasingly resembling traditional reinsurance.[120] This is felt in areas such as Florida, where Bermudan-based firms provide most of the cover via alternative products, while the leading professional reinsurers are holding back. Some have argued that the trend to transfer risk to the capital markets and the bundling of risks creates more opaque risks not dissimilar to those of the subprime crisis. There have even been warnings of a financial collapse of the reinsurance industry due to such new products.[121] But bundling risks has been the very foundation of insurance and reinsurance since their inception. Industry experts argue that fears of the reinsurance market collapsing as a

[117] For a short history see Millette et al. (2002).

[118] <http://www.artemis.bm/blog/2015/08/31/legacy-of-hurricane-katrina-reinsurance-capacity-bubble-moodys/> (accessed 15 October 2015).

[119] See Figure A.5 in Appendix.

[120] <http://www.artemis.bm/blog/2014/05/09/what-if-alternative-capital-was-indistinguishable-from-traditional-reinsurance/> (accessed 15 October 2015).

[121] Jarzabkowski et al. (2015, 178–82).

consequence of packaging risks are greatly exaggerated.[122] They stress the fact that the risks are not only fully collateralized but, unlike subprime products, ILS undergo a rigorous risk assessment. Also unlike banking, intercompany business is very restricted, preventing a contamination similar to the credit crunch.

The increased focus on the role of capital in reinsurance has left its mark on regulation. Reinsurance is a business where size, and with it capital, help distribute and even out risks on a broader level. This means that size matters exponentially, as growing size attracts even more business and risk capital becomes relatively cheaper. Smaller insurance businesses feel this in an adverse way. The smaller the insurance, the more inefficient the capital. Regulation has increasingly focused on such capital requirements. While this is understandable, it has been to the detriment of smaller insurers who, as Capie explains in Chapter 4, will be needing more risk capital support from reinsurers.

Over the past 150 years, dealing with risks has become increasingly financial in its character. This happened in two areas in particular. On the one hand, reinsurance products have become more financially sophisticated. On the other hand, as catastrophes were increasingly felt and measured to have an enormous economic impact, the business appeal of hedging such risks has grown into very big business, not only for traditional players. The value of risk per se has considerably increased with the availability of new products. Risk management has moved up a step along with the size of insured risks. Detailed evaluations of individual risks are gravitating towards larger risk categories and indices applied in alternative products.

## 1.6 Risk, Regulation, and Politics

Historically, the regulation of the reinsurance industry has never been an easy task. The technical complexity of the business, international intricacies, the invisibility of reinsurance services, and the financial success of the industry have challenged governments into adopting measures that span from an encouraging laissez-faire attitude to state appropriation and monopolization. Perhaps no other industry has been exposed to a more contrasting legislative environment. As Vec observes in Chapter 8, a general trend can, not surprisingly, be detected in net reinsurance exporting countries adopting favourable legislation. Net importing nations, on the other hand, often resorted to a variety of state interventions. These ranged from requiring deposits of risk reserves to punitive taxing of foreign companies, compulsory ceding to local reinsurance companies, and state reinsurance. More liberal regulation was often based on views that no consumer protection was required in reinsurance. Possibly, as Vec further observes, a general lack of knowledge about the industry also led to little or unspecific regulation.

[122] 'Catastrophe Bonds Pioneer Hits Back at Book' (*Financial Times*, 3 May 2015).

Considerations about systemic relevance, with repercussions on individuals, only started appearing during the current century. Vec attributes this to a partial convergence of the reinsurance industry with the banking sector.

In many markets reinsurance went largely unregulated throughout its history. As Röder points out in Chapter 7, early attempts in the seventeenth century aimed at making reinsurance compatible with existing commercial law rather than establishing a specific legal environment. Subsequently, reinsurance was often treated under legal aspects designed for direct insurance. Reinsurers thus went about creating their own framework, which, in some instances, clashed with traditional views of legal proponents, as Röder elaborates. A mutual trust environment then, as described by Pearson in Chapter 3, was imperative in maintaining a common basis for doing business. Vec, in Chapter 8, observes that this fostered a self-regulating environment which, mostly successfully, sought to keep any regulatory and legal interference at arm's length. State regulation and treating reinsurance under insurance law could, in fact, have negative effects on the development of local reinsurance industries. The USA provides one example where a little knowledge about reinsurance proved proverbially dangerous. The requirement for mono-line companies aimed at protecting end consumers. But with reinsurance it defeated its purpose as it prevented further spreading of risk and proved to be a severe hindrance to the development of a local industry.[123] Restrictions on allowing direct writing companies to assume other companies' surplus were further detrimental, and dependence on foreign reinsurance increased. Excessive regulation of marine reinsurance in the eighteenth century led to an idiosyncratic development of secondary risk hedging in England. As Clark (Chapter 2) and Pearson (Chapter 3) describe, marine reinsurance fell victim to anti-gambling legislation in 1746. This allowed co-insurance practices and Lloyd's to gradually dominate the market, and prevented the formation of a significant Continental-style reinsurance industry for decades.

Private reinsurance was also perceived as a positive force by some states. Governments inevitably function as insurers of last resort where private risk capital falls short. More liberal economies therefore had an interest in supporting private reinsurance in providing risk capital. This made even more sense if claims payments were made by foreign reinsurers. Bringing in liquidity from outside the economy where disaster struck could, to some extent, alleviate government borrowing. Reinsurance thus constitutes an important link between the insured and governments. Reinsurers have been described as 'perhaps the purest representatives of market fundamentalism as the cornerstones of political economies'.[124] Governments' support for reinsurance solutions from the private sector became reality in areas such as nuclear power. Eventually, a public–private sharing of risks was introduced to cover atomic risks, as Daston describes in Chapter 9. Also natural catastrophes, including floods, traditionally left to governments, are increasingly covered by private risk takers. But other risks such as

[123] Hotchkiss (1914). [124] Ericson and Doyle (2004, 247).

war, civil commotion, and terrorism still remain virtually uninsurable by the private sector. The most common form for states to cover such risks has been through ex post disaster relief programmes. More recently, government lending also has assumed an important role in supporting economies after disasters.

The ambivalent treatment of reinsurance by many governments is not readily explained. Poor understanding of the risk economy practised by the industry may, according to some, account for extreme state intervention. More importantly, however, both insurance and reinsurance touch on a fundamental political question about the role of the state in protecting citizens. The state combines both what has been described as a social contract as well as the fundamentals of political economies. Social insurance or welfare, in the view of François Ewald, was responsible for shifting society from having duties to having rights, creating what he termed *la société assurantielle*. Just how much insurance or reinsurance the state should provide is a never-ending political issue. Reinsurers, depending on the situation, could adopt more Rhenish arguments and support government intervention when facing risks which could not be adequately rated. In some such instances, states adopted reinsurance logic. President Roosevelt introduced state insurance and reinsurance to provide adequate cover for marine war risks in 1940.[125] The quote mentioned regarding reinsurers being the cornerstones of political economies was written in the context of discussing the establishment of a state support for the insurance industry after 9/11. After the attack, reinsurers had started excluding terrorism from their portfolios. George W. Bush attributed the economic slump in the immediate wake of 9/11 to the lack of reinsurance supply, and passed the Terrorism Insurance Act (TRIA) to provide a state reinsurance backstop for insurers.[126] The Act compelled insurers to accept terrorist risks. Foreign reinsurers, on the other hand, are, in theory, free to walk away from government sanctions. The attractive size of the US market, however, diminished the appeal of such sanctions. TRIA was supported by reinsurance representatives in order to secure a healthy direct insurance industry and also because most US proposals for state reinsurance were designed to be temporary. The idea was that this would allow the industry to catch up and develop new products to eventually replace state offerings. But with its randomness and a high probability of correlation with further terrorist attacks, terrorism still largely defies risk modelling techniques. The Act was renewed by the Obama Administration in 2015.

In some instances, reinsurance was felt to interfere with roles traditionally played by the state rather than supporting them. While governments have an interest in private industries carrying as much risk as possible themselves, they, at times, felt they were

[125] The bill was passed in 1941 and became effective as of 1942. Franklin D. Roosevelt (1942) 'Executive Order 9054 Establishing the War Shipping Administration', 7 February, in Gerhard Peters and John T. Woolley, *The American Presidency Project*: <http://www.presidency.ucsb.edu/ws/?pid=16216> (accessed 15 October 2015).

[126] George W. Bush (2002) 'Remarks on Signing the Terrorism Risk Insurance Act of 2002', 26 November, in Gerhard Peters and John T. Woolley, *The American Presidency Project*: <http://www.presidency.ucsb.edu/ws/?pid=73349> (accessed 15 October 2015).

missing out on the revenues such a business might provide, especially if premium payments went abroad. Several attempts to stem foreign dominance in reinsurance were and are still being made. The US budget plan for 2016 considered eliminating cost deduction for US insurers when reinsuring with foreign companies.[127] What mainly worried governments, especially in nations with net imports of reinsurance, was what they perceived as an imbalance of payments. Such considerations had already been brought forward by the founders of both Cologne Re and Swiss Re, who wanted to become independent of foreign reinsurance capacity. Their arguments were mostly aimed at investors but politicians later adopted their reasoning.

State insurance has a long history. Often insurance was used, and sometimes abused, for government borrowing. In the seventeenth and eighteenth centuries, tontines, a form of life annuity, were used by various European governments for short-term financing,[128] often for military purposes. Russian finance minister Sergei Witte may have been the first politician to use reinsurance to engineer the capital account of a nation. As Russia adopted the gold standard in the 1890s, he tried to curb the outflow of reinsurance payments in gold by founding a national reinsurance company.[129] The company was very short-lived due to disagreements among the founding partners. But the state also proved to be a poor manager of such an endeavour. A successor company suffered from difficulties arising from an obligation to accept defined amounts of risks, which resulted in mainly bad risks being transferred. The state example may, though, as one author argues, have led to private foundations, which, in the early twentieth century, turned Russia into a net exporter of reinsurance.[130] By 1913, the country had become number two provider of the world markets after Germany. Reinsurance continued to be of national concern during the Soviet period. From 1922 on, international financial ties were secured not only by the first international Soviet bank Ruskombank, but also by the state-owned insurance company Gosstrakh, which, besides its domestic business, insured all foreign trade and also accepted reinsurance. As the two main Russian reinsurers had defected to Denmark, Gosstrakh, in 1926, started accepting foreign reinsurance business.[131] During the peak of the Cold War, Ingosstrakh, founded in 1947 to take on foreign insurance and reinsurance business, opened offices in Soviet-influenced economies such as Egypt, Syria, and Cuba. Also, the People's Republic of China found it impossible to maintain some international ties for transport and trade without insurance, except for the years during the Cultural Revolution.[132] Foreign reinsurance provided the most efficient hedging against international liabilities in hard currencies.

[127] Department of the Treasury (2016) *General Explanations of the Administration's Fiscal Year 2016 Revenue Proposals*: <http://www.treasury.gov/resource-center/tax-policy/Documents/General-Explanations-FY2016.pdf> (accessed 15 October 2015).

[128] Weir (1989). [129] Veh (1927, 14); Petrov (2012, 224).

[130] Hollitscher (1931, 107). [131] *The Review*, 1928, 90.

[132] Interview with Wang En-Shao, former chairman of China Insurance Company in UK, 18 June 2007.

State insurance in the form of the modern welfare state had been introduced by German chancellor Otto von Bismarck in the 1880s. Rather than being an act of compassion, the move was earmarked by Bismarck's *Realpolitik*. To some degree it turned the liberal ideas of enlightenment on which insurance had been based upside down. Bismarck's idea of social insurance provided by the state was to prevent civil unrest by giving the labouring classes something to look forward too. Accordingly, state-run insurance was strongly opposed by the political left in favour of mutual insurance and alternative insurance provided by friendly societies and similar associations. Such alternatives were seen as more promising of radical and all-encompassing political change. Fascist and other totalitarian regimes, however, later embraced the idea of state welfare, as historian Robert Paxton observed in several writings. Controlling insurance and reinsurance, with some exceptions, became a hallmark of planned economies and dictatorships.[133] Italy led the way for reinsurance in 1912 when life insurers were instructed to cede 40 per cent of their business to state-owned Istituto Nazionale delle Assicurazioni. Along with financial considerations, national pride may have played a role in this as well as other cases, such as Chile, where the Caja Reaseguradora de Chile was founded in 1927 during the de facto dictatorship of General Ibáñez del Campo.[134] War in Europe may account for the high number of nationalization projects during the 1930s and 1940s.

Another wave of state interest in reinsurance started with the de-colonialization from the 1960s on. In many cases this happened at the expense of British companies, which were often victim to the anti-British sentiments in former colonies. It enabled Continental European reinsurers to profit from new markets opening up,[135] but barely any local reinsurance operations were founded initially. The UN wanted to change this and, in 1964, initiated the United Nations Conference on Trade and Development (UNCTAD) in Geneva. The same year a resolution was adopted to investigate the role of insurance and reinsurance in the economic progress of developing markets.[136] The committee for 'Improvement of the invisible trade of developing countries and financing for expansion of international trade' found that there was a lack of pooling national surplus risk locally before reinsuring it in developed countries. Local reinsurance was identified as a prerequisite for a healthy insurance industry to develop, which again was a prerequisite for a healthy economy.[137] A recommendation to support the

[133] Total or partial state monopolies of reinsurance were established in Italy (1912), USSR (1920), Chile (1927), Turkey (1929), Iran (1935), Brazil (1939), Japan (1940), Argentina (1948), and Indonesia (1967). State-run reinsurance companies were founded in Greece (1940) and France (1946). State participation (partial or total ownership) in reinsurance companies happened in Spain (1932), Portugal (1936), Mexico (1940), Egypt (1961), and Korea (1963). Projects to nationalize reinsurance were made but did not materialize in Hungary (1932), Czechoslovakia (1933), Ireland (1936), China (1937), Spain (1939), Luxembourg (1938), and Yugoslavia (1940). (Compiled from SRCA DL-04499-001 and various Swiss Re board of directors' reports.)

[134] Nationalist arguments to favour local insurance over foreign competition were often applied in various markets. See Borscheid and Haueter (2012, 189–212, 495–521, 578–98, 620–44).

[135] For Munich Re's increasing business in India and Pakistan see Bähr and Kopper (2015, 278).

[136] Couroux and Outreville (1992, 234).

[137] UNCTAD (1964, 55).

growth of local insurance and reinsurance in developing countries was presented in that year. Differing views on whether such national reinsurance operations should be state run or not (with developing countries being in favour of state monopolies and developed countries against) were not solved, but the recommendation was approved with a hundred votes in favour, one against, and twelve abstentions.[138]

The single vote against had come from the USA. The reasons for doing so do not become apparent in the discussions recorded by UNCTAD.[139] The American government had, though, expressed severe doubts over state involvement in reinsurance on their own territory already earlier on. President Truman, for example, suggested a state reinsurer to cover unemployment insurance in 1949 and another for flood damages in 1951, neither of which ever came into existence.[140] In 1955, President Eisenhower presented a recommendation to Congress to create a national reinsurance institute to cover health care.[141] The recommendation joined the ranks of many other failures in the long history of US health-care debates. Interestingly, it was not only rejected by the right and the representatives of the insurance industry, who feared, as Eisenhower expressed it, 'the camel's nose in their tent', but also by the far left, who saw a state reinsurance office as a way around state health insurance.[142] But the idea of state intervention in reinsurance never quite disappeared. The USA saw new state proposals during the Clinton era to cover natural catastrophes.[143] So far, it appears that mainly war- and terrorism-related reinsurance institutions were successful in US Congress.

[138] UNCTAD (1966, Annex I, 1–2).

[139] John A. Bushnell who served as 'international economist for the U.S. Mission in Geneva' during the 1960s, later said in an interview: 'UNCTAD staff did not seem to understand how reinsurance works. UNCTAD staff argued that reinsurance should be placed within the developing country. Of course, if there were a big disaster in a small country, all the insurance companies would be bankrupted and claims would not be covered. The advantage of placing reinsurance on a worldwide basis was precisely the spreading of risks among many countries to assure that even the biggest losses happening at the same time could be covered.' Library of Congress (1997) *The Association for Diplomatic Studies and Training Foreign Affairs Oral History Project: Interview with John A. Bushnell*, 19 December: <http://lcweb2.loc.gov/service/mss/mfdip/2007/2007bus01/2007bus01.pdf> (accessed 2 October 2015).

[140] Harry S. Truman (1949) 'Special Message to the Congress: The President's Midyear Economic Report', 11 July, in Gerhard Peters and John T. Woolley, *The American Presidency Project*: <http://www.presidency.ucsb.edu/ws/?pid=13240> (accessed 15 October 2015).Harry S. Truman (1951) 'Statement by the President Upon Signing the Flood Rehabilitation Act', 24 October, in Gerhard Peters and John T. Woolley, *The American Presidency Project*: <http://www.presidency.ucsb.edu/ws/?pid=13964> (accessed 15 October 2015).

[141] Dwight D. Eisenhower (1955) 'Special Message to the Congress Recommending a Health Program', 31 January, in Gerhard Peters and John T. Woolley, *The American Presidency Project*: <http://www.presidency.ucsb.edu/ws/?pid=10399> (accessed 15 October 2015). Eisenhower also suggested a state reinsurance program to support flood insurance in 1956. See Meier (1988, 114–15). Lyndon B. Johnson proposed a similar idea of state reinsurance in 1968. Lyndon B. Johnson (1968) 'Special Message to the Congress on Urban Problems: 'The Crisis of the Cities', 22 February, in Gerhard Peters and John T. Woolley, *The American Presidency Project*: <http://www.presidency.ucsb.edu/ws/?pid=29386> (accessed 15 October 2015).

[142] Graham (2015, 89).

[143] Brown et al. (2004, 6).

Among the abstentions in 1964 in Geneva were Switzerland and Germany,[144] the two main providers of reinsurance. In the view of large reinsurance companies, state reinsurance suffered from several drawbacks. As had already been the case with the nineteenth-century Russian reinsurer, compulsory ceding of risks led to poorer risk assessment of insurers and to a certain danger of moral hazard in ceding on mainly bad risks. Many models of state reinsurance involved primary insurers as holders of shares or other stakes. This doubled the exposure of ceding companies in case of reinsurers' defaults, as, being clients, they would lose both claims payments and, at the same time being shareholders in the reinsurance company, they would suffer from a devaluation of their shares. Another issue discussed at several UNCTAD meetings was the problem with risk distribution. Small economies and insurance markets could not provide diversified risk portfolios to local reinsurers. This was also acknowledged by representatives of the developing world. A solution was seen in cross-border pooling. This led to foundations such as the African Reinsurance Corporation, which was set up in Cameroon in 1973 by thirty-six member states on the recommendation of the African Development Bank. A similar institution, the Asian Reinsurance Corporation, was established in 1979 on the recommendation of the UN's Economic and Social Commission for Asia and the Pacific (ESCAP).

African Re and Asian Re proved more successful than the projected national reinsurers. But all such projects were heavily dependent on retrocession. This was due both to local capacity problems as well as the necessity to spread risks more globally. While national reinsurers took away business from established reinsurers, they were still forced to retrocede substantial parts of their business to reinsurers established in the global markets. Swiss Re saw both a threat and a business opportunity in this, and early on decided to participate in such institutions. It assisted in both the foundation of the Caja Reaseguradora in Chile and of Milli Reinsurance in Turkey, and acquired stakes in both operations. To some degree, state reinsurance helped alleviate a large amount of administrative work from international reinsurers by bundling risks locally. Mostly, though, reinsurers remained sceptical about accepting business from such organizations. The effect of compulsory ceding to state reinsurers was felt to have negative impact on the quality of direct writing companies, eventually preventing conducting sound business with them. This was felt in Argentina where a semi-private reinsurer, Instituto Mixto Argentino de Reaseguros (IMAR), had been founded in 1948 and transformed into the state-owned monopoly Instituto Nacional de Reaseguros (INdeR) in 1952. High acceptation levels of these organizations meant that capital requirements for insurers sank to almost zero and they could accept risks without assessing them. Combined with tax disadvantages for foreign insurers, this led to a bubble of local insurance foundations. According to *The Review*, the INdeR used its

[144] Switzerland only joined the UN in 2002 but had observer status long before and was a member of UNCTAD.

state monopoly to assume a role similar to a central bank for insurers and interfere with insurers' operations.[145]

Poor risk control and a lack of expertise in developing insurance industries were more problems identified by the UNCTAD committee. The importance of knowledge transfer and technical support from the developed world was repeatedly stressed. The committee saw a responsibility for reinsurers from developed economies to become more active in training insurance workers from developing economies.[146] A certain irony, however, became apparent in promoting national reinsurance operations which, in effect, prevented direct contact of internationally experienced reinsurers with direct writing companies. It hardly provided encouragement for reinsurers to train clients while being denied doing direct business with them. Also, it deprived the former of any first-hand information about the risk quality and prevented any corrective measures from which local companies could learn. Global reinsurers still, however, perceived there to be a vested interest in training fledgling insurance industries and thus improving the quality of underwriting—and also establishing a trust relationship with direct clients. Swiss Re, for example, had already opened the Swiss Insurance Training Centre (SITC) to transfer underwriting knowledge to developing economies in 1960. UNCTAD, however, preferred more neutral instances, and, in the 1980s, started promoting the role of reinsurance brokers in both spreading industry knowledge and supporting developing economies in finding the right reinsurance partners. More recently, governments in developing economies are directly turning to large reinsurers again to gain access to private solutions for micro-insurance and alternative reinsurance. One promising solution is seen in parametric reinsurance. Automatically triggered claims payments in such products aim at reducing time-consuming and complicated administrative work. In developing economies, such administration would often propel insurance and reinsurance costs out of proportion.

Disenchantment with state intervention started growing in the 1990s in Eastern European transition economies. Many of these fledgling economies still introduced measures to curb the outflow of reinsurance premiums by allowing foreign business only once local capacity had been used up. But, by 1997, only two countries, Russia and Romania, had briefly considered setting up a state-owned reinsurer.[147] At least in the Baltic countries local reinsurance started growing during the early transition phase, but later started shrinking again. This has been attributed to early-stage local reinsurers often being used for tax avoidance purposes, a practice which was increasingly curbed by regulatory changes.[148] While co-insurance practices also emerged in several markets, a majority of markets increasingly made use of international reinsurance. Many markets saw an abundance of small and often poorly capitalized insurers emerge, all of

[145] Blasco Martel and Rabetino (2012, 635). For market interventions by the IMAR, see Zappino (2007).

[146] UNCTAD (1964, 55); UNCTAD (1966, 11–12).

[147] Falush (1997, IV.B.8, IV.A).

[148] Leonard (2004).

which were heavily dependent on foreign reinsurance. With a subsequent investment wave of foreign and well-capitalized insurers, the need for reinsurance started diminishing again.[149] For at least the initial phase, the importance of reinsurers and brokers as knowledge transfer channels may also have been a decisive factor.[150] Currency considerations were another factor and a difficult one for state-run companies to counter. State monopolies themselves, in fact, had a long history of taking out foreign reinsurance and retrocession to hedge liabilities from foreign trade in hard currencies.[151] Reinsurance continued providing much-needed currency hedging for transition economies.

Next to national politics, geopolitics also had a massive influence on the development of reinsurance. The direct impact of wars on reinsurance business was limited. This had to do with war exclusions but also with lower industrial productivity, which reduced claims. Even life reinsurance fared economically well during wartime, as most war casualties were among young people who had not taken out life insurance. Along with monetary complications, sanctions against trading with the enemy were responsible for the large temporary shifts in global reinsurance supply. Germany, most of all nations, felt this during both world wars. The First World War, as Röder points out in Chapter 7, also marked the first direct state intervention into the idiosyncrasies of reinsurance contracts, which were nullified by the Trading with the Enemy Acts. Also, the effect of war economies on exchange rates heavily influenced the distribution of reinsurance supply and demand, as explained in Section 1.3. Trade agreements and economic unions, on the other hand, often facilitated parts of international business. In some cases they resulted in transnational oppositions to foreign reinsurers, but mostly the industry profited from trade agreements and economic unions. During the post-war era, Swiss Re, for example, expanded its global business by setting up shop in Commonwealth countries, from where it serviced other nations.

As Röder points out, the second half of the twentieth century saw new actors appearing in insurance and reinsurance regulation. The European Economic Union may have been the main political body to slowly allow reinsurance regulation to percolate. It gradually introduced a framework for facilitating cross-border insurance operations and finally opened a common European market. A first insurance directive was issued in 1973.[152] Subsequent directives had a considerable influence on abolishing die-hard insurance monopolies and state-imposed cartels in Western Europe. European Union (EU) standards, including bans on state monopolies, were also imposed on new members from Eastern Europe.[153] All this also benefited reinsurers. Not only were they now dealing with an increasingly homogenized European insurance market, but they also profited, for example, from simpler licensing requirements and simplified capital transfers. The standardization of a European legal framework, the deregulation

[149] Leonard (2004, 110). [150] Falush (1997, VII.A, VIII).
[151] Bähr and Kopper (2015, 277); Falush (1997, VII.A). [152] 73/239/EEC.
[153] Borscheid 2012e, 61.

of the insurance market, but also the coming into force of the General Agreement on Trade in Services (GATTS), and a rapid growth in equity capital provoked a consolidation wave of hitherto unseen dimensions. Reinsurance was not as much affected as direct insurance, but players from outside Europe found it easier to navigate the European markets. Notably, General Re started an alliance with the world's oldest reinsurer, Cologne Re, in 1994. Eventually, they formed a global reinsurance force in Warren Buffett's Berkshire Hathaway Inc., as discussed in Chapter 11. However, Continental European reinsurers also made more headway in the American market. Munich Re acquired American Re for USD 3.3 billion in 1996, while nine years later Swiss Re paid USD 6.8 billion for General Electrics' Insurance Solutions.

Increased regulation of the reinsurance industry has coincided with the industries increased public appearance over the last twenty years. In Chapter 8, Vec quotes German insurance academic Alfred Manes, who, in 1913, said: 'reinsurance takes place behind closed doors' (Manes 1913, 456 § 60). These doors have gradually been opened, albeit somewhat reluctantly. Governments were occasionally allowed some insight into reinsurers' business, especially when capital transfers had to be negotiated with clearing banks or licences had to be obtained. But judging from the often unfavourable treatment of especially foreign companies, the industry may not always have performed very well in lobbying their interests. This is all the more surprising as reinsurance, including foreign business, was, even by critical institutions such as the UNCTAD, seen as a vital element in the development of economies. Reinsurers' involvement in the climate debate in the 1990s, however, benefited the industry's reputation, as it credibly warned against global warming issues from an essentially entrepreneurial point of view. While the discussion at the time was more academically led, the subject has increasingly become dominated by politics, pushing reinsurers into taking a political position.

## 1.7 Risk, Responsibility, and Sustainability

The entrepreneurs who built the reinsurance industry from the nineteenth century saw risk as a profitable opportunity. This did not mean, however, that the new industry could not have a positive social value. The economist William Baumol has distinguished between entrepreneurship which had a positive outcome for societies, like innovation, which he termed productive, and entrepreneurship which had other outcomes, whether unproductive (rent-seeking) or destructive (corruption and crime).[154] Has reinsurance been beneficial to society?

[154] W. J. Baumol (1990) 'Entrepreneurship: Productive, Unproductive, and Destructive', *Journal of Political Economy* 98: 5, Part 1, 892–3.

The chapters in this volume do not directly address this question, and for the good reason that any answer would involve a critique of the capitalist system itself. Consciously taking risk is a requirement for modern capitalism. A number of scholars have suggested that the insurance industry as a whole encourages people to take on too much risk.[155] Yet if one accepts a market-oriented approach to progress, insurance and reinsurance help societies progress by facilitating the change from risk avoidance to risk taking in social and economic modern society. The insurance industry as a whole can be seen as having facilitated the movement of risk management from a personal concern to a societal contract. Reinsurance made this contract global.

The very nature of the reinsurance industry has meant that it has not been involved in some of the worst episodes in the history of capitalism. It was not a chemicals company which polluted the air, or a large employer of labour involved in bad practices. It had, therefore, limited opportunities to do bad things, though it might be regarded as supporting such practices at one remove. In Nazi Germany, Munich Re mainly profited from cancelled life insurance policies of Nazi victims.[156] Swiss Re, in turn, during the Nazi period cooperated with Munich Re and other German and Italian reinsurers in a German-initiated association to cover European large risks.[157] Many reinsurers such as Munich Re, Swiss Re, or Mercantile & General argued that stopping doing business in politically doubtful environments, such as apartheid-era South Africa between the 1950s and the 1980s, would eventually be harmful to the economy of such countries and thus to the population.[158]

Over the last 200 years reinsurers have had a special role in the capitalist system. As the industry developed, it had a vested interest in preventing excessive risks, while also providing complex societies with a mechanism to limit the damage which natural and other catastrophes could inflict. Even sceptics of multinational enterprises found the reinsurance industry useful. During the 1970s and 1980s—the high point of criticism of global corporations at the UN and elsewhere—the authors of various reports by UNCTAD and UNCTC identified reinsurance as one industry which emerging

[155] A detailed discussion of moral hazard is provided by Carol A. Heimer (1985) *Reactive Risk and Rational Action: Managing Moral Hazards in Insurance Contracts*. Berkeley, CA: University of California Press. For moral hazard in the reinsurance industry, see Doherty and Smetters (2002).

[156] Bähr and Kopper (2015, 170–2). See Bähr and Kopper (2015, 147–244) for Munich Re during the Second World War. For reinsurance (Munich Re and Swiss Re especially) in Germany during the Second World War see also Feldman (2001, 2004); Karlen et al. (2002); and Straumann (2013).

[157] Overall, however, Swiss Re's scepticism with regard to the Nazi regime prevailed. It is worth noting that the historian of Allianz singled out the position taken by Swiss Re's general manager Emil Bebler at the time as one of the few highlights of that era. Feldman (2001, 386–7, 380–3).

[158] Bähr and Kopper (2015, 315–17). Swiss Re's engagement in South Africa started in 1950. It has to be pointed out that especially Munich Re, but also Swiss Re, adopted increasingly progressive behaviours, with Munich Re renting out offices to the African National Congress (ANC) when it came to power and Swiss Re offering equal employment conditions for non-white employees. Bähr and Kopper (2015, 317); Interview, 6 October 2008, with Werner Stricker (managing director of Swiss Re Southern Africa from 1964–83) and Lenz Keel (chief executive and managing director Swiss Re Southern Africa from 1983–92).

countries could profitably deploy to assist their development.[159] Indeed, most criticism has focused on the ownership of the industry rather than its function. Many post-colonial countries considered creating their own reinsurance institutions, recognizing that the function of the industry was valuable, but that ownership by foreign private actors was not in their societal interest. However, government involvement had, usually, only limited success, except for areas which can/could not be covered by private corporations, as discussed in Section 1.6.

The high concentration levels in the industry raise questions of excessive pricing. As shown in Figure A.2 in the Appendix, the global market share of the top nine reinsurance companies was 43 per cent in 2015. As described in Section 1.5, Goshay and Sandor in the 1970s challenged the pricing of risks by reinsurers.[160] But their criticism reflected a misunderstanding of the industry, because the reinsurance buyer and seller community will always remain relatively small and limited. The true value of reinsurance should rather be seen as its ability to rate risks. Liquid markets for risk may inflate or deflate prices beyond sense. As the reinsurance business is hierarchical, the relationship between insurers and reinsurer is mainly vertical. This is evident in negotiated price finding.[161] It also means that the intra-industry connectivity is limited.[162] This again limits the potential for industry-wide shocks triggered by local events. This stands in stark contrast to banks, which depend heavily on interbank business.

It is evident that the industry has not helped itself in the past regarding its public image. It was a clubby business, at least up until the 1990s, which celebrated secrecy. There were few if any attempts to communicate with stakeholders. Reinsurers were not necessarily always nice guys. In 1965 they were described in *The Review* as: '[ . . . ] those ashen-faced, steely-eyed individuals who sit quietly in the dimly lighted, heavily carpeted rooms, smoking Benson & Hedges cigarettes in ivory holders and who announce themselves to all men as "The Reinsurers"'.[163] It is, as a result, surprising that reinsurers have more recently assumed a much higher profile, and a favourable one, as key actors in environmental sustainability. Reinsurers are now treated with growing respect by organizations otherwise critical towards global industries. Ever since Greenpeace published a pioneering report in 1993 on climate change and the insurance industry, non-government organizations (NGOs) and the reinsurance world have formed a loosely connected but rather unique interest group to create awareness

[159] E.g. UNCTC (1980) *Transnational Reinsurance Operations: A Technical Paper*. New York: UNCTC.

[160] Goshay and Sandor (1973, 59).

[161] For catastrophe risk pricing see Major and Kreps (2002).

[162] IAIS (International Association of Insurance Supervisors) (2012) *Reinsurance and Financial Stability*. Basel: IAIS, 9–10: <http://iaisweb.org> (accessed 13 May 2015). Retrocession, the ceding on of risks to other reinsurers, can, according to the IAIS, be neglected.

[163] *The Review*, 26 February 1965, 242.

for problems such as global warming.[164] The reason is a major alignment of interests, as reinsurers have a strong interest in combating global warming by limiting what can be reinsured, possibly for reinsurers more so than direct insurers, as they have the last say in underwriting climate-related risks.

Sustainability and corporate social responsibility rank high on reinsurers' agendas. Judging by the prominence of these topics on company websites, it appears, however, limited to lead reinsurers and those affiliated with large insurance companies.[165] The large global corporations may have most means to care about such problems, but in this particular industry they are also the ones who have most vested interests in taking a long-term view to tackling global threats. Most risks today are still monitored on an isolated level. Yet threat scenarios and interlinking risks matter not only to governments and the broader insurance industry but to society in general. The merging of societies, economies, and business through technology, trade, transportation and migration, communication, and investments has made risk resilience a global issue. In addition, risk is increasingly concentrated in large urban areas. The Keihin region, comprising Tokyo, Yokohama, and Kawasaki, is home to more people than live in Canada. A serious catastrophe in such a region can be expected to have severe global repercussions. Reinsurers' modelling techniques are increasingly used to prepare cities for shocks from natural and other catastrophes.

But reinsurance cannot take on such global challenges alone. The 2004 Indian Ocean Earthquake created a tsunami which killed around 280,000 people, the first disaster in this century to make it into the top ten death tolls for natural disasters so far. Also, the economic losses were huge but the insurance industry was barely affected. The disaster, however, led reinsurers to think about ways to close what has, in the meantime, become known as the 'protection gap'. In addition to targeting growth via individual insurance taken out, reinsurers are now working closer with governments.[166] But large organizations such as the UN, the World Bank, and especially the OECD, have also adopted reinsurance as an important instrument to deal with global challenges.

As Pearson concludes in Chapter 3, so-called professional reinsurance is only one of many ways to hedge risks on a secondary level. However, a case can be made that this particular component of the risk business is the one best prepared for providing a business model to help the contemporary world deal with the multiple risks it faces, from climate change and chronic water shortages, to terrorism on a global scale. Although the large reinsurers publish extensive corporate social responsibility reports, the whole business model of reinsurance could be seen as a dynamic example of the

[164] Leggett (1993): <http://www.greenpeace.org/international/en/publications/reports/leggett-insurance-climate/> (accessed 1 June 2015). For a critical view on the development of the industry's narrative of climate change see Johnson (2011, 39ff.).

[165] Such as Allianz, Munich Re, AXA, Hannover Re, Lloyd's, Partner Re, SCOR Re, Swiss Re, Zurich.

[166] Swiss Re (2015). See also Bajrektarevic and Baumer (2010).

shared value concept which Harvard Business School's Michael Porter has argued is critical for the world and for capitalism going forward. Reinsurance is a profitable business which, by its inherent nature, also produces value for society by addressing its many challenges.[167]

## Acknowledgements

The editors would like to thank Mira Wilkins for her valuable support and advice in creating this volume. We would also like to thank Hans Bühlmann and Pablo Koch for their professional reinsurance advice.

[167] M. Porter and M. K. Kramer (2011) 'Creating Shared Value', *Harvard Business Review*, January–February.

CHAPTER 2

# THE CULTURAL CONTEXT OF INSURANCE IN THE WEST

GEOFFREY CLARK

## 2.1 INTRODUCTION

TODAY, probabilistic thinking and statistical methods have so infiltrated educated cultures and economically developed societies that they seem second nature. Whether used to recommend a certain brand of chewing gum, to describe the likelihood of rain or of a scientific finding, to demonstrate the effectiveness of a medical therapy, or to summon authority on behalf of a future course of action, probabilistic arguments and statistical data are so taken for granted that their novelty, considered historically, and their exceptionality, considered epistemologically, go unnoticed in the public square. The fact that the lives, health, and fortunes of billions of people around the globe are secured through aleatory contracts variously subsumed under the catch-all 'insurance' both underscores the point that probability and statistics undergird almost every part of our modern world and highlights the importance of understanding the genesis and growth of this technique of risk management.

Insurance and related 'probabilistic practices' comprise a comparatively late chapter in the age-old human quest for material security and psychological relief from the multifarious hazards of life. Modern forms of insurance did not arise until the close of the European Middle Ages, and it wasn't until the late seventeenth century that a probabilistic revolution ushered in the use of statistical techniques and probabilistic reasoning upon which insurers could, at least in theory, rely. But in fact, practitioners of risk were surprisingly slow to respond. Insurers waited at least a century to take advantage of this new technology of risk management; even then, the actuarial foundation of their business was often more rhetoric than reality. Likewise, a full century and a half elapsed from the inception of the reinsurance business—the crowning achievement of insurantial risk-spreading—and the beginnings of its decisive growth in the mid-nineteenth century.

A critical task in writing the history of insurance therefore involves accounting for the many mental and cultural impediments that blocked the evolution of a probabilistic perspective over the *longue durée*, as well as the moral, economic, and political hurdles that retarded the emergence of a global system of risk transfer, exemplified above all in the establishment of a global secondary market of reinsured risks. Historically speaking, nothing about these patterns of thought or institutional structures was natural or obvious, however inevitable they might appear in retrospect.

## 2.2 Fortune and Fate

Insurance is a modern device, but it is based on a behaviour as old as human society itself: mutual aid. For millennia, any alleviation from the harsh realities of daily existence was likely to come from the support of the surrounding community, fellow workers, alms, or the paternalistic largess bestowed by local worthies or the state. These compensatory mechanisms assumed myriad forms. In ancient Rome, Caesar Augustus began compensating merchants from state coffers for ships lost at sea, while private means of indemnification were found by creative use of a *foenus nauticum*, or sea loan, which was forgiven in the event that goods were lost in transit. More simply, medieval guildsmen contributed to a 'common box', from which funds were paid to their infirm or unfortunate fellows. The pious made a vocation of ministering to the suffering and need of others. Early modern states maintained granaries to alleviate hunger in times of dearth. Even into the late nineteenth century, Russian lords routinely compensated their peasants for agricultural stocks lost to fire.[1] Whether mediated through a state bureaucracy, commercial contract, aristocratic society's reciprocal bonds of protection and subservience, or the horizontal solidarity of kith and kin, these manifold forms of compensation and support all took place under the twin assumptions that everyone stood on the precipice of disaster, and that a person's fortune and fate lay largely, perhaps utterly, beyond human control.

The idea that mortals were swept along on a tide of fate has had the most profound implications for European cultural and intellectual life over the millennia. For the Greeks of Homer's time only the 'blessed' gods exercised true agency. Mere mortals were their playthings and enjoyed success or suffered failure at divine whim. The classical Greeks preserved this pessimistic outlook in the story of the three Fates, who measured out men's lives on lengths of threads. The same sense of fundamental helplessness is reflected in the trope of an oracle ineluctably coming to pass whatever schemes were laid to circumvent it. In the later Christian worldview, this earthly 'vale of tears' had to be patiently endured in hopes of reward in the hereafter. Resigned acceptance of one's 'lot'—the portion and circumstances meted out by the lottery of life—registers the philosophical fatalism, spiritual acquiescence, and social

[1] C. Frierson (2002) *All Russia is Burning! A Cultural History of Fire and Arson in Late Imperial Russia*. Seattle: University of Washington Press, 182–3.

conservatism of cultures that saw virtually no prospects of a sustained improvement in humanity's moral or material condition. Hamlet may have been of an especially brittle temperament, but self-destruction seemed to him the only way to escape the 'slings and arrows of outrageous fortune'.[2]

Even for those more inclined than Shakespeare's Danish prince to embrace action and to seize control of their destinies, fortune was still seen, on balance, as an adverse force, a fickle goddess whose destructive power might, to some extent, be diminished or delayed but never entirely prevented. In Machiavelli's famous image, Fortuna is like an 'impetuous river that, when turbulent, inundates the plains, casts down trees and buildings, removes earth from this side and places it on the other; everyone flees before it, and everything yields to its fury without being able to oppose it'. Yet he allowed that, while 'fortune is the ruler of half our actions', the other half was subject to human foresight and precaution. During periods of calm, therefore, 'men can make provisions against it by dykes and banks, so that when it rises it will either go into a canal or its rush will not be so wild and dangerous'.[3] Despite Machiavelli's hopeful assertion that people (or at least circumspect rulers) had considerable power to hedge against destabilizing events, the best strategy he could offer was one that was vaguely tailored to 'time and circumstances'.

His readers may well have asked themselves what exactly it was that Machiavelli recommended as a risk management strategy—that is, beyond his notorious admonition to employ a cunning eye, a ruthless hand, and a bold will. Instead, no such systematic strategy was offered. For Machiavelli, the complexity of history's 'lessons' and the ever-shifting sands of circumstance highlighted the *particularity* of individual events rather than the *identity* of event classes. A Machiavellian science of decision and action therefore depended upon appreciating the distinctive qualities of a certain time and the specific demands of unique circumstances. This philosophical orientation led away from the notion that Fortuna's periodic inundations had an underlying regularity that might furnish a guide to the building of dykes and banks.

The instinct for security has always sought to fend off such human and natural dangers as it could, but developing a complacence in the stability of existing circumstances has almost always been viewed as dangerously presumptuous. For the ancient Greeks it led to the blindness that followed hubris and preceded a fall. As late as the Renaissance, such sentiments were still to be mistrusted. Macbeth repeats the old formula in which the witch, Hecate, brews up the king's tragic fate by instilling in him a fatal sense of security:

> He shall spurn fate, scorn death and bear
> His hopes 'bove wisdom, grace, and fear.
> And you all know, security
> Is mortals' chiefest enemy.[4]

[2] W. Shakespeare, *Hamlet*, Act 3, scene 1, line 58.
[3] N. Machiavelli (1999) *The Prince*. New York: Signet, 120.
[4] W. Shakespeare *Macbeth*, Act 3, scene 5, lines 30–3.

Life was therefore judged not only as objectively precarious, but even subjective feelings of safety and security were regarded as illusory; indeed, they were snares to trap the unwary or the proud. Given these treacherous material and psychological conditions, how could people experience anything like happiness in the modern sense of the word?

The answer, according to historian Darrin M. McMahon, is that, until the era of the Enlightenment, true human happiness was understood as capriciously awarded to a lucky few who enjoyed the favour of the gods or of fate. McMahon draws attention to the long etymological association in Indo-European languages between the word 'happy' and luck or good fortune or even fate, as in the English 'happenstance', the French *bonheur*, the German *Glück*, the Spanish *felicidad*, and the Latin *felix*.[5] In this accounting of felicity, happiness is the result of a lucky break, a chance windfall, a matching of men to hours as intoned by Henry V at Agincourt in referring to 'we happy few'.[6] In English the multiple meanings of 'fortune' map this polysemous network, in that being 'fortunate' (the beneficiary of chance circumstances) is linked with the idea of destiny ('seeking one's fortune') as well as with riches ('a fortune').

This lottery-like operation of fortune meant that happiness was an extrinsic factor of life—more like something that *happened* to a person than a condition that one could reasonably expect to achieve through one's own efforts, much less claim as a birthright. And like everything in life, its enjoyment was insecure. Classical Greeks thought that a life could be judged happy only in retrospect since, until the moment of death, the jury remained out. Christianity followed this otherworldly orientation by locating the domain of real happiness in the world of the spirit and in heaven to come, not in the worldly things of the here and now. As Jean Delumeau and Keith Thomas have shown, the church made available a lush ritual life (benedictions, the sprinkling of holy water, invocations of the saints, pilgrimages, lighting of candles, worshipping of relics, communal fasts, and so on) designed in part to inculcate a sense of security and relief, and hence deliver some measure of well-being among the faithful amidst a host of daily adversities. Ordinary, practical precautions to avert misfortune were therefore embellished with special magical rites that, for the believer, helped ward off accident, property loss, disease, death, and other natural disasters. Among Europeans running the gamut from highly educated to the completely untutored, these practices shaded gradually into other forms of prophylactic supernaturalism such remote seeing, magical healing, potions making, and astrology.[7]

After Protestantism began to prune the worship of saints and other elements of traditional Catholic piety from 'true' Christian religion, disputes continued to flare among reformers over which ceremonies should be retained and which rejected as

[5] D. M. McMahon (2006) *Happiness: A History*. New York: Grove Press, 10–11.

[6] W. Shakespeare *Henry V*, Act 4, scene 3, line 60.

[7] J. Delumeau (1989) *Rassurer et protéger: Le sentiment de sécurité dans l'Occident d'autrefois*. Paris: Fayard; K. Thomas (1971) *Religion and the Decline of Magic*. New York: Charles Scribner's Sons.

superstitious remnants of 'popery'. The form of baptism, the churching of women after childbirth, the use of holy water, the proper words to be uttered in prayer for the ill, dying, or dead were all freighted with doctrinal implications to be sure, but they functioned for Protestant and Catholic alike as crucial rites by which a community marked the passage of its members from one stage of life to another.[8] The Lord's blessings, conferred at such moments, sanctified the journey through life and, importantly, calmed the anxieties that afflicted everyone in an age lacking anaesthetics, antiseptics, reliable weather forecasts, police detectives, or much in the way to fight flood or fire. The London wood turner Nehemiah Wallington (1598–1658) may have been an exceptionally pious and anxiety-ridden man, but his diary gives voice to the acute vulnerability that his contemporaries surely all had felt at one time or another when facing the many travails of life. Wallington clearly saw what, for others perhaps, was more dimly perceived: that the events of the world were the product of a divine plan whose meaning could be decoded by those alive to God's message:

> History [ . . . ] teacheth and instructeth all those that apply their minds unto it, to govern and carry themselves virtuously and honestly in this life [ . . . ] for these high and wonderful works of God do most clearly [ . . . ] present themselves as his justice and providence [ . . . ]; for he hath a sovereign empire and predominance over all the world.[9]

This superintending providence meant that all events were divine transmissions of approbation or chastisement. Wallington therefore strained to discern the sermon being preached by God in the news of his neighbourhood, city, and nation. He interpreted a fire on London Bridge in February 1633, for example, as punishment for London's rampant 'idolatry, superstition, [ . . . ] whoredoms, adulteries, fornication, murders, oppressions, drunkenness, lying, the contempt of the Gospel with slandering', as well as for the buggery practised by a group of 'sworn brothers to it' in nearby Southwark.[10]

As long as disasters like fire were seen as the providential outcomes of sinfulness rather than as accidents whose frequency might be calculated quite independently of any consideration of the prevailing virtue or vice of the citizenry, then the emergence of a probabilistic worldview faced insuperable hurdles. Wallington's brand of providentialism, like Machiavelli's prescription for mitigating Fortuna, focused attention on the particular meaning of individual events rather on the aggregate significance of independent events.

[8] D. Cressy (1997) *Birth, Marriage and Death: Ritual, Religion, and the Life-Cycle in Tudor and Stuart England.* Oxford: Oxford University Press.

[9] Wallington quoted in P. Seaver (1985) *Wallington's World: A Puritan Artisan in Seventeenth-Century London.* Stanford, CA: Stanford University Press, 48.

[10] Seaver (1985, 49).

## 2.3 Probabilism's Historical Caesura

This point may go some way to explaining why probability theory arose so puzzlingly late in the history of human thought, and why, as a consequence, actuarial insurance, with the remarkable security it has afforded, took so long to establish itself. Historians and philosophers alike have been hard put to offer convincing arguments why probabilistic thinking was seemingly so delayed but then appeared and spread with such suddenness after the year 1660. Barbara Shapiro and Lorraine Daston have each emphasized the development of new jurisprudential standards of 'probability' (in its contemporaneous meaning as 'worthy of approval') in redefining reasonable belief and in driving mathematicians to formulate a calculus of credibility.[11] Others have focused on difficulty of detecting equiprobable outcomes in an irregular, even messy world, or on the retarding effects of an inadequate mathematical vocabulary through which probabilistic calculations might be expressed. Still others explain the delay by citing a growing philosophical or theological commitment to determinism in the age of religious reform, which discouraged the exploration of random processes. On the other hand, the rapid spread of probabilistic ideas after the mid-seventeenth century has been explained as a response to the growing economic need to fix accurate prices to annuities or insurance policies, or, less practically, to a greater tolerance for studying aleatory processes through which the divine hand could be observed. In his classic *The Emergence of Probability*, Ian Hacking largely rejects each of these approaches. He proposes instead that modern probabilism became thinkable because of the way 'probability', conceived of as 'authoritative opinion', was transposed, during the late Renaissance, from a rhetorical or discursive matrix to a new domain ruled by natural philosophy and natural theology. This new kind of 'probable' text contained 'the signs of nature, not of the written word', from which could be inferred the underlying structure and operation of the world through experiment and observation.[12]

The historian Peter Bernstein locates the earlier philosophical aversion to uncertainty at least as far back as the classical Greeks, who, he argues, were indisposed to think in terms of modern probability theory largely because they regarded verisimilitude (likeness to truth) in a pejorative light. Although, being avid gamblers, they well understood the concept of likelihood, they nevertheless prized the kind of conclusive, logical proof achievable (paradigmatically) in geometry far above experimental evidence that might lay a lesser claim upon truth, that is to say, probabilistic knowledge.[13] Although some anticipations of modern probabilistic thinking can be found thinly scattered through history prior to the seventeenth century, the old and abiding commitment to indubitable truth proved impressively resilient. Yet this very fact underscores the impressive speed with which probabilistic thinking emerged in the

[11] Shapiro (1983, 11–12, 163–226); Daston (1988, 39–48).
[12] Hacking (1975, 1–30).
[13] Bernstein (1996, 16–17).

century after Blaise Pascal and Pierre de Fermat carried out their famous correspondence on the means by which one might apportion the monetary stakes in an unfinished game. Although the problem they took up was not itself new, their method of calculating the value of outstanding chances revolutionized thinking about contingent events and uncertain outcomes. As Hacking puts it with pardonable hyperbole, 'No one could solve [problems of chance] until about 1660, and then everyone could.'[14]

The method pioneered by Pascal and Fermat for analysing uncertainty soon proved its worth for problems beyond the direct concern of gamblers. Pascal famously applied probabilistic reasoning to the question of whether one should lead a pious life. God exists or He doesn't. If not, then a life of Christian self-denial is the comparatively small price to pay for an outcome with no reward. But if He does exist, that small price purchases salvation, which is of infinitely greater value than any of the licentious delights to be savoured in this life. Pascal's wager not only supplied an additional rationale for conforming to a religious life, more importantly it furnished a new basis for all kinds of decision-making in the face of uncertain rewards and penalties.

The 'epistemological probabilism' (as Hacking terms it) of Pascal proceeded alongside the application of probabilistic notions to statistical data, notably the analyses made by John Graunt and William Petty on morbidity and mortality based on London's Bills of Mortality. This line of development reached a mature phase with the compilation of the first life table, setting out the average expected continuance of life by age cohort, published in 1693 by Edmond Halley from data obtained in Breslau (modern Wrocław). The relevance of these computations for the pricing of annuities and life insurance was immediately obvious and attracted the talents of mathematical luminaries such as Christian and Lodewijck Huygens, Nicholas Bernoulli, and Abraham de Moivre. De Moivre further supplied a method for measuring the dispersion of individual observations around their mean value, the foundation of the normal distribution, and, together with Jacob Bernoulli and Thomas Bayes, provided techniques—bordering on sorcery—for measuring the degree of uncertainty about chance occurrences even when their specific probabilities remain unknown.[15]

Yet for all their seeming power, these intellectual *tours de force* were translated into practice very slowly—puzzlingly so for most scholars who have studied how and to what extent probability theory was actually applied inside financial ministries, at insurances offices, or among physicians evaluating treatments for disease. It is perhaps not surprising that the practical impediments to the collection of systematic and reliable shipping data would have frustrated the application of statistical methods to marine insurance. The same factors may have underlain fire insurers' persistence in classifying their fire risks crudely into 'common', 'hazardous', and 'doubly hazardous' categories. But the failure by sellers of life insurance and annuities to exploit the calculations of mortality based on demographic data compiled by Petty, Halley, and their successors is more difficult to explain. Hacking highlights the problem by

[14] Hacking (1975, 5). [15] Bernstein (1996, 133).

observing that Ullpian's annuity tables, dating from the third century CE, though seemingly devoid of actuarial calculation, nevertheless formed a solid basis for annuity sales for the next millennium and a half. By contrast, the annuities designed by the Dutch and the English in the late seventeenth and early eighteenth centuries *with the benefit of probability theory and statistical techniques* often ignored basic data like the age of annuitants and carried disastrously low prices. Hacking marvels at the fact that 'this ignorant practice continued for over a century, despite the fact that the mathematicians constantly inveighed against it'.[16] Echoing this point, Bernstein notes that a century passed after Halley's publication of the first life table, 'before governments and insurance companies would take probability-based life expectancies into account'.[17] How can this delay be explained?

One line of argument stretching back to the mid-nineteenth century has presumed that early insurance and annuities businesses were too closely associated with gambling or with speculative, even fraudulent, enterprises for the prudential lessons of probability and statistics to be noticed, much less taken to heart. Over a century ago, the historian Enrico Bensa deplored the rampant gambling on lives by means of insurance that had flourished in the late seventeenth century, which he described as the 'fruit of the corruption of the time and not of the spirit of commercial speculation'.[18] Cornelius Walford, author of the massive though unfinished *Insurance Cyclopaedia*, similarly interpreted the modern insurance business as having escaped from a disreputable past, as legitimate insurance firms slowly climbed out of the semi-licit gambling rookeries and fly-by-night 'Little Goes' of the early eighteenth century.[19] A generation after Walford, Jean Halpérin revised the linear Victorian progressivism implicit in those earlier works by proposing his 'sinusoidal' history of insurance. In Halpérin's view, since the Middle Ages European society had alternated between periods when the 'instinct of social conservation' or the 'spirit of lucre and gain' predominated, with the late eighteenth century marking a swing back from speculative passions towards social solidarity.[20]

More recently, Lorraine Daston has advanced a sophisticated and more empirically grounded version of these earlier accounts, arguing that a fundamental shift in values and motives occurred in the market for insurance and annuities during the eighteenth century. For Daston, it was the emergence of a bourgeois domestic culture in the latter half of that century that engendered a heightened sense of family responsibility and an aversion to risk. This new moral sensibility in turn laid the basis for modern prudential behaviour, paving the way for the reception of probability and statistics into the market for life-contingent investments. Before that time, Daston believes, 'insurance seems to have been less prudential than reckless, fueled more by the spirit of gambling than of foresight. [...] Both insurance offices and their customers were for the most part betting on the future, not planning for it.'[21] Several pieces of evidence do appear to support her argument. It is true that, until the last quarter of the eighteenth century,

[16] Hacking (1975, 5). [17] Bernstein (1996, 87). [18] Bensa (1897, 93).
[19] Walford (1912, 2, 24). [20] Halpérin (1946, 43, 63). [21] Daston (1988, 165, 175).

insurance was a popular means for making bets of all kinds, including wagers on the longevity of the high-born or famous, the date by which a besieged city might fall, or the true sex of a cross-dressing French aristocrat. Even insurance offices that proudly advertised themselves as providing security for wives and children not only raised no objection to wagering policies but actually drafted a list of celebrity candidates they thought were particularly suitable for insuring. Daston is also right to draw attention to the fact that many annuities sold in the eighteenth century were disguised usurious loans rather than devices to secure the welfare of a dependent after the purchaser's decease.[22] Finally, there is, in the case of Great Britain at least, an attractive historical coincidence in the foundation date of the Equitable, the first life company to establish its business on an explicit actuarial basis, and the passage just a dozen years later of the Gambling Act (1774), which banned wagering policies and all other insurances in which no 'insurable interest' could be demonstrated.

On closer inspection, however, Daston's case (and perforce those of her predecessors) looks less persuasive. Although gambling insurance abounded in the early eighteenth century, there is also overwhelming evidence that policies of a modern, prudential sort were also widely taken out in the midst of this supposedly speculative era of insurance.[23] Plenty of bourgeois families existed prior to their supposed apotheosis on the eve of the Industrial Revolution, and they sought, just like their grandchildren and great-grandchildren, to indemnify themselves against loss of station and fortune. And just as prudential motives can be detected in the early life insurance market, so too can the speculative spirit be found in the era of bourgeois rectitude of the later eighteenth and nineteenth centuries. Tim Alborn has shown, for example, how life offices continued to lure customers with 'bonuses', which offered the prospect of occasional compounded returns on a portion of their paid-in premiums.[24] Acquisitive passions survived not only in the middle-class context Alborn describes, but also flourished in the growing working-class market for 'industrial' life insurance, whose modest benefits were intended mainly to finance a respectable burial. In the many cases of extended family or neighbours insuring others' lives by means of these small industrial policies, the insured's death provided a windfall by which to acquire, perhaps, new attire for the funeral, which conveniently provided a suit of Sunday best afterwards.[25]

If the boundary separating the speculative and sober phases of insurance consumption appears less than distinct, the picture grows no clearer upon examination of the extent to which mortality data were—or were not—utilized as demographic information accumulated and new, allegedly more reliable life tables were published by statisticians in the decades following Halley's pioneering work. Gerd Gigerenzer, among others, asserts that, 'eighteenth-century buyers and sellers of annuities and life insurance were no more interested in probability theory than the gamblers' since they were at heart careless thrill-seekers, not worrywarts carefully hedging against

[22] Gigerenzer et al. (1989, 25). [23] Clark (1997, 17–36).
[24] Alborn (2009, 166). See also Alborn (2002, 65–92). [25] McFall (2014, 36).

loss.[26] But to judge from the explicit or implicit mortality calculations contained in fully one-third of the prospectuses of the approximately sixty life insurance and annuity societies launched in England from 1696 to 1721, company managers did in fact draw from and occasionally cite the work of political arithmeticians in order to persuade prospective customers of the soundness of their business.[27] The Friendly Society, for instance, referred to 'the ingenious Sr. William Petty, and other mathematicians', who had calculated that, in a population 'including children, young people, aged persons, sickly and infirm, there do not die above 3 in a 100 in every year'.[28] Two other insurance projectors, George Jenkins and William Causton, similarly invoked the authority of 'Sir William Petty, and the ingenious Dr. Halley' to justify their own expectation of annual mortality at one in thirty or one in forty.[29] These early practitioners of risk did not, however, push further to discuss the differential risk of death at yearly intervals so clearly laid out in Halley's table. They likewise did not try to price their policies according to age, but instead charged one rate of premium on all insurable lives ranging in age from late childhood or adolescence to late middle age. The underlying assumption behind this pricing was that the chance of death was roughly constant for people in the middle years of life, an assumption they shared with the leading probabilists of the age including Graunt, Johan de Witt, Johannes Hudde, Leibniz, and de Moivre.[30] This seemingly perverse defiance of Halley was in fact entirely reasonable given the large margins of error surrounding all demographic data of the era, which aroused justifiable misgivings about the special relevance of age in determining a person's risk of death, and hence uncertainty about what a fair premium might be. In the face of these wide uncertainties, practitioners and theorists of risk alike understood that factors apart from age would be important indicators of mortal peril. In his *An Essay Upon Projects*, Daniel Defoe imagined a way around the confusing welter of risks to life by suggesting that life insurance companies cater to particular segments of society whose liability to accident or death could be roughly equalized:

> None can be admitted, but such whose circumstances are, at least in some degree alike, and so mankind must be sorted into classes; and as their contingencies differ, every different sort may be a society upon even terms; for the circumstances of people, as to life, differ extremely by the age and constitution of their bodies, and the difference of employment; as he that lives on shore, or a shopkeeper against a soldier, are unequal. [...] So that it is necessary to sort the world into parcels, seamen with seamen, soldiers with soldiers, and the like.[31]

[26] Gigerenzer et al. (1989, 24).

[27] Mortality calculations are presented in one-third of the approximately sixty such companies started in that period. Clark (1993, 326–7).

[28] The Friendly Society (1715, 18).

[29] Jenkins and Causton (1714).

[30] Hacking (1975, 108–10, 120–1); R. M. Jennings and A. P. Trout (1982) *The Tontine: From the Reign of Louis XIV to the French Revolutionary Era*. Homewood, IL: Richard D. Irwin, 14 n.; Alter and Riley (1986, 16–17).

[31] Defoe (1697, 118–20).

Recognizing that soldiers and seamen were in fact poor risks, insurance societies generally excluded them from admission, along with drunkards, and those who had not had smallpox or who were 'very much distempered, or distracted, and under cure'. They sometimes also excluded people from the 'marshy and unhealthy' parts of the country.[32] The utility of demographic data and probabilistic thinking were clearly not lost on practitioners of risk in the first decades of the probabilistic revolution. On the contrary, they exhibited a canny appreciation of precisely which vital statistics were really useful and reliable, and which others suggested a bogus precision that could not compete with experienced judgement in a complicated world.[33]

That reluctance to rely too heavily on rates of mortality related solely to age persisted into the late eighteenth and nineteenth centuries. Even when, in 1762, the Equitable Society established itself upon an actuarial foundation and began to charge premiums according to age at entry, its managers kept premiums well above their fair value out of an abundance of caution. Richard Price, one of the foremost statisticians of the age and later compiler of the famous Northampton table, also counselled caution, urging the Equitable to continue collecting demographic data from across England in order to reduce uncertainties about the incidence of mortality. As late as the 1830s, the actuarially fair price of a policy was still the subject of ardent debate involving the accuracy of rival mortality tables and the correct interpretation of individual companies' claims histories and estimated future liabilities. Tim Alborn has shown, indeed, that policy pricing into the late nineteenth century was based less on statistical data, which tended to indicate a floor below which price competition would be ruinous, and more on pragmatic considerations of what the market would bear.[34] The statistical basis of what was the most mathematized line of insurance remained, into the twentieth century, rather more vague than is often supposed.

The market for insurance and annuities was a major but not the only arena in which probabilistic thinking and statistical techniques were deployed in the wake of the probabilistic revolution. Medical debates also summoned—or rejected—numerical methods of analysis in judging the advisability or effectiveness of inoculation against smallpox. Beginning in the 1720s, the English physicians and mathematicians John Arbuthnot and his younger contemporary John Jurin advocated the new practice of inoculation in light of numerical calculations demonstrating, so they claimed, that people faced a much reduced risk of death as a result of smallpox inoculation compared to the chances of dying by contracting the disease naturally. Like Arbuthnot before him, Jurin derived figures from London's Bills of Mortality to illustrate the relative benefits of inoculation, but then went on to assemble a database of smallpox cases using a network of medical correspondents around the country. Whether using the London Bills or the countrywide figures, though, the data had to be adjusted in a number of ways to remove distortions owing, for example, to infant mortality, to the presence of

32 Adams (1714); The First Society of Assurance for Widows and Orphans (1705, 2).

33 For a more developed argument of these points, see Clark (1999, 114–54).

34 Alborn (2009, 103–21).

unrecorded religious dissenters, or to doubtful cases in which inoculation might not have been performed correctly or where the aetiology of an infection was questionable. Transforming the raw and imperfect data into a useable numerical table therefore required careful handling—what critics might have derided as juggling and guesswork.

Indeed, Jurin and Arbuthnot stirred a hornet's nest of criticism amongst their less mathematically enthusiastic medical colleagues. Some physicians understandably objected to inoculation against smallpox on ethical grounds since the practice required that physicians infect their patients, which seemed contrary to the Hippocratic precept of first doing no harm. Indeed, religiously doctrinaire physicians condemned inoculation as an impermissible interference in God's providence. Dr William Wagstaffe gave voice to a more bigoted line of attack in declaring inoculation to be a dangerous and misguided practice carried out by foreigners and ignorant women, and he rejected out of hand Jurin's attempt to justify inoculation through 'some obscure and improper Calculations, scarcely intelligible to any body, or if intelligible, altogether foreign to the Purpose'.[35] Most critics of Arbuthnot and Jurin's works were more temperate in their objections to the idea that statistical information could illuminate the practice of medicine, and marshalled incisive arguments against such numerical schemes. Isaac Massey, for one, rightly observed that those who received inoculation were more likely to be wealthier, to be healthier to begin with, and to receive better medical care when they did fall ill than those who were not inoculated. He concluded that the figures presented by Jurin overstated the benefits of inoculation because they did not compare like with like cases. As he explained, 'To form a just comparison, and calculate right in this case, the Circumstances of the Patients, must and ought to be as near as may be on a Par.'[36] This was exactly the point that Defoe had made about the advisability of parcelling individuals into separate insurance societies so that the qualitative attributes of members could be homogenized as far as possible. Other critics of inoculation insisted that the physician's vocation was to render care not according to abstract mathematical generalities but according to the indications presented by flesh-and-blood *patients*, each of whom possessed a particular physical constitution, history, set of habits, family, and so on. From this perspective, the process of quantification necessarily ignored the complexity of the world and always threatened to treat as equivalent cases that were in fact incommensurable.

This reluctance to place much faith in probabilistic arguments and statistical inference throughout the early eighteenth century can therefore be seen as not at all unreasonable and, in fact, as sometimes a quite sophisticated recognition that behind the tidy rows and columns of figures in the mortality and morbidity tables lay a messy backroom where the statisticians had fiddled their data in order to overcome obvious deficiencies. The delay in the use of finely graded mortality statistics in the insurance and annuities business, as well as the reluctance felt contemporaneously by many

[35] A. Rusnock (2002) *Vital Accounts: Quantifying Health and Population in Eighteenth-Century England and France.* Cambridge: Cambridge University Press, 45, 68.

[36] Rusnock (2002, 69).

physicians to embrace the practice of inoculation on the basis of numerical arguments, both point to a widely held and sober appreciation of the limits of statistical information as a guide for action in a complex world.

## 2.4 Providence, Probability, and Progress

Even if the century-long delay in the embrace of probabilistic reasoning and statistical inference had little to do with a speculative allergy to calculation as such, it is equally clear that a number of cultural and mental factors impeded a view of the world as a product of aleatory outcomes. As has already been discussed earlier in this chapter, providential thinking in early modern Europe inscribed events with a divine message, and this habit of mind inhibited a view of a probabilistic approach to the study of natural and human phenomena. But Daston and Gigerenzer and colleagues also make a compelling case that the spread of probabilism depended critically on a reconceptualization of history itself.

The Judeo-Christian understanding of humanity's situation within a biblical context joined the present to the wondrous early chapters of history in which patriarchal lifespans could last as long as Methuselah's and divine visitations and miracles filled the world. Even though Jean Calvin himself regarded the age of miracles as long past, most Europeans continued to understand the appearance of comets as portending disaster, struggled to interpret the meaning of monstrosities like two-headed calves, and saw God's judgement in great fires, floods, and earthquakes such as befell Lisbon in 1755.[37] Nevertheless, educated opinion was gradually moving away from the idea that the will of God could be directly inferred from worldly events, or even that God's hand intervened in the world at all. As early as 1619, Thomas Gataker rejected the idea that God's messages could sometimes be revealed through the outcomes of aleatory processes.[38] While that position long remained outside mainstream opinion, it steadily gained favour as the epistemological claims of natural philosophy advanced. By the mid-eighteenth century, David Hume deployed the ideas of natural law and probabilistic expectation to cast a withering doubt on the reality of all miracles—whether in the present or, especially, in the past.[39] Although Hume left intact the idea of determinate causes and rejected the reality of chance, he nonetheless conceded that, given imperfect human reason and knowledge, chance gave the appearance of operating in the world.[40] For the theologically inclined—which is to say, virtually everyone—God's 'directing

[37] Gigerenzer et al. (1989, 27); L. Daston and K. Park (1981) 'Unnatural Conceptions: The Study of Monsters in 16th and 17th Century France and England', *Past and Present* 92, August, 20–54.

[38] T. Gataker (1619) *Of the Nature and Use of Lots*. London: Ed. Griffin, 28–30.

[39] D. Hume (1977) *An Enquiry Concerning Human Understanding*. Indianapolis: Hackett, 72–90.

[40] D. Hume (1978) *A Treatise of Human Nature*. Oxford: Clarendon Press, 126.

will' still lay behind everything that happened in the universe. His intentions and messages, however, were increasingly regarded as inscrutable.

Perhaps no one walked a narrower tightrope over these murky waters than did the cleric and actuary Richard Price, who reconciled his study of the laws of human mortality with his religious commitment to divine providence by emphasizing, like Hume, the frailty of human knowledge, which gave to chance the appearance of reality:

> We are far from having a perfect knowledge of all the causes from whence events arise, and therefore cannot say how far the Divine hand may be among those causes. The uncertainty which attends all human schemes is continually observed and felt, and has given rise to the common notions of fortune.[41]

God did make use of calamities, Price allowed, in order 'to alarm and awaken men, and bring them to a sense of virtue and piety'. Yet he cautioned, 'we cannot go much further' to say that 'the calamity was designed as a judgment on the sufferers'.[42]

Price's example indicates the degree to which religious believers could (and arguably still do) entertain theories of causation not strictly compatible with one another. But in general, the gap between theological precept and insurance practice has been mediated more by pragmatic than by principled considerations. It is admittedly true that religious scruples have, in some times and places, proscribed or limited certain forms of insurance. The sixteenth-century French commercial manual *Le Guidon*, first published in the sixteenth century, stated that life insurance was 'against good morals and customs' and therefore has 'been constrained, abolished, and forbidden [ . . . ] in this country.'[43] That moral objection seems also to have formed the basis of Louis XIV's prohibition of life insurance in the 'Ordonnances de la Marine' of 1681.[44] Yet, when French merchants faced a commercial disadvantage in being debarred from insuring their slave cargoes across the Atlantic, a legal loophole was found to allow the practice while maintaining the formal prohibition.[45]

Another site of religious hostility to insurance has been described by the sociologist Viviana Zelizer in nineteenth-century America, where a moral revulsion to life (but not to fire or marine) insurance was voiced by Mennonites, Protestant Revivalists, as well as certain clergymen from established denominations like the Lutherans and Episcopalians.[46] The breadth of these religious objections, however, has recently been questioned by Sharon Murphy, who sees the widespread clerical consumption of insurance in the nineteenth century as much more eloquent testimony than the jeremiads against insurance intoned from the pulpit or in the revival tent.[47] Murphy's argument confirms my own conclusions drawn from the life insurance market of eighteenth-century

[41] R. Price (1767) 'On Providence', in *Four Dissertations*. London: Printed for A. Millar and T. Cadell, 83.

[42] Price (1767, 91).

[43] *Guidon Stile et Usance des Marchands qui mettent à la Mer* (1619). Rouen: De l'Imprimerie de Martin Le Mesgissier, 64.

[44] R.-J. Valin (1828) *Commentaire sur l'ordonnance de la marine, du mois d'aout 1681*. Poitiers: F.A. Saurin, book 3, 255.

[45] Clark (1999, 15–16).

[46] Zelizer (1979, 73–9).

[47] Murphy (2010, 7–8, 209–27).

England, where clerics were among the most enthusiastic consumers of life insurance and the loudest advocates of the 'providence'—the term now denoting a virtuous human trait—displayed by those who purchased policies for the benefit of their dependents.[48]

Care needs to be taken, therefore, in speaking about the secularizing impact of the insurance industry in particular and probabilistic thinking more broadly in the formation of modern European culture. As Peter Borscheid correctly observes, discerning the regularities in human mortality was, for many early demographers such as Johann Peter Süssmilch, a powerful demonstration of a harmonious divine order underlying nature, in much the same way that Isaac Newton's *Principia Mathematica* inspired William Derham and other natural theologians to see, in the new astronomy and mechanical physics, evidence of a wonderful, intelligent design.[49] The presumed rationality upon which the practice of insurance was based need not be understood as in conflict even with traditional forms of religion or of superstitious means of trying to avert disaster. Pierre Vilar cites the case of marine insurers in eighteenth-century Barcelona, who included in their premium payments money for masses to be said for the protection of their cargoes.[50] The cognitive dissonance they experienced was surely no greater than that of the millions today who routinely pay their insurance premiums while attending services on Friday, Saturday, or Sunday to pray that God forefend those same misfortunes. Recent research has even suggested that, today, a substantial number of people believe that taking out insurance actually reduces their risk of accident or loss.[51] It may be the case that, as the insurance executive and author Franz Kafka perceived, insurance can function as a kind of religious manipulation to ward off evil.[52]

Rather than viewing insurance as a rational technique of risk management that superseded earlier magical or religious efforts to achieve security, it may be more fruitful to follow Lucien Febvre and Jean Delumeau in seeing the growth first of marine, then of life and fire insurance as embedded in a more general intensification of a desire for security in European society that is visible from the end of the Middle Ages onwards. In this view, the rise of insurance was symptomatic of a much broader trend, illustrated also by intensified prayers for souls in purgatory, the use of the rosary, Luther's doctrine of justification by faith, Calvin's predestinarian theology, and the Puritans' telling term for a godly believer's confidence in salvation—'assurance'. Besides insurance, the quest for security led in other worldly directions as well. Delumeau suggests that, in the political sphere, it bolstered absolutism as another mechanism for enforcing civil order and property rights. In the considerably altered political and intellectual circumstances of the late eighteenth century, the demand for security ran in a politically contrary direction by deploying the authority of natural law against absolutist rule

[48] Clark (1999, 57–9, 155–69).

[49] Borscheid (2012d, 3). See also W. Derham (1713) *Physico-Theology*. London: Printed for W. Innys; W. Derham (1715) *Astro-Theology*. London: Printed for W. Innys.

[50] P. Vilar (1962) *La Catalogne dans L'Espagne modern*, vol. 3. Paris: Sevpen, 442.

[51] Tykocinski (2008, 1346–56).

[52] M. Brod (1963) *Franz Kafka: A Biography*. New York: Schocken Books, 74, 84.

in defence of life, liberty, property, and happiness, a litany most famously proclaimed in the Declaration of Independence and the Declaration of the Rights of Man.[53]

This argument does not deny that the quantitative methods and probabilistic thinking which legitimated and helped to spread insurance were not sometimes in tension with scriptural or hieratic authority. Except for a few of the most radical *philosophes*, however, who, in the eighteenth century or thereafter, has felt the need actually to overthrow the priest in favour of the actuary? Referring to the inextricable mixture of religious and rational sensibilities at work even in the minds of modern insurance customers, the *annaliste* Lucien Febvre remarked that, should an insurance agent make a house call today, no one would dare cast aspersions on the client's religious faith. The relationship between thought and action in this and other instances is too complex, Febvre believed, for any straightforward correspondence to be drawn. 'Man is not cut into slices', he offered. And history therefore 'cannot, should not be cut in two: here the events, there the beliefs.'[54]

While giving Febvre due regard on this point, it is also true that the greater confidence and optimism so characteristic of the century of the Enlightenment was partly built on improving material circumstances. Canal building and road improvement facilitated the shipment of grain to locales where crops had failed, thus alleviating famine in many countries and all but eliminating it in advanced nations like the Netherlands and Britain. Although still virulent, bubonic plague broke out with less frequency after the 1660s, the last major outbreak occurring in Marseilles in 1720. Epidemic disease, particularly smallpox, continued to prey on Europeans, but gone were the days when an eruption of plague wiped out half a city's population within a matter of weeks. A sustained upswing in the volume of inland and overseas trade, beginning in the last decades of the seventeenth century, led to unprecedented prosperity for commercial families and ultimately more creature comforts even for the working classes.[55] Sectarian strife and religious persecution persisted, but at far lower levels than in the preceding era of religious war. The extension of human sensory powers through the use of new scientific instruments and the penetrating insights of mathematical natural philosophy brought wider horizons of human knowledge into view and promised more power over the forces of nature. Literacy was rising nearly everywhere and among nearly every social group.[56] The spread of education, together with the influence of John Locke's sensationalist psychology, raised hopes that reason would eventually triumph over ignorance and superstition and humankind's lot fundamentally improve in the future.

[53] Delumeau (1989), 10–17. [54] Febvre (1956, 246).

[55] D. Roche (1987) *The People of Paris: An Essay in Popular Culture in the 18th Century*. Berkeley, CA: University of California Press; N. McKendrick, J. Brewer, and J. H. Plum (1983) *The Birth of a Consumer Society: The Commercialization of Eighteenth-Century England*. London: Hutchinson.

[56] J. Van Horn Melton (2001) *The Rise of the Public in Enlightenment Europe*. Cambridge: Cambridge University Press, 81–6.

All these material and mental developments spelled good news for the insurance industry. More coastal and overseas shipping expanded the market for marine insurance, while the growing stocks of commercial goods held in warehouses and workshops stimulated the demand for fire insurance. The gradual withdrawal of the worst epidemic diseases allowed life insurers gradually to assume greater risks and to lower policy prices. A modicum of political and social stability, as well as the reduced destructiveness (if not the prevalence) of warfare, also led to a feeling that human affairs possessed the kind of regularity upon which insurance could capitalize. It was easier to imagine that the past was prologue in the sense that experience and numerical analysis could offer a reliable guide for predicting the future.

This new, optimistic temper entailed a paradox, however, regarding the shape of history and humanity's place within it. Previously, humanity had been understood as inhabiting an inherently chaotic and unpredictable world, at the mercy of forces beyond its control and subject to harsh and unalterable realities. The human lot was as static as the world was catastrophic. But now, under the sway of the factors just outlined, a kind of 'historical uniformitarianism' emerged. Congruent with the probabilism advocated by the technicians of risk and the hopeful future proclaimed by the *philosophes* and their followers, events were assumed to be largely regular and predictable, but also embedded in a perfectible historical narrative that released humanity from its hapless monotony and made possible a differently patterned and brighter future.

No figure expressed these progressivist dreams more fervently than Antoine-Nicolas de Condorcet. In his *Sketch for a Historical Picture of the Progress of the Human Mind* (1795), a work whose idealism is perhaps only exceeded by its prescience, Condorcet describes the unbounded possibilities for human welfare made possible by the elimination of suffering and misery, the inculcation of individual happiness, and the growth of sexual, social, and political equality. Along with the spread of education, progress in the arts and sciences, greater national self-determination, and improvements to human health, Condorcet includes, as a critical component of this qualitatively better future, the establishment of insurance, annuity, and pension schemes. By these devices the mental ease previously reserved to the elite *rentier* class might be extended to all, and thereby remove the cause 'of inequality, of dependence, and even of misery, which ceaselessly threatens the most numerous and most active class'. Those evils might largely be eradicated, he explained:

> [B]y guaranteeing people in old age a means of livelihood produced partly by their own savings and partly by the savings of others who make the same outlay, but who die before they need to reap the reward; or [...] by securing for widows and orphans an income which is the same and costs the same for those families which suffer an early loss and for those which suffer it later.[57]

[57] A.-N. de Condorcet (1955) *Sketch for a Historical Picture of the Progress of the Human Mind.* London: Weidenfeld & Nicolson, 181.

Forging this social solidarity could be accomplished through either public or private means, but, however achieved, its success rested on the 'application of the calculus to the probabilities of life and the investment of money', so that the schemes may be 'formed without any real risk, once the principles for [their] proper working [ . . . ] have been widely diffused'.[58] This method of relieving the uncertainties of working families and of preventing their periodic financial disasters through a calculus of probability therefore promised to free all from the tyranny of risk and to launch society into a happier phase of history.

The 'social mathematics' of Condorcet also offered a conceptual template for the extension of probabilistic thinking to the social sciences in the nineteenth century, a process that has been described in detail by Hacking and Theodore Porter.[59] The recognition that mathematical patterns underlie contingent processes throughout human affairs brought social knowledge under the same epistemological umbrella as natural science. Paradoxically, the firmest social truths were like natural truths, to be found in statistical distributions, and, with that knowledge, human existence in a chancy world could be rendered more certain.

In this epistemological sense, chance was being thoroughly domesticated by the nineteenth century, but at the same time the practical task of spreading the risk-reducing technique of insurance encountered imposing new barriers. Condorcet had blithely adopted the Enlightenment's optimistic and cosmopolitan perspective in forecasting the progressive extension of improving institutions like insurance. Yet the penetration of insurance across cultural, linguistic, and political borders proved to be a difficult matter for insurance entrepreneurs. And even with respect to the domestic market, the industrializing economies and urbanizing societies of the early nineteenth century created ever greater concentrations of risk, thereby frustrating the efforts of insurers to safely disperse their risks. Although the insurance industry responded to such challenges in a variety of ways, a critically important method for overcoming some of these hurdles, and eventually for constructing a truly global system of risk pooling, lay in the development of reinsurance services.

## 2.5 The Rise of a Cosmopolitan Risk Culture

Through the device of reinsurance, direct insurers can transfer either a discrete risk, a specified fraction of a particular risk portfolio, or risks in excess of some retained level, to another insurer—either another direct insurer, as was more common at an earlier date, or, as the technique developed, more typically to a specialized reinsurance company. Reinsurance has therefore conferred upon retail insurers a valuable flexibility

[58] Condorcet (1955, 181). [59] Hacking (1990); Porter (1986).

in entering new markets while simultaneously limiting their underwriting exposure through the transfer of unwanted or excessive liabilities to a secondary risk market.

Reinsurance appeared in the marine insurance market in the later seventeenth century in the guise of so-called 'interest or no interest' policies. Such policies dispensed with the requirement that purchasers demonstrate a direct financial stake in the property or event to be insured. John Millar, an eighteenth-century authority on insurance law, explained that such policies created a situation in which 'the underwriter in one policy becomes the assured in another, upon the same subject, with a view of withdrawing himself from hazard'.[60] According to Millar, underwriters typically sought reinsurance when vessels they had insured were late making port, thus raising a suspicion that they concealed their private knowledge of a likely loss in order to fraudulently shift the liability to another party. The contemporary popularity of using 'interest or no interest' polices as a vehicle for gambling on shipping further tainted reinsurance, and, as a result, in 1746 parliament banned both practices by prohibiting all 'interest or no interest' policies.[61] Not all thought the ban advisable. The esteemed insurance expert, Nicholas Magens, thought the remedy 'a hard one, by depriving merchants of the power of withdrawing themselves from insurance business, when their circumstances may render it highly expedient'. But such objections could not prevail against the widely shared anxiety that 'temptation to fraud' could not be allowed to corrode the integrity of the insurance market, which rested on the 'mutual trust and confidence which subsists between assured and underwriter'.[62]

Older British firms internalized this aversion to a business that was perceived to stimulate speculation and even to fuel fraud. The historian P. G. M. Dickson has pointed, for example, to the persistent disdain exhibited by officers of the venerable Sun Insurance Office for reinsurance, which they regarded, until the very end of the nineteenth century, as not only shady but unprofitable to boot.[63] Likewise, the Royal Exchange Assurance, another old foundation, repeatedly refused opportunities to enter the reinsurance market through the first half of the century. As Clive Trebilcock, has cautioned, however, the conservative moralism exhibited by the more established British companies was not universally shared, especially by a younger generation of insurance companies like the Phoenix, the Alliance, the Guardian, and the Protector, which used reinsurance as a springboard into foreign fire markets from the 1820s onwards.[64] Nevertheless, it remains true that the most precocious and developed insurance market in the world ceded leadership of the reinsurance business to Continental firms headquartered primarily in Switzerland and in the German states.

Harold James ascribes this paradoxical failure to exploit the economic potential of reinsurance to the dominant political position of the British Empire and the robust financial condition of its insurance industry. Older methods of hedging risk through co-insurance arrangements, together with the high capitalization of the insurance sector, meant that British firms felt less need for reinsurance services.[65] Moreover,

60 Millar (1787, 232). 61 By 19 Geo. II, c. 37. 62 Millar (1787, 214–15).
63 Dickson (1960, 160–1, 176, 231). 64 Trebilcock (1985, 274). 65 James (2013b, 9).

the economic conduits laid by the British Empire lessened the considerable political and practical barriers to international growth faced by companies based in Continental Europe. As a result, specialized reinsurance companies took root earliest and most strongly in regions where the financial strains of industrialization were most acute and the concentration of accumulated risks therefore most worrisome, or where the political landscape was fragmented and the resiliency of public compensatory institutions correspondingly weaker.

The rise of reinsurance services responded to a wide variety of local, national, and global needs. Although the Cologne Re (1842–52) and the Swiss Re (1863) were founded on the heels of devastating conflagrations at Hamburg (1842) and at Glarus (1861), David Gugerli is correct to see the formation of specialized reinsurers not as a reflexive reaction to these particular disasters but as the more general consequence of a dawning consciousness of the magnitude, concentration, and complexity of risks inherent in industrial societies.[66] Considered from a more tactical perspective, reinsurance also served as a means for insurance companies operating in a fiercely competitive domestic market to cede excess risks to a foreign reinsurer rather than transfer those risks via co-insurance in the domestic market and thereby disclose sensitive proprietary information to a rival direct insurer. Likewise, in countries where economic protectionism excluded foreign firms from entering the retail insurance market, domestic companies found it desirable to reinsure their excess risks abroad, as happened in Prussia after 1837, in Russia a decade later, and particularly in Latin America later still.[67] On the other side of the equation, insurers seeking to penetrate foreign markets found reinsurance a convenient way to evade legal barriers to entry by partnering with a direct insurer abroad. Working through a domestic direct insurer also offered the possibility of reducing risks and agency costs associated with operating with incomplete information in a foreign land. So, whether inspired by keen domestic competition in financially straitened markets, by protectionist policies emplaced by developing nations, or by a countervailing effort to expand insurance services internationally, reinsurance had the ineluctable effect of binding far-flung economies and societies together. An instructive case in point is provided by the infant Soviet Union. Having deemed reinsurance irredeemably 'bourgeois', the Soviets abolished the business, only to reintroduce it in 1924 under the auspices of a state-owned entity in order to facilitate necessary foreign trade.[68] In view of the convergent outcomes of these various national policies and business strategies, the process of global economic integration and solidarity may be said to have been overdetermined through the worldwide assumption and dispersal of risks performed by the reinsurance industry.

Other types of solidarity also needed to be strengthened so that reinsurers could effectively stand as a backstop against catastrophic losses faced by primary insurers. One early weakness reinsurers had to overcome arose from the information asymmetries relative to primary insurers, who naturally had better knowledge about the risks

[66] James (2013b, 157). But see Lengwiler (2012, 147), who sees a somewhat tighter causal link.

[67] Pearson (2010, 17); Borscheid (2012d, 13).

[68] Borscheid (2012e, 46–7).

they were proposing to cede to reinsurers. This disadvantage was compounded by the pervasiveness of facultative reinsurance, in which discrete risks were offloaded onto the secondary market. In a move reminiscent of insurers' abuse of 'interest or no interest' policies in the eighteenth century, primary insurance companies in the nineteenth century preferentially saddled their reinsurers with the worst risks in their portfolios, as happened to the fledgling Swiss Re, which was pushed to the brink of bankruptcy in its first years as a result.[69] Two developments pioneered by the Munich Re helped remove this moral hazard from the reinsurance market. First, reinsurers began to negotiate more aggressively with primary insurers, aided by their growing financial stakes in the retail insurers themselves. Perhaps more importantly, reinsurers pushed hard to shift the liabilities they assumed away from facultative and towards treaty forms of reinsurance, so that whole portfolios, or some fraction thereof, were ceded by the direct insurers, thus homogenizing the risks retained by the direct insurer and those transferred to the reinsurer.[70] These measures helped build a web of trust connecting players in the direct and secondary risk markets, a powerful factor behind the growth of the reinsurance business in the late nineteenth and early twentieth centuries.

That solidarity among reinsurers and insurers (not to mention their policyholders) would be severely tested by the first major shock to the nascent international community of risk delivered by the San Francisco Earthquake of 1906. Total losses from direct earthquake damage and subsequent fires totalled about USD 400 million. Although 90 per cent of the houses in San Francisco were covered by fire policies, losses due to earthquake were excluded, as were, in some policies, fires consequent to earthquake or collapsed buildings.[71] Perhaps reflecting an understanding of these terms, the Swiss Re and other European reinsurers believed at first that their liabilities would be quite limited. Yet the hue and cry of jilted policyholders and incensed American politicians led to a reconsideration by insurers and reinsurers alike of the most advisable course of action. The British led the way by agreeing to disregard the policy exclusions and paying at least 70 per cent of the insured losses. Faced with this capitulation, the Swiss Re and other reinsurers had no alternative but to pay out claims as well.[72] While the financial strain on the insurance system was extreme—even companies as far away as Russia failed as a result—the decision by insurers to largely if not wholly honour the claims of their policyholders, and by reinsurers to pay the claims of their cedents, marked a crucial moment in the proving of the global insurance system. Not only did companies collaborate in the wake of the 1906 earthquake to standardize policy terms and conditions in order to prevent the chaos of inconsistent and overlapping claims arising from losses in San Francisco. More importantly, insurers and reinsurers came to understand that their long-term viability depended upon establishing a reputation for fair dealing that might demand a liberality of spirit and action not strictly required by a narrower assessment of legal obligation and cost. The compensatory mechanisms that came into play following the San Francisco Earthquake displayed

[69] James (2013b, 251).
[70] James (2013b, 261–2).
[71] Kobrak (2012, 287).
[72] James (2013b, 267–9).

a cosmopolitanism and international mutuality beyond the imaginings even of a Condorcet.

## 2.6 Conclusion

The history of insurance and reinsurance over the past several centuries reveals an inexorable trend towards global economic integration and social solidarity. Even though, in the twentieth century, that momentum would periodically be stalled by protectionism, revolution, and war, the long-term trajectory is unmistakable and follows the larger cultural pattern of insurance steadily working its way into the centre of modern economic, social, political life. Indeed, the global growth of reinsurance services from the early nineteenth century to the present day may be seen as the culmination of a prolonged process by which age-old forms of mutual aid and locally provided compensation have gradually been supplanted by impersonal indemnifying institutions operating according to rules-based protocols that take no heed of community identity, ethnicity, or religion. The demand for fire insurance in Russia soared, for example, after the emancipation of the serfs and the concomitant withdrawal of landlords from their traditional paternalistic role of making good their peasants' losses due to fire.[73] As those older bonds dissolved, actuarial technology stepped in to create new communities of risk that have been no less important or influential for their being largely invisible and abstract to the individuals who form them. Through the medium of international insurance networks, individuals, to a truly remarkable degree, have placed their trust and their long-term welfare not only in the hands of insurance institutions promising their decades-long fidelity, but also in a globe-encircling pool of complete strangers whose collective adherence to a behavioural code and normative regime is taken for granted. The astonishing success of this planetary network of mutual indemnification and risk reduction furnishes a powerful example of the imbricated constitutional, operating, and normative rules Douglass North has identified as both structuring and propelling the modern 'political-economic system'.[74] Indeed, Jacques Donzelot and François Ewald have located the insurance principle at the centre of the construction of the welfare state in France and Germany, profoundly reshaping jurisprudential and social notions of justice and obligation in the process. This new organizing principle—'actuarialism'—accepts the inevitability of accident and chooses on grounds of efficiency to compensate losses through means of private or public insurance rather than to assign responsibility to a liable party.[75] Insurance,

[73] Frierson (2002), 182.

[74] D. North (1981) *Structure and Change in Economic History*. New York: W.W. Norton, 203–4.

[75] F. Ewald (1986) *L'Etat Providence*. Paris: Bernard Grasset; J. Donzelot (1988) 'The Promotion of the Social', *Economy and Society* 17: 3, 395–427.

Ewald explains, is 'a type of justice under which the damage suffered by one is borne by all, and individual responsibility is made collective and social'.[76]

Without doubt, for those lucky enough to live in the countries of the developed world, individual access to insurance coverage, as well as the wider benefits of the insurance principle incorporated into the social welfare state, have fundamentally transformed expectations about what life can or should hold in store. Insurance has played a critical role in creating an unprecedented sense of security against the possibility of harm or loss. It has helped to foster a cosmopolitanism that enables trust to extend beyond the old frontiers of tribe or ethnicity or religion. It has provided an ideal socio-political balance between, in Ewald's words, 'a form of association which combines a maximum of socialization with a maximum of individualization. It allows people to enjoy the advantages of association while still leaving them free to exist as individuals.'[77] That individual freedom consists, in no small measure, of an opportunity to explore, to experiment, to expose oneself to interesting and potentially fruitful risks knowing that the mundane risks of life—fire, flood, illness, automobile accident, and the like—can be pushed into the background of worry. Insurance is a price we pay for leading more fulfilled, carefree lives far less subject to the gnawing fears that stalked previous generations. Whether the recent neo-liberal effort to resist *l'état providence* by shrinking the social safety net, rolling back the principles of actuarialism, and weaning citizens from the nanny state will ultimately prove successful is an open question, but one whose outcome will decisively shape the political, social, and cultural fortunes of the twenty-first century.

[76] Ewald (1991, 207). For other views of how the insurance industry has exerted a powerful influence over private behaviour in the modern period, see Ericson, Doyle, and Barry (2003); Clark et al. (2010).

[77] Ewald (1991, 204).

CHAPTER 3

# THE EVOLUTION OF THE INDUSTRY STRUCTURE

ROBIN PEARSON

THE economic importance of insurance to modern economies cannot be denied. In 2014, global insurance premiums amounted to USD 4778 billion, or over 6 per cent of world GDP.[1] An unknown part of this huge business was reinsured. In 2014, the fifty largest reinsurance groups had a combined gross premium income of USD 222 billion, or nearly 5 per cent of global insurance, although, as this chapter suggests this figure may belie the historic role of reinsurance in supporting the international distribution of risk.[2]

With the exception of a few standard works, the history of reinsurance has, for the most part, almost entirely failed to attract the attention of academic scholarship.[3] Only recently has a new wave of scholarship greatly extended our understanding of how reinsurance has developed in the past two centuries, although there remain considerable gaps in our knowledge.

In short, we are now in a better position to offer an overview of the industry since its earliest days. Sections 3.1 and 3.2 survey the growth of international reinsurance from its beginnings to the Second World War. Section 3.3 sketches the major trends since 1945. Section 3.4 draws some conclusions.

[1] These figures disguise wide differentials between countries and regions. In the Middle East, Central Asia, Central and Eastern Europe, insurance premiums accounted for less than 2 per cent of GDP in 2014. In 'advanced Asian markets'—Hong Kong, Singapore, Taiwan, and South Korea—the ratio was over 11 per cent. Swiss Re, *sigma*, 4, 2015, 7.

[2] Calculated from *Best's Review*, September 2015, 82.

[3] See Chapter 1, this volume.

## 3.1 Reinsurance from its Origins to the First World War

Reinsurance was practised in European marine insurance during the seventeenth and eighteenth centuries, where it co-existed alongside co-insurance and subscription insurance.[4] Ships and cargoes on the transatlantic, African, and Asian routes carried some of the largest risks of the early modern age, too large for most individuals to underwrite on their own. Thus they were ideal objects for reinsurance. In Great Britain, however, marine reinsurance ran foul of anti-gambling legislation and was banned from 1746 until 1864. This ban ensured that British marine insurance was largely conducted on a subscription basis by underwriters at Lloyds.[5]

Modern reinsurance, therefore, developed initially within fire insurance, where it took two forms: facultative reinsurance, where one fire insurance company provided a reinsurance 'facility' to another company that wished to lay off a proportion of its liability on a specific insurance or group of risks; and surplus lines treaty reinsurance, where two offices or more agreed, usually on a reciprocal basis, to exchange surplus liabilities above the limits that they were prepared to insure on specified lines of risk. Given the legal uncertainties about whether the ban on marine reinsurance also applied to other lines, the approach to facultative fire reinsurance in Britain initially remained cautious. As early as 1804, the Sun and the Imperial fire insurance offices were discussing 'reciprocal insurances' as 'the best means of promoting the mutual interest of both companies'. A year later, however, the Norwich Union Fire Insurance Society proposed to the Imperial 'to participate . . . in such insurances as may in amount exceed the sum which the Office at Norwich may wish to include in a single risk'. The Imperial declined, voicing its concern that such a device was 'not strictly legal'. Instead, the Imperial suggested 'an allocated coinsurance' arrangement, by which the Norwich Union would inform its policyholders that a policy for up to GBP 5000 could be issued

[4] Co-insurance is where the same risk is insured by two or more insurers by the issue of separate policies. Subscription insurance is where two or more insurers subscribe to insure the same risk in one policy, but often for different amounts. Ships and cargoes insured wholly within Lloyd's were insured on the latter system. However, some Lloyd's-insured risks were also co-insured by the two London marine insurance corporations, with the latter issuing their own policies.

[5] We do not know how much marine reinsurance was written outside the UK before the British proscription was lifted. It may be that most marine underwriting outside the UK was also conducted on a direct or co-insurance basis. The first specialist reinsurers in Germany in the nineteenth century did write marine and transport business. One of these, the Weseler-Rückversicherungsverein (founded in 1840 as a subsidiary of the Niederrheinische Güterassecuranzgesellschaft in Wesel), *only* wrote transport (probably river transport) reinsurance. By the end of the First World War, marine reinsurance had become a huge business. Huebner states that the eighty-eight US marine insurance companies operating in 1918 reinsured 41 per cent of their USD 174 million marine premiums. Huebner (1922, 156).

by each office 'without any additional trouble or expense'.[6] Over the next two decades, as Britain's large fire insurers faced requests to provide cover for ever-larger industrial and commercial risks, such 'allocated coinsurance agreements' multiplied.[7] This early form of risk sharing also spread to overseas business, and was the antecedent of the facultative reinsurance that developed during the second decade of the nineteenth century, legal uncertainties notwithstanding. In 1812, the Phoenix Fire Office reinsured risks that it had accepted in Jamaica with two other London offices: the Atlas and the Imperial.[8] This type of reinsurance co-existed for a while with 'allocated coinsurance', but by the 1820s reciprocal surplus lines reinsurance, both facultative and by formal treaty, had become more general.

The first reinsurance treaties were signed in England, Belgium, Germany, and France in the early 1820s.[9] This type of treaty reinsurance between direct fire insurers grew steadily in Europe, with German companies participating most frequently.[10] Of thirty-four treaties identified for the period to 1850, twenty-two involved German companies, fourteen involved British, six involved French, and a few each involved Belgian, Austrian, Russian, and Italian insurers.[11] Sixteen of these treaties were cross-border arrangements that helped distribute risk more widely and reduced the danger of revealing information about one's business to local rivals. Despite the early prominence of German companies, it is likely that other nations exported more reinsurance before 1850. In three early Franco-German and Belgian–German fire reinsurance treaties for which we have data, the average credit balances were in favour of the French and Belgian offices, and in the international treaties involving British insurers, the balances mostly lay in favour of the latter.[12] Indeed, the early reinsurance business of the large German fire insurance offices grew much more slowly than their direct business.[13]

Direct insurers employed reinsurance, first, to spread their insurance liabilities as widely as possible, geographically and by category of risk; second, to smooth out

[6] London Metropolitan Archive (hereafter LMA) CLC/B/192-18/MS 12160A/1, Imperial Insurance: Meeting Minutes of Directors, 9 May 1804; 6 March 1805.

[7] For examples, see LMA CLC/B/107/MS 16170/1, Atlas Assurance: Meeting Minutes of Directors, 27 April 1809; 9 May 1811.

[8] Clive Trebilcock suggests that 'the line between allocated co-insurance and facultative reinsurance may be rather fine'. Trebilcock (1985, 278). The key difference is that the former involves contractual relationships between all insurers and the insured, whereas the reinsurer has no contractual relationship with the insured, but only with the direct insurer. In early nineteenth-century Britain, however, this distinction was probably unclear to contemporary fire insurers, who, as noted earlier in this section, worried whether their business was also subject to the 1746 prohibition on reinsurance.

[9] Pearson (1995, 566–7).

[10] 'German' is used here in the generic sense for companies based in pre-unification German states, including Prussia, Saxony, Bavaria, Baden, Württemberg, and the city states of Frankfurt and Hamburg.

[11] Pearson (1995, 569). This total certainly does not capture all the treaties signed in this period.

[12] Calculated from Sack (1941, 119–26); Helmsen (1938). The three treaties referred to are Vaterländische Feuerversicherungs-Gesellschaft, Elberfeld/Compagnie Royale de Paris, lasting from 1829 to 1841; Colonia/La Providence, Paris, and Colonia/Compagnie Générale, Brussels, both covering 1839–42.

[13] Pearson (1995, 562).

random fluctuations in their loss ratios; and third, to enable them to increase the volume of business accepted and raise the limits they imposed on individual risks in order to make their product more attractive to consumers. Direct insurers sometimes also used reinsurance in a strategic way in order to increase their share of particular markets.[14]

In the middle of the century, the first specialist, or, as they later became known, 'professional' reinsurance companies began to appear—in Germany from the 1840s, and in Belgium, Switzerland, France, Austria, and Hungary from the late 1850s and early 1860s. Almost all of these new ventures were the progeny of direct insurance companies faced with increasing shortages of reinsurance capacity at home, and, following large urban conflagrations such as Hamburg in 1842 and Memel in 1854, becoming more aware of a need to create their own channels for reinsurance. Some of these reinsurers were restricted to accepting business only from their parent company. In some cases, such as Swiss Re, there was also a nationalist motive behind a new foundation, where promoters saw it as a means to stem the flow of reinsurance income out of their country to foreign insurers.[15] Within a few years of its foundation in 1864, the Swiss Re was reinsuring risks across Europe, North America, and Asia via a series of obligatory and facultative agreements with twenty-six partner companies.[16]

The aim of the professional reinsurance companies was to spread their risks geographically as widely and evenly as possible. By 1913, for example, just 12 per cent of Swiss Re's premium income from its seventy fire reinsurance treaties derived from Switzerland.[17] Their global distribution of business inevitably made finding solutions to the problem of monitoring—clients as well as risks—a major preoccupation for professional reinsurers.[18] This issue was exacerbated by the growing number of suppliers in the reinsurance market. In 1888, for instance, property destroyed in two huge conflagrations in the Swedish towns of Sundsvall and Umeå was reinsured by fifty-seven and forty-two companies—direct insurers and professional reinsurers—respectively.[19] With such complex webs of liability emerging between companies, international networking and cooperation among treaty partners were important in reinsurance markets at an early date. Such relations could be reinforced by face-to-face

[14] See, for example, the comments on the Liverpool, London & Globe, and Imperial insurance companies in LMA CLC/B/227/MS 21534, Heckscher & Pearson, General Foreign Letter Book, fol. 161, letter to A. Nane, Hanseatic Fire Insurance Company, 10 February 1879.

[15] Pearson (2001, 30). This was also a consideration of the promoters of the Cologne Reinsurance Company in 1842 and the Russian Reinsurance Company in 1896. Kölnische Rückversicherungsgesellschaft (1953, 12–13); Petrov (2012, 224). The Cologne promoters were also concerned about the risk of warfare hampering the ability of insurers to make claims successfully on reinsurers located in a hostile territory. See their 'Pro Memoria' of 1843, reproduced in Kölnische Rückversicherungsgesellschaft (1903, 3–5).

[16] *Preussische Versicherungs-Zeitschrift* 2, 1868, 403–4.

[17] Rohland (2011a, 47–8).

[18] On local risk inspection and the monitoring problem, as evidenced by Swiss Re records, see Chapter 1, this volume.

[19] Calculated from the data in Rohland (2011a, 93–101).

contacts between small groups of managers who were continually travelling between offices and markets. Extensive international travel, which became the identity badge of the reinsurance executive, was supplemented by frequent correspondence, telegrams, and telephone conversations between the 'captains of insurance', as Charles Simon called them, from hotel rooms, railway stations, and branch offices around the world.[20]

In addition to an extensive spatial distribution of risk, a related aim of the professional reinsurers was to control maximum retentions in order to achieve, as far as possible, a homogenous distribution of risks over a given period or underwriting cycle. To do this they required loss data from cedents over a long time period, from which they could estimate the future cost of accepting cessions, the price of retrocessions, and the level of retention.[21] Underpinning this was the maxim, already familiar before 1900, of the reinsurer 'following the fortunes' of the cedent—the latter's risks should become the former's risks through the reinsurance contract.[22] In turn, this rested upon the long-established insurance principle of *uberrima fides*, full disclosure by the cedent of any material circumstances that might affect the reinsurer's decision to enter or continue the reinsurance contract at the given price and terms.[23]

The information requirements listed eventually shaped the structure of reinsurance companies into three main units: the treaty department, responsible for the acquisition of business and the negotiation, amendment, and renewal of treaties; the accounting department, which carried out all calculations on the basis of documentation and estimates; and the technical department, which supplied the accounting department with estimates, controlled the amounts retained and retroceded, examined the losses, and carried out the actuarial work in life reinsurance.[24] In general, although underwriting margins for professional reinsurers were often low, administrative costs were also much lower than for direct insurance companies, as no expensive networks of agencies or branch offices had to be maintained to do business with the public.

Close on the heels of the first reinsurance companies came the first international reinsurance brokers. Most had their origins in shipping and general commodity trading. The most powerful reinsurance broker in the world before the First World War was the Heckscher Group, a series of interlocking partnerships that together managed an estimated mark 200 million of premiums in 1914. This may have exceeded the net premium income of the largest reinsurance company of the time, the

[20] SRCA 10.101 517.02, 8.

[21] See SRCA 10.119 090.01, R. J. Duff to the general manager of Swiss Re, 19 April 1934, enclosing the results of the New India Company's first surplus fire treaty 1920–33, and inviting the Swiss to participate in it.

[22] Rohland (2011a, 30–1).

[23] *The Review*, November 1985, 12–15. My thanks to Niels Viggo Haueter for this reference. *Uberrima fides*, 'utmost good faith', was articulated as a principle of insurance contracts between insurers and their insured by Lord Mansfield, Chief Justice of the King's Bench in London, in *Carter* v. *Boehm* [1766], reprinted in *All England Law Reports*, 183.

[24] Hollitscher (1931, 61).

Munich Re.[25] The Group commenced as a general insurance agency set up by Martin Heckscher and Carl Gustav Brauer in Hamburg in 1863. By 1900, it had sister firms for reinsurance, registered under different combinations of partners, in St Petersburg, Vienna, Berlin, and London, with branch offices in Liverpool and New York. Reinsurance brokers dealt mostly with the biggest direct insurance companies, and the powers of attorney awarded to them were broad. For example, in the notarized power given in 1875 by the Queen Insurance Company of Liverpool to Heckscher & Gottlieb of Vienna, the latter had 'unlimited powers in all matters which refer to the transaction of business in Austria-Hungary . . . ', and 'authority to make reinsurance agreements, to fix the stipulations therein and the premiums, to adjust, settle and pay losses, to effect compromises, to elect arbitrators and their umpires . . . '.[26]

Reinsurance brokers aimed to generate a large commission income through a portfolio of agencies, and to be able to place reinsurances and obtain retrocession facilities while minimizing transaction costs. They canvassed for clients and helped direct insurers enter foreign reinsurance markets with which they were unfamiliar.[27] Reinsurance brokers also had a banking function. Because they used their own funds to pay reinsurance claims and then had to demand cheques from their reinsurer clients, the ability to maintain cash flows from the latter was critical to them. The reputation of brokers with the direct insurance companies depended greatly upon their ability to settle reinsurance losses efficiently and promptly with those companies.[28] A degree of legal security from liability was also important. Brokers would not begin to negotiate reinsurance contracts on a client's behalf without a satisfactory written power of attorney. They were answerable for the honesty, efficiency, and liquidity of the reinsurers whose names they proposed to the ceding companies.[29] Thus, the reputation of reinsurance brokers also rested on their ability to set correct limits in treaties, to provide clients with an equitable distribution of risks, to keep losses down, and to deal only with respectable companies. Brokers often possessed information about markets that specialist reinsurers did not have. Consequently, at least during the late

[25] This claim is made in the firm's memorial history, privately published in 1968—Hollitscher & Gottlieb (1968, 23)—where Munich Re's net premiums (net of retrocessions) are stated to be mark 165 million in 1914. Munich Re's gross premiums in 1913–14 were mark 204 million. Kluge (2006, table 1).

[26] Reproduced in Hollitscher & Gottlieb (1968, appendix VIII).

[27] One example is the effort made by Heckscher & Pearson in 1878 to obtain, for the Second Russian Fire Insurance Company and La Fonciere Insurance Company of Paris, a share in the treaty reinsurance business from Canada ceded by the Liverpool, London & Globe Insurance Company. LMA CLC/B/227/MS 21534, Heckscher & Pearson, General Foreign Letter Book, fol. 109, letter to A. Nivert, 2 February 1878.

[28] See LMA CLC/B/227/MS 21534, Heckscher & Pearson, General Foreign Letter Book, fol. 84, letter to the Prussian Fire Insurance Company, 4 December 1877.

[29] For example, see the letter from Heckscher & Pearson to their sister firm in Berlin, enclosing the prospectus of a new company that the latter had enquired about: 'It is recently established and has a first class directorate, but our personal opinion of the Manager is not a very high one.' LMA CLC/B/227/MS 21534, Heckscher & Pearson, General Foreign Letter Book, fol. 226, letter to Messrs Heckscher & Gottlieb, 31 August 1881.

nineteenth and early twentieth centuries, the big broker firms were able to act as gatekeepers to the reinsurance business, and as enforcers of behavioural norms in the company market, maintaining the 'protocols' of the business and helping to standardize procedures, terms and conditions of treaties, and forms of risk advices and bordereaux.[30]

In the infancy of corporate reinsurance, most specialist companies remained fragile and experimental. There were difficulties in recruiting qualified managers, which some suggest may have slowed down the growth of professional reinsurance before 1914.[31] At the same time, speculative ventures popped up 'like mushrooms', only to disappear soon afterwards. At the start of 1871, for example, there were still only twelve reinsurance companies in Germany, Austria, and Switzerland, but this number more than doubled in the three boom years that followed.[32] Direct insurers also competed more fiercely for a slice of the reinsurance market. By the early 1870s, the Phoenix Assurance of London was earning 58 per cent of its huge foreign fire premium income (GBP 250,000 p.a.) from treaty reinsurance.[33] Many large British and European fire insurance companies established dedicated reinsurance bureaus, sometimes as joint ventures with other offices. There were twenty-five such bureaus in Paris in 1878, for instance, representing fourteen British, three Italian, two Swiss, and two Rumanian companies, and one each from Germany, Russia, Austria, and the USA.[34] The original function of such bureaus was to administer and broker the reinsurance risks of their firms and deal with the technical side of the business, but the bureaus soon began to accept reinsurances in their own right and became independent institutions.[35]

Over the following decades in different places, such as Belgium in 1888, reinsurance continued to suffer from minor investment bubbles, as new, often speculative, enterprises were founded overnight, and as all kinds of non-insurance institutions plunged into the market in the hope of a quick profit.[36] The UK experienced its first 'fad' for reinsurance when at least five specialist companies were founded between 1874 and

[30] On terms, conditions, and procedures of treaties, see LMA CLC/B/227/MS 21534, Heckscher & Pearson, General Foreign Letter Book, fol. 109, letter to A. Nivert, 2 February 1878; on accounting systems, LMA CLC/B/227/MS 21534, Heckscher & Pearson, General Foreign Letter Book, fols. 150–1, letter to A. Nivert, 28 October 1878; on bordereaux, LMA CLC/B/227/MS 21534, Heckscher & Pearson, General Foreign Letter Book, fol. 131, letter to the Prussian Fire Insurance Company, 9 July 1878. A bordereau was an itemized statement of risks, usually in tabular form, being ceded by a direct insurer to the reinsurer. Their use can be dated back to the earliest reinsurance treaties between British, Belgian, and French insurers in the 1820s and 1830s.

[31] Hollitscher (1931). On the difficulties faced by Swiss Re in recruiting its early managers see Straumann (2013, 248–50).

[32] Arps (1965a, 208). One paper claimed that there were sixteen reinsurance companies in Austria-Hungary alone by the start of 1873, more than in the rest of Europe together. *Deutsche Versicherungs-Zeitschrift* 14, 28 January 1873.

[33] Trebilcock (1998, 134–5, tables 2.1, 2.2).

[34] *Rundschau der Versicherungen* 28, 1878, 51–2.

[35] Hollitscher (1931). It is unclear how these bureaus related to the independent reinsurance brokers' firms that acted as agents for the direct insurers.

[36] For the reinsurance 'fad' in Belgium in 1888, see *Assecuranz Jahrbuch* 11, 1890, 389–90.

1877, but these were mostly small, poorly managed ventures that did not last. This established a pattern that lasted well into the twentieth century. Following a surge in new company foundations at the end of the First World War, the two largest British reinsurers collapsed from 'speculative' underwriting and poor marine results, and by 1927 the nine surviving reinsurance companies were described as 'lacking strength'.[37]

Some reasons have been offered as to why the British—the greatest insurance exporters of the nineteenth century—failed to develop powerful professional reinsurance companies to rival those in Zurich and Munich. Some of the large British fire insurance offices developed a distrust of European reinsurance practices, an attitude reinforced by heavy losses experienced in Russia and Austria during the 1860s and 1870s. In 1868, the manager of the Sun, Britain's oldest joint-stock insurance office, announced that his company 'do not regard reinsurance transactions with favour'.[38] The enthusiasm of the Phoenix quickly dissipated when its treaties began to deliver only heavy losses. By the end of the 1880s, the proportion of its foreign income derived from reinsurance had collapsed to 17 per cent, as treaty after treaty was cancelled. By 1914, it was below 5 per cent.[39]

In respect of developing specialist reinsurance organizations, British insurers may have suffered from the same kind of first-starter problems that several British staple industries experienced in competition with overseas rivals during the later nineteenth century. The advantages of low set-up and administrative costs, that characterized new professional reinsurance ventures in Europe, could not be matched by the large British fire insurance companies, with their already extensive agency and branch office systems strung around the world. Moreover, during the later nineteenth century, and again after the First World War, the risks were too high, and the prices and profit margins too low, on European reinsurance to induce British companies to establish reinsurance subsidiaries, when they could achieve much greater volumes of premium income on higher-rated direct business in North America and throughout the British Empire.[40] Thus, as professional reinsurance companies and brokers firms emerged in numbers in Europe, the British increasingly became net purchasers rather than sellers of reinsurance. In 1874, there were already some twenty foreign insurance companies operating in the UK, mostly writing reinsurance rather than direct business.[41] The Liverpool & London Insurance Company was reinsuring 43 per cent of its gross fire insurance premiums as early as 1856, when its agency business extended across Europe, Latin America, Africa, India, and the Far East.[42] Surviving data suggest that most UK fire insurers reinsured between 10 and 35 per cent of their gross premiums during the second half of the nineteenth century. British direct insurers thus became the most

[37] *The Review*, 1927, 939. [38] Dickson (1960, 186).
[39] Trebilcock (1998, 135, table 2.2). [40] Pearson (1995, 567–9).
[41] L. Nikisch (ed.) (1874) *Vereinsblatt für Deutsches Versicherungswesen*, vol. 2. Berlin: Mittler.
[42] Liverpool Record Office (hereafter LRO), Royal Insurance Archives, 368. ROY, J. C. Rimmer, Notes for a History of Liverpool, London & Globe, 1923.

important clients of the European reinsurance companies because their risks were truly global in distribution.

Despite the waves of reinsurance company promotions, direct insurers, rather than reinsurance specialists, continued to write the bulk of reinsurance. By 1879, when German direct insurers were reinsuring mark 45 million, or about half of their total fire business, the fire premiums earned by German reinsurance companies only amounted to mark 8.5 million, suggesting that at this stage Germany remained a net importer of reinsurance from abroad.[43] This changed following the foundation of the Munich Re in 1880 by a small group of bankers and industrialists from Bavaria and Berlin. Under the robust leadership of Carl von Thieme, a former agent of the Thuringia Assurance Company, Munich Re witnessed explosive growth, becoming the market leader within five years.[44] Thieme's strategy was based on his belief in the law of large numbers, namely that a sufficient volume and distribution of risks would ensure that loss-making treaties would be more than offset by profitable ones. In addition, by offering clients a share in Munich Re's own treaty profits—usually 10 per cent—Thieme helped to bind more closely the interests of cedents with those of the reinsurer. By the end of the century Munich Re was already expanding out of fire reinsurance into relatively new areas of reinsurance underwriting, such as accident, engineering, liability, credit and burglary reinsurance, and the reinsurance of 'substandard' lives. Munich Re also inverted the traditional relationship between parent direct insurers and their reinsurance offspring by founding direct insurance subsidiaries, or by investing in a share of other direct companies at home and abroad. The company's gross premium income reached mark 5.4 million by 1887, and mark 204.5 million by the eve of the First World War.[45] By the latter date, the aggregate fire premiums of German reinsurance companies almost equalled the total fire premiums of German direct insurers, and were over four times as great as the reinsurance income of the latter.[46]

In just over thirty years, Germany had become the world's greatest exporter of reinsurance, although professional reinsurance companies from a wide range of other nations also operated in international markets. In addition, a growing number of direct insurers from smaller countries sold fire reinsurance via general agencies or brokers, as a means of gaining access to foreign markets where they did not wish to underwrite directly. One example is the National Insurance Company of Athens, established in 1891 as Greece's first native insurance company with a modest capital of USD 500,000. Within two years of its foundation, it had appointed an agency firm in New York to write surplus line fire reinsurance.[47] Where reinsurance was concerned, there was no shortage of an adventurous, sometimes foolhardy, spirit among the smaller European nations before 1914.

[43] Gerathewohl et al. (1982, 695).

[44] The following, unless otherwise stated, is based on Bähr and Kopper (2015, 39–54).

[45] *The Review*, 1927, 930; Kluge (2006, table 1); Bähr and Kopper (2015, tables 2 and 6).

[46] Pearson (1995, table 2).

[47] *Insurance Critic* 21, June 1893, 228.

## 3.2 Crises and Change Between the World Wars

The First World War resulted in a major loss of markets in the Allied countries and the British Empire for German and Austrian reinsurers, while the Bolshevik Revolution ended the reinsurance business of Russian companies, except for a few that reconstituted themselves abroad.[48] At the same time, the inflation of property values and the risks associated with wartime economies led to soaring demand for reinsurance. The void left by the absence of the Germans was met by increasing numbers of specialist reinsurers from neutral or smaller nations such as Switzerland, Denmark, and Sweden. Table A.1 in the Appendix presents data on 275 professional reinsurance companies by date of foundation and country of origin between 1840 and 1936. The data are certainly incomplete and inexact. The table includes companies that wrote direct insurance but were described by contemporaries as undertaking 'mainly reinsurance', as well as those that were clearly pure reinsurers.[49] Nevertheless, it suffices to show how the supply of reinsurance shifted between nations during the war, and how the range of countries that gave birth to such companies expanded rapidly before and during the war, although Germany retained its early lead. 30 per cent of the companies in the table were established during the decade that straddled the First World War, with Britain, France, and Denmark hosting the largest concentrations of new reinsurance ventures. After the war and during the 1920s, the rate of new reinsurance company foundations remained higher than before 1914, while the trend towards a global diffusion of these companies among host countries continued. The 1920s also witnessed, for the first time, the emergence of an indigenous reinsurance industry in the USA. Finally, the table also reveals the slowdown in reinsurance company promotion during the depression of the early 1930s. Fewer than two new companies on average were launched each year, compared with over seven during the previous decade.

The demand for reinsurance during the First World War and the immediate post-war years could not be satisfied even by the large number of new reinsurance

[48] The US branch of the Rossiya reconstituted itself as an American enterprise, and the Salamandra set up a company in Denmark to write reinsurance outside Russia. Wilkins (2004, 91–2); Petrov (2012, 226).

[49] I have included in Table A.1 companies defined by *The Review* as doing 'mainly reinsurance', where there is no further information, but excluded those founded as direct insurers that later took up reinsurance, e.g. Sveriges Allmänna (1872) or Christiania (1847), as well as those direct insurers described as having 'substantial' reinsurance business. I have also excluded the US company Equity Fire (1909), which gave up direct writing in 1933 to operate only as a reinsurer, but returned to direct writing in 1934. I have included those companies, e.g. the three Danish companies Baltica, Rossiya, and Scandinavia, that were 'identified abroad as primarily reinsurance companies, but they hold a prominent position in the home market as direct insurers', *The Review*, 1935, 1238. Another, less important, problem with this table is that, for a small number of companies, different sources give different foundation dates, but most of these discrepancies have been eliminated by cross-checking.

companies, so direct insurers increased their activity as sellers of reinsurance, while also demanding reciprocity for the reinsurance that they ceded. When demand fell off after the war, this 'reciprocity principle' remained in many of the treaties negotiated. This put great pressure on the professional reinsurance companies, who often found it difficult to meet the insistence by direct insurers that one contract be matched against another with approximate parity. The system of reciprocity became almost universal in fire insurance and spread rapidly in accident insurance between the wars. The driver behind it was the attempt by direct insurers to maintain their volumes of premium income in the face of increasing competition in slow-growing markets. Contemporaries observed a 'wild scramble for treaty business in an attempt to maintain the premium income at all costs'.[50] Reciprocity had several important effects. First, it shifted the balance of bargaining power away from the professional reinsurance firms back towards the direct insurers.[51] Second, as business was usually between companies of different sizes, reciprocity led to an increasing fragmentation of surplus lines in treaties, in order that the volume of business reinsured by a large direct insurer would match that derived from one line of a small reinsurer's treaty. This resulted in a growing number of reinsurers participating in individual treaties, which in turn pushed up their administration costs and drove down margins. Third, because of the rising costs of reinsurance, which, ironically, reciprocity was supposed to alleviate, the reciprocal system led to what contemporaries described as the rise of a 'keen bargaining spirit' in reinsurance, in which the main aim was to secure the best deal for the moment, rather than find a solid reinsurance partner with whom to establish business relations over the long term.[52] One Norwegian insurance executive felt in 1937 that reinsurance was becoming 'more of a commercial than an insurance transaction', with much greater 'give and take' in the negotiations surrounding it.[53]

The interwar years were marked by a contraction in international trade, and by unstable financial markets that were far more prone to default than had been the case before 1914, partly due to the burden of war debts and their link to reparations payments, and partly due to the greater use of short-term lending to finance long-term capital projects.[54] A related problem was the disruption in the relation between the internal price levels in countries and the exchange value of their currencies. There were some currencies about which no one knew how much a debt or the value of an insurance policy would be worth just a few months after a transaction. Weak currencies and volatile exchange rates could make reciprocity in reinsurance expensive, especially for German reinsurers trying to pay premiums to foreign offices with a heavily

[50] *Post Magazine and Insurance Monitor* 23, 10 June 1939, 1144.

[51] *Post Magazine and Insurance Monitor* 23, 4 June 1938, 1163.

[52] *Post Magazine and Insurance Monitor* 23, 10 June 1939, 1146.

[53] *The Review*, 1937, 1208, citing Reidar Brekke, general manager of Trondhjems Forsikringsselskab. I develop an argument about this key trend in interfirm reinsurance relations in my unpublished paper 'Doing Reinsurance: From its Origins to 1938'.

[54] W. Ashworth (1987) *A Short History of the International Economy since 1850* (4th edn). London and New York: Longman, 226–53.

devalued mark. The Munich Re survived the German hyperinflation of the early 1920s mainly by maintaining a large proportion of its funds in foreign investments and real estate.[55] Establishing subsidiaries in other countries was another means of gaining valuable hard currency.[56] Exchange-rate fluctuations dogged international reinsurance through the 1920s and 1930s. Devaluation could have a capricious effect on technical underwriting results. The conversion into dollars or sterling of reinsurance premiums earned in a devalued currency could turn profits into losses and make a mockery of the principle of 'following the fortunes' of the cedent. Particularly after 1933, restrictions on the cross-border movement of currencies, imposed by many governments trying to control inflation, became an additional problem for international reinsurers. Where the latter were forced to pay premiums into local banks rather than repatriate them, such deposits rarely earned more than a nominal rate of interest.[57]

There were other external threats between the wars that had seldom been faced before 1914. For political as well as financial reasons, German reinsurance companies never recovered their pre-war position in the Anglo-Saxon markets before the depression of the early 1930s and the rise of fascism raised further concerns for foreign companies dealing with them. Elsewhere, nationalist calls for tighter controls over the operations of foreign firms created a more hostile environment for all international reinsurers.[58] In attempts to control the outflow of money abroad, some states, such as Greece and Portugal, considered nationalizing reinsurance, while the new Bolshevik government in Russia did so in 1918.[59] Between 1924 and 1946, Costa Rica, Chile, Turkey, Iran, Latvia, Brazil, and Argentina created full or partial state monopolies for reinsurance with foreign companies.[60] In Sweden, despite repeated political threats, reinsurance was not nationalized, but from 1914 to 1989, life reinsurance was dominated by a near monopoly joint-stock organization owned by the private life insurance industry. Similar quasi-monopoly reinsurers were also established in Norway and Denmark.[61]

The interwar period also saw mixed fortunes for different lines of reinsurance. The slow recovery of world trade and the decline of international shipping, together with heavy ocean marine losses, rendered marine reinsurance unprofitable. Life insurance, on the other hand, and many types of casualty and liability insurance, grew rapidly.

55 *The Review*, 28 October 1927.

56 Borscheid (2007, 131).

57 *Post Magazine and Insurance Monitor* 23, 10 June 1939, 1093.

58 On nationalist opposition to British insurers in India in the 1920s, for example, see Balachandran (2012, 450–1).

59 *The Review*, 1937, 1198; Petrov (2012, 225). In Russia, a national reinsurance company, promoted by the tariff fire insurance offices, had obtained official sanction as early as 1895, but 50 per cent of its members' surpluses were still permitted to be ceded to foreign companies. LMA, CLC/B/227/MS 21534, Heckscher & Pearson, General Foreign Letter Book, letter of 2 July 1895; Hollitscher & Gottlieb (1968, appendix XII); Petrov (2012, 224).

60 *Post Magazine and Insurance Monitor* 23, 10 June 1939, 1091; Neave (1980, 160–79); Borscheid (2007, 133); Zappino (2007). A bill for a state reinsurance monopoly was also presented to the Irish parliament in 1935. *The Review*, 1935, 1210–11.

61 Larsson and Lönnborg (2014, 2015).

Despite the continued weakness of British professional reinsurance companies, London developed as a centre for international reinsurance. Lloyds, in particular, expanded into a centre for writing reinsurance cover in the growing markets for aviation and automobile insurance, as well as liability and indemnity insurance. In 1927, 103 foreign companies from twenty-one countries were represented in the London reinsurance market by twenty-seven agency firms. The brokers Fester, Fothergill & Hartung alone had twelve companies on their books from Spain, Italy, Cuba, Japan, Czechoslovakia, Sweden, Germany, France, and Poland. By 1938, the number of companies in the London reinsurance market had risen to 118 from twenty-nine countries.[62]

Pressure for change within reinsurance also created new concerns. At the end of the war, direct insurers pressed reinsurers to curtail the use of bordereaux. Their aim was to save clerical costs, but it was also because the value of the information in bordereaux was diminishing as surplus lines in treaties were diced into ever-smaller parcels due to the reciprocity system discussed earlier in this section.[63] Generally this pressure was successfully resisted by the 'reinsurers of the old school' such as the Swiss Re, who were not keen to relinquish all knowledge of their commitments in this way. Nevertheless, quota share and facultative treaties were increasingly regarded as cumbersome. These treaties required the cedent to give the reinsurer a notice outlining the details of a risk (name of the insured, construction, occupation, rate, amount of policy, and amount retained), after which the reinsurer and cedent exchanged request notes, the cedent forwarded a copy or an extract of the original policy, and finally the reinsurer issued a guarantee note to complete the reinsurance. This was the procedure set out by the rules of the British Fire Offices Committee in 1871, and it was still largely in place in the 1930s.

Another problem for reinsurers was posed by the rise of excess-loss (XL) transactions.[64] Here the general rule was that the reinsurer paid 90 per cent of the annual claims of the cedent above an agreed amount. XL reinsurance began to become popular with direct insurers in the years before the First World War, as it helped smooth random (though not cyclical) fluctuations in their claims experience. It was difficult, however, for reinsurers to fix premium rates for the business, and difficult for them to obtain long-term treaties from cedents. For these reasons, XL reinsurance made little headway in fire insurance, although it did become widely used in automobile insurance, where the rate paid for XL cover was usually a percentage of the cedent's total motor premium income. Reinsurers took into account past claims experience and made a judgement about the underwriting ability of the ceding office. It was also usual for a top limit to be agreed, above which the cedent would bear any loss, but the whole business was hardly scientific. In 1937 a Swedish actuary found it 'not surprising that these modern forms of reinsurance are mainly effected with casual reinsurance relations of a more speculative nature'.[65]

[62] Calculated from *The Review*, 28 October 1927; 26 November 1937.

[63] *Post Magazine and Insurance Monitor* 23, 10 June 1939, 1146.

[64] *The Review*, 1937, 1220.

[65] Herman Wold, actuary of the Landsbygdens Aterförsäkringsbolag, Stockholm, in *The Review*, 1937, 1220.

One change during the interwar years did improve confidence and efficiency in the industry. The older forms of facultative reinsurance declined and became widely replaced by the obligatory first surplus treaty, the type commonly found in the Swiss Re's treaty files by the 1930s. In the older form of treaty, the direct insurer could choose whether or not to reinsure a risk, while the reinsurer was obliged to accept whatever was ceded within a defined limit. Under the obligatory first surplus treaty, the obligation worked in both directions: on the direct insurer to reinsure and on the reinsurer to accept the amounts ceded and advised by bordereaux. The great advantage of this for direct insurers was that it gave them confidence that the reinsurance would come into force at same time as their original policy, and it seems to have encouraged them to accept ever-larger amounts on the basis that reinsurance cover was something they could trust in.[66]

## 3.3 Growth, Restructuring, and the Changing Risk Environment Since 1945

The decades following the end of the Second World War witnessed complex and fundamental changes in the political, regulatory, and risk environments that global reinsurance operated in, and also in the organizational structure of the industry. After the hardships of the immediate post-war years, the industrial economies entered a period of rapid growth. American insurers focused on the huge opportunities in their home market. The number of life insurance policies sold in the USA increased threefold between 1945 and 1965. Motor and all forms of liability insurance grew even more rapidly. By contrast, in large parts of the developing world, insurers suffered from increasing difficulties in gaining access to markets. In a trend that had commenced before the war, nationalist, communist, and post-colonial governments restricted or excluded foreign insurance companies and took their insurance and reinsurance industries into state ownership. The demand for reinsurance, however, remained buoyant, not least because even nationalized reinsurance institutions found it necessary to retrocede some of their risks abroad.[67] Between 1950 and 1970, the net income of professional reinsurers grew by an average of 11 per cent a year, faster than that of direct insurers.[68] Profits, though, did not keep pace with volume. Swiss Re, for instance, operated in a narrower range of markets and lines of insurance than it had before the war. The main growth area in the 1950s was auto reinsurance, but this only

[66] See the comments of Frederick Pook, general manager of the Mercantile & General Reinsurance, London, in *The Review*, 1937, 1279.

[67] For an example, see Argentina in the early 1950s, Zappino (2007).

[68] Borscheid (2012d, 22).

generated heavy losses, while the profitability of fire reinsurance also declined. Moreover, Swiss Re found its rate of annual cancellations increasing as new reinsurance specialists from the USA and London entered the market, and as direct insurers built up their own reinsurance operations.[69]

A great deal of reinsurance, including aviation and American offshore oil industry risks, gravitated to London for the city's specialist services and its willingness to underwrite very large risks. The expansion of the London market was driven largely by the continued influx of foreign firms doing reinsurance business through UK-based brokers. By 1967, there were 220 foreign insurance companies from forty-nine countries represented in London, over four times the number that had operated in 1924.[70] Ironically, as Werner has shown, the London market increasingly failed to perform the principal function of an international reinsurance centre, namely to spread risks globally in order to provide insurers with a balanced risk portfolio. Instead of helping US insurers to lower their exposure, London actually increased their exposure by retroceding US risks back to them in large quantities, particularly in the wake of the Hurricane Betsy in 1965, the major catastrophe loss of the period. It is possible, but not yet definitively proven, that US insurers post-Betsy may have turned to European professional reinsurers for their cover because of this failure in the Anglo-US reinsurance trade.[71]

In the 1960s, the risk landscape for insurers and reinsurers began to change at an accelerating rate. It became increasingly difficult to base risk assessment on past experience. Scientific and technological change, for example in the petrochemical, plastics, and electrical industries, brought new hazards and new business opportunities. Demand for reinsurance was stimulated by the growth in large and complex risks, and by their associated disasters—nuclear power stations and radiation leaks, supertankers and oil spills, passenger jets and crashes, oil rigs and explosions. Furthermore, from the 1970s, there was a clear upswing in the frequency and scale of natural disasters. Hurricane Betsy, causing a record loss of USD 715 million, was a precursor of ever-more damaging 'big cat' events—storms, floods, earthquakes, hurricanes—to come. These included Hurricane Andrew in 1992 (USD 26.9 billion loss), Hurricane Katrina in 2005 (USD 78.6 billion), and the Japanese earthquake and tsunami of 2011 (USD 36.8 billion).[72] There were also major terrorist attacks and bombings in the USA and UK, including the attack on the World Trade Centre in 2001 (USD 25.1 billion). The years 2005 and 2011 became the two worst in history for catastrophe insurance losses. They also exposed a huge 'protection gap'—measured at USD 260 billion in 2011—between insured losses and economic losses, showing how much work insurers and reinsurers still had to do to provide adequate cover for global risks.[73]

[69] Straumann (2013, 321–2).
[70] Calculated from *The Review*, 13 January 1967.
[71] Werner (2007).
[72] Swiss Re, *sigma*, 2, 2015, table 10. All values in USD 2014. See also Table A.5.2.
[73] Swiss Re, *sigma*, 3, 2012, 10.

This cocktail of rapid technological change and a rise in the scale and frequency of catastrophic events exposed an acute lack of forecasting capability among reinsurers. The increased use of non-proportional and XL forms of reinsurance placed further technical demands on actuarial skills.[74] The need for greater in-house technical, scientific, and risk expertise became more critical to the recruitment strategies of the professional reinsurers. The largest firms also increasingly invested in computer power to support not just claims adjustment but also risk modelling. Between the 1960s and the 1980s, reinsurance moved from being largely concerned with negotiating and amending treaty contracts, to becoming a more sophisticated and complex business of risk classification, information organization, administration, accounting, and data processing.[75]

Together with increased competition, the decline of long-run treaty relations, and the growing amount of reinsurance that passed through brokers, these factors made the need for better information exchange between reinsurers more urgent. Sustained attempts at international cooperation between reinsurers commenced with the first Monte Carlo Rendezvous in 1957. This grew into a major annual event, and was supplemented in 1969 with the first formal organization of reinsurers, the Reinsurance Offices Association, and its associated publications.[76]

Between 1965 and 1986, global reinsurance premiums (measured as life and non-life premiums retained by reinsurance companies) rose from USD 5.6 billion to over USD 60 billion, growth that remained faster than ordinary insurance.[77] Western Europe and North America continued to account for most of this. This expansion, however, masked the fiercely cyclical nature of the business. The early 1970s witnessed an accelerating demand for reinsurance, while ordinary insurance capacity shrank as stock values eroded the reserves of direct insurers. US insurers increasingly sought reinsurance outside their home market, particularly in London, while European reinsurers also expanded their operations in the USA. At the same time, many direct insurers and their offshore captives were tempted into the reinsurance market by the prevailing high interest rates that promised good returns on invested reinsurance premiums, so-called 'cash flow underwriting'.[78] Many newcomers were shell companies that retained only small part of the reinsurance risk and retroceded the rest to other reinsurers. Risks thus became atomized around the world. The market became

[74] In proportional reinsurance, reinsurers take a set percentage of exposures in return for the same percentage of original premiums, minus a commission paid to cedents. In non-proportional forms of reinsurance, such as excess loss, aside from commission, the reinsurer only makes a payment to the cedent when the latter's loss exceeds a predetermined limit. In this type of business, therefore, premium turnover is lower and it is technically more difficult to estimate risk probabilities and expected losses, especially in periods of rapid inflation such as the 1970s.

[75] Straumann (2013, 328–31); Gugerli (2013, 195, 206–9).

[76] Gugerli (2013, 178–82, 199).

[77] 'Reinsurance Survey' (*Financial Times*, 8 September 1986).

[78] Straumann (2013, 332). According to New York brokers Oppenheim & Co., 'there were very few primary companies or captives that were not enticed by the wailing of the low-cost reinsurance siren'. Cited in 'Reinsurance Survey' (*Financial Times*, 8 September 1986).

overheated, reinsurance rates fell, and underwriting results worsened. This led to exits and a shrinkage in reinsurance capacity as the professional reinsurers began to cut back.

From the late 1970s to the mid-1980s, the reinsurance industry was in recession. The worst year of results occurred in 1984 when the combined ratio for reinsurers in the USA peaked at 128 per cent and over ninety firms partially or entirely withdrew from the American market.[79] This was also the period that saw the onset of the great liability crisis as long-tail APH (asbestos, pollution, and health) policies began to produce an ever-larger volume of claims, fuelled by rising levels of compensation payouts awarded by US courts. This crisis occurred in the context of increasing public concern and political activism in the USA and Western Europe about consumer protection and product liability. Public liability insurance written in the USA thirty years earlier, for instance, was hit by claims for pollution incidents, while strict and retroactive liability was imposed by US environmental regulators. The liability crisis forced direct insurers to set aside additional reserves to cover future claims, but it also made many realize that they could not provide cover for such liability insurance any more. Reinsurers suffered too. For companies such as Swiss Re, only high returns on investments kept the balance sheets in the black.[80] At Lloyd's, the response was to increase underwriting capacity by rapidly recruiting new members and to write ever-larger amounts of XL reinsurance, particularly on catastrophe risk. Many marine underwriters took their syndicates into this market even though they had little experience of the business. Some XL syndicates began to reinsure other XL syndicates, so that instead of liabilities being dispersed, they travelled round and round the same market, beginning the spiral that nearly destroyed Lloyd's in the 1990s. The spiral was kept going by the inadequate monitoring of syndicate capacity, of rates, and of the provenance of risks being insured, as well as by the conflict of interests inherent in Lloyd's structure, as managing agents and underwriters earned volume-linked commissions from too rapid expansion upon inadequate reserves.

From the mid-1980s, Lloyd's, even as it continued to expand, began tumbling towards oblivion. Outside Lloyd's, the global search for reinsurance capacity in the wake of the liability crisis led to a sharp but brief upturn in the reinsurance cycle. Rates rose and underwriting results improved. There was a revival of the use of agency firms to generate reinsurance. The new (Lloyd's-like) insurance exchanges that had appeared in New York (1980), Chicago (1982), and Miami (1983) began to write an increasing volume of direct business and reinsurance, although they soon proved unsuccessful.[81] More successfully, offshore markets, notably Bermuda, that had previously been the location of captive direct insurers placed there to benefit from tax exemption and

[79] The combined ratio, the common metric for underwriting profitability, is measured as the sum of claims paid plus expenses as a percentage of premiums. Data from 'Reinsurance Survey' (*Financial Times*, 8 September 1986).

[80] Straumann (2013, 332–3).

[81] *SunSentinel*, 18 March 1987. My thanks to Niels Viggo Haueter for this reference.

benign regulation, began to see specialist reinsurance companies forming, many of them established by US brokers.

From 1987 to the early 1990s there was another hardening of the market. A series of disasters, including oil rig explosions, earthquakes, storms, and hurricanes, triggered massive losses for those Lloyd's syndicates at the top of the XL spiral that had failed to pass on their liabilities. Over USD 8 billion was lost in the five years between 1988 and 1992 alone, the number of syndicates fell by half, and some 10,000 members were ruined. The company sector suffered less from the impact of catastrophe losses, though there were still withdrawals. Munich Re, for instance, began to exclude some Caribbean catastrophe risks and refused to cover terrorism in policies sold to UK insurers, following IRA bomb attacks in London in 1992–3. At the same time, caps were also introduced in most US proportional treaties.[82] The surge in demand and rising rates, especially for catastrophe risks, attracted a cluster of new reinsurance companies to Bermuda, which, by 2003, had captured 14 per cent of the global market.[83]

The new capital flowing into reinsurance markets in Bermuda and London, however, did not entirely resolve the shortage in reinsurance capacity that followed the tide of catastrophe losses, nor did it depress rates.[84] Retrocessions became harder to come by and brokers began to avoid placing business with small reinsurers. One outcome was the drive by reinsurance companies to increase their capital size. The logic was that well-capitalized reinsurers could better withstand catastrophe losses and would be able to cherry-pick business from those direct insurers and Lloyd's syndicates leaving the reinsurance market. Greater size also made reinsurers better able to balance their risk portfolios in a period when direct insurers were also growing in size, retaining more of their business and ceding only the largest and most complex industrial and commercial risks.[85] Consequently, a takeover wave that had begun in the mid-1980s picked up pace in the 1990s. Between 1990 and 1998 there were nineteen major reinsurance mergers and acquisitions (M&A), 13 per cent of global reinsurance volume changed hands, and the market share of the four largest reinsurance companies rose from 22 to 34 per cent.[86]

Diversification and financial innovation were two other strategies adopted by reinsurers in response to the more volatile underwriting cycle. Between 1986 and 1988, for example, Swiss Re acquired ten companies in service areas such as loss adjusting and risk inspection, captive insurance management, claims processing, and information technology (IT). By the late 1980s, its managers were speaking of 'integrated risk management' as their driving concept.[87] For all reinsurers, investment returns and investment-related products became an essential counterweight to the increasing losses made on underwriting. As the pressure on reinsurance capacity and the uncertainty of

82 'Reinsurance Survey' (*Financial Times*, 6 September 1993).
83 Holzheu and Lechner (2007, 893); Gugerli (2013, 221–2 n42).
84 'Reinsurance Survey' (*Financial Times*, 6 September 1993).
85 Stadler (1992).
86 Swiss Re, *sigma*, 9, 1998, 11; Kobrak (2012, 303).
87 Straumann (2013, 333–4).

liability on interrelated catastrophe risks grew, reinsurers sought new ways of transferring risk to the capital markets. Insurance-linked securities, especially catastrophe bonds (cat bonds), became more frequently and more successfully traded. By 2004 there were over USD 10.3 billion of insurance-linked securities outstanding and the business continued to increase rapidly through to the financial crisis of 2008.[88]

Global non-life reinsurance increased from USD 60 billion in 1990 to USD 141 billion in 2003.[89] The vast majority (84 per cent) of this business continued to be generated in North America and Western Europe. However, with the end of the Cold War, the liberalization of international trade and capital movements, and the privatization and deregulation trends in many Asian, Latin American, and former Soviet countries, emerging markets accounted for a rising proportion of global reinsurance.[90] A further series of losses from natural disasters and terrorist attacks afflicted the reinsurance industry from 1996. Lloyd's once again was badly hit due to poor management controls and poor underwriting. Where there had been over 400 Lloyd's syndicates in 1982, there were just eighty-six by 2002. The institution was saved by an injection of corporate capital with limited liability. This was introduced in 1994 as part of a wave of reforms and it rose to 80 per cent of Lloyd's capacity by the early 2000s. The old principle of self-regulation was finally abandoned in 2001 and Lloyd's came under the supervision of the UK Financial Services Authority (FSA).

Outside Lloyd's, in the hardening market of the late 1990s and early 2000s, the focus of the large corporate reinsurers shifted from expansion to a renewed concentration on core business and cost management. Diversification had reached a dead end. Synergies had not been realized and costs had increased. At Swiss Re, for example, participation in direct insurance had overburdened the management. Most of the Swiss Re's holdings in direct insurance companies were sold, the business was refocused on reinsurance, especially property and casualty reinsurance in East Asia, new insurance-linked security and asset management products were developed, and subsidiaries were integrated into the parent company.[91]

In the new century, reinsurance remains as volatile as ever. It continues to perform an essential role in proving stability to the global insurance industry and providing cover for extraordinary losses. It now shares that role with the capital markets and, in some parts of the world, also with states acting as the reinsurer of last resort for catastrophe and terrorism risks. In Japan, for example, private earthquake insurance provides USD 1.4 billion cover per loss event, while the state guarantees to pay for most of the remaining losses up to USD 66.3 billion.[92] Notwithstanding the efforts of reinsurers to restructure and extend their product, the 'protection gap' is getting wider.

[88] Holzheu and Lechner (2007, 898); James (2013, 18).

[89] Holzheu and Lechner (2007, 878).

[90] Rising from 12 to 19 per cent of non-life cessions between 1990 and 1998. Swiss Re, *sigma*, 9, 1998, 8.

[91] Straumann (2013, 335–49).

[92] Borscheid (2012d, 32). Other examples include the US Federal Emergency Management Agency, the Federal Crop Insurance Corporation, Florida's Hurricane Catastrophe Fund, the California Earthquake Authority, and the UK government's Pool Re, established in 2005 to reinsure terrorism risks.

While, between 1985 and 1995, 42 per cent of losses from natural disasters were covered by insurance, that figure had fallen to just 25 per cent by 2011.[93]

## 3.4 The Long View—Diversity and Flexibility of Reinsurance Structures

From the account given in the previous sections, how can we best summarize the main trends in the history of reinsurance since the beginning of the nineteenth century? First, the practice of reinsurance diffused from Europe to the rest of the world in a cyclical manner from the very start, through booms and slumps in provision. The number of professional reinsurance companies, and the range of countries they originated from, expanded greatly from the 1860s to the 1930s, as did the number of direct insurers trading in reinsurance. This may have been followed by some contraction between the 1930s and 1950s, although that remains speculative. Thereafter, the industry expanded again, in terms of volume, more quickly than direct insurance. Recent decades have seen an increasing concentration of the global market in the hands of the largest professional reinsurance companies.

Second, reinsurance developed in fire insurance then spread into other lines, especially from the 1880s when underwriters at Lloyds, led by the redoubtable Cuthbert Heath, pioneered new products, and when, in Europe, Munich Re developed techniques for lines such as engineering insurance that hitherto had made little use of reinsurance. The twentieth century saw the growth of all types of liability reinsurance and also a huge increase in the size and technological complexity of industrial and commercial risks that posed enormous challenges for underwriters. Together with the onset of a steep upward curve in the scale and frequency of catastrophic events from the 1970s, this led to a greater emphasis by reinsurers on expanding their scientific and technical expertise and computing capabilities and on developing mathematical risk modelling.

Third, like most other branches of the insurance industry, reinsurance developed via an extraordinarily wide range of organizational forms. It commenced with joint-stock direct fire insurance companies reinsuring among themselves. This was followed, from the 1840s, by the appearance of captive reinsurance subsidiaries, organized by direct insurers, and also by independent reinsurance companies such as the Swiss Re, some of which in turn formed their own captive subsidiary companies for retrocessions.[94] By the 1870s, there were also reinsurance bureaus, often jointly managed by several direct

[93] Borscheid (2012d, 31).

[94] The importance of retrocessions to the growth of reinsurance is difficult to exaggerate, but also difficult to measure. In Germany in 1927, for example, 36 per cent of all reinsurance premiums earned by forty-nine reinsurance companies were retroceded. Cruciger (1929, 49). On the constraints that led the Swiss Re to establish its own captive retrocession company in 1876, see Pearson (2001, 44–5).

insurers operating in foreign markets; specialist international reinsurance brokers, facilitating the transfer of reinsurance between direct insurers; and individual underwriters at Lloyds moving out of the old core marine business to write reinsurance in other lines. During the early twentieth century other vehicles for reinsurance emerged. Captive mutual and joint-stock reinsurance companies were established collectively by groups of mutual fire insurers; for example, by the cantonal fire insurance offices in Switzerland in 1911 or by Swedish rural mutual fire offices in 1936.[95] Less common, but ultimately successful, was the national, quasi-monopoly, joint-stock reinsurance company launched by Swedish life insurance companies in 1914 with the aim of diversifying their risks and reducing their dependence on foreign reinsurers.[96] Reinsurance pools were also formed, for example in aviation insurance, as direct insurance companies turned to mutual solutions for the technical problems raised by underwriting in new areas.[97] Beginning in the 1920s, then more frequently in the decades following the Second World War, many countries formed state reinsurance organizations, usually accompanied by legislation requiring private companies—principally domestic and foreign, and mainly in fire insurance—to reinsure a proportion of their business with the state organization. One might regard the insurance-linked securities traded on US exchanges during the 1990s as a further addition to this long list of vehicles by which risks have been reinsured.

Another important change that can be observed from our survey is in the forms that reinsurance took. The shift from facultative to obligatory treaty reinsurance during the middle of the nineteenth century helped reduce transaction costs and the price paid for reinsurance, and increased the number of reinsurance providers around the world. This in turn allowed risks to be more widely and evenly distributed, and helped give the international reinsurance market, for the first time, a critical mass.[98] After 1900, XL reinsurance began to appear, but became associated with the more speculative side of the industry, making most headway in some of its most fiercely competitive branches, such as automobile reinsurance. XL products continued to generate volume growth but also to create enormous problems, not least with long-tail liabilities, to the end of the century.

After the First World War, reciprocity became an established principle in the obligatory first surplus treaty, the most universal form of reinsurance between the wars. The reciprocal system reflected the power that direct insurers were able to wield over the professional reinsurance companies in treaty negotiations. As a result, some observers of the industry between the wars felt that reinsurance was becoming more 'commercial' in its nature, sharper in its business practices, with less emphasis being placed on face-to-face contact and the need to establish durable social as well as business relations between treaty partners. This 'commercialization' of reinsurance, some have argued, became still more marked with the advent of computers and the increased competitiveness and volatility of the industry since the 1960s.[99]

95 *The Review*, 1937, 1196.

96 Larsson and Lönnborg (2014).

97 *The Review*, 1937, 1196.

98 Hollitscher (1931, 59–60).

99 Neave (1980); *The Review*, 1937, 1208, citing Reidar Brekke, general manager of Trondhjems Forsikringsselskab.

There is no question that a fundamental restructuring of the reinsurance industry took place during the final third of the twentieth century. A number of factors contributed to this: the increase in market power of the largest professional reinsurers; the rise, fall, and, since 2003, recovery of Lloyd's as a major reinsurance centre; the internal transformation of the major insurance companies and also the largest broker firms into multidimensional financial groups offering a range of insurance-related services; and the creation of new reinsurance products linked to the capital markets. Behind these developments lay the transformation of the external environment caused by rapid technological change; the growth in the size and complexity of risks; and the dramatic changes in political regimes across the world, accompanied first by the closure, then, from the later 1980s, the opening up of emerging markets and their increasing integration into the global economy.

Finally, the multiplicity of vehicles for reinsurance revealed in this chapter suggests that the aggregate business of the professional reinsurance companies that emerged from the mid-nineteenth century may seriously understate the historic role of reinsurance in supporting the insurance coverage of risks worldwide. The scale and distribution of reinsurance has always been difficult to estimate. The British fire insurance companies, for instance, which were among the first in Europe to buy and sell reinsurance abroad, commonly accounted their premium income net of reinsurance, without recording the gross figure in their ledgers.[100] Data for twelve European countries in 1913 suggest that, by that date, the fire reinsurance premium income of reinsurance companies (gross of retrocessions) amounted to 25 per cent of the gross premiums of direct fire insurers and 70 per cent of their ceded premiums.[101] In other words, by the First World War, the professional reinsurance companies only accounted for a quarter of global non-life insurance, and direct insurers still sought a considerable proportion of their reinsurance beyond their ranks. As large direct insurance groups developed their own captive or internal reinsurance facilities, and as Lloyd's expanded its reinsurance operations, the proportion of global insurance ceded to professional reinsurers seems to have fallen, although without further research it is impossible to be sure about the timing of this. In 2001, direct insurers earned USD 2408 billion worldwide. Of this they ceded USD 154 billion or 6.4 per cent. 61 per cent of this went to eighteen major professional reinsurance groups, the rest was reinsured with other primary insurers and reinsurers.[102] In short, a business history of reinsurance companies can provide an important, but certainly not comprehensive, account of the development of reinsurance.

[100] This was a problem first noted by Hollitscher, when he described reinsurance as the 'Geheimwissenschaft'. Hollitscher (1931, 2).

[101] Pearson (1995, table 2).

[102] Swiss Re, *sigma*, 5, 2003, table 1.

CHAPTER 4

# THE MONETARY AND FINANCIAL ENVIRONMENT, 1860–2013

FORREST CAPIE

## 4.1 Introduction

This chapter will describe the changing monetary, financial, and macroeconomic conditions across the period within which Swiss Re, and of course all other insurers, operated. That period for Swiss Re was from its birth in the 1860s until the present day. The approach is to divide the world economy over the life of the company into four main blocks: that before the First World War; then from 1914 to 1945; next from 1945 to the beginning of the 1980s; and finally the period sometimes called the 'great moderation', from then on but culminating in the great global financial crisis that struck in 2007/8.

This introductory section sets out what the chapter does. In doing so, it will also provide some definitions to help provide focus: insurance, spreading, co-insurance, pooling, reinsurance. Then, after outlining some of the basic concepts that alert us to the need for a macroeconomic discussion, and at the same time make clear that the chapter is not concerned with microeconomic risk, it discusses the principal macro variables that insurers need to consider. The chapter then has four sections that discuss the course of the principal variables in the world economy in such a way as to indicate the changing environment with which the company had to cope. The sections are of differing lengths, largely reflecting the extent of macroeconomic activity in the period. The chapter concludes with an overview of the performance.

Reinsurers take on a portion of the risk that direct insurers wish to part with. The reinsurer might in turn pass on some of his risk to a third insurer—something known as retrocession. The balance sheet of the reinsurer has, on the liability side, a list of insurance companies from many countries and of all types—fire, car, life, and so on.

On the asset side of its balance sheet the reinsurer holds government bonds in a range of maturities and again from a range of countries. For much of the balance sheet it will want to match foreign currency liabilities with similarly denominated assets. Indeed, in many cases countries will have their own requirements that they impose on the reinsurer, ranging from complete matching to some minimum proportion. The reinsurer is also likely to hold substantial capital to cover unanticipatable losses. The nature of much of the insurance business means that these can be considerable. Natural catastrophes are unpredictable in their timing, geography, and destructive impacts. So capital will be an important consideration for the reinsurer. In support of their capital base they, like banks, have also held substantial hidden reserves in their liabilities. The hidden reserves were most commonly held in the form of undervalued assets, recorded at historic cost rather than market value.

At first glance it might seem that all insurance faces the same risks and that, other things being equal, all insurance companies should fare similarly as far as macroeconomic risks are concerned. So, for example, the direct life insurer in the post-war period when inflation was steady and rising gained from these conditions. When a life policy or, more commonly, a fixed-period endowment policy was written, it would, in 1950, be for, say, an assured sum of GBP 5000, maturing in thirty or thirty-five years' time. Annual premiums would reflect the sum and the period. However, by 1980/5, following persistent inflation, the sum to be paid out would be relatively trivial (though it would of course pay off an outstanding mortgage acquired in the 1950s). It is true that the premiums being paid over the years of the cover would also be of declining significance and, at the end, be close to trivial to the insured. But the insurer would have lost the value of the premiums only on a gently declining trend. Thus, the direct insurer gained from inflation. To the extent that increased business for direct insurers led to increased business for reinsurers, the reinsurer benefited from the same process.

And yet, in periods of volatility, the likelihood is that the reinsurer also gains. In times of increased uncertainty the direct insurer is likely to increase the amount of reinsuring he does. That being the case, the reinsurer gains again.

However, there were negatives. As David Gugerli argues in his history of reinsurance, inflation can weaken the reinsurance industry in two ways. One was not strictly economic: the 'delays in the settlement of claims resulting from complex legal proceedings surrounding large liability cases'.[1] The second was that while primary insurers could protect themselves in the way described, the reinsurer 'assumes all the losses above a certain retention on the part of the direct insurer in return for a fixed reinsurance premium'.[2]

Considerable risk will be found in financial conditions that are confronted in each country. The principal concern will centre on financial stability. Financial stability is notoriously difficult to define and hence to measure. It is perhaps easiest to think of it

[1] Gugerli (2013, 89). [2] Gugerli (2013, 89).

as the absence of financial instability, where the latter is the occurrence of financial crises. And financial crises are best defined as by Anna Schwartz as threats to the payments system.[3] If the payments system were disrupted there would be serious spillovers for the real economy. It is this externality that makes these a cause for concern for public policy. So, an instance of financial instability has macroeconomic costs and hurts innocent bystanders, 'companies which could not reasonably have been expected to anticipate them'.[4]

The macroeconomic variables that will be of most interest for the reinsurer are the following: inflation, nominal interest rates, real interest rates, income, asset prices, and exchange rates. It probably needs to be stressed that insurers, even internationally inclined insurers, were much more likely to be concerned with the microeconomic risks than with macro ones. Catastrophes were more dangerous to the industry than unanticipated alterations to interest rates.

## 4.2 Growth and Development, Mid-Nineteenth Century to 1914

Swiss Re began business in 1863. From the outset it was international in its outlook. In a sense it had to be, since its domestic territory was too limited in terms of investment opportunities and also in terms of initial business. What lay ahead for the world economy for the next fifty years, although clearly the company could not know this at the time, was a long period of relative calm. The American Civil War was raging and the Franco-Prussian War was a few years away, but when these were over there was a long period when most of the variables listed in Section 4.1 were extremely stable. There were some other wars but the period was essentially one of peace and international calm. During the eighteenth and early nineteenth centuries, insurance had spread around the world mostly in the wake of trade and migration.[5] Reinsurance at first concentrated on the growing need for fire insurance but, during the latter part of the nineteenth century, diversified into new classes of business made necessary by technical progress. But the real breakthrough of the dedicated reinsurers only happened with the full onset of globalization in the later part of the nineteenth century.

On the macro front there was, around the developed world, a growing desire for stable money and for a metallic standard. And given that Britain was at the time the most advanced economy with the greatest stability, its institutions—one of the most obviously successful being the gold standard—were admired. Britain did not suffer the

[3] A. J. Schwartz (1986) 'Real and Pseudo-Financial Crises', in F. Capie and G. Wood (eds), *Financial Crises and the World Banking System*. London: Macmillan, 11–31.

[4] W. A. Allen and G. Wood (2006) 'Defining and Achieving Financial Stability', *Journal of Financial Stability* 2: 2, 152–72, here 160.

[5] Borscheid and Haueter (2012).

financial volatility that other countries did: the gold standard seemed to have demonstrated its superiority over others and more and more countries adopted it in the latter part of the century. One clear favourable consequence was stable exchange rates.

Another consequence of the adoption of the gold standard is that, with the growing acquisition of limited gold stocks, there was a downward pressure on money supplies and hence on prices. This led to the years 1873 to 1896 being labelled 'the Great Depression', since there was the tendency at the time to associate falling prices with falls in other macro variables. But in fact the period was one of growth and prosperity, albeit with the usual cyclical pattern. The scramble for gold led, unsurprisingly, to the search for gold and, again unsurprisingly, gold was found in huge quantities in both Australia and South Africa. It followed that there were gently rising prices in the next fifteen years as money supplies grew slightly in excess of output.

Output was growing steadily and international trade was growing at a much faster pace as the world moved through the process of globalization for the first time. By some measures, the world economy was as closely integrated in the 1890s as it was later to become in the second great wave of globalization in the 1990s. It might almost be said that conditions for business were ideal. The competition and the search for new markets led, however, to a protectionist sentiment, eventually realized in rising tariffs and other obstructive measures. This was in line with a growing nationalism that ultimately resulted in the First World War. It might be said that the very success of the growing convergence contained within it the seeds of its own demise.[6]

But the main point to stress is that there was essentially remarkable stability from the 1870s to 1914 in prices and exchange rates and hence in interest rates. These all meant that financial business could take place without giving much thought to the macro conditions.

Thus, Swiss Re was born into a period of relative tranquillity that lasted until the First World War. There was the occasional shock, such as the worldwide stock market disturbances of 1873, but the main macroeconomic variables were fairly stable across these years. There would have been no particular need to develop any new strategy.

Indeed, there is little if anything to be found in Swiss Re's records throughout the nineteenth century that would point to any theoretical or applied strategy in dealing with macroeconomics. Investments were earmarked by long-term yields, such as from government and corporate bonds as well as real estate, and bills of exchange. Nearly 10 per cent of overall assets were held as cash liquidity in a simple bank account throughout the first decades.[7] Guarantee capital was provided via uncalled share capital, which made up 80 per cent of the total during Swiss Re's initial years.

Investment decisions were made by the board of directors; Zurich-based bank Credit Suisse was represented by at least one director throughout almost the entire history of

[6] K. H. O'Rourke and J. Williamson (1999) *Globalization and History: The Evolution of a Nineteenth Century Atlantic Economy*. Cambridge, MA: The MIT Press.

[7] Swiss Re started publishing their detailed investment portfolio with their annual reports from 1876 on. See also SRCA 10.108 184, Guggenbühl, 39–42.

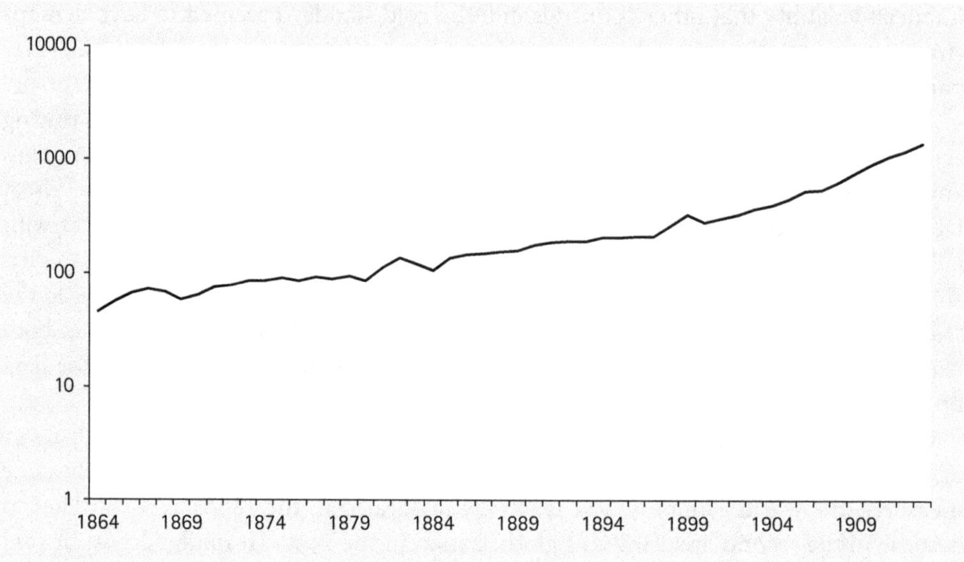


FIGURE 4.1 Swiss Re: Income from interest 1864–1914 (CHF thousand)

*Source*: SRCA 10.108 184, Guggenbühl (1939).

Swiss Re. Board minutes show that the bank representatives significantly dominated investment decisions. Close ties to the banking world were not unusual for nineteenth-century reinsurers. The oldest reinsurer, Cologne Re, was mainly financed via the Rothschild Bank in Paris, while banker Wilhelm von Finck was instrumental in the founding of Munich Re.

Such long-term investment with stable interest rates effectively shielded Swiss Re from the occasional macroeconomic disturbances during the nineteenth century. Between 1864 and 1913, income from interest was never negative and followed a long-term trend (see Figure 4.1). Accordingly, Swiss Re did not need a department collecting information on sovereigns and corporations, as for example Crédit Lyonnais did.[8]

## 4.3 Age of Turmoil, 1914–45

The world economy had really come into being in the nineteenth century with staggering flows around the world of labour, capital, and goods of every description. There were, as noted in Section 4.2, occasional disturbances, but the dominant feature

[8] M. Flandreau (2004) 'Caveat Emptor: Coping with Sovereign Risk during the International Gold Standard 1871–1913', in M. Flandreau, H. James, and C.-L. Holtfrerich (eds), *The International Financial System in the 20th Century: System and Anarchy*. Cambridge: Cambridge University Press, 17–50.

of the long period is one of steady progress, of economic development, and of considerable stability. But all of that came to a dramatic halt in the summer of 1914, and there then followed more than thirty years of international turmoil. Initially, there was an international financial crisis. That was followed by the First World War, which lasted for four years. Post-war adjustment was painful and slow, and an unsatisfactory restoration of a metallic standard lasted just a few years before the world was plunged into the greatest economic depression there had ever been. And that, of course, was followed, after some hesitant economic recovery, by the Second World War, or, as some would have it, a continuation of the First World War.

This period deserves more detailed treatment than the others, not only because so much was happening but also because it was important in light of what followed.

Financial crises in the nineteenth century (and since) followed a very similar pattern. There was a period of easy money, abundant credit, rising profits and prices, and, as the boom developed, a general state of euphoria. At some point, either insiders would decide things had gone as far as was safe and begin to get out, or central banks would see the error of easy money and raise the price bringing the boom to a sharp end. The peak would be reached and there would then be a spectacular crash. These were often closely related to the business cycle.[9]

But the financial crisis of 1914 was not like that. It came 'like a thunderbolt from a clear sky'. There had been no preceding boom or business cycle connection. It was simply panic and disruption of payments when war was declared. London was the hub of a complex interconnected world and the crisis was severe there. But it also struck in fifty other countries. Around the world, stock exchanges closed and there were runs on banks. Nowhere was spared: the USA, Europe, Latin America, and Asia all suffered. There was a flight to gold, and governments everywhere intervened to save the financial systems. The most common response was to impose a moratorium and an immediate injection of liquidity from the monetary authorities, though neither measure prevented depositors and investors from being hurt.

Within six months most stock exchanges had reopened and commercial banks were returning to an approximation of normal business, even if restrictions on financial activity were severe. The massive but variable-sized injections of liquidity resulted in different effects on prices, and hence exchange rates, that further complicated/hindered the process of international exchange. There had been no time for consultation, and in any case, not much inclination to consult among many parties given the state of international affairs.

Following the huge disruption of the international economy during the First World War it should come as no surprise to discover that the international business in insurance came to an abrupt end. Also, the pattern of trade did not recover its nineteenth-century shape nor did it grow at previous rates. And sources of imports were diverted for shipping and security reasons. The new marketing and distribution

[9] G. Gorton (1988) 'Banking Panics and Business Cycles', *Oxford Economic Papers* 40: 4, 751–81.

networks that were established were entrenched by the end of the war, and the way to economic recovery for the Europeans, further handicapped by the war, meant the situation was long lasting if not permanent. The creation of new countries (for example, from the old Austro-Hungarian and other empires), the consolidation of other countries (in, for example, the newly founded Soviet Union), and the removal of still others from what was called the international economy complicates an examination of trade but there can be no doubting its disastrous performance. Some countries were hit even harder, with primary producers heavily dependent on the US market suffering particularly.

The most important factor at work in both the growth of the 1920s and the collapse in the 1930s was American economic growth. In the 1920s, it was the chief positive element. By then clearly the largest economy in the world, it was growing strongly across the decade and primary producers of all kinds benefited enormously. But apart from that, after the initial period of post-war adjustment there was reasonable growth in some other parts of the international economy. A factor militating against growth in trade was the protectionist tendency in commercial policies. The USA had a long history of protectionism through the nineteenth century and that carried on after the war. In 1922, the Fordney–McCumber Tariff introduced some of the highest tariffs ever. The British were also guilty as, in spite of a long history of free trading, they also took some steps in the direction of protection soon after the war (safeguarding of industries legislation). There were also the problems associated with international payments (essentially floating exchange rates) to which we return in Sections 4.4 and 4.5.

In the late nineteenth century, Britain was at the centre of the foreign investment flows that were spreading ever further afield. That came to an end with the war and, after the war, the USA, having been a debtor in the late nineteenth century, emerged as the greatest creditor. In the 1920s it would lend, particularly to the Americas but also to Europe, on a large scale. A criticism at the time and soon after was that the USA carried out this investment with less care than it might—less attention to the nature of the investment that was taking place. Nevertheless, in the 1920s there were considerable flows of long-term investment around the world.

Additionally, in the opening years of the decade there was a good deal of monetary and exchange-rate chaos along with hyperinflation in much of Central Europe. With continuing uncertainty attaching to exchange rates, there were the associated substantial short-term capital flows. And also affecting short-term flows were the differential interest rates, with European and particularly German rates being well above those of the USA. But after these factors settled down in the mid-1920s, with a clearer picture of the new gold standard emerging and the Dawes Plan agreed to sort German reparations, longer-term investment began to grow rapidly. Between 1924 and 1930, USD 10 billion flowed to Europe of which USD 7 billion went to Germany. And at the same time, a foreign loan boom developed in Latin America, with an average of USD 300 million flowing each year in the mid/late 1920s.[10]

[10] C. Marichal (1989) *A Century of Debt Crises in Latin America: From Independence to the Great Depression 1820–1930*. Princeton, NJ: Princeton University Press.

All of this came to an end at the end of the 1920s. There were several reasons. The first was the developing boom on the New York Stock Exchange. Not only was there a drying up of the funds to Europe and Latin America as funds poured into the New York market, but there was also a reversal as funds were withdrawn from these territories and redirected to the USA. The second factor was the Great Depression itself. Following the American economic downturn, with trade collapsing foreign borrowers were unable to earn sufficient to service and repay their loans. This was particularly striking in Latin America where many countries were heavily dependent on the US market and reliant on one or two products.

In Europe, some of the same effects could be seen and the repatriation of capital from some of the borrowers exposed the fragility of the banking systems and culminated in the Central European banking crises. This was made worse by political uncertainty. In 1930, German political instability frightened investors, as there was a strong possibility of exchange-rate restrictions and a devaluation of the mark. In the September elections the Nazis emerged as the second largest party in the Reichstag and capital flight quickly followed. The summer of 1931 saw the banking crisis in Central Europe blow up. This was first seen in the collapse of the Credit-Anstalt in Austria in May 1931, and was quickly followed by the failure of the big Berlin bank, Danatbank or Darmstädter und Nationalbank. The political upheaval that accompanied these events produced a huge capital flight. In July, the Brüning government introduced exchange controls, and in September placed a standstill (the German Credit Agreement) on German short-term debts to overseas banks. The international debts of Austria and Hungary were subject to similar agreements.

In short, the abrupt cessation of the lending boom of the 1920s to Europe and to Latin America at the end of that decade was a calamitous event for the world economy. It contributed to the economic and political turmoil at the turn of the decade and produced further disastrous capital flight. The credit boom had turned to credit crunch.

It is impossible to understand the nature of the collapse of the international monetary system at the beginning of the 1930s without again outlining the problems the system developed in the course of the First World War and in the 1920s period of adjustment and stabilization. The gold standard had collapsed in the war. At the end of the war there was a clear desire on the part of all the principal participants to re-establish the standard and restore the world of pre-1914. But at the end of the war there were several inhibiting factors for the international monetary system. There had been a huge build-up of debt, both domestic and international. There was rapidly rising inflation in many countries, some of which would degenerate into hyperinflation. The consequences for exchange rates were catastrophic and long lasting. On top of the debt, but related, there came reparation payments imposed by the Allies on the Germans.

Early attempts at some resolution of the interlinked problems could be found in international conferences at Brussels in 1920, and in Genoa in 1922 where a resolution was passed to pursue cooperation, but the French vetoed any attempt to reopen negotiation on the German reparation question.

The wrangling involved in the attempted resolution of the debt and reparation payments rumbled on for years. The scale of the problem was huge. Inter-Allied war debt totalled USD 26.5 billion (roughly equal to twice British GDP). Most of this was owed to Britain and America. So, for example, France owed the USA approximately USD 4 billion and owed the United Kingdom USD 3 billion. Britain owed the United States USD 4.7 billion. The British were happy to settle with the USA on the understanding that they would be paid by the French. But the French needed reparations payments from Germany in order to be able to do that. The reparations imposed on Germany totalled USD 33 billion, and most of that was to be paid to Britain and France. Reparations and debt could have been linked and some netting out carried through, but the Americans, who were adamant that debts should be repaid, were equally resistant to the idea that they, the USA, should be seen to be taking reparation payments from the Germans.

In 1920 every important country had a depreciated and less than stable currency and there was a widespread desire to restore the world of pre-1914; indeed, in 1920, it seemed absolutely necessary to achieve this. The gold standard had provided a smooth means of adjustment for international trade and payments and capital flows. Under the gold standard, prices were stable, balances of payments were in equilibrium, and conditions for investors were ideal. It is not surprising that policymakers and investors alike wished to get back to that or something close to it.

There were at least two problems present in the restored standard. One was the use of foreign exchange reserves. The second was the damage to confidence that had been done as a result of Britain's weakened position and the American reluctance to take on the role that Britain had performed so well before 1914. That left a gap in international leadership.[11] With the USA reluctant to play that lead role, and international relations at a low ebb, there was little possibility of finding solutions to the problems. Things were made worse by the perversity of the two largest and dominant gold holders, France and America. America was the largest single holder of gold, with almost 40 per cent of the world's supply. But more than that, it held gold reserves far in excess of that required by its own gold legislation. Then, in the late 1920s, the Federal Reserve made things even worse when it worried about the booming New York stock market and raised interest rates. That had the effect of pulling more funds into the USA.

All of this meant that the problems the gold standard was designed to alleviate or remove had in fact worsened. France and America had growing balance of payments surpluses, while other countries, such as Britain, had persistent deficits.

Much of this story has become clear in retrospect and with the benefit of much more research. For the participants at the time, however, it would have been difficult to get a clear picture.

The chronology of the crisis between the wars is well known and agreed upon. After a certain degree of fiscal and exchange-rate stability had been achieved in the first half

[11] C. Kindleberger (1973) *The World in Depression 1929–1939*. London: Allen Lane Penguin Press.

of the 1920s, a credit boom followed in the second half. Then, after the huge capital flows peaked in 1928,[12] credit contracted and sovereign bond issues collapsed.[13] When the banking crises of Central Europe followed in 1931, currency crises emerged quickly and severe repercussions were felt around the world. Thus, while the depression is usually seen as originating in the USA, there were serious problems elsewhere that produced weakening economic conditions. But how was depression transmitted from one region to another? There were two principal means by which depression might have been transmitted: exchange rates and financial interrelatedness.

At every turn there is evidence of the domestic/international interface. While trying to stay focused on the international aspects, it is impossible to escape the domestic. Many of the responses to international difficulties were from the domestic front. Almost everywhere, regardless of the strength of the belief in free trade, domestic politics trumped any international considerations. Almost everywhere, countries resorted to protectionist devices.

This was coupled to problems in the world's monetary system—the demise of the gold standard. Gold reserves began falling sharply in the late 1920s. Some primary producers such as Argentina, Uruguay, and Australia were the first to go, and they suspended the gold standard in December 1929. But it was after the British departure from the standard in September 1931 that collapse happened. Britain had been at the centre of the system, the 'conductor of the orchestra' in the nineteenth century, and when she went there was no way for others to survive. A wave of other suspensions followed almost immediately, many of them British Empire countries or those closely linked to the British market. Other countries followed in 1932, and the USA in 1933, while some, such as Belgium and the Netherlands, hung on until 1935 and 1936. Strictly speaking, the French did not suspend the standard but devalued against gold in late 1936. The system was finished in the first half of the 1930s. It was no longer sustainable.[14]

Debt presented further problems. One approach was to default or restructure/reschedule, and that happened frequently in Latin America. In Europe, the core problem was Germany, by far the biggest debtor. With the prospects for repayment bleak in May 1931, the US President Herbert Hoover proposed a one-year moratorium on all reparation and war debts payments. The proposal was agreed to by the Allies in July of that year. There were clear positives for Germany in that it immediately relieved pressure on their budget. But, more than that, it gave them the opportunity to negotiate the cancellation of reparation payments altogether. The moratorium discriminated in favour of commercial obligations that disadvantaged France somewhat in relation to

[12] C. H. Feinstein and K. Watson (1995) 'Private International Capital Flows in Europe in the Interwar Period', in C. H. Feinstein (ed.), *Banking, Currency and Finance in Europe between the Wars*. Oxford: Clarendon Press, 94–130.

[13] Flandreau, James, and Holtfrerich (2004).

[14] D. H. Aldcroft and M. J. Oliver (1998) *Exchange Rate Regimes in the Twentieth Century*. Cheltenham: Edward Elgar Publishing.

the USA and so delayed the reaching of agreement. But at the international conference in Lausanne the following year, agreements were struck that effectively brought reparation payments to an end.

Also, an agreement was reached to a Standstill (the September 1931 German Credit Agreement) on the withdrawal of foreign credits from Germany. While these might look like moves in the direction that was desirable, there were, as is common, unintended consequences. In this case, the smaller European countries were worst affected and began losing gold reserves. To offset that, these countries sold sterling, and so put further pressure on it. The Standstill was then renewed annually from 1932 onwards. Approximately GBP 54 million was initially due to British creditors, and one-third of that was to go the clearing banks. Although the amounts for Britain were relatively small, the arrangements were seen by some as economic appeasement. But the British were inclined to go along with it for fear of something worse, such as complete moratorium.[15]

All policy became domestic centred. There was a proposal in 1931 for an Austro-German customs union, which was only defeated because of the opposition of the French. The British too considered turning the empire into a customs union. It went some way towards this goal, but achieved something less at the Imperial Conference held at Ottawa in 1932. A large number of agreements were struck between member countries favouring trade and capital flows, including Britain's preferential treatment of empire goods in the British market. The guiding principle was Britain first, empire second, and foreigners last.[16]

Countries were determined to avoid what they saw as the chaos of the early 1920s, and employ controls. In the world of managed exchange rates, apart from the stabilization funds that at least had a pretence of subtlety, other, cruder techniques were employed. The crudest was the outright prevention of currency movement—exchange controls. A long list of countries introduced some form of these as early as 1931, and, by the mid-1930s, there were thirty-four countries with some form of these in place. By the end of the decade around 30 per cent of world trade was conducted under exchange control.[17]

There also emerged currency blocs. The principal ones were the sterling area and the gold bloc. But there was also the Reichsmark bloc and there were some parallel arrangements in the Americas with the US dollar. Even in the Far East there was something like a yen bloc. Sterling was, though, by far the biggest, and extended beyond Commonwealth countries to the Middle East, Scandinavia, and parts of Latin America. While there were no formal agreements, countries pegged their currencies to sterling and kept their reserves in sterling (and often in London). Not surprisingly, there was a

[15] M. Billings and F. Capie (2011) 'Financial Crisis, Contagion, and the British Banking System between the World Wars', *Business History* 53: 2, 193–215.

[16] F. Capie (1985) *Depression and Protectionism*. London: Allen & Unwin.

[17] F. Capie (2002) *Capital Controls: A 'Cure' Worse than the Problem?* Research monograph 56. London: Institute of Economic Affairs; Aldcroft and Oliver (1998).

measure of stability from these arrangements. The gold bloc was made up of those who were determined to hold to gold—principally France, Netherlands, Belgium, and Italy, and one or two other smaller European countries. Most of these had amassed large gold reserves. These countries would, however, suffer from the depreciations that had taken place elsewhere, and it was only a matter of two or three years before they abandoned their position, in the process engaging in some 'competitive devaluation' or what later was called 'beggar-thy-neighbour' policies.

The most extreme exchange-rate measures could be found in Germany, where the principal device was bilateral exchange. The country's recent experience of hyperinflation was still all too vivid, so any policy that risked inflation was taboo. That meant that devaluation was out of the question, and indeed the Brüning government pursued deflationary policies. With 6.5 million unemployed and no foreign reserves there was always the threat that, if the Brüning government fell, either a Bolshevik or Nazi dictatorship would descend. Germany had already introduced exchange controls in July 1931. The Standstill Agreements had been predicated on Germany being able to run balance of payment surpluses. So Britain's departure from gold in September, along with all the countries which went with her, made this difficult and even impossible. Stronger measures were seen as necessary and, with Hjalmar Schacht reinstalled at the Reichsbank, a new plan was indeed produced. The plan led to the bilateralization of trade: bilateral clearing with twenty-five countries. Different mark rates were developed for each currency. Export subsidies were added and imports squeezed dramatically.

The interwar years were obviously a period of huge turmoil in the world economy. A great deal of that was political and due to war. But in spite of that there were opportunities for financial services. However, it is hard to escape the fact that there were violent swings in most macroeconomic variables across many countries. There were the hyperinflations of the 1920s and 1940s, with accompanying interest-rate and exchange-rate volatility. These are not the conditions desired by financial institutions. And how the financial world viewed all this and coped is of great interest. There are almost always opportunities. But it is more difficult to say what the appropriate strategy might have been.

The First World War brought about a fundamental shift in the geographic distribution of reinsurers. Up until the war, world reinsurance was divided into supply countries (Germany, Switzerland, Russia, and Austria-Hungary) and demand countries (France, Italy, Belgium, Netherlands, Sweden, and USA).[18] The gap left by German, Russian, and Austro-Hungarian reinsurers was filled mainly by Switzerland. Many 'mushroom' companies were founded in Germany, and also in new markets, such as Denmark, which became the new home of the two largest Russian reinsurers. Such companies profited from nominal increases in premium income but found themselves in difficulties when the monetary environment started normalizing again. Many markets, such as the USA, France, and the UK, tried to create local supply. The

[18] Arps (1970, 30); Gerathewohl et al. (1979, 778).

supply versus demand distribution was increasingly reflecting the monetary geography of harder and weaker currencies.[19]

Even for Swiss Re, the inflationary environment created difficulties. On the one hand, there were advantages in that obligations to pay out on losses had become trivial because of inflation. On the other hand, the depreciation of foreign holdings and income was massive. In 1915, Swiss Re started compiling statistics of how global assets were influenced by currencies movements. A so-called currency office was established. For the first time in the history of the company, people were employed with the main aim of handling monetary issues. Consequently, the company aimed at concentrating assets in Swiss francs and US dollars. Overall, the currency office did not appear to have significant advisory power. Throughout the war, and indeed up until 1922, Swiss Re published their reports based on pre-war parities.[20] Eventually, Swiss Re adopted a so-called 'currency congruent' strategy, stipulating that liabilities and assets in a certain market should be held in local currencies. This allowed for an overall balance sheet hedging against currency fluctuations, the first monetary strategy to be adopted in its history.

There was a fundamental shift in Swiss Re's investment strategy. As bonds provided increasingly less stability, Swiss Re turned to booming equities. Its stock holdings went from 1 per cent of the 1914 investment portfolio to 16 per cent in 1923 and over 40 per cent in 1929.[21] Financial income almost tripled during the 1920s.

Swiss Re was the only non-US reinsurer that could afford to operate in the US market during the economic upturn of the 1920s, thanks to the strong Swiss franc that allowed the deposit of the high reserves required by US authorities. This, however, led to an overexposure in US equities market that took its toll with the Great Depression. In fact, the losses proved to be more significant even than the San Francisco Earthquake.[22]

As the world economy was divided into different currency blocs in the 1930s, Swiss Re took refuge in a conservative financial policy. As in the early twenties, currency congruency was the most important measure to hedge against monetary and financial irregularities. The overall consequences of the 1930s and 1940s monetary situation were severe for the reinsurance industry. International markets gradually disintegrated and refuge was taken by direct insurers in exchanging risk portfolios amongst each other rather than ceding to reinsurers, thus creating a global shadow reinsurance market which allowed the circumvention of international capital flows. The all-important British insurance industry relied on this old practice, with the government seeing a need to support the direct insurance industry rather than the few proper UK reinsurance companies. Essentially, the UK missed the opportunity to become the world leading reinsurance market in this period despite German reinsurers disappearing from the world stage.

Inflation was also responsible for increased demand in reinsurance starting from the First World War onwards and reaching peaks during the Second World War. Not all

[19] Haegen (1956, 42–6). [20] SRCA 10.108 184, Guggenbühl, 274.
[21] SRCA 10.108 184, Guggenbühl, 331. [22] Straumann (2013).

reinsurance could be accepted by existing reinsurers and new foundations, and so, much of the reinsurance business was exchanged between direct insurers on a reciprocal basis. During the Second World War there were very few new foundations and professional reinsurers lost a lot of business to direct insurers because of inflation.

## 4.4 Golden Era to New Turmoil, 1951 to the 1980s

The Second World War brought most of the economic turmoil of the interwar period to an end, but only by the imposition of all manner of controls. In many countries price controls and exchange controls were introduced almost immediately, and these were then often the basis for what followed after the war, and in many cases lasted for decades.

It is often casually asserted that business and finance like war. New opportunities are assumed to appear. But this in fact does not seem to be the case. If anything, it is almost the opposite of what is found. Finance craves stability and war is as incompatible with stability as is possible. A recent study has argued that finance—'meaning banks, the financial services sector, insurance companies and attendant institutions [ . . . ] and their allies and affiliates in government (almost always central banks and treasury departments)—share a deeply held set of preferences regarding the basic domestic environment in which they operate [ . . . ]. In a phrase, the ideal playing field is one of macroeconomic stability.'[23] In any case, the reinsurance business suffered less in war, in part due to the exclusion of war risk in contracts, but also, as manufacturing output fell, there were fewer accidents. And life business was less affected than might be assumed since war casualties were more often among younger people who had not taken out life insurance.

Once the immediate post-war adjustments had been made in the few years up to about 1950, the world embarked on a long period of economic growth, accompanied by considerable stability from 1951 to 1973, that was later frequently referred to as the 'golden era'. Or at least the Western world or Organisation for Economic Co-operation and Development (OECD) did. Without that said, this would seem, at one level, strange. After all, the Soviet Union and its Eastern European satellites had removed themselves from the world economy. So too had China, following the success of the communist revolution of Mao Tse-tung in October 1949. But, worse than that, the Cold War had broken out with the tensions over Berlin in the late 1940s, and the whole period was characterized by tension that at various points threatened to collapse into war. The Korean War broke out in 1950, polarizing international affairs and concentrating the

[23] J. Kirshner (2007) *Appeasing Bankers: Financial Caution on the Road to War*. Princeton, NJ: Princeton University Press, 2.

tension for the following two years. War in Vietnam was almost continuous: first with the French and then later with the Americans from the 1950s until 1975. There were also related intermittent major crises over Suez and Hungary in the mid-1950s, in Cuba at the beginning of the 1960s, in Czechoslovakia at the end of the 1960s, and across much of Africa and other parts of the world during most of this period.

And yet, in spite of all this, the Western world grew as never before. Economic growth rates generally were higher than ever. There were minor 'economic miracles' in parts of Europe. International trade grew at faster rates than output. Full employment and relative price stability prevailed over most of the territory. What accounts for the growth is more difficult to say, but clearly rebuilding after wartime destruction and the postponement of investment must play some part. So too did the strong desire to open up the world economy after the inward-looking policies of the interwar years. General Agreement on Tariffs and Trade (GATT) and comparable institutions played a part. So too did the pegged exchange-rate regime that was Bretton Woods, to which we return in Section 4.4. Yet, the insurance industry did not focus on international business but rather preferred to profit from exponential growths in the respective home markets. With the exception of the Commonwealth area, most former colonial powers also lost influence with the de-colonialization process. Reinsurance was left alone to spread risks on a global basis. Despite difficulties with capital transfer and a much reduced world market, reinsurance grew much faster than insurance from the 1950s onwards.[24]

What was more important for finance was that financial repression also prevailed across most of the OECD.

Very largely in the wake of the triumph of Keynesian economics, particularly in the USA and the UK and the British Commonwealth, the role of money in the economy was downplayed. A sociological theory of inflation was held, where monopolistic companies and powerful unions were seen as responsible for pushing prices up, rather than a monetary theory that pointed to an excess of money in the system. And instead of concern with money, attention shifted to controlling credit. The measures associated with this are often (a little confusingly) called macro-prudential controls. They usually included exchange controls, interest-rate controls, and a range of devices for both limiting and directing bank lending. They appear to have been motivated as much or more by the desire to achieve and maintain financial stability by preserving the soundness of financial institutions and, at the same time, protecting the consumer. The idea was generally to protect the financial system as a whole. The control of credit was generally the main focus.

In some countries, such as, for example, Britain, this might seem puzzling since there had been remarkable financial stability for almost a hundred years. At any rate, the principal tools that were in place were controls on reserve ratios and liquid asset ratios of banks, and various devices designed in order to achieve these, such as special deposits in Britain.

[24] Reinsurance grew by 11 per cent on average year on year between 1950 and 1970. See Borscheid (2013, 102).

In the USA, Congress gave the president powers to instruct the Federal Reserve to impose credit controls on specific lenders and transactions. So, for example, after the Second World War, the Fed, in carrying out presidential and congressional mandates, deployed selective credit controls on consumer instalment loans and on residential construction loans. Some of the direction of lending had its origins in the war when shifting resources to defence and away from consumption was common. The 1969 Credit Control Act gave the Fed new and unprecedented powers to control/direct credit.

These kinds of measures could be found in most OECD countries, and were particularly strong in Europe. Across most of the continent, the period (the 'golden era') was characterized by tight regulations, non-market-oriented controls, and interventions. Generally, monetary policy was limited to keeping interest rates low (they were not believed to be significant for investment anyway) while credit resources were directed towards chosen sectors and combined with detailed regulation and rationing. The timing of the policies varied slightly from country to country but there was a remarkable similarity across many. Perhaps the most extreme case was that of France. There, a new institution, the National Credit Council, was used by the central bank to direct credit. All over Scandinavia there were similar kinds of arrangements. Denmark was a latecomer but joined the fashion in due course. In Italy, selective credit policies were in place for most of four decades following the war.

This becomes of considerable interest when we note the similarities between this period and that since the global financial crisis. The early period was one characterized by very high levels of government debt and by low interest rates, much as recently and perhaps for the foreseeable future.

From an economic point of view, the cost of credit controls in general terms, and in line with any other kinds of controls, results in a misallocation of resources—in this case a misallocation of credit. Financial innovation is obviously affected, in all probability being greatly diminished within the sector, depending on how severe and specific are the targets, and in all probability expanding outside the reach of the regulations. There is also likely to have been some state innovation such as different types of bonds. Not all of this is necessarily damaging for financial services, including insurance and reinsurance. Once the system is understood it can be adapted to. At any rate, financial repression is what dominated most of the post-war years up to the 1970s, and in some cases beyond.

In terms of the international setting, clearly the most important feature was the exchange-rate regime. At the end of the war a regime was designed at Bretton Woods. That was essentially an attempt at restoring the best features of the old gold standard and combining them with greater individual country autonomy in macro-policy. That could result in different inflation rates. So the system was one of pegged exchange rates. That is, each rate was fixed in terms of the others in the system, with the understanding that they could be moved when necessary, when differences (such as persistent differential inflation rates) opened up.

The essential idea was that the overseeing institution, the International Monetary Fund (IMF), would provide assistance to member countries to manage balance of payments in a way consistent with stable exchange rates. In fact, what came into being was a pegged-rate dollar standard. The principal obligation of member countries was to allow for free convertibility for current account transactions while capital account controls were permitted.

For industrial countries other than the USA, the system meant a par value for the currency, with the US dollar as numeraire; keeping the exchange rate within 1 per cent of this value indefinitely; and using the US dollar as the intervention currency. The growth of money supply in the long run had to be subordinated to the exchange rate and so accommodate to the US inflation rate, and current account imbalances had to be limited by using fiscal policy to offset imbalances between private saving and investment. The USA had to remain passive in the foreign exchanges, keep capital markets open, pursue an independent monetary policy, and maintain its position as net creditor by limiting fiscal deficits.[25]

The Bretton Woods arrangements are usually thought of as running from 1947 until 1971, at which point the Americans closed the gold window. But in fact, current account convertibility was not achieved until the end of the 1950s and the system was effectively over by the end of the 1960s. At that point a two-tier system came in: one private and one official. Trading in gold then began to take place and the writing was on the wall for the Bretton Woods arrangements.

The complete collapse of the arrangements came in the years 1971–3. It was in large part a consequence of loose American monetary policy from the early 1960s, worsening in the late 1960s. The inflation produced meant that the USA could no longer carry out its obligations in respect of gold parity. The devaluation of the US dollar caused an international scramble for the US reinsurance market, which had hitherto been difficult to enter due to the dollar value and excessively high reserves requirements for reinsurers.

Across the post-war period, at least after the initial adjustment and limiting the world to that part that traded freely, there was greater exchange-rate stability than there had been since the nineteenth century. There were occasional upheavals (such as the British devaluations of 1949 and 1967 when as many as thirty other countries also changed their rates). And there were pressures at other points.

There was also, as might be expected, considerable monetary stability over these same years in the developed world; even if the beginnings of less stability can be detected in these years in the behaviour of the USA and its financing of what was called the 'Great Society', and of the Vietnam War.

At the same time, it must be noted that, over much of the less-developed world, there were intermittent but serious outbursts of very rapid inflation—inflation in excess of 100 per cent per annum. That was true of many countries in Latin America and Africa and in others such as Indonesia and Israel, all of which became heavily dependent on

[25] R. I. McKinnon (1993) 'Bretton Woods, the Marshall Plan, and the Postwar Dollar Standard', in M. D. Bordo and B. Eichengreen (eds), *A Retrospective on the Bretton Woods System*. Chicago: Chicago University Press, 589–604.

foreign reinsurance. But overall exchange-rate and monetary stability can be said to have characterized the developed world.

There was also considerable financial stability over the same period, broadly the 'golden era', until the mid-1970s. There then appeared, for a variety of reasons, several large bank failures in Germany, the USA, and the UK.

This picture of stability was coming to an end in the 1970s with, first, the collapse of the Bretton Woods system and the accompanying loose monetary policies in the USA and the UK. Although Bretton Woods had collapsed, there was still a deep-seated belief in fixed exchange-rate regimes. A great deal of effort was poured into salvaging such a system (largely through the work of the Committee of Twenty (C20)). Whatever prospect that had of success, and the odds were against it given the building academic case for floating rates,[26] it also hit the buffer of surging oil prices. At the end of 1973, the oil producers' cartel raised the price of oil from USD 3 a barrel in October to USD 11.5 a barrel at the beginning of January 1974, a rise of almost 400 per cent. This had predictable differential impact on the industrial world, and it dealt the final blow to aspirations for a fixed exchange-rate regime.

There were no clear ideas on how to cope with this price shock from a macroeconomic point of view. In some cases, it was simply accommodated with the necessary monetary expansion. Inflation followed in an equally predictable fashion. Thus, a mixture of shocks and of misguided policies and policy responses resulted in the seventies being the worst decade in the experience of many developed countries.[27]

Inflation reached its highest levels ever for some of these countries either in wartime or peacetime. Output performance fell and together these became known as 'stagflation'. The first appearance of financial instability appeared from the 1930s. There were property booms and busts and share price collapses, and the worst hit sector was finance.

One consequence of the oil price rise was large increases in revenues for the oil producers, who then had the problem of doing something with them. In the main, they placed them with financial centre banks that in turn had to find profitable outlets. Much ended up in emerging market economies in Latin America. When these countries then had difficulty in repaying the loans, a major international debt problem blew up. Further oil price rises at the end of the 1970s allowed no let-up in these problems. When the borrowers had problems repaying that led to problems for the lenders at the beginning of the 1980s. The problem then became one for the developed countries, as their banks were at serious risk of failure. The threat of financial instability thus persisted into the 1980s. There were further occasional lapses in the 1980s, as in the savings and loans debacle in the USA. But that was rather readily resolved, and a growing perception developed that the authorities were learning how to handle these affairs and the markets understood what they were doing. Swiss Re's credit reinsurance,

[26] M. Friedman (1953) 'The Case for Flexible Exchange Rates', in M. Friedman (ed.), *Essays in Positive Economics*. Chicago: University of Chicago Press, 157–203.

[27] Capie (2002).

however, was seriously damaged by the tumbling real estate prices and mortgage bank failures. Credit reinsurance proved to be the reinsurance business possibly most sensitive to macroeconomic cycles.

This period does, then, cover a considerable range of experience. But, for OECD countries, it is mostly thought of as one long boom that came to an end in the1970s with the oil price rises and stagflation. Recession was common at the beginning of the 1980s.

The post-war years witnessed the disappearance of markets in the USSR, Eastern Europe, and China. Additionally, the Cold War had adverse effects on trade. At the same time, there was the re-entry of German reinsurers into the market following their country's currency reforms. There had been major exchange-rate adjustments soon after the Second World War (principally those following sterling in 1949 but others came in 1960/1). Capital controls were in place across most of the OECD, making remittance difficult. And, of course, this was a period of fairly steady inflation that began to accelerate in the late 1960s. And then, following the collapse of Bretton Woods at the beginning of the 1970s, there was further exchange-rate and interest-rate volatility.

## 4.5 Great Moderation Through Global Financial Crisis, 1980s to 2013

The upheavals of the 1970s that continued into the 1980s concentrated minds on the need for long-lasting solutions. There was, first of all, a desire for macroeconomic stability. The expression of this economically could be found in the resurgence of liberal capitalism, and politically in the election of the Reagan and Thatcher governments. The problems were identified as of being of overbearing state interference that needed reversing. Both of these administrations gave strong support to freeing up the economy—of favouring, for example, floating exchange rates and freeing capital movements from controls that had generally been in place. This was happening at the same time as the European Union (EU) began forming a single market, China started opening up, and the Soviet Empire was beginning to crumble (the single biggest possible demonstration of the failure of state direction). All this triggered the second wave of globalization, which opened up international markets for insurance companies that had concentrated largely on home markets from the First World War to the post-war boom.

The British abolition of exchange controls in 1979 was the first dramatic move by the Thatcher government on coming to power that year. Other countries soon followed suit. Exchange controls had been one of the most troubling issues for reinsurers which had maintained global networks throughout the long period of insurers focusing on local markets. Paul Volcker's appointment as Fed chairman in 1979 set the US Fed back on the road to central bank independence and the country on the road to monetary stability. More generally, there was wide-ranging debate on the means of achieving monetary stability. Control of monetary growth was seen as being central, and many experiments with targeting monetary aggregates of different kinds were pursued over the course of the 1980s.

All of this determined activity proved successful, as the developed world in particular, but also many emerging market economies, returned to the path of monetary and price stability. For almost two decades these then became the predominant characteristics of the economic environment. And while there were other elements in the story, the period of stability allowed for steady economic expansion worldwide. During the difficult times of the immediate post-war periods, when insurance was of secondary importance, its growth initially lagged behind the macroeconomic upturn. But this time the insurance industry grew faster. International business opportunities, combined with an upswing in local markets, meant that large insurers became even larger. Neo-liberal politics also proved favourable to life insurance as welfare models were increasingly challenged. The rise of equity values, furthermore, led to a market consolidation that produced insurers of a size previously unseen and large enough to retain a large portion of their risks themselves. The immense impact this had on the mass business lines of insurance was, however, felt adversely by reinsurers, as direct writing companies increasingly retained risks themselves and reinsurers were forced to concentrate increasingly on peak risks.[28]

Once the initial exchange-rate turbulence at the beginning of the 1990s had been overcome, exchange rates no longer featured as a problem. Countries in the EU took this further by aiming to bind themselves together and escape exchange-rate variation altogether in a monetary union. Whether or not this was ill-conceived is still in the process of being worked out, but it does appear that European insurers and reinsurers profited from the more open European market and the removal of some foreign exchange problems.

Of course, for those with some familiarity with the period there will be retorts that not all was well in the world. And that is true. Once we step away from the developed world we can find a great deal of monetary and financial instability. Inflation raged in countries from Serbia and Turkey to Zimbabwe. And there were also periodic outbreaks of serious financial crises in the 1990s in Russia and several countries in Asia.

But, to return to the developed world, it seemed that when potential problems appeared the authorities had learned how to deal with them. We have already alluded to the savings and loans episode. In 1987 there was a stock market crash around the world. However, due to the Fed's lead, an injection of liquidity allayed fears and was credited with steering the economy away from depression.

With most of the world then following the lead of New Zealand and Germany with inflation-targeting regimes either explicitly or implicitly there was both commitment

[28] Borscheid (2012d, 24).

and belief that inflation control was within reach. And so it seemed to have been. So far had things gone that some were prepared to talk of the death of inflation. The decade running roughly from 1993 to 2003 was christened the NICE decade—non-inflationary constant expansion.

One of the biggest changes in the world economy towards the end of the twentieth century was the emergence of economies that had long had vast potential, which, for a variety of reasons, had not been realized. By the late twentieth century, four economies in particular, Brazil, Russia, India, and China (they were given the acronym BRICs), began to realize some of their potential. These countries were not only physically large and with huge populations but they began to grow in terms of output. By 2010, after two years of deep recession in much of the OECD, these four accounted for one quarter of world output. Swiss Re opened offices in some of these markets subsequently.[29] But the influence of their growth was only seen more clearly towards the very end of the period dealt with here.

The great moderation and the NICE decade all came to a shuddering halt in the global financial crisis that broke in 2007/8. Financial crises have been relatively rare in the post-war period. The pattern for crises over the 200 years or more in which crises were present was for expectations to have been given some boost from a new investment opportunity, usually in the upswing of economic activity. Prices begin to rise, profits rise and further investment opportunities appear, and a boom develops. Increased borrowing takes place to allow more and more participants to take part. Some are then entering only to take advantage of the increasing prices. Once doubts have appeared and money tightened, the boom is over, the price of assets collapses. Banks fail as their balance sheets reflect this. So the full crisis is reached.[30]

The traditional solution to such a crisis was developed over a long period. It was for a lender of last resort to supply the necessary liquidity to the market as a whole—and not to bail out any one particular institution. The banks had to play their part by having balance sheets consistent with stability; that is, with the appropriate amount of liquid assets to cash whenever a shock struck. The underlying objective is to keep monetary growth on trend. When the panic strikes and there is a rush to cash, the money multiplier shrinks and broad money growth is at risk of collapsing (as happened in the USA in the 1930s). What the lender of last resort does is inject sufficient high-powered money into the system to offset the loss. The lender of last resort is almost invariably the central bank, as it is the institution with the ability to print money without limit. When it is clearly understood that the central bank will respond in this way, and that all those with the appropriate liquid assets will have their needs satisfied,

[29] For example, 1996: Representative Office Beijing and Escritório de Representação no Brasil Ltda; 1997: India Representative Office and Moscow Representative Office.

[30] C. Kindleberger (1996) *Manias, Panics, and Crashes: A History of Financial Crises* (5th edn). New York: Palgrave Macmillan; H. P. Minsky (1986) *Stabilizing an Unstable Economy*. New Haven, CT: Yale University Press.

that allays the panic. When such an understanding has become established it can work to prevent crises.

That pattern of crises just described was close to being repeated in the 2007/8 crisis. There are usually some different ingredients in each crisis but the mix is similar. In the case of the recent crisis, the build-up was there. A long period of easy money allowed a boom to develop. The coincidence of relative prices for consumer goods falling, as a result of the entry of China and some others into the market for these goods, simply shifted the boom to asset prices. Property and stock markets soared in the years before the collapse. This time, when some began to see that things could not continue they began to bet on the economy's demise.[31]

The insurance and reinsurance industry, with some notable exceptions, was largely unscathed during the crisis. Unlike banks, insurers and reinsurers cannot be exposed to a run on premium money. But insurance and reinsurance companies with quasi-banking activities were badly affected. As with most industry peers, Swiss Re suffered on the asset side. Prior to the financial crisis it had increased its exposure to mortgage-backed securities and asset-backed securities (MBS/ABS) from CHF 153 billion to CHF 31.2 billion. Following the freezing of the markets for high-quality subprime securities in October of 2007, the company was forced to absorb several rounds of substantial write-downs. In addition, Swiss Re suffered from severe losses from two credit default swaps. As for 2008, management had to announce a negative result amounting to CHF 1 billion—the first since the 1860s.

There was, of course, a long list of culprits in this crisis. That list ranges from politicians through regulators and rating agencies, to the banks and central banks, and on to the academics who designed the models in which such faith was placed.[32] The banks lent recklessly with ever-greater leverage—less capital and liquidity. The monetary authorities presided over excessively easy monetary conditions. The search for yield resulted in ever-more complex instruments which fewer and fewer people understood. All the signs were present except for those who believed we had entered a new paradigm, 'this time was different'. It was bound to come apart at some point.

Difficulties appeared early in the attempted resolution of the problems. One was the fact that the socialization of risk that had begun in the first half of the twentieth century had been proceeding apace. A consequence of this was that banks had grown hugely in size and many could be described as too big to fail or too important to the system to fail. As a result of the problems outlined in this chapter the whole system was at risk. Further, the traditional solution of lender of last resort was attempted after a fashion with the injection of vast amounts of liquidity in the quantitative easing programmes. But in truth the banks were not really in a position to make use of this in the appropriate way since they did not have the liquid assets required. Many were

[31] Lewis (2010).

[32] W. White (2014) *The Recent Financial Crisis*. Talk to the OMFIF (The Official Monetary and Financial Institutions Forum).

thus insolvent and beyond the care of central banks. They needed to be bought by governments.

But, in terms of the system as a whole, the problems were exacerbated by the regulatory response. Almost as soon as the crisis broke, the authorities pointed to the poor state of bank capitalization and insisted on better-capitalized banks. This might have been an appropriate position to adopt in normal times but, given that the central danger was of a collapse in broad money, the insistence on higher capital asset ratios could only mean lower lending. Either banks had to shrink their balance sheets or had to raise more capital. In both cases it is obvious this results in less lending. New capital comes from bank deposits, the key component of broad money. Thus, the injection of liquidity was, in large part, offset by the regulations on capital (also contained in new Basel rules), and so monetary growth across many countries was deficient, with predictable consequences.

The big question for reinsurers was whether they qualified as a systemic risk. Organizations close to the industry, such as the Geneva Association, found that, applying the Financial Stability Board (FSB) criteria, this appeared unlikely except for quasi-banking activities.[33] Regulation of the reinsurance industry had moved closer to banking regulation, with more severe criteria for solvency margins having already been added to the Solvency I framework in 2002. But with strong equity markets disappearing after 9/11, the fall in interest rates, and an increase in high-impact catastrophes, a new framework with a more risk-sensitive approach was perceived as necessary. Solvency II, due to come into effect in 2016, thus addresses the question of systemic relevance and effectively moves insurance regulation closer to banking regulation. Solvency II has an indirect effect on reinsurers' business in that small insurers may find it difficult to increase their solvency margins and may need to turn to large reinsurers to extend it.

Overall, the current macroeconomic environment may have a larger than ever, albeit still indirect influence on reinsurance. Low interest rates have become a continuous problem, especially for the life business, while traditional investment strategies which favoured bonds, especially government bonds, became obsolete almost overnight during the 2008 crisis. Still, reinsurance follows its own cycles, influenced mainly by large catastrophes in the wake of which the markets tend to harden. This has made reinsurance a coveted niche for large investors such as hedge or pension funds. So-called alternative capital is currently flooding the market, putting more pressure on pricing, a trend which will be hard to break without a major catastrophe.

At least reinsurance companies have profited from booming stock and mortgage markets, as central banks have pursued an expansionary monetary policy. This is, however, an unstable equilibrium susceptible to sudden changes. Investors are running the risk of being overly exposed. The moment will come when short-term interest rates start to increase, making it probable that all asset prices will plummet. Furthermore, the

[33] Geneva Association (2010, 4).

low interest-rate environment has the negative side effect that outside investors jump into the reinsurance market in order to participate from higher yields, thus increasing competition and driving down profits. New regulation and the vast surplus of capital due to the lack of profitable investments have also unleashed another wave of mergers and acquisitions. In short, the market environment has become tougher for reinsurance companies since the financial crisis.

At the time of writing, the developed world looks like it is at last on a path to recovery. There are, nevertheless, many potential hazards ahead, not least in the Eurozone. But if such hazards are contained there is still likely to be low growth across the Eurozone, with consequences for its major trading partners. But leaving aside possible hazards, we are still left with a world in which interest rates will remain low and there is a huge amount of government debt. Neither of these is likely to change in the near future. So long as there is the latter there will be pressure for the former, and until there is a reasonably long period of decent growth, the debt/income ratio will remain high.

## 4.6 Summary and Conclusion

What this chapter has sought to do is outline the range of experience of every macroeconomic kind confronted by firms trading in the international economy. Initially, in the world of the latter part of the nineteenth century, there was relative calm. Exchange rates were fixed in metallic standards and prices were stable within these. Although deflation was associated with much of this period, it was mild, barely perceptible to contemporaries and consistent with stability. Growth was steady, and capital and labour flowed in increasing quantities around the world. Finance and insurance went with them.

Leaving aside one or two regional wars and occasional episodes of the exercise of imperial power, this was a long period of peace and there appeared to be little preventing the world from sustaining ever-expanding growth and prosperity. The huge migration of labour from Europe eased population pressures there and satisfied the demand for labour in the New World. The flow of capital, largely for infrastructure, promoted economic development. There were the ups and downs of the business cycle, and periodic financial crises, as well as periods of industry consolidation, but the best summary of the period would emphasize the positive, upward, stable trends. This was a period in which international business was straightforward.

All of this was turned on its head in the First World War, and unimaginable turmoil followed through the greatest of depressions and then the next war. All macro variables experienced extremes never seen before, with hyperinflation and worthless currencies among the most obvious. Countries turned to autarky. Labour and capital flows dried up and trade in goods collapsed by 60 per cent. These were the worst of times in the international economy.

Only after the Second World War did some semblance of stability return. But it was a much smaller world economy. Growth in the OECD was faster than ever before. That was then severely disrupted in the 1970s, continuing into the 1980s, when prices, exchange rates, and growth were all badly affected. Then that interlude was followed by another period of stability that became known as the 'great moderation', only for the economy to collapse in the biggest financial crisis of all.

While it might be thought that this picture of the twentieth century meant that, for long periods, it was difficult to operate in the international economy, it is important to remember that the challenging conditions present opportunities. Furthermore, they prompt innovation, such as hedging in the foreign exchange markets. And, as already noted in Section 4.4, the movement in some variables such as inflation did not necessarily have negative outcomes for the insurance industry. That said, macro interventions such as exchange controls did have a negative impact on the industry's ability to carry out its business.

Swiss Re's performance over the long run is summarized admirably clearly by Tobias Straumann. The company grew without macroeconomic incident from its founding through to the First World War. It was particularly successful in the period 1890 to 1913. Then, remarkably, its next good growth phase was 1914 to 1929. But this is explained by the fact that its Russian and German competitors were unable to do business. The years 1930 to 1945 were relatively stagnant, and the company was forced into a 'defensive strategy'. Restrictions on capital flows were an important explanation of the situation.

Overall, the period after the Second World War until the 1980s was one of growth. There was strong macroeconomic performance until the 1970s, in spite of the financial repression that could be found in most places. But the macro environment might not tell us much. Swiss Re's success surely has more to do with its changed micro strategy, as it focused on a narrower range of business in fewer markets and relied more on investment results. The final era looked at in this chapter, from the 1980s to the financial crisis, saw Swiss Re prosper further, mostly, it seems, attributable to a mix of changed micro strategy and the benign international conditions, before suffering strains in the crisis itself.

It should be clear from what has been said thus far that an examination of Swiss Re's profits over the very long run is likely to reveal more about micro events and the firm's management than international macro conditions. There is unlikely to be any close relationship between its profits and these macro variables, except during the Great Depression of the 1930s and the recent financial crises in the 2000s.

The company's profits (as shown in Figure 4.1) grew from modest beginnings in the first twenty years of its operations to something of the order of CHF 4 million in the late 1880s. They continued on an upward trend in the next two decades (with a similar volatility), rising to over CHF 2 million before the First World War. The volatility then increased over the war and interwar years but, for the last few years of the period, they averaged over CHF 12 million. By the mid-1960s, they had more than doubled, indeed almost trebled to CHF 30 million. Thereafter, there were no losses as profits continued rising (all in nominal prices), reaching CHF 500 million in the mid-1990s and CHF 2000 million by the end of the twentieth century. But again, it needs stressing that the main thing that stands out is that it is micro events—natural disasters such as the San Francisco Earthquake—that can be picked up in the data series rather than any macro feature. The latter are more likely to have an influence on trend, but demonstrating that would require more robust data than are available.

## Acknowledgements

I would have been quite unable to produce this chapter without the guidance and assistance of Tobias Straumann and Niels Viggo Haueter. I thank them both sincerely.

CHAPTER 5

# CALCULATING THE UNPREDICTABLE

## *History of Actuarial Theories and Practices in Reinsurance*

HANS BÜHLMANN AND MARTIN LENGWILER

Actuarial science is the application of statistical and mathematical calculus on problems of insurance. Its origins stretch back into the eighteenth century. Actuarial thinking emerged as a combination of two traditions, which both had an even longer, though largely unrelated, history: the formation of probability theory in mathematics since the sixteenth century, and the expansion of insurance (in particular maritime, fire, and life insurance) whose precursors date back at least to the medieval era. The emergence and development of actuarial science can be divided into four partially overlapping periods. The first is a latency period reaching from the early seventeenth to the mid-nineteenth century. During that time, the theoretical elements of actuarial theory were already known but barely applied to insurance—a discrepancy that was partly an effect of the close cultural relation between insurance and gambling in early modern Europe. The next three periods were each marked by a constellation of new areas of actuarial practice and related theoretical innovations. The late nineteenth century saw the rise of actuarial theory in life insurance, the mid-twentieth century witnessed the application of actuarial methods in the field of non-life insurance, and, since the late twentieth century, actuaries have been co-involved, together with financial engineers, in the development of mathematical finance, which was first applied in the context of banking and the financial markets in general, and later in insurance also. Over the past two centuries, the influence of mathematical and statistical thinking to finance and insurance has constantly increased. Today, it has become a fundamental pillar.

Since the late nineteenth century, reinsurance played a special role in the history of actuarial science, in particular by acting as a platform for the formation and development of innovative actuarial knowledge. At the same time, innovations in actuarial theory and practices also affected the development of reinsurance. Since its origins in the mid-nineteenth century, commercial reinsurance dealt with all relevant branches of insurance, such as marine or transport insurance, life insurance, accident and health insurance, fire insurance, and later also motor insurance, general liability insurance, and credit insurance. Reinsurance traditionally operated on an aggregate scale and was well experienced in handling heterogeneous forms of data and their statistical analyses, often collected together with primary insurers. Thus, it soon acquired the role of a think tank of the insurance industry and became the platform where technical problems of the industry were analysed, and actuarial solutions developed and then transferred, in the form of a technical consultancy, to other insurance companies. Against this background, this chapter will also deal with the particular role of reinsurance in the history of actuarial theory.[1]

The design and modelling of insurance and reinsurance contracts played a prominent role in the development of actuarial theory. An insurance contract is the central document, in which the risk carrier (the insurance company) defines its code of conduct: the definition of the insured risk, procedures of premium and claims payment, and other technical details. Thus, insurance contracts soon became the basic object of actuarial research, and actuarial innovations often shaped the form and content of insurance contracts. The contract is for an actuary what the canvas is for a painter: the main platform on which he develops his craft. In this sense, the three periods mentioned are marked—from a reinsurance angle—by three types of reinsurance contracts: proportional contracts, which prevailed until the early twentieth century; non-proportional contracts, which gradually came to complement proportional contracts since the 1930s; and contracts based on the securitization of risks, which emerged from the 1980s onwards.

## 5.1 Judgement and Calculation: The Emergence of Actuarial Theory in the Eighteenth and Early Nineteenth Century

The basic practices of insurance (under the term of 'insurance' or other concepts), namely to provide against risks of future damages, are much older than the modern insurance industry. Annuities for example were widely known in the classical and the medieval eras. Since the fourteenth century, they were often used, de facto, as a loan contract with interest payments, a financial arrangement otherwise forbidden by the

[1] The chapter also shares a particular sensibility for the role of Swiss Re and of Swiss actuaries in general for the development of actuarial science.

papal ban on usury. More commercially oriented forms of insurance grew out of the needs of marine transport. In maritime commerce, ship owners often took out loans, which—for an additional fee—need not be fully returned if the ship suffered damage. Such forms of bottomry flourished since the thirteenth century, driven by the Crusades and the related expansion of trade relations in the Mediterranean area.[2] In the seventeenth century, early forms of fire insurance were widely established, for example in England as a reaction to the Great Fire in London 1666, but also in Continental Europe by absolutist monarchies such as Prussia or Austria or as part of local forms of self-government.[3]

In all these forms of insurance, mathematical or statistical calculation was almost completely absent. Contracts were concluded and premiums assessed on an ad hoc basis. There were no general rules on how to calculate risks, reserves, or premiums. Not mathematical formulae, but experience, intuition, and practical conventions guided the insurance practices. Companies did collect data, but without converting them into statistics.[4] In maritime insurance, the risk of loss was determined by factors like weather conditions, pirate attacks, the standards of shipbuilding, or the experience (or drinking habits!) of a captain—factors that were seen as incalculable. For Lloyd's, the famous association of underwriters founded in the seventeenth century in London, the decisive data to set the premium for maritime insurance were the famous 'Captains registers', a collection of confidential information on more than 30,000 captains, a form of data which was still in use in the early twentieth century. Insurance contracts depended on the trust of companies in their clients, not on calculation.[5]

The only exception to this absence of mathematical calculus was the early market in life insurance. In this field, statistical and probabilistic knowledge did have an influence on business practices. Technical expertise had emerged since the mid-eighteenth century and became widely accepted in the mid-nineteenth century. One important reason for this difference to other insurance branches was the relative stability of risks in life insurance, namely that of human mortality, when compared to risks in non-life insurance. Mortality statistics were already at hand in the eighteenth century, when the life insurance industry emerged, because, since the sixteenth and seventeenth centuries, many Christian churches (both Catholic and Protestant) kept registers with dates of birth, marriage, and death.[6]

In the eighteenth century, mortality statistics were increasingly analysed from the perspective of probability theory. Probabilistic calculus emerged in the seventeenth century as a mathematical form for describing numerically uncertain future events. Originally it was mainly used to measure chances in winning games of cards and dice. The correspondence between Pierre de Fermat and Blaise Pascal in 1654, for

[2] Braun (1925, 28–34); Sibbett (2004).

[3] Borscheid (1997, 37); A. Landwehr (2000) *Policey im Alltag. Die Implementation frühneuzeitlicher Policeyordnungen in Leonberg. Studien zu Policey und Policeywissenschaft*. Frankfurt am Main: Klostermann, 265f.

[4] Daston (1988, 115, 118f.).

[5] Braun (1925, 110).

[6] Daston (1988, 125–9).

example—often seen as the moment of birth of modern probability theory—typically refers to a game situation. The authors devised a mathematical method to answer the so-called 'Problem of Points', first recorded by Luca Pacioli in 1494, which consisted of finding the fair division of stakes for a sequence of games broken up before the ultimate winner was known.[7] The discoveries of de Fermat and Pascal were summarized and extended in Christiaan Huygens's book *De Ratiociniis in Ludo Aleae*, a fundamental work, published in Leiden in 1657, and considered the first textbook on life insurance mathematics.

Soon after the seminal work of de Fermat and Pascal, the next generation of mathematicians and philosophers used statistics in order to examine laws of human mortality. Important theoretical contributions came from John Graunt, who published the first study of death as a function of age, his *Natural and Political Observations upon the Bills of Mortality*, in 1662. Following Graunt's work, Edmond Halley published, in 1693, the first comprehensive and empirically founded life table, based upon the mortality statistics of Breslau (today Wrocław, Poland).[8] In the same period, Jan de Witt wrote his *Treatise on Life Annuities* (1671), one of the earliest attempts to apply probability calculus to life insurance contracts.[9]

These contributions, however, remained primarily theoretical or were addressed to government representatives. They emerged at the academic centres in countries like the Netherlands, Britain, or the German states, all with a strong tradition of universities and learned societies.[10] However, the links between these academic debates and the life insurance markets were rather weak. Early life insurance associations or companies, where they existed, were largely uninterested in the uses of probability theory and mortality statistics. In the late seventeenth century, the economic power of the Dutch and the British Empire, the related boom in international or colonial trade, and the large profits of a new wealthy middle class—merchants, but also landowners—led to the constitution of early capital markets, concentrated in economic centres such as Amsterdam, London, and Liverpool, but also Paris. The offering of government bonds, the spread of joint-stock companies, and the foundation of the stock exchanges all emerged in this crucial environment.[11]

It was in this context of concentrated wealth and an expanding commercial and bourgeois culture that insurance companies first began to flourish. This did not happen, however, in all of the leading financial centres. Amsterdam, site of the biggest banking centre in seventeenth- and early eighteenth-century Europe, focused primarily on financing international trade and issuing foreign loans, and only later on

[7] Bühlmann (1997a); Hald (1990).

[8] Daston (1988, 127).

[9] Daston (1988, 27). See also (Hald 1990, 122–30).

[10] Hald (1990, 116–43).

[11] Cassis (2010, 9–15); C. Knick Harley (2004) 'Trade: Discovery, Mercantilism and Technology', in R. Floud and P. Johnson (eds), *Cambridge Economic History of Modern Britain*, vol. 1: *Industrialisation 1700–1860*. Cambridge: Cambridge University Press, 175–9; Alborn (2004, 169).

insurance.[12] It was Britain, the second-biggest capital market after Amsterdam, which became the home of the first major insurance market in Europe. During the seventeenth century, Britain emerged as the first sizeable market for maritime, fire, and life insurance. The first associations and companies for life insurance were founded from the 1690s onwards—as many as sixty societies between 1696 and 1721.[13] But a substantial part of the insurance market—by some estimates at least 20 per cent if not the majority—consisted of purely speculative companies, offering contracts, for example, on the lives of a third person, such as famous contemporaries, on the outcome of future, often military events, or on losing in the lottery (offering a refund for the ticket expenses).[14] These 'gambling' or 'lottery insurances' were a common feature of the seventeenth-century capital market in London. The entanglement between insurance and gambling was also responsible for the widespread bans of life insurance in seventeenth-century Continental Europe (with the exception of Naples).[15]

In the early eighteenth century, business models in life insurance were still very crude. Membership to an insurance scheme was often limited to a maximum number of clients, who were charged regular premiums for administrative costs and a special contribution each time one of the insured members died. The collected money was then transferred to the survivors. Most of these companies collapsed after a certain time.[16] The insurance market—in Britain at least—moved in parallel to the swaying of the capital market.

The South Sea Bubble, for example, an investment frenzy driven by speculative hopes put into the government-protected South Sea Company, which culminated in 1720 in one of the biggest collapses of early modern capital markets, bore serious repercussions on the insurance market. Immediately before the collapse, the London market for life insurances was highly inflated—counting around 10,000 policies in 1720—and imploded to about 1,000 policies by 1750.[17] Also in other countries, like in the northern German states of Prussia or Hanover, where purely speculative institutions were rarer and where the insurance market had been dominated, since the seventeenth century, by unspeculative widows' funds, a considerable portion of these societies perished within a few years.[18]

The relevance of actuarial knowledge only gradually increased in the eighteenth century. In Britain and elsewhere in Europe, governments reacted to the catastrophic losses of the South Sea Bubble by prohibiting gambling insurances.[19] The British legislation culminated 1774 in the Gambling Act that ultimately ended the ties between gambling and insurance. Similarly, the enlightened absolutist monarchies, for example Frederic II of Prussia, began to be interested in improving the technical basis of

[12] Cassis (2010, 9–15); M. t'Hart, J. Jonker, and J. L. van Zanden (1997) *A Financial History of The Netherlands*. Cambridge: Cambridge University Press, 51–8.

[13] Clark (1999, 33).

[14] For the estimated amount of speculative contracts see (Clark 1999, 44f.); see also Daston (1988, 123).

[15] Daston (1988, 160–6).

[16] Clark (1999, 73–80).

[17] Clark (1999, 104f.).

[18] Braun (1925, 172f.); Rosenhaft (1999, 292–309, 2006, 90–113).

[19] Braun (1925, 107).

widows' funds and other insurance associations. This was the context, in which, for example, the mathematician and member of the Academy of Sciences in Berlin (later St Petersburg) Leonhard Euler (1707–1783) published an article in 1776 on the calculation of widows' pensions.[20] Thus, since the mid-eighteenth century, the tightened regulation of the insurance market led to an increased interest by insurance societies and companies in mathematical and statistical expertise.[21]

A pioneering actor in promoting the use of probabilistic and statistical methods in life insurance was the mathematician and accountant James Dodson (1716–1757).[22] Annoyed with the practice of life insurance societies to deny older applicants, for example those over forty-five, access to insurance, he developed, in a lecture given in 1756, a plan for a mathematically based insurance company, and showed how a long-term life insurance plan should be set up, in particular how premium rates constant over time (level premium rates) should be calculated and how such premiums needed to be sustained by reserves (level premium reserves).[23] The procedures described by Dodson formed the basis on which the Society for Equitable Assurances on Lives and Survivorship (later the Equitable Life Assurance Society) started business in 1762, after the premature death of Dodson. The Equitable relied heavily on the expertise of another leading figure in early actuarial theory, the mathematician and philosopher Richard Price (1723–1791), author of the *Observations on Reversionary Payments* (1771), an early standard text on life insurance mathematics. However, figures like Price only acted as consultants or secretaries of insurance associations. Only after 1775, with the installation of William Morgan (1750–1833), Price's nephew, as the first ordinary actuary of Equitable, were administrative procedures based on actuarial principles gradually installed in that company.[24] The Equitable soon became the dominating life insurer in the British market. Around 1800, this market had again risen to about 10,000 policies, half of them written by the Equitable.[25]

Under these conditions, the early nineteenth century became the incubation period for the implementation of actuarial theory in insurance practice. On the one hand, most insurance companies were still founded on a speculative or experimental basis, without much actuarial knowledge involved. In Britain for example, during the period between 1816 and 1844—described by contemporaries as the 'golden age' of life insurance—companies 'sprang up like gnats on a summer's evening and disappeared as suddenly'.[26] Figure 5.1 illustrates this speculative character of the British insurance boom of the 1840s and 1850s. Of the seventy companies founded between 1836 and 1846 (and in existence at least until 1845), only twenty-five survived until 1867. The rate of failures was even higher in the following decade. Only nineteen of the 147 companies founded between 1846 and 1855 (13 per cent) survived until 1867.

[20] Euler (1767).
[21] Daston (1988, 123, 175f.); Clark (1999, 34f.); Rosenhaft (1999, 299, 2006, 92f.).
[22] Hickmann (2004). [23] Daston (1988, 176). [24] Daston (1988, 179–81).
[25] Alborn (2009, 4); Supple (1970, 54–7). [26] Walford (1857).

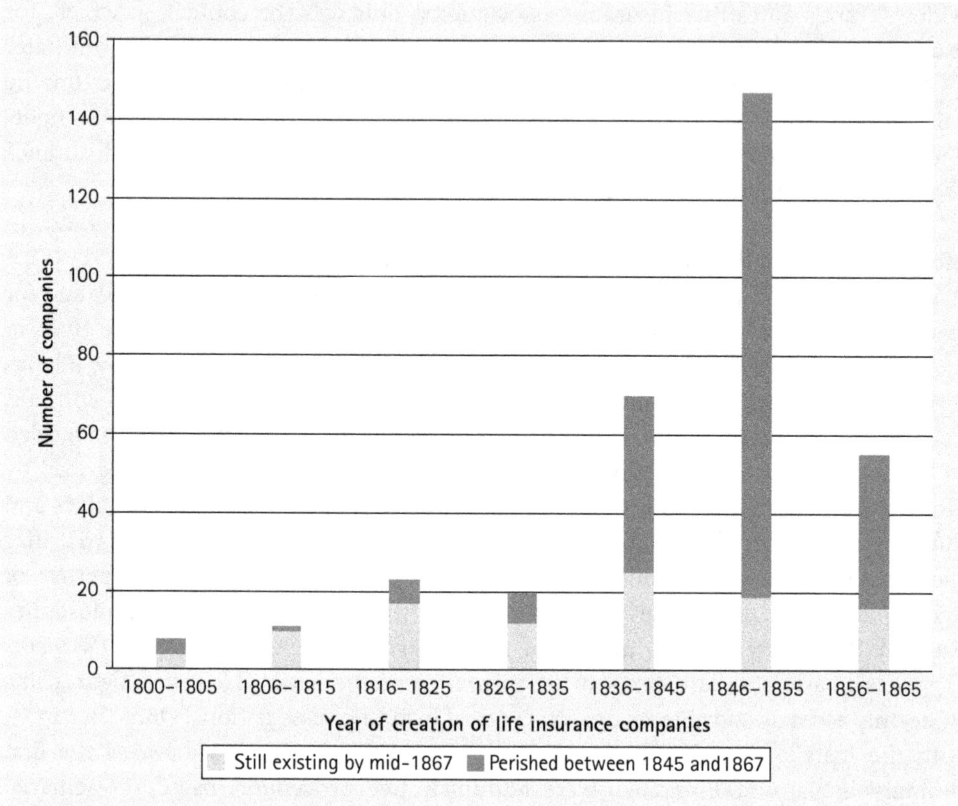


FIGURE 5.1 Boom and bust: Life insurance companies created and perished in Britain (1800–1867)

*Note*: Only those companies which existed at least until 1845 (and beyond) are counted.
*Source*: Sibbet (2004).

On the other hand, the bigger and more respected companies all started to hire actuaries, first often as secretaries for the companies' head offices, eventually mainly as responsible experts for mathematical calculations. However, even this first generation of professional actuaries hesitated to rely completely on mathematical calculus. Personal judgement, for example when selecting new clients for the company, was deemed at least as relevant for the company's success as mathematical expertise. Mere 'mechanical' calculation was seen as insufficient and unworthy of a respectable actuary. Financial success was seen as an effect of the careful and individual selection of customers—and not primarily of mathematical calculations of risk. Medical insurance officers were deemed as important for commercial success as actuaries.[27]

[27] Porter (1995, 101–3).

## 5.2 Formation of an Actuarial Profession in the Nineteenth Century

Over the course of the nineteenth century, actuarial knowledge gradually proliferated in the insurance business and contributed to stabilizing the shaky status of the industry, although slowly and only in life insurance. Three factors, partly internal, partly external to the actuarial profession, fuelled this development. First, with the large amount of unstable insurance companies perishing over a short while, more and more companies became convinced that a long-term business success depended on cautious, calculus-based policies. Second, government authorities all over Europe increased the regulation of the insurance market in the second half of the nineteenth century, mainly by establishing legal authorities for state supervision of the insurance market. Britain took the lead. The first government actuary was appointed in 1821 for the National Debt Office, but his responsibilities were in public finances, not in insurance supervision.[28] In most countries, until the 1880s, supervisory legislation was inexistent or weak. Until the 1870s, Britain had the most detailed, though still very liberal laws. The British Joint Stock Companies Act (1844) for example, only introduced compulsory registration, including the declaration of shareholders, for newly founded joint-stock companies, but put no effective government supervision in place. Even the Life Assurance Companies Act of 1870, the leading legislation internationally at that time, only asked for a moderate deposit and the annual declaration of the balance sheets to the government's Board of Trade. The government, however, had no power of inspection or supervision, as introduced consequently in other countries.[29]

More interventionist supervisory legislation was introduced later in the USA (though only on a state level, since around 1880) and in several European countries: Switzerland (1885), Germany (1901), Austria (1904), and France (1906). Although these laws did not directly demand the instalment of actuarial expertise, they had the indirect effect of making the insurance industry more sensitive towards the technical side of their business.[30] Third, actuarial theory also developed on a theoretical level, especially through the spread of mathematical statistics since the 1870s and its application to insurance practice. In Germany for example, the works of Wilhelm Lexis (1837–1914) on the use of probability theory for vital statistics—a core field of the field of mathematical statistics—opened the door for an increasingly probabilistic understanding of mortality statistics, which gradually emerged from the 1880s onwards.[31] By the end of the nineteenth century, most life insurance companies in the leading insurance markets followed solid guidelines routed in actuarial theory. Actuaries

[28] Mitchell (1974, 7).

[29] J. Taylor (2006) *Creating Capitalism: Joint Stock Enterprise in British Politics and Culture*. Woodbridge: The Boydell Press, 135–209; Freeman, Pearson, and Taylor (2012, 20–38).

[30] Lengwiler (2010, 167–86).

[31] Braun (1925, 426–30).

gradually eventually replaced medical officers as the central experts in the life insurance business for dealing with the selection of risks.[32]

As an effect of these developments, the community of actuaries transformed itself from a loose group of experts into a formally integrated profession. The actuarial profession emerged in two different forms. In the Anglo-Saxon countries the lead was with professional bodies of the insurance industry; in Continental Europe, the initiative often lay with universities. Until the mid-nineteenth century, Britain, with its advanced life insurance industry, also led the international development of the actuarial profession. Both leading organizations for actuaries were British: the Institute of Actuaries established in 1848 in London, responsible for England, Wales, and Ireland (later only Northern Ireland); and the Faculty of Actuaries founded in 1856 in Edinburgh, responsible for the Scottish insurance industry. Both institutes were closely linked to the insurance industry and dedicated to a substantial vocational—in opposition to an academic—training. Separated mainly for political and geographical reasons, they worked closely together in technical and professional issues.[33] They had a powerful influence on the life insurance industry. After the British Insurance Act of 1870, most life insurance companies appointed professional actuaries in leading management positions.[34]

In Continental Europe, actuarial knowledge was first institutionalized in the German states. Here, the development was not so much driven by professional bodies, as in Britain, but by the advanced system of research-oriented Humboldtian universities. Calls for an academization of actuarial theory were raised in Prussia and other German states as early as 1850, for example by the *Masius' Rundschau*, an insurance-related journal.[35] The University of Göttingen, an international centre of mathematics in the nineteenth and early twentieth centuries, finally became the academic centre of the new discipline. By only 1851, the mathematician and Göttingen professor Carl Friedrich Gauss (1777–1855) had written a technically advanced report on the university's *Witwen- und Waisenkasse* (widows' and orphans' pension fund), using mortality statistics and probabilistic methods. In 1895, Felix Klein (1849–1925), another leading mathematician at the University of Göttingen, launched a successful initiative for the foundation, in 1895, of the Seminar für Versicherungswissenschaften (Institute for Insurance Sciences), the first of its kind in Germany. Its founding director was the mathematician and statistician Wilhelm Lexis.[36]

At the end of the nineteenth century, actuarial science started to spread worldwide, parallel to the accelerated internationalization of the insurance industry and to the spread of life insurance to Commonwealth countries such as Canada, Australia and New Zealand, and South Africa, to South American countries, and of course to the USA, which gradually overtook Britain as the leading market for life insurance.[37] Early national organizations of actuaries were established in 1888 in the Netherlands,

[32] Porter (1986, 233–69, 2000, 226–46).
[33] Dennett (2004). [34] Braun (1925, 399). [35] Koch (1998, 144ff.).
[36] Lengwiler (2006, 80–5). [37] Braun (1925, 379–90).

1889 for both the USA and Canada, 1890 in France, 1895 in Belgium, 1897 in Italy and Australia, 1899 in Japan, 1901 in Denmark, 1903 in Germany, 1904 in Austria, Norway, and Sweden, and 1905 in Switzerland.[38] In 1895, these national actuarial associations created the International Actuarial Association (IAA), which has organized, since then, the International Congresses of Actuaries, held every three to four years.[39]

## 5.3 Actuarial Challenges in Early Reinsurance: Calculations of 'Substandard Lives'

The first specialized reinsurance companies were established since the 1850s. As a special form of contract, however, reinsurance is much older. Contracts, in which a primary insurer is ceding portions of its original policies to other primary insurers—a special type of reinsurance called co-insurance—were already known in the eighteenth century. Co-insurance mainly spread in Continental Europe and not in Britain, where, in the early eighteenth century, risk-spreading practices relied on speculative methods, for example writing specific reinsurance contracts and selling them on with higher premiums. These speculative contracts were, however, banned in 1746, as part of the legislation against gambling insurances. Indirectly, this legislation blocked the development of reinsurance in Britain.[40] Reinsurance contracts rather emerged in the German, Belgium, or Dutch centres for marine or fire insurance. In the early nineteenth century, they developed from contracts for single risks to contracts for groups of risks over a fixed period of time. At this stage, reinsurance was still a form of agreement between regular insurance companies.[41]

The growth of the reinsurance market in the early nineteenth century led to the emergence of the first specialized companies for reinsurance. The growth of towns and cities by the process of urbanization, combined with the gradual expansion of the industrial sector, boosted the values of property, convincing many owners to look for property, fire, and other forms of insurance. The expanded risks prompted insurance companies for their part to seek for reinsurance. Major fires often acted as triggering events. The Great Fire of Hamburg in 1842, the Glarus Fire, Switzerland, in 1861, and other town fires in Europe directly or indirectly led to an increased demand for reinsurance. The trend, fuelled also by the industrialization and its subsequent increase of insured values, was particularly strong in the German states.[42]

These developments ultimately led to the foundation of the first specialized reinsurance companies, also in the German states. When looking for reinsurance, German

[38] Braun (1925, 390–402).
[39] Braun (1925, 393–5).
[40] Mossner (1959, 75–7).
[41] Mossner (1959, 86f.).
[42] Mossner (1959, 94f.).

insurance companies usually ended up with foreign companies offering reinsurance services, as the latter were more established in the reinsurance market and seemed a safer bet than their younger German competitors. Also, German insurers, weary of their professional secrets, refrained from making reinsurance contracts with their closest regional competitors. Thus, in the 1830s, British, Belgian, or French insurers dominated the German market for reinsurance contracts. Some of them, however, fearing financial losses, started to demand higher reinsurance premiums from German insurers. That gave German companies a financial incentive for a national solution. In the late 1830s, some German insurers called for the foundation of a German National Reinsurance Association, in order to prevent financial drain to foreign companies. The claim was also legitimized by a form of economic patriotism. Eventually, in 1846, the first specialized reinsurance company, the Kölnische Rückversicherungs-Gesellschaft (Cologne Re), was founded; the company started business a few years later, in 1852.[43]

Actuarial research has been present, since the mid-nineteenth century, only in particular fields of reinsurance. In non-life insurance, risks were deemed too complex for mathematical calculation; statistical data was interpreted without mathematical sophistication. Instead, many decisions were based on crude statistical analysis and by pragmatic and heuristic reasoning. Modelling of catastrophic events only became an issue of actuarial theory in the middle of the twentieth century.[44] In the field of life insurance though, actuarial thinking had already become an important instrument in reinsurance since the late nineteenth century. Three topics were most prevalent: the collection and analysis of statistical data about uncommon risks in life insurance, the development of a collective theory of risk, and the question of which form of insurance contract was best to serve both the interests of clients and of insurance companies.

The statistics of uncommon risks focused primarily on the mortality of so-called 'substandard lives'—a technical term for insurance clients with grave physical ailments such as chronic heart disease, cancer, or diabetes, who applied for a life insurance contract.[45] The insurance of 'substandard lives' was sold by primary insurers. The topic, however, concerned reinsurers as well, as they typically had a substantial share in such policies. Whereas in the USA, big life insurance companies led the debate, in Continental Europe reinsurance companies engaged in calculating the specific mortality of substandard lives and developing adequate models for assessing the premiums for substandard contracts.[46]

The insurance of substandard lives was a major issue, because it touched upon a central concern of the life insurance industry: to avoid the phenomenon of 'adverse

[43] Mossner (1959, 95–8).

[44] For how reinsurance commercially coped with catastrophic risks, see Chapter 10, this volume; for the problems in calculating catastrophe risk premiums, see Gugerli (2013).

[45] For a more detailed account: Sibbett (2004), sections on substandard lives; see also Haberman (1996, 24f.).

[46] Lengwiler (2009, 95–122).

selection'. The term meant that companies with lenient selection practices, accepting all or nearly all customers for life insurance, would become especially popular among clients who were declined by other companies because of their above-average mortality risk. Thus, customer-friendly policies (with low barriers for risk acceptance) would have an adverse effect. Eventually, the company would suffer from the increased mortality among its clients and face financial losses. This financial risk stood behind the concern on adverse selection and led, during the nineteenth century, to strict selection processes in the life insurance industry, usually in the form of a medical examination. Ultimately, it was the medical officer of a company who decided whether or not to accept applicants for a new life insurance policy. Moreover, these medical concerns also initiated a new field of actuarial research: statistical mortality studies on substandard risks, which sought to quantify the relation between mortality rates and medical status, specific occupations, family histories, or places of residence.[47]

Substandard lives represented a particularly prominent group of excluded clients. Until the late nineteenth century, they were barred from any form of insurance. At the same time, progressive insurance companies saw these risks as a potential market and looked for ways to insure substandard risks, for example by adding a surcharge on the premium. The pioneering company to offer adequate insurance cover for these clients was the New York Life. In the years after 1900, its actuary, Arthur Hunter, and its chief medical officer, Oscar Rodgers, developed a standardized testing and calculation procedure—the so-called 'numerical method'—in order to evaluate the applicants' health status. The numerical method measured features like build (weight in relation to height and age), medical history of the family, occupation, personal medical history, habits (like the use of alcohol and drugs), physical condition (impairments), habitat, moral hazard (reputation, financial situation, etc.), and the plan of insurance requested by the applicant (as mortality was particularly high among people asking for short-term, speculative insurance contracts). After a simple quantification of these qualities as 'factors of extra-mortality', the method allowed for calculating additions and deductions resulting in a final surcharge to the one year rate of mortality (see Table 5.1). Thus, the rise of the numerical method also marks the increased significance of actuarial expertise in insurance companies, in contrast to the previously dominating status of insurance physicians. Mathematical know-how, combined with statistical evidence, thus enhanced and eventually replaced medical judgement. In the long run, actuarial theory gradually developed into privileged expertise within the insurance business.

In the 1930s, as more and more insurance companies began to use the numerical method, the approach was globally recognized. Most life insurance companies, but also reinsurers like Swiss Re or Munich Re, adopted it in order to measure the excess mortality—the statistical measure of premature deaths—of substandard lives.[48] In 1934, the method was officially recommended by the third international conference on substandard risks (in Prague); it thus gained quasi-official status.[49] However,

[47] Braun (1925, 412–15). [48] Coppet (1935, 106–9); Sturm (1935, 78ff.); Rudolph (1927, 327).
[49] Coppet (1935, 106–9).

**Table 5.1 The 'numerical method' in practice (1935)**

| | | | |
|---|---|---|---|
| | The calculation is made in the following manner: | | |
| | Basic figure of the average risk | 100 | |
| 1. | Build – 30 per cent overweight (debit) | +20 | |
| 2. | Family record – parents lived to be over 70 – brothers and sisters all living (credit) | | −10 |
| 3. | Occupation – banker (credit) | | −10 |
| 4. | Personal history – one attack of gout between one and two years ago (debit) | +75 | |
| 5. | Habits – rare user of alcohol (no credits allowed for habits – only debits for unfavorable ones) | 0 | 0 |
| 6. | Physical conditions - no record or report of any abnormal physical condition | 0 | 0 |
| 7. | Habitat – usually no debits or credits for applicants residing in the United States and Canada | 0 | 0 |
| 8. | Moral Hazard – favorable | 0 | 0 |
| 9. | Plan of insurance – 20 Payment Life (credit) | | −10 |
| | Numerical rating | 165 or +65 | |

*Note*: In this hypothetical example of an applicant, the person would be assessed on nine levels (points 1 to 9), with added (e.g. 'credit: −10') or deducted points (e.g. 'debit: +75') for each level measuring the deviation to the standard value (e.g. standard weight, standard family hazard etc.). The resulting sum of points (bottom line: 'numerical rating') indicates the percentage of the corrected one-year rate of mortality for this applicant (in this case: 165 per cent of a standard one year rate of mortality qx, or a surcharge of 65 per cent to qx).

*Source*: Transactions of the International Congress on Life Assurance Medicine (1935). London: Otto May, M.D., 97 f.

tarification procedures differed from country to country. In the USA and in France, insurance companies usually demanded an extra premium. In Germany and Switzerland, the insured sum was often reduced, for example to 20 per cent in the first year, to 40 per cent in the second, to 60 per cent in the third, to 80 per cent in the fourth, and 100 per cent from the sixth year onwards.[50] The task of the actuary was to develop the correct formulae for converting the excess mortality into either an appropriate extra premium or into a scale for reducing the sum insured.[51] Business approaches to insuring substandard lives were also divided into two categories. One consisted in setting up specialized companies, which focused only on this niche market. However, such companies were unpopular among potential customers as they automatically stigmatized their clientele as abnormal. Therefore, sooner or later, most of these companies perished.[52]

The other approach was promoted by reinsurers like Swiss Re or Munich Re. In these cases, regular live insurance companies insured substandard lives together with

[50] Dardel (1952, 72–4, 106f.). [51] Dardel (1952, 108). [52] Lengwiler (2009, 107–9).

healthy clients, although under a special tariff. Primary insurers then passed the rating for these contracts to the reinsurance companies. The reinsurer always accepted a major quota of such substandard policies, thus participating proportionally in premiums and claims. These participations allowed companies to constantly update statistical experience. The reinsurer thus regularly published revised rating manuals, taking into account the newest information. This model had two advantages. The clients were granted a contract with a regular insurance company and were spared any stigmatizing effect; while the primary insurers profited from the specialized knowledge of the reinsurers, based on the analysis of large pools of substandard contracts. In the long run, this proved to be the more successful recipe.[53] Eventually, more and more substandard risks were deemed insurable. Previously excluded groups, above all patients with diabetes or benign forms of cancer, were thus granted access to life insurance—a process that continued throughout the twentieth century.[54]

## 5.4 Towards a Collective Understanding of Risks in Early Twentieth-Century Reinsurance

The debate about substandard risks was mainly driven by practical needs. In the interwar period, reinsurance actuaries also worked on theoretical problems, in particular on the challenging task of reforming the so-called 'individual risk theory' and establishing a collective theory of risk. Although the final actuarial breakthrough only came in the second half of the twentieth century, ground-breaking theoretical work was already being published around 1900. Until the late nineteenth century, the problem of describing and measuring risk in insurance was usually regarded as of minor importance in life insurance. The bulk of actuarial calculation only—in probabilistic terms—referred to mean values (statistical 'averages' from a group of individual cases). If these mean values were calculated correctly, the 'law of large numbers', as already shown by Jacob Bernoulli and published in *Ars Conjectandi* 1713, would provide stability for the results of 'large' portfolios and hence for the whole insurance company. Before the rise of modern mathematical statistics through figures like Pierre-Simon Laplace, Carl Friedrich Gauss, Wilhelm Lexis, or Karl Pearson, one could indeed regard mortality tables as deterministic, as many actuaries did. There were, of course, early exceptions like Johannes Tetens (1786), Carl Bremiker (1859), and Karl Hattendorf (1868). The latter discovered that variances of gains and losses from individual policies could be added across portfolios and also over time. But the point is, that even these exceptional

[53] Gruder (1927, 288). [54] Lengwiler (2009).

thinkers modelled risk as 'bottom up', starting with the risk of the individual policy and then adding it up. It was this form of modelling that was called 'individual risk theory'.[55]

In reality, insurers were often exposed to an insurance portfolio far below the size which would allow using the law of large numbers. In fact, they were in dire need of methods to cope with small groups of risks and to quantify the fluctuations around the 'ideal' mean value. The solution to this theoretical problem was achieved in two steps: first, by the establishment of a collective theory of risk, second, by combining this new approach with the emerging probability theory. Filip Lundberg (1876–1965), a Swedish actuary, provided the seminal work for the first step. In 1909 at the International Congress of Actuaries in Vienna, he presented a new approach to insurance risk (published already in 1903 in Swedish), which was later called 'collective risk theory'. The building stones for his theory were no longer individual policies but the insurance claims, which could come from any collective (portfolio) of risks. This portfolio could be of any size, hence needed to be described by a full probability distribution (not just by its mean values, which would be sufficient for large portfolios). It is obvious that this collective understanding of risk was particularly suited for the reinsurer. Consequently, Lundberg presented his paper under the title: 'On the Theory of Reinsurance'.

However, the early works of Lundberg remained largely unnoticed. One problem was the missing link between Lundberg's risk theory and the emerging probability theory. Although Lundberg already understood insurance events as an effect of mechanisms of chance, he did not yet dispose of the tools of modern probability theory and its mathematical understanding of stochastic processes. The breakthrough in probability theory only followed in the 1930s, in particular with the publication of Andrey Kolmogorov's *Foundations of the Theory of Probability* (1933). It was left to another Swedish mathematician, Harald Cramér (1893–1985), to synthesize Lundberg's work with probability theory.[56] Technically, the new model of collective risk theory started with an initial capital and calculated the probability of losing this capital (the probability of ruin) over the long horizon. All actions by the insurer (like premium calculation, risk retention, and capitalization) were now subject to the goal of keeping the probability of ruin below a given level.

The new collective approach to risk opened up several innovative actuarial applications. First, the long-term probability of ruin was used in reinsurance to optimize the calculation of retentions, an important measure in reinsurance. Any reinsurance contract defines a division rule of financial payments—between the reinsurer and the ceding company—generated by the insured risk. The reinsurer's share is called 'surplus' or 'excess', the ceding company's share 'retention'. The problem of retention addresses the question of how much risk a ceding company may run. If the ceding company is

[55] Bühlmann (1997b, 167–9).

[56] Cramér (1930); Harald Cramér (1955) *Collective Risk Theory*. Stockholm: Försäkringsaktiebolaget Skandia.

protected by reinsurance, its probability of ruin generally decreases. The collective risk theory—as developed by Lundberg and Cramér—thus allowed the retained portion of risk to be quantified in the 1930s. Bruno de Finetti (1906–1985), at first actuary with the Generali insurance company, later mathematics professor at the University of Rome, offered, in 1940, a somewhat different approach than the one of the Scandinavian school, reflecting also the differences of risk groups. De Finetti used mean-variance optimization to find the relative values of the retention limits per risk group. Based on the same idea, Harry Markowitz developed in the 1950s a portfolio selection algorithm, which ultimately became standard in financial portfolio management.[57]

Second, approaches stemming from collective risk theory and its generalizations were used to help calculate different factors for the rating of risks. For setting a premium, both the statistical data on damages of the individual risk (the so-called loss distribution function) and also 'collateral' data of the risk to be rated, for example from the country statistics to which the individual risk belonged, were used. Before the First World War, it was still unclear how these sources of information might be measured. The answer was given by two American actuaries, A. Wayne Whitney (1918) and Francis S. Perryman (1932), who proposed a weighted average between individual claims experience and collective (collateral) data. The weight given to the individual experience was called 'credibility'. This method was developed in the interwar period in order to find proper premiums for the business of workmen's compensation in the USA.[58] Since then, credibility weighting has become a basic rating tool for most branches of insurance and reinsurance.[59]

Third, probabilistic models helped to justify methods for measuring claims reserves in reinsurance. Then, as now, claims reserves measure future payments that the risk carrier will have to make. They are an entry on the liability side of the balance sheet of a risk carrier. Moreover, they have to be assessed with a great degree of uncertainty. Particularly in reinsurance, it might take years or decades for the financial evolvement of a claim. The longer the development period, the greater the uncertainty. Since the early twentieth century, it was standard practice that an estimate of total future payments be entered in the balance sheet. In this respect, American casualty actuaries, whose society was founded in 1914 and who traditionally understood claims reserving as one of their main tasks, were particularly innovative. Since the interwar period, and until the late twentieth century, they developed a great variety of reserving procedures, most of them combinations of two basic methods: first, the so-called chain ladder method, presumably invented by accountants in the interwar period, which was later theoretically justified on the basis of a stochastic model by Thomas Mack and David Murphy (1993/4); second, the Bornhuetter–Ferguson model, named after two authors who published its algorithmic procedure in 1972.[60]

[57] De Finetti (1940); Markowitz (1952).

[58] Whitney (1918, 274–92); Perryman (1932, 65–84).

[59] Bailey (1950, 7–23); Bühlmann and Straub (1970, 111–33).

[60] Bornhuetter and Ferguson (1972, 181–95).

## 5.5 The Rise of Non-Proportional Contracts Since the 1930s

The interwar period also witnessed the rise of non-proportional contracts, marking a fundamental transformation of reinsurance contracts and related actuarial problems. Non-proportional contracts emerged from practical administrative needs as well as from a more abstract understanding of risk (no longer based on individual policies). This new understanding was driven by the collective theory of risk, which also paved the way for wider applications of probabilistic methods. The origins of non-proportional contracts stretch back into the late nineteenth century. Originally, in nineteenth-century reinsurance, contracts were almost exclusively administered in a proportional form. In these traditional contracts, the reinsurer participated in a proportion of the premium received for each policy of the cedent insurance company (minus a commission) and paid claims from each policy in the same proportion. Premiums and losses were thus shared between the insurer and the reinsurer in a fixed percentage.

In proportional reinsurance—simple in principle—the reinsurer was still faced with grave administrative problems. In life reinsurance for example, actuaries had to calculate reserves for an enormous variety of tariffs, as they differed between each ceding company and relied on different mortality tables and varying technical interest rates—an enormous task before the advent of electronic computers. Basically, the reinsurer had to record each policy ceded to him. Calculations could only be mastered by the invention of ingenious approximation methods, on which reinsurance actuaries usually spent their talents. Examples were—among others—the methods of Johannes Karup, George J. Lidstone, Julius Altenburger, and the F-method invented by Heinrich Jecklin and Hans Zimmermann at Swiss Re.[61] Similar problems were known in fire reinsurance, where proportional contracts also created substantial administrative problems. One of them was to control the accumulation of reinsured objects, for example in big cities.

Therefore, from the late nineteenth century, reinsurers tried to simplify administrative efforts by introducing more global forms of contracts. In this context, non-proportional contracts emerged as a successful alternative to proportional agreements. In non-proportional treaties, the reinsurer only owes a payment if the loss suffered by the insurer exceeds a certain amount (limit) as fixed in the contract. Thus, the loss is shared between the insurer and the reinsurer in a non-proportional form. This limit corresponds to the retention limit already mentioned. The rise of non-proportional reinsurance created new problems for the actuaries: How should reinsurance premiums be calculated? And how should retention limits be fixed?

[61] For the methods of Karup, Lidstone, Altenburger: see Zwinggi (1945, 23). For the F-method: Jecklin and Zimmermann (1950/1).

The first non-proportional contracts originated in the mid-nineteenth century among primary insurance companies in the German states who sought reinsurance from other primary insurers. In the 1880s, Lloyd's in Britain also started to sign non-proportional contracts.[62] Reinsurance companies also took up the new form of contract. Swiss Re has occasionally used so-called excess-loss (XL) treaties, one of the main forms of non-proportional contracts, since 1890.[63] However, until the turn of the century, non-proportional contracts remained rather unpopular. Primary insurers now had to cover the complete losses up to the retention limit and doubted whether the new conditions were really fair. Reinsurance companies were also sceptical, especially about the profitability of the new contracts, as the premium for XL treaties was considerably lower than that of regular proportional contracts. Accordingly, until the interwar period, non-proportional agreements remained a rare phenomenon.[64]

This only changed after the First World War, when non-proportional treaties started their lasting ascent. In the 1930s, important players in the reinsurance market—notably Lloyd's—started to push for non-proportional contracts, apparently—with many claims being handled by the ceding company alone without involving the reinsurer—to increase administrative efficiency. Another powerful force in this development was the spread of motor liability, which, in the interwar period, gradually became a major insurance branch.[65]

Despite their administrative advantages, non-proportional contracts also posed new problems. As the claims were no longer shared in a proportional way, it was unclear, in the early day of those new contracts, how premiums for the reinsurer should be calculated, how reserves assessed. In the interwar period, underwriters tried to derive premiums by looking at past averages of excess claims payments (so-called 'burning costs'), multiplying them by a 'safety factor'. This crude method could only work as long as these premiums were renegotiated every year. In addition, the ceding company would, at the end of the year, participate in the surplus created by the reinsurance treaty, if any. Gradually, it became obvious that this procedure, solely based on averages of statistical experience, would not reflect the risk character of the non-proportional reinsurance treaty. In the 1940s, actuaries started to take over modelling the full distribution of losses by a factor model, one factor being the loss frequency, the other the loss severity (size of loss). For both factors they developed probabilistic models, which then needed to be simultaneously applied to arrive at the reinsurance premium. This actuarial approach for rating non-proportional reinsurance treaties has since become standard.

[62] Golding (1927, 39); see also SRCA 10.103 067; see also letter of Thomas Witting, Swiss Re, 22 November 2010.

[63] SRCA 10.103 067, 2f.

[64] SRCA 10.103 067, 2ff.

[65] SRCA 10.103 067, 4f.

## 5.6 The Rise of Actuarial Science for Non-Life Insurance in the Post-War Decades

Since the 1950s, actuarial studies have developed in two different ways, depending on the sector concerned. Generally, the conditions for the insurance industry were favourable. With the economic boom of the post-war decades, insurance markets—and with them the opportunities for actuarial expertise—rapidly expanded worldwide. However, on a theoretical level, actuarial science profited only partly from the rising demand for its profession. In the field of life insurance, which dominated actuarial studies up to that time, actuarial knowledge did not fundamentally change; the work of actuaries in life reinsurance mainly followed traditional and standard procedures.[66] Actuarial innovations rather came from the field of non-life insurance, for example of property, liability, and casualty insurance. The expanding markets in non-life insurance, together with the relative lack of actuarial models for the calculation of such risks and the new theoretical opportunities offered by collective risk theory, eventually led to the emergence of a completely new field of actuarial theory in non-life insurance, in particular in accident and motor insurance. The effects of the Second World War on the actuarial profession accelerated this development. During the war, many actuaries, especially in countries directly involved in the war, served in the military and worked on problems of applied mathematics, especially in the areas of probability theory and statistics. After the war, they transferred their new expertise to the insurance industry.[67]

The name of 'non-life' actuary was coined in this era and explains itself from this historical context. Part of the seminal work for the application of collective risk theory on actuarial problems in non-life insurance came from Hans Ammeter (1912–1986), a Swiss actuary and manager of the Schweizerische Rentenanstalt (now Swiss Life). Also, in reinsurance, actuaries now followed the programme of non-life actuarial science, which consisted, according to Harald Cramér, of two tasks: first, to calculate the aggregate loss distribution for the collective (like the branch or the whole insurance company) in a given time period (for example, one year), and, second, to determine the long-term probability of ruin of the collective. The first approach was used for premium calculation; the second delivered a sound theoretical basis for strategic risk decisions.[68]

The emergence of a new field in actuarial science also gave rise to an organizational reshaping of the IAA (the organizer of the International Actuarial Congresses). In the 1950s, a prominent group of university professors and actuaries wanted to have more international visibility of the mathematical methods deriving from collective risk theory and from probability theory and mathematical statistics as evolved after the Second World War. The initiative was strongly supported in Scandinavia, but had also

[66] Bühlmann (1997b, 167). [67] Bühlmann (2007, 191f.). [68] Bühlmann (2007, 192–4).

enthusiastic, if not so numerous, supporters in Continental European countries. These supporters wanted to have a special international body representing their specific theoretical interest. After some struggles, the IAA agreed to establish an independent section for the new theoretical field.[69] This section was formed in 1957 and named ASTIN (Actuarial Studies in Non-Life Insurance). The same year witnessed the launch of the group's own journal, the *ASTIN Bulletin*. ASTIN had a lasting effect on actuarial science, for several reasons. On the one hand, it was a place where the influence of economics on actuarial theory became manifest. Long before the advent of mathematical finance, Bruno de Finetti, mentioned in Section 5.4, had suggested in 1957 that one should understand insurance risks not by focusing on the probability of failure but by looking at the relation between risks and the value of the firm concerned.[70] On the other hand, ASTIN successfully promoted actuarial involvement in a broad range of insurance fields. It was active in several distinct areas: in credibility theory and claims reserving, and in the calculation of extreme values (catastrophes) or of solvency margins and capital allocation.

To what extent was the history of actuarial thinking influenced by the rise of calculating machines and the computer in the post-war decades? Since the early days of electronic computing machines in the 1950s, insurance was among the first industries to buy and use computers. They were mainly used to improve the speed and productivity of administrative processes, such as the management of customer data. In this sense, the computer was a crucial instrument for accountants.[71] In the context of actuarial theorizing, however, it was, rather, an auxiliary tool. Computers were used, since the 1960s and 1970s, for the processing of mass data and for statistical analysis, for example of mortality and morbidity statistics, also for the development of investment and price indexes, relevant for the investment policies of insurance companies.[72] The calculation of actuarial formulae, however, was a different matter. Here, the computer was of minor relevance—at least until the recent trends in computer modelling. Until the 1990s, actuaries rather followed the principle of 'mind over data'.[73] Only since then has computer simulation increasingly gained importance for actuarial science.

## 5.7 Reinsurance, Actuarial Science, Mathematical Finance, and The Rise of Securitization Since the 1980s

Financial mathematics was always a sister of actuarial science, although for a long time it was considered the little sister. Traditionally, financial mathematics deals with the

[69] Bühlmann (2007, 193–5).
[70] De Finetti (1957, 433–43); see also Bühlmann (2007, 199f.).
[71] Yates (2005, 66); Dennett (2004, 63–8). [72] Dennett (2004, 68f.).
[73] Hence the title of Dennett's book *Mind over Data*: Dennett (2004, 68–70).

application of fixed compound interest calculations to determine the time value of money. Such calculations were and still are part of actuarial methods. If applied with care they can even be useful, although the idea of a fixed interest rate constant over time contradicts empirical evidence.

Since the 1950s, financial mathematics has undergone a process of tremendous change: old concepts were seen from new points of view and a rich multitude of new concepts and ideas transformed the field. This transformation is epitomized in a new name. Ultimately, the term 'financial mathematics' was replaced by the new perspective of 'mathematical finance'.

Mathematical finance emerged as a subfield of economics. Economists since the eighteenth century have given many explanations of the economic role of interest, from Eugen von Böhm-Bawerk (1851–1914), Irving Fisher (1867–1947), and Ludwig von Mises (1881–1973), to John Maynard Keynes (1883–1948). Econometricians have summarized market observations on interest rates, the so-called interest-rate term structures (tables showing the dependency of the market interest rate on the time to maturity). However, until the second half of the twentieth century, serious mathematical modelling, leading for example to the quantification of the term 'structure of interest rates', did not exist. Mathematicians (as well as actuaries) considered the financial markets as too complex to be treated mathematically and, before the advent of modern computers, calculations of high complexity had their limitations.[74]

Since the 1950s, mathematics has gradually gained a more prominent role in economics. The marriage between mathematics and economics was initiated by Léon Walras (1834–1910) and his concept of economic equilibrium, developed in 1874 and 1877 in his two-volume *Elements of Pure Economics*. The idea was revived in the 1950s by Kenneth Arrow (1921–) and Gérard Debreu (1921–2004), both of whom used modern mathematical tools and concepts. Arrow had already crystallized the idea that, in complete markets (where all agents can freely exchange goods without transaction costs), the price of any security can be viewed as adding up, over all states of the world, the claim to one unit of account in this state multiplied by the payoff of this security in this state (principle of expected value).[75] If all securities are priced in this way there is no arbitrage opportunity, in other words: no possibility of combining the

[74] D. Nitzsche (2004) 'Financial Markets', in J. L. Teugels and B. Sundt (eds), *Encyclopedia of Actuarial Science*, vol. 2. Chichester: Wiley, 701–9; K. K. Aase (2004) 'Financial Economics', in J. L. Teugels and B. Sundt (eds), *Encyclopedia of Actuarial Science*, vol. 2. Chichester: Wiley, 676–84.

[75] The remark on Arrow is based on a personal communication by Darrell Duffie, Stanford University, 13 March 2012 (by email). For Arrow's and Debreu's work: K. J. Arrow and G. Debreu (1954) 'Existence of an Equilibrium for a Competitive Economy', *Econometria* 22, 265–90; K. J. Arrow (1951) 'An Extension of the Basic Theoreme of Classical Welfare Economics', in J. Neyman (ed.), *Proceedings of the Second Berkeley Symposium on Mathematical Statistics and Probability*. Berkeley, CA: University of California Press, 507–32; G. Debreu (1959) *Theory of Value: An Anomalic Analysis of Economic Equilibrium*. New York: Wiley.

securities in a portfolio that would deliver a profit at no risk.[76] It is remarkable that the reasoning can also be turned around: absence of the possibility of arbitrage implies the construction by expected value. This dual implication in mathematically stringent form is usually attributed to Stephen Ross (1977) and J. Michael Harrison and David Kreps (1979). It was this basic principle of no-arbitrage that allowed the breakthrough in option pricing by Fischer Black and Myron Scholes (1973) and Robert C. Merton (1973). The application of the no-arbitrage principle to specific problems of pricing led to the models of Vašíček (1977), Cox–Ingersoll–Ross (1985), and Heath–Jarrow–Morton (1992).

Through this research, at first just within the discipline of economics and the environment of business schools, the new area of applied mathematics—mathematical finance—got an enormous boost. Actuaries were initially not involved in this process.

The relation between actuaries and mathematical finance was and is still complex. Mathematical finance began to be noticed in insurance, especially by reinsurance companies, from the 1980s. With the stock market boom and the rise of derivative financial products, the business of insurance companies was increasingly linked to the dynamics of capital markets. On the one side, many insurance companies substantially increased their market capitalization; on the other side, they earned a rising share of their income from investments rather than from their core business. The emerging field of mathematical finance was seen as a tool for calculating and managing the financial risks involved in these new investment policies. On the company level, the adoption of mathematical finance was mainly driven by managers and business economists. But gradually the actuarial profession also got involved.[77]

In 1988, the IAA witnessed the foundation of its second section, modelled after ASTIN but dedicated to (and called) the Actuarial Approach for Financial Risks (AFIR). Heated discussions among the leading figures of the IAA on the potentials and merits of mathematical finance in insurance had preceded this decision. Although a part of the actuarial community remained sceptic (some of them remain so today), the majority of the profession signalled, with the foundation of AFIR, its intention to integrate the new impulses from mathematical finance within its own territory of expertise. The challenge to form a new 'actuary of the third kind' combining traditional actuarial knowledge with the new perspectives delivered by mathematical finance became a driving force, particularly in the education of young actuaries.[78]

With the marriage of insurance and financial modelling, and the resulting degree of mathematical complexity, the computer gained additional importance in actuarial science. Solutions by computer simulations often became the unique way of finding solutions when analytic approaches reached their limits. However, as computer simulations seemingly mastered all mathematical complexities, they also invited the use of

[76] The principle of no-arbitrage was also already implicated in the works of Léon Walras and the Austrian School of Economics. Personal communication by Hans Föllmer, Humboldt University, 25 March 2012.

[77] Interview with Hans-Peter Würmli, Swiss Re, 16 March 2012.

[78] Bühlmann (1987).

more and more complex models. The other side of the coin is that a higher complexity of risk modelling does weaken its predictive power.

Today, the field of mathematical finance not only constitutes a new subdiscipline of actuarial science. It has also the potential of transforming classic approaches of actuarial practice, in insurance and reinsurance. Through its mathematical understanding of finance, it offers a new and refined perspective for all insurance branches exposed to the risks of financial markets. This particularly applies for traditional fields, such as life insurance and pension insurance, where considerable reserves have to be invested in the financial markets.[79] Thus, already existing insurance or reinsurance products reappeared in a new perspective. More specifically, modern solvency standards were increasingly imposing an economic, market-driven view on the balance sheets of an insurer. In this perspective, one of the main tasks of the actuary, namely calculating the needed reserves, is radically redefined. Today, actuaries also help to understand what market-consistent reserves are and what no-arbitrage means in an insurance context. The answers to these questions heavily borrow from mathematical finance.

The breakthrough for methods of mathematical finance, above all in reinsurance, came—again—from the product side: the emergence of securitization, an innovative form of tradable financial products. Today, securitization represents one innovative method to create mixed financial investments, combining insurance and banking elements. It offers a whole range of new financial products at the crossroads of banking and insurance. Securitization is characterized by the pooling of various types of debt and their payment streams as collateral for new bonds to be sold to investors via the capital markets at exchanges or over the counter.

The history of securitization stretches back into the 1970s, although the proper term only emerged in the 1980s. Securitization was made possible by a more general trend: the rise of investment banking and the relative decline of commercial banking. Since the 1970s, investment banking expanded, together with stocks, bonds, and other financial products. The first debt-backed securities, then based on mortgage loans, were issued at that time. Mortgage-related bonds were soon followed by products based on credit card debts, auto loans, or insurance-related liabilities (leading to catastrophe bonds (cat bonds))—some of these bonds were commercially successful, others not.

This trend culminated in the stock market boom of the 1980s. As capital markets were able to mobilize far more capital than insurance or reinsurance companies, securitization was seen as a way to mobilize capital to pay for mega and catastrophic risks like windstorms, earthquakes, and the like. Cat bonds were indeed the starting point for the spread of insurance-related securities. In 1992, American International Group (AIG), a major American insurance company with what some see as a particularly aggressive policy of engaging in new initiatives like the emerging market of securities, proposed the first cat bond, designed to cover against wind and earthquake risks (the bond was withdrawn before issued).[80] A few months later, in the aftermath of

[79] Interview with Hans-Peter Würmli, Swiss Re, 16 March 2012.

[80] For a history of AIG, see Shelp and Ehrbar (2009).

Hurricane Andrew, the Chicago Board of Trade, a stock exchange responsible for the future and options exchange and particularly innovative in designing new investment products, proposed and issued a series of cat bonds and thus helped spread the idea of insurance-related securities. Again, the new products were primarily pushed by financial specialists and their search for new investment products beyond classical assets. Actuaries only played a minor role, mainly as providers of the data (in forms of loss indices), based on which securities were designed. Although a few of the bonds failed and produced losses for the investors (for example, in cases related to Hurricane Katrina or the collapse of the World Trade Center in September 2001), insurance-related securities continued to develop. In recent years, they even entered new areas, for example with bonds based on mortality and longevity risks in life insurance, or with bonds based on health-care risks.[81] Another driving force for the spread of securitization, especially within insurance companies, was a structural transformation of financial corporations. With the increasing integration in the 1990s of banking and insurance business under the roof of 'bancassurance', actuaries got more and more active in jointly modelling insurance risks and investment risks. The trend to bancassurance started in the late 1980s and replaced the hitherto loose forms of cooperation between banks and insurers. It was partly motivated by hopes for increased efficiency and profits of the industry—a hope which, ultimately, did not materialize. After 2000, the trend lost its previous momentum.[82]

In the early days of securitization, the reinsurance industry opinion was split on the new market. Because of its perspective to cover for mega risks, securitization threatened to marginalize reinsurance companies in their core market—pessimists already predicted the nearing end of reinsurance itself. Whereas some reinsurers like AIG (formally an insurance company with a strong reinsurance branch) embraced the new approach and took an active part in its development, companies like Swiss Re or Munich Re saw securities rather as a competing product and remained sceptical, at least at the beginning. Swiss Re entered the market reluctantly in the mid-1990s, but then quickly changed into an active and even leading innovative promoter of securitization, for example by launching longevity bonds.[83] Like most actors in this field it did not only sell such products but used them also as investment vehicles. Beyond this direct involvement, reinsurance also participated indirectly in the new market. Reinsurance actuaries often acted as experts on catastrophic and other risks, and provided, as consultants for commercial banks and other bond issuers, the necessary indices for the construction of securities.[84]

Since the beginning of the financial crisis in 2007, derivative financial products such as securitization have been increasingly criticized and sometimes identified as being

[81] Interview with Morton Lane, Lane Financial, 22 December 2011.

[82] For Germany, see Borscheid (2012c, 65f.); for Switzerland: Lengwiler (2012, 165f.).

[83] Interview with Hans-Peter Würmli, Swiss Re, 16 March 2012; interview with Morton Lane, Lane Financial, 22 December 2011.

[84] Interview with Hans-Peter Würmli, Swiss Re, 16 March 2012; interview with Donald McKenzie, 2006.

responsible for the economic downturn. Of course, since 2007, the global economy witnessed not just one, but several crises: a crisis of the US mortgage market in 2007/8, a subsequent international banking crisis, a sovereign debt and/or government spending crisis, mainly in Western European countries, and, since 2009, the monetary crisis of the euro, the single currency of the European Union (EU).[85]

Securitization has mainly been blamed in the context of the 'subprime crisis': the collapse of a sector of the US mortgage market. Even for this limited phase of the crisis, the causes are manifold, and securitization was criticized together with a complex cluster of other factors—such as extremely low interest rates since 2001, lenient lending practices in the emerging market for 'subprime' mortgages, and failing rating agencies—for leading to the collapse of a substantial part of the mortgage market and thus undermining the financial system as a whole.[86] What had happened? After the US Federal Reserve reacted against the 2001 crisis by slashing interest rates to a record low, stock markets and mortgage markets started a boom period, with dangerous effects. The quick expansion of the subprime loan market in particular, partly backed by complex and increasingly intransparent derivative products, proved a highly explosive mix. When the Federal Reserve, in 2004/5, started to act against rising inflation risks by increasing interest rates, it caused a disastrous chain reaction. Many lenders in the subprime market could no longer pay their rising mortgages and the market quickly collapsed. As an effect, some derivative products (like mortgage-backed securities and credit default swaps) had no longer a market value. Other products (like credit default swaps) were threatening to trigger enormous payments to the contracting parties. For insurance and reinsurance companies, the engagement in asset-backed securities often proved disastrous. In 2008, AIG nearly went bankrupt and was only saved by a multi-billion dollar bailout from the Federal Reserve and the government of the USA. Swiss Re also took a very substantial loss for writing down part of its asset portfolio.[87]

Was the boom in derivative products—or securitization—ultimately responsible for the economic collapse? Some analysts find it questionable to exclusively blame the derivative instruments—or even the mathematical formula behind them. They see the problem of derivative products rather in their application and in related business practices: in the lack of corporate control, or outright fraudulent management practices, and in common overconfidence in the accuracy of mathematical models. A better acknowledgement of the uncertainties in assessing the risks of derivative products and of the difficulties in assessing their adequate price might have helped prevent some aspects of the crisis.[88]

[85] For the US subprime and banking crisis see J. E. Stiglitz (2010) *Freefall: America, Free Markets, and the Sinking of the World Economy*. New York: Norton; Lewis (2010); Gorton (2010); see also the official US government report: USPSI (2011). For a historiographical view on the crisis: C. M. Reinhart and K. Rogoff (2009) *This Time is Different: Eight Centuries of Financial Folly*. Princeton, NJ: Princeton University Press.

[86] USPSI (2011).

[87] Shelp and Ehrbar (2009); Lengwiler (2012, 164f.).

[88] Föllmer (2009); Donelly and Embrechts (2010).

The issue is still open, and a consensus on how to prevent similar abuses of financial products and its catastrophic consequences has not (yet) evolved. One thing at least seems clear: in the foreseeable future, the insurance industry, including its finance-related activities, will need more rather than less expertise in actuarial science and mathematical finance.

## Acknowledgements

For comments and advice we would like to thank Mira Wilkins (Florida International University), Geoffrey Jones (Harvard Business School), Robin Pearson (Hull), Welf Werner (Bremen), Darrel Duffie (Stanford University, Menlo Park, CA), Hans Föllmer (Humboldt-University, Berlin), Theodore Porter (UCLA, Los Angeles), Morton Lane (Lane Financial LLC, Wilmette, IL), Paul Embrechts (ETH Zurich), Thomas Witting (Swiss Re, Munich), Hans-Peter Würmli (Swiss Re, Zurich), Niels Viggo Haueter (Swiss Re, Zurich), David Gugerli (ETH Zurich), and Daniela Zetti (ETH Zurich).

CHAPTER 6

# THE RISE AND DECLINE OF TREATY REINSURANCE

## *Changing Roles of Reinsurers as Financial Service Providers*

ALEXANDROS-ANDREAS KYRTSIS

## 6.1 The Reinvention of Reinsurance in the Nineteenth Century

> The trade of insurance gives great security to the fortunes of private people, and, by dividing among a great many that loss which would ruin an individual, makes it fall light and easy upon the whole society.
>
> In order to give this security, however, it is necessary that the insurers should have a very large capital.[1]

When Adam Smith was alluding to the insurer's need for capital, he could not have anticipated the future role of reinsurers as financial service providers. Although the financial intricacies of risk management lay beyond the horizon of even the brightest minds of the early years of the Industrial Revolution, it is likely that people like Smith were aware of how reinsurance could cope with the capital shortages caused by a period of high claims. The ban of this kind of coverage of marine risks for companies operating from British soil since 1746 and for more than a century, and the habit of spreading risks with the 'names' system used by Lloyd's, might have kept Smith from having a closer look at the reinsurers' craft.[2] But the fact that reinsurance, contrary to

[1] A. Smith ([1776] 1976) *An Inquiry Into the Nature and Causes of the Wealth of Nations*. Oxford: Oxford University Press, 757.

[2] Mossner (1959, 75–8); Pearson (1995, 560–1, 2012, 67–9).

insurance, was not mentioned in *The Wealth of Nations* was perhaps mainly due to the way his contemporaries understood the problems of insurability. At the end of the eighteenth century, and until the middle of the nineteenth, the handling of risks depended for the most part on mutuality and pools, and not on spreading these among various organizational entities.[3] Some of the exceptional insurance risks, for instance of sea transport, could be reinsured by those who were ready to gamble. The perceived likelihood of major insurance events was a source of high profit for those who were ready to provide protection to insurers in exchange for premium; but it could be a cause of ruin as well.

The reluctance of insurance companies to issue policies or to expand their business did not solely depend on their fear of disproportional claims after an insurance event. When the demand for insurance took off in the nineteenth century (as a consequence of rising economic performance, urbanization, and the subsequent changing attitudes towards the risks to which families and enterprises were exposed),[4] the direct companies were faced with a rather paradoxical problem that influenced their underwriting capacities. Growing marketing, sales, and administrative costs under conditions of fierce competition in expanding insurance markets could easily upset the balance sheets of the companies. This applied especially to the smaller and younger ones, the survival of which was conditional upon fast business growth. The mismatch between the fluctuating revenue and the attached costs, on top of which indemnities also had to be added, was a challenge that made many insurers consider slowing down the issuance of new policies.[5] The difficulty of handling growing volumes of contracts caused a dilemma: they had either to reject customers independently of the character of risks they were seeking to insure, or, alternatively, risk collapse because of the unaffordable administrative costs and the financial burden that the frantic issuance of policies might imply. This contradiction became, increasingly, an inherent factor in the changing dynamics of insurance markets in Europe and in the USA for about a century preceding the First World War. Indeed, today insurers still struggle with similar problems, which require capital injections and capital relief. Because of the widespread awareness of this complication among insurers, the search for appropriate solutions became a vital issue. As Ernst Froelich observed, these solutions could not be found along the lines of the so-called 'net line' or 'names' system prevailing in London. According to

[3] T. Corbet (1841) *An Inquiry into the Causes and Modes of the Wealth of Individuals, or the Principles of Trade and Speculation Explained; In Two Parts*. London: Smith, Elder & Co., 100–2; A. Birnie (1962) *An Economic History of Europe 1760–1939*. London: Methuen, 220–6.

[4] According to Daron Acemoglu's and Fabrizio Zilibotti's model, economic actors decide between saving, investment in low-risk and low-return activities, and high-risk and high-return activities. The latter are the ones that promote change towards higher levels of economic performance (Acemoglu and Zilibotti 1997, 711). The more economic momentum depends on high-risk activities, the more insurance is required, and, from a certain level of exposure, reinsurance also becomes a necessary condition. For the relation between growth and insurance in the nineteenth century, see also Borscheid (2012a, 39–44); Mossner (1959, 82–4); Arps (1965a, 383–4); Pearson (2004, 315–22). See also Zelizer (1978); Anderson, Eriksson, and Lindmark (2010); Anderson and Lindmark (2010).

[5] Lengyel (1927, 1–5).

this system, the placement of large risks could be easily conducted on a short notice and within highly responsive and spatially dense social networks of wealthy businessmen. The lack of such opportunities on the Continent, where a large number of much smaller commercial, maritime, and financial centres were scattered across a wider geographical space, called for a different approach.[6] The difficulties of exploiting social proximity caused by distance—in times in which even the invention of the telegraph was not enough to replace direct contact between business interlocutors—made the search for structured services necessary. The need for formal contracting between insurers and reinsurers, who were based in far-flung places and who had no preceding close connections was made apparent. This factor of social and spatial distance also posed a problem of transaction costs in cases where each risk had to be assumed and treated separately.

The contractual and operational innovations of reinsurers in the nineteenth century that emerged as a response to these new challenges paved the way for new services, first, in the form of 'treaty reinsurance', and, much later, at the end of the twentieth century, in the form of 'financial reinsurance'.[7] The bankers played a rather marginal role in this, as insurers did not rely decisively on direct or indirect lending to boost their operations. The insurance business as such did not create collateral beyond its tangible and intangible assets, and thus raising working capital with bank credit remained marginal.[8] And attempts at raising additional shareholder capital rarely improved

[6] The point was made in the 1950s by Ernst Froelich, a general manager of Swiss Re, in a paper delivered before the London Institute of Insurance in which he juxtaposed the Continental system to the British one, practised mainly by Lloyd's. *The Review*, 1957, 1315–22.

[7] Innovations as forms of adaptive response to pressures and changes in the sense discussed by Joseph A. Schumpeter (J. A. Schumpeter (1947) 'The Creative Response in Economic History', *Journal of Economic History* 2: 2, 149–59) emerged in the case of reinsurance as a consequence of passive reinsurance, i.e. from the demand for reinsurance and the prescription of contract provisions by direct companies. Creative responses as a result of active reinsurance originating from the marketing and product or service management efforts of reinsurers have been minimal since the interwar period due to operational path dependencies and lock-ins related to the techniques of treaty reinsurance, with the exception of the methods and techniques of catastrophe risk assessment (see Section 6.11).

[8] Banks made capital available for the establishment of new insurance (and reinsurance) companies (Wandel 1998, 59–61), but they remained reluctant to grant credit for the expansion of the insurance business. For instance, the minutes of the meetings of Swiss Re's board of directors (hereafter BoD) show that only minimal credit was taken, and this only for certain non-critical lines of operating costs (SRCA, Meeting minutes of Swiss Re's BoD 1864–1940). The relevance of insurance for economic development, especially in Germany, can be inferred from the fact that foundation capital for insurance and reinsurance was more available than for industrial enterprises (S. Wolff (1915) *Das Gründungsgeschäft im deutschen Bankgewerbe*. Stuttgart: J. G. Cotta'sche Buchhandlung, 98–105; J. Kocka (1978) 'Entrepreneurs and Managers in German Industrialization', in P. Mathias and M. M. Postan (eds), *The Cambridge Economic History of Europe*, vol. 7, part I. Cambridge: Cambridge University Press, 492–589, here 536), although this trend reversed after 1900 (Kocka (1978, 565–70)). Concerning the difficulty of regarding the mitigation of risks by taking other risks, as practised by the insurers (and reinsurers), as collateral, it is worth noting the following: many economists and financial analysts point out the fact that collateral for bankers in the case of enterprises does not depend only on material assets, but also on expectations from the control of its revenue streams. Beyond material collateral, what counts is the controllability and transparency of the borrowers' action. See discussion of this topic in J. Stiglitz and

the availability of financial resources.[9] Using reinsurance to reduce retention therefore became a familiar method of smoothing the finances of the direct companies. But this only made sense if reinsurance premiums remained affordable. The cost of ceding primary risks had to be held within certain limits to support the robustness of the insurer. This meant reinsurers could not rely on high rates to expand their business, but needed flourishing direct companies.

In this respect, premiums were not set solely as a consequence of the bargaining power of reinsurers. Rising operating and transaction costs, resulting in reliable risk assessment, as well as from actuarial work required by each life reinsurance contract, was one of the main preoccupations of reinsurance managers and actuaries. Initially much of reinsurance was offered by the direct companies themselves and, later in the nineteenth century, by their specialized reinsurance departments. The norm for the reinsurance business was that separate decisions were made for each risk that was offered for cession.[10] Ceding was conducted exclusively on a facultative basis. But if each separate risk had to be cautiously assessed, and correspondingly the reinsurance scheme calculated every time anew, the transaction costs would soar, at least as long as information-processing capacities remained low.[11] New contractual practices and new financial technologies were required. If reinsurance was to be conducted technically on a running basis (and in contractual terms also on an obligatory basis, binding the reinsurer to assume certain categories of risks), and not on a facultative basis (allowing the reinsurer to turn down contracts), the financial agreements and the assessment of risks also had to be suitably adjusted.[12] Reinsurance contracts had to provide for the

A. Weiss (1981) 'Credit Rationing in Markets with Imperfect Information', *American Economic Review* 71: 3, 393–410; Evans and Jovanovic (1989); D. W. Diamond and R. G. Rajan (2000) 'A Theory of Bank Capital', *Journal of Finance* 55: 6, 2431–65. The assets that can be captured by a lender in case of default would have been, in the case of insurance risks, policies, not production factors. As S. J. Lengyel (1927, 1–3) explains, estimating the assets of insurers as a function of the policies issued is extremely difficult, and the same applies to their reserves, also to their hidden reserves. Taking reinsurance signals more risk taking, and thus is a negative signal for bankers.

[9] The stock exchange has never been a significant source either of direct lending nor of positive signalling effects resulting from shareholder value. Insurers were mainly judged by their ability to respond to claims, and thus from their balance sheet reserves. Raising capital through the stock exchange was rarely a strategic move, although attempts to cope with high claims by selling packages of their own shares was not unusual (Arps 1965a, 457, 626–9, 638–9). Furthermore, plunging equity prices after a major insurance event was more often the case than booming shareholder value because of a lack of threats to the insurer (Arps 1965a, 653). However, direct companies have always been more aggressive in investing and managing assets than reinsurers, who tended to have a very low percentage of their turnover employed for asset management. This conclusion can be easily drawn from the longitudinal study of company profiles of reinsurance companies. Also, the study of the minutes of the meetings of the Swiss Re BoD between 1880 and 1960 records an explicit reservation towards making the company's financial strategy dependent upon direct lending from the stock exchange. On the financial management of insurers see contributions in: Cummins and Lamm-Tennant (1993).

[10] At the end of the 1850s there was only one specialized reinsurance company, Cologne Re (Kölnische Rückversicherungs-Gesellschaft, founded in 1846). Masius (1857, 7–8).

[11] On the evolution of the adoption of information technologies in the insurance industry: Yates (2005).

[12] Gugerli (2013, 158–9).

build-up of technical reserves at the reinsurer, and, at the same time, allow the direct companies to reduce their liabilities and thus make them financially strong enough to pay premiums to the reinsurers. This meant that the reinsurer had to estimate the financial risks for separate groups of material risks and the conditions under which these financial risks could be shared between the direct insurer and the reinsurer.[13] Bundling risks and assessing the exposure that was expected from groups of risks became a business and operational necessity.

But the assessment of exposures corresponding to groups of risks, contrary to those of separate risks that had to be ceded in the facultative way, required new methods and techniques for screening and monitoring the operations of the insurance companies. It is obvious that this kind of reinsurance contracts made long-term and concordant inter-firm relationships necessary. In what was to be called 'treaty reinsurance', the dominant practice of the direct insurers was to seek reinsurance contracts that covered a large set of risks, often whole insurance portfolios, the duration of which could extend into several decades. This continuity was clearly facilitating the overall insurability of risks to which the direct insurer was exposed. It created a spectacular stability in commercial relationships that was not easy to find in other branches of the economy.[14] Short-term disruption and consequent cancelation of contracts was, however, not rare. In spite of occasional conflicts, the stability of reinsurance relationships facilitated continuity both in terms of contracting techniques and financial technologies. This created a favourable organizational and operational environment for standardization.[15] Such effects can be mostly observed in the cases where quota-share treaty reinsurance methods were applied. Quota-share agreements were mostly open-ended or at least on very long terms.[16] This meant that, in the case of treaty reinsurance, which was based on obligatory treaties, the situation was totally different from the practices adopted

[13] Pfeiffer (1975, 20–1).

[14] Under these circumstances, the reinsurer had to follow the fortunes of the ceding company for the duration of the treaty relationship. This requires a highly confidential and symbiotic relationship, which makes treaty reinsurance, according to many expert views, more of an associational relationship than typical insurance. Ehrenberg (1885, 15–16, 43–5, 48–50); Herrmannsdorfer (1921, 25–9); Mossner (1959, 14). For an opposite view according to which reinsurance treaties always have the character of an insurance policy, see Rau (1901, 320–1). The symbiotic relationships were often complemented or sometimes even triggered by the shareholder interests of a reinsurer who acquired stocks of insurance companies. There have also been companies, like Munich Re, which not only purchased shares, but created a new direct insurance company and subsequently controlled it, as is the case of Allianz: Arps (1965b, 7–14). But, independently of the way one interprets the character of this relationship, the issue behind treaty reinsurance is the problem of information, combined with psychological propensities and the question of trust. The wordings in an internal paper of Swiss Re are very characteristic in this respect: 'For the reinsurer there is an added difficulty in that he must make up his mind on how far he can rely on the ceding company's estimates. The way estimates are made and claims handled and reported may vary from company to company. Some managers have a tendency to be over-optimistic. They may be so by nature or it may be conceivable that such optimism is inspired by the knowledge that reinsurers, as a rule, base their excess premiums quotations to a large extent on the loss experience of the company and that if a favourable experience is shown the company may get its cover cheaper' (SRCA 10.146 212.04, How to Establish and Follow Excess Loss Reserves). Concerning the relationship between technical and legal issues in the practice of reinsurance, see Villotte (1927).

[15] Carl (1990, 237); Hürlimann (1931, 3).

[16] Carl (1990, 121–2).

among those agents offering predominantly facultative coverage, especially if the latter implied transfers of tail or peak risks to the reinsurer.

## 6.2 Specialists in Strategic Financial Partnership

How financial risks have been shared is of central importance. As Fritz Herrmannsdorfer stressed, the motives for opting for quota-share reinsurance contracts were never of a purely technical nature.[17] More frequently than not, they originated from economic and financial considerations. Quota-share reinsurance implies a sharing of risks between the direct insurer and the reinsurer in which non-proportional effects are excluded or separately treated.[18] Quota-share (proportional) reinsurance was, since the take-off of insurance markets in the nineteenth century, for the most part applied to accident, liability, hail, and transport reinsurance. But it was also always important in cases of rapid growth of business. Although many obligatory treaties included partly or entirely non-proportional agreements, the quota-share element supported the sharing of risks between the two parties.[19] In the case of non-proportional reinsurance, the indemnification of the damage is overtaken by the reinsurer above a certain level and is indexed according to a previously agreed pattern or layers. The latter is crucial as, usually, non-proportional reinsurance is an arrangement on top of a proportional agreement. In contrast to quota share, claims are attributed to each separate risk and the contractual obligations are defined with reference to a period of time (such as a year or the duration of the contract).[20] For many companies, this was not the preferred way of transferring certain categories of risks. The most effective way for creating convenient conditions of sharing risks between the direct insurer and the reinsurer is obligatory quota-share reinsurance. The obligatory–proportional reinsurance services bind the two parties to each other in a much stronger sense than any kind of facultative reinsurance agreements.[21] This is mostly the case with quota-share treaty reinsurance contracts.[22]

Treaty reinsurance was not the only element that defined the relationship between the direct insurer and its reinsurer, although in many cases it was the bulk around which reinsurance programmes were flexibly developed. The deep commercial relationships often resulted in diverse and heterogeneous reinsurance programmes that included various components and modules. Treaties were occasionally a mix of contractual elements, partly on a facultative and partly on an obligatory basis.[23] The

[17] Herrmannsdorfer (1927, 70). [18] Liebwein (2009, 70).
[19] Bourthoumieux (1998, 1367–84). [20] Liebwein (2009, 168).
[21] Pfeiffer (1975, 24). [22] Carl (1990, 121–2).
[23] The obligatory–facultative form of treaty was, by 1865, an accepted practice. See references to treaties in the meeting minutes of Swiss Re's BoD of 18 July 1865: SRCA 10.107 758.

contractual and financial technologies of the reinsurer were thus absorbing a variety of risks. Furthermore, the continuity and relative standardization that could be observed in the case of long-term treaty reinsurance did not totally rule out conflicts and instabilities. As already pointed out in Section 6.1, contracts were often cancelled or prematurely terminated, and hard renegotiations of their terms were not a rare incident.[24] Litigation was almost irrelevant in all these cases, though arbitration was regarded useful, if rarely used. Negotiations could be painstaking and imply harsh arguments, but it was rarely the case that the parties could not find a solution within the confines of their own social and organizational networks. Relationship issues arose mostly from changing economic conditions that affected insurance markets and business plans. The business objectives were generally openly agreed and cases of moral hazard or reinsurers' opportunism were rare.[25] After a period of trial and error, which lasted approximately from the 1820s until the 1870s, the mature and sophisticated contractual structures of treaty reinsurance could be easily adapted to the diverse needs of the companies so that additional lawyers were seldom needed. As many commentators observe, most prominently Cecil E. Golding, by the mid-nineteenth century the refinement of contracts and their technical excellence, within both the few specialized reinsurance companies and in the reinsurance departments of direct companies, were admirable.[26]

Treaty reinsurance contracting required, in addition, a lot of financial and managerial knowledge.[27] This led to innovation in the financial services provided by the reinsurers and new organizational models. The main role of reinsurers as financial service providers was always that they could offer capital relief. Reinsurance treaties enabled the removal of capital necessary for hedging risks from the direct company's balance sheet. But this was not enough for insurers facing the problem of taming their

[24] Moosbrugger (1964). [25] *The Review*, 1957, 1315–22.

[26] The techniques—actuarial, financial, contractual—did not emerge out of nowhere; they relied on traditions and experiences that reached back to earlier forms of securitization of commercial transactions. The perfection of these contracts has raised the question among several authors as to whether these had a longer tradition than initially thought (Golding (1931); Gerathewohl et al. (1979, 758–9)). The traditions of commercial loans and the financial instruments which have accompanied these must have had a prominent role in the shaping of ideas about transactional and contract architectures, mathematical and quasi-mathematical techniques that actuaries were using, but also on styles of negotiation in which their development and use was embedded (P. G. M. Dickson (1967) *The Financial Revolution in England*. London: Macmillan; L. Neal (1990) *The Rise of Financial Capitalism: International Capital Markets in the Age of Reason*. Cambridge: Cambridge University Press; J. H. Munro (2000) 'English "Backwardness" and Financial Innovations in Commerce with the Low Countries 14th to 16th Centuries', in P. Stabel, B. Blondé, and A. Greve (eds), *International Trade in the Low Countries (14th–16th Century): Merchants, Organisation, Infrastructure*. Leuven: Garant, 105–67; C. Wennerlind (2011) *Casualties of Credit. The English Financial Revolution 1620–1720*. Cambridge, MA: Harvard University Press; Bronzin (1908); Davis and Etheridge (2006)). Although Erwin Hürlimann regarded reinsurance as an activity that was much less scientific than direct insurance (Hürlimann 1931, 22–3), the impact of actuarial, accounting, and financial technologies on reinsurance operations was significant. This can be seen also in the structure of reinsurance contracts that are clearly much more strongly influenced by the mathematical than the legal culture of the time.

[27] Carl (1990, 265–7, 271–2).

operating costs. Ceding commissions, deposits of a percentage of reinsurance reserves with the primary insurer, expense allowances, as well as sharing of profits between the insurer and the reinsurer, became crucial parts of financial agreements incorporated in the obligatory treaties.[28] These arrangements could be found also in the facultative cases, but the en masse agreements on such matters had a quite different meaning for business planning on both sides. The resulting financial mechanisms were of central importance; especially before methods of capital surplus relief on the basis of securitized alternative risk transfers (ARTs) became common practice.[29]

The idea of treaty reinsurance made the existence of dedicated reinsurance companies a necessity. By the end of the nineteenth century they were highly skilled firms, managing huge business streams and guaranteeing the maximum possible stability of the insurance industry, whilst also producing quite respectable profits for most of the time until the First World War.[30] Their ability to do this was due to the fact they could set up and efficiently manage complex reinsurance programmes, at the core of which there was, in the most cases, a kernel of treaty reinsurance around which various other reinsurance services were built.[31] The fact that specialized reinsurance companies did not immediately emerge can be traced back to the lack of a sufficient understanding of the operational requirements of such services.[32] This can be made clear through the fact that, initially, many direct companies went for ceding risks on a running basis with other competitor direct insurers. Alternatively, many direct insurers founded their own reinsurance companies, in the belief that the insurance of the insurers was more or less similar to direct insurance.[33] The realization that running or obligatory reinsurance implies a different kind of risk assessment and, in particular, a closer look into the internal organization, management, and accounting of the ceding company, created, not unexpectedly, problems in the contracts among competitors who were unwilling to

[28] According to Ludwig Arps (1965a, 213), sharing risks became the most crucial aspect of the new style of reinsurance that prevailed at the end of the nineteenth century, and put, in many cases, commissions and allowances at a much lower priority. Arps distinguishes four dimensions that defined the reinvention of reinsurance: (a) the tendency towards the substitution of facultative by obligatory reinsurance; (b) the tendency towards profit sharing instead of commissions and allowances; (c) increasingly proportional instead of non-proportional ceding; (d) widely spreading risks both geographically and according to insurance classes. On the management of flows of payments by the reinsurance companies see Thiemermann (1993).

[29] The development of securitized capital relief methods will be discussed in the Section 6.11.

[30] The profitability of specialized reinsurance companies varied. We can also compare the pre-First World War with the interwar period. The comparison shows a better performance in the first case. Kopf (1929, 30–43).

[31] Roos (1964). [32] Hürlimann (1931, 4–7).

[33] At the end of the nineteenth century, we can observe the reverse tendency, namely that the reinsurers founded their own direct companies, producing revenue streams for the reinsurer. A typical case was Munich Re, which founded Allianz (see Gugerli 2013, 167). But, more usually, reinsurers sought to control direct companies through the acquisition of stock. On the strategy of creating or enabling or enhancing premium revenue through participation in the direct insurer's capital see SRCA 10.107 968, Notiz zur Frage unserer Orientierung im deutschen Geschäft; SRCA 10.107 968, Bericht über die Sanierung des Anker in Wien. This practice of share acquisition prevailed gradually after the end of the nineteenth century. On this topic: Le Blanc (1939, 99–102).

share the information that any sensible risk assessment would require.[34] Understanding the commercial tactics and the internal organizational life and qualities of the personnel of the ceding company was of critical importance. The direct companies had many reasons not to disclose information to their competitors. Seeking partners abroad, in order to avoid transferring risks on a running basis to competitors who might demand confidential information, often led to operational difficulties. The understanding of the business and of the efficiency of the ceding company required proximity. But proximity was not easy given the need to spread risks geographically by having them assumed by different insurers and reinsurers in various countries. Much of the work of monitoring contract partners has been done, since the end of the nineteenth century, by travelling actuaries and other reinsurance managers, who can discuss issues on site.

## 6.3 Regional and National Differences

Ceding insurance risks abroad attracted the attention of economic policymakers. In the years of economic nationalism that overwhelmed especially the newly developing powers, like Germany and Italy, but also Russia, this method of risk transfers was increasingly regarded as a disadvantage for the national economy. Founding its own national champion in reinsurance was regarded by many in Continental Europe, from about 1840, as a patriotic priority.[35] But in spite of the patriotic tone expressed by proponents of the development of reinsurance activities or in most foundational documents of reinsurance companies, it is highly unlikely that the private capital invested in this business neglected the market opportunities. However, the readiness to create favourable conditions for insurability through specialized reinsurance companies was not always without opposition. Some authorities that could not or were unwilling to understand the mechanics of reinsurance were hindering the development of specialized reinsurance companies.[36] But in the years following the economic and financial crises of the 1870s the new model prevailed. The landscape of successful independent reinsurance companies was proof of this. Neither of the two—treaty reinsurance and specialized reinsurance companies—could work effectively without the other. Two interdependent innovations emerged out of this. A contractual innovation, treaty reinsurance, that was defining the relationship on the basis of which insurance and financial innovations were made possible; and an organizational innovation, the independent reinsurance company, that emerged out of new business and operational necessities.

[34] See, for this, Hürlimann (1931, 7–10); Arps (1965a, 206–10).

[35] Hürlimann (1931, 4); Sack (1941, 134).

[36] See Prussia in the middle of the nineteenth century, but also much later regulation (see American Actuaries).

It was in the German-speaking regions of Europe that treaty reinsurance obtained the greatest significance, and it is also there that the first specialized reinsurance companies appeared. Actually, the first known attempt to adopt running reinsurance was in 1821 in the Low Countries. But the treaty between the Dutch Compagnie Royale d'Assurance Contre l'Incendie and the Belgian Compagnie des Propriétaires Réunis was closer to mutual insurance than running reinsurance as it developed in later years. The first really obligatory treaty, in spite of the inclusion of facultative elements, is considered to be the transfer of fire insurance risks of the Württembergische Privat-Feuer-Versicherungs-Gesellschaft to the Elberfelder Vaterländischen Feuerversicherungs-Gesellschaft. This 1829 treaty, which was of a non-proportional character, remained in force for seventy-three years. The arbitration clause in the treaty attributed to the document a legal character in the strict sense, though the mechanisms of litigation were never activated.[37] From the point of view of the economic historian it is interesting to draw attention to the width of the insurance portfolio and the variety of risks that were ceded. Economic geographers might be impressed by the aspect of spatial diversification, although this was not an unusual practice in post-Napoleonic Europe. As in most cases of similar contracts that we know of from this period, French, Belgian, and British insurers were also involved.[38]

The bearers of political power and the state had an interest in the mitigation of risks—the perception of which might have slowed down the improvement of overall economic performance. In this sense, for Continental Europeans, especially for Prussians, the logic of reinsurance coverage was embedded in a desire to catch up with British industrialization. The sentiment of lagging behind others drove concerted action.[39] The rapid pace of economic change that was imposed to a great extent by the state also altered the risk consciousness of large parts of society.[40] Protecting the new wealth of the expanding bourgeois and middle classes, invested in property and other valuable objects, as well as the protection of the standard of living of the descendents in case of death of the earning member of the family raised the readiness to pay for fire and life insurance. Concerning economic nationalism, it is worth noting that insurance (and reinsurance) issues were part of the political debate, especially in Germany, and this had to do with the protection of wealth and the improvement of risk calculation, allowing entrepreneurs and investors to contribute to national socio-economic development. But it had also a direct political meaning. Lack of insurance combined with social inequality implied that accumulation of potential risk could

37 Golding (1931, 62–6); Mossner (1959, 88–92).

38 Pearson (1995, 561); Trebilcock (1985, 274–5); Mossner (1959, 85–94, 97).

39 Kocka (1978, 531). See also the discussion on the relationship between financial networks and forced industrialization in A. Gerschenkron (1965) *Economic Backwardness in Historical Perspective.* New York: F. Praeger.

40 On economic change and the new wealth in Germany: R. H. Tilly (1978) 'Capital Formation in Germany in the Nineteenth Century', in P. Mathias and M. M. Postan (eds), *The Cambridge Economic History of Europe*, vol. 7, part I. Cambridge: Cambridge University Press, 382–441.

undermine the legitimacy of the political system.[41] The potential ruin of insurers became a matter of public concern, and not just for reasons related to the protection of the rights of the individual insured. Drawing attention to the politics of risk perception can help us explain why the specialized reinsurance companies and treaty reinsurance developed mainly in Germany, although French companies played a significant role during the initial phases. The typical case of a reinsurance company that relied on core competencies and core business around treaty reinsurance was the Munich Re (Münchener Rückversicherungs-Gesellschaft), although other companies had paved the way to this operational model, like Cologne Re and Swiss Re.[42] The former's ascent to world champion on the eve of the First World War was characteristic for this industry. It is not just coincidence that a German company had the lion's share of the market; and the same applies to the fact that most of the other companies with significant market power came from the German-speaking countries or had strong ties with Germany and Austria-Hungary. The bond of the dominant reinsurance companies with German social, economic, and political history also played a role in the gradual decline of treaty reinsurance in the aftermath of the First World War.

## 6.4 Putting Reinsurance History into Perspective

The focus on treaty reinsurance and the workings of specialized reinsurance companies shifts the interpretation of the history of reinsurance, highlighting some disregarded aspects. For the most part, the narrative has been driven almost exclusively by spectacular insurance events, most prominently by urban conflagrations and later by storms, like hurricanes. Furthermore, the tales about how relationships between direct companies, reinsurers, and retrocessionaires evolve are restricted to the focus on front-office activities, and rarely take a look into the back-office operations. Specialized reinsurers were disproportionally small organizations when compared to the primary insurance companies, and thus they attracted little attention, either from the public, or from those interested in the development of techno-organizational settings. In the reinsurance companies, a relatively small number of people could manage seemingly mythical amounts of capital that were allocated to cover a spectacular palette of risks.

[41] It is characteristic that there have been debates about the national importance of insurance and thus also of reinsurance in Germany, and that part of this debate was influenced by the question whether insurance and reinsurance should be state or privately owned. Wagner (1881, 106–8); Schramm (1884, 14–17); Arps (1965a, 63–98); F. Stern (1979) *Gold and Iron: Bismarck, Bleichröder, and the Building of the German Empire.* New York: Vintage Books, 224.

[42] Arps (1965a, 647–9); Pearson (1995, 561).

But this was not visible.[43] Even less visible was the technical ingenuity of the actuaries and of other members of the staff of reinsurance companies. The functional differentiation between front and back office was operationally often blurred, and this was definitely the case during negotiations of important treaties. But the calculus on which the contracts and their structure relied, and the monitoring of operational payment flows, was the product of the silent toil of highly knowledgeable back-office operators. Their work made possible the avoidance of ruin and financial mismanagement of the direct companies, to which not only treaty-related services were offered, but invaluable informal consultancy services as well.

In this sense, peak risks, and their often devastating consequences, made up only a small part of the sequence of events that shaped the development of this industry. Of course, we should not infer from this that major catastrophes have not had a decisive impact. The famous dramatic urban conflagrations and the aftermath of hurricanes are discrete incidents that play a role in the economic history of risk governance, the understanding of which is often obstructed by a veil of emotions. For the public, the fear of financial ruin due to physical disasters might influence one's ability to cope with risk exposures far more strongly than the intricacies of the financial bottlenecks and the dilemmas of managing insurance companies. In this sense, the public ignores the technicalities of back-office processes. The attention can be more easily attracted by acts of God, as major disasters that triggered major insurance events were called. These led to broad metaphysical reflections, contrasting the supposed banality of practical responses in the event of such shattering occurrences. There is a parallel here with political history, where developments are described by regime change and revolution and the more subtle trends and processes go unnoticed.

In this sense, it could be asked how the capital investment required by reinsurers would have been justified without these catastrophes that shook the public? Even so, the aggregate overall insurability of risks was more a matter of normal than of exceptional peak risks. Risk governance, in fact, would have been paralysed if the possible impact of normal risks not being managed had been understood. Of course, treaty reinsurance could not deliver the emotion-laden stories of natural catastrophes. Thus, it is logical and understandable that many major companies such as Cologne Re (the first specialized professional reinsurance company, 1846) and Swiss Re (1863) were founded a few years after great fires (Hamburg 1842 and Glarus 1861). The 1858 Christiania fire in Norway and the 1888 Umeå and Sundsvall city fires in Sweden also had a significant impact on the development of reinsurance business.[44] The San Francisco blaze of 1906 that followed the earthquake caused deep changes in certain fields of insurance and reinsurance. This said, it was actually the emergence of treaty reinsurance as a combined insurance and financial service, offering risk coverage by spreading risks among various entities and individuals, which played a vital role. From

[43] Tobias Straumann's title for his history of Swiss Re (*The Invisible Giant*) is well chosen. Straumann (2013).

[44] Kopf (1929, 48–52).

this perspective, financial reinsurance, which emerged at the end of the twentieth century, extended this combination of insurance and financial services, by distributing risks in the financial markets. If we take a long-term perspective in the examination of the development of financial technologies, then it was treaty reinsurance, transferring risk through the global insurance networks, that guaranteed insurability.[45] Treaty reinsurance offered, as the complexity theorists might say, the attractors that created order in fluid, complex international networks of risk transfer. It created conditions of stability, but at the same time of vulnerability within the reinsurance industry. For this kind of dynamic was highly sensitive to the features of economic and financial geographies.

## 6.5 Risk Transfers in a Fragmented World

> Before 1914 the earth had belonged to all. People went where they wished and stayed as long as they pleased. There were no permits, no visas, and it always gives me pleasure to astonish the young by telling them that before 1914 I travelled from Europe to India and to America without passport and without ever having seen one.[46]

In reality, treaty reinsurance was a belle époque business.[47] Its golden era was the period 1880–1914. It created a stable, though less lucrative part of reinsurance programmes, which counterbalanced exposure to the transfer of more volatile and high-impact risks.[48] The geographical diversification of risks in a globalized economy was critical for this. But after the First World War, the free movement the privileged people of the early twentieth-century era of globalization enjoyed belonged to a 'world of yesterday'. As barriers were erected, the economic and financial geography of the world radically altered. The segmentation of the insurance and financial networks and the regulatory and legal strains imposed upon them made the management of en masse ceding of risks a tough and perilous exercise. Only a few of the largest companies could

[45] Baruch Berliner distinguishes nine criteria of insurability: (a) randomness of the loss occurrence; (b) maximum possible loss; (c) average loss amount upon occurrence; (d) average period of time among occurrences; (e) insurance premium; (f) moral hazard; (g) public policy; (h) legal restrictions; (i) cover limits. Berliner (1982, 3–4).

However, the limits to insurability depend also on the availability of the contractual and techno-organizational enablers of appropriate financial technologies.

[46] S. Zweig (1943) *The World of Yesterday: An Autobiography*. London: Cassell & Co., 308.

[47] Between 1880 and 1913, the volume of insurance in Germany grew six times, whereas the volume of reinsurance grew twenty-seven times, which also implied a transfer of higher percentages of insurance premiums to the reinsurers. Arps (1965a, 644–7).

[48] It is highly interesting that the golden era of quota-share treaty reinsurance is, at the same time, the era of the increasing exposure of both direct insurers and reinsurers to peak risks, which emerged from the simultaneous coupling of risks and the rise of asset values between 1880 and 1914. See Arps (1965a, 645).

maintain their old relationships, built on contracts running for decades. Much of the business of those headquartered in the countries that lost the war was redirected to companies with more favourable standing in the new political conditions. The privileged firms were also not spared the post-war turbulence. They tried hard to cope with inflation and currency risks, as well as with deposit and credit regulations and capital controls imposed by protectionist regimes. This made the flow of payments between the cedent and the reinsurer extremely difficult.[49]

Economic fragmentation and the consequent difficulties for cross-border transactions, which also led to deposit and licensing problems, were decisive for post-war development. The requirement to deposit part of the agreed premiums with the cedent emerged as a consequence of local insurers attempting to detach the management of new risks from international volatility. Further, currency risk problems arose. And high inflation made the non-proportional part of treaties a nuisance. All these negative factors brought about quite messy conditions in the insurance and reinsurance markets,[50] in contrast with the years between the 1870s and 1914, when the gold standard prevailed. At this time, barriers to all kinds of trans-border mobility were, if not removed, at least minimized, and the stability of exchange rates practically eliminated currency risks.[51]

The fragmentation of the world after 1914 made the life of the established reinsurers extremely difficult. Without smooth international operations, without seamlessly spreading risks among various places with different configurations of risks, and without the flexibility of transactions within worldwide networks, the basic concepts on which this industry had been built since inception, and since the institutionalization of treaty reinsurance as their core competency, began to falter. These developments influenced, in the first place, the specialized companies that were relying on treaty reinsurance as their core business. The decades before this turn to adverse conditions were, however, of decisive importance for the shaping of the reinsurance business and its impact on the development of the advanced capitalist economies.

[49] Andreoli (1932); Arps (1970, 47–9); Netzel (2003, 50–1). The problem was not only the barriers, but the political and legal instability, which exposed reinsurance operations to enormous risks. For instance, because of the ban on reinstatement of debt to Germany and Austria following the Peace Treaty, there was uncertainty for years whether the deposits that the reinsurer left to the direct company would be accepted as operational transfers or be declared as illegal forms of debt. At the same time, governments, in the spirit of protectionism, not only raised the amount of deposits, but also the question of whether foreign reinsurance companies should be allowed to create local subsidiaries in the form of legal entities. Invaluable information on these issues: SRCA 10.125 020.02, Mitteilungen des Revisionsbureaus. Zur Frage der Autarkie in der Rückversicherung: SRCA 10.125 020.02. Mitteilungen des Revisionsbureaus. Die Behandlung der unechten Fremdwährungsversicherungen im Abrechnungsverkehr.

[50] On the exposures to higher risks of non-proportional reinsurance treaties under conditions of higher inflation see Horvath (1975).

[51] G. M. Gallarotti (1995) *The Anatomy of an International Monetary Regime: The Classical Gold Standard 1880–1914*. New York and Oxford: Oxford University Press, 18.

Although the philosophy of the industry during the period 1870 to 1914 never ceased to play a role in the industry, treaty reinsurance was never again to have the same role. The collapse of the German Reich and of the Russian Empire, in which important reinsurance centres were located, were not negligible developments.[52] For instance, Rossiya, one of the big companies of the prewar, relocated to Denmark and to the USA,[53] and Munich Re shrank and restricted its activities to a much narrower geography, seriously reducing its treaty portfolio. The well-crafted operational model of the ravaged German companies continued, despite the harm done to their international networks. But others expanded their business along similar lines. Swiss Re, for example, was already well established. It was located in a neutral country and could exploit the advantages of this status. The industry changes after 1919 show to what extent the German disaster, and more generally the European disaster, played a significant role, among other factors, in the gradual decline of classical treaty reinsurance. This process was to last from the 1920s until the 1980s. From an economic point of view, it must be noted that it was not only German companies which depended on German economic development, but also Austrian, Swiss, and in many cases French and Belgian companies—these were thus all affected by the devastating developments. Even risk transfer in the USA relied on large German companies like Munich Re, which held a significant share of the market.

Alongside this geographical fragmentation, these first years after the war also lacked stability. The problem in this relatively short period between the armistice and the end of hyperinflation in 1924 was not insurability as a consequence of demand for coverage, but rather lack of insurance appetite.[54] Premium volumes were very low, with a relatively small number of policies issued yearly and an insufficient dispersion of intercorrelated risks. This drove many insurers and the recklessly daring smaller reinsurers to higher risk exposure.[55] But after 1924, the insurance markets regained momentum and, remarkably, kept growing into the 1930s, despite the 1929 crash. The desire for reconstruction was visible in the improvement of cities like Paris, Vienna, Berlin, New York, or Rome.[56] Even the restrictions to international travelling were relaxed. Still, the few illusory years of better prospects in the 1920s left an imprint on much of the dynamics of the economy and society. The speculative impulse and the short-termism of the period shaped dominant attitudes.[57] It also gave plenty of

[52] On the impact of the passage from the Russian Empire to the Soviet Union see Petrov (2012, 228–30).

[53] Rossiya was reconstituted in Denmark out of its Danish subsidiary, to which it managed to transfer most of its assets and its portfolio, and in the USA out of its American subsidiary: Haegen (1956, 44); Kopf (1929, 73). Similar developments can be observed in the case of the dissolution of Austria-Hungary, where companies that operated as champions at the level of empire became national champions in the separate countries that emerged after the First World War: Haegen (1956, 44). On Russia and the Russian reinsurance companies, as well as on the reinsurance industry in Austria-Hungary, see Hollitscher (1931, 105–18, 124–5).

[54] Borscheid (2013, 73–4).

[55] Andreoli (1932, 9–10); Arps (1970, 123–4).

[56] Zweig (1943, 240–1).

[57] J. K. Galbraith (2009) *The Great Crash 1929*. Boston, MA: Mariner Books, 66–87.

opportunity for speculation and arbitrage, and this created a highly unfavourable interplay between moral hazard and opportunism that permeated the relationships between insurers and reinsurers.

It was not solely the imbalances caused by the currency issues that undermined the stable relationships needed for beneficial treaty reinsurance. Companies residing in countries with weak currencies struggled to contract with companies operating from strong currency countries.[58] This was another reason that transformed old relationships and urged many direct companies to seek a reformulation of their reinsurance programmes. There was a tremendous pressure to transform obligatory and quota-share treaties into facultative and non-proportional, with a growing tendency towards ceding excess of loss.[59] Besides, long-term coverage based on automatically or tacitly renewable contracts was not in vogue any more. These were trends that prevailed for direct companies despite the implied higher transaction and administrative costs. Few reinsurers could satisfy these needs without sliding into recklessness. Much of the business was shifting away from the dedicated companies towards the direct companies assuming more and more reinsurance on a facultative basis.[60] Many direct insurers sought to manage their risk through the establishment of pools. Various forms of ad hoc mutual insurance took much of the business away from the specialized companies. The few big specialized reinsurance companies that could keep an edge by expanding the sophistication of their information collection and other techniques, worked with considerably tighter financial management due to diminishing revenue margins and higher exposure to background and accounting-related operational risks.[61]

Inflation, and the implied currency risks, increased the fluidity and volatility of reinsurance environments. As Ernst Andreoli, a Swiss reinsurance accountant, stressed, this often undermined the trust between insurers, reinsurers, and retrocessionaires.[62] The subsequent deterioration of trust led to an unprecedented interest in the formal and legal aspects of the treaties, though this could not do much to avert crises of relationships among companies. The opportunities to speculate or to conduct arbitrage with currency prices in the international reinsurance business was, in the interwar period, greater than ever, and insurance protection against the volatility of currency prices was in no sense an efficient antidote, as it left enough space for non-transparent operations.[63] The principle that maintained the relationships between the direct

[58] Andreoli (1932, 9). [59] Hürlimann (1931, 5–6); Gugerli (2013, 178–83).

[60] On direct insurers in the role of reinsurers see Prölss (1964a).

[61] Improving the internal organization of the financial and accounting units, as well as their ability to cope with more demanding asset management requirements and improve monitoring of the financial profiles of the treaty portfolio, was a constant preoccupation of reinsurers, especially in the 1920s and early 1930s. See the minutes of the meetings of Swiss Re's BoD, especially between 1924 and 1935. Also SRCA 10.146 212.02, Revisionsbureau. Seine bisherige Tätigkeit und künftige Organisation.

[62] Andreoli (1932, 21).

[63] Besides, there was a tremendous effort to deal with currency risks with special kinds of currency portfolio insurance. Many insurers and reinsurers chose not to assume such risks, but the market grew nevertheless, though with unsatisfactory results. For the ramifications of actions reinsurers were taking

companies and their reinsurers was that neither of the two parties would exploit the financial schemes attached to the insurance agreements to gain a disproportional benefit, especially if this was at the cost of the other party. This changed in the unstable economic environment after the First Wold War. The tendency to manipulate the accounting of non-technical reserves, created not only distrust, but also additional risks. It was also difficult for reinsurers to present their assets and their financial profile so that they could signal financial strength, and thus enhance their bargaining power. The appetite to complement technical reserves with hidden reserves grew, but with exposure to the financial markets through more aggressive asset management, this was not always successful.[64]

In spite of much financial ingenuity, overall the complications remained. The disadvantages caused by protectionist regimes could not be easily overcome.[65] But, also, administrative and acquisition costs in multinational insurance and reinsurance operations came under the strain of complex accounting dependent on currency volatility. The principle that, in reinsurance or retrocession, the currency in which premiums or indemnity were paid was to be the currency of the underlying direct insurance policies became common practice, especially during the high inflation of the early 1920s. As Andreoli notes, this practice was not accepted everywhere, with the most notable example of Britain, where sterling was used for all kinds of contracts.[66] Adopting the currency of the direct insurance premiums created order due to increased standardization of operations, but also led to a burdensome fragmentation of reinsurance operations. For the direct insurer, this was not a big problem. But, for the reinsurance portfolios, including a homogeneous class of risks that came from different jurisdictions implied that policies that were covered by treaty reinsurance had to be indexed ex post or, in the best case, regrouped. Running obligatory contracts, and especially the quota-share ones, thereby often lost their initial character. They became unstable subcontracts that produced risk heterogeneity.

in this context see the internal confidential report of Swiss Re circulated on 14 October 1919: SRCA 10.116 652.02. Relevant information can be found also in SRCA 10.149 770.01.

[64] For the case of Swiss Re see Straumann (2013, 283–94; 2014).

[65] The 'closed-border' economic policies infected almost all major industrial powers. The French case is characteristic: nationalization of insurance in France (law of 25 April 1946 passed with 487 against 63 votes in the parliament) and the establishment of the state-owned Caisse Central de Réassurance (CCR) totally altered the conditions of business. Reinsurers had similar problems to face in the Soviet Union. On the French case see also Straus (2012). The retention (at least partially) of rights and the continuation of contacts required painstaking negotiations, often backed by governments undertaking persistent diplomatic efforts. SRCA 10.107 970.

[66] Andreoli (1932, 21).

## 6.6 Risk Heterogeneity and the Tyranny of Facultative Ceding

Reinsurers had to accept ever-more non-proportional and especially excess-loss (XL) business. This in turn resulted in an increased use of retrocession; not always successfully. Retrocession is something that reinsurers tend to avoid, because the sharing of risks implies the sharing of profit: the latter being more probable if risks had been previously made visible to both sides. This is why, when proportional contracts prevailed in the portfolio of a reinsurer, retrocession, or pooling, was not the first option. However, in the strains of the interwar period, when there was a massive shift from proportional to non-proportional reinsurance, retrocession became a critical issue. As retrocession had to do with the bad and mostly abnormal risks the reinsurers were assuming, other reinsurers or direct companies were highly reluctant to go into the business of retrocession or pooling, unless they could receive considerable premiums. The disadvantages of this situation for the specialized reinsurers were obvious. Moreover, it had a side effect of accelerating the decline of treaty reinsurance. The more reinsurers had to share risks and profit (the latter on a continuous basis because of the transfer of premium to their retrocessionaires), the less they had available in financial resources to transfer to the direct companies.

As has already been noted in Section 6.1, the specialized reinsurance companies functioned as lenders of 'first resort' to their clients, the direct companies, in order to help them increase the volume of their business—a practice that was based on the expectation of subsequent premium transfers. Like the banks, they lent in order to develop the appetite of their clients for further pecuniary transfers. The conditions that were created by non-proportional and especially by XL reinsurance meant a severe blockage of this mechanism. This was a decisive factor in the first and perhaps most significant push in the decline of treaty reinsurance during the interwar period. Attempts to boost non-technical reserves through asset speculation exposed the companies to the volatilities and consecutive plunges of the stock exchanges. The general volatility or the shrinking of asset values after 1929 also made management of hidden reserves almost impossible. Practically, as things evolved in the interwar period, there was no other choice left to the reinsurers than to gamble with various forms of non-proportional contracts; this was necessary to retain a sensible level of competitive parity. In effect, contracting no longer offered the same benefits but it could not be refused if reinsurers wanted to stay afloat in the financial and insurance networks.

Many experienced and powerful companies who had an insightful understanding of the evolution of risk tried to counterbalance the problem by improving their own housekeeping. Technical accounting developed in this respect but, without reliable and cost-effective information technology (IT), this activity was connected to the increase in underwriting and risk assessment costs. The improvement of internal organization and disciplined financial management saved many of the companies who had to sail in the rough seas of the interwar period.[67]

The European crisis of reinsurance companies also influenced US developments, where the trends were moving in similar directions, but with a much faster and stronger swing. The USA was to become the new trendsetter, influencing other economies. The characteristics of the post-First World War American boom, to which the 1929 crash put an end, had a notable impact on the shaping of the American insurance and reinsurance markets, and this caused international reverberations. Previously insurers had to cope with the risks of big ventures. For the most part, large risks were originating from the risk exposures of larger enterprises. However, the risk tolerance of the managers of the American large companies was decreasing fast. They were now less inclined to act as daring adventurers, preferring to be cautious and responsible managers of the assets entrusted to them. As the American historian William E. Leuchtenburg observed, contrary to the usual preconceptions about American social and economic life, people were not inclined to establish new businesses. They rather sought a place in the fast-growing corporate bureaucracies. Alfred Chandler drew attention, in his seminal work, to the significance of the birth of the big corporations that followed the organizational patterns of the railway companies.[68] But what Leuchtenburg was pointing to was the divorce between ownership and control and the role of the salaried businessmen, for whom ownership of stocks was not a significant factor. This altered risk perception and risk management attitudes, and thus influenced the corporate demand for insurance and reinsurance.[69] Household demand was also showing an upward development, fuelled by the spectacular increase in insurance advertising in the USA. The market power of American companies could also be seen from the variety of nationalities to which insurance coverage was provided.[70]

[67] Swiss Re internal report of 4 July 1927 authored by Ernst Andreoli: SRCA 10.146 212.02, Buchhaltung, Zentrales Rechnungswesen, Organisation, Revision, Statistik. Compatibility of accounting systems between reinsurers and simplification of administrative procedures is part of discussions and negotiations among directors. Often, expenses and additional premiums, under separate categories and thus implying accounting complications, are taken into consideration by means of weighing additional revenue with relatively marginal significance against administrative costs. See for instance SRCA 10.123 990.03.

[68] A. D. Chandler Jr (1977) *The Visible Hand: The Managerial Revolution in American Business*. Cambridge, MA, and London: Harvard University Press; A. D. Chandler Jr (1978) 'The United States: Evolution of Enterprise', in P. Mathias and M. M. Postan (eds), *The Cambridge Economic History of Europe*, vol. 2. Cambridge: Cambridge University Press, 70–133.

[69] 'The businessman [he means the hired manager or salaried executive] was less interested in risk and more in stability.' W. E. Leuchtenburg (1958) *The Perils of Prosperity 1914–1932*. Chicago: University of Chicago Press, 199. These 'businessmen', as organizational men, were significantly segregated from the free-floating individual speculators that John K. Galbraith describes in his book on the crash of 1929. They also belonged to different social networks from the bankers. Their strategies were shaped by the structure of the enterprises entrusted to them by the owning shareholders.

[70] Kobrak (2012, 289–96).

The coupling of the European insurance and reinsurance business with the American had a far-reaching influence across the Atlantic. American companies had been, up to this point, extensively influenced by European business and organizational models, not least treaty reinsurance. The geographical direction was now reversed. Ideas and methods of organizing the business moved from the New to the Old Continent. This was also a result of intensified transatlantic business connections. The USA has always been an important market, especially for European reinsurers. But since the end of the First World War and the brief economic recovery of the 1920s, no reinsurer could have a reasonable international standing without having access to the American insurance markets, so there was no lack of demand for their services.

But the insurance industry in the USA followed different patterns to that in Europe. Direct companies assumed many of the risks others among their competitors could not retain. This certainly went in parallel with connections to the Continental European reinsurance industry, mostly through the subsidiaries of the European companies and the gradual adoption of the European reinsurance model in the eve of the First World War. But as American insurers became significant players at a global scale (the outcome of this process became apparent well after the Second World War[71]), they either raised the percentage of retention or took over much of the reinsurance business through their own specialized departments.

Involvement in the USA drove European reinsurers into difficult territory in which old and tested skills were not a guarantee of success. In the few good years before the crash, direct companies, especially in the USA, had accumulated enough technical reserves to confidently raise the percentage of retention. Moreover, they created pools or other forms of mutual coverage or conducted reinsurance on an ad hoc basis. They chose risks selectively and recklessly, without hesitation, to assume excess of loss, without sufficient risk management. Direct companies, which followed a more cautious approach to their reinsurance lines, were also carving out the better, less intercorrelated risks that would have been bundled in broader obligatory treaties. This frustrated the dedicated reinsurers as they faced the extreme, abnormal risks, which also implied highly correlated underlying risks.

A top manager of Swiss Re, the company with the largest market share, reported from his travels in the USA between May and July 1935 how the contours of this changing world of insurance and reinsurance were shifting.[72]As Paul Alther observed, after having thorough consultations with the local representative of his company, there was a lot of pressure to take on facultative XL business that would expose the reinsurer to excessive risks without having any real idea of how to assess this exposure. The situation for his company and its market share was good when compared with that of competitors. It had a dominant position among foreign reinsurers active in the USA. The bleak side of the situation had to do with the general economic conditions. Recession was waning in 1935, but enterprises and households were still reluctant to

[71] More details on the internationalization of the American insurance industry in Wilkins (2011).

[72] SRCA 10.107 969.

pay for insurance beyond the necessary minimum they could afford. Similar attitudes applied to the insurers, who often preferred taking on risks recklessly in order to increase their premiums without investing in reinsurance coverage. If they opted for risk transfers they would probably try to create conditions of mutuality among the direct companies so that premium could return as retrocession. This meant that reinsurance pools became a common solution to the coverage problems of US direct companies.

As direct insurance companies covered risks they did not wish to retain, treaty reinsurance was undermined, since the mutually protected direct companies remained competitors in the insurance markets, unwilling to open their books to the ones who assumed their risks. The natural result of this was that short-term facultative contracting became the dominant practice. As discussed, direct insurers sought to mostly cede their excessive exposures and thus tried to convince the reinsurers to assume XL risks and agree upon potentially dangerous contracts. Many direct insurers sought to cancel long-standing treaty reinsurance coverage with a quota-share bulk and shift to ceding excess of loss. The smaller risks, which needed distributing, were preferably ceded in a facultative way to other direct companies who offered reinsurance coverage. Trying to significantly raise the volume of premium through facultative contracts, and especially through excess of loss, implied high research and transaction costs, making a good return questionable. As Alther stresses in his report, insurers and reinsurers who could be more or less successful in technical matters, and who could avoid false assessment of risks, had to pay for highly experienced and expensive underwriting experts and technical staff. This infrastructure existed in the headquarters of the big European companies, but without proximity to local operations. Development of local subsidiaries with comparable capacities was not a viable option as there was not a sufficient volume of risky facultative contracts to justify such expenses. According to this report by Alther, it is clear that his company was trying hard to retain the key revenue stream from its treaty reinsurance business but that this was no longer possible.

How to reorient the business was not clear. David Gugerli, who has used this report in the discussion of the problems that excess of loss posed to the reinsurers in the interwar period, observes that the technical prerequisites to assess risks were not available at this stage.[73] The non-life branches were relying on rather flawed mathematical foundations. This was primarily the case with XL reinsurance until well after the Second World War. There was nothing available that could easily replace the solid foundations of treaty reinsurance and offer the security which allowed reinsurers to accommodate the less assessable and risky contracts in a reinsurance portfolio.

[73] Gugerli (2013, 178–83).

## 6.7 Waning Bargaining Power

For obvious reasons, proportional ceding would have been preferable for the reinsurers. But this method no longer provided the same stability and security as in the period 1880–1914. Admittedly, quota-share and obligatory treaties had been much more resistant than non-proportional and facultative ones to inflationary movements and subsequent currency risk. But, as already stressed in Section 6.5, under the fluid conditions of the interwar period they had to suffer from risk heterogeneity. The subversion of trust among companies again increased transaction costs in the turbulent environment of the post-First World War era. Reports by reinsurance practitioners themselves show the difficulties that the long period of transformation after the 1873 crisis brought, as the business and operational models of this first period of increasingly organized and regulated capitalism changed.

The negotiation of contracts that took place in the 1930s between Swiss Re and its almost fully owned Viennese life insurance company, the Anker, were characteristic in this respect. The discussions revolved around the long-term quota-share and obligatory contracts arranged decades ago. Quota-share reinsurance contracts, if not packaged on a running basis in treaty reinsurance, imply high transaction costs. With obligatory treaties, the transfer of information on policies could be standardized with short statements containing crucial aspects of the accounting and the risk covered, as well as the reporting obligations included in the contract—in reinsurance terminology, with the so-called bordereaux.[74] Simplifying or even skipping the processing of separate policies enabled a significant reduction of operating costs. The fact that separate ceding of quota-share contracts would require a tremendous amount of work for the ceding direct insurer, and that these costs were to be shared with the reinsurer, was put forward as an argument against going for excess of loss. But quota share had to be combined with the obligatory element. This is directly expressed in a note sent by the Anker to Emil Bebler, a director of Swiss Re in February 1927. This perspective created a dilemma for both parties, but with consequences that were about to become more critical for the reinsurer.[75] The question that had to be answered was whether the whole of the life insurance portfolio should be ceded with quota-share reinsurance on a running basis, or whether the portfolio should be split between old and new business, the latter part transferred into non-proportional contracts. The sequence of negotiations shows how discussions progressed more generally among insurers and reinsurers. Astonishingly, the fact that Swiss Re was the main shareholder of Anker didn't ease negotiations. In fact, comments became more direct on such issues as shareholder value. For instance, the reinsurer as a shareholder was interested in overall shareholder value and therefore tended to be more relaxed and rather inclined to give way in premium negotiations and around contract terms.

[74] Mossner (1959, 85). [75] SRCA 10.149 770.01.

The exchange of arguments between Swiss Re and the Anker continued well into the 1930s. Ten years of correspondence after this first exchange of arguments allows us to follow the preoccupations of Continental insurers and reinsurers as to the significance and the financial value of treaty reinsurance. Continental reinsurers have, for the most part, preferred treaty reinsurance. If the reinsurers could signal that they were powerful enough and the signals were well perceived, they could force the counterparty to accept quota-share and obligatory treaties as a precondition for accepting the non-proportional and facultative ceding. But the relationships between companies were increasingly influenced by fierce competition and the variable and fuzzy balance of power between insurers and reinsurers. In the years of recovery from the First World War and then hyperinflation, efforts to re-establish favourable conditions for treaty reinsurance ended up mostly in failure. The situation did not improve in the relatively short economic recovery of the 1920s. And it remained unchanged well after the great crash of the New York Stock Exchange in 1929, and in the years before the disaster of the Second World War.

The relationship between companies never really improved and distrust poisoned the climate of negotiation and transactions. The well-established and powerful reinsurers sought to continue their old obligatory and quota-share treaties, even if they had to repackage the reinsurance programmes in which these were embedded or change the terms of the old contracts. This included Swiss Re, which benefited from its Swiss neutral status, but German reinsurers as well, who could regain ground in spite of the burdens imposed by the Versailles Treaty. The unwillingness of direct insurers to retain the old contract architectures, in cases where they could not insert even greater portions of non-proportional and facultative elements, is clear through the many letters exchanged in this period and in the minutes of various meetings. For instance, in the case of the dispute between Swiss Re and Anker, the latter tried hard to find wording that might have supported a more flexible approach, shifting the financial benefit towards the direct company. The reinsurer tried hard, but not always successfully, to retain the usual wording, which retained the balance in the flow of payments and in the obligation for reinstatements, embedded in the reinsurance agreements from the pre-First World War period.

These conflicts brought to the foreground the division between direct insurance and dedicated reinsurance companies, even in cases where reinsurers had acquired the direct company. Under such circumstances, the direct insurers felt more vulnerable than the reinsurers, who could allegedly sell the shares of the direct company to any potential investor, a view expressed in the confidential exchange of arguments between associated insurers and reinsurers. It was argued that the reinsurer should account for both treaty revenue and the dividends or the probable returns from selling equity. The rationale was that favourable conditions offered by the reinsurer, such as improved deposit terms, better commissions to cover operating costs, and, most importantly, a better mix in the reinsurance programmes containing more XL contracts, would raise shareholder value for the reinsurer. The specialized reinsurance companies felt obliged to increasingly succumb to such pressures, without always having the opportunity to calculate the risks. Against this background, one can better understand what one of the top reinsurance managers of the interwar period, Erwin Hürlimann, really meant when he was talking of the gamble that was driving the reinsurance business.[76] As a general manager, and later chairman of the board of directors of Swiss Re, he had to cope with the incredible pressure to assume non-proportionally ceded risks that were often impossible to assess. Like many of his colleagues, he was forced to live with the expectations of those who were not ready to realize the dreadful uncertainties of their times.

## 6.8 The Road to Financial Reinsurance

> The primary companies are offering fiercely competitive products and the reinsurer has very little margin left to make a profit. So what did the reinsurer have to do in many cases? He entered the financial reinsurance marketplace, because it is an area where you can make good profits and where you take on very little risk. So, from a reinsurer's standpoint, financial reinsurance is important, but it is probably only a temporary solution to the real problem which is underlying our industry.[77]

After the end of the Second World War, and in the following decades of spectacular economic growth, reinsurance companies were faced with new pressures. Old habits and mindsets were put to the test. New reliable and trustworthy practices that could respond to the challenges were not easily found. But, as in all situations of crisis, the innovative potential of industries was underestimated. As in the second half of the nineteenth century, at the turn of the twentieth to the twenty-first century a new wave of changes caused a major reshuffling in many of the most dynamic companies. This time the responses were not solely adaptive, but creative as well, and brought about new forms of active reinsurance. Market-driving companies invented and imposed new reinsurance products and services and made a pivotal contribution to the innovations that transformed global finance from the early 1990s. The American actuary Oscar Scofield could not anticipate the spectacular development of financial risk management techniques and their significance for the transformation of the reinsurance companies who had to adapt to the convergence of insurance and financial markets. At the same time, he did not realize that the new world of financial reinsurance would bring new background risks, tacitly transferred from the opaque world of investment banking. But, most importantly, what was difficult to realize was that the financial technologies of structured finance had strong affinities with the approach of treaty reinsurance. Financial reinsurance was, in many respects, a protean metamorphosis of the financial logic that was inherent in treaty reinsurance contracting and operations. Mathematical

[76] Hürlimann (1931, 5–7).

[77] Oscar R. Scofield (quoted in Greenberg et al. (1986, 2616)).

portfolio theory and the esoteric mathematical risk analysis techniques created a new language, the use of which obstructed access to old financial wisdom. Many things that were regarded as totally novel could be found in the operations of insurers and reinsurers. No doubt, the mathematical techniques they used until the 1960s were rather primitive compared to later developments. But the essence of the new operational approach was already present in the earlier workings of reinsurance.

The reinvention of the industry under the circumstances of the post-war years was not easy. The internal dynamics of the big companies were bound to have established operating traditions and mindsets. Many systemic obstacles were difficult to unblock. Besides, with few exceptions, to which perhaps Swiss Re and Erwin Hürlimann personally belonged, the world of reinsurance was almost totally segregated from the world of banking. It therefore took a long time for the workings of investment banking to attract the attention of reinsurers. For many decades, the focus of the reinsurers was on problems of insurability as defined by physical risks and the probable claims that these may imply. And the financial focus of the reinsurers was strongly influenced by the management of reserves. The more dynamic and aggressive asset management that could be observed in the case of many direct companies was not characteristic of the dominant reinsurers. In this, they followed the dominant corporate habits, according to which, until the 1990s, what counted was the primacy of operating revenue and the underestimation of non-operative revenue streams produced by asset management. As long as the perception of the financial risk exposure was regarded as a consequence of the aggregate financial risk originating from the company's reserves, it was very difficult to switch to a different perspective. The turn occurred in the 1990s. The repackaging of reinsurance services that were now bundled with innovative financial services which were created by the reinsurers themselves was a kind of liberation from a long period of crisis, in spite of the new kinds of risk exposures that had to be managed with painstaking care.

The legacy of the problems of the interwar period remained alive well into the Cold War era. The Second World War had made everything worse for the reinsurers. Business was not only disrupted because of the hostilities. The insurance and reinsurance networks were regarded from all sides as sources of information leaks, and the fact that managers and operators had developed close relationships across boundaries made their loyalty suspect. For instance, the American Trading with the Enemy Act (passed by President Woodrow Wilson in 1917 and still in power when the Second World War began) was in no way compatible with the nature of the interwoven contract arrangements of the reinsurers, as everything had to be restricted in parcelled jurisdictions: any country, or company, that was doing business with others that were doing business with the enemy was regarded as hostile.[78]

As has already been discussed in Section 6.5, the crisis of the early twentieth-century globalization, the consecutive waves of economic instability after the First World War,

[78] For the impact of the Trading with the Enemy Act on international business see Wilkins (2004, esp. 47, 452).

and also the later developments in the insurance markets after the Second World War, posed a real threat to the model of risk governance that was relying on reinsurance programmes, with a kernel of treaty reinsurance. The idea of seeking stability through treaty reinsurance persisted well into the 1990s. Only with the financial innovations of the end of the twentieth century and the spread of computer-processing capacity, which radically altered the conditions of non-proportional reinsurance operations, was it possible to make the business less dependent on reinsurance programmes built around obligatory and quota-share modules. Financial reinsurance solutions gradually replaced treaty reinsurance as the stabilizing core of reinsurance programmes.

## 6.9 New Core Competencies

It took about seven decades, from the early 1920s until the early 1990s, for the processes of transformation of reinsurance to bring to the surface new, recognizable contours. This transformation of the business also saw a radical transformation of the core competencies of the big reinsurance companies. What reinsurance could do, that neither the direct insurers nor the investment bankers could, rested in the assessment of natural catastrophes and of high-impact technological risks. This kind of risk assessment was combined with sophisticated financial management and the fine-tuning of financial innovations. Through this, the proprietary competitive advantages and the core competencies of reinsurers shifted from the combination of contracting with financial instruments towards the combination of catastrophe forecasting with financial instruments. This meant also a shift from innovative internal accounting and the distribution of risks among various insurance and reinsurance organizations, towards distributing risks through the financial markets. Instead of spreading risks through networks of organizations, the risks were placed in a wide variety of portfolios.[79] This doesn't mean that all the old reinsurance services and traditional practices had been totally abandoned. The various elements constituting the palette of products and services now appeared in different configurations.

The road to financial reinsurance had its origins in the changing balance of power in the insurance and reinsurance markets of the 1950s and 1960s. At first, reinsurers

[79] This portfolio aspect can be better observed in the case of multiple trigger products (MTPs), which really detach finite reinsurance from traditional reinsurance programmes. As J. David Cummins and Mary A. Weiss explain (Cummins and Weiss 2009, 511): 'Going even further beyond conventional reinsurance policies are multiple-trigger products (MTPs). [ . . . ] For example, an MTP might cover the cedent for catastrophic hurricane losses that occur simultaneously with an increase in market-wide interest rates. The cedent would thus be protected against having to liquidate bonds at unfavorable prices to pay losses resulting from the catastrophe but would not have to pay for protection covering circumstances where a catastrophe occurs when securities market conditions are more favorable. In effect, MTPs combine conventional reinsurance protection and financial derivatives in a single, integrated contract . . . '.

adopted an increasingly defensive stance. In several aspects the situation looked like a re-enactment of the middle of the nineteenth century. Initially, it was once more the high growth rates of the insurance industry that created new pressures on the companies and caused a crisis in their business and operating models. But very soon, in early 1960s, the fast-growing and increasingly powerful direct insurers could build considerable reserves and gain access to capital markets, and thus their demand for proportional reinsurance waned rapidly. Direct companies increasingly opted for mutual coverage on a facultative basis, and thus for the exclusion of specialized reinsurers, driving the reinsurers into different market niches. Many direct companies, especially in the USA, also created their own reinsurance departments.[80]

The macroeconomic environment posed a different kind of challenge. Inflation once more raised the risk exposure originating from proportional contracts, though not to post-First World War levels.[81] Proportional and obligatory contracts, on the other hand, suffered initially from the lack of growth. Nevertheless, in the boom years of the 1950s and 1960s, the business of reinsurance programmes built around treaty reinsurance could not recover. In this sense, Les Trente Glorieuses were not as successful for reinsurance as for other industries.[82] This can also be traced back to the geopolitical divisions of the post-war era. New forms of geographical fragmentation emerged. The reshaping of international relations created new barriers to business. The East–West division, the enlargement of the communist bloc, and the Cold War intensified the problem that emerged in the interwar period with the creation of the Soviet Union. A third push in the change of the economic and financial geography was to come when the system of developmental stratification of the 1960s started crumbling. Events accelerated after the oil crisis of 1973. But the decentralization of the world system that it implied came six years later, with the breakdown of modernization and the Balkanization of the international system, signalled by the Iranian Revolution. The Iranian Revolution revealed what was to become clearly visible in the first decade of the twenty-first century, namely that the development of the world system could not be based on an increasing cultural homogeneity, in spite of technological convergence (in the use of technologies, not in their production). The fragmentation of the international economic system that emerged between the end of the 1940s and the early 1980s was later followed by a financial globalization. The new trends in finance as the new homogenizing element at a global scale created new conditions both for the investment in and insurance of assets.

To the extent that reconstruction after the Second World War was progressing, values of assets also increased everywhere around the parts of the world where insurance was more or less institutionalized. The rise in demand for insurance protection could not be satisfied without corresponding reinsurance coverage. This, however, didn't necessarily automatically ensure a smooth expansion of reinsurance business. Direct insurers in many places, especially in the USA grew very strong, and this meant

[80] Kobrak (2012, 299). [81] SRCA 10.107 979.

[82] Gugerli (2013, 147–53, 184–97); Straumann (2013, 318–35). See also SRCA 10.107 978.

that they could operate with much higher levels of retention and without the need to pay for reinsurance. This gave them greater flexibility in their tariff wars. The growth years from 1950–70 expanded the volume of premiums without precedence, and this went hand in hand with higher concentration in the industry, also due to the repeal of the legislative restrictions for multi-line insurers after 1949 that were inhibiting the development of the insurance markets in the USA. Although multi-line insurers faced a concentration of risks that had to be spread with reinsurance, this didn't boost coverage programmes based on treaty reinsurance. The various non-life risks and their facultative ceding with non-proportional, mostly XL, techniques, created—beyond the usual insurance risks—various operational risks to the reinsurers. Reactions to these problems varied between the USA and Continental Europe. In Europe, practices of stricter formality with higher levels of transparency prevailed in the negotiations and in the process of contracting. For instance, 'off-shoring' of risk transfers and placement of assets destined for the financial management of treaties in legal entities located in tax havens was less frequent.[83] Also, relationship management did not imply direct involvement in the business of the direct insurer, as was often the case in the USA. Even the old-style practices of treaty reinsurance, in spite of habits of 'organizational forensics', was done from an external approach and thus was combined with a certain degree of aloofness, unless the reinsurer had acquired a respectable percentage of shares of the direct insurer. It is very interesting that this aloofness implied a stricter contracting and operational culture within the Continental European companies.

Post-war growth had also another side effect that caused predicaments for reinsurance and also accelerated the gradual abandonment of treaty reinsurance. The expansion of the consumption of manufacturing products and of the provision of services created new liability problems, especially in the USA, but increasingly in Western European societies too. Product liability, especially for machines and devices destined for wider use, as well as for other consumption goods (such as automobiles, pharmaceutics, and others) changed the insurance landscape. New lines emerged also from the insurance of liabilities of lawyers, physicians, engineers, and, in many cases, of managers (as in the case of risky technical projects).[84] Another issue was the emergence of consecutive liability crises as the result of the massive expansion of consumption and the growing sensitivity for pollution and health issues. These went hand in hand with new forms of risk aversion because of the constantly rising standard of living. The issues that arose from exposure to asbestos belong in the same category of liability problems. The coupling of various risks in the sense that has been discussed by Charles Perrow,[85] and the proximity of objects with higher values in densely populated areas or

[83] The captive business implied loss of revenue streams for the established reinsurers. See, for this, SRCA 10.107 979. Furthermore, the habits and the work ethics of those involved in the captive business, who were not at all interested in long-term and symbiotic relationships between companies, were totally different from those familiar to traditional reinsurers. In the captive business, commercial opportunism and neglect of reciprocity was the rule. Sloppiness and year-end targets in unstable connective networks were central elements of the business culture in places like the Bahamas. Duffy (2004, 100).

[84] Gerathewohl et al. (1979, 829–30). [85] Perrow (1984, 62–100).

in new forms of warehousing and transport, or the materials with new features that bear new risks, also created new exposures that have radically altered the financial profiles of insurance and, consequently, of reinsurance portfolios related to production and logistics.[86]

Actually, the need to provide cover for oil exploitation and drilling operations was to become one of the drivers of major change in the business. London insurers were the main developers of alternative solutions that became the precursors of finite risk reinsurance. The other origin of finite reinsurance—or financial reinsurance as it is often called because of its importance for capital relief and other financial functions—has been various conflicts between firms and regulators in the USA since the late 1970s. The extraction of fuel and of other raw materials had, however, other implications beyond this. Nuclear technology highlighted peak risks with an enduring impact. Raw materials and fossil fuel implied long-distance transport and thus exposure to higher transport risks. Shipping changed its shape and hull problems opened new chapters in insurance. But also drilling per se was a problem that insurers could not properly handle.[87] These developments changed the role of reinsurance and created new conditions of premium and service competition. Besides, the new pressures of passive reinsurance imposed by the direct insurers strongly implied an increase in facultative and non-proportional reinsurance agreements. This meant a strain that was difficult to manage under conditions of IT that did not enable the minimization of calculative and transaction costs.

Insurance needs arising from the massive expansion of the automobile markets and the unprecedented multiplication of insurance policies should not be underestimated as a factor that transformed both insurance and reinsurance markets. This trend was also the result of state legislation, originating first in the interwar USA and then embracing the whole world after the 1950s. Automobile insurance posed a threat to traditional business models that was not easily seen at the beginning.[88] Compulsory automobile insurance, growing since its inception, even before the First World War, created many headaches for reinsurers. Until the 1950s, the markets remained rather limited in volume. But when the numbers exploded, in spite of the instabilities that the ceding of these risks was implying, reinsurers could not ignore the demands of the direct insurers. The losses caused from this multiplication of policies were considerable for the direct insurers, affecting the reinsurers as well.[89] The motor insurance markets have been highly volatile from the start and did not lend themselves to long-term stable reinsurance contracts. The origins of these dynamics were to be found in the way direct insurance was marketed and contracted. As Robin Pearson observes:

> Motorists had little brand loyalty and high street brokers and garage agents offered insurance at every point of vehicle repair or sale. As well as competing on price, rivalry between companies focused on glossy and imaginative advertising

[86] SRCA 10.107 975, Meeting minutes of Swiss Re's BoD, 5 April 1967.

[87] Kyrtsis (2011). [88] Gerathewohl et al. (1979, 829). [89] *The Review*, 1957, 1315–22.

campaigns that were far more ambitious than anything the insurance industry had yet attempted in terms of marketing.[90]

For the reinsurer, this kind of insurance could be nothing other than a facultative business with extreme rate competition. XL reinsurance for motor liability insurance was adopted at a fast pace in the post-war era.[91] Archival evidence shows the worries of the industry. For example, the managers of the Erste Allgemeine Unfall- und Schadenversicherungs-Gesellschaft in Vienna were among those alarmed by this development. The constant policy changes, even for long-term contracts, were a real nuisance. But tough competition made them accept unfavourable terms. Retention levels lowered and they sought to cede as much as they could to their reinsurers. Reinsurers accepted the business to maintain parity, though, ex post, it proved disastrous. Fundamentally, they could not escape the dilemma of either turning down clients or assuming practically uninsurable risks.[92]

All in all, insurance became extremely important for contemporary lifestyles and thus also a factor of political legitimacy. The emotions that transactions in this domain implied could not be ignored by the state. The various product and services offered by reinsurance companies, and the growing links between insurance companies and banks (the latter being a sector that underwent massive deregulation after the abolishment of the Bretton Woods agreement) meant also a de facto, though indirect, deregulation of the insurance and reinsurance markets. For the politicians and the authorities this posed a threat, especially in cultures like the USA that tended to be highly litigious. While the deregulation of the financial markets progressed, the regulatory efforts intensified. These pressures were not always compatible with the business models in the insurance and reinsurance industry. Well-intended legislative interventions created rigidities, arising from a lack of mutual understanding between enterprises and regulators or from risk perceptions driving practices on both sides. The result was attempts to evade legal restrictions and regulations by spotting loopholes and by adopting informal procedures to protect themselves from excessive legal and institutional risks. The regulators, on their part, tried to introduce and implement tighter measures. They were destined finally to lose, but, in the meantime, this meant a massive adaptation of the business of all branches of financial services to the ramifications imposed by these regulatory battles.

The regulatory and tax issues had a crucial impact on developments and for the operational responses of both insurers and reinsurers. Until the late 1970s, there was a lot of quota-share contracts, including on an obligatory basis to help smaller insurance companies—and also the bigger ones—to cope with capital strains caused by acquisition expenses and (partly) regulatory-imposed reserve requirements. Competition, and especially the so-called term-wars in life insurance, was a factor, especially in the USA, that upset the balance sheets of insurance companies and thus made them search for mutual relationships with reinsurers. Reinsurers had, further, to find ways to respond

[90] Pearson (2012, 78). [91] Straumann (2013, 323). [92] SRCA 10.121 116.04.

appropriately to tax code advantages or disadvantages.[93] But there were many other factors that brought about this change, which led to what was to be called financial reinsurance or finite reinsurance. Sensitivity and alertness to financial issues increasingly defined the priorities of managerial action; the worries of the staff of the companies are clearly visible through a glance in the archives.

## 6.10 Bridges Between Traditional and Financial Reinsurance

Reinsurers certainly felt that problematic accident and non-life reinsurance required a revenue stream from asset management. For many managers it was necessary, even in the late 1970s, to achieve a minimum of such earnings and to protect them from exchange-rate volatilities.[94] This was a sign that reinsurers, who used to be extremely reserved concerning speculative asset management, were becoming much less reluctant to expose their portfolios to the risks of the financial markets in order to seek a higher yield. This was also the case, as we have seen in Section 6.5, in the interwar period, mostly with very mediocre success, to say the least. But the financial markets developed differently from the 1970s, and thus the appetite to hedge the financial risks of non-proportional reinsurance with more aggressive asset management seemed to be justified. As we can read in a then-confidential report on the American reinsurance business found in the Swiss Re archives, written as early as 1971, 'The reinsurance business is involved in producing and supplying investable funds. Results in the reinsurance business, therefore, are importantly affected by conditions and trends in the money markets.'[95] Such an utterance in the previous decades would have meant a reference to problems and handicaps, such as the ones that became critical in the post-First World War era, and much less so in the era of the international monetary regime that was imposed by the Bretton Woods agreement. As no exact date is indicated on the document, it is hard to say whether this confidential report was authored as a response to the famous speech by President Richard Nixon in August 1971, in which he denounced the support of the USA in the post-war system of exchange-rate stability. It is, however, clear that the wording reverberates a sense of these new developments. The pressure came, of course, from the need to cope with the financial risks that abnormal material risks implied, which combined with the lower retention and the uneven risk-sharing strategies of the direct companies.[96] Furthermore, many non-proportional treaties implied long-tail effects and this also raised the need for reserves that could be built counter-cyclically to negative occurrences.

[93] Jennings (2008, 22–3). [94] SRCA 10.107 982. [95] SRCA 10.125 590.01.
[96] SRCA 10.107 977, Enclosure 2 of the meeting minutes of Swiss Re's BoD.

It is, however, obvious that this changing awareness of the issue wouldn't have been enough without new opportunities to hedge in the financial markets. As we can read in the same confidential report:

> It does not seem likely that there will be any change in the pattern of low influx of capital into the insurance business. A future growth of the primary insurance business will have to be financed through additional profits and reinvestment of earnings. The lack of capital inflow will tend to support the use of proportional reinsurance for surplus relief purposes. Such market need for loans of capital should increase [the reinsurers'] market opportunities.[97]

This is a revealing passage because it shows that, in 1971, the increasing importance of finance in reinsurance services was already at the doorstep. But at the same time we can observe an insistence to stick with traditional reinsurance with obligatory treaties.

A detachment from the prevailing views was needed. Surplus relief was part of traditional structured finance, but in the context of treaty reinsurance the corresponding schemes of financial management did not rely on speculating in the financial markets. The convergence of the work of the actuaries with that of the asset managers and the investment bankers was definitely in sight, but reluctance remained. How fast things were moving became apparent when, in the late 1980s, the Chicago Board of Trade approached Swiss Re to provide expertise in the development of commodity bonds, the predecessors of catastrophe bonds (cat bonds) that became fashionable after the middle of the 1990s.[98] But existing patterns were still followed. In spite of the growing tendency to give in to the pressure of the direct companies that increasingly wanted to cede their risks with facultative and non-proportional treaties, often on a short-term basis, the preservation of traditional obligatory or proportional long-term treaties was still alive. Well into the 1980s, the special care to expand and ameliorate services for treaty clients was central to senior management.[99] The by-no-means unjustified view prevailed among the older and the more senior staff that facultative reinsurance operations implied higher costs and of course risks that were more difficult to manage than preserving or entering treaty business. There was thus still a hope that, as it was the habit since the turn of the nineteenth to the twentieth century, the facultative market could be transferred into treaty arrangements.

The strategic value of such efforts proved, however, to be rather questionable. Mergers of insurance companies and trans-border alliances in the process of European economic integration allowed insurers to increase retentions. Similar trends also prevailed in the USA with the 'multi-liners' and the growth of insurance giants. Old obligatory or proportional treaties were either not renewed, or were more and more frequently packaged in insurance programmes dominated by facultative and non-proportional coverage of the direct risks.[100] In a report addressed to the Swiss Re general management

[97] SRCA 10.125 590.01. [98] Straumann (2013, 338).
[99] Straumann (2013, 338); SRAC 10.125 590.01.
[100] SRAC 10.107 977, Geschäftsverlauf und Ausgangslage.

on 18 January 1968 by two unidentified actuaries, the formulation goes as follows: 'Increasingly the non-proportional business proves to be the key to the entire treaty connection.'[101] Besides, active reinsurance and the influence of terms by the reinsurers was more difficult in the industrial nations, while in the developing world it was easier, unless blocked by the nationalization of insurance or reinsurance, the preference of national players, or the facilitation of monopolies. Retrocession was another significant unfavourable parameter. The capacity needs of the direct companies put a strain on the potency of the reinsurers who had to further cede assumed risks to a retrocessionaire. Difficulties in this domain resulted in trying to counterbalance retrocession with even more sophisticated marketing functions.[102] But it was not only the risk attitudes and the financial conditions that were rapidly moving in an unfavourable direction. The marketing styles and the channels of distribution of insurance products and services also changed. The role of the brokers had, in this respect, a profound impact. The increasing number of brokerage firms since the late 1960s brought about forms of intermediation that were by no means compatible with the intimate financial relationships prevalent since the nineteenth century. More aloof forms of financial services began to prevail. The community of interests and the intertwining of organizational networks were more apparent in the common development and sharing of knowledge as well as of technical standards, which also embraced contracting techniques. As increased reinsurance capacity emerged from the domination of non-proportional reinsurance, technical operations became gradually more important than the social ties which had driven the earlier reinsurance networks.

The operational reinvention of the reinsurance industry led to trans-company consultations and solution-finding processes that significantly altered the business. Reorganizations began about 1964. The big reinsurers started building specialized teams of experts who could assess and handle risks on the basis of advanced scientific and technical knowledge, differing from traditional 'front-office' (or 'travelling actuaries' who conducted auditing and organizational inspection on site) or back-office actuaries.[103] In 1967, meetings and conferences occurred that clearly questioned the old operational style of those who remained attached to traditional treaty reinsurance. In spite of fierce commercial competition, all the major reinsurers decided to amplify the development of scientific and technical knowledge that might cope with the new risks and approaches.

It is highly interesting in this respect, that all technical and scientific aspects (in terms of natural science and mathematics) were embedded in the interplay with organizational and contractual know-how. The mapping of technical and scientific aspects onto legal ones, and in turn onto contract clauses, was one of the main issues at

[101] SRCA 10.146 212.04, Some Thoughts on Methods and Procedures in Establishing Loss Reserves in Fire & Casualty Reinsurance.

[102] Record of discussions on peak risks and the consequent need of intensified marketing combined with augmented technical capabilities in SRCA 10.107 979.

[103] SRCA 10.107 977, Enclosure 2 of the meeting minutes of Swiss Re's BoD.

the epicentre of the potential new modalities of operational action. Financial aspects of the contracts, such as the specification of tariffs or reserves, were to be assessed in correspondence with levels of risk exposure. Statistics and accounting, especially technical accounting issues, were minutely handled. One of the issues was to define the minimum requirements that might influence the financial parameters of contract architectures, especially with regard to modifications and when they had to be shifted towards excess of loss. Risk assessment and risk management and their contractual translation should leave behind the era of rules of thumb that raised the suspicion of arbitrary exposures and enter a scientific era, creating a sense of reliability for clients. It is no coincidence that this 'scientification' of the industry created signalling instruments in the form of publications, many of which were destined for the wider public of investors and managers, but some of which projected the spirit of technicalities that were addressed to the scientifically versed actuary. These developments have been, as one may easily understand, most significant in non-life reinsurance.[104]

In simple terms, financial reinsurance or finite reinsurance (as it is most commonly referred to in the non-life segment) focuses on the financial management and not on the risk transfer linked to insurance events. In other words, leverage events and innovative accounting are the most significant aspects of these financial products and services. Financial reinsurance seeks to give solutions to the direct insurer that can reduce the risk-based capital requirements. Furthermore, it can improve the tax efficiency of reserves by reinsuring non-deductible deficiency reserves on the basis of sound financial management, in parallel with the minimization of legal risk.[105] These forms of structured finance address a wide range of financial objectives for the direct companies and were offered as services by the reinsurers, years before investment bankers came up with their sophisticated financial instruments. This shouldn't be unexpected given the actuarial techniques and the accounting techniques that the specialized reinsurers in particular were using in order to manage complex reinsurance programmes with an obligatory kernel. Treaty reinsurance had offered many of the ideas that were later integrated in structured finance. Actually, the management of complex long-term treaties had been the genuine predecessor to structured finance.

Through financial reinsurance the limits of insurability could be expanded, though in some cases by shifting risks from insurance events into credit events. The technique differed from treaty reinsurance mainly because the latter was spreading risks among organizations, whereas financial reinsurance was spreading risks among organizationally detached portfolios. This gave the opportunity to go beyond what traditional reinsurers considered a limit to insurability, namely the correlation or the high impact of tail risks. Higher correlated insurance risks could now, as the belief was, be hedged by lower correlated risks spread across portfolios of financial instruments. The various forms of securitization that are used in the context of financial reinsurance could also facilitate regulatory arbitrage as well as the collateralization of low-frequency but

[104] SRCA 10.107 975, Meeting minutes of Swiss Re's BoD, 6 February 1968.

[105] Leblanc (2003, 17).

high-impact risks.[106] ART or structured insurance is one of the main aspects of financial reinsurance, and cat bonds, as we will see in Section 6.11, are a core aspect of this kind of financial technology. However, as the argument goes here, there are also similarities, the main being that financial reinsurance, as with treaty reinsurance, was a way to create a stable kernel for a complex, adaptive, but inherently unstable system of operations.

This was not, however, understood from the beginning, and many actuaries, as discussed, resisted these practices. The transfer of risk either to cope with legal risks arising from regulatory pressures, or for economic reasons related to balance sheet amelioration, was not easily accepted by the guilds of actuaries who represented the core teams of the operational staff both in insurance and reinsurance.[107] There was a lot of soul-searching among the actuaries, who had to go through an identity crisis before they were able to realize that the industry had to change. The topics and the arguments in a panel discussion carried out among American actuaries in the early 1980s are highly illuminating. It is interesting that, in this discussion, what prevail are the taxation issues and regulatory issues to which we have already referred. They see in these the origins of the necessity of financial reinsurance.[108] At the stage at which this discussion took place, the participants were unable to envision the new forms of reinsurance. They tended to believe that the new financial solutions would not continue to be applied for very long. They deemed them as being related to short-term regulatory strains, many of which were traced back to political responses to the risk perceptions of consumers and politicians.[109] This sceptical stance was the result of a partial understanding of the industry to which they belonged. Because of a lack of historical knowledge, not unusual among the insiders of every industry, they believed that what was being done in the context of finite reinsurance was a novelty of the era of securitization. In reality, what they were faced with was a re-exploitation of the finest reinsurance traditions.

Of course, many aspects of the techniques of spreading risks and the economic and legal entities among which risks were distributed changed over time. But the essence remained in many respects the same. This was crucial for an understanding of the history of reinsurance. Much of this history depends on the rise and decline of treaty reinsurance, the function of which was gradually taken over by financial or finite reinsurance. As Kai-Uwe Schanz and Prakash Shimpi stress in a passage of paramount importance in this context:

[106] Cummins and Trainar (2009). [107] Greenberg et al. (1986).

[108] Greenberg et al. (1986, 2598).

[109] See Greenberg et al. (1986, 2601). As Eugene Copeland, one of the participants of the 1986 panel discussion organized by the American Society of Actuaries stated: 'Regulators have a legitimate and very understandable interest in surplus relief reinsurance. The sole reason for their existence is to protect the policyholders and help assure the solvency of insurance companies. [ . . . ] Unfortunately, some aspects of the resulting measures and those now being considered are, in my opinion, an over-reaction to the perceived problems.'

> Finite risk reinsurance (or finite re) is based on the same instruments as traditional reinsurance. However, the essential characteristic of finite products, in particular the assumption of limited risk by the reinsurer, the multi-year period of the contracts, the sharing of the result with client, and the explicit inclusion of future investment income in the stipulation of the price, offer additional possibilities that are encountering growing interests among corporations. Among other things, finite products can: (a) stabilise reinsurance costs and the availability of capacity; (b) smooth fluctuations in results; (c) expand underwriting capacity; (d) provide (partial) protection against as yet unreported claims; and (e) optimise the balance sheet.[110]

'Future investment income' is the expression that makes the difference. This turn can be more explicitly observed in the risk management technique which is called ART, or in the cases where the intertwining of the transfer of risks that depend on insurance events is combined with the transfer of risks that depend on credit events, as is the case with cat bonds. The inefficiencies of the insurance markets are thus corrected by the expected efficiencies of the financial markets, the undulations of which are regarded as non-correlated. In other words, it was expected that the reinsurance cycles would not coincide with the cycles of the financial markets.[111]

## 6.11 Financial Instruments as Symbols of a New Era

Cat bonds, as they are commonly known, symbolize the new era. These are independent tradable instruments, but they can also constitute parts (ingredients) of reinsurance packages or programmes. At this point we will skip the technical details; their exposition would not be of great relevance here. It suffices to point to the function of cat bonds: catastrophe-linked securities provide capital when a low-frequency high-impact event triggers a payout. These highly efficient mechanisms, if triggered, require capital that corresponds to less than half of 1 per cent of the US stock and bond markets.[112] The assumption here is that the financial markets can absorb the financial burden of such peak risks through chains of risk transfer. The volume of the cat bonds market is not as big as one might think, but it is rather stable and resilient. Volume of issuance and of transactions is not the main criterion for the significance of a financial technology, and in this sense what applies to treaty reinsurance, with its variable volume over time, applies also to cat bonds and to financial schemes built around these. The most important aspect about this instrument is, however, that it relies on a configuration of skills, knowledge, and operational elements that cannot be easily acquired apart from by

[110] Schanz and Shimpi (2001, 132).
[111] Cummins and Weiss (2009, 394, 502).
[112] Cummins and Weiss (2009, 394–5).

large, specialized reinsurance companies. Cat bonds should be regarded as the emblematic financial instruments that show the specific traits of the convergence of the reinsurance markets with the financial markets.

The other instruments that were tightly related to financial reinsurance well before the cat bonds had been invented are so-called 'captives'. There are reinsurance commentators who see captives as one of the main origins of financial reinsurance. They connect their history with solutions offered by Lloyd's. Indeed, there are various origins of the development of financial reinsurance that made necessary a convergence between insurance and financial markets. For instance, there are reports locating the first appearance of financial solutions to solve the capital problems of insurers and reinsurers in the early 1960s.[113] For some of these, Lloyd's syndicates' dispatch of money overseas, to be placed in special legal entities in tax-light jurisdictions from where tax-optimization activities were also facilitated as part of reinsurance premium management, was one of the first such activities. Captives, as legal entities, have been very similar to what special purpose vehicles (SPVs) have been in later decades, after the 1990s, for the investment bankers. They were a refuge for shifting risks off-balance sheet. We have mentioned the Lloyd's practices, which, according to many commentators, are the early origin of financial reinsurance. But captives pre-date the Lloyd's practices. A property engineer and fire insurance expert turned insurance broker found the way to transfer risks into legal entities, located in jurisdictions where the quality and the level of legal risk exposure made this possible. As noted, coping with legal and regulatory issues without triggering adverse legal action, as seen in the case of the captives, was one of the most important motivations for financial innovations in the insurance markets, as with investment banking. Of course, this inclination arose from the perception that innovative financial management was subject to unnecessary and not totally sensible restrictions. This perception arose, to a great extent, from the strains created by the high tail-risks or from other forms of peak risks of non-proportional reinsurance and the anticipated financial consequences of insurance events.[114]

These new reinsurance instruments created a new mix of reinsurance programmes and thus, although the idea of having an attractor in the middle of the complexity of dynamic networks was retained, the character and the effects of attractors changed. This can be traced back to the fact that the risks were now predominantly spread into the financial markets. One main difference between the new kernels of reinsurance programmes that emerged in the 1990s as opposed to the reinsurance programmes of the late nineteenth century that were based on treaty reinsurance, is the following: traditional reinsurance was, in its initial form, the foundation of wealth creation. In contrast, financial reinsurance became a method of protection for already accumulated wealth. It protected portfolios, not industrial ventures or household plans, from the inhibiting factors that excessive risk perception might imply. In contrast to traditional reinsurance, it became a protector of the money economy and not of the so-called real

[113] IAIS (2006). [114] Bernard and Tian (2009, 723); Cummins and Weiss (2009, 501).

economy. The peak risks that emerged did not result from the exposure of utilities, but rather from the exposure of bubble-based portfolios.

Few organizations beyond the bigger reinsurers had the knowledge and the skills that allowed them to take up these challenges and transform them into business models and efficient operations. In the early 1970s, in a period when the plethora of problems of reinsurers seemed to be insurmountable, new signs for development came from two areas. These were the assessment of catastrophe risks and the capital relief problems of direct insurers, both areas to which reinsurers were sensitive and had appropriate knowledge. The combination of non-life insurance mathematics with the assessment of big catastrophe risks became an area of expertise in the big reinsurance companies. And capital relief issues have always been part of treaty reinsurance—the tradition of which still remains alive in the reinsurance business. It is no coincidence that the Chicago Board of Trade approached Swiss Re to develop commodities bonds in the 1980s. And it is also no coincidence that, in the late 1970s and in the early 1980s, when, due to taxation issues, direct insurance companies searched for the appropriate financial innovations that might enable capital relief, it was the reinsurance companies that found the solutions and started offering services. It was these that evolved into financial reinsurance or finite reinsurance. There was no indication whatsoever that any of those in the insurance or reinsurance industry at this time had realized that these new tasks would lead to new solutions and services. And even later, in the late 1980s, when these services started crystallizing and thus became a visible part of what reinsurance companies could offer to their clients, very few realized their importance. When all this started in the 1980s, no expert in the field could imagine the radical reconfiguration of the palette of services that would gradually push into the shadow the core of traditional reinsurance, namely treaty reinsurance.

## Acknowledgements

I owe many thanks to David Gugerli, who pushed me into the fascinating adventure of trying to understand the history of reinsurance, and to Niels Viggo Haueter for his encouragement, invaluable advice, and continuous practical assistance. Niels and his colleagues within the Swiss Re Corporate History Team and the company's historical archives, Anne-Katrin Becker, Salvatore Novaretti, and Jörg Zimmer, were always ready to help me spot the right archival material. The generosity of Swiss Re and of the Institute of History of Technology at the Swiss Federal Institute of Technology (ETH) enabled me to spend the time needed for my archival and bibliographical research in Zurich.

CHAPTER 7

# FROM GENTLEMEN'S AGREEMENT TO JUDICIAL INSTRUMENT

## *The History of Contract Practice and Conflict Resolution in Reinsurance*

TILMANN J. RÖDER

## 7.1 Introductory Remarks

THIS chapter deals with contract practice and conflict resolution—both in and out of court—in reinsurance business. It is structured according to key periods in the evolution of reinsurance law, which—while not entirely congruent—can be aligned to certain periods of economic and social history.

Aside from major economic and social upheavals such as industrialization, urbanization, and globalization, individual catastrophic events and the occurrence of novel loss patterns have also helped to shape contract law and the customary forms of conflict settlement within the industry. The economic repercussions of the devastating fires of Hamburg (1842) and Glarus (1861), for example, were the inspiration behind the first reinsurance companies. The earthquake/fire catastrophe of San Francisco (1906) gave rise to an initial attempt by the industry to standardize contract clauses on a global scale. In the 1980s, the hefty legal disputes concerning asbestos-related health damage that raged in the USA reached the reinsurance industry, resulting not only in a noticeable tightening of regulation, but also in a change in the conflict culture that existed between primary insurance companies and the reinsurance industry. The prior reticence of either side to instigate court proceedings diminished considerably, with disputes increasingly waged in public. While initially responding to the terrorist attack of 9/11 with exclusion clauses, the reinsurance industry was not averse to close cooperation with numerous governments in an attempt to find a way of dealing with the phenomenon in its latest dimension. All of these examples have constituted a fundamental learning curve for the industry and have conspired to shape the evolution of the reinsurance contract and how the industry deals with conflicts.

Law has been a constituent part of reinsurance since time immemorial—contracts are concluded and settled all the time. What is noticeable, however, is that the law has rarely, if ever, developed along similar lines to domestic and international private and commercial law. One reason is that most countries showed little interest in the fundamentals of the reinsurance contract until well into the 1980s, exerting at most an indirect influence in the form of various supervisory systems and regulations.[1] Key impulses came from natural science, economics, and mathematics, and the reinsurance industry had to ensure that it was up to speed with the latest findings in these disciplines.[2] It was often a matter of translating risk calculations into actual clauses in contracts. An unusual but significant exception to the rule was the drafting of new contractual quotes for Muslim business partners in the 1980s, the aim being to tap into lucrative new markets. The specialist legal know-how required here came from Islamic scholars who would assess draft contracts—frequently with normative effect—and monitor business practices.

Any examination of the question of how contract practice and conflict culture in reinsurance evolved, what role legal expertise played in this development, and how this knowledge was generated and changed over time, is a complex undertaking. At this point, we should mention the four most important findings. First, continuity in terms of all the salient features of the reinsurance contract appears to have existed since the second half of the nineteenth century. Second, several constant factors have shaped the evolution of contract practice, such as the desire, for various reasons, to keep the state at arm's length. Third—and closely related to the above—the principle of avoiding litigation, to which the industry preferred arbitration, has been a recurrent theme in the history of conflict in reinsurance. Fourth, differences between legal regimes appear to be less important than differences between the conflict cultures in the respective countries.

## 7.2 Precursors and Early Forms

It is not an easy task to shed light on the origins of reinsurance and, thus, of the reinsurance contract. Archiving contracts for posterity was the last thing on the minds of the traders who conceived these business models. The common assumption that reinsurance grew out of maritime insurance—the oldest line of insurance business—seems plausible.[3] We know of agreements—compatible in functional

[1] See Chapter 8, this volume. [2] Chapter 5, this volume. [3] Staring (1993, chapter 1, 5).

terms with modern reinsurance—dating back to the fourteenth century that served to mitigate the perils of sea transport by transferring, rather than spreading, some of the risk.[4] So these were not co-insurance agreements, which were actually of much greater practical importance in the field of maritime insurance than reinsurance until well into the nineteenth century.[5]

The earliest sovereign regulation governing maritime reinsurance came in the form of the Antwerp costuymen (1609) and then, under King Louis XIV of France, in the significant Ordonnance de la Marine (1681). Both laws expressly permitted reinsurance; the Ordonnance also included provisions governing reinsurance premiums and outlawed overinsurance and double insurance, which had been identified as the first steps towards fraud. These examples were followed by similar regulations in other European countries.[6] That said, the main purpose of these new bodies of law was to consolidate existing customary commercial law (*lex mercatoria*) in the field of insurance and reinsurance, rather than to implement new legislation.

Increasing references to maritime reinsurance in the legal literature of the following decades give an indication of the spread and growing importance of this line of business in Europe and North America.[7] But it had yet to be established as a judicial instrument and was open to considerable abuse, which goes some way to explaining its prohibition by the British Crown by way of the Marine Insurance Act of 1745. Exceptions were permitted only in cases where a reinsurer would assume the risks of an insolvent insurance company.[8] This was not reinsurance in the true sense of the word (the insurance of one insurer by another), but rather a case of the 'reinsurer' assuming risk as the new contractual partner of the original insured. Nonetheless, this procedure was commonly referred to as reinsurance in commercial and judicial practice for decades. The British prohibition of maritime reinsurance was not rescinded until 1864.[9] It remained a somewhat exceptional phenomenon; in most European countries and in North America it was always permissible to transfer insured risks to third parties.[10]

[4] The oldest known reinsurance agreement was a contract concluded in 1370, which, although designated a contract of sale, was actually an arrangement between the insurers to transfer part of the risk. See Gerathewohl et al. (1979, 698–701) for more information on this and other cases from the fourteenth and fifteenth centuries.

[5] Gerathewohl et al. (1979, 710).

[6] Terminazioni of Venice (from 1705 onwards); Hamburger Assekuranz- und Haverei-Ordnung (1731); Ordinance of Bilbao (1738); Prussian Civil Code (1794). See Gerathewohl et al. (1979, 717–23) for further examples.

[7] Some of the earliest literature to discuss reinsurance includes: *Guidon Stile et Usance des Marchands qui mettent à la Mer* (1619). Rouen: De l'Imprimerie de Martin Le Mesgissier; R.-J. Valin (1766) *Nouveau commentaire sur l'ordonnance de la marine, du mois d' août 1681*. La Rochelle: Chez Jerôme Legier; B. Emerigon (1783) *Traité des Assurances et des Contrats à la Grosse*. Marseille: J. Mossy; J. Park (1787) *A System of the Law of Marine Insurance*. London: Printed by His Majesty's law printers for T. Whieldon; J. G. Büsch (1792) *Theoretisch-praktische Darstellung der Handlung in deren mannigfaltigen Geschäften*. Hamburg: Hoffmann; S. Marshall (1802) *A Treatise on the Law of Insurance*. London: Printed by A. Strahan.

[8] Mossner (1959, 76).

[9] See Staring (1993, chapter 1, n24).

[10] See, for example, J. Kent (1928) *Commentaries on American Law*. New York: O. Halsted, 226.

## 7.3 Emergence of the Basis of the Modern Contract, 1820–80

The period around 1820 is significant inasmuch as it marks the point at which reinsurance—previously the reserve of the maritime world—began to spread to other lines of business. Indeed, the first fire reinsurance agreements in both Europe and the USA can be traced back to around 1820.[11] Internationally, however, maritime business continued to dominate.

Equally significant was the emergence of treaty reinsurance, later also known as 'general' or 'obligatory' reinsurance, where the contractual terms and conditions for a multitude of risks are stipulated in advance. This is the opposite of 'individual' reinsurance, later known as 'specialty' or 'facultative' reinsurance. In treaty reinsurance, the risks were outlined according to general criteria and only submitted individually after the contract was concluded. The historian David Gugerli is justified in calling these developments in contract structure the 'most important structural changes' in reinsurance business of the nineteenth century.[12] But it was decades before treaty reinsurance became established. Sophisticated contracts comprising complex portfolios of risks remained the exception until the end of the nineteenth century.[13] Until well into the nineteenth century, most archived agreements were, to say the least, concise; there are cases where the respective parties made do with a simple note and the reinsurer's signature on the original insurance policy.[14] This could only have been an example of individual risks being reinsured on a facultative basis. But there were other reasons for the apparent decision to dispense with more comprehensive written documentation. Reinsurance contracts were largely freely negotiable, their structure and execution being subject only to very few external and internal influences.

External and, in particular, state influences rejected the idea of freedom of contract that spread from Britain from around 1770 onwards.[15] Judges, lawmakers, administrators, and economists such as Adam Smith advocated the dismantling of restrictive, status-driven, and mercantile economic regimes.[16] These were replaced by a system whereby the parties to a contract were at liberty to structure their agreements independently.[17] Around 1820, the notion of freedom of contract occupied a central

[11] See Chapter 3, this volume. [12] Gugerli (2013, 166).

[13] Golding (1931, 3–6). [14] Staring (1993, 7).

[15] P. S. Atiyah (1979) *The Rise and Fall of Freedom of Contract*. Oxford: Clarendon Press.

[16] Atiyah (1979, 226); e.g. A. Smith (1776) *An Inquiry into the Nature and Causes of the Wealth of Nations*. London: W. Strahan and T. Cadell.

[17] H. K. Will (1994) *Notice und Reasonableness. Instrumente der Vertragskontrolle im Common Law des 19. und 20. Jahrhunderts*. Berlin: Duncker & Humblot, 30, 33.

position in British and Anglo-American common law,[18] in the French *codes*,[19] and in the formal, deductive German system of civil law.[20] This contributed to reducing regulation of both the insurance industry and the basis of its contracts.

Internal, corporate influences on contract design remained slight too, as the concept of risk analysis had yet to make a breakthrough in the insurance industry and actuarial theory.[21] There is also an important societal factor to bear in mind. The insurers who were busy concluding contracts with each other all belonged to the same social class, and their correspondence shows that many of them were even friends. What is more, they were far less accountable to third parties with an economic interest in their business than they were after the spread of the stock corporation. In the prevailing spirit of mutual trust, they were apt to dispense with comprehensive written documentation and rely on 'gentlemen's agreements' instead.[22]

The increasing interest by legal authors in reinsurance in the late eighteenth and early nineteenth centuries is a clear indication of its growing importance in international business practice. The specific features of the reinsurance contract began to crystallize in the specialist literature of the time. Although these contracts were designed to transfer risk, they did not constitute a direct contractual relationship between the insured and the reinsurer.[23] Another salient feature, namely the obligation on the part of the primary insurer to retain a part of the overall risk, did not appear until during the course of the nineteenth century.

Until the middle of the century, however, co-insurance and reciprocal reinsurance among primary insurers encroached on the reinsurance industry's position as an autonomous segment and slowed its development. Many primary insurers evidently believed that tying themselves to a reinsurer would jeopardize their own autonomy. But cooperation with other primary insurers harboured risks too, as this was an ideal opportunity to gain an insight into another company's business practices.[24] Ultimately, however, the rapid growth in urban and industrial risks pushed primary insurers to the limits of their business capacity. The devastation wreaked by catastrophes such as the

[18] Pound (1909, 454, 456ff.); Will (1994, 28).

[19] *Code civil des Français* (1804), *Code de procédure civile* (1806), and *Code de commerce* (1807). The Code civil was applicable in the Kingdom of Italy from 1806; in the Confederation of the Rhine (as Badisches Landrecht) from 1810, and also partially in Poland, Luxembourg, Holland, Belgium, and—in a more modified form—in Romania from 1863; in Portugal from 1867; and in Spain from 1888/9.

[20] A uniform system of civil rights did not exist in nineteenth-century Germany, but a cross-territory debate on jurisprudence was ongoing. In the 1850s, Austrian jurisprudence also endorsed the German historical school.

[21] Chapter 5, this volume.

[22] Gugerli (2012, 27). See, for example, R. H. Tilly (1995) 'Unternehmermoral und -verhalten im 19. Jahrhundert. Indizien deutscher Bürgerlichkeit', in J. Kocka (ed.), *Bürgertum im 19. Jahrhundert*, vol. 2: Wirtschaftsbürger und Bildungsbürger. Göttingen: Vandenhoeck & Ruprecht, 35–64.

[23] Klaus Gerathewohl cites several examples of agreements dating from the seventeenth to the early nineteenth century, which, although referred to as 'reassurance', did not display the key attributes of a reinsurance contract. Gerathewohl et al. (1979, 713–14).

[24] Gugerli (2012, 15, 18).

fires of Hamburg (1842), Memel (1854), Glarus (1861), and Chicago (1871) propelled many insurance companies into bankruptcy. This was the opportunity for reinsurance companies—invariably boasting the new legal structure of a stock corporation and, for the most part, well capitalized—to assert their business model.[25] Because some risks even exceeded the capacity of reinsurance companies, they would offload risks to other, third-party carriers. Thus, the practice of retrocession came about almost at the same time as reinsurance was established.[26]

The availability of ever-more novel insurance models contributed to the spread of reinsurance: in around 1843 Italian companies concluded a maritime reinsurance treaty;[27] a German–Italian hailstorm reinsurance contract from 1854 is known to exist; in Switzerland, a life reinsurance contract was signed in 1844; and a corresponding German–Swiss treaty exists from the year 1858. These were invariably proportional reinsurance contracts where the reinsurer received a certain share of the premiums as recompense for paying a corresponding share of the indemnification in the event of a loss. However, founded as it was on the specific details of the primary insurance contracts, this system proved unworkable when insurance companies began to expand certain lines of business—notably life and fire insurance—and make them available to the mass market. Reinsurance actuaries were simply unable to examine the contents of tens of thousands of primary insurance contracts. Alexandros-Andreas Kyrtsis fittingly refers to this time as a 'period of trial and error'.[28] For this reason, actuaries and mathematicians developed the method known as non-proportional reinsurance, where the reinsurer was obliged to pay only when the loss had exceeded a certain limit. Within this basic model, a further distinction was drawn between 'surplus' reinsurance and 'excess of loss' (XL) reinsurance treaties. Their actuarial calculations were then incorporated into the treaty wordings. Although non-proportional reinsurance was not used very much during the nineteenth century, it became the leading model in the twentieth.[29] The idea of standardizing reinsurance contracts also emerged. Although never implemented, the concept was mooted for use in life reinsurance in around 1873.[30]

The perpetual emergence, transformation, bifurcation, and disappearance of contract types is best described using the theory of evolution of the legal academic and sociologist Niklas Luhmann. According to his theory, law evolves in three stages: irritations give rise to variations, followed by selection, and then stabilization.[31] In the case of reinsurance, irritations can be external events such as disasters, as well as the emergence of new forms of primary insurance or internal developments such as

[25] See Gerathewohl et al. (1979, 711, 727ff.).

[26] Gerathewohl et al. (1979, 763ff.) cites a German–Belgian retrocession agreement of 1860.

[27] Gerathewohl et al. (1979, 769); Ehrenberg (1885, 18ff., 24ff.), alludes to the fact that treaty reinsurance in the maritime class of insurance had now begun.

[28] Chapter 6, this volume.

[29] Chapter 5, this volume; Gerathewohl et al. (1979, 761f.) refers to an XL reinsurance treaty of 1857 and other examples in later years. In Great Britain, they also became more popular in the motor vehicle and accident lines of business at the end of the nineteenth century.

[30] Gerathewohl et al. (1979, 770).

[31] Luhmann (1970).

actuarial innovations. Companies respond to these 'irritations' by continually adapting existing contracts or developing new ones—'variations' in the language of evolution theory—only very few of which, however, are actually used in large numbers in the long term. In practice—at least in an ideal scenario—the most suitable contract types are selected and this results in a period of stabilization that will last at least until the next irritation occurs. Although these theoretical terms are not applied universally in this chapter, the underlying ideas are alluded to every now and then.

As with the development of contract types, the continual transformation of individual clauses and wordings can be described in evolutionary terms too.[32] An interesting point to note is the industry-specific language that emerged in the course of the nineteenth century. It was clearly more important for the parties to express mutual feelings of trust than to insist on precise legal wordings; *utmost good faith* or *uberrima bona fides* is a good example. Lawyers in Continental Europe would argue that the notion of good faith cannot be bettered anyway. When used by the reinsurer, the wording was a diplomatic way of reminding the insurer of its duties of disclosure and due diligence—meaning that it was actually based on the age-old principle of commercial prudence. Lawyers found expressions such as 'follow the fortunes' even more confusing. The term 'cession', commonly used to describe the reinsurance process, differs uniquely from the ancient legal term of 'cessio', which refers to the process of transferring an outstanding debt to a new creditor. The industry's euphemistic 'provisional notice of cancellation' still makes the hair of a self-respecting lawyer stand on end,[33] as notices of cancellation must always be issued unconditionally for the sake of legal certainty. These and many similar expressions came about because, in the defining decades of the industry, contracts were worded not by lawyers but by specialist traders acting as insurers ('underwriters') and brokers, who could assume that, even in the event of a dispute, their agreements would not come under the scrutiny of a judge or lawyer but be examined by an arbitration court consisting of experienced businessmen like themselves. Even today, court judgements that provide guidance on the interpretation of individual clauses and wordings are few and far between. The rulings of an arbitration court concern only the parties involved and are not usually published.[34]

At this point, we can examine three of the observations made initially. First, despite the ongoing and, in some phases, rapid evolution of contract types, all the main elements of the reinsurance contract crystallized between 1820 and 1880. Essential features were the relevant risk (to be defined as accurately as possible), the beginning and the end of the period of liability, and the reinsurance premium. Gradually, provisions governing the late or inadequate payment of premiums, accounting, and settlement; duties of disclosure by the primary insurer and rights of control on the part

[32] Examples of standard wording of the nineteenth century include 'follow the fortunes' and 'to pay as may be paid thereon'. *The Review*, 1961, 1424.

[33] Frey (1989, 295–7).

[34] The emergence of a unique, industry-specific expression is characteristic of less regulated international industry sectors such as commodities and securities trading, as well as reinsurance.

of the reinsurer; errors and omissions; courts of arbitration; applicable law; and other aspects requiring regulation were added.[35] Other difficult legal questions emerged for the first time or appeared in a new form, such as the filtering through of losses adjusted by the primary insurer to the reinsurer.[36] This issue of a reinsurer's obligation to indemnify the insurer when the latter had paid a claim as a gesture of goodwill (where the original insured did not have a valid claim) led to conflicts. Also, the importance of the systematic distinction between 'insurance of fixed sums' and 'indemnity insurance', and that between life and non-life insurance, were recognized and incorporated into contract design.[37] By around 1880, treaty or obligatory reinsurance, which is not as old as facultative reinsurance in historic terms, could be considered mature in the legal sense.[38] With that came the development of reinsurance technique, the modern foundations of which were established in the years leading up to 1880.[39]

Second, several factors came to light between 1820 and 1880 that were to have a lasting effect on contract design. Worthy of mention is the distance the reinsurance industry maintained between itself and the authorities of the countries in which the companies were based or from which they operated. Both sides contributed to this situation. Beyond the implementation of general social, commercial, and fiscal rules and regulations, governments showed little interest in reinsurance business as it did not affect the vulnerable layperson, at least not directly. At the same time, reinsurers did not trust that government agents had the in-depth, up-to-date knowledge of the business necessary to make appropriate decisions. They preferred to shape their own contracts, thereby applying the principle of contractual autonomy, which was barely contested until well after the middle of the century.

This point leads us to the third observation, namely the tendency to avoid litigation apparent between 1820 and 1880.[40] The archives of reinsurance companies contain hardly any references to judicial proceedings from this period. If an action was brought, it was the primary insurers who went to court for the simple reason that, in most disputes, they were demanding money from the reinsurers and not vice versa.[41] Aside from the alleged ignorance of judges with regard to the economic and technical fundamentals of the business, and the length and cost of proceedings, a significant reason for wanting to avoid the law courts was the fact that insurers and reinsurers always tended to form interest groups and were economically much more dependent

35 See Gerathewohl et al. (1979, 766f.).

36 The 'follow the fortunes' clause was debated in an early court judgement: *Western Assurance Company of Toronto* v. *Poole* [1903] 1 King's Bench Division 376.

37 It was not until the twentieth century that the distinction between life and property/casualty ('P&C') became established.

38 Golding (1931, 90). Gugerli mentions quota-share reinsurance contracts developed by Munich Re in the 1880s: Gugerli (2012, 25).

39 For example, Ehrenberg (1885), the first German-language monograph.

40 See also Chapter 8, this volume.

41 A rare but important example is the judgement in the case *New York Bowery* v. *New York Fire Ins., New York*, before the Supreme Court in 1837, in which the court confirmed the legality of a fire reinsurance contract by falling back on principles of maritime reinsurance.

on one another than partners in other businesses such as banking or commerce. Insurers needed reinsurers because it was often only with their help that they could meet the needs of their own clients for comprehensive insurance protection and develop new markets without the risk of bankruptcy should there be an accumulation of losses. In turn, reinsurers made a living from primary insurance business and the trust bestowed upon them by insurers.[42] As a result of this economic symbiosis, insurer and reinsurer would operate closely as partners, not just in regular business such as the appraisal of new risks, but also in the event of a loss. Reinsurers would provide primary insurers with the benefit of the specialist knowledge acquired in the course of their increasingly international business, which gave the insurers security and an edge over the competition.[43]

From this position of joint interest, the parties to the contract would endeavour to settle conflicts themselves and not to resort even to the services of an arbitrator, whom they preferred to a state judge in any case. For instance, the arbitration clause contained in the first known German reinsurance treaty concluded in 1829 between the Stuttgart-based Württembergische Privat-Feuer-Versicherungs-Gesellschaft and the Elberfeld-based Vaterländische Feuerversicherungs-Gesellschaft was not used once during the seventy-three-year term of the contract.[44] That said, arbitration clauses spread across all markets during the course of the nineteenth century; a contract referred to by Cecil Golding between Riunione Adriatica di Sicurtà and Compagnie d'Assurances contre l'Incendie La France of 1850 serves as another early example.[45]

## 7.4 Development as a Judicial Instrument: Contract and Conflict, 1880–1960

The period between 1880 and 1960 was shaped by events in world history that left a mark on the reinsurance industry too. The two world wars in particular resulted in dramatic slumps in international business. However, they were of little relevance to the development of the basic elements of the reinsurance contract.

As the decades passed, contract types and their content evolved further. Ever-more insurable risks were identified and then marketed by primary insurers with the support of the reinsurance industry: accident, motor, burglary, windstorm, credit, and baggage insurance, to name but a few examples. Although reinsurers were involved in the development of these product innovations to some degree, the design and structure of the contracts with primary insurers remained largely unchanged despite the diversity of subject matter. Indeed, it was not until the 1920s that the reinsurance contract was further developed in a systematic manner.[46]

[42] For the importance of trust, see, in particular, Chapter 3, this volume.

[43] Gerathewohl et al. (1976, 409f.).

[44] Mossner (1959, 88ff.).

[45] Golding (1931, 68).

[46] Gerathewohl et al. (1979, 763).

In the early years of the new century, XL contracts became extremely popular as a consequence of the urban disasters of Baltimore (1904), San Francisco (1906), Valparaiso (1906), Kingston (1907), and Messina (1910).[47] During this period, the reinsurance industry experienced a surge in international popularity, as it also did between and after the two world wars; this coincided with lawyers of varying provenance starting to exert an influence on contract design and conflict resolution. Key supply countries in which reinsurance companies maintained headquarters included Germany, Switzerland, Austria-Hungary, and Russia, while France, Italy, Belgium, the Netherlands, and Sweden were the countries from which demand was greatest. Reinsurance did not become widespread in England until the early twentieth century. Specialist reinsurers found it difficult to gain a foothold there due to the popularity of reciprocal or 'mutual' reinsurance among insurance companies, in particular in the field of maritime insurance, and as a result of the strong market presence and considerable flexibility of Lloyd's underwriters. North American primary insurance companies initially accepted offers from foreign reinsurers. Only in the wake of the urban conflagrations of Baltimore and San Francisco, which resulted in many fire insurance companies filing for insolvency, did businessmen in the USA establish the first domestic reinsurance companies.[48]

The example of the earthquake-triggered fire disaster of San Francisco demonstrates how single events can influence insurance law. At the start of the twentieth century, California was regarded as a gold mine, including by fire insurers. Business there was deemed to be 'exceptionally favourable', giving rise to 'substantial profits' for the participating companies.[49] The prospect of big profits had attracted many insurance companies to the West Coast. At the start of 1906, 114 fire insurance companies were competing with one another in the state of California.[50]

But the mood of optimism came to an abrupt halt on 18 April 1906, when a tremendous earthquake shook the emerging conurbation of San Francisco to its core. Entire streets collapsed. Soon afterwards, several fires broke out, which destroyed virtually the entire city within the space of two days.[51] The first serious reports put the insured losses in San Francisco at between USD 250 and 300 million.[52] Although the fire insurance and reinsurance companies immediately initiated loss settlement, the process was soon beset by considerable problems. In many cases, it emerged that the validity of insurance claims could not be ascertained clearly from the respective contracts, which invariably excluded losses due to force majeure through various wordings. As early as 30 April 1906, representatives of twenty reinsurance companies,

[47] Golding (1931, 5–6). [48] Gerathewohl et al. (1979, 779).

[49] *Österreichische Versicherungs-Zeitung* (1906a, 122).

[50] Insurance Commissioner of the State of California (1906, 5).

[51] On the course of the disaster: Kennedy (1908).

[52] 'Total Insurance Risk amounts to USD 250,000,000: *Sixty Per Cent*' (*New York Herald*, European Edition (Paris) of 21 April 1906), 2; *The Review* (quoted from *Der Versicherungsfreund und volkswirtschaftliche Post* of 20 April 1906, 6).

from Germany, Austria-Hungary, Italy, Denmark, Switzerland, Russia, and France,[53] met in Frankfurt am Main for a crisis meeting, declaring that they would recognize only those claims of affiliated insurers where there was a 'strong legal obligation' to do so.[54]

Not all of the fire insurance companies yielded to this pressure. Some, including many wealthy British companies, decided to pay all claims—even the legally dubious ones. A second group tried to pay no more than it considered itself obliged to pay. Although in many cases these companies were forced to go to court, some succeeded in stabilizing their precarious financial situation. A third group of companies needed to deploy all available financial reserves in order to keep their business going. In many cases, this only worked if the insured clients were prepared to accept an unfavourable settlement for the sake of preserving the company's solvency.[55] The other companies had either already gone bankrupt or were deferring payment ahead of their inevitable demise.[56] Nevertheless, by the end of 1906, the majority of the 90,000 or so insured and reported fire claims had been regulated. On the basis of what we know today, total property losses amounted to more than USD 400 million,[57] between USD 235 million and 265 million of which were picked up by the insurance industry.[58] In total, at least 243 companies were involved directly or indirectly in compensation payments,[59] of which at least nineteen went bankrupt.[60] The reinsurers' share of the net loss indemnified by insurance companies was 36 per cent.[61]

It was obvious to everyone involved and to all observers that the bewildering array of liability and exclusion clauses had made it much more difficult to assess obligations in individual cases and the legal and financial situation in general. Insurers needed to decide whether they were willing to pay for earthquake-related fire losses of this nature in the future. Four reinsurance company directors seized the initiative in this regard: Charles Simon of Swiss Re, Heinrich Gruenwald of Cologne Re, Carl Thieme of Munich Re, and B. Lindner of Badische Rück- und Mitversicherungs-Gesellschaft (Stuttgart).[62]

[53] The participating companies were: Badische Rück- und Mitversicherungs-G., Erste Böhmische Rück, Europa, La Fondiaria, Hamburg, Hamburg-Bremer Allgemeine Rück, Kölnische Rück (Cologne Re), Minerva Retrocessions- und Rückversicherungs-G., Münchener Rück (Munich Re), Nordisk, Nye Danske, Oberrheinische, Prudentia, Rheinisch-Westfälische Rück, Rossiya, Salamandra, Schweizerische Rück (Swiss Re), Skandinavia, Societé Anonyme de Réassurances contre l'Incendie. Some companies are missing from archived documents, while others are included: Gladbacher Rück, Skandia, Süddeutsche Rück, Westdeutsche, Wiener Rück. SRCA 10.144 425.02; SRCA 10.144 430.02 drafts and draft letters.

[54] Masius' Rundschau (1906, 226ff.).

[55] Österreichische Versicherungs-Zeitung (1906), 276; Mackenzie 1907, 251 ff.

[56] A. M. Best Company 1907; the loss liquidator Horace F. Atwood (quoted from Österreichische Versicherungs-Zeitung (1906b, 195, 208)); *La Semaine. Chroniques, Finances, Assurances*, 2 December 1906, 6.

[57] An American civil engineer put the total loss at USD 420 million, 20 million of which was attributable directly to the earthquake, 400 million to the conflagration. Freeman (1932, 663).

[58] Mackenzie (1907, 251ff.); Österreichische Versicherungs-Zeitung (1906b, 235).

[59] A. M. Best Company (1907, 6); Österreichische Versicherungs-Zeitung (1906c, 319).

[60] Mackenzie (1907, 251ff.), cites fifteen American and four European companies.

[61] Röder (2012, 95).

[62] Statistics from (Jahn 1912, sheet 66ff.).

Their stated aim was to introduce a standard clause with global applicability that would clarify the situation regarding the exclusion of catastrophe losses from fire insurance policies. They did this by comparing more than a thousand fire insurance policies that they had sent to them by business partners from around the world. In the middle of 1907, the four directors repaid the favour by publishing a brochure in four languages setting out the criteria for an ideal 'earthquake clause', and recommending that these criteria be implemented by local insurance companies and associations.[63] While the latter acted on the proposal in countries such as France, Spain, and Portugal, the idea was rejected by Dutch and British insurers, who took the opposite approach and offered to assume earthquake risks globally against payment of an additional premium with a view to reinforcing their market position. In some markets, including California, legislators intervened by stipulating contractual content or impeding and even banning the use of exclusion clauses in order to avoid imposing an extra financial burden on the population and the public sector in the event of a disaster. The initiative to reform insurance clauses desired by the reinsurance industry also failed in countries in which public insurance institutions and/or mutual companies predominated, such as in Switzerland.[64]

It can be asserted that the San Francisco disaster triggered a sea change in the way reinsurers approached contract law. Reinsurers had long since recognized the need for worldwide legal standards in their business and had become adept at implementing these over the heads of national legislators, essentially by making their own law. The following decades would see reinsurers employ this talent for transnational self-organization time and again, with the aim of standardizing specific contractual elements on a global basis.

The San Francisco disaster was a remarkable event in terms of conflict resolution too. Whereas hundreds of actions were brought by those insured against the fire insurance companies, legal disputes between primary insurers and reinsurers were few and far between, and this was also the case in the wake of the devastating urban disasters of Valparaíso, Kingston, and Messina. The reasons are manifold. Reinsurers were generally sceptical of the state courts as they had little confidence in the ability of judges to grasp the complex business issues involved. What is more, since conflicts between insurers and reinsurers often took place on the international stage, there was uncertainty as to which laws should be applied. The universal conflict-of-law regime of private international law that sets out which of several possible civil or commercial law systems should apply in a specific case was still in its infancy and subject to much debate.[65] In addition, major court cases would potentially have given rise to an increase in state interference in the reinsurance industry, leading to a raft of new laws and administrative regulations. By contrast, the practice of resolving conflicts autonomously offered a string of benefits: the parties involved could reach an agreement by themselves or choose an arbitrator acquainted with what was customary in the

[63] Röder (2012, 147–9). [64] Röder (2012, 151–288).

[65] G. Kegel (1995) *Internationales Privatrecht* (7th edn). Munich: Beck, 170ff.

industry. By doing so, they could avoid revealing the details of their business to a court and, thus, to the competition, and save themselves a lengthy legal battle that could take years to be resolved. Only when it was a question of pure survival would a company's directors depart from this strategy. A highly spectacular case saw a group of claimants and fire insurers make the trip from San Francisco to Europe in order to conduct negotiations directly with the relevant insurers and reinsurers and take the matter to court if necessary. In order to increase political and public pressure, they took along the mayor of the devastated city for good measure—up to then, a completely inconceivable strategy.[66]

The First World War marked a turning point. Just when reinsurance had established itself as an important element in an increasingly complex global economic environment, the warring factions forced companies to revoke reinsurance contracts with business partners in countries they were now fighting against.[67] After the war, the peace treaties retroactively sealed the fate of cross-border reinsurance, and existing business ventures were run off under supervision. Although, in legal terms, this constituted massive interference by international law in contract law, it was soon followed by the realization that it was causing financial distress to all parties involved. Nevertheless, restrictions in contractual freedom remained; the era of unfettered economic liberalism had come to an end.[68] This was especially the case in the fledgling Soviet Union. Although the ban on reinsurance had been lifted in 1922, the country was subject to strict regulation, and this had repercussions in terms of contract content too.[69] The observation that old practices count for little when it comes to economic survival was borne out once again during the rampant inflation of the 1920s, when primary insurance and reinsurance companies occasionally resorted to the law courts to ascertain who was to bear the excessive foreign exchange losses.[70]

The Second World War had a similar impact on the reinsurance industry. Once again, all contracts concluded with business partners in enemy countries were rendered invalid; 1947 saw the general annulment of all contracts concluded by German reinsurers with foreign business partners and vice versa. Reflecting developments after the First World War, however, this interventionist policy was rescinded in 1949/50 in order to prevent economic damage to all parties involved.[71] The increasing East–West confrontation at the start of the 1950s also saw a temporary suspension of contractual relations between reinsurers and primary insurers on either side of the Iron Curtain. That said, the political, economic, and social upheavals of the first half of the twentieth century had remarkably little impact on the law of contract. Events happening around the world were reflected in only a small number of new clauses; even war

[66] *La Semaine, Chroniques, Finances, Assurances*, 18 November 1906, 8; *Österreichische Revue* (1906, 280).

[67] Gerathewohl et al. (1979, 780f.).

[68] Gugerli (2012, 34ff.).

[69] Seraphim (1926, 5).

[70] On the litigation proceedings of an English insurance company against a French reinsurer before the Paris Court of Appeal: *Die Rückversicherung* (1926, 32). See also Chapter 6, this volume.

[71] Gerathewohl et al. (1979, 808).

mortality was not excluded from life insurance policies and the associated reinsurance agreements.[72]

In the post-war period, the reinsurance contract continued its transformation into a complex judicial instrument. As legal doctrines began to penetrate contract law and specific content became standardized, the characteristic 'patchwork' nature of the contract apparent at the turn of the twentieth century, with its repeated amendments and supplements, began to disappear in a slow and lengthy process that is still ongoing. In an essay written in 1949, the German lawyer Erich Prölss refers to several particularly well-known standard contracts and clauses used on the international stage.[73] The aim was to enhance legal certainty for both parties to a contract in the grey area between acceptable risk and incalculable peril. Corporate law departments began to expand, and there was a conspicuous increase in the number of legal publications in this field.[74] As before, however, the topic interested only very few academics; reinsurance law remained an exotic subject in university law faculties.

Little is known about the role played by brokers in the development of the insurance contract and in the resolution of disputes. It is known that specialist reinsurance brokers were heavily involved in the London insurance market. The contracting parties trusted that their brokers would propose advantageous financial and legal conditions, as the economic historian Robin Pearson succinctly summed up:

> They were answerable for the honesty, efficiency and liquidity of the reinsurers whose names they proposed to the ceding companies. Thus the reputation of reinsurance brokers also rested on their ability to set correct limits in treaties, to provide clients with an equitable distribution of risks, to keep losses down, and to deal with only respectable companies. Brokers often possessed information about markets that specialist reinsurers did not have. Consequently, at least during the late nineteenth and early twentieth centuries, the big broker firms were able to act as gatekeepers to reinsurance business, and as enforcers of behavioural norms in

[72] Gerathewohl et al. (1979, 788f.).

[73] These were the English codifications of the principles of facultative fire reinsurance business (Rules of the Fire Offices' Committee for the Regulation of Guarantee Transactions in Fire Insurance Business and Rules for the Regulation of Guarantee Transactions by Guarantees issued in the United Kingdom); the Standard Form of Reinsurance Agreement of the Surety Association of America applicable to the facultative fidelity and surety business of its members; Lloyd's maritime reinsurance policy; the arbitration clause of the Internationaler Transport-Versicherungs-Verband (ITVV); the Wiener Rückversicherungs-Klausel of the ITVV, which also dealt with war risks; and a standard clause stipulating that certain content be included in the bordereaux of hull reinsurance contracts (origin unknown). The ITVV's General Terms and Conditions of Facultative Reinsurance of 1923 had not been a success. Prölss (1964b, 90f.).

[74] Important monographs are contained in: B. de Mori (1936) *Le contrat de reassurance. Etude de droit compare.* Rome: Inst. internat. pour l'unification du droit privé; S Crisafulli Buscemi (1938) *La riassicurazione.* Naples: E. Jovene; R. Van de Casteele (1952) *La réassurance au point de vue juridique.* Paris: L'Argus; C. E. Golding (1937) *The Law and Practice of Reinsurance.* London: Buckley Press; E. Prölss (1965) *Beiträge zum Rückversicherungsrecht.* Karlsruhe: Verlag Versicherungswirtschaft.

> the company market, maintaining the 'protocols' of the business and helping to standardise procedures, terms and conditions of treaties, and forms of risk advices and bordereaux.[75]

Although the contracting parties were at liberty to accept or reject these conditions, it can be assumed that the brokers' proposals were indeed often accepted and thus had a normative effect.[76] The practice of issuing merely a slip containing the essential aspects of the insurance acceptance (the risk, the premium due, the term, and the period of liability) also emanated from the London brokers. Weeks, even months, would go by before the details of the agreement were set down in the wording. In order to ensure at least a modicum of legal certainty until the wording was ready, brokers would often refer to standard 'London market' clauses on the slip.

Arbitrators also played a role, at least indirectly, in the development of basic contract structures. In the event of a dispute between the insurer and the reinsurer, it was usually the responsibility of the arbitrator to resolve the matter in compliance with the law. Arbitration was based on the content of the contracts (provided this did not contravene mandatory legal norms), as well as on the international usages and customs of the business. In reaching a decision, the arbitrator would always examine the individual clauses and his interpretation would enable the reinsurer to judge whether his business practices were in keeping with the law, judicial usage and custom, and the other elements of the contract. If this was not the case, the clauses could be amended for future contracts—another example of the evolution of the basis of contracts.

The phenomenon of standardizing contract content was only recognized quite late on in its historical context. It forms a parallel with the standardization of technology and the 'normalization' of patterns of human behaviour in the disciplinary systems—schools, barracks, factories and offices, hospitals and asylums, and so on—as described by Michel Foucault.[77] Common to all these processes is the definition of and subsequent strict orientation to a given norm, be it a physical scale unit, a typewriter keyboard, a production process, a specific dress code or code of conduct, or, in our case, a legally watertight standard clause—theoretically applicable in all legal jurisdictions—for the exclusion of earthquake losses, such as the one developed by Charles Simon and his colleagues in 1907.[78] It is always interesting to note who or what was the driving force behind standardization. If the issue was deemed to be of particular importance to the citizens of a country, governments would insist on demonstrating their regulatory sovereignty. But, with technical matters, governments would often rely on the ability of trade associations and professional bodies to organize, standardize, and regulate the matter themselves.[79] Governments recognized the huge importance of primary

[75] Chapter 3, this volume.

[76] For information on recent reinsurance brokerage practice, see, for example, MacGillivray (1988, 527f.).

[77] See M. Foucault (1975) *Surveiller et punir. Naissance de la prison*. Paris: Gallimard, 152ff., 186, and 189f; Ewald (1990, 138–61).

[78] Röder (2012, 5ff.).

[79] See Vec (2006).

insurance in the personal lives of individuals at an early stage, and it was subject to statutory regulation in many countries in the late nineteenth/early twentieth centuries. By contrast, they considered reinsurance to be more of a technical matter than a social one, and were content, as before, to leave the development of contract law and the formulation of international standards to companies, science, and legal practice.

At this point, we can examine two of the observations made initially. It is a fact that certain factors continuously shaped the evolution of the contract, albeit in varying degrees of intensity. There are five key factors and these can be summarized as follows:

First, early reinsurance contracts were characterized by a patchwork approach, resulting from a continuous need to calibrate agreements in line with claims experience, for example, or due to a change in the cession and retrocession structure. Although the scope for flexible change diminished with the onset of standardization and the legal systematization of contract content, it did not disappear altogether.

Second, a continuous process of juridification of reinsurance can be observed, and this manifested itself in contracts becoming ever larger. In the context of the history of ideas, the juridification of reinsurance is one aspect of the secularization of risk in modern societies.[80]

Third, contract law evolved essentially by way of exclusion clauses, at least between 1880 and 1960. A number of companies responded to newly identified loss factors—some of which were discovered by spectacular loss events or disasters, others revealing themselves only gradually through scientific research (such as the damaging effect on health of smoking)—in the form of exclusions. Other companies, however, would selectively promote the absence of exclusions in their contracts in an effort to counter the aggravated risk by acquiring new customers.

Fourth, the deployment of increasingly hazardous technology led to the industrialized societies becoming more and more aware of risk during the course of the nineteenth century. They responded by adopting ever-more complex strategies in order to avert these perils and manage the risk in hand. This, too, contributed to the juridification of insurance, manifesting itself in the form of increasingly complex contract law.

The fifth factor is the tendency of the reinsurance industry to keep the state at arm's length for the reasons mentioned in Section 7.4. State agents were to have no influence on the fundamental design and structure of contracts, as reinsurers considered self-regulation to be more appropriate and more effective. An increase in regulation, especially in the USA, was evident only from the 1980s onwards, but this should not be overestimated.

The related finding, namely that the reinsurance industry is inherently averse to litigation, was confirmed in the period from 1880 to 1960 too. In 1937, an author introduced a brief report on important rulings made in English, French, German, Italian, and American courts in the preceding decades with the following words:

> Modern re-insurance is so largely governed by the arbitration clause that it may come as a surprise to many of the younger generation of re-insurance men to find

[80] This observation was made by David Gugerli.

> that case law has decided, in one country or the other, many of the problems governing the relations between ceding offices and their re-insurers.[81]

The New York Convention of 1958 merely served to bolster international arbitration.[82] However, the differences in national conflict cultures were becoming more marked. While European market players tended to adopt a more collaborative approach to resolving disputes, American companies preferred to take a more confrontational stance and were less averse to taking matters to court or going public. After the Second World War, groups of specialist lawyers who wanted to expand the field of insurance litigation for their own profit began to emerge in the USA. The National Association of Claimants' Compensation Attorneys (NACCA) and the International Association of Insurance Counsel employed state-of-the-art methods to convince juries of the merits of their cases:

> Today the tools of the damage suit lawyer include blackboards, chalk, artificial limbs, neurological skeletons, colored plastic torsos and every other part of the human body. The use of such eye-appealing evidence feeds the human desire for the sensational. Juries are no different than other humans—the more dramatic the case, the less the monotony, the greater the impact on the emotions and the longer remembered.

In the interest of perfect preparation, they would read the opposing side's publications, for example the *NACCA Law Journal* or the *Insurance Counsel Journal*, and would even attend their opponents' congresses and training seminars.[83] In the decades that followed, the conflict culture within the industry moved far beyond the borders of the USA.

## 7.5 Contract Law in the Vortex of Globalization and New Risks: Developments Since 1960

The period from the 1960s onwards was characterized by globalization, accompanied in part by the challenge of having to adapt to other legal frameworks. What is more, new risks—notably in the fields of health, the environment, and terrorism—led to changes in contract law.

[81] *The Review*, 1937, 1201–3.

[82] The New York Convention on the Recognition and Enforcement of Foreign Arbitral Awards ('New York Convention') was ratified at a conference of the United Nations (UN) in 1959 and came into force in 1959.

[83] Morse (1953, 14–16).

Industrial globalization, that began with de-colonization and received added impetus at the end of the Cold War thanks to the establishment of liberal economic policies in many parts of the globe, was, in the eyes of reinsurers, a golden opportunity to develop new areas of business. In the former colonies that had gained independence (in 1960, eighteen countries gained independence in Africa alone), new insurance markets and systems emerged, mainly under the aegis of companies from the former colonial states that had operated in these regions prior to independence. These companies now passed on their business links with European reinsurers to the newly founded local firms. In addition, numerous private- and public-sector initiatives were launched, with the aim of building autonomous reinsurance systems. As had been the case in many other countries previously, the emerging nations were also faced with the question of state intervention. In many cases, governments took control of existing reinsurance companies or set up new monopolies.[84] Regional cooperation initiatives also bore fruit in some cases, notably the African Reinsurance Corporation, which was founded in 1977 by member states of the Organization of African Unity in collaboration with the African Development Bank.[85] Research into the effects of this trend on reinsurance contract law has yet to be conducted. The same goes for natural catastrophes—but increasingly also accidents in industrial plants—in emerging countries striving to improve living standards for a growing population through rapid industrialization.[86]

The legal repercussions of entry into Islamic territories are, on the other hand, well known. In the post-war years, the insurance and reinsurance industries made particularly rapid inroads into the Gulf States, which were experiencing an oil-based economic boom, as well as into North Africa and South Asia. However, apart from commercial insurance with its European origins that was now penetrating many markets, there existed the ancient Islamic form of insurance known as *takaful* that was already practised in many an Islamic society. *Takaful* is a cooperative, non-profit system of compensation for unforeseen losses paid for out of a fund to which people agree to donate small regular contributions. As such, *takaful* is not unlike cooperative insurance, which is also founded on the idea of mutuality. But *takaful* is much older—it was possibly already being practised at the start of Islamic civilization in the seventh century—and it complies strictly with the rules of Islamic law. At least when interpreted strictly according to conservative Islamic principles, *takaful* prohibits several elements of commercial underwriting. These include profit-oriented agreements based on uncertainty (*gharar*), gambling (*maisir*), and interest payments (*riba*), although it is debatable whether the latter applies generally, or only to usurious interest. In the course of the modernization of Islamic societies, businessmen, in collaboration with Islamic legal scholars, started to develop new *takaful* models that provided similar functions to Western insurance while complying with Islamic Shari'ah law. This development has its origins in the religiously conservative Sudan of the late 1960s; important centres

84 For information on the relationship between reinsurance and politics, see Chapter 1, this volume.

85 Gerathewohl et al. (1979, 832, 836).

86 See Chapter 10, this volume.

were subsequently established in Malaysia and Pakistan too. The prohibition of commercial insurance was confirmed in a series of legal opinions and court judgements,[87] while others legitimized the new *takaful* models.[88] This led to an upswing in the *takaful* industry, which continued to offer new insurance models, such as motor, accident, property, liability, marine, building, health, family (life) *takaful* cover, while commercial primary insurers were obliged to withdraw from many markets. The Islamic legal councils did, however, grant *takaful* institutions special dispensation to collaborate with commercial reinsurers by applying the principle of 'necessity' (*darura*).[89] Although most providers of reinsurance cover did not come from the region, the Iraq Reinsurance Company, which was founded in 1960, proved a rare exception to the rule. However, from the end of the 1970s onwards, beginning in Sudan, *retakaful* institutions emerged that practised reinsurance in compliance with the rules of Islamic jurisprudence. This meant that the principle of necessity could no longer be used as justification for special dispensations.[90] To avoid being squeezed out of the markets of the Middle East, North Africa, and South Asia, conventional reinsurance companies developed their own *retakaful* models and had them certified by standard institutes such as the Islamic Financial Services Board (IFSB) in Malaysia or the Accounting and Auditing Organization for Islamic Financial Institutions (AAOIFI) of Bahrain, which allowed them to preserve or establish operations in many Muslim countries.[91] Such companies included market leader Hannover Re, which ran international operations from Bahrain, and Swiss Re and Munich Re with their respective offices in Kuala Lumpur. *Retakaful* providers also emerged in the region in the form of Saudi Re (in Riyadh), Kuwait Re (in Kuwait), Trust Re (in Bahrain), ACR Retakaful (in Malaysia), Emirates Re (in Dubai), Africa Retakaful (in Cairo), and many more. A characteristic feature and a mandatory requirement in many countries is the close involvement of Islamic legal scholars in the form of Shari'ah advisory boards, whose job it is to monitor existing business operations and develop innovative business products while ensuring that new and existing contract models comply with the Shari'ah.

[87] *Fatwa* issued in judicial conference held in Mecca in Shaban 1398 AH (1978 CE); unanimous decision by Muslim scholars in seminar held in Morocco on 6 May 1972; *fatwa* issued by National Religious Council of Malaysia in 1972; verdict of the Supreme Court of Egypt on 27 December 1926; unanimous resolutions and *fatwa* by '*ulama* in the Muslim League Conference in Cairo in 1965; *fatwa* of Islamic Fiqh Academy (OIC) 1985: 'The commercial insurance contract [ . . . ] which is commonly used by commercial insurance companies, is a contract, which contains major element of risk, which voids the contract and, therefore, is prohibited (*haram*) according to the Shariah.'

[88] *Fatwa* issued by Higher Council of Saudi Arabia in 1397 AH (1976 CE) in favour of Islamic model; *fatwa* issued by the Fiqh Council of Muslim World League in 1398 AH in favour of Islamic insurance; *fatwa* issued by the Fiqh Council of the Organization of the Islamic Conference in 1405 AH in favour of insurance under Islamic model; the Grand Counsel of Islamic Scholars in Mecca, Maja Al-Fiqh, approved the *takaful* system in 1985 as the correct alternative to conventional insurance in full compliance with Shari'ah; Act of 1984 authorized by the '*ulama* and government of Malaysia.

[89] Arbouna (2000, 335ff.).

[90] That said, some authors still opine that justification based on *darura* is still valid, e.g. Rahman, Ahmad, and Buang (2011, 11768ff.).

[91] Akoob (2009, 143ff.).

It is not an isolated case that Islamic law resulted in wholesale adjustments to the practice of insurance and reinsurance and to the relevant laws of contract. Jewish and orthodox Christian law also prohibit usurious interest, and this was the subject of debate in the Middle Ages in connection with maritime insurance in particular.[92] In modern times, followers of both these religions also developed insurance systems and contractual bases founded on mutuality.[93] In practice, however, they were far less important than the Islamic *(re)takaful*.

Another crucial development since the 1960s has been the emergence of new risks (or in some cases, established risks occurring in unprecedented intensity or scale) that have led to changes in both contract law and conflict culture in reinsurance. Health risks such as the carcinogenic effect of the building material asbestos, environmental risks such as hurricanes occurring in densely populated areas, and terrorism, the destructive force of which reached an unprecedented level on 9/11, resulted in huge compensation payments on the part of insurance and reinsurance companies alike. Some insurers and reinsurers attempted to protect their companies, at least for the future, by introducing exclusion clauses, while others went on the offensive by actually accepting the same risks—essentially the same policy adopted by certain market players after the earthquake-related fire disaster of San Francisco.

The heated legal disputes concerning asbestos-related health impairments that raged, above all, in the USA,[94] reached the shores of the reinsurance industry in the 1980s, resulting not only in a raft of new and robust regulations but also in an acceleration of the pace of change in the conflict culture of the insurance industry. In the 1970s, scientists had provided evidence of the damaging effect of asbestos, confirming what had been suspected for decades.[95] Reinsurers soon realized that a global epidemic was in the offing because asbestos has been mined in countries as far apart as Brazil, Colombia, Canada, South Africa, Russia, Greece, Italy, and Turkey for global use in the construction industry. In the USA, the first class actions—that is, a form of lawsuit where a plaintiff sues a defendant on behalf of a larger number of persons who have been injured by the same defendant in the same way—against companies that had produced or processed asbestos came in the 1980s.[96] Regardless of the outcome of the class action, the defending company and its liability insurers faced huge expenses from the outset. By 2000, companies that used to manufacture or use asbestos, and their insurers/reinsurers, had paid out more than USD 50 billion in claims in the USA alone, with around 200,000 further court cases pending and considerably more in the pipeline. With considerable tactical skill, attorneys exploited the opportunities presented by American procedural law to have their cases heard in the court or jurisdiction considered most likely to provide a favourable judgement (a strategy known as 'forum

[92] See, for example, Passamaneck (1974); Nehlsen-von Stryk (1986).

[93] Odierno (2012, 53ff.).

[94] The risk trio of asbestos, pollution, and health became infamous under the acronym APH claims.

[95] Detailed information in McCulloch and Tweedale (2008).

[96] See, for example, the study conducted by Cologne Re (1988).

shopping'), to aggregate promising cases with less promising ones in a mass action in the hope of obtaining a successful outcome for each and every plaintiff, to target a number of defendants simultaneously in order to transfer liability to the next company when the preceding one becomes insolvent (one US asbestos manufacturer after another went bankrupt as a result of litigation), and, if possible, to sue for additional punitive damages.[97] Lawyers' and other procedural expenses frequently ran to twice the amount actually paid out in damages to the plaintiff.[98] That being the case, primary insurers and reinsurers not only attempted to exclude from future cover any loss or damage arising from the negative effects of asbestos, but also found themselves having to go to court in order to defend their interests more than ever before.[99] Although, as a rule, companies would join forces to defend their case, there were several cases of litigation between insurers and reinsurers, which once again reflects the departure from the previous consensus of avoiding state jurisdictions.[100] Another forensic instrument—albeit not a wholly new one—with which to litigate directly against reinsurers is the practice of 'fronting', which refers to the possibility of cutting the claim through to the reinsurer if the primary insurer becomes insolvent.[101] It proved almost impossible for reinsurers to redress the damage caused by the loss of confidentiality when managing conflicts.

As early as the 1970s, reinsurers recognized the causal link between the rise in the number of environmental risks, as borne out by loss statistics, and the anthropogenic warming of the Earth's atmosphere, otherwise known as the 'greenhouse effect'.[102] The devastation wreaked by catastrophes such as Hurricane Betsy (1965) and Hurricane Andrew (1992) in the USA, and the floods in Thailand (2011), gave rise to debates, largely led by the reinsurance industry, on whether to include or exclude certain individual risks. Questions of causation arose during claims liquidation that attracted varying responses, depending on the legal jurisdiction—a phenomenon reinsurers had already experienced at the turn of the century. In the wake of the destruction of New Orleans caused by Hurricane Katrina (2005), the question arose as to whether or not certain losses were the result of the windstorm itself (insured) or of the flood waters

[97] AAA (2001, 3f.).

[98] The legal academic Christopher Edley (Jr) reckoned that, 'of every dollar paid by defendants, over sixty cents goes to the lawyers. Adding the overhead costs of both the judicial and the insurance systems, asbestos litigation consumes two dollars of society's resources in order to deliver a single dollar to people who were exposed.' Edley (1999, 5).

[99] This was reflected in literature. For the end of the 1990s, see the comprehensive groundwork study of Anderson, Stanzler, and Masters (1997).

[100] Jericho (1988, 289ff.).

[101] Hall (2001, 22). In the case *Joel S. Ario* v. *Swiss Reinsurance America Corp., Pa. Commw. Lexis 737* (Pa. Commw. Ct., 21 December 2007), the court set out the limits of fronting against reinsurance companies. A distinction should be drawn between the term fronting when referring to a tactic in litigation (as used here), and the same word used to describe a business tactic employed by a reinsurance company when it assumes a risk in its entirety.

[102] Munich Re was probably the first company to call the risk by this name in a 1973 publication entitled 'Flood / Inundation'.

forced into the city by the hurricane (not insured).[103] This almost exactly mirrored the situation in San Francisco after the earthquake of 1906, where the debate centred on whether the earthquake (not insured) or the resulting fires (insured) caused the losses.[104]

The decisive strategic response of the reinsurance industry to the statistically proven increase in natural catastrophes since the early 1990s came in the form of tradable financial products (securitization). By combining their own expertise in major risks—for example, in the field of nuclear energy[105]—with the latest findings in actuarial science and the options provided by investment banking, reinsurers were able to allocate capital on a scale previously unheard of in conventional reinsurance. A presentation of the resulting catastrophe bonds (cat bonds) and their implementation in contracts would be beyond the scope of this chapter, however.[106]

The risk posed by international terrorism manifested itself on a previously unimaginable scale in the attack on the World Trade Center in New York on 9/11. The event, which affected risks in almost all lines of insurance business simultaneously, gave rise to a multitude of complex legal questions for the attorneys involved. One major dispute centred on the question of whether the attack constituted one or two loss events: as the iconic building comprised two distinct towers, the leaseholder demanded indemnification of twice the sum insured, which was twice as much as the twenty-two insurance companies—among them Swiss Re with a major share—were prepared to pay. In addition, there were the payouts on the life insurance policies of tens of thousands of victims who were either inside the World Trade Center itself or in the aircraft that were flown into the towers, not to mention buildings, motor, and countless other insurance policies. Indemnified losses ultimately totalled some USD 40 billion.

After 9/11, insurance companies introduced various changes in order to combat the new threat, including a limitation or complete exclusion of liability for losses arising from terrorist acts.[107] Recognizing that the insurance industry would not survive further attacks on this scale, some countries elected to support their insurers by assuming some of the risks. Insurance and reinsurance companies also cooperated with state authorities when it came to developing new indemnification systems. In the USA, the Terrorism Risk Insurance Act (TRIA) of November 2002 guarantees support to insurers via the shared public compensation of insured losses resulting from acts of terrorism as defined in the Act. Thus, the government began to exert an influence—albeit indirectly—on contract structure, and to some degree assumed the role of a reinsurer.

Reinsurance business became more judicial and forensic than ever before in the early years of the twenty-first century, as the asbestos claims and the repercussions of 9/11

[103] 'By Wind or by Water' (*The Economist* (US edition), 19 July 2007).

[104] Röder (2012, 54 ff.). [105] See Chapter 9, this volume.

[106] For more information on securitization, see Chapter 5, this volume; on cat bonds, see Chapter 10, this volume.

[107] Everett (2002/3, 175ff.); Kendall (2002, 569ff.); Wolgast (2007, 146ff.).

showed only too well.[108] At Swiss Re, lawyers work mainly in the following departments: Contracts & Wording, Legal & Compliance, and Regulatory Affairs, as well as in Claims. As a result, contract content has become even more standardized and comprehensive model reinsurance contracts are no longer unusual.[109] An important innovation in the field of conflict resolution has been the creation of umbrella arbitration organizations. An entity worthy of note is ARIAS—the Reinsurance and Insurance Arbitration Society of the Association Internationale de Droit des Assurances (AIDA) founded in 1960—which has introduced its own arbitration clause and operates from several locations around the globe.[110] Although, as before, litigation is not a common form of conflict resolution, it is still a legitimate option for American primary insurers in disputes with reinsurers,[111] and legal precedent rulings are serving to consolidate international customary law.[112] Other differences in the judicial and conflict cultures of the USA and Continental Europe that have had an effect on claims settlement and, at least indirectly, on contract design, also came to light through novel claims scenarios. Reinsurers responded to these claims with remarkable flexibility, as indeed they did when adapting the basis of their contracts to the *takaful* concept in Muslim regions.

## 7.6 Closing Remarks

Although the reinsurance contracts of the early twenty-first century may seem far removed from those of the late nineteenth, their basic concept remains the same. In the course of the twentieth century, new types of reinsurance contract appeared in other lines of business, largely as a result of the introduction by primary insurers of new business models and, above all, of countless new clauses based on experience gleaned from everyday practice, especially from loss events: an unstoppable evolution of law. Reinsurance contract law has proved itself to be extremely flexible and reinsurers more than capable of adapting to the characteristic forms of conflict resolution in the

[108] Nützi (2000, 50f.). [109] And also *The Review*, July–August 2004, 33.

[110] Merkin (2007, 308, 445ff.).

[111] 'Love on the Rocks' (*The Economist*, 19 March 2003). The London legal expert Clive O'Connell alludes to the more litigious nature of US society compared with the British culture of conflict. *The Review*, May 2003, 25.

[112] The most important court rulings during this period came from the UK; for example, *Insurance Co. of Africa* v. *SCOR (UK) Reinsurance Co. Ltd*, Court of Appeals 1985 on the reinsurer's obligation to 'follow the settlements'; *Forsikringsaktieselskapt Vesta* v. *Butcher*, House of Lords 1988 on the applicable law; *Pan Atlantic Insurance Co. Ltd* v. *Pine Top Insurance Co. Ltd*, House of Lords 1994 on the primary insurer's duty to disclose all material information, *Axa Reinsurance UK PLC* v. *Field*, Court of Appeals 1996 and *Hill* v. *M&G Re*, House of Lords 1996 on the definition of a loss event; and *Charter Reinsurance Co. Ltd* v. *Fagan and Others*, House of Lords 1996 on the reinsurer's obligation to 'follow the settlements' in the event of the insurer's insolvency.

respective regions of operation.[113] At the same time, the principles of avoiding legal disputes and maintaining a distance to the state became less important. The characteristic patchwork nature of the ever-changing contract—a feature until well into the twentieth century—failed to survive the continuing juridification of insurance that is still ongoing today. However, risk awareness, which first emerged in the nineteenth century, continues to expand into the world's industrial and post-industrial societies, and even beyond into the countries of the Global South, under the shadow cast by the destruction of the natural environment, the scarcity of resources, and population growth. With its specific contract and conflict culture, reinsurance has become an element in the complex system of loss prevention and risk management, and must nowadays cooperate with far more industry players than would have been conceivable just a few decades ago.

## Acknowledgements

Niels Viggo Haueter, Geoffrey Jones, and David Gugerli, along with many of the volume's authors and Swiss Re employees, made important contributions to this chapter through their suggestions and constructive criticism, and our heartfelt thanks go to all of them. I am also deeply grateful to the translator, Karen Rudd Gloor, for her marvellous work.

[113] Overall, the reinsurance business throughout the twentieth and twenty-first centuries can (with few exceptions) be characterized as being rather adaptive than innovative. See Chapter 1, this volume.

CHAPTER 8

# REINSURANCE LAW AS AN AUTONOMOUS REGULATORY REGIME?

## *Resistance to Codification and Avoidance of State Jurisdiction in the Twentieth Century*

MILOŠ VEC

THE law of the global reinsurance industry is a unique, normative order, formed, above all, by the relationships between reinsurers and the reinsured. Characteristic of this normative order in the twentieth century was the interest of parties engaged in international activities in, first, keeping contracts as free as possible from statutory requirements and, second, keeping disputes resulting from breaches of contract out of state courts. Instead, they preferred to resolve disputes privately through arbitration. The autonomy of the parties in terms of both the legislative framework and enforcement is thus of considerable importance. These regulatory liberties might also constitute a desirable goal in other areas of commercial law. In the reinsurance law of Continental Europe in the twentieth century, however, they already seem to have been implemented to a particularly far-reaching extent.

The trends towards juridification, state intervention, and bureaucratization that are often observed in other areas of law have not had the same kind of impact in the reinsurance industry as elsewhere. This was certainly the case in Continental European law at any rate, and this is used in Section 8.3 by way of example to illustrate global developments. Legal developments took a different course here from other areas of commercial law, with juridification and state intervention initially absent. The perception of reinsurance law, over many decades in the twentieth century, as a kind of bastion of liberalism may also have had something to do with legislators' original apparent lack of interest in treating reinsurance as a separate sector of industry or in concerning themselves with its specific nature. The absence of regulation may be attributable not only to legal policy but also to a lack of knowledge about the industry.

Not until towards the end of the twentieth century, under the influence of globalization and given the trend towards reinsurers increasingly acting or being seen as financial service companies, did the premises change. Reinsurers became closer to banks and were subject, not least in Continental Europe, to an increasing amount of regulation. The reinsurers attempted to resist this both with arguments derived from their earlier sense of identity and expressions of interest in legal policy with which the industry sought to defend its autonomy.

This chapter is concerned with reinsurance law as an autonomous regulatory regime in this sense. Legal developments in Germany and Switzerland, in particular, are at the centre of this, and this contribution follows the pattern of developments there. It investigates the regulatory framework of the state for the reinsurance industry and describes the strategies used by the reinsurers to resist the attempts of the state and other players to create such a mandatory normative framework. Above all, it discusses the purpose of and the forms taken by the resistance to regulation and court rulings in the twentieth century. What form of autonomy did develop here, and why were the international players involved able to get what they wanted in terms of legal policy to such a large extent? Essentially, this involves describing reinsurance law as a unique regulatory regime. Reinsurance law is described against the backdrop not just of developments in civil law but also, in particular, various forms of state-run economy and the emergence of the modern interventionist state.[1]

## 8.1 Reinsurance as a Modern Regulatory Regime

### 8.1.1 Regulatory Regime, the Interventionist State and Juridification

When reinsurance law is described as a modern 'regulatory regime', this term refers to a system of (legal) rules and provisions established by the state or other authorities to regulate certain economic activities. Peter M. Lencsis defines 'business or trade regulation' as 'the imposition of specific governmental controls or standards upon business activities which would otherwise be governed only by the decisions of the business owners, the forces of the marketplace, and general law'.[2]

The regulatory regime is thus defined by the control and enforcement of the authorities: the standards of control and the regulatory requirements originate with the state or a government authority; at any rate, they have not developed on the

[1] M. Stolleis (1989) 'Die Entstehung des Interventionsstaates und das öffentliche Recht', *Zeitschrift für neuere Rechtgeschichte* 11, 129–47.

[2] Lencsis (1997, 1).

autonomous initiative of the parties involved. To this extent, the regulatory regime is semantically close to the interventionist state. This term describes 'a political system or judicial regulatory regime in which the state intervenes to a significant extent in the legal relationships between private actors'.[3]

As far as commercial law is concerned, this intervention seems to be the norm. Commercial relationships are one of the areas in which developments have led to talk of the 'juridification' of relationships in society.[4] Juridification was perceived in three forms: the tendency to create statutory law to cover all eventualities, the tendency to take disputes to court, and bureaucratization.[5] It was clearly associated with the expansion of the modern interventionist state and the increase in government spending and criticized from a liberal point of view.

Legal historians have not systematically researched the extent to which there were patterns of development here that ran contrary to the expansion of the modern interventionist state in the development of commercial law in the nineteenth century. The juridification theory thus suffers from an empirical deficit that can also be attributed to the weakness of the historical sociology of law and the absence of historical expertise in political science. Only now, following globalization, do phenomena in which a certain legal autonomy has developed in particular branches of society (*lex mercatoria*, *lex sportiva*, 'Code and other Laws of Cyberspace'[6], etc.) appear to be coming into the focus of civil law,[7] and, in particular, of legal theory.[8] These are the subject of lively discussion. There is much debate, in particular, about the degree of autonomy of the relevant sets of rules and regulations from the state.[9]

## 8.1.2 'Self-Regulation' and 'Regulated Self-Regulation'

The 'self-regulation' model, which emphasizes the autonomy of the parties involved, can be understood as an antonym to the 'interventionist state' or a state-dominated 'regulatory regime'. Fields of reference for legal history are trading and insurance.[10]

[3] Vec (2011, col. 1279).

[4] F. Kübler (ed.) (1984) *Verrechtlichung von Wirtschaft, Arbeit und sozialer Solidarität. Vergleichende Analysen*. Baden-Baden: Nomos Verlag.

[5] Voigt (1980, 15–37).

[6] This is the title of a book by L. Lessig (2000) *Code and Other Laws of Cyberspace*. New York: Basic Books.

[7] A. Röthel (2007) 'Lex mercatoria, lex sportiva, lex technica. Private Rechtsetzung jenseits des Nationalstaates?', *JuristenZeitung* 62, 755–63, here 755.

[8] G. Teubner (1996) 'Globale Bukowina. Zur Emergenz eines transnationalen Rechtspluralismus', *Rechtshistorisches Journal* 15, 255–90.

[9] Kadelbach and Günther (2011, 9–48).

[10] K. O. Scherner (2011) 'Handelsrecht: Selbstregulierung und Regulierung beim Eisenbahnfrachtgeschäft und im Versicherungswesen in der ersten Hälfte des 19. Jahrhunderts', in P. Collin and G. Bender (eds), *Selbstregulierung im 19. Jahrhundert—zwischen Autonomie und staatlichen Steuerungsansprüchen*. Frankfurt am Main: Vittorio Klostermann, 195–229; A. Cordes and

However, recent research in the field of legal history has revealed that pure self-regulation is virtually never found; the normal case in the nineteenth and twentieth centuries, in which the parties were granted a particularly high degree of freedom, was 'regulated self-regulation', which is found in many fields of commercial and employment law,[11] but also in environmental and technology law.[12]

This 'regulated self-regulation' is 'a form of interweaving of state regulation and social self-regulation combined with powerful organised interest groups'.[13] Consequently, a defining characteristic of 'regulated self-regulation' is that 'state and private organisations' are closely interwoven.[14] This was evident even before the emergence of the modern interventionist state in the last quarter of the nineteenth century. Even in the first half of the nineteenth century, considered to be a liberal period, in which there was evidence of 'diverse forms of social organisation emerging given the new scope for freedom of action', these forms of organization were hardly ever completely autonomous, as research in the field of the history of law has recently revealed: 'It became clear that, even at that time, self-regulation almost never occurred without the involvement of the state.'[15]

### 8.1.3 Interpenetration of Public and Civil Law

One of the significant aspects of the discovery of 'regulated self-regulation' in jurisprudence in the last decade has been the insight into the interpenetration of public and civil law in the modern age. The examination of the genesis of the modern

S. Dauchy (eds) (2012) *Eine Grenze in Bewegung/Une frontière mouvante. Öffentliche und private Justiz im Handels- und Seerecht/Justice privée et justice publique en matières commerciales et maritimes (Schriften des Historischen Kollegs 81)*. Munich: De Gruyter Oldenbourg.

[11] G. Bender (2006) 'Regulierte Selbstregulierung. Der Fall Tarifautonomie', in M. Vec, M.-T. Hütt, and A. M. Freund (eds), *Selbstorganisation. Ein Denksystem für Natur und Gesellschaft*. Cologne: Böhlau Verlag, 335–71; P. Collin (2015) 'Regulierte Selbstregulierung der Wirtschaft. Neue Normierungsstrukturen im späten 19. und frühen 20. Jahrhundert', *Zeitschrift für Neuere Rechtsgeschichte* 37, 10–31.

[12] M. Kloepfer, C. Franzius, and T. Weber (2002) *Technik und Recht im wechselseitigen Werden. Kommunikationsrecht in der Technikgeschichte (Schriften zum Technikrecht 4)*. Berlin: Duncker & Humblot.

[13] K. Groh (2012) 'Gesellschaftliche Selbststeuerung?', in P. Collin et al. (eds), *Regulierte Selbstregulierung im frühen Interventions- und Sozialstaat (Studien zur europäischen Rechtsgeschichte, 270)*. Frankfurt am Main: Vittorio Klostermann, 33–52, here 33. See also the outline by P. Collin (2011) '"Gesellschaftliche Selbstregulierung" und "Regulierte Selbstregulierung". Ertragreiche Analysekategorien für eine (rechts-)historische Perspektive?', in P. Collin et al. (eds), *Selbstregulierung im 19. Jahrhundert. Zwischen Autonomie und staatlichen Steuerungsansprüchen (Studien zur europäischen Rechtsgeschichte 259)*. Frankfurt am Main: Vittorio Klostermann, 3–31.

[14] P. Collin et al. (eds) (2012) *Regulierte Selbstregulierung im frühen Interventions- und Sozialstaat (Studien zur europäischen Rechtsgeschichte 270)*. Frankfurt am Main: Vittorio Klostermann, vii–x, here vii.

[15] P. Collin et al. (2012, vii).

interventionist state shows that it was possible to overcome certain systemic weaknesses through functional cooperation between otherwise dichotomous fields of law,[16] and regulated self-regulation seems to be a fitting example of this crucial cooperation. 'Supportive and protective civil law and public law'[17] have a control function for both the state and society that was not part of the programme of the classical codifications of the long nineteenth century.

However, if certain fields, such as reinsurance law, were able to systematically avoid the juridification of the interventionist state, it raises the question all the more sharply as to which motives were behind this evolution and why it was possible to resist, at least partially, the norm-establishing/rule-making environment of the modern interventionist state.

## 8.1.4 Fields of Investigation in Reinsurance Law

The hypothesis that there were hardly any fields within economy in which there was pure self-regulation will form the backdrop for the examination of reinsurance law. The primary aim will be to analyse the attempts of the state to establish norms or legal provisions as well as the strategies of the reinsurers in the absence of such legislation.

Developments in German and Swiss reinsurance law in the late nineteenth and early twentieth centuries will be examined. The reason for selecting these two countries and Continental European law is that, in terms of both legal and economic aspects, they are essential in the development of the reinsurance industry.[18] In addition to the leading role played by Swiss and German reinsurance companies in the global industry right up to the present day, there were also the efforts of the state to establish norms: the strategies of the state's legislative bodies have often been compared in the literature, albeit partially due to their proximity in time and their similarity in terms of content.[19] The key developments in the contract law regime took place here, above all: 'The history of treaty insurance is located in the German speaking world, from where it spread in all important industrial countries and beyond. [ . . . ] for much of the story the Germans and the Swiss have been the protagonists.'[20] Both countries have always had highly developed legal cultures in which the self-regulation strategies of the reinsurers and the regulatory environment have been subject to particularly close examination by jurists. The epoch being examined can be considered as the period in which the industry underwent its formation phase, which David Gugerli has defined as being the period between 1860 and 1960;[21] it was not just the (internal) organization of the reinsurance industry that developed during this period but also the legal framework.

[16] Stolleis (1989).

[17] J. Rückert (2003) 'Das Bürgerliche Gesetzbuch. Ein Gesetzbuch ohne Chance?', *JuristenZeitung* 58, 749–60.

[18] Pearson (1995, 559); Kopf (1929, 28).

[19] Herzfelder (1913, col. 568).

[20] Chapter 6, this volume.

[21] Gugerli (2013, 154–83).

## 8.2 THE SOURCES OF REINSURANCE LAW

In order to examine the issue of juridification and state intervention and their absence, to a large extent, in German and Swiss reinsurance law, the sources of reinsurance law in the twentieth century will be outlined briefly here. No attempt will be made to cover everything, nor will the approach be systematic.

### 8.2.1 Fragmentary Special Legal Framework

Examining reinsurance law reveals, on the one hand, a variety of legal sources. On the other hand, however, some particular features are evident that are characteristic of the regulatory regime. Historically, there is evidence of initial legal regulation as early as the pre-modern period, in the course of the juridification of (marine) insurance.[22] Gerathewohl, author of a comprehensive manual of reinsurance law, conjectures that it can be assumed 'that the laws and regulations of individual countries do in no way constitute new legislation; instead they were only intended and able to provide a more public and secure framework of international customary law'.[23] Accordingly, juridification was based on actual commercial (legal) practices. However, the term *international* customary law appears unsuitable for this, since this suggests an element of agreement between countries; practice, however, is indicative of a transnational concept and points to an older understanding, as it existed in *ius gentium*, that is, customary law held *in common* by all peoples.[24]

More comprehensive legislation was enacted for the first time in the context of the wave of rational legal codification. A number of paragraphs are devoted to reinsurance law in the General State Law for the Prussian States of 1794 (ALR T.II Tit 8 Section 13b §§ 2016–2023 'Von der Rückversicherung'). However, this trend towards juridification by partial or overall codifications was not continued around 1900 during the second wave of codification.

On the contrary, as a glance at the legal situation in Germany shows, reinsurance law remained exempted from the regulations of codifications and other statutory law. William Lewis, professor of law in Greifswald, took a comparative approach in 1889 and established that the statute law did not provide any particular norms for this type of treaty at all.[25] Erich R. Prölss, a lawyer and member of the management board of

[22] On the history of reinsurance in the Middle Ages and the pre-modern period, see Mossner (1959).

[23] Gerathewohl et al. (1979, 723).

[24] J. Schröder (2000) 'Die Entstehung des modernen Völkerrechtsbegriffs im Naturrecht der frühen Neuzeit', in S. Byrd, J. Hruschka, and J. C. Joerden (eds), *Die Entstehung und Entwicklung der Moralwissenschaften im 17. und 18. Jahrhundert (Jahrbuch für Recht und Ethik 8)*. Berlin: Duncker & Humblot, 47–71.

[25] Lewis (1889, 112).

Bayerische Rückversicherungs AG and Rühag Rückversicherungs-AG in Munich, declared in 1942: 'There are generally no provisions in law at all to prevent international reinsurance from being restricted by national legislation.'[26] Similarly, Hans H. Frey noted in 1979 with reference to Swiss law: 'The reinsurance treaty is a contract that is not regulated by law.'[27]

The General German Commercial Code (ADHGB) of 31 May 1861 mentioned (marine) reinsurance in Articles 782 and 783. Pursuant to Article 783 of the ADHGB, the 'risk assumed by the marine insurer (reinsurance)' could be the object of marine insurance pursuant to Article 782 of the ADHGB. In addition, there was a further explicit mention of the reinsurance relationship in Article 868, para. 3, of the ADHGB; however, this merely provided for the commencement of a term in the event of the abandonment of a right: 'In reinsurance, the abandonment term begins at the end of the day on which abandonment is declared by the insured to the reinsured.' The new German Commercial Code (HGB), which came into force on 1 January 1900 at the same time as the German Civil Code (BGB), adopted these provisions in §§ 778, 779, and in § 864, para. 3, HGB. Those were the only explicit provisions relating to reinsurance. Following the Act on the Reform of the Insurance Contract Law of 23 November 2007 (VVG),[28] these three provisions (and with them the legal definition of reinsurance in § 779 HGB) are now no longer applicable.

In § 116 of the Act on the Supervision of Insurance Undertakings (VAG) of 12 May 1901,[29] which regulated the insurance industry in terms of public law, it was stated that undertakings involved exclusively in reinsurance, with the exception of mutual insurance associations, required neither admission nor supervision. However, on the basis of a further clause of § 116 of the Insurance Contracts Act (VVG), the ordinance of the Federal Council (Bundesrat) on the supervision of domestic private reinsurance companies was enacted on 18 June 1908.[30] This stipulated that domestic reinsurance companies were subject to the regulations on accounting and reporting.[31] Although the imperial supervisory authority (Kaiserliches Aufsichtsamt) subsequently issued regulations on accounting and reporting, it held back when it came to enforcing them, in the interests of maintaining secrecy and promoting the competitiveness of the German companies.[32] The supervision of reinsurance companies thus remained significantly less rigorous than that of primary insurers.[33]

§ 186 of the Imperial VVG of 1 January 1910 stipulated that the provisions of this Act were not applicable to marine insurance or reinsurance. This was a 'purely negative provision'.[34] This German provision had a Swiss counterpart in Article 101 of the Swiss Insurance Contracts Act of 2 April 1908: 'This act is not applicable: 1. to reinsurance

[26] Prölss (1942a, 9).
[27] SRCA 10.158 903.03, Dr H. Frey, Aspekte des Rückversicherungs-Vertragsrechts, 1.
[28] Bundesgesetzblatt BGBl. 2007 I, 2631. [29] Reichsgesetzblatt RGBl. 1901, 139.
[30] Reichsgesetzblatt RGBl. 1908, 409. See Kössler (2008, 40–4).
[31] The original regulations can also be found in their entirety in Hanzlik (1911, 9).
[32] Hagen (1920, 140). [33] Kössler (2008, 44).
[34] Hagen (1920, 141); similarly Jahn (1912, 17).

treaties; [ . . . ] Only the provisions of the Code of Obligations are applicable to these treaties.'

This legislation was subsequently augmented by a number of further provisions without fundamentally changing the picture. Consequently, reinsurance law was largely not explicitly regulated by statutory law;[35] legislation was decidedly fragmentary, and, moreover, limited to defining which provisions should not be applicable. Instead, other norms took on great significance. Victor Ehrenberg and Walther Plass listed in 1908 respectively 1910 the types of legal sources for reinsurance law: agreement between the parties, customary law, the nature of the matter at hand, and, finally, civil and commercial law.[36] This sequence makes it clear that the primary focus is on the autonomy of the parties in shaping their legal relationships; accordingly, reinsurance law was primarily contract law.[37] The legal experts Ehrenberg and Plass mentioned statute law last among the sources of reinsurance law, not only due to the absence of specific provisions but also because the applicability of general norms of civil law is contingent on many factors. After all, it is necessary to clarify first which provisions of general civil law or commercial law can be applied by analogy to the reinsurance industry.

## 8.2.2 Analogous Application of Laws and General Legal Principles

This analogous application of general provisions has been the subject of much controversial debate in legal literature. The lack of specific provisions for reinsurance raised the difficult question as to whether the silence of the legislation represented a real gap that could be filled, or whether the application of analogy was ruled out because these general provisions were not appropriate for the particular nature of this industry. Application by analogy of the VVG,[38] HGB,[39] and general insurance law,[40] has repeatedly been considered as a potential source of law.

This constellation explains why so much has been written in the literature on reinsurance law about the fundamental categorization of the reinsurance treaty. Questions have been asked there about the 'essence',[41] the 'nature',[42] the '*nature of the matter*',[43] the 'legal nature',[44] the 'juridical nature',[45] and the 'juridical character'[46] of this particular

[35] See for instance *The Review*, 1961, 1420; and recently, along the same lines, Looschelders (2012, 1).
[36] Ehrenberg (1908, 1); Plass (1910, 3). [37] See Chapters 6 and 7, this volume.
[38] Heise (1932, 18, 32); Ehrenberg (1908, 11). [39] Lewis (1889, 108).
[40] See Ehrenberg (1885, 3).
[41] Ehrenzweig (1886, 176); Rau (1901, 314, 319); Lewis (1889, 112, 123); Obermayer (1912, 2).
[42] Lewis (1889, 114, 116, 126); Hagen (1920, 142); Hanzlik (1911, 16); Herrmannsdorfer (1924, 17, 41); Heise (1932, 2–6, 18); Moldenhauer (1924, cols 1045–78 (1055)); Ehrenberg (1885, 37–50).
[43] Gruenwald (1904, 276; emphasis in the original). Prölss (1942b, 121).
[44] Heun (1926, 115); Hasenclever (1935, 8); Prölss (1942b, 118).
[45] Schäfer (1900, 2). [46] Lewis (1889, 113, 125); Hanzlik (1911, 17, 24, 30–50).

contractual obligation. Depending on the type of contract to which the law of reinsurance was similar, it was possible to fall back on the 'basic principles',[47] 'principles',[48] or 'general principles'[49] of general insurance law, for example.

In other words, the low level of explicit juridification created the need to close the gaps in the system by falling back on general doctrines, on legal principles. As so often, they were needed in order to establish in as concrete a manner as possible—despite or because of their abstract nature—which form justice should take.[50] However, this did not only happen within the national framework. Particularly in such a transnational industry as reinsurance, legal principles ensured the universality of provisions, filled gaps, and set values. In other words, they were multifunctional.

### 8.2.3 Case Law

In addition to the insignificant nature of the role played by statutory law, the absence of a further source of law is also conspicuous in this overview: case law. Ehrenberg noted as far back as 1885 that case law was 'almost entirely absent' as a source of law for reinsurance.[51] There are barely any court judgements referred to in legal literature.[52] When there is recourse to case law in Germany, the judgement of the Reichsgericht (Supreme Court) of 6 March 1903 (RGZ 55, 86) is repeatedly cited. There are so few cases involving reinsurance that the court judgements that do exist are often quoted.[53] Private arbitration awards made or legal opinions requested are not really available for law-making purposes because they are not published.[54] More recent legal studies confirm that there is a 'lack of relevant court judgements'.[55]

### 8.2.4 Customary Law

Finally, customary law, which is repeatedly specified as a source of law,[56] is also associated with technical difficulties. Indeed, the regular recurrence of contract clauses is considered to be an expression of customary law,[57] and imitation is understood to be

[47] Hanzlik (1911, 24).

[48] Lewis (1889, 108, 112); Moldenhauer (1901, 19–49, 145); Hanzlik (1911, 23); Prölss (1954, 613 § 186, section 2).

[49] Hagen (1920, 141).

[50] J. Rückert (2003) 'Das BGB und seine Prinzipien. Aufgabe, Lösung, Erfolg', in M. Schmoeckel, J. Rückert, and R. Zimmermann (eds), *Historisch-kritischer Kommentar zum* BGB, vol. 1: *Allgemeiner Teil §§ 1–240*. Tübingen: Mohr Siebeck, 34–122, before § 1, margin n5.

[51] Ehrenberg (1885, 4). [52] Vahldiek (1954, 1–16). [53] Hagen (1920, 142).

[54] SRCA 10.160 179.04, Dr H. Frey, Rechtliche Aspekte des Rückversicherungsvertrages, 7.

[55] Mankowski (2002, 1177); see also recently Looschelders (2012, 1).

[56] SRCA 10.160 179.04, Dr H. Frey, Rechtliche Aspekte des Rückversicherungsvertrages, 3.

[57] Lewis (1889, 108); Ehrenberg (1908, 37).

a pattern-forming system.[58] Prölss enthused in 1942 about the uniquely global, norm-establishing strength of contractual practice: 'Since the methods and requirements of reinsurance are largely the same all over the world, *reinsurance practice can be substituted for uniform reinsurance law throughout the world* to an extent that scarcely exists in any other field.'[59]

However, identifying commercial (legal) practices is particularly difficult in the reinsurance industry. There are two factors responsible for this: first, the lack of publicity and transparency of the treaties and, second, the evidently low level of standardization of the treaty wording.

The low level of publicity as an obstacle to identify commercial (legal) practices is reflected in a variety of phenomena. It is often stated in the commercial and legal literature that the reinsurance industry conducts its business far from the public eye.[60] The pioneer of insurance studies, Alfred Manes, declared frankly: 'In short, reinsurance takes place behind closed doors.'[61] The court of appeal judge and member of the judicial council, Otto Hagen, who approvingly quoted Manes in this context in 1920,[62] confirmed that:

> [T]his form of insurance business takes place as good as completely away from the focus of public attention. In practice, only companies' own employees and the employees of the reinsured undertakings (i.e. the closed insurance world) come into contact with it; in the meantime, state supervision has become effective only within narrow limits; legal disputes are dealt with almost entirely by means of arbitration proceedings.[63]

Hagen noted in 1920 that these are 'treaties to which there is otherwise no regular public access'.[64] This limited publicity received by agreements reached through private autonomy is one of the key reasons why identifying the provisions of customary law is beset with particular difficulties.[65]

There is also a second factor. If one believes the evidence of the literature, the level of standardization in reinsurance treaties at the beginning of the twentieth century was not particularly high (in contrast to general insurance law).[66] The reinsurers do not appear to have used pre-formulated general terms and conditions with their policyholders,[67] or at least not systematically.[68] In 1920, Hagen asserted the following:

[58] Ehrenzweig (1881, 75).
[59] Prölss (1942a, 10; emphasis in the original). Similar: Prölss (1942b, 129).
[60] Schäfer (1900, 1); Herrmannsdorfer (1924, v); *The Review*, 1965, 210–12; Pfeiffer (1994, 16).
[61] Manes (1913, 456 § 60). [62] Manes (1913, 456 § 60).
[63] Hagen (1920, 138). [64] Hagen (1920, 142 n17).
[65] Looschelders (2012, 1). [66] Scherner (2011, 220).
[67] SRCA 10.160 179.04; Pfeiffer (1994, 16–18). On the legal history of general terms and conditions see P. Hellwege (2010) *Allgemeine Geschäftsbedingungen, einseitig gestellte Vertragsbedingungen und die allgemeine Rechtsgeschäftslehre (Jus Privatum 148)*. Tübingen: Mohr Siebeck.
[68] Mainardi (1925, 64–7): there are 'general conditions for facultative reinsurance business of the Internationaler Transport-Versicherungs-Verband'. Their exceptional character is stressed by Prölss (1942b, 127).

> Reinsurance differs from other branches of insurance in terms of how it regulates itself; in that general conditions of insurance are not usual in the same way that they are elsewhere; instead of standardised general conditions, contractual relationships within the reinsurance area are regulated on a case by case basis by unique treaties.[69]

The Cologne professor of insurance law, Paul Moldenhauer, noted: 'The conditions of insurance found in other branches of insurance are unknown in reinsurance. [...] *In general, however, reinsurance treaties are agreed as required in each specific case,* although *certain types* do emerge over time.'[70] The English reinsurance doyen Cecil Edward Golding declared in 1937:[71] 'there is no standardised form of wording applicable even to treaties of the same kind, for ceding companies use such wording as is best adapted to their needs and this is not always the same, whether as between companies in the same country or in different countries'.[72]

Where there are references to general conditions of insurance in reinsurance law, it is noted that these general terms and conditions are not made public.[73] Discretion and even secrecy was thus part of the way business was done in an industry that did not reveal its instruments of self-regulation. There were only the initiatives to increase cooperation and coordination in the reinsurance business, which finally enforced the standardization of the contractual handling of clients from the 1970s onwards under the banner of increased industry integration.[74]

This discretion and secrecy as well as the absence of general terms and conditions also explain why the literature on reinsurance law is avowedly devoted to the collection and reproduction of individual reinsurance treaties,[75] or even individual clauses.[76] In view of the low level of publicity given to the industry's practices, these have an important role to play in terms of documentation, and they close a gap in the scientific debate. The recording and reprinting of the settlements between parties is the prerequisite for being able to establish general customary law and deal with legal issues in the context of actual business practices. The Austrian insurance law expert Adolf Ehrenzweig declared in 1881 that such collections of material were necessary for an understanding of the law.[77] In 1900, Wilhelm Schäfer referred to the necessity of making use of records and internal company information.[78] Modern training and educational material also include such collections of authentic contract clauses.[79] In other words, the collection of material was already recognized as a method around a hundred years ago and has become established in the scientific discourse about reinsurance law.

[69] Hagen (1920, 142). [70] Moldenhauer (1924, col. 1066; emphasis in the original).

[71] There is a brief appreciation of Golding at: <http://www.insurancehalloffame.org/laureateprofile.php?laureate=34> (accessed 12 February 2013).

[72] Golding (1937, 72). [73] Ehrenberg (1885, 5). [74] Gugerli (2013, 196).

[75] See, for example, Diamantidi (1918, 65); Mainardi (1925, 53); Golding (1937, 221–54); Pfeiffer (1994, 91).

[76] Manes (1913, 465 § 61). [77] Ehrenzweig (1881, 75). [78] Schäfer (1900, 2).

[79] SRCA 10.160 179.04, PM/WT (Koordination), 'Principles of Reinsurance', cover page: '[This article] is compromised exclusively of quotations from reinsurance treaties.'

A variety of sources of law thus exist in reinsurance law, but there are certain characteristics stressing the difference to other fields of commercial law. There is a conspicuous absence of special laws and case law. Instead, reference is made in many cases to the will of the parties involved. Prölss made the following comment in generalizing about the VVG: 'Reinsurance is regulated only by means of treaties.'[80] Frey noted the following for his reinsurance course at Swiss Re in 1979: 'The reinsurance treaty is by far the most important source of law.'[81] Where there are gaps to be filled, it is necessary to fall back on general legal principles or selected norms of general insurance law or the general law of obligations.[82]

## 8.3 Resistance to Codification and Avoidance of State Jurisdiction

In its moderate pluralism, this system of sources of the law reflects a relatively high degree of autonomy for economic actors in Continental European law; the reinsurance industry has evidently been able to largely resist being affected by ongoing codification efforts, there has been supervision by the authorities only to a limited extent, and it has not dealt with its conflicts primarily in the state courts.

The questions discussed in Sections 8.3.1 and 8.3.2 as to the motives behind resistance to codification and avoidance of the courts began to arise when legislators first discovered and articulated an interest in regulating the reinsurance industry. This is not a matter of course. Observations in the USA in the period before 1914 even indicate that the reinsurance industry and its particular features were not necessarily perceived any differently from the rest of the insurance industry.[83] This recognition on the part of legislators required them to work their way into the particular problems and practices of an industry that was not at all noticeable in the contract business, nor did it attract any public attention through its activities. Not until legislators began to take notice of the reinsurance industry at this time did reinsurers come under pressure to resist being included in ongoing codification efforts.

### 8.3.1 Avoidance of the Law?

One could interpret this legal policy strategy of the reinsurers as reflecting a general aversion to law as an instrument of regulation. Indeed, in portrayals of the reinsurance

80 Prölss (1954, 613 § 186, section 2).

81 SRCA 10.158 903.03, Dr H. Frey, Aspekte des Rückversicherungs-Vertragsrechts, 2, and SRCA 10.160 179.04, Dr H. Frey, Rechtliche Aspekte des Rückversicherungsvertrages, 2.

82 Description for Swiss law in Salzmann (1967, 277–89).

83 Hotchkiss (1914, 1–3).

industry both by insiders and outsiders, reference has been made regularly to the key role played by 'trust' in business practice.[84] Manes, for example, emphasized that 'the whole reinsurance industry is built on mutual trust to an extremely large extent'.[85] Rau noted in 1901 that: 'there can be no other contract that relies on the goodwill and honesty of the parties involved as much as the reinsurance treaty'.[86] The latest research into the history of the industry also stresses this aspect: 'Reinsurance is often characterized as a business built on personal relationships, goodwill and mutual trust.'[87]

These evocations of trust, goodwill, and honesty also refer to the binding force of social norms with which the actors involved are obliged to comply. Conventions and conferences, such as the ones held in Monte Carlo since 1957, also serve this purpose.[88] In other words, the reinsurance industry is understood as a closed system as far as possible and is presented (also rhetorically) in such a way that it is possible to make clear distinctions both internally and externally.

However, the law should not be automatically kept out of agreements and conflict settlements; these should not rely on a moral, ethical sense of duty alone. After all, the self-organization and self-regulation strategies of reinsurers were evidently based on law as a normative order—just not on statute law.[89] This very specific regulatory regime was to be constructed on the basis of contracts or treaties and general terms and conditions rather than laws. The reinsurance industry was thus not prejudiced against the legal normativity as such; instead, the industry's preference was clearly to create its own law, which would apparently take the place of statute law. However, the embedding of the reinsurance treaty in the general legal framework was not discussed, and no issue was made of the interfaces between statutory law and the law created by the industry itself.

## 8.3.2 Resistance to Codification and the Associated Arguments

In the course of the twentieth century, the protagonists involved in the reinsurance industry rejected statute law and supervision by state authorities with great unanimity. The fundamental positions are adopted again on a regular basis when new codification efforts are made; at the same time, the long-standing debates about juridification turn the focus onto the business and legal interests involved. The debate about the draft legislation on insurance contracts serves as an example. In the early years of the twentieth century, the regulation of the (primary) insurance market was discussed.

[84] Ehrenberg (1885, 28); Jahn (1912, 45); SRCA 10.160 179.04, Dr H. Frey, Rechtliche Aspekte des Rückversicherungsvertrages, 5; Stahl and Meyenburg (2006, 201); Pfeiffer (1994, 16); Gugerli (2013, 158, 168).

[85] Manes (1913, 468 § 61).

[86] Rau (1901, 416).

[87] Chapter 3, this volume. Similarly: Milligan-Whyte and Veed (1989, 124).

[88] Gugerli (2013, 152, 178ff.).

[89] Abramovsky (2008, 25).

As far as the reinsurers were concerned, the inclusion of their industry in the draft legislation was the sensitive issue.

The opinions of Heinrich Gruenwald, a director of Kölnische Rückversicherungs-Gesellschaft in Cologne, were prominent in discussions of the legislation in the first decade after 1900. In 1903, Gruenwald explicitly attacked not just the contents of the draft legislation; he also rejected the suggestion that the reinsurance industry should be included in the planned provisions at all:

> It follows from all this that the legislation does not create a satisfactory situation for the reinsurance industry, and it is therefore understandable that the industry *does not wish to be subjected* to such legislation. However, even if it were to be asked whether the position adopted by the reinsurance industry towards this legislation could be different if the provisions involved were to match its needs more closely, the answer, given the experience of practice, would have to be no.[90]

That was fighting talk designed to resist the juridification of the business relationships of reinsurers; they should not be affected by the juridification of the primary insurance relationship.

Gruenwald took the view that the juridification of the reinsurance industry was wrong in principle:

> As far as the reinsurance companies involved are concerned, there is absolutely *no* need in practice for the statutory regulation of reinsurance; its absence thus far has not been perceived as a problem in any way in business life. They see no need at all for any codification of the law affecting their line of business, and they see no benefits of any kind from such codification, only numerous disadvantages resulting from the new necessity to anxiously ensure, when drafting their treaties and in all their business activities, that all provisions of the law that have to be regarded as inappropriate for their business are excluded or altered.[91]

A strategy for preventing the reinsurance industry from being subjected to the planned provisions against its wishes was thus formed: the parties involved would eliminate the provisions of the legislation as far as possible from the private, autonomous agreements concluded between themselves. This indicated that it would be possible to lawfully thwart the normative offerings of legislators designed to regulate the reinsurance industry and replace them with provisions agreed by the parties themselves.

In a contribution to a journal in 1954, L. Tytens from Brussels (presumably a representative of the reinsurance industry) declared: 'It is a pity that laws and regulations must be enacted in connection with reinsurance because this to a certain extent alters the nature of reinsurance.'[92] Tytens argued against any form of state intervention, whether it took the form of monopolization, control, or legislation, because 'reinsurance is best left alone from all official interference'.[93] The arguments that

[90] Gruenwald (1904, 278; emphasis in the original).
[91] Gruenwald (1904, 278; emphasis in the original).
[92] *The Review*, 3 December 1954, 1168.
[93] *The Review*, 3 December 1954, 1170.

were developed around 1900 during the discussions of the proposed legislation proved to be salient for many years. Decades later they were employed again in new debates about regulation.

Gruenwald's arguments have been quoted extensively in this section and presented as representative, but there was, of course, an opposing standpoint. This was formulated by Moldenhauer, a lecturer at the commercial college (Handelshochschule) in Cologne, who argued in favour of the juridification of the reinsurance industry in the context of the draft legislation on insurance contracts. He pleaded for 'the establishment of certain principles of reinsurance law that are still being disputed in the courts or by some companies'.[94] He added that this should be done on the principle 'that the legislation exercises prudent moderation, only regulates where it is absolutely necessary and does not seek to establish principles for arrangements or issues that are still in the process of development'.[95]

Of course, Moldenhauer did not win the argument; the efforts to introduce juridification failed, and the draft provisions were removed from the VVG. The German reinsurance industry was thus able to assert its normative ideas in this case at least. The arguments put forward by the industry also come up in earlier and later discussions of legal policy for the purpose of resisting codification.

#### *8.3.2.1 No Consumer Involvement*

The main argument and standard justification put forward by the reinsurers for the absence of state intervention is that any involvement of legislators with the aim of offering material protection would be inappropriate. Justifications for state intervention, as in typical consumer protection constellations,[96] could not be brought forward either by the state or interest groups. That is because it was not possible to identify a need to protect a supposedly weaker contracting party in the context of reinsurance—in contrast to social insurance, for example.[97] Both parties in reinsurance are insurance companies, as stated in the justification for the draft VVG (Begründung zum Entwurfe), and are thus 'generally business customers and, as such, sufficiently able to ensure that their interests are protected'.[98] The following appeared in the *Handwörterbuch der Staatswissenschaften* (a pocket dictionary of political science) of 1901: 'Provisions of the state against mismanagement, as deemed to be necessary these days in most types of primary insurance involving greater or lesser degrees of intervention, would be entirely superfluous and unnecessarily restrictive in reinsurance because transactions are only conducted between parties experienced in business.'[99] In 1903, Ehrenberg emphasized that the parties were 'members of groups with business

[94] Moldenhauer (1904, 281). [95] Moldenhauer (1904, 282).

[96] M. Vec (2009) 'Consumer Protection (Medieval and Post-Medieval Roman Law)', in S. Katz (ed.), *The Oxford International Encyclopedia of Legal History (ELH)*, vol. 2. New York: Oxford University Press, 169–73.

[97] Neumann (1911, 80).

[98] Quoted from Hanzlik (1911, 12). [99] Emminghaus (1901, 474).

expertise'.[100] Frey noted around 1980: 'Primary insurers and reinsurers are informed, competent contracting parties; there is no reason for legislation to protect the weaker party.'[101] Swiss Re stated in 2010 that: 'Reinsurance clients are sophisticated counterparties such as insurers, brokers or other reinsurers.'[102] This was designed to undermine arguments in favour of legislative intervention seeking to correct any asymmetry in terms of the information available to the parties or their negotiating power. This argument has been much used by reinsurers, but it is not necessarily a convincing one because there was indeed asymmetry in the information available to contracting parties: the reinsurers had more comprehensive, more 'global' data, whereas the primary insurers knew their own business model better than the reinsurers. There was thus plenty of scope to debate asymmetries.

Unlike in countless other fields of civil law, however, the reinsurance industry was largely able—operating under the banner of consumer protection—to resist these efforts to turn away from the liberal model of private autonomy and classical private law based on freedom and equality and instead to establish binding minimum standards and make instruments available for their compulsory enforcement.[103] However, consumer protection was of no significance in the reinsurance business, and interventions in the interests of a group of people who could be said to be in need of protection did not seem relevant.

### 8.3.2.2 *The Ideal of 'Elasticity'*

A further theme in the arguments against juridification and, at the same time, an indication of the reinsurers' ideas, was the ideal of 'freedom of movement'. Ehrenburg spoke about this and also used the term 'elasticity' in this context.[104] This is not an economic term in this case but an ideal in jurisprudence describing the relationship between legal norms and socio-economic change.

The reinsurers thus resisted restrictions that would entail the enactment of statute law. Instead, they demanded flexibility and adaptability. The ideal that inspired such an approach to jurisprudence, with an antipathy to primary legislation, was evidently based primarily on the desire to facilitate business development.[105] According to the reinsurers, the state could best achieve this by refraining from putting in place statutory provisions. Enforcement and state intervention, on the other hand, were also rejected for macroeconomic reasons. In a speech to the Insurance Institute in London in 1954,

[100] Ehrenberg (1903, 204).

[101] SRCA 10.160 179.04, Dr H. Frey, Rechtliche Aspekte des Rückversicherungsvertrages, 2.

[102] Swiss Re (2010, 39).

[103] M. Schmoeckel (2007) 'Grundlagen der Verbrauchergeschäfte', in M. Schmoeckel, J. Rückert, and R. Zimmermann (eds), *Historisch-kritischer Kommentar zum BGB*, vol. 2: *Schuldrecht. Allgemeiner Teil, 2. Teilband §§ 305–432*. Tübingen: Mohr Siebeck, 1581–667 before §§ 312ff.; M. Schmoeckel (2007) 'Besondere Betriebsformen', in M. Schmoeckel, J. Rückert, and R. Zimmermann (eds), *Historisch-kritischer Kommentar zum BGB*, vol. 2: *Schuldrecht. Allgemeiner Teil, 2. Teilband §§ 305–432*. Tübingen: Mohr Siebeck, 1668–707 §§ 312–21f.

[104] Ehrenberg (1903, 205).

[105] Vec (2006, 280–91).

Werner Nierhaus of Munich Re warned: 'Private companies, managers in the spirit of free enterprise, will always be more enterprising, flexible, and efficient than governmental insurance offices with their red-tape methods. Any state intervention is contrary to the very nature of our profession.'[106] The liberal economic principles expressed here led to legislation being regarded as restricting freedom and as rigid.

On the other hand, the desire for flexibility and adaptability meant that adjustments could be made to suit the economic needs of reinsurers but also of economies, something that would not be possible with legislation, given its rigidity and binding nature. The numerous references to the technological and economic change that the reinsurance industry had to,[107] and still has to, deal with ('technological progress and the increasing level of interconnectedness in the economy and society';[108] growing and new kinds of risks[109]) also had a purpose in terms of legal policy. As far as those who spoke for the reinsurance industry were concerned, these provided evidence of why the establishment of standards that do not change with time can only hinder business activity and be deleterious to the common good and so were thus dismissed. According to this view, it was not possible to cope with far-reaching technological and economic changes when saddled with rigid legislation; instead, (only) self-regulation could provide the scope for normative flexibility desired by the industry which a legislative form of normativity would only threaten. This much talked about adaptability or flexibility should be pursued, it was said, by avoiding legislation and promoting self-regulation. Frey acclaimed the effects of resisting codification around 1980: 'The absence of rigid statutory regulation has given reinsurers the opportunity in practice to adapt reinsurance treaties to serve the changing needs of primary insurers and develop new forms of treaty.'[110]

### 8.3.2.3 *Internationalism*

Finally, there are repeated references in the literature on reinsurance law to the internationalism of the industry and its treaties.[111] This internationalism was also used in arguments put forward to support the legal policy strategy of preventing legislation. Gruenwald wrote in 1903: 'The majority of primary [insurance] companies seek to achieve their business objectives primarily by exploiting their *domestic* market, whereas reinsurance is predominantly *international*.'[112]

Gruenwald concluded from this that legislation was dysfunctional and that, if it came to codification, international activities and national regulation would be in

[106] *The Review*, 14 December 1956, 1228. [107] *The Review*, 1968, 3; Böcker (1935, 41).

[108] Mumenthaler (2005, 1). [109] *The Review*, 14 December 1956, 1222.

[110] SRCA 10.160 179.04, Dr H. Frey, Rechtliche Aspekte des Rückversicherungsvertrages, 2.

[111] Vallebona (1889, 135); Ehrenzweig (1880, 24); *The Review*, 3 December 1954, 1148; Mainardi (1925, 35); *The Review*, 14 December 1956, 1227; *The Review*, 9 December 1949, 925. Research also emphasizes the reinsurance industry's 'strong international orientation right from the start', see Werner (2010).

[112] Gruenwald (1904, 279; emphasis in the original).

conflict, and this would even be detrimental to achieving the objectives of the legislation:

> The reinsurer, on the other hand, could expect the legislation to regulate only its contractual relationships in the German market, in other words relationships that often play no greater role in the company than those with companies in any other geographical area. Here, too, this regulation would be of extremely minor significance to the reinsurer's most important kind of contractual relationships, namely obligatory treaties, and possibly of no significance at all.'[113]

Nierhaus also stressed this point in his speech in London in 1954:

> From this [the international nature of reinsurance] necessarily follows that any restriction interfering with the free play of forces and with the possibility of covering risks on a world-wide basis will seriously jeopardise the capacity and efficiency of reinsurers. [ . . . ] This unpleasant topic embraces all state interventions ranging from measures taken to protect the domestic markets to establishing state insurance offices.'[114]

The state also had to give this conclusive argument serious consideration. That is because companies with international activities were indeed exposed to very different legal systems and diverging provisions. Consequently, legislation implemented within a national framework would only have a partial impact on them, regardless of the motivation behind it. In other words, the possible abandonment of juridification had the potential to reflect helplessness on the part of legislators. This had structural causes and resulted from the mismatch between national legislation and international business activities.

Unfair treatment could also be argued: the international nature of activities would result in German reinsurers within Germany being subject to a stricter regime, whereas their foreign competitors would be able to operate in the global market free of these constraints. This unfair treatment would thus result in disadvantages and have a negative impact on the companies and the national economy. An appeal was therefore made to legislators on behalf of domestic companies to fulfil their protective, beneficial role, and attempts were made to persuade them not to engage in any norm-setting activity. The justification for the draft VVG explicitly rejected the imposition of constraints on the freedom of contract of reinsurers through compulsory provisions, with the aim of ensuring 'the insurer's scope for adapting its conditions of insurance to suit legislation and conditions in other countries'.[115]

Conversely, it must also be considered that some unfair treatment of reinsurers by national legislation was intentional and thus the desired effect of the legislation. Wherever there was a desire to favour domestic reinsurers, it was possible to close the domestic market to foreign companies through legislation. Just because this did not happen in either Germany or Switzerland does not mean that it did not happen

[113] Gruenwald (1904, 279). [114] *The Review*, 14 December 1956, 1227.
[115] Quoted from Hanzlik (1911, 12).

elsewhere in the world in the twentieth century, far from it. Particularly in planned economies, there was a tendency to protect domestic markets from global competition and/or bring foreign companies, in particular, under control.

### *8.3.2.4 Result: Relatively Successful Resistance to Regulation*

As far as the reinsurers were concerned, there were thus a whole series of arguments against statutory regulation of reinsurance law in the VVG. With hindsight, however, it is possible to read them as position statements that went well beyond the specific circumstances involved, and canonized a powerful array of weaponry supporting the cause of resistance to juridification of which the industry has repeatedly been able to make use. Gruenwald concluded that the inclusion of reinsurance in codification was neither in the public interest nor in anyone's private interests:

> Thus while I dispute that regulating the reinsurance industry through legislation is in the *private* interest of those involved, I can feel even more confident in my belief that it is also not in the *public* interest because I know that in this respect I essentially share the same view as a recognised authority in this specific field, namely Professor *Ehrenberg*.[116]

This and similar pleas for self-regulation have been relatively successful in the history of German and Swiss reinsurance law.[117] In the consultations that took place during the drafting of the VVG, German legislators accepted Gruenwald's arguments, and the second draft (submitted to the Federal Council (Bundesrat) in March 1905), as well as the draft submitted to the Reichstag in November 1905, made reference to the differences between reinsurance and other forms of insurance and ensured the former were not subject to the same provisions. The reinsurance industry was thus able to avoid juridification of its activities for many decades to a greater extent than other industries. Ehrenberg noted in 1903 that the interest groups were able to celebrate great success.[118] He saw this by no means as a shortcoming of this field of law; on the contrary. The fact that this particular constellation also enabled legal scholars to shape this field of law by their interpretations and complements undoubtedly contributed to this view.

According to the insurance law expert, Ehrenberg, in 1903, and the court of appeal judge and member of the judicial council, Hagen, in 1920, regulatory loopholes should be closed by analogy through case law and, above all, jurisprudence.[119] In Switzerland, too, parallel interventions by reinsurers can be found;[120] they prevented

[116] Gruenwald (1904, 280; emphasis in the original).

[117] Reinsurers have made these kinds of pleas all over the world. See, for example, *The Review*, November 1986, 5. The focus of this contribution is primarily on the history of German and Swiss reinsurance law. It is not claimed to be global in scope.

[118] Ehrenberg (1903, 204).

[119] Ehrenberg (1903, 211); in agreement with him: Gruenwald (1904, 280). See also Hagen (1920, 138).

[120] See, for example: Bemerkungen schweizerischer und auswärtiger, in der Schweiz konzessionierter Feuer-, Transport- und Rück-Versicherungsgesellschaften zu dem von Herrn Professor Dr H. Roelli im Auftrage des Bundesrates ausgearbeiteten Entwurfe zu einem Bundesgesetz über den

the reinsurance treaty from being regulated in the planned VVG as provided for in the draft legislation.

These disputes took place against the backdrop of the regulatory regime of comparatively liberal states and in the context of Continental European law in non-totalitarian periods. The premise in both Germany and Switzerland was the legitimacy and legality in principle of a private-sector reinsurance industry with international activities as well as private autonomy.[121] The industry was concerned to protect this private autonomy from being interfered with by legislators or bureaucrats. This premise could by no means be taken for granted in an international comparison. Attempts were repeatedly made to restrict freedom of contract and even to nationalize reinsurance companies during the course of the twentieth century and in numerous different countries. These followed economic cycles and, above all, changes of political system in individual economies (between the wars, for example).[122] Nationalization changed the business models and forms of economic activity of the reinsurers.[123] Attempts to nationalize reinsurers were, of course, castigated and rejected in the juridical literature relating to reinsurance law even more sharply than mere efforts to introduce regulation in certain areas.

## 8.3.3 Self-Regulation of Conflicts and Avoidance of State Jurisdiction

The self-regulation of the industry through private autonomous norm establishment and the conclusion of treaties has been complemented by autonomous conflict resolution through arbitration tribunals. This has been the norm historically.[124] It has remained typical for reinsurance treaties right up until the present day,[125] and evidence of this can also be found in German reinsurance treaties before the twentieth century:[126] 'The reinsurance industry has enjoyed the relative neglect of the courts for centuries.'[127]

Versicherungsvertrag, St. Gallen 1897 [Comments by Swiss and foreign fire and transport insurers and reinsurers with authorisation to work in Switzerland on the draft Insurance Contracts Act drawn up by Professor Dr H. Roelli on behalf of the Federal Council, St. Gallen 1897].

[121] S. Hofer (2001) *Freiheit ohne Grenzen? Privatrechtstheoretische Diskussionen im 19. Jahrhundert (Jus Privatum 53).* Tübingen: Mohr Siebeck.

[122] *The Review*, 11 October 1929, 978; Hollitscher (1931, 12, 93); *The Review*, 1932, 177; Gugerli (2013, 176); *The Review*, 4 October 1968, 1140.

[123] *The Review*, 26 February 1965, 226.

[124] Manes (1913, 468 § 61); Diamantidi (1918, 33); Mainardi (1925, 50); Hagen (1920, 138); Prölss (1954, 613 § 186, section 2); *The Review*, January 1988, 23.

[125] Jericho (1988, 289); Biagosch (2007, 2008); Gerathewohl et al. (1976, 583); Nonna and Strassberg (1986, 586–611); Labes (1996).

[126] Gerathewohl (1979, 766).

[127] Milligan-Whyte and Veed (1989, 122).

Ehrenberg noted in 1903 that it was extremely rare for the reinsured to take legal action in the courts.[128] Gruenwald stated with pride in 1903 that Kölnische Rückversicherungs-Gesellschaft had never, in the previous fifty years, had a dispute with any of its reinsured that ended up in court.[129] This statement was repeatedly quoted in the subsequent literature,[130] because it puts a figure on the extent to which the courts were avoided. In addition, Mossner wrote about an arbitration clause from 1829 that was never used in the seventy-three years for which the treaty containing it remained in force.[131]

This approach of institutionalizing arbitration tribunals as the instrument of conflict resolution in the industry was clearly so widespread that, in some cases, the decisions of these tribunals were recorded in a standardized form. In 1925, Riccardo Mainardi provided evidence of 'arbitration tribunal provisions for disputes based on reinsurance treaties of the Internationaler Transport-Versicherungs-Verband'.[132] Arbitration promises to be a more efficient, more practice-based way to reach decisions.[133]

The autonomy of the reinsurance industry in terms of conflict regulation is also reflected in its internal training literature. This instructs those entering the industry in conflict resolution, by presenting case-based training using either fictitious or authentic cases. The sample resolutions—often written by hand on the records that are available—outline the key points of the correct answers or arbitration tribunal decisions.[134] However, in contrast to typical legal training or educational material, the resolutions are provided without any reference to legal foundations.[135] The resolution is evidently based on an assessment of the treaty situation, taking legal ethics and general principles of insurance law into account, without having to fall back on normative statutory provisions.[136]

## 8.4 Outlook: Bringing the State Back In?

The picture painted in this chapter primarily describes a particular national (mainly German but also Swiss and Austrian) regulatory framework, and is limited to a number of decades in the late nineteenth and early twentieth centuries; in other words, the

[128] Also Ehrenberg (1903): 'It was extremely rare for the reinsured to take legal action in the courts' (quoted from Gruenwald (1904, 278)).

[129] Gruenwald (1904, 278).

[130] Hanzlik (1911, 2).

[131] Mossner (1959, 92, 93ff.).

[132] Mainardi (1925, 67–9).

[133] Jahn (1912, 47); Biagosch (2007, 2008).

[134] SRCA 10.158 903.03, Dr H. Frey, Aspekte des Rückversicherungs-Vertragsrechts.

[135] SRCA 10.160 179.04, RV-Fachausbildung.

[136] SRCA 10.160 179.04, RV-Fachausbildung.

initial phase of the organization of the reinsurance industry. Accordingly, the Continental European legal system was the point of reference, and the focus was on periods in which the legitimacy and legality in principle of a private-sector reinsurance industry with international activities was accepted, and in which there was a fear of juridification, above all, by parliament and national bureaucracies; on the other hand, these national institutions themselves were revealed to be powerless against a very international industry.

However, new protagonists have come into play since then. The European Union (EU) is establishing its own norms, and these are also applicable to reinsurers. Reinsurers were not initially included in the regime of directives relating to insurance law because they focused only on primary insurance.[137] This picture changed with the directive 2005/68/EC on reinsurance,[138] which was transposed into German law on 1 February 2007 as the eighth amendment of the Insurance Supervision Act and the Financial Services Act (8th VAG amendment). Reinsurance companies based in Germany are thus subject to a requirement to have approval and legal and financial supervision by the German Federal Financial Supervisory Authority (BaFin). This introduction of reinsurance supervision was apparently in line with the wishes of international financial market institutions. These sought to stabilize international financial markets and improve the supervision of reinsurance companies after 9/11.[139] At the same time, previously highly disparate national systems of regulation were standardized,[140] and this tightened provisions relating to the supervision of reinsurance companies. The reasons for doing this included, in addition to security aspects, the desire to improve the economic strength and competitiveness of European insurers in the global market. Further regulation is also coming into play, such as the Dodd–Frank Wall Street Reform and Consumer Protection Act, Solvency II, and Basel III, whose impact on the reinsurance industry is also the subject of lively debate.[141] As a result, there is therefore a whole host of legal provisions establishing norms in the various fields of activity, depending on the location of the reinsurance company.[142]

The years from 1980 to 2010, which represented the third phase of the organizational development of the reinsurance business, were characterized, accordingly, not just by deregulation and liberalization in the global economy,[143] but also, in particular, by new impetus in terms of regulation.

[137] Mankowski (2002, 1177).

[138] Directive 2005/68/EC, Council Directives 73/239/EEC, 92/49/EEC, as well as Directives 98/78/EC and 2002/83/EC.

[139] Galahn (2007, 390).

[140] Falush (1997, § IV A and *passim*).

[141] Fürer (2011); Webel (2010); Osetrova (2007).

[142] Wang (2002). An exemplary overview in SRCA 10.166 961.04, Pierre Ozendo, Information on Reinsurance Regulations.

[143] Gugerli (2013, 152, 210ff., 217, 225).

This wave of regulation was observed by reinsurers with considerable concern in some cases.[144] The arguments employed to resist regulation were to some extent similar to those used in the period examined here: the specific differences from the industries particularly affected by regulation already or about to be affected were highlighted: 'But financial institutions differ greatly from one another and it is important their unique characteristics are taken into account when new regulations are developed.'[145] These distinctions were drawn and continue to be drawn, above all, to the banking sector: 'The business model of insurers is fundamentally different from that of banks. [...] Excessive regulations may also create competitive distortions. [...] traditional business industry is very unlikely to become the source of systemic risk.'[146] It thus becomes clear that the reference point of the comparison has shifted. Instead of differentiating reinsurance from the insurance industry and consumer protection, which seemed threatening around 1900, it is now being differentiated from the banks[147]—with reinsurance and primary insurance currently both being put in the same category: 'The main purpose of insurance regulation is to protect policy holders. This is in contrast to banking regulation, which—besides protecting depositors—aims to maintain the stability of the financial system.'[148]

The justification for resistance to juridification and control has thus changed: the objective remains the same, it is just the comparison parameters that have changed. Instead of differentiating reinsurers from (primary) insurers, they are differentiated from banks in order to avoid becoming the victim of intervention by governments and states.

This strategy of resisting regulation has not been entirely successful, and reinsurers are now increasingly subject to juridification. This is underlined by the observations made initially about the relationship between self-regulation and state intervention. The field of reinsurance is becoming subject to a process of regulation and juridification in which a variety of actors are engaged in normative activity. Accordingly, it is not possible to identify a pattern of pure self-organization and self-normalization of the reinsurance industry; here, too, the state and communities of nations are creating the framework. It is not possible, then, to speak of a completely (private) autonomous regulatory regime. The self-regulation that takes place here is not entirely free of the state's influence. As so often in modern regulatory regimes, the private sector and state are both playing a role in shaping regulation, and both public and civil law are involved.[149] The degree of freedom involved does seem to be comparatively high, depending on where you set the reference points of the comparison. However, this process has not concluded, and the new international and transnational actors, in

144 'Swiss Re gegen strengere Regeln: Rückversicherung warnt vor Folgen für die Realwirtschaft' (*Frankfurter Allgemeine Zeitung*, 10 December 2009), 24.

145 Swiss Re (2010, 37).

146 Swiss Re, *sigma*, 3, 2010, 1.

147 *Versicherungstag in Berlin—Seitenhiebe gegen Banken* (Der Platow Brief, 19 November 2010), quotes Munich Re CEO Nikolaus von Bomhard.

148 Swiss Re, *sigma*, 3, 2010, 2.

149 Collin et al. (2012, vii).

particular, are striving to establish norms,[150] thus lending legitimacy to their existence and causing them to collaborate and compete with other regulatory institutions: 'In the age of globalisation, decisions are being taken before our eyes involving nation states, world state and partially systemic internal policy about a new design for regulation, a coming normative order.'[151]

[150] See *The Review*, June 2002, 11: 'numerous international organisations and bodies whose actions will affect them [re/insurers] too'.

[151] G. Bender (2012) 'Tarifautonomie, Regulierte Selbstregulierung, Korporatismus', in P. Collin et al. (eds), *Regulierte Selbstregulierung im frühen Interventions- und Sozialstaat (Studien zur europäischen Rechtsgeschichte 270)*. Frankfurt am Main: Vittorio Klostermann, 53–67, here 56.

CHAPTER 9

# WHAT IS AN INSURABLE RISK? SWISS RE AND ATOMIC REACTOR INSURANCE

LORRAINE DASTON

## 9.1 Introduction: An Entirely New Kind of Risk

In January 1956, representatives of insurance firms from ten West European countries met in Paris to discuss 'a new and important risk' and whether this 'new danger, this new hazard could be included in a policy'.[1] The twenty-one delegates constituted the Groupe de Travail du Risque Atomique, which was established by the Comité Européen des Assurances on the initiative of Swiss Re. Swiss Re quickly assumed the leadership of the working group and guided the formulation of the insurance guidelines at both the national and international level, as European insurers navigated between the International Atomic Energy Agency (IAEA),[2] the Organization for European Economic Cooperation (OEEC),[3] and a patchwork of national regulatory laws.[4] The key role played by Swiss Re in making atomic risks insurable is surprising on

[1] SRCA 10.158 622.01, Comité Européen des Assurances, 41 (translated quote). The countries represented were: Austria, Belgium, Denmark, Finland, France, Great Britain, Italy, the German Federal Republic, Sweden, and Switzerland.

[2] The IAEA resulted from the United Nations (UN) conference on the Peaceable Uses of Atomic Energy held in Geneva in August 1955, and began operations in 1957.

[3] The OEEC was founded in 1948 to help administer the Marshall Plan in Europe. In 1961 it was reorganized (and expanded) into the Organization for Economic Development.

[4] The IAEA was an agency of the UN and the Nuclear Energy Agency (NEA) was an agency of the Organisation for Economic Co-operation and Development (OECD). The alphabet soup of acronyms was made still more confusing by the fact that, in different languages, the same agency was known by different abbreviations: e.g. IAEA in English, but IAEO in German. On the history of the IAEA, see

several counts, not least because some in its own higher echelons at first responded to the prospect of insuring atomic reactors with the utmost wariness,[5] to the point of wondering whether any kind of insurance made sense in the atomic age.[6] Yet only a decade later, members of Swiss Re's board of directors were invoking atomic reactor insurance as a model for dealing with all kinds of other problematic risks,[7] from ever-bigger airplanes to ever-more-frequent hurricanes.[8] A *sui generis* risk that defied all the rules of responsible insurance had been tamed.

How did this happen—and happen so quickly? Formidable challenges loomed in 1956: there were no statistics upon which to base probability estimates of the risks of peaceable uses of atomic energy and the harms to persons and damage to property in the case of a serious accident were potentially unlimited—both in terms of costs and duration. Additionally, the risks were multiple and complex, from the shipping of radioactive materials to the disposal of waste products with half-lives longer than all of recorded human history. Meanwhile, relevant scientific knowledge about atomic energy and engineering know-how about building reactors changed on an almost daily basis. And that was only the beginning of the conundrums confronting the European insurers. They also had to coordinate (and try to influence) the legal frameworks of multiple countries, all of which were in the process of drafting their own regulations for the use of atomic energy, with notably different aims (for example, private versus state ownership of reactor facilities).

Then there was the emergent layer of international regulatory bodies: European Atomic Energy Community (EURATOM),[9] the OEEC, and the IAEA with interests

D. Fischer (1997) *History of the International Atomic Energy Agency: The First Forty Years*. Vienna: IAEA; H.-F. Meyer (2007) 'Die Geschichte der Internationalen Atomenergie-Organisation IAEO', in D. Schiefer, W. Sandtner, and W. Rudischhauser (eds), *50 Jahre Internationale Atomenergie-Organisation IAEO. Ein Wirken für Frieden und Sicherheit im nuklearen Zeitalter*. Baden-Baden: Nomos, 10–29.

[5] Reactors to generate power by nuclear fission were, of course, only one of the applications of atomic energy that required insurance: other risks included shipping of radioactive materials, the use of radioisotopes in industry and medicine, nuclear-powered vessels, and the disposal of nuclear waste. See V. Göthel, G. Voigt, and W. Burkart (2007) 'Atomenergie zum Nutzen von Umwelt und Gesundheit', in D. Schiefer et al. (eds), *50 Jahre Internationale Atomenergie-Organisation IAEO. Ein Wirken für Frieden und Sicherheit im nuklearen Zeitalter*. Baden-Baden: Nomos, 121–35. However, since reactor accidents were potentially the most catastrophic in their consequences, discussions of liability insurance revolved around that topic.

[6] SRCA 10.107 770, Meeting minutes of Swiss Re's board of directors (hereafter BoD), 1 September 1953, 207; 8 May 1954, 226. These early hesitations emphasize the difficulty of separating the risks from war- and peacetime applications of atomic energy.

[7] The technical name for such insurance is now Nuclear Installation Insurance, covering not only the reactor but the fuel cycle as well. (I am grateful to Sebastiaan Reitsma, former head of Nuclear Energy Risks at Swiss Re, for this clarification.) However, since both primary and secondary sources customarily refer to atomic reactor insurance, I shall follow that usage in order to avoid confusion.

[8] SRCA 10.107 772, BoD, 14 December 1965, 5 (hurricanes); 15 March 1966, 5 (airplanes).

[9] EURATOM was created in 1957 as an extension of the European Coal and Steel Community, with the aim of promoting the development of nuclear power in Europe and coordinating the initiatives of member states.

that diverged as often as they converged. Because atomic energy had been first deployed for military purposes, much technical information about the effects of exposure to radioactivity, control, and cooling techniques for nuclear reactions, and other relevant matters, was classified and largely in the hands of foreign powers (the USA and the Soviet Union). Markets, never absent from any insurance deliberations, exerted pressures in this case as well, especially since US insurance firms, with the help of Congress, had stolen a march on the Europeans by participating in Atomic Energy Commission (AEC) deliberations within months of the Atomic Energy Act becoming law in August 1954. Finally, insurers, constitutionally averse to state involvement in their business, were forced to enlist the state in this exceptional case as insurer of last resort.

The reconceptualization of atomic reactors as insurable risks, and indeed as a paradigm of how to insure other catastrophic risks, was therefore a remarkable feat. It stretched (and sometimes snapped) analogies with past precepts and practices of the modern insurance industry. Moreover, as those involved in hammering out the guidelines for this new kind of insurance insisted time and time again, the implications extended to almost every other form of standard insurance, from life to fire to accident. A nuclear accident, for example, changed the very meaning of 'accident', since the slow, cumulative effects of radioactive contamination on both people and physical plant lacked the defining element of 'suddenness' that ordinarily applied to such policies. What would happen to shipping insurance if two vessels carrying fissile materials, or even powered by nuclear engines, collided? What health insurance for workers in atomic plants (not only reactors but also laboratories and hospitals using radioisotopes) would cover conditions such as leukaemia that were diagnosed decades after exposure to radioactive sources and in only hypothetical causal connection to that episode? And, the biggest headache of all, how could the premiums for liability insurance even be estimated, much less damages paid, without reserves that dwarfed anything even the reinsurance business had ever before contemplated? No wonder insurers in several countries, including Switzerland and Germany, at first took refuge in exclusionary clauses that banished all risks relating to atomic energy from their policies.

Yet the collective mood of European insurers shifted very quickly in the early 1950s. The foreseeable exhaustion of fossil fuels (and the rising costs, political as well as financial, associated with cartels and scarcity), the prospect of falling still further behind the USA in the applications of atomic energy, the dazzling possibilities of applications for everything from cancer treatments to submarines to watches, and, last but not least, the prestige of keeping pace with the research and peaceful uses of atomic energy, even if excluded from competing with the two great powers, the USA and the Soviet Union, in the realm of nuclear weapons—all these factors changed minds and attitudes towards what remained insurance *terra incognita*.

Europe, rather than individual nation states, became the player in this new world race to exploit atomic energy. 'Wedged between the power blocks, Europe has pulled itself together in a collaboration in the field of nuclear energy', observed the Bern-based trade journal *Schweizerischer Versicherungskurier* approvingly, apropos of the founding of the Conseil Européen de Recherche Nucléaire (CERN) laboratory in the environs of Geneva in 1954.[10] Atomic fitness became a proxy for a modern, dynamic economy. In 1969, one German industrialist went so far as to suggest that export economies without nuclear power plants might be at a disadvantage, 'since the potential customers have less confidence in that country's capabilities'.[11] As the enormity of the risks entailed in the commercial development of atomic energy was evident from the outset, it was clear that no private concern could afford to invest in this area without at least liability insurance.[12] State and private-sector pressure on the insurance industry intensified. By 1955, even the reluctant Swiss Re was feeling the heat: 'in European and American industrial circles the criticism of the hesitations of the insurance companies [in the area of liability insurance for atomic reactors] grows ever louder'.[13]

That Swiss Re would figure so centrally in pushing European insurance companies towards an acceptance of atomic energy risks was anything but inevitable. These developments become comprehensible only against the background of American initiatives, culminating in the Price–Anderson Act of 1957 (see Section 9.2). Thanks to the prodding of Swiss Re (and especially its financial and staff support of the Comité d'Études du Risque Atomique (CERA)), European insurers followed suit with astonishing speed and coherence (Section 9.3). The American and European approaches to the novel risks of atomic energy ultimately transformed ideas of what could be an insurable risk (Section 9.4). The critical period for the developments examined in Sections 9.2 and 9.3 was roughly 1946 to 1960; only Section 9.4 looks forward and backward (and then selectively) to identify precedents and consequences of insurance for atomic energy risks.

## 9.2 Making up the Numbers: The US Congress Confronts the 'Insurance Problem'

In December 1953, US President Dwight D. Eisenhower delivered an address to the General Assembly of the United Nations (UN) that announced a dramatic (and rhetorically calculated) shift in American nuclear policy. Although the USA, already

[10] Belser (1958, 131) (translated quote).

[11] H. Klarr (1970) 'Current Problems of Nuclear Insurance from the Point of View of Industry', in International Atomic Energy Agency, *Insurance for Nuclear Installations: Reports and Documents Resulting from a Panel of Experts Convened by the International Atomic Energy Agency in Vienna, 24–28 November 1969*. Vienna: IAEA, 63. Klarr was quoting with approval the opinion of a former West German Minister for Atomic Power, Professor Siegfried Balke.

[12] SRCA 10.158 627.02, Special Committee for Nuclear Energy, Report 25 June 1956, 15.

[13] SRCA 10.107 923, BoD, 5 July 1955, 265 (translated quote).

embarked on an atomic arms race with the Soviet Union, would continue research, development, and manufacture of atomic weapons, it would, Eisenhower revealed, now also support the creation of an International Atomic Energy Agency to oversee peaceful applications of atomic energy: 'Experts would be mobilized to apply atomic energy to the needs of agriculture, medicine, and other peaceful activities. A special purpose would be to provide abundant electrical energy in the power-starved parts of the world.'[14] Eisenhower's 'Atoms for Peace' speech was aimed at domestic as well as international audiences. By 1953, the nightmarish associations of atomic energy with weaponry powerful enough to destroy all of human civilization had been cemented in the minds of the American public by articles in the popular press about the deadly effects of bombardment and radioactive fall-out, memoirs of Hiroshima and Nagasaki after August 1945, what-if novels, and apocalyptic films.[15] There was no way of putting the genie back in the bottle, but leaders in politics, science, and industry hoped that an 'atoms-into-ploughshares' programme would go some way towards rehabilitating the reputation of atomic energy, and with it, those who had been involved in the development of its more bellicose applications. Visions of atomic utopias countered those of atomic dystopias: flourishing agriculture, plentiful cheap energy, cures for disease, and atomic-powered everything versus mushroom cloud explosions, devastation, and hideous suffering.[16] The Atomic Energy Act of 1954, which expanded the powers of the AEC (established in 1946 as a state monopoly on fissionable materials needed for military use) to include the promotion and regulation of the private applications of atomic energy, profited from and added to the momentum of this initiative.

Because the US military had worked closely with private contractors to realize the Manhattan Project, the state monopoly on atomic energy had never been fully state-run. The young AEC continued this policy, working closely with firms such as Westinghouse and General Electric to design prototype nuclear reactors. Thus, even before it became legally possible for the AEC to grant licences and regulate the civilian use of atomic energy, it had developed a close working relationship with the companies best positioned to take advantage of new opportunities in this area. By 1953, partly at the urging of the Congressional Joint Committee on Atomic Energy (JCAE), then conducting hearings on the private development of atomic energy, and partly under pressure

[14] D. D. Eisenhower, 'Atoms for Peace', 8 December 1953, § 70: <http://voicesofdemocracy.umd.edu/eisenhower-atoms-for-peace-speech-text/> (accessed 13 February 2013). On the context of the speech, see I. Chernus (2002) *Eisenhower's Atoms for Peace*. College Station, TX: Texas A&M University Press; J. Krige (2006) 'Atoms for Peace, Scientific Internationalism, and Scientific Intelligence', *Osiris* 21, 161–81.

[15] See, for example, S. C. Zeman (2012) '"To See Things . . . Dangerous to Come To": Life Magazine and the Atomic Age in the United States 1945–1965', in D. van Lente (ed.), *The Nuclear Age in Popular Media: A Transnational History 1945–1965*. New York: Palgrave, 53–78.

[16] A great deal has been written on the political, scientific, and commercial motives for the shift in emphasis to the civilian uses of atomic energy. For a broad historical overview from the discovery of X-rays in 1895 to the hopes for fission reactors as of 2009, see M. Chauvin (2009) *De l'atome au nucléaire. Un siècle de prouesses scientifiques et d'enjeux politiques*. Québec: Presses internationales Polytechnique.

from the newly established Atomic Industrial Forum, whose membership spanned business and academia, the AEC initiated drafting legislation to make private atomic energy initiatives legal. Joint Committee legal counsel George Norris Jr became involved, patterning the new law on the 1934 Federal Communications Act. After extensive Joint Committee hearings at which industry representatives testified to their eagerness to become involved in the promotion of atomic energy, Congress passed the Atomic Energy Act in August 1954, empowering the AEC to license and regulate the atomic energy industry.[17]

But there was not a word about liability insurance in the 1954 Atomic Energy Act. On the face of it, the omission is puzzling. As many critics of the Atomic Energy Act have pointed out, the AEC was charged not only with regulating but also promoting a civilian atomic energy industry. It was to smooth the way for private business, providing technical expertise and flexible regulation—much to the dismay of competitors providing power from coal, gas, and other more traditional fuels, who considered such kid-glove treatment to be tantamount to a government subsidy.[18] Yet leaders of the key firms had made it perfectly clear during the Joint Committee hearings leading up to the passage of the Atomic Energy Act that no company would invest in reactors until the problem of liability insurance was solved. Francis McCune, of General Electric's Atomic Products Division, testified to Congress that no power company would build a reactor until adequate liability insurance was available, where 'adequate' clearly exceeded the amount that private insurance companies were willing to underwrite.[19] Until the 'insurance problem' could be solved, there would be no nuclear industry—and the insurance companies showed no signs of budging.

In 1955–6, the Joint Committee received various reports concerning the insurance problem: from the Atomic Industrial Forum, the McKinney Panel of Eminent Citizens, the Legislative Drafting Project of Columbia University, the Insurance Study Group of ten executives of fire and casualty insurance companies summoned by the AEC, and the AEC itself. Roughly speaking, the options on the table were as follows: completely private insurance (favoured by the AEC); some combination of private insurance and government indemnity (the latter for a far larger amount than the former, but both limited—favoured by the insurance industry); and an unlimited government indemnity (favoured in the Columbia report). In 1956, some sixty US insurance companies banded together to form two pools: the Mutual Atomic Energy Liability Underwriters (MAELU) and the Nuclear Energy Liability Insurance Association (NELIA).[20] But

[17] G. T. Mazuzan and J. S. Walker (1984) *Controlling the Atom: The Beginnings of Nuclear Regulation 1946–1962*. Berkeley, CA: University of California Press, 7–31.

[18] J. V. Rees (1994) *Hostages of Each Other: The Transformation of Nuclear Safety since Three Mile Island*. Chicago: University of Chicago Press, 28–32; C. Martinez and J. Byrne (1996) 'Science, Society and the State: The Nuclear Project and the Transformation of the American Political Economy', in J. Byrne and S. M. Hoffmann (eds), *Governing the Atom: The Politics of Risk*. New Brunswick, NJ: Transaction Publishers, 67–102.

[19] Johnson (1986, 44–5).

[20] Two additional pools, the Nuclear Energy Property Insurance Association (NEPIA) and the Mutual Atomic Energy Reinsurance Pool (MAERP), were formed to provide property coverage for

even though these pools were willing to offer third-party liability insurance for damages up to USD 60 million (a colossal sum by the standards of the day, four times the amount of any other kind of coverage then offered), the nascent nuclear industry held out for further government guarantees.[21] The AEC rejected government reinsurance of the insurance industry as undue meddling in the private insurance market, although the Bureau of the Budget briefly revived the possibility in its review of 1957 draft legislation (on the analogy of a flood-relief bill then under discussion in Congress).[22]

This was the impasse that confronted the Joint Committee in its attempts to draft supplementary legislation that would solve the insurance problem. Although the probability of a catastrophic nuclear accident was, experts agreed, very small, the damages if such an accident *did* occur were very big—and no one had any idea how to quantify 'very small' and 'very big'. Government-run atomic reactors boasted an excellent safety record to date, yet experience with reactors was far too limited to provide reliable statistics. Even if a bomb-like nuclear explosion was ruled out, a major reactor accident could not only destroy the entire expensive plant but also poison the local population and contaminate the surrounding area for decades through the spread of dangerous radiation.

A report (known as WASH-740), commissioned by the AEC from Brookhaven Laboratory and submitted to Congress in March 1957, estimated the property damages caused by such an accident near a major city at USD 7 billion, with 3400 deaths and 43,000 injuries—albeit with a probability of such an accident set at one in a billion per reactor.[23] But whenever pressed by members of the Joint Committee, AEC commissioners admitted that all such numbers were speculative. 'Though I speak with an air of certainty', waffled chemist and commissioner Willard Libby, 'I am not sure that these figures are absolutely the upper limits of maximum possible loss.'[24] Some members of Congress worried that anything less than unlimited indemnity for citizens affected by such accidents might be unconstitutional. Against this background, the nuclear industry clamoured for 'nothing short of complete indemnification' as a precondition for building and operating reactors.[25]

After yet more reports and hearings of the Joint Committee, plus some fierce political wrangling, Congress passed the Price-Anderson amendment to the Atomic Energy Act in September 1957. Its compromise solution to the insurance problem

nuclear facilities. These pools did not require additional government indemnity assurances. JCAE (1974, 368–9); and (for the premiums charged by NELIA and MAELU) (376–7). NELIA and MAELU did not actually start writing insurance policies until 1957: Butler (1957).

21 Johnson (1986, 46–50). 22 Mazuzan and Walker (1985, 109–10, 116–17).

23 P. A. Greenberg (1996) 'Safety, Accidents, and Public Acceptance', in J. Byrne and S. M. Hoffmann (eds), *Governing the Atom: The Politics of Risk*. New Brunswick, NJ: Transaction Publishers, 127–75, here 145.

24 Willard Libby to Senator Clinton Anderson, Joint Committee on Atomic Energy hearings, May 1956 (quoted in Mazuzan and Walker (1984, 114)).

25 Mazuzan and Walker (1984, 106–7).

supplemented the USD 60 million coverage of the two private insurance pools with a government indemnity of USD 500 million. The latter figure seems to have been more or less snatched from thin air, as a 'common sense' midpoint between unlimited government indemnity and none whatsoever. As Senator Clinton Anderson, chairman of the Joint Committee later explained, 'in suggesting $500 million [we were] [ . . . ] trying to [ . . . ] get some figure that would not frighten the country or Congress to death and still solve the problem [ . . . ]'.[26] The AEC surrendered its recommendation of unlimited government indemnity (although Price-Anderson left open the possibility of special legislation should compensation beyond the limit be deemed necessary). In return, the Joint Committee abandoned the idea of government reinsurance. A minimal annual fee charged to the atomic energy licensees for the government indemnity mollified the Bureau of the Budget, which was concerned that otherwise a something-for-nothing precedent would be established in government-industry dealings. Finally, all parties to the Price-Anderson Act regarded its provisions as tentative, to be revised in light of subsequent experience: a sunset clause on the indemnity and limited liability provisions forced Congress to review them by 1 August 1967.[27]

## 9.3 Herding Cats: Swiss Re, CERA, and the European Insurers

No insurance company with significant concerns in the US market could overlook the efforts of their American colleagues to organize themselves into pools to provide unprecedented amounts of liability coverage and to lobby Congress for favourable provisions in the Price–Anderson amendment to the Atomic Energy Act. Already in April 1956, over a year before the passage of the Price–Anderson amendment, William E. Belser, director of the CERA staffed and financed by Swiss Re, was pressurizing Matheus Klaas, president of the New York-based Swiss Re North American Corporation, for information about what was going on in American circles: Could Klaas get hold of a copy of the McKinney report? What about the relevant AEC publications?[28]

Even European insurers less attentive to overseas developments could hardly ignore the huge Geneva conference on the peaceful uses of atomic energy in August 1955,[29] in

[26] Quoted in Johnson (1986, 49).

[27] In 1967, the Price-Anderson Act was revised to expedite damage claims procedures in case of an accident and once again extended for a ten-year period, to compel Congress to conduct another review of its provisions in light of experience. JCAE (1974, 277–98).

[28] SRCA 10.158 628.01, W. E. Belser to M. Klaas, 14 April 1956; M. Klaas to W. E. Belser, 19 April 1956. Klaas apologized for his inability to get the desired information 'aus erster Hand' (from the source) and warned that orders placed in February to the US Government Printing Office took a long time to be fulfilled.

[29] SRCA 10.107 771, BoD, 10 December 1957, 3. As of 1957, Swiss Re had reinsurance relationships with forty-four North American insurance companies.

which around two thousand participants from seventy-three nations listened to scientific papers and marvelled at the swimming-pool reactor specially flown over from Oak Ridge, Tennessee, and set up in the grounds of the Palais des Nations.[30] The Swiss government, suitably impressed, bought the reactor, which was later installed in Würenlingen (canton Aargau) and administered by Reaktor Aktiengesellschaft (Reaktor AG) for research purposes. By September 1955, Swiss Re's board of directors had commissioned a report from physicist Paul Scherrer of the Swiss Federal Institute of Technology (ETH) Zurich (and a founder of Reaktor AG) on the risks posed by atomic reactors, proposed the creation of a central depot for all relevant publications, and pronounced the question of insuring atomic risks to be now 'acute'.[31]

Only a few months before, in December 1954, Swiss Re's board of directors had been contemplating exclusionary clauses for all risks related to atomic energy, and its earlier discussions on the subject in 1953 had questioned the possibility of cleanly distinguishing military and peaceful uses of atomic energy.[32] Its volte-face on the question of insuring atomic energy risks was in part driven by projected Swiss energy demands, in part by pressures on direct insurers, especially in the USA ('It is impossible to exclude certain risks covered by direct insurers from the reinsurance contract'[33]), and in part by a certain pride in Swiss Re's status as a world leader in the field. At the 1955 Vienna congress of European insurance companies, Swiss Re assumed the presidency of the newly established study group on atomic energy risks. By the autumn of 1955, Swiss Re, first in the person of board member Dr Paul Guggenbühl and later in that of CERA director Belser, was discreetly but firmly steering European insurance policy in the matter of atomic risks.

'Steering' perhaps exaggerates the degree to which Swiss Re was able to muster its colleagues in other European countries into anything like a coherent formation. As Belser admitted to his American colleagues at the Atomic Industrial Forum in 1957, the European insurers were hampered by a patchwork of national legislation, contrasting plans and paces for the development of atomic energy, and at least three different international bodies (the OEEC, the IAEA, and EUROATOM), all attempting to shape the insurance framework according to their own lights:

> In Europe, unfortunately, we have not yet progressed so far [as the Price–Anderson amendment]. [ . . . ] If you did not already know, I should, to my regret, have to tell you that these 19 [European] states each have their own legislation and rules of their own in the field of third-party liability, or at least that differences become apparent as soon as we look more closely at their legal institutions in this field.[34]

[30] J. A. Hall (1987) 'The International Atomic Energy Agency: Origins and Early Years', *IAEA Bulletin* 2, 47–54, here 50. See also J.-C. Favez and L. Mysyrowicz (1987) *Le Nucléaire en Suisse. Jalons pour une histoire difficile*. Lausanne: Editions l'Age d'Homme, 84–90.

[31] SRCA 10.107 770, BoD, 6 September 1955, 263–4.

[32] SRCA 10.107 770, BoD, 13 December 1954, 245; 1 September 1953, 206–7.

[33] SRCA 10.107 770, BoD, 9 May 1955, 256 (translated quote).

[34] Belser (1957a, 1–2). At the end of his article, Belser provided a chart of the different provisions in various European countries, from the standpoint of exceptions and limitations of liability.

However, the fact that Belser was able to represent European insurers as a group at the New York conference was already a minor triumph of diplomatic manoeuvring. At the first meeting of the Groupe de Travail du Risque Atomique in January 1956, Swiss Re had not only made sure to orient discussion with a memorandum on the topic; its representative Guggenbühl repeatedly reassured the delegates that the purpose of the meeting was only an exchange of views and information whenever they lost their way in the maze of different national laws and constantly changing atomic technologies. It was Guggenbühl who was appointed 'chef rapporteur' (which perhaps allowed him to smooth over certain Franco-German tensions in the minutes), and it was Guggenbühl who suggested that 'an office of documentation' be created in order to work out detailed proposals that could not be expected to emerge from meandering discussion. And, finally, it was Guggenbühl who offered the services of Belser and Belser's secretary, Walter Diehl, to run the proposed office—to be lodged at and paid for by Swiss Re, to the tune of about CHF 250,000 per annum.[35]

Subsequent meetings of the Commission Permanente du Risque Atomique debated such questions as limits to liability (with the British defending the high end and the Italians the low), limits to duration of claims period after an accident, and how to deal with the transportation of nuclear material. Members groped for the right analogies to bridge old and new risks: Perhaps the historic British decision to limit liability for the shipping industry? Or aviation? Or tried-and-true fire insurance? They compared notes and exchanged information. These meetings certainly contributed something to the creation of a European community of insurers, if rarely to a European consensus. But almost all of the actual coordination emanated from the office of CERA at Swiss Re. It was Belser who gathered the documents, drafted the position papers, attended conferences, conducted correspondence, and published articles in French, German, and English in trade journals and the popular press.

Keeping a weather eye on developments in the USA, Belser worked out arguments to push reluctant European governments to pass legislation that would solve the insurance problem along Price-Anderson lines. How could American firms deliver nuclear products to Europe without knowing what liabilities they were incurring? And, given the size of most European countries, it was illusory to believe that the effects of a nuclear accident would stop at national boundaries: pan-European coordination would be essential. It was the responsibility of the state to insure the welfare of its citizens, which in turn depended on the availability of plentiful, affordable energy—which almost no European country could guarantee from its own sources and, in any case, would be exhausted worldwide in the foreseeable future. In such a situation, the state must be prepared to shoulder additional burdens in order to make the development of atomic energy possible and profitable. Unlimited liability for proprietors of nuclear power plants would strangle the new industry in its cradle; so would too long a claims

[35] SRCA 10.158 622.01, Groupe de Travail du Risque Atomique, Minutes of meeting held 16–17 January 1956, Paris, 9, 14, 18 (passages struck out in pencil concerning the exchanges between Artom and Gruse), and SRCA 10.107 772, BoD, 1 September 1964, 13.

period following the accident. And it was the state that should assume liability for damages that exceeded the amount that national pools could cover—not only because the insurance companies could not possibly come up with such enormous sums (Belser quoted the USD 7 billion figure from the AEC report), but also because it was the responsibility of every civilized state to come to the aid of its citizens in the case of a natural catastrophe—and atomic energy could wreak havoc equal to that of natural forces.[36]

When not trying to consolidate divergent opinions among the insurers, lobby their governments (including the Swiss) to pass more accommodating and uniform legislation, as well keep tabs on the Americans, Belser was doing battle with the OEEC, which had its own ideas about the best way to organize European liability insurance for atomic energy risks. On at least one crucial issue, the OEEC sided with the operators of reactors against the insurers: Should liability insurance be offered per installation or per incident? The OEEC favoured the latter, but the insurers were four-square behind the installation option: 'Insurers can only grant the high cover demanded once per installation: it is not impossible that the same installation may cause one or more severe accidents within a short period, while in addition the same event may cause further losses in other branches of insurance.' After an accident, it would, under the installation model, be up to the insurers (and reinsurers) to decide whether or not to renew coverage, after 'the cause of damage had been clarified'.[37]

Both American and European insurers fretted about how to make sure that reactor operators adhered to the highest safety standards: Belser flagged this as an unsolved problem in a presentation to the Swiss Re board of directors in 1962.[38] Indeed, it still vexes the nuclear industry, insurers, and governments after accidents at Three Mile Island (1979), Chernobyl (1986), and Fukushima (2011).[39] But Belser failed to persuade the OEEC to alter its recommendations to the IAEA, resulting in a confused compromise in which the 1963 Vienna Convention on Civil Liability for Nuclear Damage (Article VII) provided for insurance on a per-incident basis but insurance cover was in fact available on a pro-installation basis for a limited period of time.[40]

A recurrent theme among the insurers was the possibility of enlarging the national pools into at least pan-European if not global pools. Since the late nineteenth century, reinsurers like Swiss Re had pioneered the international distribution of risk.[41] Given

[36] Belser (1957b, 22). Most of Belser's papers were circulated to interested parties in typescript, rather than officially published, a model also used by the Atomic Industrial Forum.

[37] SRCA 10.158 622.01, Comité Européen des Assurances, Memo addressed to the IAEA, 18 August 1959, 5.

[38] SRCA 10.107 772, BoD, 4 September 1962, 10.

[39] Rees (1994, 11–26); E. D. Blandford and M. M. May (2012) *Lessons Learned from 'Lessons Learned': The Evolution of Nuclear Power Safety after Accidents and Near-Accidents*. Cambridge MA: American Academy of Arts and Sciences.

[40] IAEA (International Atomic Energy Agency) (1970) *Insurance for Nuclear Installations*. Vienna: IAEA, 44; Meier (1965, 70).

[41] Rohland (2011a, 49–52); Röder (2012, 26–44).

the immensity of the potential damages of a major reactor accident, spreading the risk more broadly appealed from a strictly technical point of view, just as the international standardization of regulations and liability provisions did on grounds of simplicity and efficiency. Above these hard-headed calculations, however, often hovered a vision of an international community bound in solidarity by the peaceable uses of atomic energy, a vision first conjured in Eisenhower's 1953 'Atoms for Peace' speech. What became the IAEA was originally intended to receive contributions of fissionable materials from governments all over the world in order to pursue peaceful applications of atomic energy. EURATOM translated these hopes to Europe and promoted atomic energy cooperation as the first step towards the creation of a 'United States of Europe':

> Euratom in itself is nothing else than the application of the federal method [i.e. the creation of a federal community of European nations] to the field of atomic energy. It is the pooling of resources—the particular resources being our scientific abilities and the industrial capacity that is present in Europe.[42]

But internationalization of both pools and regulations foundered on the shoals of specificity—not only of national legal systems but also of the risks themselves. When the French and Italian delegates proposed a 'super-pool' (or at least a common schedule of premiums) at the May 1959 meeting of the Commission Permanente du Risque Atomique, the Swiss representative was dismissive: 'A central tarification is not acceptable. One must be able to take into account the special circumstances of every individual case.'[43] As late as June 1956, in his memorandum to the OEEC, Belser seems to have considered seriously the possibility of pan-European pools and perhaps even cooperation with non-European markets, especially in the USA.[44] International pools for other forms of insurance, such as shipping and aviation, also proved impossible to achieve, despite Swiss Re's efforts in these areas: 'To produce international solidarity among European insurers seems impossible.'[45] The quick succession of European conventions on 'Third Party Liability in the Field of Nuclear Energy'—Paris (29 July 1960), Brussels (31 January 1963), and Vienna (21 May 1963)[46]—bears witness to the difficulty of Belser's task in coordinating the European insurers among themselves as well as with American insurers on the one hand, and with international bodies such as the OEEC, EURATOM, and the IAEA, on the other.

[42] M. Kohnstamm (1957) 'Some Problems Facing the European Atomic Energy Community', in Atomic Industrial Forum, *The 1957 Nuclear Industry: Problems and Progress*. New York: Atomic Industrial Forum, 1–7, here 4. Max Kohnstamm, a Dutch diplomat, is identified as secretary-general, Action Committee for a United States of Europe.

[43] SRCA 10.158 622.01, Commission Permanente du Risque Atomique, Minutes of meeting held 11–12 May 1959, Milan, 5 (translated quote).

[44] SRCA 10.158 627.02, Special Committee for Nuclear Energy, Report 25 June 1956, 28.

[45] SRCA 10.107 772, BoD, 15 March 1966, 41 (translated quote).

[46] A. Bette, J. M. Didier, R. Fornasier, and R. M. Stein, *Compensation of Nuclear Damage in Europe* (Brussels: 1965), contains the texts of the conventions, with commentary. For the text of the Brussels 1963 Supplementary Convention, see <http://www.oecd-nea.org/law/nlbrussels.html> (accessed 11 May 2016); see also Meier (1965, 92–3).

The pillars of Belser's detailed position papers—limited claims period (he suggested ten years), channelling all damages to the operator of the nuclear installation, limited liability for the insurers, supplemental and much greater government indemnity in the case of a catastrophic accident—resembled those of the Price–Anderson amendment. But Belser's justification shifted the pattern of emphases from the American debates, which had focused on incentives to private industry to take over the development of atomic energy and on keeping government intervention in the private insurance market to a minimum. The European insurers also worried about the state muscling in on their business and accepted the principle that sufficient insurance guarantees were the precondition for the existence of an atomic energy industry. However, in the foreground stood not the sanctity of private enterprise but the responsibilities of the state: to its citizens and to the insurers themselves. The former had a right to prosperity, stability, and safety; the latter to special protections because the risks of atomic energy defied every rule of sound insurance. There were no reliable statistics about the frequency and severity of accidents, no reliable estimates of damages in case of accidents, and no recourse to reinsurance according to the rules of the national pools. The insurance industry, which, since the late eighteenth century, had anchored its reputation in sound statistics and prudent fiscal planning,[47] would have to throw its customary caution to the winds in order to underwrite the literally incalculable new risks. In his articles, lectures, and position papers, Belser hammered this point home: the insurers had '*adopted a positive attitude towards these still unknown risks. Nevertheless the demands they will have to meet must not be contrary to the business that has been conducted successfully on sound lines and in accordance with long established practice.*'[48] Despite their dread of state involvement,[49] it was only with state-legislated liability limits and supplements that the insurers were willing to embark on a voyage in uncharted seas without a compass.

## 9.4 No Fault and Whose Fault: A New Model for Catastrophic Risks

In September 1964, upon Belser's retirement, Swiss Re returned the directorship of CERA to the Comité Européen des Assurances and looked back with satisfaction on its shepherding role in creating a European framework for the insurance of atomic energy risks. By then, the 'entirely new risk' of a decade ago had become a 'typical example for

[47] Daston (1988, 172–87).

[48] SRCA 10.158 627.02, Special Committee for Nuclear Energy, Report 25 June 1956, 15 (emphasis in the original).

[49] The threat of the *Verstaatlichung* of insurance is a recurring theme in the discussions of the Swiss Re BoD in the 1950s and 1960s—whether the risk in question was hurricane damage, airplane crashes, or auto accidents.

newly emergent risks. It is part of the mission of insurance to investigate and not simply reject such risks. In this way private insurance can maintain its leading role.'[50] In subsequent years, Swiss Re board of directors' members returned to the atomic energy case as a model for other catastrophic risks, such as hurricanes (after Hurricane Betsy cost the company over CHF 20 million in 1965–6), riots and civil unrest (after damages caused by the Los Angeles riots of 1965), and earthquakes (reluctantly reinsured for fear of losing business, especially in the lucrative US market). In each case, discussion veered between the view that Swiss Re would do better to wash its hands entirely of such potentially ruinous risks and the retort that it was all a matter of getting the numbers right and pricing premiums accordingly. The atomic energy model straddled these extreme positions, as a way of insuring potentially enormous risks under the protection of a government-dictated ceiling for damage claims.[51]

Yet, despite its rhetorical role as a happy medium in these discussions, liability insurance for atomic energy risks remained a wild venture from the standpoint of traditional insurance practices. The estimates for the probabilities of a major accident and the resulting damages were as much the result of guesswork in 1966 as they had been in 1956—and indeed long thereafter. In the USA, regulatory policies advocating defence-in-depth reactor design had been repeatedly criticized by scientists, environmentalists, and even by the responsible government agencies as inadequate. The 1972 Reactor Safety Study (known as WASH-1400) commissioned by the AEC fared no better. Using probabilistic risk assessment (PRA) and fault-tree analysis (originally developed by Bell Laboratories and Boeing Company in the 1960s to estimate the risk of an inadvertent firing of a Minuteman intercontinental ballistic missile), the authors of WASH-1400 produced reassuring estimates of the very low probability (*circa* one in a billion) of a catastrophic reactor accident.[52] However, a 1978 review of WASH-1400 by the Nuclear Regulatory Commission concluded: 'we are unable to define whether the overall probability of a core melt given in WASH-1400 is high or low, but we are certain that the error bands are understated'.[53] Damage estimates were equally wobbly, especially since reactors originally sited in relatively sparsely populated areas had, over time, come to be surrounded by more densely settled communities. Contrary to the insurers' expectation, the numbers did not solidify with experience. Yet insurers remained sanguine: a 1964 report on the involvement of the American insurance industry in both military and civilian uses of atomic energy opined that 'it is ironic that the most destructive instrument devised by man should have proved to be one of the safest of large-scale insurance risks'.[54]

Swiss Re's insouciance about the risks of atomic energy may, in part, be explained by the fact that national pools did not practise reinsurance, leaving Swiss Re's main

[50] SRCA 10.107 772, BoD, 1 September 1964, 13.

[51] SRCA 10.107 772, BoD, 4 December 1965, 5–6; 18 October 1966, 5–8.

[52] See Keller and Modarres (2005, 271–85, esp. 274–84) on WASH-1400 and its critics.

[53] Quoted in Greenberg (1996, 147); see also Johnson (1986, 73–8).

[54] *Travelers 100 Years* (1964, 110). I am grateful to Dan Bouk for bringing this article to my attention.

business apparently unaffected. It is striking to see how little trace the worst reactor accidents left in the deliberations of its board of directors, which was otherwise obsessively attentive to every disaster that might deplete its reserves. Even the January 1969 accident in Lucens, Switzerland, which Swiss Re had, in 1962, co-insured for CHF 75,000 (out of a total of CHF 500,000 assigned to the Swiss insurance pool[55]), went unremarked in its minutes. The board's only response to the Three Mile Island accident in Pennsylvania on 28 March 1979 was a tirade about the 'atomic psychosis' that moved the American (and Swiss) public to exaggerate such risks out of all proportion,[56] and once again to congratulate itself on Swiss Re's position as a 'leader' in atomic energy insurance: 'On the basis of its own decades-long pioneer work and experience with atomic risks, SR is convinced that hardly any other technological area can boast such a high level of safety.'[57] The board was willing to put its money where its mouth was and increase the amount covered per risk to CHF 35 million—evidence that, even when Swiss Re was directly involved in insuring atomic energy risks, alarms no longer sounded and anxiety levels stayed flat.

In retrospect, the trajectory of Swiss Re's attitude towards atomic energy risk anticipates a larger rethinking of catastrophic risks that began at latest in the 1980s. Throughout the 1960s and 1970s, technological disasters loomed large in the worst-case imaginings of insurance executives: oil spills, factory explosions, dangerous side effects of medications and consumer products, airplane crashes, mayhem on the highways. At a 1967 press conference, Dr Walter Diehl, vice chairman (*stellvertretender Direktor*) of Swiss Re, highlighted the greatest risks currently facing the insurance industry: the relentless rationalization of manufacture, taxing human capacity beyond its limits; big, expensive ships and planes; dense geographic concentration of insured goods; increase in crime; rising negligence.[58] Not one single natural cause of insured damages made Diehl's list of misfortunes.

This was, in large part, because natural catastrophes like hurricanes, volcanoes, and earthquakes had been expressly excluded from insurance contracts[59] (albeit with mixed success when disaster actually struck, as Swiss Re and other insurance companies discovered to their chagrin in the case of the 1906 San Francisco Earthquake[60]). Exceptions to this strategy occurred only under intense political or economic pressure—often both in combination, as when Swiss Re and other insurers were dragged kicking and screaming into hurricane and coastal flood insurance in the

[55] SRCA 10.107 772, BoD, 20 February 1962, 11.

[56] Perhaps the BoD had in mind popular anti-reactor demonstrations at Kaiseraugst in 1975, which caused a political uproar in Switzerland. See Favez and Mysyrowicz (1987, 147–66).

[57] SRCA 10.107 776, BoD, 26 June 1979, 16.

[58] SRCA 10.166 133.00.66, W. Diehl, 'Grossrisiken und Grossschäden in der modernen Versicherung und Rückversicherung', press conference, 18 April 1967.

[59] SRCA 10.106 683.08. See for example the sceptical discussion of earthquake insurance in 'Insurance and the Economic Consequences of Earthquakes'.

[60] Röder (2012, 45–95).

USA under the threat of otherwise being excluded from that market altogether.[61] The combination of rarity, unpredictability (both in terms of frequency and severity), the immensity of the damage potential, and the impotence of all human foresight and power to avert the event made natural disasters paradigm examples of what, since Roman times, had been called *vis maior* (*force majeure*, *höhere Gewalt*, acts of God): events that made all precautions and prudence futile and therefore suspended ordinary contractual liability.[62]

What the debate over atomic energy risks foreshadowed was a new way of thinking about catastrophes that blurred the line between the natural and man-made—and made all of them, even the most devastating, potentially insurable. Human culpability was most certainly at issue in all discussions of atomic energy risks, from the design of reactors to the exhaustive reports that followed every accident. But in all other respects, the catastrophic reactor accident resembled an earthquake or volcano: rare, unpredictable, and almost unimaginably destructive of life and property. In all such cases, there were only the most speculative estimates of frequency, intensity, and damages: the traditional distinction between a quantifiable 'risk' and an amorphous and uncertain 'danger' melted away. Belser grasped this point when he likened state responsibilities in the case of a reactor accident to those borne in the case of a natural disaster: 'Whenever these [by human means uncontrollable natural] forces are unleashed, then every civilized state intervenes to help the victims. Now we are confronted with an energy equal to that of natural forces in its dangerous potential.'[63] In less polemical contexts Belser also acknowledged the glaring disanalogy: human beings chose to build reactors; they did not choose to suffer earthquakes. For just that reason, he advised a Japanese colleague that any reactors built in earthquake-prone zones would have to be able to withstand '*any* earthquake, even the worst'. Ordinarily, explained Belser, the 'Act of God' clause would exclude liability for damages due to 'flood, windstorm, typhoon, lightning and, of course, earthquake'. But, he continued, reactors were a different matter: 'In the case of reactors, however, people felt that with regard to "Acts of God", the liability of the operator should only then not be engaged when the "Act of God" is of such a character *that it could not in any way be expected to happen*.'[64]

What Belser could not have foreseen were two developments that undermined traditional 'Act of God' exclusions, starting in the 1980s. On the one hand, new approaches to risk management and financial investment (e.g. catastrophe (or cat) bonds) lowered resistance to insuring rare and unpredictable natural catastrophes.[65] On the other, social scientific and political analyses increasingly emphasized the element of human culpability in making natural disasters even more disastrous. Recent sociological

[61] SRCA 10.157 104.02, E. A. G. Manton, 'U.S.A. Natural Catastrophe', October 1985.

[62] See the specifications of the International Chamber of Commerce Force Majeure Clause 2003: <http://www.derecho.uba.ar/institucional/competencia_arbitraje_iic_force_majeure_and_hardship_clauses_2003.pdf> (accessed 11 May 2016).

[63] Belser (1957b, 22) (translated quote).

[64] SRCA 10.158 622.02, W. E. Belser to K. Imamura, 23 April 1959.

[65] Chapter 10, this volume.

studies of natural disasters like the hurricanes that periodically wreak havoc in southern Florida in the USA or the heatwaves that killed scores of people in North America and Europe in 1995 and 2003 point out that mighty financial interests encourage reckless building along hurricane paths and that equally mighty political interests trap the poor and the elderly in the hottest parts of big cities.[66] Nor is this the view of just a minority of activists and alarmists. The title of a collection recently published by the World Bank and the UN points the direction in which the new wind is blowing: *Natural Hazards, Unnatural Disasters: The Economics of Effective Prevention*.[67]

Within this new scheme of things, sharp lines no longer divide 'natural' from 'man-made' catastrophes: there are only catastrophes, more or less frequent, more or less unpredictable, more or less costly. Within the complex mathematical models of major insurance and reinsurance companies, the risks of a hurricane of Katrina proportions or a fiscal collapse of Lehman Brothers proportions are fungible, all grist for the simulation's mill. The radius of reasonable foresight has lengthened: governments can now be held responsible (and in some cases liable) for damages due to unmaintained infrastructure, unenforced building codes, inadequate warning and rescue systems, imprudent zoning laws. If more people die in Iran or Pakistan than in Los Angeles or Tokyo when earthquakes of the same force strike, then it is now considered to be someone's fault—usually the corrupt officials who took bribes to overlook unsafe buildings on illegal sites.[68]

Against this background, the once *sui generis* risks of atomic energy no longer seem anomalous. Around 1960, the hybrid of human agency and devastating natural forces, liability and unpredictability, seemed unprecedented. But, by 1990, such amphibious catastrophes were a widening category. All disasters were to some extent natural; all were also to some extent man-made.

By establishing a 'Cat Peril Team' to model all such catastrophes, Swiss Re seemed perfectly in step with these developments: instead of the mechanical and chemical engineers who had staffed the Abteilung Technik und Spezialsparten (technical department and special lines, known as 'TS' in internal memoranda) in the 1960s and who were, first and foremost, concerned with damage prevention,[69] it is statisticians, financial experts, and other scientists with mathematical modelling and computer simulation skills who now dominate Swiss Re's approach to risk management. Instead of journeying to Libya to inspect an oil refinery first hand to assess risk of fire and explosion, as the TS engineers once did, the modellers develop sophisticated scenarios that blend data about the value of insured property, the volatility of the bond market, and the 50,000-year cycle of tropical cyclones.[70] From the standpoint of modern risk

[66] Steinberg (1997, 414–38); Klineberg (2005).

[67] World Bank/United Nations (2010). [68] Kellenberg and Mobarak (2011, 297–312).

[69] In 1979, Swiss Re's risk management group consisted of four chemical engineers, one electrical engineer, one building engineer, one mechanical engineer, one physicist (charged with computers and 'risk models'), one economist, and three secretaries. See SRCA 10.166 820.00.011.

[70] SRCA 10.118 490.00.038, Swiss Re Cat Peril Team, 19.

management techniques, a risk is a risk is a risk, whether it is a big bank collapse, a Force 5 hurricane, or a major nuclear reactor accident. All are parameters to be estimated and brought into quantitative alignment with another by the assumptions of the mathematical model.

Mathematical models co-exist with ever-more exacting analyses of human responsibility. A recent stock-taking of the prospects for atomic energy after the 2011 Fukushima reactor accident in Japan emphasized prevention and responsibility:

> It is not possible to anticipate or prevent all accidents, but it is noteworthy that most of the serious accidents that have affected the nuclear industry were in fact anticipated by engineers, operators, or managers, and yet were still not prevented. This fact is specifically true of Fukushima, where Japan's nuclear safety agency had warned against siting the backup generators on low ground.[71]

Paradoxically, the risks of atomic reactors have thus become paradigmatic for two apparently contradictory approaches: the no-fault, homogenizing estimates of the modellers (backed up by legislation that caps liability in the absence of reliable numbers), and the whose-fault, finger-pointing condemnations of experts and the general public. If atomic reactor risks paved the way to thinking about many other catastrophes as natural–man-made hybrids, all similarly insurable, they have also once again become *sui generis*, straddling the line between no fault and whose fault.

## Acknowledgements

My thanks to Niels Viggo Haueter and Jörg Zimmer, who were my gracious hosts and guides in the Swiss Re Company Archives. For critical comments and suggestions, I am grateful to Dan Bouk, Markos Carelos, David Gugerli, Geoffrey Jones, Sebastiaan Reitsma, Welf Werner, Mira Wilkins, and Daniela Zetti.

[71] K. Marvel and M. May (2011) *Game Changers for Nuclear Energy*. Cambridge, MA: American Academy of Arts and Sciences, 5.

# CHAPTER 10

# NATURAL CATASTROPHES AND THEIR EFFECTS ON REINSURANCE

WELF WERNER

From the downfall of Pompeii to the reactor accident at Fukushima, natural catastrophes have always attracted particular attention. However, the catastrophes that have occurred around the world in recent decades have had an immediate bearing on an ever-greater number of people. Modern mass media confront societies around the world with a deluge of images and news stories that let them share in the enormous suffering caused by such events, almost as they happen. In addition to how they are perceived, it is possible the actual causes of such catastrophes have also changed over time. Global climate change is largely attributable to emissions, to which various regions of the world contribute in varying degrees and by which they are affected in widely differing ways. For the sociologist Ulrich Beck, the general globalization process has created a global risk society in which transnational interdependencies reduce the importance of national states.[1]

This perspective is only one example of the increased scientific interest in natural catastrophes. For many years, historians did not view such events as a theme in themselves, but since around 1985 they have attracted a high level of interest within the field of environmental and global history, given their varied interfaces to culture, society, and politics.[2] An economic perspective has attracted less attention in this process. Since the Great Depression of the 1930s, the key focus of economists looking at global crises and catastrophes has been on the man-made catastrophes that belong to the economic cycle. The most recent global and European financial crisis has further strengthened this view of catastrophes.

Against this background, it is hardly surprising that the close relationship between insurance and natural catastrophes has yet to attain importance among economists.

[1] Beck (2007). [2] Schenk (2007, 9–31).

The multifaceted knowledge of this topic has largely remained the preserve of specialists in the insurance industry's companies, corporate publications, and specialist press. All of these sources offer a great deal of evidence that reinsurance has played an important role in the management of natural catastrophes since its inception in the rapidly expanding insurance markets of the second half of the nineteenth century. Nevertheless, what reinsurers actually do has generally remained a mystery, given that the large majority of the business is conducted with direct insurers, rather than with citizens and companies. The only inkling of how such financial transactions functioned would not arise until the industry was pushed to its limits by singular, major catastrophes. More information has only become available in recent decades. The growing public interest in natural catastrophes has coincided with an increased readiness on the part of major global specialist reinsurers such as Swiss Re and Munich Re to provide an insight into their activities as part of their increasingly professional corporate communications. Since the 1970s, numerous reinsurers have regularly published market reports and publications on individual risk events.

At the time of the establishment of major professional reinsurers in the late nineteenth century, the most important major loss events were city fires, such as the conflagration that followed the 1906 San Francisco Earthquake. In the twentieth century, other events such as earthquakes, hurricanes, and floods led reinsurers to different parts of the world. The global giants of the catastrophe field, such as Munich Re, were exposed to a particular concentration of earthquakes on the Pacific coasts of Asia and America, in Central Asia, and, to a lesser extent, the Mediterranean. With the exception of Africa, tropical hurricanes occur in many equatorial regions and with particular frequency in the Caribbean, the south-western USA, and the Asia-Pacific region. Floods occur along many rivers. In coastal regions, they are especially frequent after tropical storms, winter storms, and tsunamis.[3]

Nevertheless, reinsurers' operating activities overlap with these hotspots only to a limited degree. Since the late nineteenth century, the main focus of reinsurers' activities has been the USA, followed at some distance by Western Europe. Compared with the number, intensity, and devastation of the catastrophes in Asia in the twentieth century, reinsurance had a relatively modest penetration, remaining largely confined to Japan. This meant that reinsurers' activities and the reporting that accompanied it followed a familiar pattern. In global history, a new and flourishing branch of historical research, the tendency of historians and others to neglect regions beyond the North Atlantic has been characterized as 'Eurocentrism'. Through its conscious focus on world regions outside the North Atlantic and their experience with events of global importance, the many contributions to global history have greatly inspired the more traditional branches of historical research for quite a few decades now.[4]

[3] Munich Re (2011a).

[4] D. Sachsenmeier (2011) *Global Perspectives on Global History: Theories and Approaches in a Connected World.* Cambridge: Cambridge University Press.

However, the heavy concentration of reinsurance activities around the shores of the North Atlantic and Japan were in no way the result of a limited intellectual horizon of the reinsurance industry. Rather, the reinsurers' geographical focus highlights one of the most important features of the nexus between reinsurance and natural catastrophes. Reinsurers get involved in the complex events surrounding such catastrophes only if a variety of conditions are met over which they have little or no influence. Reinsurers play a part in managing catastrophes in various countries and regions of the world only if: (a) these catastrophes cause the destruction of significant property values; (b) these losses were also insured by direct insurers in market-oriented economies; and (c) these insurers were also reinsured in one way or another against such risks. In the twentieth century, these preconditions were met by only a few countries, containing a small minority of the world's population.

The following sections will show that reinsurers' role as the insurers' insurers meant that they were predestined to be involved in highly developed insurance markets. These markets had comparatively rare loss events that entailed enormous impact when they did occur and required the development of specific technical knowledge to assess them. Because of their countless business contacts with direct insurers, reinsurers found themselves the conduit for diverse information on major loss events, which direct insurers active at a national or regional level would only collect on a discrete and partial basis. In this sense, the cover of major loss occurrences was closely connected with the second characteristic of this type of financial business, namely its cross-border focus, resulting from its foreign branches and international trading ties.

Section 10.1 looks at the special connection between natural catastrophes and the highly developed reinsurance markets of the present day. Then, the role of reinsurers in the city fires of the late nineteenth and early twentieth century is reviewed, alongside the fires caused by the San Francisco Earthquake in 1906 (Section 10.2). In Sections 10.3 and 10.4, the spotlight falls upon the development of reinsurance for natural catastrophes in the Atlantic and other global regions. Finally, in Section 10.5, questions are posed as to how far reinsurers, through their increasing involvement beyond the North Atlantic, have already entered into the global risk society, and whether in the future they can maintain their role as specialists in the insurance of large-loss events.

## 10.1 Present-Day Catastrophes and Markets

It was a long journey from the initial experiences with the city fires of the late nineteenth and early twentieth centuries to today's complex markets for catastrophe risks with their differentiated information and instruments. While a plethora of information has become available in recent years and decades in the form of corporate publications, in the past, business journals such as *National Underwriter* in the USA and *The Review* in the UK seldom reported on the role played by reinsurers in natural catastrophes. Nevertheless, the focal points of financial reporting have largely stayed the same over the years. Two topics remain at the heart of regularly published analyses: first, the description of loss events and their causes, including the calculation of economic and insured losses and fatalities, and, second, the effects of these events on the reinsurance markets, particularly on their profitability, capital adequacy, and conditions regarding new treaties. Subjects covered by the reports also include questions concerning the reduction of losses and loss avoidance.

Since 1968, Swiss Re has regularly reported on a wide range of aspects of international and reinsurance markets in its publication *sigma*, which appears several times a year and whose studies are regularly referenced in scientific publications and the mass media. Since 1969, the company has issued an edition of this series devoted to the topic of natural and man-made catastrophes at the start of each year.[5] The report for 2010 is based on forty years of data stretching back to 1970.[6] At the same time, 2010 was a year of exceptionally high global losses, which well illustrates the current status of the nexus between reinsurance and catastrophe. The review by *sigma* begins by listing important events and trends and noting that the year, with its 304,000 fatalities, USD 218 billion of economic losses, and USD 43 billion in insured losses, was in seventh place since 1970 in terms of the level of insured losses. The economic losses were 60 per cent higher than the previous year, but remained lower than 2005, which marked the apex of the 40-year period of observation in terms of insured losses, with three hurricanes in the south-western USA—Wilma, Rita, and, in particular, Katrina.

The natural catastrophes that had a particular impact in 2010 in terms of insured losses were earthquakes in Chile (USD 8 billion) and New Zealand (USD 4.5 billion), the winter storm Xynthia in north-western Europe (USD 2.8 billion), another storm in the USA (USD 2.2 billion), and floods in Australia (USD 2.1 billion). The report looks at the extent of earthquake losses and considers their long-term development. While seismic activity remained unchanged overall, economic losses have risen since 1970, due to increasing concentrations of populations and property values in earthquake-prone urban regions. Nevertheless, measures such as improved building standards, good infrastructure, and professional crisis management helped to reduce losses. The review of the year's most important trends and events concludes with the reminder that, despite various prevention measures, it is impossible to avoid all risks, meaning that making financial provisions remains a necessity in the world's catastrophe-prone regions.[7]

The main part of the report reveals further interesting insights into the specific relationship between reinsurance and natural catastrophes at the present time, for example, the relative importance of natural catastrophes vis-à-vis man-made catastrophes, the second-most important form of major loss occurrences. The number of

[5] Swiss Re, *sigma* 1, 2011. For Swiss Re's numerous special editions on individual major loss events see <http://www.swissre.com/library/>.

[6] For the latest figures see Appendix.

[7] Swiss Re, *sigma* 1, 2011, 1.

natural catastrophes did not greatly exceed the number of man-made catastrophes, with 167 events versus 137 (based on the definitions defined by Swiss Re) in 2010, which was also the case in the previous years. The consequences of the natural catastrophes were, however, considerably more serious, accounting for 92 per cent of insured losses and 98 per cent of fatalities.[8] Alongside earthquakes, storms, and floods, the other major causes of natural catastrophes that regularly result in claims payments are heatwaves, drought, bush fires, cold, frost, and hail, the latter accounting for only around 1 per cent of total insured losses in 2010.[9] The report also provides numerous reminders that the impact of natural catastrophes on reinsurance portfolios varies tremendously in different regions of the world, as can be seen by comparing the details of economic and insured losses in North America and Latin America. While 75 per cent of economic losses were insured in North America in 2010, that figure was only 15 per cent in Latin America and the Caribbean, despite the fact that the economic implications of those losses were of much greater significance for Latin America and the Caribbean than for the USA, as is proven by a comparison of economic losses and gross domestic product (GDP).[10] While economic losses amounted to 13 per cent of GDP in the USA, the corresponding figure for Latin America and the Caribbean was 110 per cent.[11]

However, there are also significant differences in reinsurers' share of natural catastrophes within each continent, region, and country. While a high proportion of losses caused by natural catastrophes have traditionally been insured in Europe, there were two major loss occurrences in 2010 in which insurance played a relatively minor role.[12] Heatwaves and forest fires in Russia resulted in economic losses of USD 15 billion. The report gives no details on the insured losses associated with this event, for the simple reason that there was no cover worthy of note. The consequences of the volcanic eruption in Iceland in the spring of 2010, which received much media attention due to the ash clouds that lingered over Europe and the North Atlantic for weeks, were also uninsured. While this event caused no noteworthy property damage, it did result in considerable losses in the form of business interruption, particularly for the airlines, which either lacked or had inadequate insurance for such an event. In contrast, the coverage levels for the floods in France and the winter storm Xynthia were high, with between 60 per cent and 70 per cent of the economic losses being covered by the insurance companies respectively.[13]

The number of lives lost as a result of natural catastrophes also varies enormously. The 220,000 fatalities resulting from the earthquake in Haiti represented more than 2 per cent of the entire population of the Caribbean. The event was the second-most deadly earthquake in the period under review, behind a quake in Tangshan, China, in 1976. As only USD 100 million of the USD 10 billion economic loss was insured, it had

[8] Swiss Re, *sigma* 1, 2011, 1, 14. [9] Swiss Re, *sigma* 1, 2011, 14, own calculations.
[10] Swiss Re, *sigma* 1, 2011, 6, own calculations. [11] Swiss Re, *sigma* 1, 2011, 4.
[12] Swiss Re, *sigma* 1, 2011, 7, 24. [13] Swiss Re, *sigma* 1, 2011, 17, 20, own calculations.

scant impact on 2010 claims payments.[14] The situation was similar with the heatwave and forest fires in Russia: low claims payments contrasted with high losses of life. The event led to 56,000 fatalities. The earthquakes in Chile and New Zealand, where insurers had to meet claims amounting to USD 8 billion and USD 4.5 billion respectively, in contrast cost only 562 lives in the case of the former and none in the case of the latter. Looking at the experiences of earthquakes over the past twenty years, the report states that the deadliest events occur in the world's growth regions, while quakes in industrial regions result in the highest insured losses, such as the Northridge Earthquake (USA, 1994), the earthquakes in Concepción (Chile, 2010), Darfield (New Zealand, 2010), and Kobe (Japan, 1995).[15]

Swiss Re's report concludes with some lessons that can be learnt from past earthquakes. The comparatively small number of fatalities in Chile and New Zealand can be explained first and foremost by building regulations and their strict monitoring.[16] The fact that both events caused significant property damage shines a light on the importance of secondary loss agents or losses not directly caused by ground tremors. Such agents were insufficiently accounted for in the risk models used by the insurance industry in 2010. The earthquake in Chile was followed by a tsunami. In New Zealand, the shocks led to an effect known as soil liquefaction: diminished cohesion of the soil that can cause significant damage to buildings and roads. In contrast with the earthquakes in Chile and New Zealand, the quake in Haiti shows that questions of catastrophe management will remain a major challenge for developing and emerging countries. As there is no insurance market for earthquake risks in many of these countries, the main focus is on preventative measures, such building regulations. To this end, Swiss Re includes an earthquake map for Haiti in its report, based on its own calculations, which can help the reconstruction process minimize future earthquake damage.

In the regularly published reports on the World Catastrophe Reinsurance Market, the US reinsurance broker Guy Carpenter focuses primarily on the effects of major loss events on reinsurance markets, with a particular focus on contract pricing and conditions.[17] Besides the catastrophes which, due to the September publication date of the report, are generally only covered if they occur in the first six months of each year, the focus lies on the trends in claims payments, the capital adequacy of the reinsurers, and the terms of new treaties, which are significantly impacted by both the trends in claims payments and the capital adequacy. In addition, other current factors influencing the reinsurance of major loss occurrences are regularly reported on, such as developments in the markets for catastrophe bonds (cat bonds) and in the catastrophe models used by the insurance industry. Another section of the 2010 report is concerned with the effects of changes to the regulatory framework on the activities of the market, particularly in connection with the introduction of the Solvency II European solvency and equity capital rules and the proposals to change the tax laws in the USA.

[14] Swiss Re, *sigma* 1, 2011, 6, 15.
[15] Swiss Re, *sigma* 1, 2011, 12.
[16] Swiss Re, *sigma* 1, 2011, 12f.
[17] Guy Carpenter (2010).

For the contract pricing and conditions, it identifies an average price erosion of 6 per cent for new treaties signed in the first half of 2010, resulting from an overcapitalization of the markets of up to USD 20 billion. By way of contrast, the prices of excess of loss treaties and facultative risks in Chile rose by between 50 per cent and 70 per cent.[18] With regard to the further development of contract pricing and terms, the report notes that even one major loss event is enough to reverse market trends. It was difficult to forecast the conditions of future new treaties and, in particular, the treaties to be concluded with effect from 1 January 2011, it reports, as the hurricane season in the USA was just beginning and had been predicted to be active, and the development of the markets depended on the degree to which reinsurers' capital would be impacted by major loss events by the end of the year. An event in the magnitude of USD 23–30 billion would stabilize the markets, while an event of more than USD 50 billion would lead to a significant correction of the conditions. Important factors for the markets for cat bonds were loss trends and, in particular, the course of the hurricane season in the USA. According to the report, eight cat bond issues were completed in the second quarter of 2010, increasing the cat bond market's risk capital by USD 2.05 billion, of which USD 1.7 billion was on storm damage in the USA alone.[19] The introductory overview concludes with the statement that a low price level and changes to the regulatory framework would make agreeing contract conditions more difficult for reinsurers in the near future.

## 10.2 City Fires and the San Francisco Earthquake

The know-how contained in today's reports developed, during the course of the twentieth century, from a series of highly varied experiences with major loss occurrences. Of the two historical roots of reinsurance, marine insurance and fire insurance, it was the development of fire insurance in Western Europe and North America in the nineteenth century in particular that led to know-how in dealing with major loss occurrences.[20] Industrialization and urban migration led to city fires becoming an important existential threat, despite these being caused not just by forces of nature, but, to a large extent, by unfavourable planning regulations and human negligence. It must also be remembered that city fires played a significant role before the development of fire insurance and reinsurance. The chronicles of catastrophes in Western Europe include the fires in London (1666), Lisbon (1775), and Hamburg (1842), with only the fire in Lisbon being the result of a natural catastrophe.[21] The high population density in the area meant that the latter catastrophe, addressed by authors such as

[18] Guy Carpenter (2010, 11). [19] Guy Carpenter (2010, 14).
[20] Gerathewohl et al. (1982, 649ff.); Kopf (1929, 29ff.). [21] Koch (1966); Sofonea (1997).

Voltaire, Kant, and Goethe, and caused by an earthquake, led to extraordinary losses and numerous fatalities, despite the fact that the earthquake itself was not particularly powerful.[22] It was following the fire in Hamburg, which broke out in a warehouse, and spread quickly on account of the dry spring weather and strong wind, that the question of adequate reinsurance protection began to gain traction, against the background of a well-developed fire insurance industry. The first independent specialized insurer, Kölnische Rückversicherungs-Gesellschaft (Cologne Re), was founded in 1846, four years after this event. Almost concurrently, the Aachen Reinsurance Company came into being as a subsidiary company of the Aachen and Munich Fire Insurance Company. The impact of the Hamburg Fire and the ensuing claims settlement regulations had been a decisive factor in the setting up of the special purpose reinsurer.[23] The foundation and early development of Swiss Re, set up in 1863, was also closely connected with city fires, such as that in the Swiss city of Glarus (1861) and the Swedish city of Sundsvall (1888), as well as the San Francisco Earthquake (1906). Another important motive for the establishment of Swiss Re and other professional reinsurers was the effort to minimize premium payments to foreign companies.[24]

In the USA, it was the fires in Chicago (1871), Boston (1872), and Baltimore (1904) that increasingly raised the demand for reinsurance cover.[25] As elsewhere, these events focused attention on the limited capacity of direct insurers and also the problem of the accumulation of losses at companies whose business activities were regionally limited. The city fires that took place from the 1870s onwards led to extensive public discussions about insurance and its capabilities, unlike those in the early years of the USA. This was due largely to the fact that the country had quickly caught up in the amount invested in per capita insurance premiums. The emerging economic power drew level with the UK in 1880, despite the fact that, only thirty years previously, US per capita insurance premiums had been only a sixth of those in the UK.[26] Unlike the UK, the legality of reinsurance treaties had already been confirmed by the New York's Supreme Court in 1837. Nevertheless, compared with Europe, in the USA, few specialist reinsurers were set up by Americans until well into the twentieth century.[27] While there was no formal legal challenge to conducting reinsurance treaties in the USA, two other legal barriers to the insurance business generally put the development of reinsurance in specialized reinsurance companies in the USA at a disadvantage. Regulation, which is organized on the state level in the USA, hindered not only multiline, but also nationwide, business activities: two crucial prerequisites for building healthy reinsurance portfolios. As a result, reinsurance cover was largely provided by American direct insurers in the form of co-insurance.

[22] Koch (1966, 29); Sofonea (1997, 3ff.).

[23] Friedrich Adolph Brüggemann, under whose leadership the Aachen and Munich Fire Insurance Company developed into the largest fire insurer in Germany, travelled to Hamburg in 1842 to settle a claim and, based on his experiences there, decided to set up his own reinsurance subsidiary. See Gerathewohl (1982, 689f.).

[24] Rohland (2011a, 2011b, 153–69).

[25] Koch (1966, 18); Kopf (1929, 58ff.).

[26] Pearson (2004, 366) (quoted from Kobrak (2012, n41)).

[27] Kopf (1929, 58, 72).

The public discussions on the role of insurers and reinsurers in major loss occurrences peaked for the first time in the wake of the 1906 San Francisco Earthquake. The quake had a defining influence on how insurers and reinsurers dealt with major loss occurrences, an influence that extended far beyond the borders of the USA.[28] In the early morning of 18 April, several seismic shocks hit San Francisco. Buildings collapsed and the inhabitants sought safety in the higher areas of the city. The consequences of the earthquake were worse than the quake itself: numerous fires broke out in different parts of the city, culminating in a three-day-long conflagration. Collapsed chimneys and unattended fire-places caused the fires, with leaking gas pipes fuelling the flames. Damage to the water pipes meant that many hydrants were not functioning. The fire department sought to control the fires by demolishing entire rows of houses and using controlled explosions. When the fire was finally extinguished on the morning of 20 April, four fifths of the city (corresponding to an area of 30 $km^2$) had been destroyed. The official number of fatalities was approximately 500, but later estimates put the death toll at 3000. Property losses were estimated between USD 300 million and 500 million. Following intensive legal wrangling, the insurance industry met claims of USD 235 million, equivalent to one hundred times the 1906 premium volumes for fire insurance in San Francisco.[29] Around 90 per cent of the approximately 25,000 destroyed buildings had been insured against fire.[30]

The San Francisco Earthquake is worthy of note for two closely related reasons, namely the complex wrangling about the paying out of claims relating to earthquake clauses in the fire insurance policies and the presence of numerous European insurers and reinsurers. As contemporaries and many later sources attest, insurers from 'around the world' were involved in settling the claims.[31] The event made clear what insurance experts already knew: the general globalization process that took place at the end of the nineteenth century had had a particularly strong impact on US fire insurance, like many other branches of the insurance business.[32]

The fact that British insurers had had a significant presence in the city fires in Chicago and Boston in the early 1870s led to 25 per cent of all US fire insurance being in the hands of British suppliers by 1881.[33] In San Francisco, foreign fire insurers had a market share of around 50 per cent by the turn of the century and foreign companies played a significantly larger role in reinsurance business treaties, with a market share of around 90 per cent across the USA as a whole by 1918.[34] For the first time, the San

[28] The San Francisco Earthquake has also attracted a great deal of attention in literature over the years. See, for instance, Bertogg et al. (2005); Koch (1966, 10ff., 1969, 137–77); Munich Re (2006); Pearson and Lönnborg (2007); Sofonea (1997, 5ff.).

[29] Bertogg et al. (2005, 12). [30] Bertogg et al. (2005, 10).

[31] Röder (2006); Rohland (2011a; Borscheid and Haueter (2012).

[32] Pearson (1995, 551–71); Wilkins (1989). Also, see, in particular, the contributions of Wilkins, Pons, and Borscheid in Borscheid and Pearson (2007).

[33] Wilkins (2009, 337) and Wilkins (1989, 529) (quoted from Kobrak (2012, n49, n51)).

[34] Bertogg et al. (2005, 10) and *Best's Insurance News*, 15 August 1917, 33–7 (quoted from Kobrak (2012, n76)).

Francisco Earthquake and the ensuing disputes focused the attention of citizens, companies, courts, and politicians on the extraordinarily high level of foreign penetration. Insurers and reinsurers had concluded policies with different conditions, in line with those operating in their home countries, and there were also differences in the way the claims were settled. San Francisco revealed not only an advanced stage of globalization in one of the key sectors of the US financial services sector, but also the lack of any harmonization of legal policy and framework conditions. However, the situation within the USA itself was extremely complicated, due to the fact that the individual states were responsible for regulating the insurance industry.

Most fire insurance policies contained earthquake clauses that excluded earthquake damage in one form or another. While insurers saw these as exempting them from any obligation to pay out claims, there were hundreds of legal cases in which those insured put forward the case that the exclusion did not apply to the San Francisco Earthquake, as the majority of buildings had been destroyed by the fire storms that raged for several days, which meant that the quake was not the direct cause of the losses.[35] The legal altercations also revolved around the 'Fallen Building Clause' contained in New York Standard Fire Insurance policies that had originally been introduced to prevent insurance fraud. This policy clause removed the obligation to indemnify in cases where buildings had already collapsed before they could burn down. For the courts, this raised the question of how extensive the collapse needed to be to justify overruling the fallen building exclusion clause. The business relationships maintained by reinsurers with numerous cedents and other reinsurers via retrocession instruments meant that all these claims and legal cases brought a wide range of information on losses, policy conditions, and claims settlement regulations together. Although reinsurers had, as a rule, worded their exclusions from earthquake damage more clearly than the direct insurers, they remained responsible for a significant proportion of the losses incurred, which generally had grave consequences for their business results. With net claims payments of CHF 4.3 million compared with earned premiums of CHF 11.4 million in the non-life sector, the San Francisco Earthquake remains, to this day, the largest loss event in Swiss Re's history.[36] It was not alone, as the majority of primary insurers were also obliged to meet significant claims payments. Although the legal wrangling about entitlement to benefits took three years to resolve, the vast majority of the 90,000 notified claims were settled within a year of the loss occurrence.

Settling the claims was far from the final chapter in the story of the San Francisco major loss event. Once the immediate consequences of the event had been brought under control, the question arose of whether the mishmash of different policy clauses that had come to light following the quake should be simplified to make

[35] Röder (2006, 69). [36] Bertogg et al. (2005, 14).

regulating future major losses easier and thus give insurers and those insured a firmer foundation for new policies and the obligations arising from them. In an interesting study of legal history, Tilmann Röder shows that, in the absence of international organizations concerned with the harmonization of national regulations, fewer governmental bodies were trying to establish a uniform earthquake clause in the aftermath of the San Francisco Earthquake than were internationally operational insurers and, in particular, reinsurers.[37] Röder compares the efforts of these companies regarding the events in San Francisco with issues such as the harmonization of screws, bolts, and threads, or the introduction of voluntary rules for the interpretation of contracts in international trade, such as the well-known free on board (FOB) commercial clause. He asks whether the case of the earthquake clause gave rise to a *lex mercatoria*, and follows in particular the efforts of four reinsurers to ensure that earthquake risk continued to be strictly excluded from fire insurance policies or subject to an additional premium. The objective of this initiative was to ensure that fire and earthquake risks remained insurable and to create more transparency with regard to the scope of liability of fire policies.[38] In conclusion, the author states that a uniform international *lex mercatoria* or similar transnational legal structure did not come into being. Strict exclusions would not have been enforceable in internationally oriented markets subject to a high level of competitive pressure such as the Netherlands and the UK. Nevertheless, Röder considers that the efforts to harmonize legislation regarding earthquake exclusion clauses were the harbingers of a development in which the legal framework became increasingly independent of state actors.[39]

The San Francisco Earthquake brought to light the diversity and breadth of relationships held by the international reinsurance industry. It spelt out what had sounded rather theoretical when uttered by the leading global specialist reinsurers such as Swiss Re in 1863 or Munich Re in 1880: the reinsurance of major risks is closely linked to the international orientation of the business activities of these companies and their involvement in a variety of insurance lines.[40] In 1929, Edwin W. Kopf, an early chronicler of reinsurance, summarized the ideas of a prominent co-founder of the Munich Reinsurance Company in these words:

> Thieme's internationalism was based on the idea of smoothing out the effects of purely local fluctuations in business, climatic and operating conditions. Losses on one branch of the business in one country could be counterbalanced by gains on another branch in the same country. Or losses on all lines in one country would be compensated by gains on all lines in another country. The internationalisation of reinsurance was, in his opinion, the first step toward the atomisation and the widespread distribution of risk.[41]

[37] Röder (2006). [38] Röder (2006, 51f.). [39] Röder (2006, 227f.).
[40] Gerathewohl (1982, 694, 697). [41] Kopf (1929, 32).

## 10.3 An Atlantic World

The San Francisco Earthquake made the in-balances between supply and demand in the global reinsurance market clear, a situation that remained steady for much of the twentieth century. The USA was particularly exposed to natural catastrophes, due to the earthquake risks on the West Coast and regular, recurring hurricanes in the south-east. In the rapidly developing US economy, these catastrophes also caused the destruction of a significant volume of insured assets, which meant that the USA was, by global standards, an important market when it came to demand for catastrophe cover. In contrast, a significant proportion of the international reinsurance industry was concentrated in Western Europe, in the form of Continental specialist reinsurers and Lloyd's of London. At the outbreak of the First World War, the countries most involved in the reinsurance industry were Germany, Switzerland, Austria-Hungary, and Russia. Germany alone accounted for 67 per cent of premium income of independent reinsurance companies.[42]

Two world wars and the economic crisis of the 1930s reinforced again the fact that the international reinsurance markets were significantly impacted by developments in Western Europe and North America. Like the rapid development of globalization over the nineteenth century, the destruction of international economic relationships that took place between 1914 and 1945 had its global epicentre in the North Atlantic region.[43] This was true both for reinsurers and for many other internationally oriented companies. As a result, quite a few changes occurred in the global market shares of European professional reinsurers and their home countries.[44] Moreover, the companies were preoccupied with specific challenges such as inflation and exchange-rate changes, and interruptions to international business resulting from war or the consequences of the peace treaties.[45] Natural catastrophes took a back seat role in business reports and journals of the time, not least because they occurred less frequently in the years between 1914 and 1945. In an overview of the major natural catastrophes of the twentieth century that were of particular relevance to insurance published in the British journal *The Review*, the only natural catastrophe in the USA to happen during this period was the Great Miami Hurricane of 1926.[46] A study of the long-term development of tropical hurricanes in the USA showed that while there was a cluster of particularly deadly events of this type between 1914 and 1945, the period was

[42] Gerathewohl (1982, 727) and Kopf (1929, 33) (quoted from Holland (2009, 22)).

[43] M. D. Bordo, A. M. Taylor, and J. G. Williamson (eds) (2003) *Globalization in Historical Perspective*. Chicago: University of Chicago Press.

[44] Haegen (1956, 42).

[45] Borscheid (2007, 129–41); Gerathewohl (1982, 729–54). See also the case study on Swedish marine and reinsurance in the interwar period: Petersson (2011).

[46] *The Review*, July–August 2004, 24–5.

nevertheless below average compared with the long-term trend of the twentieth century in terms of the economic losses that these caused.[47]

In contrast to the period between 1914 and 1945, the post-war period was characterized by extraordinarily steady economic growth. The rapid and fairly stable rise in prosperity formed a background against which the enormous suffering and considerable destruction caused by natural catastrophes played out. This applied not only to the public reporting of major loss events such as Hurricane Betsy in 1965, which attracted considerable attention as an insidious threat to lives and property, but also for professional communications from the insurance industry, in which these events contrasted sharply with a market trend largely unaffected by political and macroeconomic influences. Unlike any other phase of development of the reinsurance industry in the USA, the idea became established in the decades following the Second World War that the markets and their strongly cyclical nature were driven primarily by natural catastrophes. However, the phase during which there was an almost undivided focus on natural catastrophes came to an end in the early 1970s. Developments such as the transition to flexible exchange rates, a phase of pronounced high interest rates, the rapid growth of offshore centres such as Bermuda, the increasing integration of insurance and banking markets, and numerous financial innovations meant that it again became clear to reinsurers that they would have to tackle some very varied factors and influences.

Hurricane Betsy, which in August 1965 struck land along the coasts of Florida and Louisiana at wind speeds of up to 256 km per hour, destroyed property values amounting to USD 3 billion in only a few hours, and was for many years the largest and most spectacular major loss event in the post-war period.[48] The *National Underwriter* began its annual review of the development of the US reinsurance market with the words: 'The reinsurance business will never be the same—after the event of Betsy. The market both here and overseas still reels from the shock of it [ . . . ].'[49] As is the case with other similar loss events, Betsy is described in the business journal not simply in terms of the absolute numbers of fatalities, and economic and insured losses, but also through a variety of information on meteorological and construction-related aspects of the calamity, in particular also due to its influence on the development of the combined loss ratio, *a ratio* regularly used by *National Underwriter* and other business journals to compare a year's insured losses with the sum total of premiums and operating costs. As can be seen in Figure 10.1, the combined ratio rose following the 1965 hurricane to a level of 1.08, moving between 0.96 and 1.0 in years where there was no particular accumulation of major loss events. Betsy not only made apparent the huge influence that tropical hurricanes have on the otherwise steady growth of the US reinsurance markets, but, in the same way as the San Francisco Earthquake, provided the impetus for further consideration of the business relationships of the international reinsurance markets.

[47] Blake and Landsea (2011, tables 2, 3b, 7. 11).

[48] *The Review*, July–August 2004, 24–5.

[49] *National Underwriter*, 1966, 46.

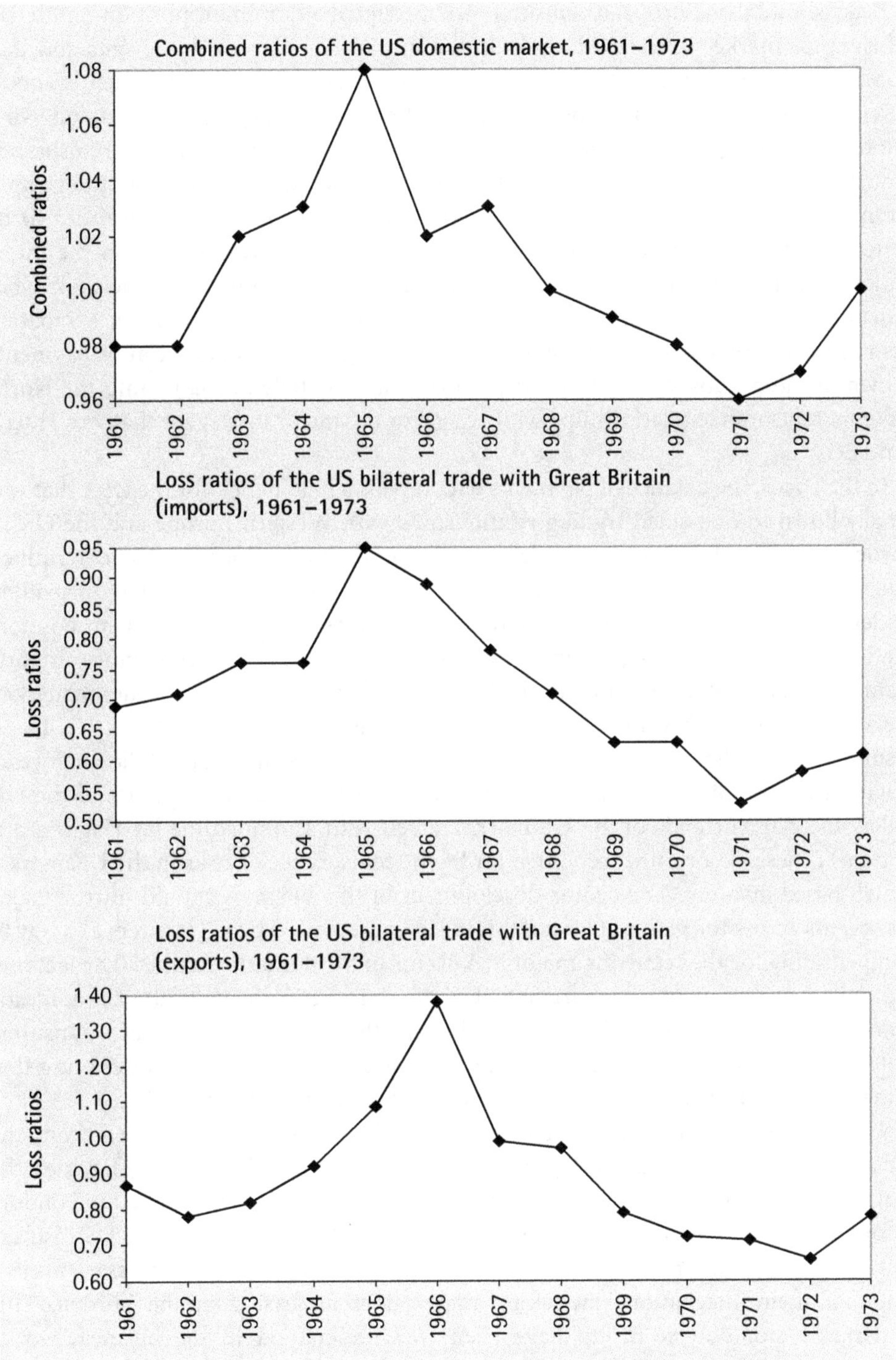


FIGURE 10.1 Combined ratios of the US market and the bilateral trade relationships between the USA and the UK, 1961–1973

*Source*: Werner (2007).

Betsy shows that European reinsurers still occupied a dominant position on the US reinsurance market in the mid-1960s in the insurance of major loss events and that domestic insurers remained inexperienced when it came to handling such events.[50] After the end of the Second World War, there had been an expectation that, following the renewed collapse of a large proportion of its European rivals, the US reinsurance industry would follow the example of numerous other US industries and develop a strong presence on the national and international markets. In 1949, in order to be better able to track the progress of the domestic competitive position on the international reinsurance markets, the US Department of Commerce undertook what remains an unconventional step of posting reinsurance transactions as a separate item in the national balance of payment statistics. The premium and claims payments shown in these statistics can be used to obtain more detailed insights into the North Atlantic reinsurance relationships with regard to the major loss event that was Hurricane Betsy.

In the 1950s, the balance of payments data reveals a high deficit for the USA that was largely down to one-sided trading relationships with Western Europe and the UK in particular.[51] The development of claims in international business can be determined due to the fact that claims and premium payments are listed separately, providing evidence of the difficulties encountered by US insurers in their dealings with London, the international reinsurance centre. As might be expected, US reinsurance imports from the UK over the 1960s mirror the trajectory of claims on the US domestic market. Hurricane Betsy makes a clear impact on the reinsurance of US risks by UK-based insurers, as do the lesser major loss events in the preceding and following years (Figure 10.1, middle). The surprising thing is that US reinsurance exports to the UK follow the claims trends of the US market, albeit with a minor time lag (Figure 10.1, bottom). These exports are accounted for by the reinsurance of risks in the UK market by US-based insurers. The claims development of this business should mirror major loss events across the globe, at least if this business were used by US insurers as a way of compensating for the recurring major loss events in the domestic market. The fact that the claims development of exports matches the claims experience of the US domestic market allows only one conclusion to be drawn—that it was US risks that US insurers were writing, particularly in the reinsurance centre of London.[52] It is interesting that these exports generate markedly higher loss ratios than the imports.

The development of claims in international business, as can be seen from the separate figures for losses and premiums in Figure 10.1, show the difficulties the American insurers had in dealing with the international reinsurance market in London. In other words, by writing reinsurance business on the London market, US insurers suffered an aggravation of the negative consequences of domestic major loss events as a result of their international activities, rather than an easing of the burden. This remarkable situation seems to have been well understood in the business world.

[50] Werner (2007). [51] Werner (2007, 19ff.). [52] Werner (2007, 13f.).

Examining the particular relationship between the US insurance industry, in which specialist reinsurers continued to play a subordinate role compared with direct insurers, and the London reinsurance market (and in particular, Lloyd's of London), the business journal *Best's Fire and Casualty News* draws the following conclusions with regard to Hurricane Betsy:

> By 1960 there were a great many American companies interested in accepting reinsurance—some on a businesslike basis and many not. Under the pressure of this buyer's market, the underwriting syndicates in London were anxious to increase their own ability to serve their customers across the world. One device that was developed in order to provide additional capacity was the parcelling out of participations in excess contracts to insurers in the U.S. This was done by numerous Lloyd's syndicates and also by members of the London company market. Acceptance of such business became quite a status symbol [in the USA], especially for unsophisticated insurance company officers. The natural result of this development was that when unfavourable experience developed in the U.S., many insurers found that they were not only paying substantial losses on their own direct policies but they were also sharing to a much greater degree than they had anticipated in such catastrophe losses through the excess contracts written for underwriters in London's market. Betsy was the crowning blow, and many of the insurers who had decided to experiment in the reinsurance field withdrew—blowing on their burned fingers as they did so![53]

The tropical cyclones, which in later years caused extraordinarily high losses in the USA, were Hurricane Andrew (1992), with insured losses of USD 27 billion, and Hurricane Katrina (2005), with insured losses of almost USD 80 billion. While Andrew drew consideration largely because of its impact on the insurance industry, Katrina seared itself into the US public consciousness primarily as a result of Washington's unfortunate crisis management and the city of New Orleans. From the early 1990s onwards, these two major events, in conjunction with a particular accumulation of similar medium-sized and smaller loss events, increasingly led public opinion and opinion within the industry to suspect that the intensity and number of natural catastrophes had significantly increased and were the consequences of climate change. However, various scientific studies of long-term hurricane trends revealed that the prime cause for the ever-increasing loss amounts in the USA seemed to be the rapid growth in population in areas particularly affected by the storms rather than any change in the number and intensity of the storms themselves. Various studies examined the question of what losses would have been incurred had past events occurred in the recent past, taking into account the changes in the concentration of demographics and assets. From this vantage point, it is the 1970s and 1980s that stand out in the twentieth century due to an accumulation of particularly serious natural catastrophes. These findings coincide with the fact that the meteorological data reveals that these two decades witnessed the worst weather events.[54]

[53] Kelly (1967, 16–22). [54] Pielke and Landsea (1998); Blake and Landsea (2011).

The trend towards higher economic and insured losses over the last twenty years is primarily the result of a population shift towards the parts of the country particularly affected by storms. The fact was that the south-western USA had been experiencing particularly strong economic growth for a considerable period. While the region had been sparsely inhabited at the beginning of the twentieth century compared with other parts of the country, a large proportion of the economic development during and after the Second World War had been concentrated there. Economic activity shifted from the industrialized Frost Belt in the north-eastern states to the Sun Belt, which included both the south-west and the south-east of the country. The demographic changes in the population of Florida illustrate the extraordinary dynamism of this process. Between 1900 and 2000, the state moved from position thirty-three in the list of most populated individual states to fourth place.[55] The rise of the south-western USA is not solely due to the shift from an industrial society to a service and technology society, but also to the ageing population and an associated annual influx in the winter months due to the agreeable climate.

Earthquakes, the second major natural catastrophe to which the USA is particularly prone, have led to much lower losses than hurricanes in the twentieth century. This is true not only of the USA, but also globally, with earthquakes accounting for only around a tenth of the claims payments arising from major loss events in the second half of the twentieth century.[56] Although such events are far less frequent, they nevertheless have the capacity to cause far more destruction. The San Francisco Earthquake left no room for doubt in the USA that California is particularly exposed to these natural catastrophes. Despite this, the population growth in the West Coast's main metropolitan areas, such as San Francisco and Los Angeles, considerably outstripped the average. California, Florida, Texas, and New York accounted for 38 per cent of the total population growth over the twentieth century in the USA.[57] Following a number of smaller quakes, such as Long Beach (1933), San Fernando (1971), and Loma Prieta (1989), the destructive power of earthquakes reappeared in earnest in 1994 with the Northridge Earthquake, which reached 6.9 on the Richter scale.[58] Its epicentre was the San Fernando Valley, 32 km north-west of Los Angeles. With its fifty-seven fatalities and economic losses of USD 53 billion, the quake was the most expensive to date both in the USA and globally. The insured losses, at around USD 21 billion, were considerably less than the economic losses, mainly due to the low penetration of earthquake insurance in California. For residential buildings, the penetration was only around 30 per cent to 40 per cent, considerably below the roughly 90 per cent penetration of storm loss coverage in Florida.[59] That insured losses make up a comparatively low proportion of the economic losses of earthquake risks is down to higher retentions,

[55] F. Hobbs and N. Stoops (2002) *U.S. Census Bureau, Census 2000 Special Reports, Series CENSR-4: Demographic Trends in the 20th Century*. Washington, DC: US Government Printing Office, 7.

[56] Insurance Services Office (1994, 43).

[57] Hobbs and Stoops (2002, 24).

[58] Insurance Services Office (1994, 22–4).

[59] Munich Re (1994, 13); Insurance Services Office (1994, 14f.).

which not only reduce the share of the economic loss borne by the insurer, but also encourage policyholders to prevent losses. It must also be remembered that, despite the fact that the losses that occurred in Northridge were high by global standards, such an event by no means represents the worst-case scenario for the US West Coast.[60] Were a larger event, comparable with the 1906 San Francisco Earthquake, to occur, economic losses would be many times higher. Studies conducted in the 1990s for earthquakes in San Francisco and Los Angeles estimated property values of USD 170–225 billion. The median probability of occurrence is estimated to be a hundred years.[61]

The two major loss events, Andrew and Northridge, helped to ensure the rapid spread of computer-based catastrophe models in the insurance industry from the mid-1990s onwards, various models having been developed as early as the 1980s.[62] The Insurance Services Office in Santa Barbara, California, had produced an initial risk model based on earthquake maps and land-use plans as early as 1929.[63] All of these models are based on the determination of numerous factors such as the probability of occurrence of the events, their severity and location, the anticipated losses and the insured losses.

When developing models, earthquakes with a comparatively low probability of occurrence but especially high loss potential represent the greatest challenge, particularly with respect to global hotspots such as San Francisco, Los Angeles, and Tokyo. As relatively little information is available from the past about these natural catastrophes, the trends need to be carried forward in the form of stochastic models, a task increasingly undertaken by specialist providers such as Applied Insurance Research, Risk Management Solutions, and EQE International. Despite all the progress that has been achieved in the forecasting of natural catastrophes and their effects with the help of catastrophe models in recent years and decades, the question of whether the market takes sufficient account of such forecasts remains. As the market reports discussed in Section 10.1 of this chapter show, the calculation of premiums on the reinsurance markets depends in particular on the reinsurers' loss experience and employment of capital in the recent past. During periods with few loss events, reinsurers generally experience significant pressure on prices. Moreover, major catastrophe losses are prone to underestimation when similar loss events only occurred some considerable time ago.

The effect that Hurricane Andrew had on the insurance industry highlights a further important dimension of the interrelationship between the insurance markets and natural catastrophes. The storm led to the collapse of eleven insurers and a third of all the Lloyd's syndicates.[64] Together with the 9/11 terrorist attack and Hurricane Katrina, it unleashed a controversy about the strong cyclical pattern of the reinsurance markets and raised questions about insufficient market capacities. Such discussions, in which the possibility of government market intervention is generally raised at some

[60] Munich Re (1994, 13).
[61] Risk Management Solutions (1995, 3).
[62] Chapter 9, this volume.
[63] Bertogg et al. (2005, 20).
[64] Insurance Services Office (1994, 20).

point, have taken place at regular intervals in the history of insurance and reinsurance. The vehemence with which it was expressed in the USA at the beginning of the twenty-first century attained a new quality, not least because it embodied a range of completely different concerns. The terrorist attack on the World Trade Center encroached on vital American security interests. The increase in natural catastrophe losses impacted on the global topic of climate change. The rise of the cat bond markets, which became apparent in the late 1990s, opened up new perspectives for avoiding capacity constraints, which relied on the increasing convergence between the insurance and banking markets. The discussion about market cycles and insufficient capacity featured not only voices from the insurance industry, but also a significant number from government bodies and international organizations, and was reflected in the scientific literature of the insurance industry and in banking publications.[65]

David Durbin, an author from the world of business, uses the major loss events, the strong cyclical patterns, and the development of the cat bond markets as an opportunity to deal with the structures of the global markets for catastrophe protection.[66] He examines the global revenues of accumulated loss per event insurance (cat XL) in 2000, where the underlying risks per definition are catastrophe-related.[67] He shows that global demand at the end of the twentieth century continues to be shaped by demand from the USA, followed, by some considerable remove, by Japan, the UK, Canada, Australia, and Mexico.[68] In the industrialized nations, cover varies tremendously by natural catastrophe, with far less coverage of earthquakes than storm and water damage. He states that prices are dependent on strong cycles associated with past loss events and do not necessarily reflect the underlying risk situation. There could be significant price variations in very short periods, such as the 50 per cent variation over the five-year period 1994 to 1999.[69] Cat bonds, which came into being as part of the general convergence of banks and the insurance industry, could help dampen these fluctuations. While these markets are still relatively small in volume, they have considerable potential for development. He further states that it is in the interests of insurers, who accounted for 35 per cent of the total volume issued, to engage in the new markets and thereby mobilize additional capital.[70]

An extensive survey, conducted in the USA in 2004 in the wake of the terrorist attack on the World Trade Center by the Government Accountability Office (GAO) on behalf of the US Congress, examined the question of what regulatory requirements existed in European countries and the USA for the insurance and reinsurance of major loss events. According to the authors, the provision of sufficient capacity in the (immediate) aftermath of major loss events depends not only on the development of cat bond markets, but also on numerous other factors. These include the measures of assistance

[65] See OECD (2011); US GAO (2005); Cummins (2007, 179–220); Cummins and Weiss (2009, 493–545); Nell and Richter (2005).

[66] David Durbin was head of Group Management at Swiss Re in 2001.

[67] Durbin (2001, 297–309).

[68] Durbin (2001, figure 3, 301).

[69] Durbin (2001, 302f.).

[70] Durbin (2001, figure 9, 306).

from institutions established by individual states, for example the Florida Hurricane Catastrophe Fund (FHCF) and the California Earthquake Authority (CEA), the tightening up of building regulations in especially affected areas, the further development of risk models, the increasing of retentions, and the founding of additional reinsurers specialized in catastrophe insurance in Bermuda.[71] A general tax concession for provisions relating to natural catastrophes and terrorist attacks would not necessarily improve the ability of the US insurance industry to pay out claims.[72] A very diverse range of measures are employed in Europe, with strong state involvement in the insurance of terrorism losses in particular.

Overall, the USA remained so dominant as a reinsurance market at the beginning of the twenty-first century that it, as is evidenced in the market reports referred to in Section 10.1 of this chapter, clearly tops the global premium payments chart for natural catastrophes. This is, to a considerable extent, due to the fact that the relative economic loss of influence of the USA since the post-war years was accompanied by a large-scale internal migration to regions at particular risk of natural catastrophes. Other factors also play a part. The turbulent globalization of the financial markets at the turn of this century is giving rise to widespread discussions regarding new developments for reinsurance and other financial services, with the USA being used as an example. Subjects under debate include the catastrophe model, the question of insufficient capacities for catastrophe losses, the role of the state in insurance and reinsurance markets, new financial instruments such as cat bonds, and the trend towards offshoring. The US insurance markets for major losses are, at the beginning of the twenty-first century, starting to display a particular 'structural power' of the kind that political economists describe for the US banking markets—despite the continuing high concentration of specialist reinsurers in Western Europe.[73]

## 10.4 Global Risk Society

While the global reinsurance markets of the twentieth century were heavily shaped by US demand and European supply, other regions of the world have gained in importance in recent decades against a background of the rapid expansion of globalization and the formation of new growth centres; in part, this is merely because natural catastrophes happening outside of the North Atlantic area have attracted more public and professional attention due to the improved flow of information. As can be seen in *sigma* 1, 2011, a large proportion of the worst natural catastrophes in terms of fatalities over the period 1970–2010 occurred in Asia and in developing and emerging countries. Of the forty events, twenty-seven occurred in Asia and accounted for 75 per cent of

[71] US GAO (2005, 4). [72] US GAO (2005, 7).

[73] E. Helleiner (2011) 'Understanding the 2007–2008 Global Financial Crisis: Lessons for Scholars of International Political Economy', *Annual Review of Political Science* 14, 67–87, here 78f.

global fatalities, while thirty-seven occurred in the developing and emerging countries as a whole, accounting for 97.6 per cent of deaths worldwide. Globally, by far the most important causes of natural catastrophes involving very high number of fatalities were earthquakes, at twenty-one of forty events, followed by storms (eight), floods (five), and heatwaves (three).[74]

As can also be seen in the above-mentioned issue of *sigma*, the forty natural catastrophes with the highest number of fatalities between 1970 and 2010 only rarely led to high claims payments. There can be no doubt, however, that these catastrophes generally entailed considerable economic losses. Insofar as we accept the United Nations' (UN's) definition of exceptionally large disasters, which are defined by assessing the amount of damage and comparing it to the locally and regionally available resources for self-help, many of the most deadly natural catastrophes also certainly disrupt a particularly large proportion of the fundamental and material requirements for existence.[75]

Looking at the catastrophes from the perspective of claims payments rather than fatalities gives us another picture entirely.[76] This viewpoint, which is important for both insurers and reinsurers, brings into focus different events with a completely different regional distribution. As stated in Sections 10.2 and 10.3 of this chapter, it is North America—and the USA in particular—that head up the table, followed by Europe and Japan. The proportion of insured losses from the forty most serious events accounted for by North America is 75.8 per cent, followed by Europe with 14.3 per cent, Asia with 6.3 per cent, and South America with 2.3 per cent. Claims payments in Asia are almost entirely accounted for by Japan. The rest of Asia, global hotspot of the largest natural catastrophes, barely features when it comes to claims payments. The situation is similar with regard to the developing and emerging countries as a whole, accounting as they do for only 2.3 per cent of global insured property values. As the industrialized nations are the focal point of claims payments, North American hurricanes top the list, accounting for nineteen of the events, followed by Western European winter storms and floods, which were the causes of eleven more of the forty events.

Of course, looking at the world's largest natural catastrophes in terms of fatalities and insured losses gives no more than an indication of the global distribution of the very many types of loss events and their impact on lives, property, and insurance markets. Nonetheless, this comparison makes it plain that, from the point of view of insurance and reinsurance, the world cannot be said to have come together in a single global risk society. Looking further afield than the strongly integrated North Atlantic risk markets, we see various very different 'global risk societies', each with a relatively

[74] Man-made catastrophes are also taken into account in table 9 in Swiss Re *sigma* 1, 2011, as per the original Swiss Re data. However, they play a very minor part, accounting for just one event, an accident at a chemical company in Bhopal, India.

[75] Munich Re (2011b, 45).

[76] Man-made catastrophes are also taken into account in table 8 in Swiss Re *sigma* 1, 2011, in line with the original Swiss Re data. The only such event to appear in the table is the 9/11 terrorist attack.

undeveloped international network. The differences in the way that natural catastrophes are handled are particularly stark when we compare Asia with North America. While Asia is exposed to by far the largest natural catastrophes from a humanitarian point of view, with the exception of Japan, insurers and reinsurers play little or no role in their management. North America's natural catastrophes, which are of far less significance in terms of their humanitarian dimensions, are, in contrast, insured and reinsured to a very high degree.

What additional patterns can we discern in the diverse large claim events? Let us first look at Europe. Although the accumulation of natural catastrophes involving a particularly high number of fatalities is, at 5.9 per cent, not particularly striking, there are some catastrophes that are plainly of global significance in their scale, such as an earthquake in Turkey in 1999 and three heatwaves in 1976, 1999, and 2010, each claiming between 6000 and 56,000 victims.[77] The comparative high claims payments were primarily the result of winter storms and floods in north-western Europe.[78] The high level of claims payments in Western Europe, and increasingly also in Central Europe, can, as in the USA, be largely explained by the generally high insurance density. An additional factor is that the region has the highest concentration of specialized insurers in the world. Looking back at all the natural catastrophes of the twentieth century of particular significance to the insurance industry, *The Review* names six events that were largely confined to Western Europe: the earthquake in Avezzano, Italy (1915); a North Sea storm surge that primarily affected the Netherlands and the UK (1953); a wind storm in the UK (1987); the winter storm Daria, which caused damage in many regions of Western Europe (1990); the winter storms Anatol, Lothar, and Martin, whose worst effects were felt in Denmark, Germany, Switzerland, and Spain (1999); and a flood in Central Europe, with the Czech Republic, Austria, and Germany worst affected (2002).[79]

As the forest fires in Russia and the ash clouds from Iceland in 2010 demonstrated, there are considerable differences in the participation of insurance in the economic losses caused by natural catastrophes between individual European countries. A flood that affected the Czech Republic, Poland, and Germany in 1997 provides a further example that, even in regions with well-developed insurance and reinsurance markets, by no means all natural catastrophes have high levels of loss cover.[80] The heavy rainfall at the start and middle of July 1997, caused by the two low-pressure systems Xolska and Zoe, brought torrential rainfall of up to 200 litres per square metre. Southern Poland and eastern areas of the Czech Republic each suffered flooding covering 6000 km$^2$, representing 2 and 8 per cent of the respective countries. Some 1500 towns and villages and numerous city centres were flooded, along with entire industrial areas. Along the courses of the Oder and Morava, hundred-year water levels were exceeded by up to two metres. The region had last suffered similar extreme flood disasters in 1736, 1854, and 1903.

[77] Swiss Re, *sigma* 1, 2011, table 9.
[78] Swiss Re, *sigma* 1, 2011, table 8.
[79] *The Review*, July–August 2004, 24–5.
[80] See Hausmann and Hux (1997).

Germany was less affected, as the flood waves had already reached their peak in the Czech Republic and Poland. In addition, the rescue services had longer to prepare, to strengthen dams and take other measures. The waters finally receded after three weeks, leaving behind 100 dead and 300,000 evacuees. The total economic loss was around DM 7 billion, only around 15 per cent of which was insured. The comparatively low claims payments of DM 1.2 billion can be explained by the fact that many of those affected did not consider themselves to be under threat or could not afford cover. In addition, there was extensive uninsurable damage to roads, bridges, and other kinds of infrastructure. Despite the comparatively low claims payments, the 1997 floods endangered numerous insurers who had not had sufficient time to accumulate sufficient reserves since the fall of the Berlin Wall in 1989. Reinsurers, who were just as quick to establish themselves in the Czech Republic, Poland, and East Germany as the direct insurers, bore around 50 per cent of the claims payments in the three states. As what can be done to improve flood control systems is limited by cost considerations, one of the most important lessons that came out of the flood, in the report from Swiss Re, was the need to improve risk maps. Unlike storms or earthquakes, according to Swiss Re the areas at risk of flooding can generally be well defined. Such maps barely existed prior to the occurrence of the loss event, mainly due to political reasons.[81] Communications between insurers and reinsurers could also have been significantly better in these young insurance markets. Contractually agreed timetables, on which primary insurers totalled loss occurrences only within the first 168 hours of the loss event, proved problematic for both insurers and reinsurers. The flooding lasted several weeks and caused numerous identified loss events, with the result that primary insurers had to bear their retentions many times over and were also able to pass a higher proportion of their loss burden onto reinsurers.[82]

As noted in Section 10.3 of this chapter, the most serious natural catastrophes are concentrated in Asia, but, with the exception of Japan, these losses are either insufficiently covered or not covered at all by insurance or reinsurance. This is because either the insurance penetration rate of these markets is extremely low or, as in the case of China, practically no insurance market exists in the private sector. While natural catastrophes in Asia accounted for around three quarters of all global fatalities between 1970 and 2010, with the exception of the four events in Japan, the continent scarcely appears in the claims payment table. This situation is reflected in the forty-year and also in the hundred-year summary in *The Review*, where comparatively few events in Asia appear: the 1923 Great Kanto Earthquake in Yokohama and Tokyo, a cyclone in Bangladesh in 1970, the 1976 Tangshan Earthquake, and the Kobe Earthquake in Japan in 1995. In the last ten years, the most important addition to the list would be the 2011 reactor accident in Fukushima.

The 1970 cyclone in Bangladesh and the 1976 Tangshan Earthquake demonstrate how natural catastrophes can give rise to devastating humanitarian catastrophes in

[81] Hausmann and Hux (1997, 6–8). [82] Hausmann and Hux (1997).

highly populous yet economically poor regions, and the remarkable gulf that has existed between them and the insurance and reinsurance markets in the twentieth century. The cyclone in Bangladesh was the largest windstorm catastrophe of the twentieth century.[83] On 12 November 1970, a tropical cyclone hit the coastal region of Chittagong and Khulna. The result was that around 70 per cent of the country was underwater for several weeks. The death toll lay between 300,000 and half a million. The economic losses, estimated at USD 63 million, give an insufficient indication of the scope of the humanitarian catastrophe that developed as a consequence of the storm and flooding. The event, which, together with the Tangshan Earthquake, tops the list of the most deadly global natural catastrophes, led to no insured losses. As one of the poorest countries on earth, the insurance market in Bangladesh remains extremely undeveloped.

The Tangshan Earthquake took place on 28 July 1976 at 4 a.m. and registered 7.8 on the Richter scale.[84] The epicentre of the quake was 11 km below the centre of Tangshan, a city with a multimillion population. Within seconds, the city was almost completely destroyed. Seismological measuring stations, set up following the 1966 Xingtai Earthquake, had failed to detect any prior indication of the quake. The harrowing consequences were 650,000 dead and destruction or severe damage to around 85 per cent of all buildings. The economic losses were estimated at around USD 5.6 billion.[85] In the absence of private insurance companies, it was down to government bodies to alleviate the losses and suffering.

The first indications of increased involvement by the insurance industry in the management of natural catastrophes in Asia came only at the end of the twentieth century, despite the fact that Southeast Asia had, since the late 1970s, become the most important growth region in the world, causing a considerable increase in insurance density in many places. As *sigma* 1, 2011, shows, only in the last ten years have particularly deadly natural catastrophes in Asia begun to lead to claims payments. Excluding Japan, such events include the earthquake in Iran (1990), hurricanes in India and Bangladesh (1999), an earthquake centred on India, Pakistan, and Nepal (2001), quakes and the tsunami in Indonesia (2004, 2006), and an earthquake in China (2008). Nonetheless, the claims payments for these six events, amounting to around USD 2.8 billion, remain extremely low by global standards.[86]

Japan, a highly developed industrialized country, differs greatly from the picture of Asia as a whole and must be considered separately. It is characterized by an extremely high accumulation of natural catastrophes combined with a highly developed market economy with a high insurance density, where enormous assets are concentrated in very small areas, unlike anywhere else in the world. Here too, the insurability of natural catastrophes has its limits, with difficult-to-calculate earthquake risks and tsunamis at the forefront of the threats. The small country has suffered four events associated with particularly high claims payments in the last forty years, only one of which involved

[83] *The Review*, July–August 2004, 24–5.
[84] Yong et al. (1988, vii, 1–51).
[85] *The Review*, July–August 2004, 24–5.
[86] Swiss Re, *sigma* 1, 2011, table 9.

very high fatalities. These were Hurricane Mireille (1991) with fifty-one victims and USD 9 billion in claims payments, the Kobe Earthquake (1995), which led to 6425 deaths and USD 3.5 billion in claims payments, and Hurricane Bart (1999) with twenty-six victims and USD 5.3 billion in claims payments.[87] A fifth event of global dimensions occurred after 2010: an earthquake in 2011 that caused the Fukushima reactor accident, led to 15 840 fatalities and caused insured losses of USD 35 to 40 billion.[88] The events of 2011 again show that, despite the enormous efforts devoted to early warnings and earthquake-resistant buildings, even industrialized nations are unable to avoid major catastrophes. The catastrophes in Japan in recent decades have been considerably larger in scope than those in the USA, although, taking the twentieth century as a whole, there has been a certain similarity between the two states regarding unusual earthquakes. For the USA, these were the 1906 San Francisco Earthquake and the 1994 Northridge Earthquake, which stand out from the various other similar occurrences due to the extraordinarily high level of losses, while, for Japan, these were the Great Kanto Earthquake and the Kobe Earthquake, which occurred in 1923 and 1995, quite close in time to the events in the USA.

The Great Kanto Earthquake, though often mentioned in conjunction with the quake in San Francisco, was much larger in its extent, despite there being some parallels in the course the disaster took and with regard to the controversy surrounding claims payments.[89] The event, which destroyed the port city of Yokohama and extensive areas of neighbouring Tokyo on 1 September 1923, led to a fire storm in which 210,000 buildings burnt down. In total, some 105,000 lives were lost. Newspapers were soon reporting insurance claims amounting to JPY 2.2 billion. Later studies showed that the insured assets amounted to JPY 3.3 billion.[90] The event exposed the weaknesses of the underdeveloped insurance system. Japanese non-life insurers had assets of only around JPY 200 million, not least because the presence of foreign insurers had been declining since the start of the twentieth century. As in the USA, there were also disputes about the earthquake clauses in the policies. However, in Japan the government intervened on behalf of those insured. Shortly after the event, it obliged domestic insurers to meet 10 per cent of all losses, as well as offering loans to those insurance companies unable to meet their obligations from their own resources. With few exceptions, such as the Tokio Marine Insurance Company in particular, insurers had no choice but to make full use of this offer. The claims payments amounted to JPY 1.5 billion, with the insurance industry meeting 0.5 per cent of all economic losses and the government meeting 4.3 per cent.[91]

Despite the payments being quite low when compared with the economic losses, the government's intervention spared the insurance industry from a serious loss of image and allowed it to improve its future prospects.

[87] Swiss Re, *sigma* 1, 2011, table 8. [88] Munich Re (2012, 8).

[89] However, there is comparatively little information on the Great Kanto Earthquake in Western sources. For example, Kopf devotes only a few sentences to the development of reinsurance in Japan in his much-quoted history of reinsurance. See Kopf (1929, 56).

[90] Yoneyama (2009, 11). [91] Yoneyama (2009, 18).

Foreign fire insurers also initially refused to pay out claims. However, as part of the government programme, twenty-six of the twenty-eight foreign insurers, among them Swiss Re, issued voluntary payments amounting to one year's premium.[92] There was only limited international reinsurance for fire damage. The total volume of reinsurance treaties amounted to JPY 750 million, only 10 per cent of which came from foreign companies.[93] In marine insurance, the situation was entirely different, as there was little controversy surrounding payment obligations. Of the approximately JPY 16 million in insured losses, around 60 per cent was covered by foreign reinsurance companies.

There is no mention of natural catastrophes in South America and Africa in the hundred-year review in *The Review*. Africa does not appear at all, not even its most serious catastrophes of the past forty years in terms of either fatalities or insured losses. In contrast, catastrophes in South America comprised 7.4 per cent of all fatalities and 2.3 per cent of all insured losses. Events with exceptionally numerous fatalities were the earthquakes in Peru (1970) and Guatemala (1976), and a volcanic eruption in Colombia in 1985. Of these three catastrophes, which ranked among the ten deadliest events in the period under review, only the earthquake in Guatemala led to claims payments from insurance companies, although these were of modest proportions. The only event in South America associated with considerable claims payments in the period analysed was the aforementioned 2010 earthquake in Chile. In addition, the climate phenomenon El Niño received plenty of global attention in the late 1990s.[94] A similar phenomenon led to a 12 per cent fall in GDP in Peru in 1983 due to losses in the fisheries and agricultural industries.[95]

When we look at Africa, we can see that natural catastrophes are only one of several existential challenges facing emerging nations. Humanitarian catastrophes, which occur frequently in sub-Saharan Africa, can be caused by war, civil war, corruption, or other factors. Natural catastrophes that occur particularly frequently include drought and floods. While both events are very frequent, they seldom reach the dimensions of a major loss event. Drought in particular is a natural occurrence that develops relatively gradually over long periods and so rarely appears in the statistics on major catastrophes. In countries such as Botswana, Burkina Faso, Chad, Ethiopia, Kenya, Mauritania, and Mozambique, catastrophic drought is ever present.[96]

There may well be other problems of comparability in the statistics on natural catastrophes and their consequences, for instance in relation to the notably high figures for fatalities in Western Europe as a result of heatwaves. This phenomenon is simply not recorded in the statistics for subtropical or tropical regions that face such heatwaves more frequently. The nations south of the Sahara also give us a good example of why the insurance of natural catastrophes does not play a greater role in many emerging countries. As well as having limited means with which to protect against natural catastrophes and numerous other substantive threats, the literature also lists access to

[92] SRCA 10.143 874.02, Earthquake in Japan. [93] Yoneyama (2009).
[94] See Trüb (1998). [95] UNEP (2002, 285). [96] UNEP (2002, 276).

international assistance as a factor that reduces willingness to take measures to protect against natural catastrophes. For instance, the focus of the World Bank's assistance measures for natural catastrophes is on sub-Saharan Africa and South America, which together account for around half the measures undertaken.[97] Another, possibly more fruitful, path to better insurance coverage for low income countries could be micro-insurance, a large variety of practices which are in accordance with established insurance principles. However, the development of such schemes, is—on a global scale—still in its infancy.[98]

## 10.5 Review and Outlook

Natural catastrophes have diverse effects on reinsurance. Major loss events such as city fires played an enormous part in the formation and establishment of specialist reinsurers in the late nineteenth century. In later years, events such as the San Francisco Earthquake also gave an important impetus to the definition of the tasks of specialized insurers in national and international insurance markets and to adapting to the constantly changing framework conditions. While the most important question for companies is the degree to which natural catastrophes can be taken into account in insurance contracts, the focus in recent years and decades has been on developing complicated stochastic models to determine the probability and loss potential of catastrophes. The results of these analyses have, however, not always had sufficient impact on pricing policy in the highly competitive reinsurance markets, whose pronounced cycles are the result of natural catastrophes.

From the very beginning, the international focus of the activities of the reinsurers was a factor in the close relationship between reinsurance and natural catastrophe. Their cross-border activities put these companies in a position to gather experience on relatively rare major loss events and ensure that their risk portfolios were internationally balanced. As is the case in other industries, the reinsurers' cross-border activities did not result in an equivalent network of international business relationships. In the diverse global risk society, the contradictions in the insurance and reinsurance of natural catastrophes were primarily due to differences in the level of economic development of economies and insurance markets, factors over which the reinsurers had no direct influence. The differences between North America and Asia highlight the contradictions in the global risk economy. While the USA dominated demand for catastrophe insurance in the twentieth century, due to its high concentrations of assets and frequent natural catastrophes, a large proportion of the reinsurance available was concentrated in the hands of internationally active specialist reinsurers in Western Europe. The majority of global cross-border reinsurance business remains

[97] Parker (2006, 13).

[98] For more information on current activities see <http://www.microinsurancenetwork.org>.

concentrated in the Organisation for Economic Co-operation and Development (OECD) states bordering the North Atlantic.

Asia, where the majority of the most serious natural catastrophes of the twentieth century occurred, was of little significance in the portfolios of the internationally active specialist reinsurers. As is the case in many parts of Africa and Latin America, this is due to the generally low level of development of the insurance markets and the absence of competitive prevention measures in state-dominated economies. This situation has only begun to change in the last ten years, during which time insurers and reinsurers in Asia and South America have occasionally appeared in tables of claims paid for natural catastrophes, although these payments were low both by global standards and in comparison with the economic losses.[99] While the economic rise of Southeast Asia is leading to an integration of insurance markets, it is doing so with something of a time lag. The merging of the risk markets of Asia and the North Atlantic, and of the industrialized and emerging nations, will remain one of the great challenges of the twenty-first century. Reinsurers will certainly play an important part in this process, although these companies will face numerous challenges other than natural catastrophes. In the twentieth century, they had to cope with global economic crises and world wars and, from the 1970s onwards, events such as exchange-rate fluctuations, high interest periods, and the general globalization of the financial market. A rapidly changing regulative environment, the convergence of banking and insurance markets—such as in the case of cat bonds—offshore movements, and increased demand for financial planning services are only some of the numerous influences on business that the companies will need to remain on top of. Of course, reinsurers also needed to focus on their mass business, rather than only spectacular major loss events.

The question of what role natural catastrophes and the globally accumulated know-how relating to the insurance of these events should occupy in their business transactions is one that reinsurance companies will need to re-examine at regular intervals. In the past, there were also considerable changes and unusual economic situations that affected the priority that reinsurers gave to natural catastrophes. Although numerous twentieth-century sources leave no doubt that there is a close relationship between natural catastrophes and reinsurance, professional reinsurers have publicly focused on this aspect of their business activities only over the past thirty years or so, since around the 1980s, during which time a growing need for business communications coincided with an increased interest in natural catastrophes by the public and scientists.[100]

One of the few constants of reporting on reinsurance markets and natural catastrophes is the finding that the threats are getting bigger, a view largely shared by insurance and reinsurance companies and numerous other voices. Observers of catastrophes and events in the markets have always been firmly convinced that they were entering a new age that posed greater challenges. This analysis of the current situation persists to this

[99] There is a future-oriented analysis of both of these global regions in Guy Carpenter (2012).

[100] For example, natural catastrophes were not among the key topics addressed in Gerathewohl's extensive work. See Gerathewohl (1982).

day and, given factors such as climate change and population growth, may even be justified. For such reasons, reinsurers will in future come under great pressure to address the topic of natural catastrophes. Nevertheless, they face numerous other current challenges. The global and European financial crises show clearly that the global economy has left the stability of the post-war decades behind.[101] Insurers and reinsurers, like many other companies, are faced by a difficult-to-predict environment. The cost of saving the insurance company American International Group (AIG) during the US subprime mortgage crisis was USD 182 billion. As Swiss Re notes in an annual review on natural and man-made catastrophes, the losses incurred by the collapse of this one insurance company are several times higher than the claims paid out by the insurance industry for the most serious global natural catastrophes.[102]

[101] Werner and Pierenkemper (2002).

[102] Swiss Re, *sigma* 2, 2009, 39 (quoted from Borscheid (2010)).

# CHAPTER 11

# CONTINUITY AND CHANGE IN REINSURANCE 1990–2016

ROMAN LECHNER, NIELS VIGGO HAUETER, AND LAWRENCE KENNY

A review of reinsurance market developments from the 1990s on is faced with an interesting conundrum. On the one hand, the fundamental business model of reinsurance appeared relatively unchanged through this period. On the other hand, industry leaders perceived a fundamental transformation in how business was conducted. There were various attempts to bring it closer to the financial markets, and the industry underwent radical change through mergers and acquisitions (M&A), new technology, and shifts in capital sources. Also, a major shift in corporate cultures took place against the background of a rapidly globalizing business environment. While the globalization of corporate cultures was not specific to reinsurers it may be argued that their already very international business model allowed such changes to happen at an impressive pace.

Another factor that changed during this period was the risk landscape. The opening of the twenty-first century saw a man-made catastrophe that dwarfed everything before it, whilst, in 2005, the so-far most financially devastating natural catastrophes happened. It was not the nature of risk per se that changed but the size of reinsured risks, their frequency, and the interdependence of reinsured risks in reinsurers' portfolios. Up until the late twentieth century, the reinsurance industry had adapted to a constantly changing risk landscape but had not been fundamentally changed by it. Supply and demand changes in the industry had mainly been caused by political events such as wars, regulation, and shifting economic power, as well as by economic circumstances such as exchange rates and inflation. The late 1980s and early 1990s may have been the first time that risks started causing severe changes in the way risk was distributed in the market. The task here is therefore to map how this changing risk landscape reshaped the distribution of risk business among existing and new players and, with this, redefined the roles of the respective stakeholders. The hypothesis developed is that the scale and concentration of risks faced by the industry led to an increasing level of interdependency between the different sectors of the market as they sought to satisfy client demand, and deal with increasing concentration in values and globalization. What appeared to be very different models of operation between brokers, global reinsurers, and Bermudan funds emerged as parts of an intricate ecosystem satisfying the increasing appetite to manage risk effectively.[1]

The reinsurance market, then, increasingly came to act as a subtle ecosystem that absorbs risks and adapts to a changing risk landscape. As with most ecosystems, there was considerable competition, but also a significant amount of collaboration and mutual dependency as market players and their clients sought to optimize the diversification of risks at the best price. In this way, it is noticeable that major reinsurers were some of the early movers in both introducing alternative capital and setting up a new class of reinsurers, the so-called class of ninety-two, in Bermuda, and that the latter would never have thrived without the considerable influx of talent from the London market in the 1990s. Of course, this was never a zero-sum game as the operators in the market were often public companies and also needed to grow to satisfy their shareholders, but such growth had to be profitable—the objective was not to accumulate more capital per se, but to allocate capital at a good rate of return and store reserves to cover losses.

Whilst this chapter, therefore, is structured on rather traditional lines, considering the different market sectors and approaches to reinsurance, the major events that shaped the market and the rise of alternative capital, there is also an attempt to consider how the reinsurance industry overall adapted to the challenge of providing cover for clients as the risk landscape evolved.

## 11.1 Basic Market Structure

Broadly speaking, two major approaches to the market of reinsurance have developed since the nineteenth century. The first can be described as the *Continental* approach, championed by the market-leading companies of Continental Europe and, in particular, Germany and Switzerland, where the first professional reinsurance companies emerged. This approach aimed at offering a full service relationship with clients, tailoring packages and bringing considerable risk expertise to bear on the clients' issues. This meant that price finding was negotiated rather than prices being determined by a liquid secondary market for risks. A unique feature of reinsurance was that larger size and global reach allowed companies to spread risks more efficiently, requiring less reserve capital per risk. The largest, Swiss Re and Munich Re, had already established a lead position in the nineteenth century, which they were, on the whole,

[1] See Gugerli (2013) for a comprehensive historical study of cooperation and competition in the reinsurance industry.

able to maintain. They soon started playing a special role in setting standards both in risk assessment and pricing. Eventually, this resulted in the two companies being considered 'lead reinsurers'. Other 'follow' reinsurers participating in ceded risks would often rely on the risk assessment and the pricing of the lead reinsurers. This distinction of 'lead' and 'follow' reinsurers was later expressed as first- and second-tier reinsurers. For over a century, lead reinsurers sought to be present in all segments of the market and manage globally diversified portfolios. Only more recently did the next tier, such as Hannover Re, SCOR (Société Commerciale de Réassurance), and General Re, the subsidiary of Berkshire Hathaway, internationalize on a larger scale and establish a strong presence in Europe, often through M&A, such as in the case of General Re taking over Cologne Re. These companies focused more on specific segments, flexibly managing their capital allocation according to market pricing, and have by now gained a combined market share of some 30 per cent in property and casualty reinsurance and 70 per cent in life and health reinsurance.[2]

The second approach was more *market-based*. Lloyd's had already championed this model in the seventeenth century when risks were traded in coffee houses. Eventually, this evolved beyond Lloyd's into a web of specialists organized around brokers and the processes of pricing and risk transactions. By the mid-twentieth century, this became known as the 'London market'. Brokers would negotiate a reinsurance programme on behalf of clients, having analysed the risks, structured the contract, and reviewed the market potential. Over the period under discussion, there was a substantial consolidation among the insurance and reinsurance brokers, so that, by 2015, the leading three reinsurance brokers together had come to command about three quarters of the brokered reinsurance market.[3]

Around the turn of the century, brokers sought to broaden their role from pure brokerage to extended services, including structured solutions. Ultimately, their strategy increasingly led to a full service offering to the client, so that the reinsurer potentially became a supplier of a capacity-driven, capital-based product. However, in practice, brokers and large reinsurers often shared a symbiotic relationship, working with clients to analyse, structure, and place their risks in a collaborative way. The top brokers also adopted the advances in data management and modelling to mobilize the market data they collected as part of their daily business and make it available to clients. Not only were there efficiency gains through automatization, it was also hoped the improved access to market data and analytics would bind in clients and improve bargaining power with cedents and reinsurers. Well over half of US property and casualty reinsurance came to be intermediated by brokers by the middle of the first decade of the twenty-first century.[4] The markets of London and Bermuda continued to

[2] See Figures A.2.1 and A.2.2 in Appendix.

[3] The three leading reinsurance brokers: Aon Benfield, Guy Carpenter (part of Marsh & McLennan Companies (MMC)), and Willis Re.

[4] Holzheu and Lechner (2007, 888).

hold to the broker model into the new century, whilst, in Continental Europe, direct customer contacts between cedents and reinsurers still dominated.

Brokers formed part of what was traditionally called the London market, where ninety-six Lloyd's syndicates and more than fifty small to medium-sized reinsurance companies provided insurance and reinsurance cover. But, from the 1990s, Bermuda developed into a major location for broker-related reinsurance companies. This was heavily influenced by its closeness to the vast US market and the attraction of an advantageous legal and tax framework.[5] Bermuda developed into the funnel for the new flexible capital that first emerged in the early 1990s in response to the high prices available in the natural catastrophe market. After 9/11, a new wave of capital flowed into casualty and primary insurance as well, and the entrepreneurial Bermudan market began to be characterized by a focus on digital operations and computer modelling to facilitate transactions. The most prominent Bermudan players acquired a market share of around 15 per cent.[6] Recently, however, Switzerland, especially Zurich, has emerged as a main reinsurance hub for specialized reinsurers, attracting players from Bermuda and the Cayman Islands looking to move closer to their European clients.[7]

Apart from a significant number of smaller, more locally and regionally focused players, the national reinsurers also stood out. As described in the Introduction to this volume, countries with net imports of reinsurance in particular had started founding state-run reinsurers in the early twentieth century, often with a monopoly position. More recently, some of them were partly or completely privatized, Korean Re, for example, as early as 1978 when the fledgling economy started thriving. IRB (Brazilian Re) is currently state-owned after a planned initial public offering (IPO) in 2015 was cancelled due to market turmoil. China Re undertook an IPO in Hong Kong in 2015. The General Insurance Corporation of India (GIC Re) remained state-owned, leaving a mix of former monopoly reinsurers and privatized players with roughly 8 per cent of the market.[8] In 2012, China Re and Korean Re entered the league of top ten reinsurance companies,[9] gaining respective market shares of around 3 per cent in 2014 with property and casualty (P&C) gross premiums of around USD 5 billion each.[10] Despite being relatively large in premium income, former monopoly or state-run reinsurers were often not globally diversified, but all of these players have become capable of further expansion into the international reinsurance industry.

Whilst one can describe these approaches to reinsurance separately, in practice they became very interlinked. Large brokers increasingly developed their risk expertise and tapped into the core competencies of large reinsurers. Continental reinsurers expanded their presence in London and Bermuda and continue to work with state-owned

[5] Cummins (2008). [6] See Figure A.2.2 in Appendix.

[7] 'Rückversicherung. Der Fluch der Karibik' (*Die Handelszeitung*, 2 December 2010).

[8] See Figure A.2.1 in Appendix.

[9] 'Global Reinsurance Capital Hits Record Levels' (*Reuters News*, 4 September 2012).

[10] A. M. Best (2015) '"It is Not Your Father's Reinsurance Market Anymore": The New Reality', Special report on global reinsurance, 2 September, 8. Market size is estimated by Swiss Re, Economic Research & Consulting, see also Appendix.

insurers, while Bermuda-based players developed strong links in the US and London market. Increasingly, a client might also work with both a broker and a Continental-style reinsurer, with both collaborating to find the most appropriate arrangement for the risks under scrutiny. A major driver of how the client chose to work was the complexity of the solution they required. Tailored solutions required greater analytical and underwriting capabilities, generally only found at the major reinsurers, sometimes at the top brokers or at a speciality reinsurer focused on a specific niche.

The market events from 1990 to 2016 led to an ebb and flow in the development of each of these market approaches, and it is in their division and confluence that the overall market is best described. It may also be helpful to indicate that, by market events, we are reviewing events that helped to shape the marketplace for reinsurance in this period, rather than a purer perspective on the changing risk landscape. Indeed, should be noted that, although new risks emerged, the toolbox of instruments used by reinsurers to structure the contractual covering of the risks, such as excess of loss, remained relatively stable, other than the insurance-linked security (ILS) and alternative capital markets that will be discussed separately. The next sections of this chapter go on to review the main drivers and events that impacted the development of the reinsurance market through this period.

## 11.2 Search for Scale, Market Liberalization, and Technological Advance

Several long-term trends came together in the 1990s to lead to a major shift in the strategy of insurers and reinsurers. As financial markets deregulated and electronic trading began to link financial centres in real time across time zones, there was a recognition that there was only space for a few companies to act as real global operators with leading positions in the major markets and strong representation elsewhere. As in many industries, this led almost inevitably to a process of consolidation within the global reinsurance market. Within the industry it was noticeable that rating agencies also placed a value on size and diversification, with the larger players remaining relevant to major corporates and insurers as their own industries consolidated. Well-capitalized very large players were perceived as presenting a lower risk of default should a major catastrophe occur. But size was not enough, the other watchword was *focus*. This meant insurers divesting their positions in reinsurance and vice versa to create more coherent companies with a global footprint.

Throughout the 1990s, access to many Latin American and Asian markets was liberalized, but the increasing ease of operating across borders was perhaps most clearly seen in the liberalization of the European market in 1995. The shift from national supervision of insurers towards solvency controls led to a major deregulation and an intensification of cross-border activity as a single transnational trading market was created. Coordination of insurance supervision across Europe also improved with the founding of the International Association of Insurance Supervisors (IAIS) in Basel in 1994. The General Agreement on Trade in Services (GATS) of 1995 reflected these moves on a global stage, and eased access to and accelerated changes in some other domestic markets as regulation slowly harmonized across borders, although it at no point became uniform.

As the markets were deregulated there was also a transformation in technology. The roll-out of the Internet made communication in all areas cheaper, faster, and more straightforward. A company could be run internationally in real time with instant access to internal and public sources of information. As processing power improved and data sources became available, more complex risk simulations could be made, particularly for natural catastrophe modelling and asset allocation. Technology also facilitated the extension of the ecosystem of players active in the marketplace. Small and niche risk consultants and modellers could use telecommunications to extend their reach internationally, creating virtual bureaus as required, with their gap in relation to major players shrinking, as they could acquire risk intelligence online at decreasing costs. Brokers and some clients could outsource elements of the risk management process to these newer players, as the flow and importance of timely risk information accelerated.

## 11.3 Mergers and Acquisitions

The external drivers of M&A around strategic scale and reach and liberalization of markets were matched by events within the reinsurance market, ensuring that size and focus became imperatives. The liability crisis 1985/6 in the USA,[11] man-made disasters like the explosion of Piper Alpha in 1998 and the Exxon Valdez oil spill in 1989, as well as a number of large-scale storms (Hurricane Hugo in 1989, Winterstorm Daria in 1990, Typhoon Mireille, and in particular Hurricane Andrew, in 1992) highlighted how exposures for property and other types of cover were increasing. Ceding companies required access to higher reinsurance capacities as the scale of risks and potential losses grew. They also put greater emphasis on security and the financial rating of reinsurers, partly because they were facing uncollectible debts from smaller insolvent reinsurers. Many smaller suppliers of reinsurance, among them reinsurance departments of primary insurers, withdrew from the market.

As a consequence, professional reinsurers sought to increase their own size and scale, in order to profit from improved pricing and be able to supply higher capacities, whilst

[11] See Berger, Cummins, and Tennyson. (1992).

not neglecting diversification. A wave of M&A followed between 1994 and 1998. In non-life reinsurance, 1996 proved to be a highpoint in terms of value traded, with companies comprising around 13 per cent of global market share finding new owners.[12] The top four players grew their share from 22 per cent in 1990 to 29 per cent in 1996, and about 34 per cent in 1998.[13]

The wave of reinsurance M&A activity began with the intercontinental acquisition of the long-standing Cologne Re (then worldwide number five) by the leading US company and worldwide number four, General Re. At the end of the 1980s, when its non-US business was only 5 per cent of turnover,[14] General Re had already expressed an ambition to be a leading reinsurer internationally. The opportunity presented itself as the bank Sal. Oppenheim wanted to sell its majority share to strengthen its own capital base. Sal. Oppenheim had been one of the founders of Cologne Re in 1846. In 1995, another leading US reinsurer, Employers Re,[15] itself owned since 1984 by General Electric, acquired the leading German reinsurers Aachen Re (from Generali) and Frankona (from Gerling). Here also, the sale was motivated by a desire to strengthen the core business, for Generali expansion as a direct insurer, and for Gerling its own brand. Frankona was, in any case, separately run from Gerling, the majority owner. A movement in the opposite direction followed when Munich Re acquired American Re for the then enormous sum of USD 3.3 billion, making Munich Re the third largest reinsurer in the USA. American Re was owned until 1992 by Aetna Life and Casualty, and then by the leveraged buy-out firm Kohlberg Kravis Roberts & Co. (KKR).[16]

Each of the transactions tended to follow the same pattern. The purchaser wanted to broaden its geographical reach in order to build a focused global portfolio. The seller wanted to strengthen its own core business and therefore divest its reinsurance arm. But these transactions were only the tip of the iceberg. Swiss Re strengthened its position in life reinsurance through the purchase of Mercantile & General Re (M&G) (1996) and Life Re (1998). In 1998, Berkshire Hathaway, the diversified conglomerate created by Warren Buffett, acquired the fourth-largest reinsurer, General Cologne Re, for the record sum of USD 22 billion. This acquisition marked the end of the M&A wave of the 1990s, as well as the rise of Berkshire Hathaway to the top tier of global reinsurers.

Before the General Re acquisition, Berkshire Hathaway (BH) had already been in the reinsurance business. Well furnished with the capital backing of the BH Group, its main subsidiary, National Indemnity, had been focusing on transactions that would require very large underwriting capacities, which other players could not devote to a single risk. A well-known example in the super-catastrophe business comes from 1996,

[12] For a comprehensive list see Holland (2009, 25–6). [13] Swiss Re, *sigma* 9, 1998, 11.

[14] General Re Corporation (1997) *Annual Report 1996*, 10.

[15] Employers Re, later on rebranded as General Electric Insurance Solutions (GEIS), was acquired by Swiss Re in 2005/6.

[16] <http://www.fundinguniverse.com/company-histories/american-re-corporation-history/> (accessed 13 December 2015).

when National Indemnity provided the newly founded Californian Earthquake Authority with a USD 1 billion cover over a four-year period.[17] A second field of activity was the retroactive business that is the assumption of a certain loss portfolio from an insurer, where the ceding party would neutralize the risk of losses on claims reserves, but also the chance of a positive development. The largest transaction had been the acquisition of the claims reserves of Lloyd's run-off entity Equitas for USD 7 billion in 2007.

The process of integrating acquired or merged businesses became a major requirement for the leading reinsurers. Previously, international expansion had been achieved through extensive travels and, later, the creation of stand-alone subsidiaries. Such local offices were often in better positions to satisfy local regulation and solvency demands for risk reserves deposits to be made on a country-by-country basis. Requirements varied considerably from market to market and this, combined with the relative independence of local subsidiaries, had led to rather heterogeneous international company structures. In the late 1990s, Swiss Re led the way for reinsurers to adapt their organizational structures to a globalizing environment, creating what they termed a 'one company approach'. This consisted of a single brand applied throughout global markets, marking the end of its traditional company name, the Schweizerische Rückversicherungsgesellschaft.[18] The Münchener Rückversicherungsgesellschaft became Munich Re in 2009. Possibly more importantly, by the mid-1990s, the companies began to consider their capital base as more integrated, with the potential to move capital internationally to take advantage of attractive business or product segments. They also began to tackle the difficult issues of legacy information technology (IT) systems to simplify data and information management internationally.

During the mid-2010s, the process of consolidation continued to impact smaller generic reinsurers and brokers whose capital ratings were not strong especially. Firms in the industry needed to offer something more than capital, whether specialist niche expertise, global reach, or strong client relationships—preferably all of these—to remain relevant to clients. In addition, some Bermudan-based firms sought to diversify away from reinsurance by investing in the primary specialty markets.

## 11.4 The Soft Market of the Late 1990s

The second half of the 1990s saw a fall in reinsurance prices as a capacity shortage moved to one of excess capital. Losses were lower than anticipated and the number of major catastrophe events was also relatively low. The direct insurance sector had been consolidated, resulting in larger and better-capitalized players with less need for reinsurance cover, but still they needed more sophisticated solutions in mature markets

[17] Berkshire Hathaway (1997) *Annual Report 1996*.

[18] Straumann (2013, 336ff.).

such as Europe and the USA. Demand for reinsurance capacity in emerging markets such as Latin America and Asia, however, was growing.[19] At the same time, both primary insurers and reinsurers were recording enormous investment profits, especially from rising stock markets. Insurers were at that time heavily engaged in stocks, with not just their own capital but also part of their technical reserves invested. In particular, huge profits were made at the end of the 1990s with the internet share bubble. The euphoria from this success led to some insurers perceiving themselves less as managers of insurance risks and more as fund managers successfully investing in rising stock markets.[20] As the internet bubble burst in 2000 and the US stock market fell, however, the business model based on rising stock markets showed its vulnerability.

But the lure of the capital markets for reinsurers went deeper than a question of investment returns or the concerns of insurers to safeguard their client access, as banks looked to broaden their product range to include insurance, creating a bancassurance business model primarily driven by benefits in sales and distribution.[21] The real attraction for reinsurers was in *risk* transfer. Rather than a reinsurer holding a client's risk on their own balance sheet, the vision was to act as a gateway to the broader capital markets, packaging and transferring the risk to third parties. With this model, the reinsurer's balance sheet would be transformed from a storage room of risk reserves to a revolving door opening out to the capital markets. Some of the traditional reinsurer's risk assessment and underwriting skills would be required to package the client's risks, with the diversification happening via the vast liquidity of the capital markets.[22] The offering a reinsurer could make would now be much broader, as their own capital would be freed up to address other needs the client had in managing their balance sheet.[23]

This acceleration in the use of capital implied a transformation in how the reinsurer operated. It also required a shift in skills and mindset that only the most sophisticated were willing to contemplate. The sources for this desire to shift business model were

[19] Swiss Re (2004, 9).

[20] Accelerated growth in financial services in the USA, for example, was, overall, much more pronounced in securities and credit intermediation from the 1980s on, while insurance had shown a steady growth since the 1940s. See R. Greenwood and D. Scharfstein (2012) 'The Growth of Modern Finance': <http://www.people.hbs.edu/dscharfstein/growth_of_modern_finance.pdf> (accessed 21 December 2015).

[21] <https://www.scor.com/en/sgrc/insurance-market/item/2228-analysis-of-bancassurance-and-its-status-around-the-world.html?lout=sgrc> (accessed 21 December 2015). For a differing view see <http://www.sueddeutsche.de/wirtschaft/der-kunde-wuenscht-es-einfach-nicht-bank-und-versicherung-passen-nicht-zusammen-1.919789> (accessed 21 December 2015).

[22] 'It is easy to imagine, then, insurance companies underwriting insurance policies effectively acting as originators, sourcing and selling those risks to the capital markets much as interest rates and credit risks are traded today.' Swiss Re (1996) *Re-thinking Risk Finance*. Zurich: Swiss Re, 25.

[23] 'The client's risk map and risk financing objectives build the foundation for structuring a solution that will require not only expertise in underwriting and corporate finance, but also legal, tax and accounting skills.' Swiss Re (1996, 20).

relatively easy to locate. Reinsurers had, since at least the 1970s, a concern that their market position would be weakened by their clients' increasing scale and access to cheap capital, and that this would lead to increasing self-insurance.[24] The understanding of capital efficiency had increased significantly in the reinsurance industry during the early 1990s,[25] especially among the market leaders. But at the same time they faced pressure from analysts and commentators in the financial world due to their business model being too capital intensive and exposed to major losses. Offering diversification through the capital markets, it was hoped, would remove these concerns and allow reinsurers to compete with banks in terms of their return on capital.

Although an elegant theory, the practicalities of making this type of risk transfer a reality were significant. Swiss Re investigated various approaches to bringing reinsurance and banking activities closer together in the mid-1990s. Analogies between modern financial products and reinsurance offerings were already being investigated in the late 1980s.[26] The result was a special unit, *New Markets*, dedicated to Alternative Risk Transfer (ART), that looked to pioneer Swiss Re as a 'wholesale financial services provider', which, from 1999 on, even included the investment banking firm Fox-Pitt Kelton.[27]

## 11.5 Bermuda

This British colony in the North Atlantic, a two-hour flight from Boston in the USA, first became known as a haven for captives and then, in 1985/6, for specialized liability insurers, among others ACE and XL Capital.[28] Industrial companies, in response to the liability crisis, founded these in an attempt to provide affordable cover for themselves. The pre-existing security of British law and governance was supported by carefully crafted regulation and a highly responsive and collaborative approach to those wishing to do business on the island. It was after Hurricane Andrew struck southern Florida in August 1992, leading to damage in excess of USD 16 billion (or around 27 billion in 2014 prices),[29] that the role of Bermuda changed. As reinsurance prices hardened, the island's attractive tax and regulatory structures led to the creation of new start-ups specializing in natural catastrophe cover. Eight companies were founded, known as the Bermuda Class of 1992, with combined capital of USD 4 billion.[30] With Bermuda's changing role the world of reinsurance also changed, as a significant part of this capital inflow came from outside the established reinsurance market. Investors included reinsurers, insurers, brokers, investment banks, and private investors. A large part

[24] Swiss Re (2004, 9). [25] See Chapter 1, this volume.

[26] Marbacher (1989); also Swiss Re, *sigma* 7, 1992. See also Chapter 1, this volume.

[27] Swiss Re (2004, 13).

[28] See Cummins (2008) for a detailed economic analysis of the Bermudan insurance market.

[29] Swiss Re, *sigma* 2, 2015, 41. [30] Cummins (2008, table 7.5).

was provided by direct insurers. Rather than extending cover in their own books, they preferred investing in reinsurance start-ups in order to profit from advantageous market conditions. The companies focused on writing short-term, high-margin business that took advantage of favourable prices. Of the Bermuda Class of 1992, two independent companies, Partner Re and Renaissance Re, survived a period of consolidation. Renaissance Re remained focused on the catastrophe market and achieved outstanding results over the following decades. Partner Re diversified, mainly through the acquisition of European companies, including Société Anonyme Française de Réassurances (SAFR), Winterthur Re, and Paris Re, becoming one of the top ten reinsurers worldwide.

In addition to the favourable tax regime, Bermuda benefited from being a pure business-to-business location for the insurance industry, simplifying supervision and regulation and separating it largely from the long-running liability and consumer protection issues of the neighbouring US market. A licence could be applied for in one of four classes, from the relatively simple single parent captive to the right to trade in excess liability and property catastrophe business. Each class had distinct solvency stipulations, but the calculation of loss reserves and premiums was lightly regulated.

After 9/11, Bermuda again benefited from the shift in market prices and was the domicile for the majority of start-up reinsurers. Over USD 8 billion in fresh capital was raised within a few months of 11 September 2001, and invested in new ventures.[31] Again, as in the Bermuda of the early 1990s, start-ups were often funded by insurers, reinsurers, investment banks and private equity investors, and through public placements.[32] In addition to its position in catastrophe cover, Bermuda saw some of its new players also move into casualty and specialty insurance and reinsurance. Despite its isolated location, Bermuda became quickly interconnected with the London market, as a natural place to deal in large international risks. In this sense it is important to see Bermuda as part of an international network of re/insurance centres, although it developed a new idiosyncratic business model which some see as based less on the face-to-face interaction prevalent in the London market and more on the negotiating approach of Continental reinsurers, offering tailor-made solutions for individual clients.[33]

## 11.6 The London Market and Lloyd's Crisis in the 1990s

Historically, London has been the most important marketplace for transacting international insurance and reinsurance. Although the so-called *London market* is often

[31] Holzheu and Lechner (2007, 886). [32] Cummins (2008, table 7.5).

[33] <http://www.cassknowledge.com/sites/default/files/article-attachments/trading-risk-cass-knowledge.pdf> (accessed 23 May 2016).

equated with Lloyd's, insurance companies outside of Lloyd's have also played a major role. In 2014, London market participants wrote GBP 48 billion (USD 80 billion) in premiums, about half of which was reinsurance business, of which 25 billion was written by the Lloyd's syndicates, and 23 billion by insurance companies organized by the International Underwriting Association (IUA).[34] In 2016 there were forty-six active ordinary members of IUA and a similar number of affiliated and associated members, while Lloyd's consisted of ninety-six syndicates offering insurance and reinsurance cover.

The focus fell particularly on Lloyd's at the beginning of the 1990s, as the 300-year-old institution underwent far-reaching reforms to avoid collapse. Between 1988 and 1992, the Lloyd's syndicates accumulated losses of more than GBP 8 billion. The losses originated from marine and energy insurance, including the explosion on the Piper Alpha oil rig and various oil tanker disasters; natural catastrophes stemming from US hurricanes and European winter storms; and from US liability claims. The situation was aggravated by the infamous London market spiral, the practice of mutual retrocession between syndicates.[35]

The board of Lloyd's had no choice but to act, setting in place a series of reforms that shaped the trajectory of the market. First, it began to admit corporate capital in 1994, in order to reverse the decline in underwriting capacity felt as some individual names withdrew. This was particularly urgent as competitors were harvesting the hard market conditions. Operating on a limited liability basis, by 2004 corporates accounted for 88 per cent of the total capacity of GBP 15 billion.[36] Figure 11.1 illustrates the development of Lloyd's capacity, measured in USD billions.

Second, a clear distinction between future business and the period of losses was marked by transferring the ongoing liabilities from before 1993 to a new company. Equitas was formed in 1996 with initial capital of GBP 11.2 billion.[37] Finally Lloyd's initiated a number of reforms to update their corporate governance and increase transparency, improving the financial security of the whole market.

Unable to grasp the business opportunities the hard market after Andrew offered, the combined market share of the Lloyd's syndicates fell from 7 per cent to 4 per cent between 1992 and 1996.[38] The years following the reforms were characterized by a relative stagnation in terms of overall capacity, combined with a significant structural change towards corporates as capital providers and a rapid consolidation, with the number of syndicates declining from four hundred in 1991 to eighty-six in 2002.[39] However, starting with the hard market in 2002, the underwriting capacity at Lloyd's

[34] IUA, *London Company Market Statistics Report 2015*, 1: <http://www.iua.co.uk/IUA_Member/Publications/London_Company_Market_Statistics_Report.aspx> (accessed 14 December 2015).

[35] See Bain (1998).

[36] Holzheu and Lechner (2007, 895).

[37] For a comprehensive discussion on the reconstruction and renewal plan, see <http://corporate.findlaw.com/corporate-governance/the-lloyd-s-reconstruction-and-renewal-a-success-story-or-is-the.html> (accessed 10 February 2016).

[38] Holzheu and Lechner (2007, 895).

[39] Swiss Re, *sigma* 3, 2002, 20.

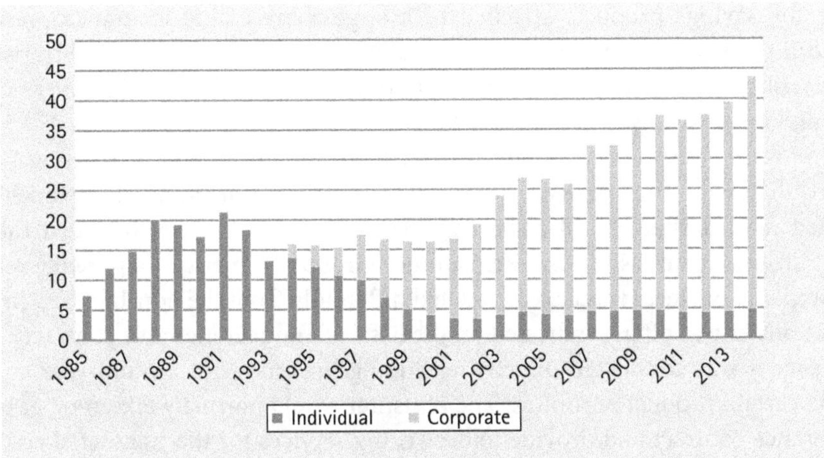


FIGURE 11.1 Lloyd's capacity, 1985–2014, in USD billion

*Source*: Lloyd's Statistics, a statistical guide to the Lloyd's market, various editions: Member capacity by year of account, 1993–2014; Statistics relating to Lloyd's, 2001: Capacity by traditional market 1985–1992. <http://www.lloyds.com/the-market/tools-and-resources/resources/statistics-relating-to-lloyds>. Original figures are converted into USD at 1 January 2016 foreign exchange rates.

also started to expand again, and Lloyd's regained its traditional role in the international re/insurance segment. By 2014, the P&C reinsurance market share of the Lloyd's syndicates was at a similar level to before the crisis, at around 8 per cent.

## 11.7 Life Reinsurance

The life reinsurance segment also experienced some structural changes starting in the mid-1990s. First, there was strong reinsurance demand in the USA and the UK. In both markets, but to a lesser extent in the UK, competitive pressures were forcing primary insurers to increase efficiency. Part of this process was to move away from a vertically integrated business model to focus on distribution. Consequently, they outsourced underwriting and mortality risk to reinsurers. On the supply side, there was an increasing interest in life reinsurance, because results from the more consistent cash flow of life premiums were smoother than other lines of business. Consequently, large composite reinsurers began to scale up their life portfolio.

Although the growth in the life sector outperformed that of the non-life sector throughout the 1990s and at the start of the 2000s, the life reinsurance market overall remained much smaller than the non-life reinsurance market.[40] This was mainly

[40] See Holzheu and Lechner (2007, 883).

because the savings products attached to a large share of life insurance premiums required little or no reinsurance. Life reinsurance mostly covered mortality risk, but covered risks were increasingly extended to include morbidity, disability, critical illness, and longevity risks.

Life reinsurers also consolidated; however, the period of high activity was more extended than with non-life. By 2014, the six largest life reinsurance companies had a combined market share of 88 per cent.[41] The top five reinsurers included the four largest European composites, and Reinsurance Group of America—a pure life reinsurance company. Business was also conducted differently from the non-life part. In P&C, the risk transfer was often syndicated on the basis of annual renewable contracts, in life reinsurance it was conducted directly, excluding brokers, with a multi-year contract based on certain product portfolios. The reinsurer would normally take 100 per cent of a reinsurance contract and provide underwriting services for the transacted risks.

## 11.8 The 9/11 Shock and the Hard Market

The terrorist attack of 9/11 in New York sent severe shock waves through the reinsurance industry. Beyond the issue of managing the huge losses, two factors were critical. First, terrorism had been covered in most contracts as a matter of course. As the scale and unpredictability of terrorism events became apparent, it meant it would not be possible for an insurer to set an affordable premium on future contracts. Many reinsurers started excluding terrorism risks. Second, a new level of cumulative losses was experienced, where a whole series of claims from fire, life, business interruption, aviation, and liability occurred at the same time. The Insurance Information Institute estimated the total losses from 11 September 2001 to be over USD 30 billion. This included USD 9.6 billion in property claims, USD 11 billion in business interruption claims, USD 3.5 billion in aviation liability claims, USD 4 billion in other liability claims, and USD 3.4 billion in claims from other lines of business.[42]

The terrible events of 9/11 spotlighted the concentration of high values in an area such as Manhattan and the potential knock-on effects of major losses in a single area. One result was a recognition that the insurance industry needed to be clear about the limits of their coverage and, in particular, clarify with other stakeholders, such as governments and regulators, how risks and potential losses would be mitigated by the state playing its role as 'insurer of last resort'.[43] In November 2002, the Terrorism Risk

[41] See Figure A.2.1 in Appendix.

[42] Hartwig, Stewart, and Wilkinson (2004). For 2014 inflated values see <http://www.iii.org/fact-statistic/terrorism>.

[43] For an analysis of these effects on the entire property and casualty industry see Swiss Re, *sigma* 4, 2002.

Insurance Act (TRIA) was introduced in the USA to clarify the role of the government in underpinning insured losses in the face of terrorist attack.[44] It was consistently renewed for specified periods by government during this period.[45] While some countries already had similar facilities in place, for example, the UK and Spain, which had faced terrorist attacks earlier from the Irish Republican Army (IRA) and the Basque Euskadi Ta Askatasuna (ETA), other countries introduced new covers like Extremus in Germany and Gestion de l'Assurance et de la Réassurance des Risques Attentats et Actes de Terrorisme (GAREAT) in France.

Despite the unprecedented and completely unexpected size of the insured losses, the re/insurance industry remained remarkably stable, and without major defaults. There were a number of voluntary market exits, but, importantly, there was no general unavailability of reinsurance coverage. As some players exited the market, an improvement in prices also made entry attractive.[46] Along with more than USD 20 billion of new capital raised by incumbent reinsurance companies, a number of Bermuda-based start-ups received an additional USD 9 billion.[47] Strategic sponsors of the start-ups included large insurers and insurance brokers, particularly for the short-tail property lines of business.[48]

The 9/11 shock wave hit an industry that was already at the trough of a very severe soft market after the US liability crisis of mid-1980, with industry-combined ratios of 117 per cent and 114 per cent for 1999 and 2000 (see Figure 11.2). The additional loss burden took the combined ratio to 131 per cent, and, overall, a negative return on equity (ROE) of -3 per cent,[49] before these high underwriting losses were compensated by asset returns. Faced by mounting underwriting losses and declining equity markets, reinsurers had already begun to seek better rates at the January 2001 renewals, but after 9/11 and the resulting capacity shortage, huge rate increases were widespread over all geographic regions and lines of business, in primary insurance as well as in reinsurance. Rate increases of 100 per cent were not uncommon: some specialty lines such as aviation even tripled.[50] Consequently, the profitability of new underwritten business

[44] See Congress of the United States, Congressional Budget Office (2005) *Federal Terrorism Reinsurance: An Update*, January, Washington, DC: <https://www.cbo.gov/sites/default/files/109th-congress-2005-2006/reports/01-05-terrorism.pdf>.

[45] See Congress of the United States, Congressional Budget Office (2015) *Federal Reinsurance for Terrorism Risk in 2015 and Beyond*, June, Washington, DC: <https://www.cbo.gov/sites/default/files/114th-congress-2015-2016/workingpaper/50171-TRIA_Working_Paper_1.pdf>.

[46] For a discussion of the effects of state intervention versus a natural rebound of the markets see J. R. Brown J. D. Cummins, C. M. Lewis, and R. Wei (2004) 'An Empirical Analysis of the Economic Impact of Federal Terrorism Reinsurance', *Journal of Monetary Economics* 51, 861–98: <http://business.illinois.edu/ormir/JME%20TRIA.pdf>.

[47] Holzheu and Lechner (2007, 886).

[48] Short-tail businesses are all classes of business in which claims are reported and settled in a relatively short period of time (e.g. most classes of property business).

[49] Swiss Re, Economic Research & Consulting, based on a market aggregate of the financials of the leading international reinsurance companies.

[50] Price indices are not generally available, but some London market insurance companies such as Amlin provide overviews of renewal rating indices of their own book. Amlin (2015) *Annual Report 2014*, 53.

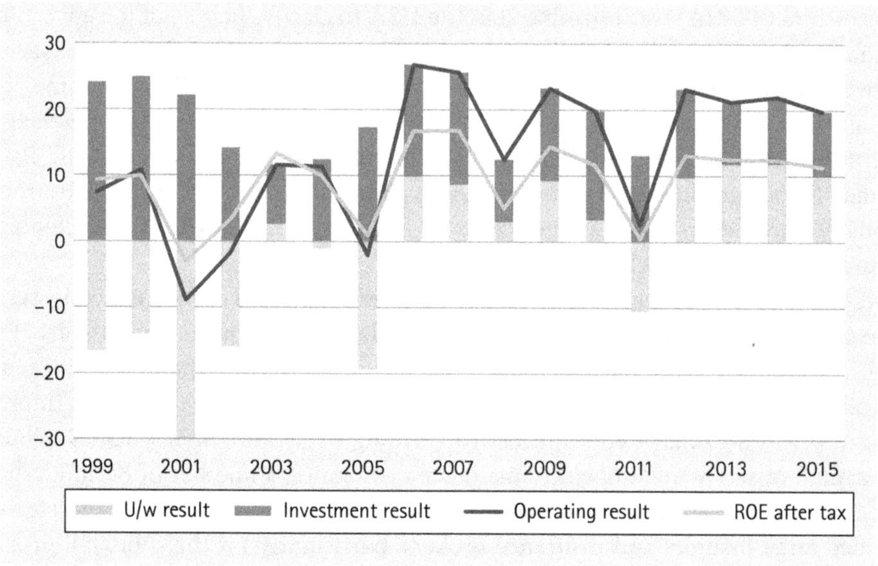


FIGURE 11.2 Profitability of the P&C reinsurance market, 1999–2015

*Source*: Swiss Re, Economic Research & Consulting, market aggregate based on the financials of the leading international reinsurance companies.

of insurers and reinsurers soared, but heavy claims from business written during the soft market years put a drag on results for 2002 and partially for 2003 and 2004. Eventually the soft market years receded, and a period with strong underwriting results followed, which were only interrupted by large natural catastrophe losses.

## 11.9 The 2004/5 Hurricanes and their Impact on Modelling

More than a decade after Hurricane Andrew, and after a period of relative calm, 2004 and 2005 brought consecutive record-breaking hurricane seasons. Whilst Andrew led to insured losses of USD 27 billion (at 2014 prices), most of them in Florida, the four large hurricanes making landfall (Ivan, Charlie, Frances, and Jeanne) caused USD 32 billion at 2014 prices in the USA and in the Caribbean. And the following year, the Hurricanes Katrina, Rita, and Wilma (KRW) accrued losses of USD 106 billion. Out of the ten most costly hurricanes in the USA, six occurred in 2004 and 2005.

Apart from devastation and significant human and economic loss, each catastrophe—and in particular large ones—had its own specific qualities, influencing how governments, the public, and the re/insurance industry would attempt to learn and adapt for future events. Hurricane Andrew was characterized by very high wind-speed. On the other hand, the record damage caused by Katrina, and also most of the damage by Rita, was due to storm-surge flooding in built-up coastal areas.

The complexity of estimating losses that might be triggered by a natural catastrophe event added to the challenge of both the independent and reinsurer modellers, who were trying to map out their frequency and severity through time. In particular, the hurricanes of 2004/5 exposed serious deficiencies in the existing catastrophe models by both independent vendors and re/insurance companies. Prior to Katrina, for example, modelling relied heavily on lessons drawn from Andrew in 1992, but this proved disastrous in 2005, as Andrew's low storm surge had led to this type of risk being underestimated in the modelling scenarios.[51] According to Guy Carpenter, the models underestimated the actual losses by between 30 per cent and 60 per cent. Afterwards, this led to considerable model revision and improved data collection, and much debate in the industry about the calibration of the models. The result was an increased awareness of far higher exposures for the re/insurance industry, leading to higher rates of natural catastrophe cover.[52] Figure 11.3 illustrates the fluctuation of property catastrophe prices between 1990 and 2016.

The development of both reinsurer and independent models played a key role in the growth of the industry. The increasing robustness of the models grew reinsurers' confidence in offering natural catastrophe cover, including to emerging markets and government agencies, and supported a more flexible approach to their allocation of capital to take advantage of favourable prices in the market. Independent vendor models gave players in alternative capital more transparency about the underlying risks they might invest in, significantly reducing the uncertainty of the market, especially for new players. Finally, for brokers, independent models reduced the knowledge gap compared to global reinsurers, moving the larger brokers further towards a broad service model for clients. This said, the models remained an approximation of what might occur, acting as a valuable risk management tool but not as an accurate guide to short-term activity in natural catastrophes.

One area where the complexity of modelling natural events became apparent was the influence of climate change. Based on the scientific evidence available, the reinsurance industry has been an early advocate of both reducing carbon emissions and taking steps to adapt to the inevitable effects of global warming.[53] It was one of the few industries whose models reached out into the post-2050s, when the forecast effects of rising sea levels and shifts in precipitation and temperature would potentially lead to major shifts in population and loss of insured values. Whilst it was too simple to predicate every increase in flooding or hurricane activity to the effects of man-made emissions,

[51] <http://blog.willis.com/2015/08/10-years-on-the-evolution-of-modeling-since-katrina/> (accessed 17 March 2016).

[52] <http://www.guycarp.com/content/dam/guycarp/en/documents/dynamic-content/Ten-Year_Retrospective_of_the_2004_and_2005_Atlantic_Hurricane_Seasons_Part_2.pdf> (accessed 17 March 2016).

[53] See SRCA 000586. Also Haufler (2009, 247–8).

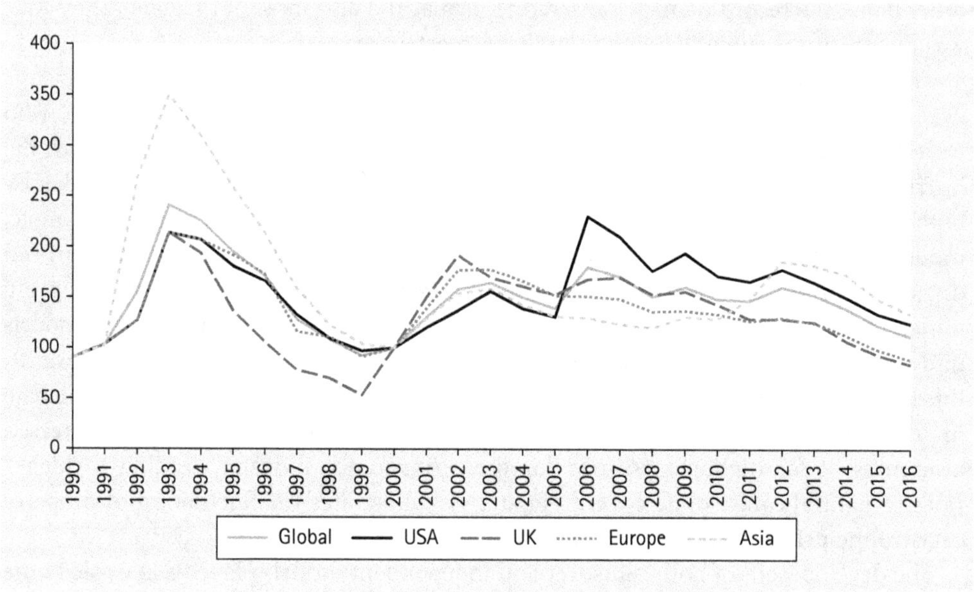


FIGURE 11.3 Property catastrophe price index, by region, 1990–2016

*Note*: Original data is rebased to 2000 = 100; the global series were adjusted for the period until 2000 by using a weighted average of the regional indices.

*Source*: Guy Carpenter <http://www.gccapitalideas.com/2016/01/06/chart-global-property-catastrophe-rol-index-1990-to-2016/>; <http://www.gccapitalideas.com/2016/01/06/chart-regional-property-catastrophe-rol-index-1990-to-2016/>.

reinsurers remained in the vanguard of those seeking to understand the long-term cycles of our weather systems, and actively attempted to apply the latest prudent scientific evidence to their modelling approaches.

## 11.10 Emerging Markets

As in many other industries, both primary insurers and reinsurers looked to emerging markets for future growth, particularly after 1995 when the market opened following the introduction of the GATS. Since the nineteenth century, spreading risks geographically had always appealed to the reinsurer because of the benefits of risk diversification. But as global economic growth began to rely more heavily on the fast-growth markets of Latin America and Asia there was recognition of a long-term requirement to be present in these markets. At the beginning of the 1990s, the emerging markets played a relatively small role both in terms of demand and supply. During the 1990s, the share of ceded premiums in non-life reinsurance oscillated around 10 per cent. By 2014, the share was 26 per cent, mainly driven by a strong development of Chinese reinsurance business. Whilst Chinese premiums increased from virtually zero to 9 per cent globally, the non-Chinese emerging market premiums rose to a global share of cessions of 17 per cent by the mid-2010s.[54] In life, the relative weight of the emerging markets remained very low; only in the mid-2010s did their combined share reached the 10 per cent threshold.[55] Again, the Chinese contribution to this growth was considerable, despite increasing volatility within the economy and the potential for more subdued growth.

The logic of servicing this broad economic growth was simple but the reality was more complex. As an increasingly wealthy middle class evolved, and corporations grew in scale and complexity, they proved slower to purchase insurance than their Western neighbours. This so-called protection gap, the part of potential losses uncovered by re/insurance, could partially be ascribed to different cultural approaches to managing risk, such as the role of families offering support at the time of a death instead of life insurance or of expectations of governments intervening after natural disasters.[56] However, it left many players hopeful of further growth, despite difficult regulatory conditions in some countries and enormous competition both domestically and internationally.

Global institutions such as the World Bank and the Bank for International Settlements (BIS) highlighted the macroeconomic impact of unmitigated disasters. The BIS found that the uninsured part of losses impact the macroeconomy negatively, while insured losses from catastrophes could be 'inconsequential or even positive for economic activity'.[57] This prompted reinsurers to increase work with governments to develop solutions for underinsured areas both in emerging and mature markets.[58] Also, non-government organizations (NGOs) started investigating the impact of insurance on the resilience of emerging markets.[59]

## 11.11 Financial Crisis

The financial crisis of 2008 is well documented. Beginning with the subprime crisis in 2007, it culminated in the default of Lehman Brothers on 15 September 2008, the largest bankruptcy in the USA, of USD 600 billion. Almost immediately, interbank

[54] Swiss Re, Economic Research & Consulting.

[55] Swiss Re, Economic Research & Consulting.

[56] For growth issues of the reinsurance industry in emerging markets see Bajrektarevic and Baumer (2010).

[57] Goetz von Peter, Sebastian von Dahlen, and Sweta C. Saxena (2012) *Unmitigated Disasters? New Evidence on the Macroeconomic Cost of Natural Catastrophes*, BIS Working Papers 394, December: <http://www.bis.org/publ/work394.htm> (accessed 24 March 2016). For World Bank and reinsurance see World Bank (1995, 2002).

[58] Swiss Re, *sigma* 5, 2015; Swiss Re (2015).

[59] See, for example, University of Cambridge Institute for Sustainable Leadership (2015) *Insurance Regulation for Sustainable Development*: <http://www.cisl.cam.ac.uk/publications/latest-publications/policy-brief-insurance-regulation-for-sustainable-development> (accessed 24 March 2016).

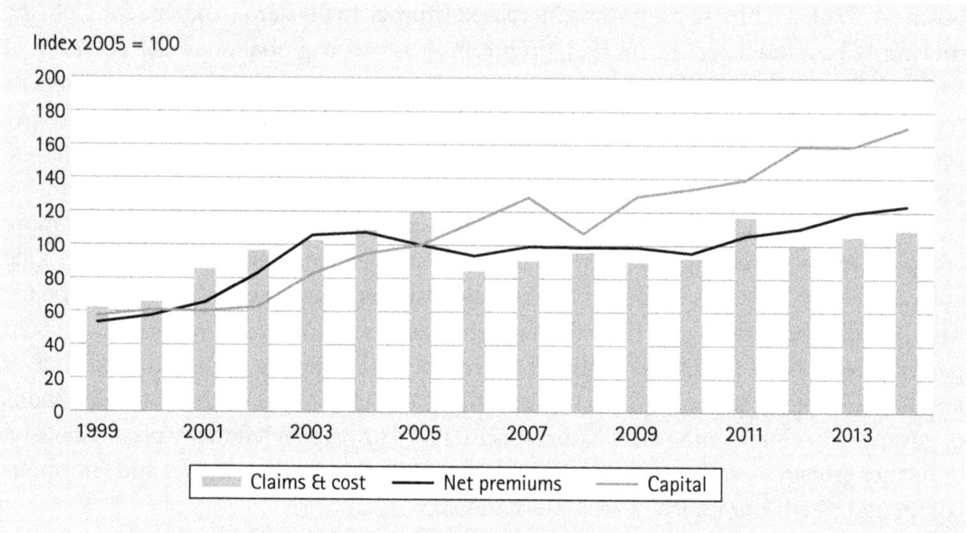


FIGURE 11.4 Global P&C reinsurance: Net premiums, underwriting expenses (claims, commissions, administrative expenses), and capital, 1999–2015

*Source*: Swiss Re, Economic Research & Consulting, market aggregate based on a sample of around twenty leading reinsurance companies.

lending came to a standstill and the shadow banking system collapsed. Only a massive bailout by the Federal Reserve and other central banks prevented the international finance system from a complete collapse, but a severe recession—with global repercussions—was inescapable.

As Figure 11.4 shows, the reinsurance sector did not go unscathed. Between the end of 2007 and 2008, the value of invested assets declined by 12 per cent and the capital base shrank by 19 per cent.[60] Like the primary insurance sector, most reinsurers could withstand this setback because of the significant excess capital they had accumulated since 2003. Global reinsurance capacity had been reduced, but not depleted by the financial crisis and, by 2008, solvency was back to 2005 levels. However, reinsurers were also decreasing their risk appetite, as obtaining new post-event capital was difficult and expensive. The prevailing climate also made on-balance-sheet capital invested in low-risk and highly liquid assets much more attractive.

The crisis had its most severe impact on companies that had been drawn towards more speculative strategies, such as covering complex financial products. This led to the failure of the American International Group (AIG) and a major disruption at Swiss Re.[61] Most companies, however, had remained wedded to the core reinsurance business model and emerged relatively unscathed.

60 Swiss Re, Economic Research & Consulting database. Market aggregate based on a sample of around twenty leading reinsurance companies.

61 Straumann (2013, 349–50).

Being part of the financial sector, re/insurers were inevitably involved in discussion around systemic risks ('too big to fail') and the need to identify so-called SIFIs—systemically important financial institutions. Not least, this was triggered by the fact that, the day after the collapse of Lehman Brothers, the insurance giant AIG received a USD 85 billion bail-out: the largest in history at that time, only surpassed by the rescue measures for the government-sponsored mortgage lenders Fannie Mae and Freddie Mac. A closer look to the AIG case,[62] however, reveals that it was not the core insurance activities that triggered the company crisis, but the financial products section. This was offering default protection (credit-default swaps) to collateralized debt obligations (CDOs) with enormous potential payouts, perceived as highly unlikely to occur before the financial crisis hit. Indeed, the insurance institutions which failed or were bailed out in 2008 and 2009 were either mono-liners providing bond insurance or bancassurance conglomerates which suffered due to their banking business. A report by the Geneva Association (a think tank of the insurance and reinsurance industry) found that neither insurers nor reinsurers per se posed a systemic risk, while some of their non-core activities, such as 'derivatives trading on non-insurance balance sheets' and 'mismanagement of short-term funding from commercial paper or securities lending' had the potential to create systemically relevant risks.[63]

Interestingly, in one sense the financial crisis led to a renewed confidence in the fundamental insurance and reinsurance business model.[64] It became increasingly apparent that banks and insurance companies operated with different models. Insurance was based on a contract where premiums were paid in return for cover should a loss event occur and the insurer was obliged to put aside reserves to cover these risks. The risk of a major liquidity failure was therefore much lower, with the settlement of claims taking longer and the processes of interbank overnight and on-demand lending absent. In effect, this meant there could be 'no-run' on the insurance company as could occur with a bank, as investors withdraw their capital.

In the case of reinsurers it was seen that the individual reinsurers' balance sheets were not systemically connected in the same way as banks. They may have shared in taking a proportion of an individual reinsurance risk as part of the ecosystem of sharing risk through the reinsurance marketplace, but there was no interbank market or shadow bank relationship in normal business.[65] Each reinsurer was responsible for paying losses from the capital reserves they apportioned for a risk. In this sense, the events of 2008 highlighted how the reinsurance ecosystem focused on taking the risk of the insurer or client and spreading it through the marketplace to avoid overexposure. This is important for the hypothesis of reinsurance as a resilient ecosystem, and in part explains the longevity of the role of the reinsurer, namely that the dominant connection

[62] See R. O'Harrow Jr and B. Dennis (2008) 'The Beautiful Machine', *Washington Post*, 29 December.

[63] Geneva Association (2010, 4).

[64] See, for this discussion, IAIS (2012) *Reinsurance and Financial Stability*. Basel: IAIS, 10: <http://iaisweb.org>.

[65] See also IAIS (2012).

within the market is not among the different reinsurers, trading packaged risks among themselves without sight of the underlying exposure, but between the client and the reinsurer involved in a contract.

## 11.12 Alternative Capital

Alternative capital or capacity is a term used to describe collateralized insurance cover, including ILS or catastrophe bonds (so-called 'cat bonds').[66] It is a means to directly transfer re/insurance risk to the wider capital market, or later to investors, omitting the potential capacity limitations of the traditional re/insurance industry as experienced in the aftermath of events such as Hurricane Andrew and 9/11. For an investor, it created a new asset class where it was possible to invest directly in a specific re/insurance risk, as opposed to investing in re/insurance carriers, which not only included a widespread portfolio of different risks, but also asset management risks, legacy portfolios, and operating and corporate strategy risks.

Although the basic idea of implementing an ILS transaction was simple and understandable, in practice it was complex and demanding. The risk-ceding party had to set up a special purpose reinsurance vehicle (SPRV), providing the reinsurance cover and issue securities to investors to receive the necessary capital funds. Importantly, as the investor had to allocate 100 per cent of the capital to this risk for the period it was covered, there was no diversification benefit. ILS were particularly successful in the property catastrophe area because they dealt with peak risks that were not easily diversified by smaller reinsurers, and were short tail in the sense that funds were only tied up for the period of the cover. In addition, independent natural catastrophe models had matured to allow for a fairly transparent assessment of the risk.

Hannover Re issued the first cat-linked security transaction in 1994—a USD 85 million bond.[67] However, it took more than a decade until the ILS capacity started to become actually perceptible in the reinsurance market, outside of the pioneering participants. A similar ILS product on the life side was called extreme mortality risk. It covered issuers of securities against pandemic risks that could trigger a high number of life insurance contracts.[68]

Another form of alternative capacity, which slowly overtook cat bonds after 2010 as the most important source of alternative capital, was collateralized reinsurance (CR). CR developed strongly as capital collected in specialized cat risk funds exceeded the

[66] See P. Trainar (2014) *Alternative Capital in (Re)Insurance*. Munich: The Geneva Association: <https://www.genevaassociation.org/media/887425/ga2014-ie70-trainar.pdf>. A good overview is also provided by: <http://thoughtleadership.aonbenfield.com/Documents/20150909-ab-securities-ils-annual-report-2015.pdf>.

[67] See Swiss Re, *sigma* 4, 2009.

[68] Life ILS also includes securities to finance acquisition costs instead of buying reinsurance cover from the capital markets, so-called embedded value transactions.

supply of cat bonds from re/insurers. Again, funds were invested into SPRVs that were either stand-alone or sidecars to existing reinsurance entities. They offered 'traditional' reinsurance cover, just with the important difference that security is provided via a 100 per cent collateralization. Brokers played a critical role in ensuring that stand-alone SPRVs had market access by distributing CR capacity to cedents. However, in order to be successful, CR entities required underwriting expertise to the same extent as traditional follower reinsurers, again highlighting the interconnections within the reinsurance ecosystem.

Only history will tell us whether this growth in alternative capital was a product of low returns in other asset classes and limited losses due to a relatively low number of recent natural catastrophes. Certainly it appeared there was an important shift in the natural catastrophe market, placing enormous pressure on players whose function was to simply offer capital when the market conditions are hard, as their service became increasingly commoditized.

## 11.13 Conclusion

Although the stresses and strains of the post-crisis economic downturn created difficult market conditions for all international business, it can be said that the reinsurance sector emerged from this difficult period with a renewed confidence in its fundamental business. The ecosystem of the industry as a whole was seen to be quite flexible and robust, despite the considerable consolidation and shifts in practice. A product palette that remained relatively unchanged and well understood, whilst enterprise risk management supported improved stewardship, supported this robustness. The reinsurance sector was also able to respond to a changing risk landscape, where terrorism and global warming tested the limits of insurance and shone a spotlight onto the role of government and international agencies in managing global risk.

Risks also grew in scale, interconnection, and concentration, and it was these factors, enabled by technology and globalization, which reinforced the emergence of an ecosystem of service providers, clustered around different ways of helping clients manage their risks. The main models of the Continental and broker approaches both thrived, leading to considerable competition and collaboration according to client requirements. Importantly, their interdependency was not a systematic risk because their primary relationship was mediated through the client and not through interconnections in competitor balance sheets or intercompany lending. In particular, the attraction of diversifying risks through the broader capital markets was much better understood, namely using existing reinsurance approaches to package risks, creating a new asset class for investors, rather than shifting to a model of financial engineering akin to an investment bank.

The ecosystem has proven relatively resilient in the face of major catastrophes, with advances in alternative capital and computer modelling further adding to its robustness. Such catastrophes include the large accumulation in 2011, with earthquakes in Japan and New Zealand and floods in Thailand. Indeed, it could be argued that these twenty-five years saw the industry undergo an existential renewal. It moved from a reactive fear of becoming irrelevant to global clients in the 1990s, with their own access to cheap capital to manage their risks, to a renewed confidence in its ability to quantify and absorb risks through its core product offering.

# APPENDIX

**Table A.1 Specialist reinsurance companies by country and year of foundation, 1840–1936**

| | 1840–1849 | 1850–1859 | 1860–1869 | 1870–1879 | 1880–1889 | 1890–1899 | 1900–1909 | 1910–1919 | 1920–1929 | 1930–1936 | Totals |
|---|---|---|---|---|---|---|---|---|---|---|---|
| Germany | 2 | 2 | 4 | 11 | 13 | 4 | 6 | 12 | 16 | 1 | **71** |
| Belgium | | 1 | | | 1 | | 1 | 2 | 3 | 1 | **9** |
| Hungary | | | 1 | | | | | 1 | | | **2** |
| Switzerland | | | 3 | 1 | | | 1 | 3 | 3 | | **11** |
| Austria | | | 1 | 2 | 1 | 1 | 1 | | | | **6** |
| Russia | | | | 1 | | 2 | 1 | | | | **4** |
| Sweden | | | | 1 | 1 | 3 | 1 | 2 | 1 | 1 | **10** |
| UK | | | | 5 | | | 6 | 12 | 1 | | **24** |
| France | | | | 1 | 1 | 2 | 5 | 11 | 6 | 1 | **27** |
| Denmark | | | | 1 | 1 | 5 | 2 | 20 | | | **29** |
| Netherlands | | | | | 1 | | | | 2 | | **3** |
| Bulgaria | | | | | | 2 | | | 1 | 1 | **4** |
| Italy | | | | | | 1 | | 4 | 4 | 1 | **10** |
| Finland | | | | | | 1 | 1 | 2 | 2 | 1 | **7** |
| Latvia | | | | | | | 1 | | 1 | | **2** |
| Spain | | | | | | | 1 | 3 | 1 | | **5** |
| USA | | | | | | | 1 | 5 | 21 | 3 | **30** |
| Norway | | | | | | | | 2 | | | **2** |
| Japan | | | | | | | | 3 | 1 | | **4** |
| Poland | | | | | | | | 2 | 1 | | **3** |
| Argentina | | | | | | | | | 3 | 1 | **4** |
| Portugal | | | | | | | | | 2 | 1 | **3** |
| Danzig* | | | | | | | | | 1 | | **1** |
| Chile | | | | | | | | | 2 | | **2** |
| Greece | | | | | | | | | 1 | | **1** |
| Turkey | | | | | | | | | 1 | | **1** |
| **Totals** | **2** | **3** | **9** | **23** | **19** | **21** | **28** | **84** | **74** | **12** | **275** |

*Note*: This table takes no account of exits.

* Danzig was a free city-state under League of Nations protection 1920–39.

Table compiled by Robin Pearson. See also footnote 49 in his chapter.

*Sources*: Calculated from Hollitscher (1931); Cruciger (1926, 1929); various company references in the following German, UK, and US newspapers and periodicals: *Deutsche Versicherungszeitung*; *Rundschau der Versicherungen*; *Post Magazine*; *Assecuranz Jahrbuch*; *Insurance and Commercial Magazine*; *Insurance Times*; *Insurance Critic*; and the national reinsurance surveys in *The Review*, 28 October 1927, 8 November 1929, 29 November 1935, 26 November 1937.

**Table A.2 Number of reinsurance company foundations by country, 1850–1930**

| | 1850–1859 | 1860–1869 | 1870–1879 | 1880–1889 | 1890–1899 | 1900–1909 | 1910–1919 | 1920–1929 | 1930 | Totals |
|---|---|---|---|---|---|---|---|---|---|---|
| Argentina | | | | | | | | 3 | | 3 |
| Austria | 1 | 1 | | 1 | | 1 | | | | 4 |
| Belgium | 1 | | | | | 1 | 1 | 1 | | 4 |
| Bulgaria | | | | | | | | 1 | | 1 |
| Canada | | | | | | | | 2 | | 2 |
| Czechoslovakia | | | 1 | | | | | | | 1 |
| Denmark | | | | 1 | 2 | | 10 | | | 13 |
| Finland | | | | | | | 2 | 1 | | 3 |
| France | | | | 1 | 1 | 2 | 4 | 3 | | 11 |
| Germany | 2 | 1 | 3 | 2 | 1 | 2 | 2 | 14 | | 27 |
| Holland | | | | 1 | 2 | | | 1 | | 4 |
| Hungary | | 1 | | | | | 1 | | | 2 |
| Italy | | | | | 1 | | 2 | 3 | | 6 |
| Japan | | | | | | 1 | 3 | 3 | | 7 |
| Norway | | | | | | | 4 | | | 4 |
| Poland | | | | | | | | 1 | | 1 |
| Portugal | | | | | | | 1 | | | 1 |
| Spain | | | | | | 1 | 3 | 1 | | 5 |
| Sweden | | | | 1 | 2 | 2 | 4 | 1 | | 10 |
| Switzerland | | 2 | 1 | | | | 2 | 1 | | 6 |
| UK | | | | | | 5 | 10 | | | 15 |
| USA | | | | | | 1 | 6 | 20 | 1 | 28 |
| **Totals** | **4** | **5** | **5** | **7** | **9** | **16** | **55** | **56** | **1** | **158** |

*Note*: This table contains only reinsurance companies which still existed when the second edition of Golding's book was published in 1931.

*Source*: Golding (1931, 121).

Table A.3.1 Top 15 reinsurance companies for 1929

| Rank | Company | Country | Net premium in GBP m | Net premium in USD m [1] | Net premium in USD m, 2015 prices [2] |
|---|---|---|---|---|---|
| 1 | Munich Re | Germany | 9.75 | 47.30 | 654.0 |
| 2 | Swiss Re [3] | Switzerland | 6.87 | 33.40 | 462.0 |
| 3 | Prudentia [4] | Switzerland | 2.66 | 12.90 | 178.0 |
| 4 | Cologne Re | Germany | 2.04 | 9.90 | 137.0 |
| 5 | Rossia of America | USA | 1.99 | 9.67 | 134.0 |
| 6 | Salamandra [5] | Denmark | 1.42 | 6.91 | 95.5 |
| 7 | European General | USA | 1.32 | 6.41 | 88.6 |
| 8 | Skandinavia [5] | Denmark | 1.31 | 6.37 | 88.0 |
| 9 | General Re | USA | 1.10 | 5.33 | 73.7 |
| 10 | Baltica [5] | Denmark | 1.09 | 5.28 | 73.0 |
| 11 | Française de Réassurance | France | 1.03 | 4.98 | 68.8 |
| 12 | G.-K. Rheinische Rück | Germany | 0.90 | 4.36 | 60.3 |
| 13 | International | USA | 0.89 | 4.32 | 59.7 |
| 14 | Frankona Re | Germany | 0.84 | 4.09 | 56.5 |
| 15 | Christiania General [5] | Norway | 0.84 | 4.07 | 56.2 |

*Notes*: [1] Converted with: http://www.measuringworth.com/exchange/ using the CPI/RPI.
[2] Converted with: http://www.measuringworth.com/uscompare/ using the CPI.
[3] Includes also: Swiss Re USA a/c (GBP m 0.92).
[4] Includes also: Prudentia USA a/c (GBP m 1.08).
[5] These Scandinavian companies are also primary insurers.

*Source*: *The Review*, 21 November 1930, 1109.

Table A.3.2 Top 15 reinsurance companies for 1938

| Rank | Company | Country | Net premium in GBP m | Net premium in USD m [1] | Net premium in USD m, 2015 prices [2] |
|---|---|---|---|---|---|
| 1 | Munich Re [3] | Germany | 15.56 | 76.10 | 1280.0 |
| 2 | Swiss Re [4] | Switzerland | 10.82 | 52.90 | 889.0 |
| 3 | Cologne Re | Germany | 2.82 | 13.80 | 232.0 |
| 4 | European General | USA | 2.18 | 10.60 | 178.0 |
| 5 | Gerling Konzern Rück | Germany | 1.85 | 9.03 | 152.0 |
| 6 | Cie. Generales Accidents [5] | France | 1.77 | 8.66 | 146.0 |
| 7 | Frankona Re [6] | Germany | 1.58 | 7.71 | 130.0 |
| 8 | Employers Re | USA | 1.47 | 7.19 | 121.0 |
| 9 | Bavarian Re | Germany | 1.27 | 6.23 | 105.0 |
| 10 | Aachener Rück | Germany | 1.24 | 6.06 | 102.0 |
| 11 | General Re | USA | 1.19 | 5.82 | 97.8 |
| 12 | G.K. Rheinische | Germany | 1.19 | 5.82 | 97.8 |
| 13 | Skandinavia [5] | Denmark | 1.18 | 5.78 | 97.1 |
| 14 | Mercantile & General | UK | 1.03 | 5.06 | 85.0 |
| 15 | Hamburg-Bremer Rück | Germany | 1.02 | 5.01 | 84.2 |

*Notes*: [1] Converted with: http://www.measuringworth.com/exchange/ using the CPI/RPI.
[2] Converted with: http://www.measuringworth.com/uscompare/ using the CPI.
[3] Figure from 30 June 1939.
[4] Includes also: Swiss Re USA a/c (GBP m 1.18).
[5] Includes some direct business.
[6] Figure from 30 June 1938.

*Source*: *The Review*, 24 November 1939, 1067–8.

**Table A.3.3 Top 15 reinsurance companies for 1952**

| Rank | Company | Country | Net premium in GBP m | Net premium in USD m [1] | Net premium in USD m, 2015 prices [2] |
|---|---|---|---|---|---|
| 1 | Swiss Re [3] | Switzerland | 39.81 | 111.00 | 990.0 |
| 2 | Munich Re | Germany | 16.16 | 45.10 | 402.0 |
| 3 | Caisse Centrale | France | 9.13 | 25.50 | 227.0 |
| 4 | North American Casualty | USA | 8.56 | 23.90 | 213.0 |
| 5 | General Re | USA | 7.55 | 21.10 | 188.0 |
| 6 | Mercantile & General | UK | 6.49 | 18.10 | 161.0 |
| 7 | Employers Re | USA | 5.36 | 15.00 | 134.0 |
| 8 | American Re | USA | 5.29 | 14.80 | 132.0 |
| 9 | North Star | USA | 4.98 | 13.90 | 124.0 |
| 10 | Nord Africaine | Algeria | 4.69 | 13.10 | 117.0 |
| 11 | Instituto de Reaseguros | Brazil | 3.86 | 10.80 | 96.3 |
| 12 | Reinsurance Corporation | UK | 3.50 | 9.77 | 87.1 |
| 13 | Cologne Re | Germany | 3.44 | 9.59 | 85.5 |
| 14 | American Reserve | USA | 3.30 | 9.21 | 82.1 |
| 15 | Storebrand [4] | Norway | 3.16 | 8.84 | 78.8 |

*Notes*: [1] Converted with: http://www.measuringworth.com/exchange/ using the CPI/RPI.
[2] Converted with: http://www.measuringworth.com/uscompare/ using the CPI.
[3] Includes also: Swiss Re USA a/c (GBP m 11.72).
[4] Includes some direct business.

*Source*: *The Review*, 4 December 1953, 1655–6.

**Table A.3.4 Top 15 reinsurance companies for 1965**

| Rank | Company | Country | Net premium in USD m | Net premium in USD m, 2015 prices [1] |
|---|---|---|---|---|
| 1 | Swiss Re Group | Switzerland | 473.4 | 3550 |
| 2 | Munich Re | Germany | 336.6 | 2520 |
| 3 | American Re | USA | 125.5 | 941 |
| 4 | General Re | USA | 123.0 | 923 |
| 5 | Caisse Centrale de Réassurance [2] | France | 100.1 | 751 |
| 6 | Gerling Re Group | Germany | 93.4 | 701 |
| 7 | Mercantile & General Group | UK | 72.5 | 544 |
| 8 | Cologne Re | Germany | 56.0 | 420 |
| 9 | Frankona Re | Germany | 53.5 | 401 |
| 10 | Employers Re | USA | 53.4 | 401 |
| 11 | Instituto Nacional de Reaseguros [3] | Argentina | 41.3 | 310 |
| 12 | Bavarian Re | Germany | 38.3 | 287 |
| 13 | Française de Réassurances | France | 37.4 | 281 |
| 14 | Union Re | Switzerland | 25.7 | 193 |
| 15 | Victory Group | UK | 24.9 | 187 |

*Notes*: [1] Converted with: http://www.measuringworth.com/uscompare/ using the CPI.
[2] State enterprise.
[3] State enterprise; 1964 figure.

*Source*: *International Insurance Monitor*, April 1967, 90.

**Table A.3.5 Top 15 reinsurance companies for 1980**

| Rank | Company | Country | Net premium in USD m | Net premium in USD m, 2015 prices [1] |
|---|---|---|---|---|
| 1 | Munich Re | Germany | 3559.2 | 10200 |
| 2 | Swiss Re Group [2] | Switzerland | 2754.7 | 7920 |
| 3 | General Re Group | USA | 948.4 | 2730 |
| 4 | Gerling Group [3] | Germany | 823.3 | 2370 |
| 5 | Mercantile & General Re Group | UK | 543.8 | 1560 |
| 6 | Cologne Re | Germany | 531.4 | 1530 |
| 7 | SCOR | France | 495.3 | 1420 |
| 8 | Frankona Re | Germany | 442.0 | 1270 |
| 9 | Employers Re | USA | 383.3 | 1100 |
| 10 | American Re | USA | 364.4 | 1050 |
| 11 | Prudential Re | USA | 322.0 | 925 |
| 12 | Toa Fire & Marine Re [4] | Japan | 296.9 | 853 |
| 13 | Bavarian Re | Germany | 288.8 | 830 |
| 14 | INA Re | USA | 287.6 | 826 |
| 15 | NRG | The Netherlands | 271.0 | 779 |

*Notes*: [1] Converted with: http://www.measuringworth.com/uscompare/ using the CPI.
[2] Includes reinsurance subsidiaries, also with Bavarian Re.
[3] Includes reinsurance subsidiaries.
[4] Year ended 31 March 1981.

*Source*: *International Insurance Monitor*, April/May 1982, 4.

**Table A.3.6 Top 15 reinsurance companies for 1990**

| Rank | Company | Country | Net premium in USD m | Net premium in USD m, 2015 prices [1] |
|---|---|---|---|---|
| 1 | Munich Re | Germany | 8245.0 | 14900 |
| 2 | Swiss Re | Switzerland | 5633.8 | 10200 |
| 3 | Employers Re | USA | 2639.0 | 4780 |
| 4 | General Re | USA | 2065.0 | 3740 |
| 5 | Cologne Re | Germany | 1879.3 | 3400 |
| 6 | Hannover Re | Germany | 1664.4 | 3010 |
| 7 | SCOR | France | 1629.4 | 2950 |
| 8 | Generali | Italy | 1540.6 | 2790 |
| 9 | Gerling Globale Re Group | Germany | 1391.9 | 2520 |
| 10 | Mercantile & General Re | UK | 1371.3 | 2480 |
| 11 | Skandia International | Sweden | 1211.4 | 2190 |
| 12 | NRG | The Netherlands | 1205.5 | 2180 |
| 13 | Frankona Re | Germany | 1134.5 | 2050 |
| 14 | Tokio Marine & Fire | Japan | 927.9 | 1680 |
| 15 | American Re | USA | 921.5 | 1670 |

*Note*: [1] Converted with: http://www.measuringworth.com/uscompare/ using the CPI.

*Source*: *Reactions*, 16 March 1992, based on Standard & Poor's data.

Table A.3.7 Top 15 reinsurance groups for 1996

| Rank | Group | Country | Net premium in USD m | Net premium in USD m, 2015 prices [1] |
|---|---|---|---|---|
| 1 | Munich Re | Germany | 11028.9 | 16600 |
| 2 | Swiss Re | Switzerland | 10013.8 | 15100 |
| 3 | General & Cologne Re | USA | 6661.2 | 10100 |
| 4 | Employers Re | USA | 4573.0 | 6900 |
| 5 | Lloyd's | UK | 4174.0 | 6300 |
| 6 | Allianz | Germany | 3944.7 | 5950 |
| 7 | Generali | Italy | 3915.4 | 5910 |
| 8 | Zurich Re | Switzerland | 3348.0 | 5050 |
| 9 | Hannover Re | Germany | 3250.1 | 4900 |
| 10 | Gerling Global Re | Germany | 2328.7 | 3510 |
| 11 | SCOR | France | 2275.0 | 3430 |
| 12 | AXA Re | France | 1344.2 | 2030 |
| 13 | Transatlantic | USA | 1142.5 | 1720 |
| 14 | Winterthur | Switzerland | 1133.6 | 1710 |
| 15 | Everest Re | USA | 1042.9 | 1570 |

*Note*: [1] Converted with: http://www.measuringworth.com/uscompare/ using the CPI.

*Source*: Standard & Poor's: *Global Reinsurance Highlights*, 1998, 8.

Table A.3.8 Top 15 reinsurance groups for 2005

| Rank | Group | Country | Net premium in USD m | Net premium in USD m, 2015 prices [1] |
|---|---|---|---|---|
| 1 | Munich Re | Germany | 22602.8 | 27400 |
| 2 | Swiss Re [2] | Switzerland | 21203.6 | 25700 |
| 3 | Berkshire Hathaway Re | USA | 10041.0 | 12200 |
| 4 | Hannover Re | Germany | 9190.8 | 11100 |
| 5 | GE Insurance Solutions [2] | USA | 6697.0 | 8120 |
| 6 | Lloyd's | UK | 6566.8 | 7960 |
| 7 | XL Re | Bermuda | 5012.9 | 6080 |
| 8 | Everest Re | Bermuda | 3972.0 | 4810 |
| 9 | Reinsurance Group of America | USA | 3863.0 | 4680 |
| 10 | PartnerRe | Bermuda | 3615.9 | 4380 |
| 11 | Transatlantic Re | USA | 3466.4 | 4200 |
| 12 | Tokio Marine & Nichido Fire Insurance | Japan | 2789.3 | 3380 |
| 13 | SCOR | France | 2691.8 | 3260 |
| 14 | Odyssey Re | USA | 2301.7 | 2790 |
| 15 | Korean Re | Korea | 1946.7 | 2360 |

*Notes*: [1] Converted with: http://www.measuringworth.com/uscompare/ using the CPI.
[2] In 2006, Swiss Re acquired GE Insurance Solutions.

*Source*: Standard & Poor's: *Global Reinsurance Highlights*, 2006, 24.

Table A.3.9 Top 15 reinsurance groups for 2010

| Rank | Group | Country | Net premium in USD m | Net premium in USD m, 2015 prices [1] |
|---|---|---|---|---|
| 1 | Munich Re | Germany | 29269.1 | 31800 |
| 2 | Swiss Re | Switzerland | 19433.0 | 21100 |
| 3 | Berkshire Hathaway Re | USA | 14669.0 | 15900 |
| 4 | Hannover Re | Germany | 13652.2 | 14800 |
| 5 | Lloyd's | UK | 9762.1 | 10600 |
| 6 | SCOR | France | 8141.3 | 8840 |
| 7 | Reinsurance Group of America | USA | 6659.7 | 7230 |
| 8 | PartnerRe | Bermuda | 4705.1 | 5110 |
| 9 | Everest Re | Bermuda | 3945.6 | 4280 |
| 10 | Transatlantic Re | USA | 3881.7 | 4210 |
| 11 | MS&AD Holdings | Japan | 3587.4 | 3890 |
| 12 | Korean Re | Korea | 2803.0 | 3040 |
| 13 | Tokio Marine Group | Japan | 2617.2 | 2840 |
| 14 | NKSJ Holdings | Japan | 2526.1 | 2740 |
| 15 | General Ins. Corp. of India | India | 2321.4 | 2520 |

*Note*: [1] Converted with: http://www.measuringworth.com/uscompare/ using the CPI.

*Source*: Standard & Poor's: *Global Reinsurance Highlights*, 2012, 50.

Table A.3.10 Top 15 reinsurance groups for 2014

| Rank | Group | Country | Net premium in USD m [1] |
|---|---|---|---|
| 1 | Munich Re [2] | Germany | 37761 |
| 2 | Swiss Re | Switzerland | 31640 |
| 3 | Hannover Re [2] | Germany | 15100 |
| 4 | Berkshire Hathaway Re | USA | 14919 |
| 5 | SCOR | France | 12324 |
| 6 | Lloyd's | UK | 10416 |
| 7 | Reinsurance Group of America [3] | USA | 8670 |
| 8 | China Reinsurance Corporation | PRC | 7857 |
| 9 | PartnerRe | Bermuda | 5720 |
| 10 | Everest Re | Bermuda | 5257 |
| 11 | Great West Lifeco | Canada | 3809 |
| 12 | Korean Re | Korea | 3582 |
| 13 | Transatlantic Re | USA | 3410 |
| 14 | General Insurance Corporation of India [4] | India | 2216 |
| 15 | Axis Capital Holdings Limited | Bermuda | 2127 |

*Notes*: [1] Between 2014 and 2015 there was hardly any inflation.
[2] Net premium written data not reported, net premium earned substituted.
[3] Figure taken from Standard & Poor's: *Global Reinsurance Highlights*, 2015, 58.
[4] Fiscal year-end 31 March 2015.

*Source*: *Best's Review*, September 2015, 82.

**Table A.4 Insurance and reinsurance, 1990–2014: Premiums written in USD bn and real premium growth, life versus non-life**

| | Primary insurance | | | | Reinsurance | | | |
|---|---|---|---|---|---|---|---|---|
| | Premiums written, life | Premiums written, non-life | Real premium growth, life | Real premium growth, non-life | Premiums written, life | Premiums written, non-life | Real premium growth, life | Real premium growth, non-life |
| 1990 | 743 | 665 | 0.8% | 1.8% | 8 | 66 | 0.4% | 15.5% |
| 1991 | 808 | 705 | 2.9% | 1.4% | 8 | 71 | 0.2% | 2.5% |
| 1992 | 906 | 764 | 5.8% | 3.0% | 9 | 79 | 2.3% | 5.5% |
| 1993 | 1012 | 801 | 6.4% | 4.1% | 10 | 83 | 7.8% | 6.2% |
| 1994 | 1108 | 848 | 3.4% | 1.5% | 11 | 92 | 7.7% | 5.7% |
| 1995 | 1231 | 920 | 5.2% | 1.6% | 12 | 104 | 2.6% | 3.7% |
| 1996 | 1204 | 920 | 2.6% | 0.6% | 13 | 99 | 9.1% | −5.8% |
| 1997 | 1241 | 899 | 8.0% | 0.9% | 14 | 95 | 10.3% | −2.6% |
| 1998 | 1296 | 893 | 6.0% | −0.1% | 16 | 94 | 11.6% | −0.3% |
| 1999 | 1444 | 919 | 7.6% | 1.7% | 18 | 101 | 15.6% | 6.4% |
| 2000 | 1551 | 938 | 10.0% | 3.9% | 22 | 108 | 18.4% | 8.4% |
| 2001 | 1470 | 984 | −1.5% | 5.7% | 24 | 119 | 9.8% | 10.4% |
| 2002 | 1565 | 1105 | 3.0% | 9.1% | 27 | 134 | 11.7% | 8.9% |
| 2003 | 1717 | 1273 | −0.3% | 5.9% | 32 | 149 | 9.8% | 3.8% |
| 2004 | 1905 | 1391 | 3.1% | 2.2% | 37 | 140 | 8.3% | −11.2% |
| 2005 | 2023 | 1430 | 4.6% | −0.2% | 40 | 136 | 3.2% | −6.1% |
| 2006 | 2160 | 1534 | 4.2% | 3.8% | 42 | 144 | 1.6% | 2.0% |
| 2007 | 2455 | 1662 | 5.8% | 1.3% | 45 | 155 | 1.7% | 0.4% |
| 2008 | 2437 | 1756 | −6.4% | −0.7% | 48 | 165 | 1.0% | 0.5% |
| 2009 | 2366 | 1711 | −0.7% | 0.2% | 48 | 161 | 3.8% | 0.6% |
| 2010 | 2517 | 1785 | 3.0% | 1.9% | 51 | 163 | 2.5% | −1.9% |
| 2011 | 2619 | 1939 | −3.0% | 1.9% | 57 | 189 | 4.4% | 9.5% |
| 2012 | 2625 | 1976 | 2.0% | 2.6% | 55 | 195 | −3.2% | 2.7% |
| 2013 | 2545 | 2049 | −1.8% | 2.7% | 56 | 202 | 0.8% | 2.1% |
| 2014 | 2655 | 2124 | 4.3% | 2.9% | 57 | 213 | 1.4% | 4.3% |

*Note*: Local currency values are converted at market exchange rates.

*Source*: Swiss Re Economic Research & Consulting.

Figure A.1 Global reinsurance: Gross premiums written by region, 2013

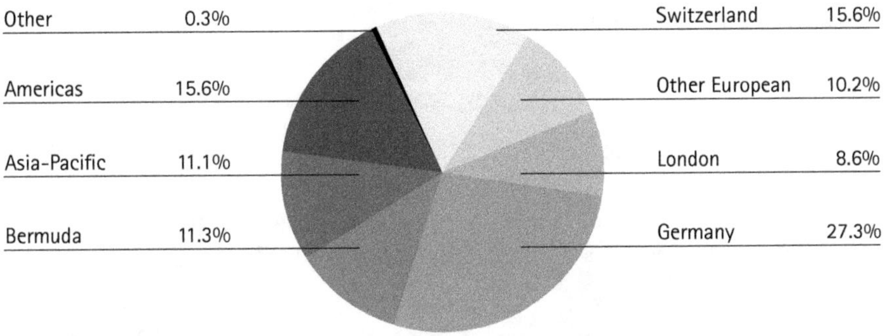


*Note*: Based on A. M. Best's Top 50 Ranking of global reinsurers. Region determined by ultimate parent's domicile. Americas includes USA, Canada, and Latin America. Americas GPW includes Berkshire Hathaway subsidiaries National Indemnity and General Re Corp.

*Source*: A. M. Best Company – used with permission.

Figure A.2.1 Reinsurance market 2014: Life and health

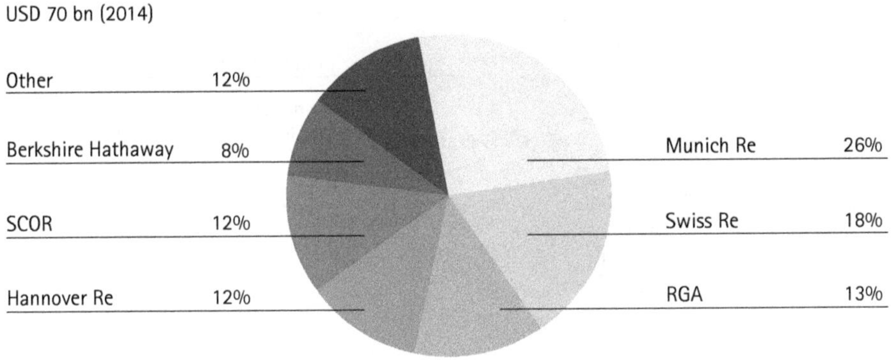


*Source*: Swiss Re Economic Research & Consulting.

Figure A.2.2 Reinsurance market 2014: Property/casualty

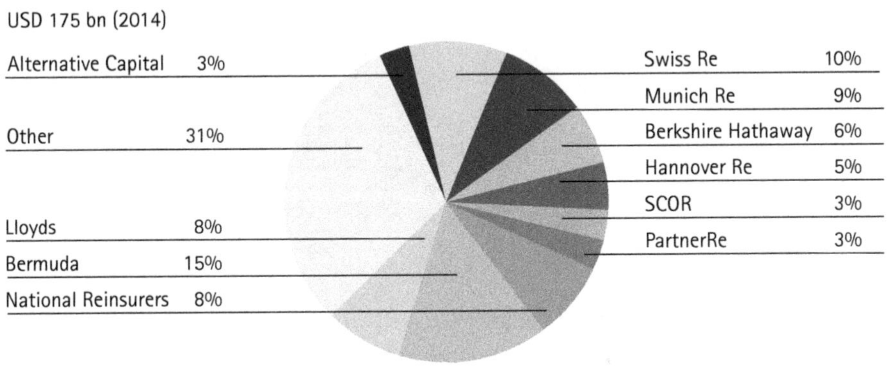


*Source*: Swiss Re Economic Research & Consulting.

## Geographical origin of cessions to reinsurance companies, 2014

Figure A.3.1 Life premiums ceded by region, 2014

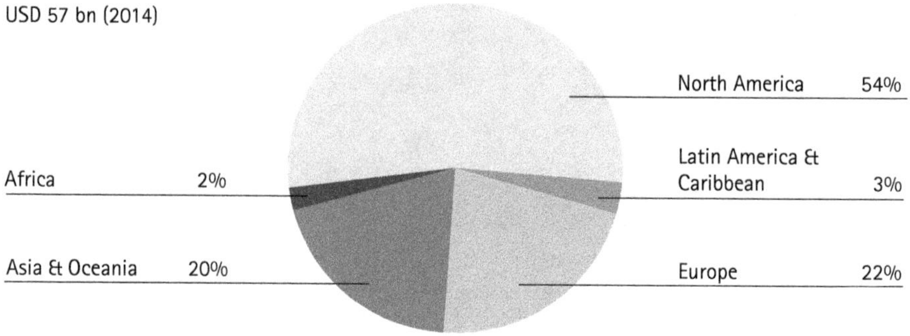


*Source*: Swiss Re Economic Research & Consulting.

Figure A.3.2 Non-life premiums ceded by region, 2014

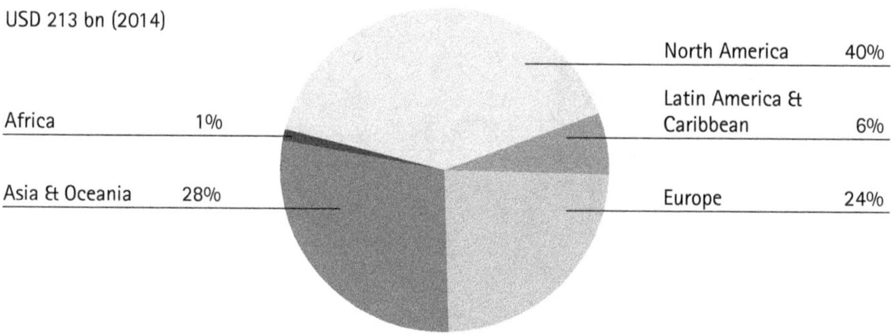


*Source*: Swiss Re Economic Research & Consulting.

Figure A.3.3 Overall premiums ceded by region, 2014

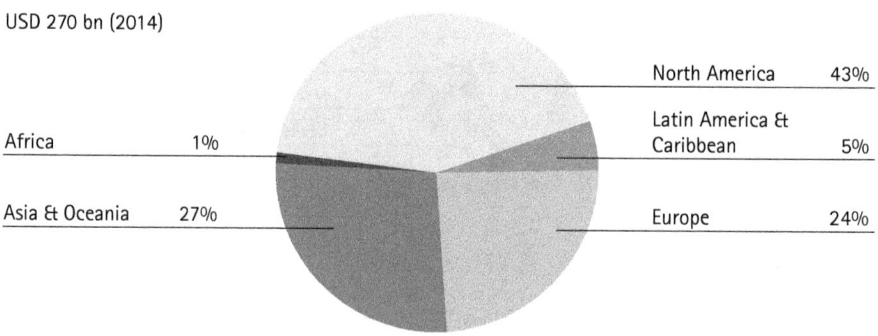


*Source*: Swiss Re Economic Research & Consulting.

Figure A.4 Cat bond notional by year, 1997–2015

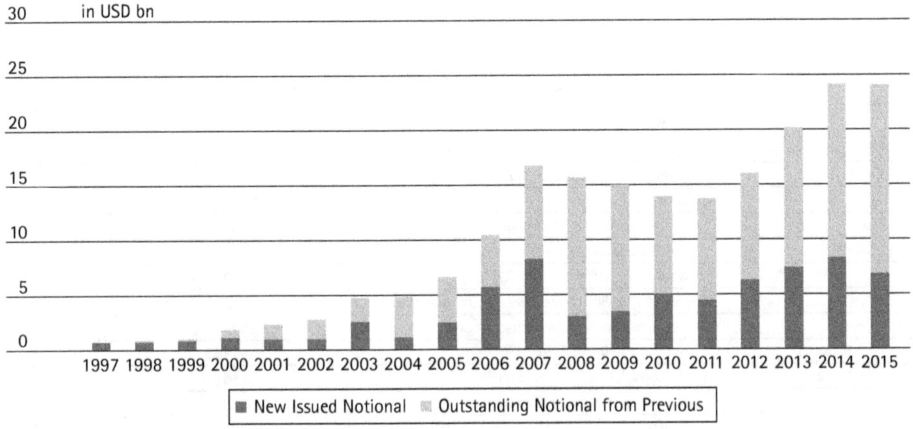


*Note*: Past performance is no guarantee of future results.

*Source*: Swiss Re Capital Markets.

Figure A.5 Swiss Re Global Cat Bond Index Total Return versus Barclays US High Yield and S&P 500 Total Return, 2002–2015

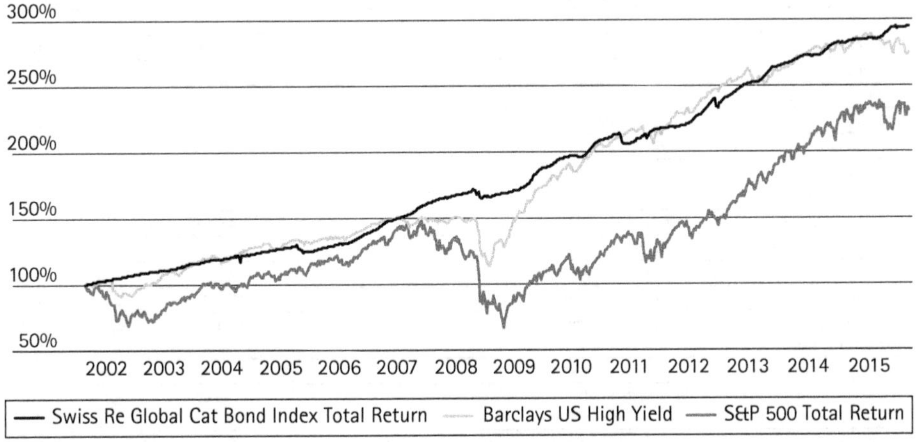


*Note*: Swiss Re Global Cat Bond Index Total Return, calculated by Swiss Re Capital Markets, is a market value-weighted basket of natural catastrophe bonds tracked by Swiss Re Capital Markets, calculated on a weekly basis; past performance is no guarantee of future results. This index tracks the aggregate performance of all catastrophe bonds issued under Rule 144A. The index captures bonds denominated in any currency, all rated and unrated cat bonds, outstanding perils, and triggers. Life and health cat bonds are not contained within the index.

*Sources*: Swiss Re Capital Markets; underlying data for 'Barclays US High Yield', is Barclays US Ba High Yield Index via Barclays Live website; underlying data for 'S&P 500 Total Return' is S&P 500 Total Return Index via Bloomberg website; underlying data for 'Swiss Re Global Cat Bond Index Total Return' is based on indicative prices only.

## Table A.5.1 Natural catastrophes and man-made disasters: The 100 most costly events in terms of economic losses, 1970–2014

| Year | Country | Event | Economic loss (in USD m, 2015 prices) | Insured loss (in USD m, 2015 prices) | Victims |
|---|---|---|---|---|---|
| 2011 | Japan | Earthquake ($M_W$ 9.0) triggers tsunami; aftershocks, landslides | 221 189.22 | 36 864.87 | 18520 |
| 2005 | USA, Gulf of Mexico | Hurricane Katrina; storm surge, damage to oil rigs | 169 861.58 | 79 663.48 | 1836 |
| 2008 | China | Earthquake ($M_W$ 7.9) in Sichuan; aftershocks | 137 115.60 | 403.28 | 87449 |
| 1995 | Japan | Great Hanshin Earthquake ($M_W$ 6.9) in Kobe | 128 110.33 | 3 843.31 | 6425 |
| *2001* | *USA* | *Terror attack on WTC, Pentagon, and other buildings* | *127 128.62* | *25 129.31* | *2982* |
| 2012 | USA, Caribbean | Hurricane Sandy; massive storm surge | 72 230.48 | 36 115.24 | 237 |
| 1994 | USA | Northridge Earthquake ($M_W$ 6.7) | 70 327.71 | 24 454.86 | 61 |
| 2010 | China | Floods, mudslides caused by heavy monsoon rain | 56 875.94 | 827.09 | 2490 |
| 2011 | Thailand | Floods caused by heavy monsoon rains | 48 450.97 | 15 799.23 | 815 |
| 1992 | USA, Bahamas | Hurricane Andrew; floods | 44 746.36 | 27 016.67 | 65 |
| 2008 | USA, Caribbean | Hurricane Ike with winds up to 195 km/h | 44 641.76 | 22 343.26 | 193 |
| 1998 | China | Massive flooding along Yangtze River | 43 602.03 | 437.76 | 3656 |
| 2004 | Japan | Chuetsu Earthquake ($M_W$ 6.6); strong aftershocks | 36 717.11 | 750.25 | 39 |
| 1980 | Italy | Earthquake ($M_W$ 6.9); aftershocks | 33 959.17 | 115.12 | 2914 |
| 2010 | Chile, South Pacific Ocean | Earthquake ($M_W$ 8.8) triggers tsunami; over 200 aftershocks | 32 591.25 | 8 691.00 | 562 |
| 1995 | China | Drought in north-eastern China | 30 581.23 | 0.00 | 0 |
| 1999 | Turkey | Earthquake ($M_W$ 7.6) in Izmit | 28 444.20 | 1 422.21 | 19118 |
| 1988 | Armenia | Earthquake ($M_W$ 6.8) | 28 043.37 | 0.00 | 25000 |
| 2004 | USA, Caribbean, Barbados et al. | Hurricane Ivan; damage to oil rigs | 27 590.95 | 16 179.98 | 119 |
| 2005 | USA, Mexico, Jamaica, Haiti et al. | Hurricane Wilma; torrential rain, floods | 24 350.87 | 15 247.58 | 53 |
| 1976 | China | Earthquake ($M_W$ 7.6) | 23 321.45 | 0.00 | 255000 |
| 1995 | North Korea | Floods | 23 321.10 | 0.00 | 68 |
| 2008 | China | Snowstorms, freezing rain across the country | 22 012.70 | 1 313.30 | 130 |
| 1994 | China | Severe drought | 21 985.65 | 0.00 | 0 |
| *2010* | *Gulf of Mexico, USA* | *Explosion on Deepwater Horizon oil rig* | *21 727.50* | *1 086.38* | *11* |
| 2011 | New Zealand | Earthquake ($M_W$ 6.1); aftershocks | 21 065.64 | 16 852.51 | 185 |
| 2004 | USA, Cuba, Jamaica et al. | Hurricane Charley | 20 066.14 | 10 096.86 | 36 |
| 1999 | Taiwan | Chi-Chi Earthquake ($M_W$ 7.6) | 20 053.16 | 1 422.21 | 3400 |
| 1993 | USA | Mississippi floods | 19 678.13 | 1 685.46 | 45 |
| 2005 | USA, Gulf of Mexico | Hurricane Rita; floods, damage to oil rigs | 19 412.75 | 12 252.26 | 34 |
| 1989 | USA, Puerto Rico et al. | Hurricane Hugo | 18 446.28 | 8 738.48 | 71 |
| 1998 | USA, Caribbean | Hurricane Georges; floods | 17 440.81 | 5 974.93 | 600 |
| 1991 | Japan | Typhoon Mireille/No. 19 | 17 399.00 | 9 822.68 | 51 |
| 2003 | France, Italy, Germany et al. | Heatwave and drought in Europe | 17 376.15 | 1 623.94 | 35000 |
| 1996 | China | Severe monsoon floods | 17 127.02 | 582.25 | 1529 |
| 1999 | Switzerland, UK, France et al. | Winter storm Lothar | 17 066.52 | 8 248.82 | 110 |
| 2013 | Germany, Czech Republic et al. | Floods: damage to houses, infrastructure, and farmland | 16 818.29 | 4 204.57 | 25 |
| 2004 | Indonesia, Thailand, Sri Lanka et al. | Earthquake ($M_W$ 9.0); tsunami in Indian Ocean | 16 303.74 | 2 508.27 | 220000 |
| 2010 | Russia | Wildfires caused by drought and prolonged heatwave | 16 295.63 | 0.00 | 130 |
| 2012 | USA | Drought in the Corn Belt | 15 477.96 | 11 350.50 | 123 |
| 1990 | Iran | Earthquake ($M_W$ 7.4); landslides | 14 506.02 | 208.52 | 40000 |
| 1976 | Italy | Earthquake ($M_W$ 6.4); aftershocks | 14 455.14 | 4.16 | 922 |
| 2002 | Germany, Czech Republic et al. | Severe floods | 13 821.53 | 3 040.74 | 52 |
| 1989 | USA | Loma Prieta Earthquake ($M_W$ 6.9) | 13 380.61 | 1 835.06 | 63 |
| 2004 | USA, Bahamas | Hurricane Frances | 13 068.08 | 6 305.36 | 50 |
| 1980 | Algeria | Earthquake ($M_W$ 7.1) | 12 950.53 | 0.00 | 4500 |
| 1990 | France, UK et al. | Winter storm Daria | 12 148.79 | 8 466.55 | 95 |
| 2007 | Germany, UK, et al. | Winter storm Kyrill; winds up to 190 km/h, floods | 11 426.24 | 6 966.29 | 54 |
| 1999 | USA, Bahamas | Hurricane Floyd; heavy rain, floods | 11 377.68 | 4 013.86 | 78 |

| | | | | | |
|---|---|---|---|---|---|
| 2012 | Italy | Earthquake ($M_W$ 5.9); aftershocks (Event 1) | 11 067.92 | 1 091.30 | 7 |
| 2008 | USA | Iowa and Midwest Flooding | 11 006.35 | 0.00 | 22 |
| 2008 | USA, Caribbean | Hurricane Gustav with winds up to 240 km/h; floods | 11 006.35 | 3 411.97 | 165 |
| 2008 | Myanmar (Burma), Bay of Bengal | Tropical Cyclone Nargis with winds up to 215 km/h | 11 006.35 | 3 411.97 | 138300 |
| 2004 | USA, Caribbean, Haiti et al. | Hurricane Jeanne; floods, landslides | 10 589.91 | 4 831.91 | 3034 |
| 2011 | USA | Major tornado outbreak; 349 tornadoes, hail | 10 532.82 | 7 688.96 | 321 |
| 2013 | China | Typhoon Fitow | 10 465.82 | 1 152.42 | 12 |
| 2000 | Japan, South Korea | Tokai floods due to heavy rain; landslides | 10 240.85 | 1 362.80 | 18 |
| 1993 | China | Floods in south-eastern China | 9 938.45 | 0.00 | 1000 |
| 1993 | USA, Canada, Cuba | Winter storm ('1993 Storm of the Century') | 9 871.86 | 3 236.93 | 303 |
| 1996 | China | Floods | 9 537.26 | 0.00 | 1200 |
| 2011 | USA | Major tornado outbreak (180); winds up to 405 km/h, hail | 9 479.54 | 7 425.64 | 177 |
| 1998 | India, Bangladesh, Nepal | Floods caused by monsoon rains; landslides | 9 083.76 | 0.00 | 2861 |
| 1985 | Mexico | Earthquake ($M_W$ 8.0) | 9 033.21 | 1 042.12 | 9500 |
| 1990 | Switzerland, Germany | Winter storm Vivian | 9 030.98 | 5 785.47 | 64 |
| 2004 | Japan, South Korea | Typhoon Songda/No. 18 | 8 993.24 | 4 496.62 | 45 |
| *2003* | *USA, Canada* | *Power blackout due to old electricity lines affects 50m people* | *8 704.10* | *231.77* | *0* |
| 1983 | USA | Hurricane Alicia | 8 544.04 | 1 943.53 | 21 |
| 2010 | Haiti | Earthquake ($M_W$ 7.0); aftershocks | 8 542.17 | 108.64 | 222570 |
| 1999 | Spain, France, Switzerland, Italy | Winter storm Martin | 8 533.26 | 3 413.30 | 57 |
| 1992 | USA | Hurricane Iniki | 8 442.71 | 2 701.67 | 6 |
| 2000 | North Korea | Tropical storm '12'; heavy damage to infrastructure | 8 255.33 | 0.00 | 42 |
| 2000 | North Korea | Typhoon and torrential rains; 29000 homes destroyed | 8 255.33 | 0.00 | 40 |
| 2012 | China | Floods caused by heavy torrential rains | 8 254.91 | 144.46 | 149 |
| 2011 | USA, Canada, Bahamas et al. | Hurricane Irene; torrential rainfall, extensive flooding | 8 004.94 | 6 117.50 | 53 |
| 2009 | France, Spain | Winter storm Klaus; winds up to 170 km/h, heavy rain | 7 921.04 | 3 504.59 | 25 |
| 1995 | USA, Mexico, Gulf of Mexico et al. | Hurricane Opal; floods | 7 773.70 | 3 895.44 | 77 |
| 1987 | France, UK et al. | Storm and floods in Europe | 7 712.88 | 6 462.14 | 22 |
| *2002* | *North Atlantic, Spain, Portugal* et al. | *Oil tanker* Prestige *breaks in two (no insured loss)* | *7 601.84* | *39.52* | *0* |
| 1979 | USA | Hurricane Frederic; storm surge | 7 512.97 | 2 607.72 | 5 |
| 1997 | Poland, Czech Republic, Germany et al. | Floods after heavy rain | 7 379.43 | 2 361.42 | 100 |
| 1990 | Japan | Typhoon Flo/No. 19 | 7 253.01 | 426.11 | 40 |
| 1988 | Mexico, Jamaica, Haiti, USA, Venezuela | Hurricane Gilbert | 7 251.79 | 2 187.38 | 360 |
| 1983 | USA | South-east drought | 7 142.36 | 0.00 | 0 |
| 1999 | Japan | Typhoon Bart/No. 18 | 7 111.05 | 5 745.53 | 26 |
| 1999 | Venezuela | Floods, mudflows, and landslides | 7 111.05 | 312.89 | 10000 |
| 2003 | South Korea | Typhoon Maemi with winds of up to 210 km/h | 7 078.23 | 648.39 | 131 |
| 2014 | India | Cyclone Hudhud | 7 006.99 | 633.04 | 68 |
| 2010 | Pakistan | Floods caused by heavy monsoonial rains | 7 004.11 | 488.87 | 1985 |
| 1995 | China | Severe floods | 6 996.33 | 108.83 | 1200 |
| 2013 | China | Earthquake ($M_W$ 7.0) | 6 915.71 | 25.43 | 198 |
| 2002 | UK, Italy, Germany, Czech Rep. et al. | Severe floods accross Europe (event 1 of 2) | 6 910.77 | 1 382.15 | 71 |
| 2011 | China | Floods causes by heavy monsoonal rains; landslides | 6 741.00 | 205.39 | 350 |
| 2010 | New Zealand | Earthquake ($M_W$ 7.0); over 300 aftershocks | 6 735.53 | 5 431.88 | 0 |
| 2001 | USA | Tropical Storm Allison; heavy rain, floods | 6 690.98 | 4 822.69 | 43 |
| 1977 | Romania | Earthquake ($M_W$ 7.2) | 6 569.44 | 0.00 | 1578 |
| 1979 | USA, Dominican Republic, Puerto Rico | Hurricane David; flooding | 6 533.01 | 401.42 | 1100 |
| *1989* | *USA, North Pacific Ocean* | *Oil tanker* Exxon Valdez *hits a riff and spills crude oil* | *6 499.15* | *210.27* | *0* |
| *1986* | *Ukraine, Belarus* | *Explosion at Chernobyl nuclear power plant* | *6 483.14* | *0.00* | *30* |
| 2011 | Australia | Floods caused by heavy rains | 6 478.95 | 2 375.61 | 22 |
| 2003 | USA | Snowstorms; hail | 6 437.95 | 463.53 | 6 |

*Victims*: Dead and missing.
$M_W$: Moment magnitude scale.
*Source*: Swiss Re Economic Research & Consulting and Cat Perils.

## Table A.5.2 Natural catastrophes and man-made disasters: The 100 most costly insurance losses, 1970–2014

| Year | Country | Event | Economic loss (in USD m, 2015 prices) | Insured loss (in USD m, 2015 prices) | Victims |
|---|---|---|---|---|---|
| 2005 | USA, Gulf of Mexico | Hurricane Katrina; storm surge, damage to oil rigs | 169 861.58 | 79 663.48 | 1836 |
| 2011 | Japan | Earthquake ($M_W$ 9.0) triggers tsunami; aftershocks, landslides | 221 189.22 | 36 864.87 | 18520 |
| 2012 | USA, Caribbean | Hurricane Sandy; massive storm surge | 72 230.48 | 36 115.24 | 237 |
| 1992 | USA, Bahamas | Hurricane Andrew; floods | 44 746.36 | 27 016.67 | 65 |
| *2001* | *USA* | *Terror attack on WTC, Pentagon, and other buildings* | *127 128.62* | *25 129.31* | *2982* |
| 1994 | USA | Northridge Earthquake ($M_W$ 6.7) | 70 327.71 | 24 454.86 | 61 |
| 2008 | USA, Gulf of Mexico, Caribbean et al. | Hurricane Ike with winds up to 195 km/h | 44 641.76 | 22 343.26 | 193 |
| 2011 | New Zealand | Earthquake ($M_W$ 6.1); aftershocks | 21 065.64 | 16 852.51 | 185 |
| 2004 | USA, Caribbean, Barbados et al. | Hurricane Ivan; damage to oil rigs | 27 590.95 | 16 179.98 | 119 |
| 2011 | Thailand | Floods caused by heavy monsoon rains | 48 450.97 | 15 799.23 | 815 |
| 2005 | USA, Mexico, Jamaica, Haiti et al. | Hurricane Wilma; torrential rain, floods | 24 350.87 | 15 247.58 | 53 |
| 2005 | USA, Gulf of Mexico | Hurricane Rita; floods, damage to oil rigs | 19 412.75 | 12 252.26 | 34 |
| 2012 | USA | Drought in the Corn Belt | 15 477.96 | 11 350.50 | 123 |
| 2004 | USA, Cuba, Jamaica et al. | Hurricane Charley | 20 066.14 | 10 096.86 | 36 |
| 1991 | Japan | Typhoon Mireille/No. 19 | 17 399.00 | 9 822.68 | 51 |
| 1989 | USA, Puerto Rico et al. | Hurricane Hugo | 18 446.28 | 8 738.48 | 71 |
| 2010 | Chile, South Pacific Ocean | Earthquake ($M_W$ 8.8) triggers tsunami; over 200 aftershocks | 32 591.25 | 8 691.00 | 562 |
| 1990 | France, UK et al. | Winter storm Daria | 12 148.79 | 8 466.55 | 95 |
| 1999 | Switzerland, UK, France et al. | Winter storm Lothar | 17 066.52 | 8 248.82 | 110 |
| 2011 | USA | Major tornado outbreak; 349 tornadoes, hail | 10 532.82 | 7 688.96 | 321 |
| 2011 | USA | Major tornado outbreak (180); with winds up to 405 km/h, hail | 9 479.54 | 7 425.64 | 177 |
| 2007 | Germany, UK, et al. | Winter storm Kyrill; winds up to 190 km/h, floods | 11 426.24 | 6 966.29 | 54 |
| 1987 | France, UK et al. | Storm and floods in Europe | 7 712.88 | 6 462.14 | 22 |
| 2004 | USA, Bahamas | Hurricane Frances | 13 068.08 | 6 305.36 | 50 |
| 2011 | USA, Canada, Bahamas et al. | Hurricane Irene; torrential rainfall, extensive flooding | 8 004.94 | 6 117.50 | 53 |
| 1998 | USA, Caribbean | Hurricane Georges; floods | 17 440.81 | 5 974.93 | 600 |
| 1990 | Switzerland, Germany | Winter storm Vivian | 9 030.98 | 5 785.47 | 64 |
| 1999 | Japan | Typhoon Bart/No. 18 | 7 111.05 | 5 745.53 | 26 |
| 2010 | New Zealand | Earthquake ($M_W$ 7.0); over 300 aftershocks | 6 735.53 | 5 431.88 | 0 |
| 2004 | USA, Caribbean, Haiti et al. | Hurricane Jeanne; floods, landslides | 10 589.91 | 4 831.91 | 3034 |
| 2001 | USA | Tropical storm Allison; heavy rain, floods | 6 690.98 | 4 822.69 | 43 |
| 2004 | Japan, South Korea | Typhoon Songda/No. 18 | 8 993.24 | 4 496.62 | 45 |
| 2013 | Germany, Czech Republic et al. | Floods; damage to houses, infrastructure, and farmland | 16 818.29 | 4 204.57 | 25 |
| 2003 | USA | Thunderstorms, tornadoes, hail, flash floods | 5 407.87 | 4 126.72 | 51 |
| 1999 | USA, Bahamas | Hurricane Floyd; heavy rain, floods | 11 377.68 | 4 013.86 | 78 |
| 2013 | Germany, France | Hailstorms | 4 905.33 | 3 903.24 | 0 |
| 1995 | USA, Mexico, Gulf of Mexico et al. | Hurricane Opal; floods | 7 773.70 | 3 895.44 | 77 |
| 1995 | Japan | Great Hanshin Earthquake ($M_W$ 6.9) in Kobe | 128 110.33 | 3 843.31 | 6425 |
| 2009 | France, Spain | Winter storm Klaus; winds up to 170 km/h, heavy rain | 7 921.04 | 3 504.59 | 25 |
| 1999 | Spain, France, Switzerland, Italy | Winter storm Martin | 8 533.26 | 3 413.30 | 57 |
| 2008 | USA, Caribbean | Hurricane Gustav; winds up to 240 km/h, floods | 11 006.35 | 3 411.97 | 165 |
| 1993 | USA, Canada, Cuba | Winter storm ('1993 Storm of the Century') | 9 871.86 | 3 236.93 | 303 |

| | | | | | |
|---|---|---|---|---|---|
| 2010 | France, Germany, Belgium et al. | Winterstorm Xynthia; winds up to 160 km/h | 4 590.89 | 3 043.76 | 64 |
| 2002 | Germany, Czech Republic et al. | Severe floods | 13 821.53 | 3 040.74 | 52 |
| *1988* | *UK* | *Explosion on platform* Piper Alpha | – | *2 964.59* | *167* |
| 1991 | USA | Forest fires which spread to urban areas; drought | 4 523.74 | 2 957.83 | 26 |
| 2001 | USA | Hail storm, multiple tornadoes, flash floods | 4 148.41 | 2 944.03 | 3 |
| 2014 | USA | Severe thunderstorms, large hail | 3 703.70 | 2 938.32 | 0 |
| 2010 | USA | Thunderstorms, tornadoes, hail, floods | 4 345.50 | 2 933.21 | 0 |
| 2007 | UK | Floods caused by heavy rain | 4 264.70 | 2 843.13 | 4 |
| 2003 | USA, Canada | Hurricane Isabel | 5 150.36 | 2 804.50 | 56 |
| 2002 | North-west Europe | Winterstorm Jeanett with winds up to 160 km/h | 4 146.46 | 2 764.31 | 37 |
| 1996 | USA | Hurricane Fran | 5 135.31 | 2 745.64 | 39 |
| 1999 | Denmark, Sweden et al. | Winterstorm Anatol | 3 555.53 | 2 708.43 | 20 |
| 1992 | USA | Hurricane Iniki | 8 442.71 | 2 701.67 | 6 |
| 1979 | USA | Hurricane Frederic; storm surge | 7 512.97 | 2 607.72 | 5 |
| 2012 | USA | Severe storms, 75 tornadoes | 3 095.59 | 2 579.66 | 42 |
| 2012 | USA | Thunderstorms, large hail, 38 tornadoes, heavy rains | 3 095.59 | 2 579.66 | 1 |
| 2005 | Switzerland, Germany, Austria et al. | Rain, floods, and landslides | 4 221.88 | 2 576.06 | 49 |
| *1989* | *USA* | *Explosion in petrochemical plant* | – | *2 532.76* | *23* |
| 1990 | France, Germany, Netherlands et al. | Winterstorm Herta | 3 641.40 | 2 526.22 | 28 |
| 2004 | Indonesia, Thailand, Sri Lanka et al. | Earthquake ($M_W$ 9.0); tsunami in Indian Ocean | 16 303.74 | 2 508.27 | 220000 |
| 2014 | Japan | Snowstorm | 5 005.00 | 2 504.69 | 26 |
| 2014 | France, Germany, Belgium | Wind and Hailstorm Ela | 3 462.04 | 2 434.81 | 6 |
| 2011 | Australia | Floods caused by heavy rains | 6 478.95 | 2 375.61 | 22 |
| 1997 | Poland, Czech Republic, Germany et al. | Floods after heavy rain | 7 379.43 | 2 361.42 | 100 |
| 1995 | Caribbean et al. | Hurricane Luis | 3 886.85 | 2 332.11 | 16 |
| 2005 | Denmark, Sweden et al. | Winterstorm Erwin; floods | 3 676.29 | 2 289.83 | 18 |
| 2007 | UK | Floods caused by heavy rain | 3 411.76 | 2 274.51 | 3 |
| 2010 | Australia | Tropical cyclone Tasha; Floods caused by heavy rains | 5 567.94 | 2 227.18 | 1 |
| 2002 | USA | Multiple tornadoes, large hail, flash floods | 2 766.07 | 2 206.27 | 7 |
| 1988 | Mexico, Jamaica, Haiti, USA, Venezuela | Hurricane Gilbert | 7 251.79 | 2 187.38 | 360 |
| 1974 | USA | 148 tornadoes (23 EF4 and 7 EF5) in 17 states | 4 806.22 | 2 183.78 | 315 |
| 2006 | USA | Thunderstorms, tornadoes, winds up to 240 km/h, hail | 2 350.85 | 2 174.53 | 27 |
| 2010 | USA | Thunderstorms, winds up to 130 km/h, hail, tornadoes | 3 259.13 | 2 172.75 | 3 |
| 1976 | Germany, UK, Belgium et al. | Winterstorm Capella | 5 413.91 | 2 115.59 | 82 |
| 1999 | USA | 70 tornadoes in the Midwest, hail, floods | 2 844.42 | 2 111.98 | 55 |
| 2011 | USA | Thunderstorms, 46 tornadoes, winds up to 210 km/h, hail | 3 159.85 | 2 106.56 | 9 |
| 2011 | New Zealand | Earthquakes ($M_W$ 5.2 and $M_W$ 6.0) | 3 159.85 | 2 106.56 | 1 |
| 1983 | USA | Winter storm, cold wave | 2 380.79 | 2 095.09 | 500 |
| 2003 | USA | Thunderstorms with large hail | 2 703.94 | 2 066.58 | 0 |
| 2012 | USA | Derecho storm with winds up to 146 km/h; tornadoes, hail | 3 095.59 | 2 063.73 | 28 |
| 1973 | USA | Flooding along the Mississippi | 5 339.34 | 1 975.02 | 33 |
| 1970 | USA, Cuba | Hurricane Celia | 3 171.89 | 1 966.25 | 31 |
| 1998 | USA | Severe hailstorm, thunderstorms, tornadoes | 2 906.80 | 1 954.82 | 1 |
| 1983 | USA | Hurricane Alicia | 8 544.04 | 1 943.53 | 21 |
| 2013 | Canada | Floods | 4 785.87 | 1 914.35 | 4 |
| 1998 | Japan, Philippines | Typhoon Vicki/No. 7 | 2 180.10 | 1 855.40 | 12 |
| 1989 | USA | Loma Prieta Earthquake ($M_W$ 6.9) | 13 380.61 | 1 835.06 | 63 |
| 2013 | USA | Severe thunderstorms, tornadoes (EF5 tornado in Moore, OK) | 3 051.05 | 1 806.22 | 27 |
| 2007 | USA | Thunderstorms, tornadoes, winds up to 130 km/h, flash, floods | 3 427.87 | 1 800.47 | 23 |

*(continued)*

**Table A.5.2 Continued**

| Year | Country | Event | Economic loss (in USD m, 2015 prices) | Insured loss (in USD m, 2015 prices) | Victims |
|---|---|---|---|---|---|
| 1998 | Canada, USA | Winter storm (North America Ice Storm) | 6 421.19 | 1 779.66 | 44 |
| 1995 | USA | Thunderstorms, heavy rains, large hail, tornadoes | 3 575.90 | 1 764.63 | 21 |
| 2012 | USA | Thunderstorms, hail, 27 tornadoes, straight-line winds | 2 063.73 | 1 754.17 | 0 |
| 2014 | Mexico | Hurricane Odile | 3 259.31 | 1 701.70 | 6 |
| 1993 | USA | Mississippi floods | 19 678.13 | 1 685.46 | 45 |
| 1992 | USA | Slow-moving winter storm (Downslope Noreaster) brings floods | 5 065.63 | 1 682.04 | 19 |
| 2014 | USA | Winter storm | 2 502.50 | 1 671.17 | 21 |
| 2012 | USA, Caribbean | Hurricane Isaac | 3 393.80 | 1 650.98 | 40 |
| 2013 | USA | Thunderstorms, tornadoes, hail | 2 034.03 | 1 642.48 | 1 |

*Victims*: Dead and missing.
$M_W$: Moment magnitude scale.
EF4 and EF5: Second highest and highest categories on Enhanced Fujita scale.
*Source*: Swiss Re Economic Research & Consulting and Cat Perils.

**Table A.5.3 Natural catastrophes and man-made disasters: The 100 worst events by victims, 1970–2014**

| Year | Country | Event | Economic loss (in USD m, 2015 prices) | Insured loss (in USD m, 2015 prices) | Victims |
|---|---|---|---|---|---|
| 1970 | Bangladesh | Storm and flood catastrophe | 548.74 | – | 300000 |
| 1976 | China | Earthquake ($M_W$ 7.6) | 23 321.45 | – | 255000 |
| 2010 | Haiti | Earthquake ($M_W$ 7.0); aftershocks | 8 542.17 | 108.64 | 222570 |
| 2004 | Indonesia, Thailand et al. | Earthquake ($M_W$ 9.0); tsunami in Indian Ocean | 16 303.74 | 2 508.27 | 220000 |
| 2008 | Myanmar (Burma), Bay of Bengal | Tropical cyclone Nargis with winds up to 215 km/h | 11 006.35 | – | 138300 |
| 1991 | Bangladesh | Tropical cyclone Gorky | 45.03 | 3.60 | 138000 |
| 2008 | China | Earthquake ($M_W$ 7.9) in Sichuan; aftershocks | 137 115.60 | 403.28 | 87449 |
| 2005 | Pakistan, India, Afghanistan | Earthquake ($M_W$ 7.6); aftershocks, landslides | 6 369.87 | – | 74310 |
| 1970 | Peru | Earthquake ($M_W$ 7.9) triggers massive avalanche and floods | 3 489.07 | – | 66000 |
| 2010 | Russia, Czech Republic | Heatwave with temperatures up to 40 degrees Celsius | 1 174.38 | – | 55630 |
| 1990 | Iran | Earthquake ($M_W$ 7.4); landslides | 14 506.02 | 208.52 | 40000 |
| 2003 | France, Italy, Germany et al. | Heatwave and drought in Europe | 17 376.15 | 1 623.94 | 35000 |
| 2003 | Iran | Earthquake ($M_W$ 6.5) destroys 85% of Bam | 2 446.42 | – | 26271 |
| 1978 | Iran | Earthquake ($M_W$ 7.7) in Tabas | – | – | 25000 |
| 1988 | Armenia | Earthquake ($M_W$ 6.8) | 28 043.37 | – | 25000 |
| 1985 | Colombia | Volcanic eruption on Nevado del Ruiz triggers lahars | 506.74 | – | 23086 |
| 1976 | Guatemala | Earthquake ($M_W$ 7.5) | 4 581.00 | 312.34 | 22300 |
| 2001 | India, Pakistan | Earthquake ($M_W$ 7.6) in Gujarat | 6 021.88 | 133.82 | 19737 |
| 1999 | Turkey | Earthquake ($M_W$ 7.6) in Izmit | 28 444.20 | 1 422.21 | 19118 |
| 2011 | Japan | Earthquake ($M_W$ 9.0) triggers tsunami; aftershocks, landslides | 221 189.22 | 36 864.87 | 18520 |
| 1999 | India | Tropical cyclone 05B with winds up to 260 km/h | 3 555.53 | 142.22 | 15000 |
| 1977 | India | Tropical cyclone in Andrah Pradesh | 1 663.76 | – | 14204 |
| 1998 | Honduras, Nicaragua et al. | Hurricane Mitch in Central America | 6 176.95 | 581.36 | 11683 |
| 1985 | Bangladesh | Tropical cyclone in Bay of Bengal | – | – | 11069 |
| 1971 | India | Odisha cyclone; flooding in Bay of Bengal and Orissa state | 182.55 | – | 10800 |
| 1999 | Venezuela | Floods, mudflows, and landslides | 7 111.05 | 312.89 | 10000 |
| 1985 | Mexico | Earthquake ($M_W$ 8.0) | 9 033.21 | 1 042.12 | 9500 |
| 1993 | India | Earthquake ($M_W$ 6.4) | 459.16 | 0.39 | 9475 |
| 2013 | Philippines, Viet Nam, China, Palau | Typhoon Haiyan; storm surge | 5 085.08 | 518.68 | 8135 |
| 1976 | Philippines | Earthquake ($M_W$ 7.1); tsunami in Moro Gulf | 157.75 | – | 7079 |
| 1995 | Japan | Great Hanshin Earthquake ($M_W$ 6.9) in Kobe | 128 110.33 | 3 843.31 | 6425 |
| 1991 | Philippines | Typhoon Thelma (Uring) | 67.22 | – | 6304 |
| 1976 | France | Heatwave, drought | – | – | 6000 |
| *1984* | *India* | *Accident in chemical plant; methyl isocyanates released* | *1 072.13* | – | *6000* |
| 2006 | Indonesia | Earthquake ($M_W$ 6.4); Bantul almost completely destroyed | 3 526.27 | 47.02 | 5749 |
| 2013 | India | Floods caused by heavy monsoon rains | 1 118.72 | 508.51 | 5748 |
| 1976 | Indonesia | Earthquake ($M_W$ 7.1) | – | – | 5422 |
| 1972 | Iran | Earthquake ($M_W$ 6.6) in Fars | – | – | 5374 |
| 1974 | Pakistan | Earthquake ($M_W$ 6.0) | 15.64 | – | 5300 |
| 1972 | Nicaragua | Earthquake ($M_W$ 6.3) | 5 889.86 | 765.68 | 5000 |
| 1987 | Ecuador | Earthquakes ($M_W$ 6.1 and $M_W$ 6.8); oil pipeline damaged | 3 126.84 | 1 396.66 | 5000 |
| 1980 | Algeria | Earthquake ($M_W$ 7.1) | 12 950.53 | – | 4500 |
| 2007 | Bangladesh, India | Cyclone Sidr in Bay of Bengal; floods | 1 335.73 | – | 4407 |
| *1987* | *Philippines* | *Ferry* Dona Paz *collides with oil tanker* Victor | – | – | *4375* |
| 1972 | Iran | Storms and snow in Ardekan | – | – | 4000 |
| 1976 | Turkey | Earthquake ($M_W$ 7.9) in Van | – | – | 4000 |
| 1998 | Afghanistan | Earthquake ($M_W$ 6.5) in Takhar | – | – | 4000 |
| 2006 | Netherlands, Belgium, France | Heatwave in Europe | – | – | 3865 |
| 1978 | India | Severe floods caused by monsoon rains | 599.48 | – | 3800 |
| 1998 | China | Massive flooding along Yangtze River | 43 602.03 | 437.76 | 3656 |
| 1999 | Taiwan | Chi-Chi Earthquake ($M_W$ 7.6) | 20 053.16 | 1 422.21 | 3400 |

*(continued)*

**Table A.5.3 Continued**

| Year | Country | Event | Economic loss (in USD m, 2015 prices) | Insured loss (in USD m, 2015 prices) | Victims |
|---|---|---|---|---|---|
| 2004 | Haiti, Dominican Rep., Puerto Rico | Floods after torrential rains | – | – | 3344 |
| 1978 | Reunion | Tropical cyclone | – | – | 3200 |
| 1997 | Vietnam, Cambodia, Thailand | Typhoon Linda | 885.53 | 7.38 | 3078 |
| 2004 | USA, Caribbean, Haiti et al. | Hurricane Jeanne; floods, landslides | 10 589.91 | 4 831.91 | 3034 |
| 1981 | Iran | Earthquake ($M_W$ 7.2) in Kerman | – | – | 3000 |
| 1981 | Iran | Earthquake ($M_W$ 6.6) in Golbas | – | – | 3000 |
| *2001* | *USA* | *Terror attack on WTC, Pentagon, and other buildings* | *127 128.62* | *25 129.31* | *2982* |
| 2010 | China | Earthquake ($M_W$ 6.9); aftershocks | 110.45 | 0.64 | 2960 |
| 1980 | Italy | Earthquake ($M_W$ 6.9); aftershocks | 33 959.17 | 115.12 | 2914 |
| 2005 | Indonesia | Earthquake off Nias Island ($M_W$ 8.6) | – | – | 2905 |
| 1998 | India, Bangladesh, Nepal | Floods caused by monsoon rains, landslides | 9 083.76 | – | 2861 |
| 1982 | Yemen | Earthquake | – | – | 2800 |
| 1974 | Bangladesh | Flood | – | – | 2500 |
| *1981* | *India* | *Passenger train derails and falls into river Bagmati* | – | – | *2500* |
| 2010 | China | Floods, mudslides caused by heavy monsoonal rain | 56 875.94 | 827.09 | 2490 |
| 1992 | Indonesia | Earthquake ($M_W$ 5.7) triggers tsunamis | 168.85 | – | 2484 |
| 1988 | Bangladesh | Floods | – | – | 2379 |
| 1998 | Afghanistan, Tajikistan | Earthquake ($M_W$ 5.9) | – | – | 2300 |
| 1975 | Turkey | Earthquake | – | – | 2300 |
| 2003 | Algeria | Earthquake ($M_W$ 6.8) | 6 437.95 | 41.98 | 2266 |
| 1998 | Papua New Guinea | Seaquake ($M_W$ 7.0) triggers tsunami | – | – | 2183 |
| 1995 | Russia | Earthquake ($M_W$ 7.0) | 99.71 | – | 2032 |
| 2005 | Pakistan | Cold wave: heavy rain, snow, mudslides, avalanches; dams burst | – | – | 2029 |
| 1996 | India | Tropical cyclone; severe damage to cropland | 2 403.11 | – | 2000 |
| *2002* | *India* | *Social unrest after arson attack on train* | *2 266.09* | *12.43* | *2000* |
| 2002 | Afghanistan, Pakistan | Earthquake ($M_W$ 6.1) | 131.72 | 52.69 | 2000 |
| 1974 | Honduras | Hurricane Fifi | – | – | 2000 |
| 2010 | Pakistan | Floods caused by heavy monsoon rains | 7 004.11 | 488.87 | 1985 |
| 1981 | Portugal | Heatwave | – | – | 1906 |
| 2012 | Philippines | Typhoon Bopha | 930.74 | – | 1901 |
| 1982 | Mexico | Eruption of volcano El Chichón | – | – | 1900 |
| 2002 | India, Bangladesh, Nepal | Cold wave with temperatures falling to near freezing | – | – | 1892 |
| 1992 | Pakistan, India | Floods caused by monsoon rains | 1 110.81 | – | 1884 |
| 1983 | Mexico | El Chichón Volcano explosive eruption (pyroclastic flows) | – | – | 1879 |
| *2002* | *Gambia, South Atlantic* | *Overloaded ferry* Le Joola *sinks in stormy waters* | – | – | *1863* |
| 2005 | USA, Gulf of Mexico | Hurricane Katrina; storm surge, damage to oil rigs | 169 861.58 | 79 663.48 | 1836 |
| *1993* | *Haiti* | *Overloaded ferry* Neptune *sinks in storm* | – | – | *1800* |
| 2010 | China | Mudslide caused by heavy rains | 824.29 | 2.92 | 1765 |
| 1991 | China | Floods, landslides | 13.05 | – | 1729 |
| 1986 | Cameroon | Mount Cameroon Volcano eruption with lethal gas release | – | – | 1700 |
| 2005 | Mexico, Guatemala, El Salvador et al. | Hurricane Stan; heavy rain, floods, and landslides | 2 487.26 | 253.58 | 1690 |
| 1990 | Philippines | Earthquake ($M_W$ 7.7) | 670.27 | 100.54 | 1666 |
| 2004 | India, Bangladesh | Floods and landslides caused by monsoon rains | 4 176.27 | – | 1630 |
| 1997 | Kenya | Floods; many rivers burst their dykes | 920.93 | – | 1600 |
| 1980 | India | Floods | – | – | 1600 |
| 2004 | Philippines | Tropical storm Winnie; flashfloods, landslides | 94.06 | – | 1593 |
| 1977 | Romania | Earthquake ($M_W$ 7.2) | 6 569.44 | – | 1578 |
| 1984 | Philippines, China | Typhoon Ike (Nitang); winds up to 220 km/h | 255.49 | – | 1538 |
| 1996 | China | Severe monsoon floods | 17 127.02 | 582.25 | 1529 |

*Victims*: Dead and missing.
$M_W$: Moment magnitude scale.
*Source*: Swiss Re Economic Research & Consulting and Cat Perils.

**Table A.6 Thresholds for insured losses and casualties (at 2014 prices)**

| | | |
|---|---|---|
| **Insured losses (claims):** | | |
| | Maritime disasters | USD m 19.6 |
| | Aviation | USD m 39.3 |
| | Other losses | USD m 48.8 |
| *or* Total losses: | | USD m 97.6 |
| *or* Casualties: | | |
| | Dead or missing | 20 |
| | Injured | 50 |
| | Homeless | 2000 |

*Source*: Swiss Re Economic Research & Consulting and Cat Perils.

**Figure A.6 Number of natural catastrophes and man-made disasters, 1970–2014**

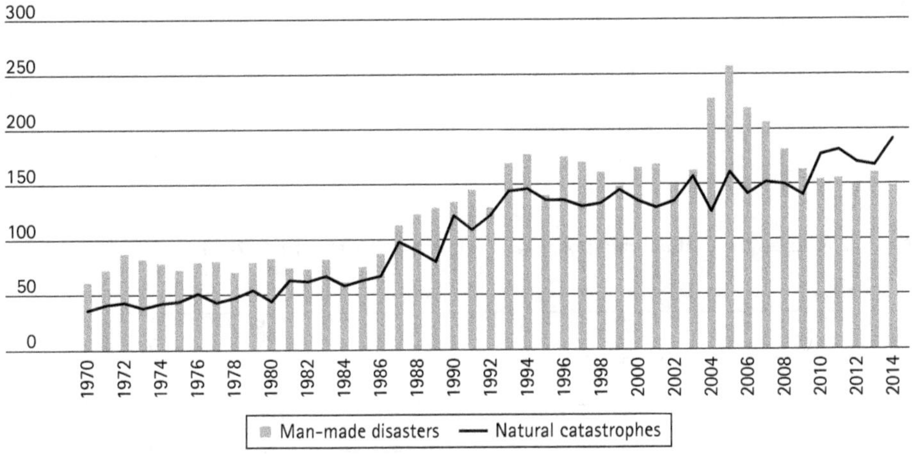


*Source*: Swiss Re Economic Research & Consulting and Cat Perils.

**Figure A.7 Number of victims from natural catastrophes and man-made disasters, 1970–2014**

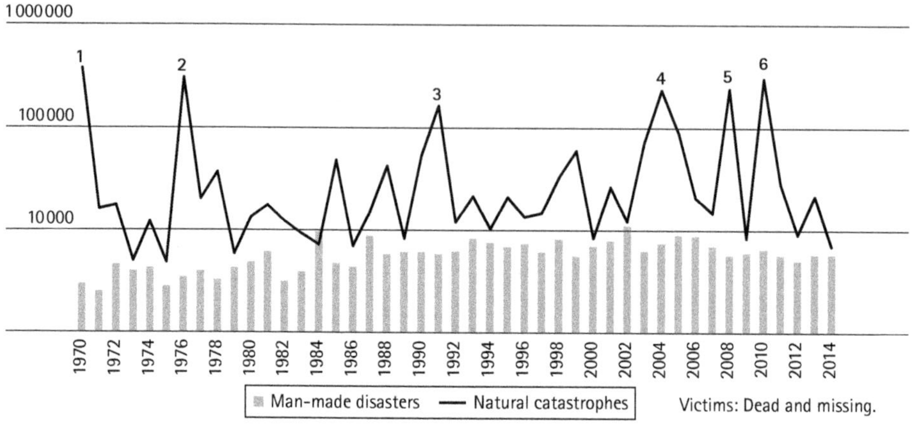


1 1970: Flood catastrophe in Bangladesh
2 1976: Earthquake in China
3 1991: Tropical Cyclone Gorky in Bangladesh
4 2004: Earthquake and tsunami in Indian Ocean
5 2008: Tropical Cyclone Nargis in Myanmar, earthquake in China
6 2010: Earthquake in Haiti

*Note*: Scale is logarithmic: number of victims increases tenfold per band.

*Source*: Swiss Re Economic Research & Consulting and Cat Perils.

**Figure A.8 Insured losses from natural catastrophes and man-made disasters, 1970–2014**

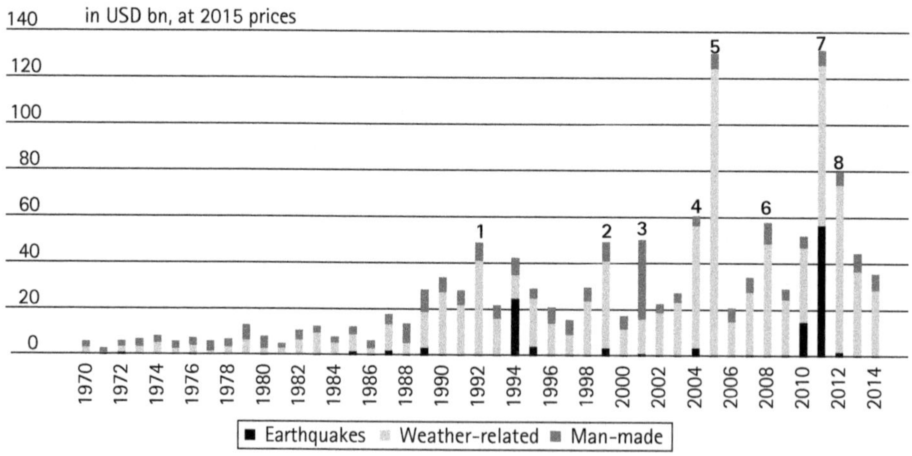


1 1992: Hurricane Andrew
2 1999: Winterstorm Lothar
3 2001: 9/11
4 2004: Hurricanes Ivan, Charley, Frances
5 2005: Hurricanes Katrina, Rita, Wilma
6 2008: Hurricanes Ike, Gustav
7 2011: Earthquakes in japan and New Zealand; Thailand flood
8 2012: Hurricane Sandy

*Source*: Swiss Re Economic Research & Consulting and Cat Perils.

Figure A.9 Insured versus uninsured losses from natural catastrophes, 1970–2014

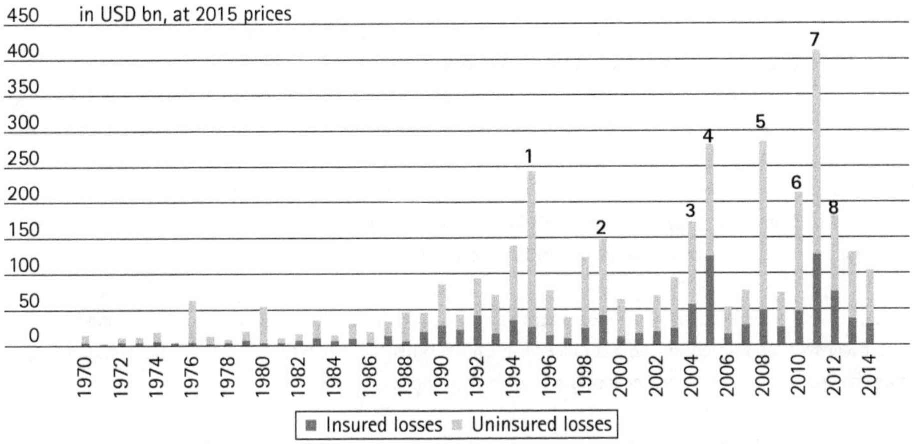


1 1995: Great Hanshin Earthquake
2 1999: Winterstorm Lothar
3 2004: Hurricanes Ivan, Charley, Frances
4 2005: Hurricanes Katrina, Rita, Wilma
5 2008: Hurricanes Ike, Gustav; earthquake in China
6 2010: Earthquake in Chile; floods in China and Pakistan
7 2011: Earthquakes in Japan and New Zealand; Thailand flood
8 2012: Hurricane Sandy

*Source*: Swiss Re Economic Research & Consulting and Cat Perils.

Figure A.10 Insured versus uninsured losses from natural catastrophes and man-made disasters, 1970–2014

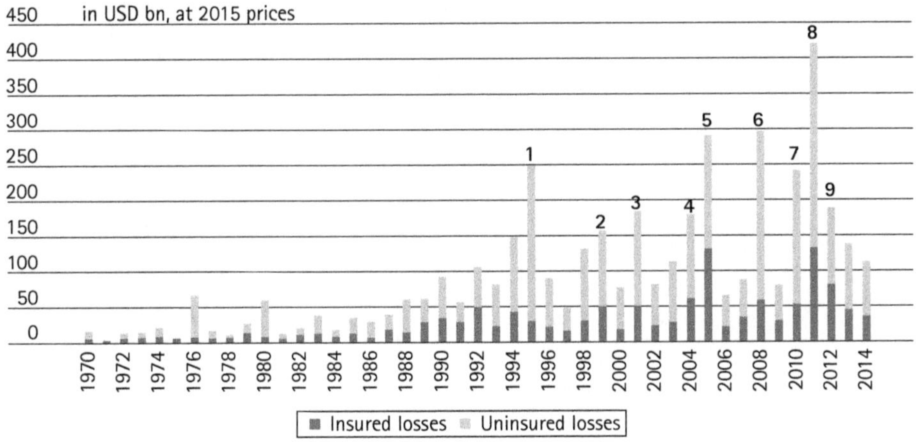


1 1995: Great Hanshin Earthquake
2 1999: Winterstorm Lothar
3 2001: 9/11
4 2004: Hurricanes Ivan, Charley, Frances
5 2005: Hurricanes Katrina, Rita, Wilma
6 2008: Hurricanes Ike, Gustav; earthquake in China
7 2010: Earthquake in Chile; floods in China and Pakistan
8 2011: Earthquakes in Japan and New Zealand; Thailand flood
9 2012: Hurricane Sandy

*Source*: Swiss Re Economic Research & Consulting and Cat Perils.

## Explanatory notes to Tables A.5.1.–A.6. and Figures A.6.–A.10.: Natural catastrophes and man-made disasters, 1970–2014

*Natural catastrophes:* The term 'natural catastrophe' refers to an event caused by natural forces. Such an event generally results in a large number of individual losses involving many insurance policies. The scale of the losses resulting from a catastrophe depends not only on the severity of the natural forces concerned, but also on man-made factors, such as building design or the efficiency of disaster control in the afflicted region.

*Man-made disasters:* This section categorizes major events associated with human activities as 'man-made' or 'technical' disasters. Generally, a large object in a very limited space is affected, which is covered by a small number of insurance policies. War, civil war, and war-like events are excluded.

*Insured losses:* 'Losses' refer to all insured losses except liability. Leaving aside liability losses, on the one hand, allows a relatively swift assessment of the insurance year; on the other hand, however, it tends to understate the cost of man-made disasters. Life insurance losses are also not included.

*Selection criteria:* Swiss Re's *sigma* has been publishing tables listing major losses since 1970. Thresholds with respect to casualties—the number of dead, missing, severely injured, and homeless—also make it possible to tabulate events in regions where the insurance penetration is below average. Table A.6. details the loss thresholds for the reporting year 2014, which were applied in this compilation.

# Glossary

| | |
|---|---|
| ART/Alternative Risk Transfer | Refers to non-traditional ways of insuring risks such as transferring them to financial markets to securitize them in the form of, e.g., catastrophe bonds. |
| Bancassurance | Partnership between a bank and an insurance company. Most often with the bank being a point of sales for insurance products. |
| Bordereaux | Lists of insured risks provided by the ceding party to the reinsurer. |
| Captive | Insurance companies owned by large corporations insuring only or mainly their own risks. |
| Cat Bonds | Cat bonds or catastrophe bonds are securities that are linked to natural catastrophe risks and which are transferred to investors on the financial markets. |
| Cession/to cede | Used to describe the transfer of a risk to an insurer or reinsurer. |
| Cedent | Insurer reinsuring with another party. |
| Co-insurance | Sharing of risks among several parties including insurers and sometimes reinsurers. |
| Deposit | Also called *fonds de roulement*. Part of or entire reserves or premium payments being administered by the ceding party. |
| EVM | Economic value management. |
| Excess of Loss | Most common form of non-proportional reinsurance, which defines indemnification of the insurer above a fixed self-retention. Sometimes used synonymous with non-proportional reinsurance. |
| Facultative Reinsurance | Reinsurance of individual, usually large risks accepted on a case-by-case basis as opposed to reinsuring an entire portfolio of risks. |
| Financial Reinsurance | Also called fin re or finite re (for non-life reinsurance). Form of reinsurance which takes capital management into account. Sometimes used for reinsurance products primarily aimed at managing capital and sometimes used to describe the capital management element in more traditional products. |

| | |
|---|---|
| Follow the Fortunes | Clause used in reinsurance which stipulates that if the insurance company pays out on losses, the reinsurers has to indemnify the cedent. |
| *Fonds de Roulement* | See Deposit. |
| IBNR | Provision for claims incurred but not reported by the balance sheet date. |
| ILS/Insurance Linked Securities | A collective term for securities such as cat bonds or life and health securities. |
| Long-tail Liability | Liability for claims, such as health claims from asbestos, which take a long time to become known and settled. |
| Micro-insurance | Used in developing markets to insure small risks with low premiums. |
| Moral Hazard | The taking on of excessive risks because one is insured. |
| MPL | Maximum possible loss. |
| Non-Proportional Reinsurance | Reinsurance contract which applies when losses exceed a certain limit. |
| Obligatory Reinsurance | See Treaty Reinsurance. |
| OTC | Over-the-counter selling of financial products such as ILS. |
| Parametric Insurance | A form of insurance or reinsurance which guarantees payment based on a defined triggering event (parametric trigger). |
| Proportional Reinsurance | Reinsurance contract where the reinsurer participates with a defined percentage in all claims. |
| Quota Share | Form of proportional reinsurance in which a defined percentage of all risks assumed by the primary insurer in a specific line is reinsured. |
| Reciprocity | Mutual exchange of risks between insurers and sometimes between insurers and reinsurers. |
| Retrocession | Ceding part of a risk or the entire risk on to another reinsurer. |
| Treaty Reinsurance | Participation of the reinsurer in certain sections of the insurers' business as agreed by treaty, as opposed to single risks (see also Facultative Reinsurance). |
| *Uberrima Fides* | Literally 'utmost good faith'. Used in reinsurance to indicate that the ceding party should disclose all risk-relevant information. |
| XL | See Excess of Loss. |

# Select Bibliography

Note: this Select Bibliography contains references relevant to the book's main theme of reinsurance. Other, more tangential, references are given in the various chapter footnotes.


AAA (American Academy of Actuaries) (2001) *Overview of Asbestos Issues and Trends*. Washington, DC: American Academy of Actuaries.

Abramovsky, A. (2008) *Reinsurance: The Silent Regulator?* Syracuse, NY: Syracuse University Press.

Acemoglu, D. and Zilibotti, F. (1997) 'Was Prometheus Unbound by Chance? Risk, Diversification, and Growth', *Journal of Political Economy* 105: 4, 709–51.

Adams, W. (1714) *The Company of London Insurers, on the Lives of Men, Women, and Children*. London: British Library 8225.a.31.

Akoob, M. (2009) 'Reinsurance and Retakaful', in S. Archer, R. A. A. Karim, and V. Nienhaus (eds), *Takaful Islamic Insurance: Concepts and Regulatory Issues*. Singapore: John Wiley & Sons, 143–69.

Alborn, T. L. (2002) 'The First Fund Managers: Life Insurance Bonuses in Victorian Britain', *Victorian Studies* 45: 1, Autumn, 65–92.

Alborn, T. L. (2004) *Conceiving Companies: Joint Stock-Politics in Victorian England*. London: Quinn.

Alborn, T. L. (2009) *Regulated Lives: Life Insurance and British Society 1800–1914*. Toronto: University of Toronto Press.

Alter, G. and Riley, J. C. (1986) 'How to Bet on Lives: A Guide to Life Contingent Contracts in Early Modern Europe', *Research in Economic History* 10, 16–17.

A. M. Best Company (1907) *Special Report upon the San Francisco Losses and Settlements*. New York: A. M. Best.

Anderson, E. R., Stanzler, J. S., and Masters, L. S. (1997) *Insurance Coverage Litigation*. Hoboken, NJ: John Wiley & Sons.

Andersson, L. F. and Lindmark, M. (2010) 'All Fired Up: The Growth of Fire Insurance in Sweden 1830–1950', *Financial History Review* 17: 1, 99–117.

Andersson, L. F., Eriksson, L., and Lindmark, M. (2010) 'Life Insurance and Income Growth: The Case of Sweden 1830–1950', *Scandinavian Economic History Review* 58: 3, 203–19.

Andreoli, E. (1932) *Die Bedeutung der Währungsprobleme in der Versicherung und Rückversicherung*. Berlin: Carl Heymann.

Arbouna, M. B. (2000) 'The Operation of Retakaful (Islamic Reinsurance) Protection', *Arab Law Quarterly* 15: 4, 335–62.

Arps, L. (1965a) *Auf sicheren Pfeilern. Deutsche Versicherungswirtschaft vor 1914*. Göttingen: Vandenhoeck & Ruprecht.

Arps, L. (1965b) *Wechselvolle Zeiten. 75 Jahre Allianz Versicherung 1890–1965*. Munich: Allianz Versicherungs-AG.

Arps, L. (1970) *Durch unruhige Zeiten. Deutsche Versicherungswirtschaft seit 1914*, vol. 1: *Erster Weltkrieg und Inflation*. Karlsruhe: Verlag Versicherungswirtschaft.

Arps, L. (1976) *Durch unruhige Zeiten. Deutsche Versicherungswirtschaft seit 1914*, vol. 2: *Von den Zwanziger Jahren zum Zweiten Weltkrieg*. Karlsruhe: Verlag Versicherungswirtschaft.

Bähr, J. and Kopper, C. (2015) *Munich Re. Die Geschichte der Münchener Rück 1880–1980*. Munich: C. H. Beck.

Bailey, A. L. (1950) 'Credibility Procedures: Laplace's Generalization of Bayes' Rule and the Combination of Collateral Knowledge with Observes Data', *Proceedings of the Casualty Actuarial Society* 37, 7–23.

Bain, A. (1998) *Insurance Spirals and the Lloyd's Market*. Glasgow: University of Glasgow, Department of Economics.

Bajrektarevic, A. and Baumer, C. (2010) 'Climate Change and Reinsurance: The Human Security Issue'. Paper presented at Fifth Viennese Conference on South East Asian Studies: Human Security in South-East Asia, Vienna, 28–9 May.

Balachandran, G. (2012) 'India: From a Colonial Outpost to a Leading Market', in P. Borscheid and N. V. Haueter (eds), *World Insurance: The Evolution of a Global Risk Network*. Oxford: Oxford University Press, 444–71.

Beck, U. (2007) *Weltrisikogesellschaft*. Frankfurt am Main: Suhrkamp.

Belser, W. E. (1957a) 'Present Position of Reactor Owners in Europe in Respect to Third Party Liability and Insurance', in Atomic Industrial Forum, *The 1957 Nuclear Industry: Problems and Progress*. New York: Atomic Industrial Forum, 1–28.

Belser, W. E. (1957b) 'Die Stellung der Versicherung zu den Risiken der Kernenergie', *Wirtschaftspolitische Mitteilungen* 13, 1–29.

Belser, W. E. (1958) 'Die Gefahren des Atomzeitalters', *Schweizerischer Versicherungskurier* 13: 5, 127–35.

Bensa, E. (1897) *Histoire du contrat d'assurance au moyen age*. Paris: Albert Fontemoing.

Berger, L. A., Cummins, J. D., and Tennyson, S. (1992) 'Reinsurance and the Liability Insurance Crisis', *Journal of Risk and Uncertainty* 5, 253–72.

Berliner, B. (1982) *Limits of Insurability*. Englewood Cliffs, NJ: Prentice Hall.

Bernard, C. and Tian, W. (2009) 'Optimal Reinsurance Arrangements under Tail Risk Measures', *Journal of Risk and Insurance* 76: 3, 709–25.

Bernstein, P. (1996) *Against the Gods*. New York: John Wiley & Sons.

Bertogg, M., Guatteri, M., and Castaldi, A. (2005) *A Shake in Insurance History: The 1906 San Francisco Earthquake*. Zurich: Swiss Re.

Biagosch, A. (2007) 'Wie das Trübe in Rückversicherungsverträgen zu klären ist. Zahl der Schiedsverfahren nimmt zu. Von einem Petersburger Seminar der DIS', *Versicherungswirtschaft* 23, 1 December, 2008.

Bindenagel, J. D. (ed.) (1999) *Washington Conference on Holocaust-Era Assets, November 30–December 3, 1998: Proceedings*. Washington, DC: US Government Printing Office.

Blake, E. and Landsea, C. W. (2011) *The Deadliest, Costliest, and Most Intense United States Tropical Cyclones from 1851 to 2010 (and Other Frequently Requested Hurricane Facts) (NOAA Technical Memorandum NWS NHC-6)*. Miami: National Hurricane Center.

Blasco Martel, Y. and Rabetino, R. (2012) 'Argentina: The Changing Fortunes of the Argentinian Insurance Market', in P. Borscheid and N. V. Haueter (eds), *World Insurance: The Evolution of a Global Risk Network*. Oxford: Oxford University Press, 620–44.

Böcker, T. (1935) '*Die Einheitsversicherung. Unter Berücksichtigung ihres Verhältnisses zur Rückversicherung*'. Doctoral Thesis, Göttingen University, Dortmund.

Bonβ, W. (1995) *Vom Risiko. Unsicherheit und Ungewissheit in der Moderne*. Hamburg: Hamburger Edition.

Bornhuetter, R. L. and Ferguson, R. E. (1972) 'The Actuary and IBNR', *Proceedings of the Casualty Actuarial Society* 59, 181–95.

Borscheid, P. (1997) *275 Jahre Feuersozietäten in Westfalen. Vorsprung durch Erfahrung*. Münster: Westfälische Provinzial-Versicherungen.

Borscheid, P. (2007) 'A Globalisation Backlash in the Inter-war Period?', in P. Borscheid and R. Pearson (eds), *Internationalisation and Globalisation of the Insurance Industry in the 19th and 20th Centuries*. Marburg: Philipp University of Marburg, 129–41.

Borscheid, P. (2010) 'Mit Sicherheit leben. Zur Geschichte und Gegenwart des Versicherungswesens', *Zeithistorische Forschungen* 7, 188–202.

Borscheid, P. (2012a) 'Far East and the Pacific: Overview', in P. Borscheid and N. V. Haueter (eds), *World Insurance: The Evolution of a Global Risk Network*. Oxford: Oxford University Press, 415–43.

Borscheid, P. (2012b) 'Latin America and Caribbean: Overview', in P. Borscheid and N. V. Haueter (eds), *World Insurance: The Evolution of a Global Risk Network*. Oxford: Oxford University Press, 559–77.

Borscheid, P. (2012c) 'Insurance, Expansion, and Setbacks', in P. Borscheid and N. V. Haueter (eds), *World Insurance: The Evolution of a Global Risk Network*. Oxford: Oxford University Press, 37–66.

Borscheid, P. (2012d) 'Introduction', in P. Borscheid and N. V. Haueter (eds), *World Insurance: The Evolution of a Global Risk Network*. Oxford: Oxford University Press, 1–34.

Borscheid, P. (2012e) 'Europe: An Overview', in P. Borscheid and N. V. Haueter (eds), *World Insurance: The Evolution of a Global Risk Network*. Oxford: Oxford University Press, 37–66.

Borscheid, P. (2013) 'Global Insurance Networks', in H. James (ed.), *The Value of Risk: Swiss Re and the History of Reinsurance*. Oxford: Oxford University Press, 23–144.

Borscheid, P. and Haueter, N. V. (eds) (2012) *World Insurance: The Evolution of a Global Risk Network*. Oxford: Oxford University Press.

Borscheid, P. and Pearson, R. (2007) *Internationalization and Globalization of the Insurance Industry in the 19th and 20th Centuries*. Zurich and Marburg: Philipp University of Marburg.

Bourthoumieux, J. (1998) 'La Réassurance proportionnelle', in F. Ewald and J.-H. Lorenzi (eds), *Encyclopédie de l'assurance*. Paris: Économia, 1367–84.

Braun, H. (1925) *Geschichte der Lebensversicherung und der Lebensversicherungstechnik*. Nürnberg: Koch.

Bronzin, V. (1908) *Theorie der Prämiengeschäfte*. Leipzig: Franz Deuticke.

Brown, J. R. et al. (2004) *An Empirical Analysis of the Economic Impact of Federal Terrorism Insurance*. Cambridge, MA: National Bureau of Economic Research.

Bühlmann, H. (1987) 'Actuaries of a Third Kind?', *ASTIN Bulletin* 17: 2, 137–8.

Bühlmann, H. (1997a) *Mathematische Paradigmen in der Finanzwirtschaft*. Zurich: ETH.

Bühlmann, H. (1997b) 'The Actuary: The Role and Limitations of the Profession since the Mid-19th Century', *ASTIN Bulletin* 27: 2, 165–71.

Bühlmann, H. (2007) 'The History of ASTIN: Invited Lecture at the 50 Years Anniversary of ASTIN', *ASTIN Bulletin* 37: 2, 191–202.

Bühlmann, H. and Straub, E. (1970) 'Glaubwürdigkeit für Schadensätze', *Mitteilungen der Vereinigung schweizerischer Versicherungsmathematiker* 70, 111–23.

Butler, R. (1957) 'Liability Insurance in the United States', in Atomic Industrial Forum (ed.), *The 1957 Nuclear Industry: Problems and Progress*. New York: Atomic Industrial Forum, 2–6.

Carl, U. (1990) *Probleme der organisatorischen Gestaltung der Rückversicherungsunternehmung*. Karlsruhe: Verlag Versicherungswirtschaft.

Carter, R. L., Lucas, L. D., and Ralph, N. (2000) *Reinsurance* (4th edn). London: Reactions Publishing Group in association with Guy Carpenter & Co.

Cassis, Y. (2010) *Capitals of Capital: The Rise and Fall of International Financial Centers, 1780–2009*. Cambridge: Cambridge University Press.

Chilchinsky G. and Heal, G. (1998) 'Managing Unknown Risks: The Future of Global Reinsurance'. <https://mpra.ub.uni-muenchen.de/8820/1/MPRA_paper_8820.pdf> (accessed 12 June 2015).

Clark, G. et al. (eds) (2010) *The Appeal of Insurance*. Toronto: University of Toronto Press.

Clark, G. W. (1993) 'Life Insurance in English Society and Culture 1695–1775'. Doctoral Thesis, Princeton University, New Jersey.

Clark, G. W. (1997) 'Life Insurance in the Society and Culture of London 1700–1775', *Urban History* 24: 1, May, 17–36.

Clark, G. W. (1999) *Betting on Lives: The Culture of Life Insurance 1695–1775*. Manchester: Manchester University Press.

Cologne Re (1988) *Asbestos-Related Claims in the U.S.A.: Impact on the Reinsurance Industry*. London: Cologne Re.

Coppet, L. (1935) 'Contribution to Discussion', in O. May (ed.), *Transactions of the International Congress on Life Assurance Medicine*. London, 106–9.

Couroux, M. and Outreville, J. F. (1992) 'The Development of Insurance Markets of Developing Countries: UNCTAD's Activities in the Field of Human Resources Development', *Geneva Papers on Risk and Insurance* 17: 63, April, 232–43.

Cramér, H. (1930) 'On the Mathematical Theory of Risk', in *Skandia Jubilee Volume*. Stockholm: Centraltryckeriet, 7–84.

Cruciger, G. (1926) *Die Praxis der Rückversicherung*. Munich: Vitalis Verlag.

Cruciger, G. (1929) *Was muss jeder Versicherungsbeamte insbesondere auch der Werbebeamte im Aussendienst von der Rückversicherung wissen? Eine kurze Einführung in das Wesen und die Technik der Rückversicherung*. Munich: Vitalis Verlag.

Cummins, J. D. (2007) 'Reinsurance for Natural and Man-Made Catastrophes in the United States: Current State of the Market and Regulatory Reforms', *Risk Management and Insurance Review* 10: 2, 179–220.

Cummins, J. D. (2008) 'The Bermuda Insurance Market: An Economic Analysis', 6 May 2008. <http://www.bermuda-insurance.org/pdf-downloads/CumminsReport08.pdf> (accessed 31 May 2016).

Cummins, J. D. and Lamm-Tennant, J. (eds) (1993) *Financial Management of Life Insurance Companies*. Boston, MA: Kluwer.

Cummins, J. D. and Trainar, P. (2009) 'Securitization, Insurance, and Reinsurance', *Journal of Risk and Insurance* 76: 3, 463–92.

Cummins, J. D. and Weiss, M. A. (2009) 'Convergence of Insurance and Financial Markets: Hybrid and Securitized Risk-Transfer Solutions', *Journal of Risk and Insurance* 76: 3, 493–545.

Dacy, D. C. and Kunreuther, H. (1969) *The Economics of Natural Disasters: Implications for Federal Policy*. New York: Free Press.

Dardel, E. de (1952) 'Les risques aggravés en assurance sur la vie', *Schweizerische Versicherungszeitschrift* 20: 3/4, 65–74, 104–10.

Darroch, J. and Kipping, M. (2012) 'Canada: Taking Life Insurance Abroad', in P. Borscheid and N. V. Haueter (eds), *World Insurance: The Evolution of a Global Risk Network*. Oxford: Oxford University Press, 252–73.

Daston, L. (1988) *Classical Probability in the Enlightenment.* Princeton, NJ: Princeton University.

Davis, M. and Etheridge, A. (2006) *Louis Bachelier's Theory of Speculation.* Princeton, NJ, and Oxford: Princeton University Press.

De Finetti, B. (1940) *Il problema dei pieni (Giornale Istituto Italiano 11).* Rome: Istituto Italiano degli Attuari.

De Finetti, B. (1957) 'Su un impostazione alternativa della teoria collettiva del rischio', in *Transactions of the XVth International Congress of Actuaries*, vol. 2. New York: Mallon, 433–43.

De Morgan, A. (1868) 'Some Account of James Dodson, F.R.S', *Journal of the Institute of Actuaries and Assurance Magazine* 14: 5, October, 341–64.

Debreu, G. (1959) *Theory of Value: An Anomalic Analysis of Economic Equilibrium.* New York: Wiley.

Defoe, D. (1697) *An Essay upon Projects.* London: Printed by R. R. for Tho. Cockerill.

Dennett, L. (2004) *Mind over Data: An Actuarial History.* Oxford: Institute of Actuaries.

Diamantidi, A. N. (1918) *Handbook on Reinsurance.* London.

Dickson, P. G. M. (1960) *The Sun Insurance Office 1760–1960.* Oxford: Oxford University Press.

*Die Rückversicherung* (1926) 'Rückversicherung und Währungsverschlechterung', *Versicherung und Geldwirtschaft* (with supplement *Die Rückversicherung* 8), 5.

Doherty, N. and Smetters, K. (2002) *Moral Hazard in Reinsurance Markets.* Working Paper 9050. Cambridge, MA: National Bureau of Economic Research.

Donelly, C. and Embrechts, P. (2010) 'The Devil is in the Tails: Actuarial Mathematics and the Subprime Mortage Crisis', *ASTIN Bulletin* 40: 1, 1–33.

Douglas, M. and Wildavsky, A. (1982) *Risk and Culture: An Essay on the Selection of Technological and Environmental Dangers.* Berkeley, CA: University of California Press.

Duffey, R. B. and Saull, J. W. (2008) *Managing Risk: The Human Element.* Chichester: Wiley & Sons.

Duffy, C. R. (2004) *Held Captive: A History of International Insurance in Bermuda.* Toronto: Oakwell Boulton.

Durbin, D. (2001) 'Managing Natural Catastrophe Risks: The Structure and Dynamics of Reinsurance', *Geneva Papers on Risk and Insurance* 26: 2, April, 297–309.

*The Economist* (2003) 'Love on the Rocks: Arguments between Insurers and Reinsurers', *The Economist*, 19 March.

*The Economist* (2007) 'By Wind or By Water', *The Economist (U.S. Edition)*, 19 July.

Edley, C. (1999) 'Prepared Statement Concerning H.R. 1283: The Fairness in Asbestos Compensation Act'. Hearing before the Committee on the Judiciary House of Representatives 106th Congress, 2nd session, Washington, DC.

Ehrenberg, V. (1885) *Die Rückversicherung. Festschrift der Rostocker Juristen-Fakultät für Georg Beseler.* Hamburg and Leipzig: Leopold Voss.

Ehrenberg, V. (1903) 'Die gesetzliche Regelung der laufenden Versicherung', *Zeitschrift für die gesamte Versicherungswissenschaft* 3, 203–11.

Ehrenberg, V. (1908) *Das künftige Rückversicherungsrecht (Veröffentlichungen des Deutschen Vereins für Versicherungs-Wirtschaft 15).* Berlin: Mittler.

Ehrenzweig, A. (1880) 'Aphorismen über Rückversicherung', *Assekuranz-Jahrbuch* 1, 24–42.

Ehrenzweig, A. (1881) 'Der Rückversicherungsvertrag und seine Usancen', *Assekuranz-Jahrbuch* 2, 75–91.

Ehrenzweig, A. (1886) 'Vertragsrecht und Rückversicherungs-Betrieb', *Assekuranz-Jahrbuch* 7, 172–202.

Emminghaus, A. (1901) 'Rückversicherung', in J. Conrad et al. (eds), *Handwörterbuch der Staatswissenschaften* (2nd edn). Jena: Fischer, 472–5.

Erdönmez, M. (ed.) (2004) *Trends und Herausforderungen in der Rückversicherung. Perspektiven der Praxis*. St. Gall: Verlag Institut für Versicherungswirtschaft der Universität St. Gallen.

Ericson, R. V. and Doyle, A. (2004) *Uncertain Business: Risk, Insurance, and the Limits of Knowledge*. Toronto: University of Toronto Press.

Ericson, R. V., Doyle, A., and Barry, D. (2003) *Insurance as Governance*. Toronto: University of Toronto Press.

Euler, L. (1767) 'Sur les rentes viagères', *Mémoires de l'Académie des sciences de Berlin* 16, 165–75.

Evans, D. and Jovanovic, B. (1989) 'An Estimated Model of Entrepreneurial Choice under Liquidity Constraints', *Journal of Political Economy* 97: 4, 808–27.

Everett, D. J. (2002/3) 'Comment, The "War" on Terrorism: Do War Exclusions Prevent Insurance Coverage for Losses Due to Acts of Terrorism?', *Alabama Law Review* 54: 1, 175–91.

Ewald, F. (1990) 'Norms, Discipline, and the Law', *Representations* 30, 138–61.

Ewald, F. (1991) 'Insurance and Risk', in G. Burchell, C. Gordon, and P. Miller (eds), *The Foucault Effect: Studies in Governmentality*. Chicago: University of Chicago Press, 197–210.

Falush, P. (1997) *Development of Reinsurance Markets in the Economies in Transition*. Paris: OECD.

Febvre, L. (1956) 'Pour l'histoire d'un sentiment: Le besoin de securité', *Annales: Économies, Sociétés, Civilisations* 11: 2, 244–7.

Feldman, G. D. (2001) *Die Allianz und die deutsche Versicherungswirtschaft 1933–1945*. Munich: C. H. Beck.

Feldman, G. D. (2004) 'Competition and Collaboration among the Axis Multinational Insurers: Munich Re, Generali, and Riunione Adriatica 1933–1943', *Financial History Review* 10, 165–94.

Felix, O. (2015) 'FX Risks in the Interwar Period: How did Swiss Re React to Its New Financial Risk Exposure?' Master's Thesis, History Department, Graduate Institute of International and Development Studies, Geneva.

The First Society of Assurance for Widows and Orphans (1705) *Assurance for Widows and Orphans*. London: Guildhall Broadsides 11.87.

Föllmer, H. (2009) 'Alles richtig und trotzdem falsch? Anmerkungen zur Finanzkrise und zur Versicherungsmathematik', *Mitteilungen der DMV* 17: 3, 148–54.

*Försäkringsaktiebolaget Skandia* (1955) 'Collective Risk Theory', in Skandia (ed.), *Försäkringsaktiebolaget Skandia 1855–1955*. Stockholm: Försäkrings-AB Skandia, 92.

Freeman, J. R. (1932) *Earthquake Damage and Earthquake Insurance*. New York: McGraw-Hill.

Freeman, M., Pearson, R., and Taylor, J. (2012) *Shareholder Democracies? Corporate Governance in Britain and Ireland before 1850*. Chicago: University of Chicago Press.

Frey, H. H. (1989) 'Geschriebenes und ungeschriebenes Recht der Rückversicherung', *Schweizerische Versicherungszeitschrift* 57: 9, 293–301.

The Friendly Society (1715) *Land Security, for Establishing a Perpetual Insurance on Lives of Men, Women, and Children*. London: British Library 8225.a.27.

Fürer, G. (2011) 'Why Getting Regulation Right is Paramount', *Financial Times*, 4 July.

Galahn, G. (2007) 'VAG-Novelle. Bald neue Möglichkeiten für Rückversicherer', *Versicherungswirtschaft* 6, 15 March, 390.

Gaulding, J. (1995) 'Race, Sex, and Genetic Discrimination in Insurance: What's Fair?', *Cornell Law Review* 80: 6, September, article 4.

Geneva Association (2010) *Systemic Risk in Insurance: An Analysis of Insurance and Financial Stability*. Geneva: Geneva Association.

Gerathewohl, K. et al. (1976) *Rückversicherung. Grundlagen und Praxis*, vol. 1. Karsruhe: Verlag Versicherungswirtschaft.

Gerathewohl, K. et al. (1979) *Rückversicherung. Grundlagen und Praxis*, vol. 2. Karlsruhe: Verlag Versicherungswirtschaft.

Gerathewohl, K. et al. (1982) *Reinsurance: Principles and Practice*, vol. 2. Karlsruhe: Verlag Versicherungswirtschaft.

Gibson, R., Habib, M., and Ziegler, A. (2007) *Financial Markets, Reinsurance, and the Bearing of Natural Catastrophe Risk*. Zurich: Swiss Finance Institute, University of Zurich.

Gigerenzer, G. et al. (1989) *The Empire of Chance: How Probability Changed Science and Everyday Life*. Cambridge: Cambridge University Press.

Golding, C. E. (1927) *A History of Reinsurance with a Sidelight on Insurance*. London: Waterlow & Sons.

Golding, C. E. (1931) *A History of Reinsurance with a Sidelight on Insurance* (2nd edn). London: Waterlow & Sons.

Golding, C. E. (1937) *The Law and Practice of Reinsurance*. London: Buckley Press.

Gorton, G. (2010) *Slapped by the Invisible Hand: The Panic of 2007*. Oxford: Oxford University Press.

Goshay, R. C. and Sandor, R. L. (1973) 'An Inquiry into the Feasibility of a Reinsurance Futures Market', *Journal of Business Finance* 5: 2, 56–66.

Graham, J. M. (2015) *We Are Against Socialized Medicine, But What Are We For? Federal Health Reinsurance, National Health Policy, and the Eisenhower Presidency*. Missoula, MT: University of Montana Scholar Works.

Graumann, M. (1999) *Organisationstheoretische Untersuchung der Rückversicherungsunternehmung*. Berlin: Duncker & Humblot.

Greenberg, A. D. et al. (1986) 'Financial Reinsurance: Panel Discussion', *Record of Society of Actuaries* 12: 4A, 2597–627.

Grossmann, M. (1964) 'Rückversicherung vor 100 Jahren', *Schweizerische Versicherungszeitschrift* 31, 385–401.

Group of Thirty (2006) *Reinsurance and International Financial Markets*. Washington, DC: Group of Thirty.

Gruder, O. (1927) 'Die Versicherung anormaler Leben in Österreich', in S. H. Jarvis (ed.), *Transactions of the 8th International Congress of Actuaries, London 27th to 30th June 1927*, vol. 4. London: Layton, 283–307.

Gruenwald, H. (1904) 'Rückversicherung', in A. Manes (ed.), *Kritik des Gesetzentwurfs über den Versicherungsvertrag. Berichte und Debatten auf der Mitglieder-Versammlung des Deutschen Vereins für Versicherungs-Wissenschaft am 10., 11., 12. Dezember 1903 (Veröffentlichungen des Deutschen Vereins für Versicherungswissenschaft 2)*. Berlin: Mittler & Sohn, 272–80.

Gugerli, D. (2012) 'Cooperation and Competition: Organization and Risks in the Reinsurance Business 1860–2010'. Unpublished manuscript, Zurich.

Gugerli, D. (2013) 'Cooperation and Competition: Organization and Risk in the Reinsurance Business 1860–2010', in H. James (ed.), *The Value of Risk: Swiss Re and the History of Reinsurance*. Oxford: Oxford University Press, 147–233.

Guy Carpenter (2010) *World Catastrophe Reinsurance Market 2010*. New York: Guy Carpenter.

Guy Carpenter (2012) *Cold Spots Heating Up: The Impact of Insured Catastrophe Losses in New Growth Markets*. New York: Guy Carpenter.

Haberman, S. (1996) *Landmarks in the History of Actuarial Science (Actuarial Research Paper 84)*. London: Faculty of Actuarial Science & Insurance, City University London.

Hacking, I. (1975) *The Emergence of Probability*. Cambridge: Cambridge University Press.

Hacking, I. (1990) *The Taming of Chance*. Cambridge: Cambridge University Press.

Haegen, P. L. van der (1956) *Der Internationale Rückversicherungsmarkt unter besonderer Berücksichtigung des Schweizerischen Angebots*. Berne: Herbert Lang & Cie Verlag.

Hagen, O. (1920) 'Begriff und Rechtsgrundlagen der Rückversicherung', *Zeitschrift für die gesamte Versicherungswirtschaft* 20, 137–60.

Hald, A. (1990) *A History of Probability and Statistics and their Applications before 1750*. London: Wiley.

Hall, R. M. (2001) 'Fronting: Business Considerations, Regulatory Concerns, Legislative Reactions and Related Case Law', *XII Mealey's Reins. Rep.* 14. <http://www.robertmhall.com/articles/frontingdoc.htm> (accessed 23 May 2016).

Halpérin, J. (1946) *Les assurances on Suisse et dans le monde*. Neuchâtel: Editions de la Baconnière.

Hanzlik, A. (1911) *'Die juristische Natur der Rückversicherung'*. Doctoral Thesis, Leipzig University, Leipzig.

Hartwig, R. P., Stewart, G., and Wilkinson, C. (2004) *Terrorism, Insurance, and the United States Government*. New York: Insurance Information Institute.

Hasenclever, W. (1935) *'Risikoverschiebung bei der Rückversicherung'*. Doctoral Thesis, Heidelberg University, Charlottenburg.

Haueter, N. V. (2012) *How Swiss Re Evolved*. Zurich: Swiss Re.

Haufler, V. (1997) *Dangerous Commerce: Insurance and the Management of International Risk*. Ithaca, NY: Cornell University Press.

Haufler, V. (2009) 'Insurance and Reinsurance in a Changing Climate', in H. Selin and S. D. VanDeveer (eds), *Changing Climates in North American Politics: Institutions, Policymaking, and Multilevel Governance*. Cambridge: The MIT Press, 241–62.

Hausmann, P. and Hux, I. (1997) *Die Überschwemmungen in Tschechien, Polen und Deutschland: Aus der Katastrophe lernen*. Zurich: Swiss Re.

Head, G. L. (1982) 'Continuing Evolution of the Risk Management Function and Education in the United States', *Geneva Papers on Risk and Insurance* 7: 23, April, 180–6.

Heise, H.-J. (1932) *'Die Rückversicherung als Haftpflichtversicherung'*. Doctoral Thesis, Jena University, Ellrich.

Helmsen, W. (1938) *'Die Rückversicherung. Studien zu ihrer Geschichte, Bedeutung und mathematisch-technischen Behandlung'*. Doctoral Thesis, University of Munich, Hildesheim.

Herrmannsdorfer, F. (1921) *Wesen und Behandlung der Rückversicherung*. Munich: Piloty & Loehle.

Herrmannsdorfer, F. (1924) *Wesen und Behandlung der Rückversicherung* (2nd edn). Munich: Piloty & Loehle.

Herrmannsdorfer, F. (1927) *Technik und Bedeutung der Rückversicherung*. Munich: Piloty & Loehle.

Herzfelder, E. (1913) 'Rückversicherung', in A. Manes (ed.), *Versicherungslexikon. Ergänzungsband für die Jahre 1908–1912*. Tübingen: Mohr, cols 568–81.

Heun, W. (1926) 'Die Auswirkungen der partiarischen Abrede bei den Rückversicherungs- und Retrozessionsverträgen auf die Geschäftsführung des Zedenten', in Reichsverband der Deutschen Volkswirte (ed.), *Festgabe für Otto Prange. Beiträge zu Theorie und Praxis des Versicherungswesens dargebracht von Berufskollegen, Freunden und Schülern unter Mitarbeit von Hans Gustav Argus et al. (Schriften des Reichsverbandes der Deutschen Volkswirte 6: Volkswirtschaft und Privatwirtschaft, Reihe B: Beiträge zu Theorie und Praxis des Versicherungswesens 1–20).* Berlin: Verlag des Reichverbandes, 115–36.

Hickmann, J. (2004) 'History of Actuarial Science', in J. L. Teugels and B. Sundt (eds), *Encyclopedia of Actuarial Science*, vol. 2. Chichester: Wiley, 838–47.

Holland, D. M. (2009) 'A Brief History of Reinsurance', *Reinsurance News* 65, February, 4–29.

Hollitscher & Gottlieb (1968) *Über 100 Jahre Rückversicherungsvermittlung.* Vienna: Privately published.

Hollitscher, C. H. von (1931) *Internationale Rückversicherung (Veröffentlichungen des Deutschen Vereins für Versicherungs-Wissenschaft 48).* Berlin: E. S. Mittler & Sohn.

Holzheu, T. and Lechner, R. (2007) 'The Global Reinsurance Market', in J. D. Cummins and B. Vernard (eds), *Handbook of International Insurance: Between Global Dynamics and Local Contingencies.* New York: Springer, 877–902.

Horvath, E. (1975) *L'influence de l'inflation sur la réassurance non-proportionelle des branches non-vie.* Bienne: Anderegg-Guenin.

Hotchkiss, W. H. (1914) 'Reinsurance and Retrocession as Affecting and Affected by our American Insurance System: Extension of Remarks of William H. Hotchkiss, (former Superintendent of Insurance of New York) at the National Convention of Insurance Commissioners held at Chicago Ill, April 15, 1914'. Original typescript, the Insurance Library Association of Boston (no archive identification number).

Huebner, S. S. (1922) *Marine* Insurance. New York: D. Appleton.

Hürlimann, E. (1931) *Remarks on Reinsurance Past and Present.* London: Waterlow & Sons.

IAIS (International Association of Insurance Supervisors) (2006). *Issues Paper on the Regulation and Supervision of Captive Insurance Companies.* Basel: IAIS.

Insurance Commissioner of the State of California (1906) *39th Annual Report.* Sacramento, CA: Insurance Commissioner of the State of California.

ISO (Insurance Services Office) (1994) *Catastrophes: Insurance Issues Surrounding the Northridge Earthquake and Other Natural Disasters (ISO Insurance Issues Series Study).* New York: Insurance Services Office.

Jahn, W. (1912) '*Studien über Rückversicherung und deren Statistik*'. Doctoral Thesis, Ludwig Maximilian University of Munich, Berlin.

James, H. (2013a) 'Introduction: The Insuring Instinct', in H. James (ed.), *The Value of Risk: Swiss Re and the History of Reinsurance.* Oxford: Oxford University Press, 1–22.

James, H. (ed.) (2013b) *The Value of Risk: Swiss Re and the History of Reinsurance.* Oxford: Oxford University Press.

Jarzabkowski, P., Bednarek, R., and Spee, P. (2015) *Making a Market for Acts of God: The Practice of Risk-Trading in the Global Reinsurance Industry.* Oxford: Oxford University Press.

JCAE (Joint Committee on Atomic Energy) (1974) *Selected Materials on Atomic Energy Indemnity and Insurance Legislation.* Washington, DC: Government Printing Office.

Jecklin, H. and Zimmermann, H. (1950/1) 'Reserveberechnung auf Basis hyperbolischer Interpolation. Ergänzende Bemerkungen. Weitere Ergänzungen zur F-Methode', *Mitteilungen der Vereinigung schweizerischer Versicherungsmathematiker* 50: 2, 179–96/51: 1–2, 37–52, 137–63.

Jenkins, G. and Causton, W. (1714) *A Proposal for Settling Jointures and Granting Annuities: After the Rate of 40 l. per Cent. Per Annum.* London: British Library 8235.a.49.

Jennings, R. (2008) 'Titans of Reinsurance: Joe Kolodney', *Reinsurance News* 62, 20–4.

Jericho, E. (1988) 'Insurance and Reinsurance Disputes', *Defense Counsel Journal* 55: 3, July, 289–96.

Johnson, J. W. (1986) *Insuring against Disaster: The Nuclear Industry on Trial.* Macon, GA: Mercer University Press.

Johnson, L. (2011) 'Insuring Climate Change? Science, Fear, and Value in Reinsurance Markets'. Dissertation, University of California, Berkeley, CA.

Kadelbach, S. and Günther, K. (2011) 'Recht ohne Staat?', in S. Kadelbach and K. Günther (eds), *Recht ohne Staat? Zur Normativität nichtstaatlicher Rechtsetzung (Normative Orders 4).* Frankfurt am Main: Campus, 9–48.

Kader, H. A. et al. (2010) 'The Determinants of Reinsurance in the Swedish Property Fire Insurance Market during the Interwar Years 1919–39', *Business History* 52: 2, 262–84.

Kahane, Y. (1977) 'Determination of the Product Mix and the Business Policy of an Insurance Company: A Portfolio Approach', *Management Science* 23: 10, 1060–9.

Karlen, S. et al. (2002) *Schweizerische Versicherungsgesellschaften im Machtbereich des 'Dritten Reichs'.* Zurich: Chronos.

Kellenberg, D. and Mobarak, A. M. (2011) 'The Economics of Natural Disasters', *Annual Review of Resource Economics* 3, 297–312.

Keller, W. and Modarres, M. (2005) 'A Historical Overview of Probabilistic Risk Assessment Development and its Use in the Nuclear Power Industry: A Tribute to the Late Professor Norman Carl Rasmussen', *Reliability Engineering and System Safety* 89, 271–85.

Kelly, A. B. (1967) 'Insurance Capacity in the Changing Reinsurance Market', *Best's Fire and Casualty News*, 16–22.

Kendall, J. (2002) 'The Incalculable Risk: How the World Trade Center Disaster Accelerated the Evolution of Insurance Terrorism Exclusions', *University of Richmond Law Review* 36, 569.

Kennedy, L. J. (1908) 'The Progress of the Fire in San Francisco April 18th–21st: As Shown by an Analysis of Original Documents'. Master's Thesis, University of California, Berkeley.

Kleeberg, J. M. (2003) 'From Strict Liability to Workers Compensation: The Prussian Railroad Law, the German Liability Act, and the Introduction of Bismarck's Accident Insurance in Germany 1838–1884', *New York University Journal of International Law and Politics* 36, 53–132.

Klineberg, E. (2005) *Heat Wave: A Social Autopsy of Disaster in Chicago.* Chicago: University of Chicago Press.

Kluge, H. (2006) 'Der Einfluss des Geschäfts der "Allianz" auf die Entwicklung der "Münchener Rückversicherungs-Gesellschaft" in deren ersten fünfzig Jahren (1880–1930)', *Jahrbuch für Wirtschaftsgeschichte* 61, 217–46.

Knight, F. H. (1921) *Risk, Uncertainty, and Profit.* New York: Houghton Mifflin.

Knight, F. H. (1951) *The Economic Organization.* New York: Augustus M. Kelley.

Knight, F. H. (1957) *Risk, Uncertainty and Profit* (8th edn). New York: Kelley & Millman.

Kobrak, C. (2012) 'USA: The International Attraction of the US Insurance Market', in P. Borscheid and N. V. Haueter (eds), *World Insurance: The Evolution of a Global Risk Network.* Oxford: Oxford University Press, 274–308.

Koch, P. (1966) *Große Katastrophen der Versicherungsgeschichte (Schriftenreihe des Seminars für Versicherungsbetriebslehre an der Universität München 28).* Munich: Institut für Versicherungswirtschaft.

Koch, P. (1969) 'Auswirkungen von Katastrophen und Großschäden in historischer Sicht', *Zeitschrift für die gesamte Versicherungswissenschaft* 58, 137–77.

Koch, P. (1998) *Geschichte der Versicherungswissenschaft in Deutschland.* Karlsruhe: Deutscher Verein für Versicherungswissenschaft.

Kölnische Rückversicherungsgesellschaft (1903) *Rückblick auf die Entstehung und die Entwicklung des Geschäftes der Kölnischen Rückversicherungsgesellschaft in Köln.* Cologne: Kölnische Rückversicherung.

Kölnische Rückversicherungsgesellschaft (1953) *100 Jahre Kölnische Rückversicherungs-Gesellschaft.* Cologne: Dumont.

Kopf, E. W. (1929) *Notes on Origin and Development of Reinsurance.* New York: Globe Printing Company.

Kössler, N. (2008) *Die Versicherungsaufsicht über Rückversicherungsunternehmen. Vom Reichsgesetz von 1901 bis zur Richtlinie über die Rückversicherung (Schriften zum Versicherungs-, Haftungs- und Schadensrecht 15).* Hamburg: Kovac, 40–4.

Kyrtsis, A.-A. (2011) 'Insurance of Techno-Organizational Ventures and Procedural Ethics: Lessons from the Deepwater Horizon Explosion', *Journal of Business Ethics* 103: supplement 1, 45–61.

Labes, H. W. (1996) *Schiedsgerichtsvereinbarungen in Rückversicherungsverträgen.* Frankfurt am Main: Lang.

Lane, M. (ed.) (2002) *Alternative Risk Strategies.* London: Risk Waters Group.

Larsson, M. and Lönnborg, M. (2014) *SCOR Sweden RE: 100 Years of Swedish Re(insurance) History.* Stockholm: Dialogos Förlag.

Larsson, M. and Lönnborg, M. (2015) 'Organising Risk Management in Sweden: The Life Reinsurance Market'. Paper presented at the XVIIth World Economic History Congress, 3–7 August, Kyoto.

Le Blanc, H. (1939) *La réassurance au point de vue économique.* Paris: Librairie Général de Droit et de Jurisprudence.

Leblanc, R. (2003) 'Year-End Capital Management Using Financial Reinsurance', *Reinsurance Section News* 51, 17–19.

Leggett, J. (1993) *Climate Change and the Insurance Industry: Solidarity among the Risk Community?* Greenpeace. <http://www.greenpeace.org/international/en/publications/reports/leggett-insurance-climate> (accessed 1 June 2015).

Lencsis, P. M. (1997) *Insurance Regulation in the United States: An Overview for Business and Government.* Westport, CT: Quorum Books.

Lengwiler, M. (2006) *Risikopolitik im Sozialstaat. Die schweizerische Unfallversicherung 1870–1970.* Cologne: Boehlau.

Lengwiler, M. (2009) 'Double Standards: The History of Standardizing Humans in Modern Life Insurance', in M. Lampland and S. L. Star (eds), *Standards and their Stories: How Quantifying, Classifying, and Formalizing Practices Shape Everyday Life.* Ithaca, NY, and London: Cornell University Press, 95–122.

Lengwiler, M. (2010) 'Competing Globalizations: Controversies between Private and Social Insurance at International Organisations (1900–1960)', in R. Pearson (ed.), *The Development of International Insurance.* London: Pickering & Chatto, 167–86.

Lengwiler, M. (2012) 'Switzerland: Insurance and the Need to Export', in P. Borscheid and N. V. Haueter (eds), *World Insurance: The Evolution of a Global Risk Network.* Oxford: Oxford University Press, 143–66.

Lengyel, S. (1927) *Die Bilanzen der Versicherungsunternehmungen.* Berlin: Leopold Weiss.

Leonard, A. (2004) 'Reinsurance Issues in the Baltic Countries', in OECD (ed.) *Insurance in the Baltic Countries.* Paris: OECD, 105–41.

Lewis, M. (2010) *The Big Short: Inside the Doomsday Machine.* New York: Norton.

Lewis, W. (1889) *Lehrbuch des Versicherungsrechts.* Stuttgart: Enke.

Liebwein, P. (2009) *Klassische und modern Formen der Rückversicherung*. Karlsruhe: Verlag Versicherungswirtschaft.

Looschelders, D. (2012) 'Grundfragen des deutschen und internationalen Rückversicherungsrechts', *Versicherungsrecht-Aufsätze* 1, 1 January, 1–9.

Luhmann, N. (1970) 'Evolution des Rechts', in R. Lautmann, W. Maihofer, and H. Schelsky (eds), *Jahrbuch für Rechtssoziologie und Rechtstheorie* vol. 1: *Die Funktion des Rechts in der modernen Gesellschaft*. Bielefeld: Bertelsmann, 3–22.

Luhmann, N. (2003) *Soziologie des Risikos*. Berlin: Walter de Gruyter.

MacAlister-Smith, P. (1985) *International Humanitarian Assistance: Disaster Relief Actions in International Law and Organization*. Dordrecht: Martinus Nijhoff Publishers.

McCulloch, J. and Tweedale, G. (2008) *Defending the Indefensible: The Global Asbestos Industry and its Fight for Survival*. Oxford: Oxford University Press.

McFall, L. (2014) *Devising Consumption: Cultural Economies of Insurance, Credit and Spending*. Abingdon and New York: Routledge.

MacGillivray, E. J. (1988) *MacGillivray and Parkington on Insurance Law: Relating to All Risks other than Marine*. London: Sweet & Maxwell.

Mackenzie, R. K. (1907) 'The San Francisco Earthquake and Conflagration', *Journal of the Federation of Insurance Institutes* 10, 251–79.

MacMinn, R. D. (2005) 'On Corporate Risk Management and Insurance', *Asia-Pacific Journal of Risk and Insurance* 1: 1, 97–119.

Mainardi, R. (1925) *Die Rückversicherung* (2nd edn). Berlin: Verlag Deutsche Versicherungs-Presse.

Major, J. A. and Kreps, R. E. (2002) 'Catastrophe Risk Pricing in the Traditional Market', in M. Lane (ed.), *Alternative Risk Strategies*. London: Risk Waters Group, 201–20.

Manes, A. (1913) 'Die internationalen Verflechtungen des Versicherungswesens. Ein Überblick', *Weltwirtschaftliches Archiv* 2, 1 January, 102–10.

Manes, A. (1922) *Versicherungswesen (Teubners Handbücher für Handel und Gewerbe)* (2nd edn). Leipzig: Teubner.

Manes, A. (1924) *Versicherungswesen* (4th edn). Leipzig and Berlin: Teubner.

Manes, A. (1930) *Versicherungs-Lexikon*. Berlin: E. S. Mittler & Sohn.

Mankowski, P. (2002) 'Internationales Rückversicherungsvertragsrecht', *Versicherungsrecht-Aufsätze* 28, 1 October, 1177–88.

Marbacher, J. (1989) 'Makro- und mikroökonomische Aspekte der Rückversicherung', *Schweizerische Versicherungszeitschrift*, 57, September, 273–91.

Markowitz, H. (1952) 'Portfolio Selection', *Journal of Finance* 7, 77–91.

Masius, E. A. (1857) *Systematische Darstellung des Gesamten Versicherungswesens*. Leipzig: Theodor Thomas.

*Masius' Rundschau* (1906) 'On the San Francisco Disaster: Declaration by 20 European Reinsurance Companies, Frankfurt am Main 30.4.1906', *Masius' Rundschau* 18, 226.

Mayers, D. and Smith Jr, C. W. (1982) 'On the Corporate Demand for Insurance', *Journal of Business* 55, 281–96.

Mayers, D. and Smith Jr, C. W. (1987) 'Corporate Insurance and the Underinvestment Problem', *Journal of Risk and Insurance* 54, 45–54.

Mehr, R. I. and Hedges, R. A. (1963) *Risk Management in the Business Enterprise*. Homewood, IL: R. D. Irwing.

Meier, K. J. (1988) *The Political Economy of Regulation: The Case of Insurance*. Albany, NY: State University of New York Press.

Meier, L. (1965) 'Die Atomversicherung. *Grundzüge und technische Rückstellungen*'. Doctoral Thesis, University of St. Gallen, Zurich.

Mener, A. S. (2007) 'Disaster Response in the United States of America: An Analysis of the Bureaucratic and Political History of a Failing System', *College Undergraduate Research Electronic Journal*, 10 May.

Merkin, R. (ed.) (2007) *A Guide to Reinsurance Law*. London: Routledge.

Millar, J. (1787) *Elements of the Law Relating to Insurances*. Edinburgh: Printed for J. Bell, Parliament-Close.

Millette, M. et al. (2002) 'Securitization of Life Insurance Business', in M. Lane (ed.), *Alternative Risk Strategies*. London: Risk Books, 395–426.

Milligan-Whyte, J. and Veed, M. C. (1989) 'Bermudian, English and American Reinsurance Arbitration Law and Practice and Alternative Dispute Resolution Methods', *Tort & Insurance Law Journal* 25, 120–49.

Mitchell, R. B. (1974) *From Actuarius to Actuary: The Growth of a Dynamic Profession in Canada and the United States*. Chicago: Society of Actuaries.

Moldenhauer, P. (1901) 'Die laufende Versicherung', *Zeitschrift für die gesamte Versicherungswissenschaft* 1: 19–49, 141–64.

Moldenhauer, P. (1904) 'Rückversicherung', in A. Manes (ed.), *Kritik des Gesetzentwurfs über den Versicherungsvertrag. Berichte und Debatten auf der Mitglieder-Versammlung des Deutschen Vereins für Versicherungs-Wissenschaft am 10., 11., 12. Dezember 1903 (Veröffentlichungen des Deutschen Vereins für Versicherungswissenschaft 2)*. Berlin: Mittler & Sohn, 281–6.

Moldenhauer, P. (1924) 'Rückversicherung', in A. Manes (ed.), *Versicherungslexikon* (2nd edn). Berlin: Mittler & Sohn, cols 1045–78.

Moosbrugger, M. E. (1964) 'La technique des négociations en réassurance', *Schweizerische Versicherungszeitschrift* 31, 377–85.

Morgan, M. J. (ed.) (2009) *The Impact of 9/11 on Business and Economics: The Business of Terror. The Day that Changed Everything?* New York: Palgrave Macmillan.

Morse, R. G. (1953) "The Reinsurance Companies' Viewpoint of the Recent Trend toward High Verdicts', *Insurance Counsel Journal* 20, January, 14–16.

Mossner, B. (1959) *Die Entwicklung der Rückversicherung bis zur Gründung selbständiger Rückversicherungsgesellschaften*. Berlin: Duncker & Humblot.

Mumenthaler, C. (2005) 'Die Versicherungswirtschaft braucht das Knowhow der Ingenieure', *Infoflash. Informationsbulletin der Gruppe IngCH Engineers Shape our Future* 28, November, 1.

Munich Re (1973) *Flood/Inundation*. Munich: Munich Re.

Munich Re (1984) *1880–1980: 100 Years of Munich Re*. Munich: Munich Re.

Munich Re (1994) *Das Erdbeben von Northridge in Kalifornien am 17. Januar 1994 (Topics Schadenspiegel 37)*. Munich: Munich Re.

Munich Re (2006) *The 1906 Earthquake and Hurricane Katrina: Similarities and Differences—Implications for the Insurance Industry*. Munich: Munich Re.

Munich Re (2011a) *NATHAN. Weltkarte der Naturgefahren. Version 2011*. Munich: Munich Re.

Munich Re (2011b) *Topics Geo. Naturkatastrophen 2010. Analysen, Bewertungen, Positionen*. Munich: Munich Re.

Munich Re (2012) *Topics Geo. Naturkatastrophen 2011. Analysen, Bewertungen, Positionen*. Munich: Munich Re.

Murphy, S. A. (2010) *Investing in Life: Insurance in Antebellum America*. Baltimore, MA: Johns Hopkins University Press.

National Underwriter (1966) *Annual Analysis of the American Reinsurance Market, 9 December.* Chicago: National Underwriter Co.

Neave, J. (1980) *Speaking of Reinsurance . . .* Brentford: Kluwer Publishing.

Nehlsen-von Stryk, K. (1986) *Die venezianische Seeversicherung im 15.Jahrhundert.* Ebelsbach: R. Gremer.

Nell, M. and Richter, A. (2005) 'Catastrophic Events as Threats to Society: Private and Public Risk Management Strategies', in M. Frenkel, U. Hommel, and M. Rudolf (eds), *Risk Management: Challenge and Opportunity.* Berlin: Springer, 321–40.

Netzel, C. (2003) 'Grundlinien der Entwicklung der Versicherungsmathematik und verwandter Gebiete in den letzten hundert Jahren', in K. Wolfsdorf and E. Helten (eds), *100 Jahre Organisation der Versicherungsmathematiker in Deutschland.* Karlsruhe: Verlag Versicherungswirtschaft, 41–107.

Neumann, R. (1911) 'Die Rückversicherung auf dem Gebiete des sozialen Versicherungswesens', *Zeitschrift für die gesamte Versicherungswissenschaft* 11, 80–90.

*New York Herald* (1906) 'Sixty Per Cent', *New York Herald (European Edition)*, 21 April, 2.

Nonna, J. M. and Strassberg, J. E. (1986) 'Reinsurance Arbitration: Boon or Bust', *Tort & Insurance Law Journal* 22, 586–611.

Nurkse, R. (and Brown, W. A.) (1944) *International Currency Experience: Lessons of the Inter-War Period.* New York: Columbia University Press.

Nützi, K. (2000) 'Contract Services', *Swiss Re Magazine* 1, 50–1.

Obermayer, G. (1912) '*Die Rückversicherung*'. Doctoral Thesis, Friedrich-Alexander Universität Erlangen, Borna-Leipzig.

Odierno, H. S. (2012) 'Faith-Based Risk-Sharing Structures', in S. O. Gönülal (ed.), *Takaful and Mutual Insurance: Alternative Approaches to Managing Risks.* Washington, DC: World Bank, 53–65.

OECD (Organisation for Economic Co-operation and Development) (2011) *Risk Awareness, Capital Markets and Catastrophic Risks.* Paris: OECD Publishing.

OECD (Organisation for Economic Co-operation and Development) (2014) *OECD Reviews of Risk Management Policies: Boosting Resilience through Innovative Risk Governance.* Paris: OECD Publishing.

Okuyama, Y. (2008) *Critical Review of Methodologies on Disaster Impact Estimation: Background Paper Prepared for the World Bank–UN Assessment on the Economics of Disaster Risk Reduction.* Niigata: International University of Japan.

Okuyama, Y. and Sahin, S. (2009) *Impact Estimation of Disasters: A Global Aggregate for 1960 to 2007.* Washington, DC: World Bank.

Osetrova, A. (2007) *Die Regulierung des Versicherungsmarkts unter besonderer Berücksichtigung der Solvabilitätsvorschriften (Versicherungswissenschaft. Schriftenreihe des Vereins zur Förderung der Versicherungswissenschaft 31).* Karlsruhe: Verlag Versicherungswirtschaft.

*Österreichische Revue* (1906) 'Die Schadensliquidation von San Francisco', *Österreichische Revue*, 280.

*Österreichische Versicherungs-Zeitschrift* (1906a) 'Das amerikanische Pacific- und kalifornische Feuerversicherungsgeschäft in den letzten 6 Jahren', *Österreichische Versicherungs-Zeitschrift*, 122.

*Österreichische Versicherungs-Zeitschrift* (1906b) 'On the Situation in San Francisco', *Österreichische Versicherungs-Zeitschrift*, 276.

*Österreichische Versicherungs-Zeitschrift* (1906c) 'Report Compiled by a Loss Liquidator in San Francisco', *Österreichische Versicherungs-Zeitschrift*, 306.

Paiva Abreu, M. de and Tâmega Fernandes, F. (2012) 'Brazil: The Resilience of the Brazilian Insurance Market', in P. Borscheid and N. V. Haueter (eds), *World Insurance: The Evolution of a Global Risk Network*. Oxford: Oxford University Press, 578–98.

Parker, G. (2013) *Global Crisis: War, Climate Change and Catastrophe in the Seventeenth Century*. New Haven, CT: Yale University Press.

Parker, R. S. (2006) *Hazards of Nature, Risks to Development: An IEG Evaluation of World Bank Assistance for Natural Disasters*. Washington, DC: World Bank.

Passamaneck, S. M. (1974) *Insurance in Rabbinic Law*. Edinburgh: Edinburgh University Press.

Pauly, M. V. (1968) 'The Economics of Moral Hazard: Comment', *American Economic Review* 58: 3, part I, 531–7.

Pearson, R. (1995) 'The Development of Reinsurance Markets in Europe during the Nineteenth Century', *Journal of European Economic History* 24: 3, 557–72.

Pearson, R. (2001) 'The Birth Pains of a Global Reinsurer: Swiss Re of Zürich 1864–79', *Financial History Review* 8: 1, 27–47.

Pearson, R. (2004) *Insuring the Industrial Revolution: Fire Insurance in Great Britain 1700–1850*. Aldershot: Ashgate.

Pearson, R. (2010) 'Introduction: Towards an International History of Insurance', in R. Pearson (ed.), *The Development of International Insurance*. London: Pickering & Chatto, 1–24.

Pearson, R. (2012) 'United Kingdom: Pioneering Insurance Internationally', in P. Borscheid and N. V. Haueter (eds), *World Insurance: The Evolution of a Global Risk Network*. Oxford: Oxford University Press, 67–97.

Pearson, R. and Lönnborg, M. (2007) 'Swedish Insurance Companies and the San Francisco Earthquake of 1906', in P. Borscheid and R. Pearson (eds), *Internationalisation and Globalisation of the Insurance Industry in the 19th and 20th Centuries*. Zurich and Marburg: Philipp University of Marburg, 27–41.

Perrow, C. (1984) *Normal Accidents: Living with High-Risk Technologies*. New York: Basic Books.

Perryman, F. S. (1932) 'Some Notes on Credibility', *Proceedings of the Casualty Actuarial Society* 19, 65–84.

Peter, G. von, Dahlen, S. von, and Saxena, S. (2012) *Unmitigated Disasters? New Evidence on the Macroeconomic Cost of Natural Catastrophes*. Basel: Bank for International Settlement.

Petersson, G. J. (2011) 'Insurance and Cartels through Wars and Depressions: Swedish Marine Insurance and Reinsurance between the World Wars (Umeå Studies in Economic History 44)'. Doctoral Thesis, Umeå University, Umeå.

Petrov, Y. A. (2012) 'Russia: Early Expansion, State Involvement, and Re-Emergence of the Insurance Industry', in P. Borscheid and N. V. Haueter (eds), *World Insurance: The Evolution of a Global Risk Network*. Oxford: Oxford University Press, 213–36.

Pfeiffer, C. (1975) *Einführung in die Rückversicherung*. Wiesbaden: Gabler.

Pfeiffer, C. (1994) *Einführung in die Rückversicherung. Das Standardwerk für Theorie und Praxis* (4th edn). Wiesbaden: Gabler.

Pielke, R. A. and Landsea, C. W. (1998) 'Normalized Hurricane Damages in the United States 1925–95', *Weather and Forecasting* 13: 3, 621–31.

Plass, W. (1910) '*Die Besonderheiten der Rückversicherung in den einzelnen Versicherungszweigen*'. Doctoral Thesis, University of Göttingen, Hamburg.

Porter, T. M. (1986) *The Rise of Statistical Thinking 1820–1900*. Princeton, NJ: Princeton University Press.

Porter, T. M. (1995) *Trust in Numbers: The Pursuit of Objectivity in Science and Public Life*. Princeton, NJ: Princeton University Press.

Porter, T. M. (2000) 'Life Insurance, Medical Testing, and the Management of Mortality', in L. Daston (ed.), *Biographies of Scientific Objects*. Chicago: University of Chicago Press, 226–46.

Pound, R. (1909) 'Liberty of Contract', *Yale Law Journal* 18: 7, May, 454–87.

Power, M. (2007) *Organized Uncertainty: Designing a World of Risk Management*. Oxford: Oxford University Press.

Prölss, E. R. (1942a) *Zwischenstaatliches Rückversicherungsrecht*. Rostock: Hinstorff.

Prölss, E. R. (1942b) 'Rechtsgrundlagen des Rückversicherungsvertrages', *Zeitschrift für das gesamte Handelsrecht und Konkursrecht* 109, 113–41.

Prölss, E. R. (1954) *Versicherungsvertragsgesetz* (8th edn). Munich: C. H. Beck.

Prölss, E. R. (1964a) 'Der rückversichernde Versicherer', *Schweizerische Versicherungszeitschrift* 31, 366–77.

Prölss, E. R. (1964b) 'Standardisierung von Rückversicherungsverträgen', in E. R. Prölss (ed.), *Ansichten der Rückversicherung*. Karlsruhe: Verlag Versicherungswirtschaft, 89–102.

Rahman, A. Ab, Ahmad, W. M. W., and Buang, A. H. (2011) 'Can a Takaful Company Reinsure with a Reinsurance Company?' *African Journal of Business Management* 5: 30, 11768.

Rau, H. (1901) 'Die Rückversicherung der Gegenwart', *Zeitschrift für die gesamte Versicherungswissenschaft* 1, 298–321, 399–419.

Risk Management Solutions (1995) *What if a Major Earthquake Strikes the Los Angeles Area? (Topical Issues Series)*. Menlo Park, CA: Risk Management Solutions.

Rivera, J. D. and Miller D. S. (2006) 'A Brief History of the Evolution of United States' Natural Disaster Policy', *Journal of Public Management & Social Policy* 12: 1, spring, 5–14.

Röder, T. J. (2006) *Rechtsbildung im wirtschaftlichen 'Weltverkehr'. Das Erdbeben von San Francisco und die internationale Standardisierung von Vertragsbedingungen 1871–1914*. Frankfurt am Main: Klostermann.

Röder, T. J. (2012) *From Industrial to Legal Standardization 1871–1914: Transnational Insurance Law and the Great San Francisco Earthquake*. Leiden and Boston, MA: Brill and Martinus Nijhoff Publishers.

Rohland, E. (2011a) *Sharing the Risk: Fire, Climate and Disaster, Swiss Re 1864–1906*. Lancaster: Carnegie Publishing.

Rohland, E. (2011b) 'From Wood to Stone: The Risk Management of Swiss Re in the Sundsvall Fire 1888', *Environment and History* 17, 153–69.

Roos, J. C. (1964) 'Die Dienstleistungen des Rückversicherers', *Schweizerische Versicherungszeitschrift* 31, 401–14.

Rosenhaft, E. (1999) 'Mich als eine Extraordinarium. Die Witwe als widerstrebendes Subjekt in der Frühgeschichte der Lebensversicherung', in U. Arnold, P. Meyers, and U. C. Schmidt (eds), *Stationen einer Hochschullaufbahn. Festschrift für Annette Kuhn*. Dortmund: Edition Ebersbach, 292–309.

Rosenhaft, E. (2006) 'But the Heart Must Speak for the Widows: The Origins of Life Insurance in Germany and the Gender Implications of Actuarial Science', in M. Gray and U. Gleixner (eds), *Formatting Gender: Transitions, Breaks and Continuities in German-Speaking Europe 1750–1850*. Ann Arbor, MI: University of Michigan Press, 90–113.

Rudolph, K. (1927) 'Die Versicherung Minderwertiger Leben in Deutschland', in S. H. Jarvis (ed.), *Transactions of the 8th International Congress of Actuaries, London 27th to 30th June 1927*, vol. 4. London: Layton, 322–9.

Sack, W. (1941) *Die deutsche Rückversicherung in der Entwicklung (Veröffentlichungen des Institutes für Versicherungswissenschaft an der Universität Leipzig 6)*. Leipzig: Felix Meiner.

Salzmann, H. (1967) 'Der Rückversicherungsvertrag im Schweizerischen Privatrecht', in E. Frey et al. (eds), *Ausblick und Rückblick. Festschrift für Erich R. Prölss zum 60. Geburtstag*. Munich: C. H. Beck, 277–89.

Schäfer, W. (1900) '*Die Feuerrückversicherung*'. Doctoral Thesis, Heidelberg University, Heidelberg.

Schanz, K.-U. and Shimpi P. A. (2001) 'Finite Risk Reinsurance', in P. A. Shimpi (ed.), *Integrating Corporate Risk Management (Swiss Re New Markets Series)*. New York: Texere, 132–51.

Schenk, G. J. (2007) 'Historical Disaster Research: State of Research, Concepts, Methods and Case Studies', *Historical Social Research* 32: 3, 9–31.

Schramm, C. (1884) *Für und wider die Verstaatlichung des Versicherungswesens*. Zurich: J. Schabelitz.

Seraphim, P. H. (1926) 'Rückversicherungsverträge der russischen Reichsversicherungsgesellschaft mit ausländischen Versicherungsgesellschaften', *Versicherung und Geldwirtschaft* (with supplement *Die Rückversicherung* 1), 5.

Serini, H. (1910) 'Ein Streifzug durch die Haftpflichtversicherung der Vereinigten Staaten', *Zeitschrift für die gesamte Versicherungswirtschaft* 10, 31–56.

Shapiro, B. J. (1983) *Probability and Certainty in Seventeenth-Century England*. Princeton, NJ: Princeton University Press.

Shelp, R. K. and Ehrbar, A. (2009) *Fallen Giant: The Amazing Story of Hank Greenberg and the History of AIG* (2nd edn). Hoboken, NJ: Wiley & Sons.

Shimpi, P. A. (ed.) (2001) *Integrating Corporate Risk Management (Swiss Re New Markets Series)*. New York: Texere.

Shiu, E. S. W. (1993) 'Asset/Liability Management: From Immunization to Option-Pricing Theory', in J. Cummins and J. Lamm-Tennant (eds), *Financial Management of Life Insurance Companies*. Boston, MA: Kluwer, 151–66.

Sibbett, T. (2004) 'History of Insurance', in J. L. Teugels and B. Sundt (eds), *Encyclopedia of Actuarial Science*, vol. 2. Chichester: Wiley, 848–61.

Smith, B. D. and Stutzer, M. (1995) 'A Theory of Mutual Formation and Moral Hazard with Evidence from the History of the Insurance Industry', *Review of Financial Studies* 8: 2, summer, 545–77.

Smith, C. W. (1993) 'Corporate Risk Management and the Insurance Industry', in J. Cummins and J. Lamm-Tennant (eds), *Financial Management of Life Insurance Companies*. Boston, MA: Kluwer, 125–49.

Sofonea, T. (1997) *Drei grosse historische Erdbeben aus der Sicht der Versicherung (Schriftenreihe des Seminars für Versicherungsbetriebslehre an der Universität München 94)*. Munich: Versicherungswirtschaftlicher Verlags- und Beratungsdienst.

Stadler, E. (1992) 'Der Rückversicherungsmarkt. Entstehung und aktuelle Entwicklungen', *Versicherungsrundschau* 47: 12, December, 386–95.

Stahl, A. and Meyenburg, B. (2006) 'Fit für das internationale Parkett. Duty of Utmost Good Faith und Avoidance im englischen Rückversicherungsrecht', *Versicherungswirtschaft* 3, 1 February, 201.

Staring, G. S. (1993) *Law of Reinsurance*. Rochester, NY: Clark Boardman Callaghan.

Steinberg, T. (1997) 'Do-It-Yourself Deathscape: The Unnatural History of Natural Disaster in South Florida', *Environmental History* 2, 414–38.

Steinberg, T. (ed.) (2006) *Acts of God: The Unnatural History of Natural Disaster in America*. New York: Oxford University Press.

Straumann, T. (2010) *Fixed Ideas of Money: Small States and Exchange Rate Regimes in Twentieth-Century Europe*. Cambridge: Cambridge University Press.

Straumann, T. (2013) 'The Invisible Giant: The History of Swiss Re 1863–2013', in H. James (ed.), *The Value of Risk: Swiss Re and the History of Reinsurance*. Oxford: Oxford University Press, 237–352.

Straumann, T. (2014) 'The Discreet Charm of Hidden Reserves: How Swiss Re Survived the Great Depression', in P. Clement, H. James, and H. Van der Wee (eds), *Financial Innovation, Regulation and Crises in History*. London: Pickering & Chatto, 55–64.

Straus, A. (2012) 'France: Insurance in the French Financial Networks', in P. Borscheid and N. V. Haueter (eds), *World Insurance: The Evolution of a Global Risk Network*. Oxford: Oxford University Press, 118–42.

Sturm, J. (1935) 'Methoden der Risikobewertung', in O. May (ed.), *Transactions of the International Congress on Life Assurance Medicine*. London, 29–81.

Supple, B. (1970) *The Royal Exchange Assurance: A History of British Insurance 1720–1970*. Cambridge: Cambridge University Press.

Swiss Re (2004) *Capitalising on Change: How Swiss Re has Built a Global Firm*. Zurich: Swiss Re.

Swiss Re (2010) *The Essential Guide to Reinsurance*. Zurich: Swiss Re.

Swiss Re (2011) *The Fundamentals of Insurance-Linked Securities*. Zurich: Swiss Re.

Swiss Re (2015) *Closing the Protection Gap: Disaster Risk Financing, Smart Solutions for the Public Sector*. Zurich: Swiss Re.

Thiemermann, M. (1993) *Rückversicherung und Zahlungsströme. Ein Beitrag zur Finanzwirtschaft von Rückversicherungsunternehmen*. Bergisch Gladbach: Verlag Josef Eul.

*Travelers 100 Years* (1964) 'Into the Atomic Age', in *Travelers 100 Years*. Hartford: The Travelers Insurance Companies, 109–11.

Trebilcock, C. (1985) *Phoenix Assurance and the Development of British Insurance*, vol. 1: *1782–1870*. Cambridge: Cambridge University Press.

Trebilcock, C. (1998) *Phoenix Assurance and the Development of British Insurance*, vol. 2: *The Era of the Insurance Giants 1870–1984*. Cambridge: Cambridge University Press.

Trüb, J. (1998) *El Niño 1997/98. Dem Phänomen auf der Spur*. Zurich: Swiss Re.

Turner, B. A. (1978) *Man-Made Disasters*. London: Wykeham.

Tykocinski, O. E. (2008) 'Insurance, Risk, and Magical Thinking', *Personality and Social Psychology Bulletin* 34: 10, October, 1346–56.

UN Human Rights Council (2014) *Promotion and Protection of the Rights of Indigenous Peoples in Disaster Risk Reduction, Prevention and Preparedness Initiatives: Study by the Expert Mechanism on the Rights of Indigenous Peoples*. New York: United Nations.

UNCTAD (United Nations Conference on Trade and Development) (1964) *Proceedings of the United Nations Conference on Trade and Development: Final Act and Report*. New York: United Nations.

UNCTAD (United Nations Conference on Trade and Development) (1966) *Progress Reports on the Programme of Work on Invisibles—Insurance and Reinsurance: Reinsurance Policy and Operations in Developing Countries. Report of the Expert Group on Reinsurance*. New York: United Nations.

UNEP (United Nations Environment Programme) (2002) *Global Environment Outlook*, vol. 3: *Past, Present and Future Perspectives*. London: Earthscan Publications Ltd.

UNHCR (United Nations High Commissioner for Refugees) (2001) 'The Wall Behind Which Refugees Can Shelter: The 50th Anniversary of the 1951 Geneva Refugee Convention', *Refugees Magazine* 2: 123, 2001.

US GAO (United States Government Accountability Office) (2005) *Catastrophe Risk: U.S. and European Approaches to Insurance Natural Catastrophe and Terrorism Risks*. Washington, DC: US Government Accountability Office.

USPSI (United States Senate Permanent Subcommittee on Investigations) (2011) *Wall Street and the Financial Crisis: Anatomy of a Financial Collapse*. Washington, DC: US Senate Permanent Subcommittee on Investigations.

Vahldiek, W. (1954) *Rückversicherung, Seeversicherung, Versicherungsaufsichtsgesetz*. Berlin: De Gruyter.

Vallebona, S. (1889) 'Die Rückversicherung, ihr Wesen, ihre Wichtigkeit, ihre internationale Verbreitung und ihre Einschränkung im Kriegsfall', *Assekuranz-Jahrbuch* 10, 131–8.

Vec, M. (2006) *Recht und Normierung in der Industriellen Revolution. Neue Strukturen der Normsetzung in Völkerrecht, staatlicher Gesetzgebung und gesellschaftlicher Selbstnormierung (Studien zur europäischen Rechtsgeschichte 200, Recht in der Industriellen Revolution 1)*. Frankfurt am Main: Vittorio Klostermann.

Vec, M. (2011) 'Interventionsstaat', in A. Cordes, H. Lück, and D. Werkmüller (eds), *Handwörterbuch zur Deutschen Rechtsgeschichte* (2nd edn). Berlin: Erich Schmidt, cols 1279–83.

Veh, R. von (1927) *Das Versicherungswesen Estlands. Seine Entwicklungsmöglichkeiten und sein Rückversicherungsproblem (anwendbar für sämtliche Randstaaten) mit Hinweis auf die 100jährige Tätigkeit der ehemaligen Russischen Versicherungs-Aktiengesellschaften*. Tallinn: Magnus Keller.

Verhoef, G. (2012) 'South Africa: Leading African Insurance', in P. Borscheid and N. V. Haueter (eds), *World Insurance: The Evolution of a Global Risk Network*. Oxford: Oxford University Press, 325–45.

Villotte, C. (1927) *Nature technique et juridique de la réassurance*. Brive: Chastrusse Frères.

Voigt, R. (1980) 'Verrechtlichung in Staat und Gesellschaft', in R. Voigt (ed.), *Verrechtlichung. Analysen zu Funktion und Wirkung von Parlamentarisierung, Bürokratisierung und Justizialisierung sozialer, politischer und ökonomischer Prozesse*. Königstein: Athenäum, 15–37.

Wagner, A. (1881) 'Der Staat und das Versicherungswesen', *Zeitschrift für die gesamte Staatswissenschaft* 37, 102–72.

Walford, C. (1857) *The Insurance Guide and Hand-Book*. London: Layton.

Walford, C. (1912) 'Historical Review of Life Assurance in Great Britain and Ireland' [supplement], in H. W. Andras (ed.), *The Insurance Guide and Handbook* (5th edn). London: Charles and Edwin Layton, 2, 24, 26.

Wallace, E. K. (2000) 'The Needs of Strangers: Friendly Societies and Insurance in Late Eighteenth Century England', *Eighteenth-Century Life* 24: 3, 53–72.

Wandel, E. (1998) *Banken und Versicherungen im 19. und 20. Jahrhundert*. Munich: R. Oldenburg.

Wang, H.-C. (2002) *Fundamentals of Reinsurance Regulation from a Comparative Perspective (Essays in International Financial & Economic Law 41)*. London: The London Institute of International Banking, Finance & Development Law Ltd.

Webel, B. (2010) *The Dodd–Frank Wall Street Reform and Consumer Protection Act: Insurance Provisions*. Washington, DC: Congressional Research Service.

Weir, D. R. (1989) 'Tontines, Public Finance, and Revolution in France and England', *Journal of Economic History* 49: 1, 95–124.

Werner, S. (2009) '*Rückversicherung in der Weltwirtschaftskrise. Performanceanalyse professioneller Rückversicherungsunternehmen in der Schaden- und Unfallversicherung 1924–1935*'. Master's Thesis, Ludwig Maximilian University, Munich.

Werner, W. (1993) *Die späte Entwicklung der amerikanischen Rückversicherungswirtschaft*. Berlin: Duncker & Humblot.

Werner, W. (2007) 'Hurricane Betsy and the Malfunctioning of the London Reinsurance Market: An Analysis of Transatlantic Reinsurance Trade 1949–1989', *Financial History Review* 14: 1, 7–28.

Werner, W. (2010) 'Multilateral Insurance Liberalization 1948–2008', in R. Pearson (ed.), *The Development of International Insurance (Financial History Series 5)*. London: Pickering & Chatto, 85–101.

Werner, W. and Pierenkemper, T. (eds) (2002) *Wirtschaftspolitik nach dem Ende der Bretton Woods-Ära (Jahrbuch für Wirtschaftsgeschichte 1)*. Berlin: Akademie Verlag.

Whitney, A. W. (1918) 'The Theory of Experience-Rating', *Proceedings of the Casualty Actuarial Society* 4, 274–92.

Wilkins, M. (1989) *The History of Foreign Investment in the United States to 1914*. Cambridge, MA: Harvard University Press.

Wilkins, M. (2004) *The History of Foreign Investment in the United States 1914–1945*. Cambridge, MA: Harvard University Press.

Wilkins, M. (2009) 'Multinational Enterprise in Insurance: An Historical Overview', *Business History* 51: 3, 334–63.

Wilkins, M. (2011) 'Multinational Enterprise in Insurance: An Historical Overview', in P. J. Buckley (ed.), *Business History and International Business*. London: Routledge, 28–57.

Wolgast, M. (2007) 'Global Terrorism and the Insurance Industry: New Challenges and Policy Responses', in T. Brück (ed.), *The Economic Analysis of Terrorism*. London: Routledge, 146–72.

Woo, G. (2002) 'Quantifying Insurance Terrorism Risk', in M. Lane (ed.), *Alternative Risk Strategies*. London: Risk Waters Group, 201–20.

World Bank (1995) *The World Bank Primer on Reinsurance*. Washington, DC: World Bank.

World Bank (2002) *Social Reinsurance: A New Approach to Sustainable Community Health Financing*. Washington, DC: World Bank.

World Bank/United Nations (2010) *Natural Hazards, Unnatural Disasters: The Economics of Effective Prevention*. Washington, DC: World Bank Publications.

Yates, J. (2005) *Structuring the Information Age: Life Insurance and Technology in the Twentieth Century*. Baltimore, MD: Johns Hopkins University Press.

Yoneyama, T. (2009) 'The Great Kanto Earthquake and the Response of Insurance Companies: A Historical Lesson on the Impact of a Major Disaster', *Hitotsubashi Journal of Commerce and Management* 43: 1, 11–26.

Yoneyama, T. (2012) 'Japan: The Role of Insurers in the Rapid Modernization of Japan', in P. Borscheid and N. V. Haueter (eds), *World Insurance: The Evolution of a Global Risk Network*. Oxford: Oxford University Press, 495–521.

Yong, C. et al. (eds) (1988) *The Great Tangshan Earthquake of 1976: An Anatomy of Disaster*. Oxford: Pergamon Press.

Zappino, J. S. (2007) *El Instituto Mixto Argentino de Reaseguros: La Formación de un Mercado Nacional de Seguros (1946–1952)*. Buenos Aires: Ediciones Cooperativas.

Zelizer, V. A. (1978) 'Human Values and the Market: The Case of Life Insurance and Death in 19th-Century America', *American Journal of Sociology* 84: 3, 591–610.

Zelizer, V. A. (1979) *Morals and Markets: The Development of Life Insurance in the United States*. New York: Columbia University Press.

Zwinggi, E. (1945) *Versicherungsmathematik*. Basel: Birkhaeuser.

**SRCA (Swiss Re Company Archives, Zurich)**

SRCA 10.101 517.02, Simon, C., Bilder und Figuren aus vergangenen Zeiten, 8 December 1933; 14 December 1934.

SRCA 10.103 067, Early Catastrophe Excess of Loss Covers in the U.S. and England, 1981.

SRCA 10.106 683.08, Insurance and the Economic Consequences of Earthquakes.

SRCA, Verwaltungsratsprotokolle/Meeting minutes of Swiss Re's Board of Directors (BoD), 1864–1940.

SRCA 10.107 758, Meeting minutes of Swiss Re's BoD, 21 March 1865–9 April 1977.

SRCA 10.107 770, Meeting minutes of Swiss Re's BoD, 1 September 1953; 8 May 1954.

SRCA 10.107 770, Meeting minutes of Swiss Re's BoD, 1 September 1953; 13 December 1954.

SRCA 10.107 770, Meeting minutes of Swiss Re's BoD, 9 May 1955.

SRCA 10.107 770, Meeting minutes of Swiss Re's BoD, 6 September 1955.

SRCA 10.107 771, Meeting minutes of Swiss Re's BoD, 10 December 1957.

SRCA 10.107 772, Meeting minutes of Swiss Re's BoD, 20 February 1962.

SRCA 10.107 772, Meeting minutes of Swiss Re's BoD, 4 September 1962.

SRCA 10.107 772, Meeting minutes of Swiss Re's BoD, 1 September 1964.

SRCA 10.107 772, Meeting minutes of Swiss Re's BoD, 4 December 1965; 18 October 1966.

SRCA 10.107 772, Meeting minutes of Swiss Re's BoD, 14 December 1965; 15 March 1966.

SRCA 10.107 772, Meeting minutes of Swiss Re's BoD, 15 March 1966.

SRCA 10.107 776, Meeting minutes of Swiss Re's BoD, 26 June 1979.

SRCA 10.107 923, Meeting minutes of Swiss Re's BoD, 5 July 1955.

SRCA 10.107 968, Notiz zur Frage unserer Orientierung im deutschen Geschäft, 1924.

SRCA 10.107 968, Bericht über die Sanierung des Anker in Wien, 10 June 1927.

SRCA 10.107 969, Alther, P., Amerika Reise, 23 May–10 July 1935.

SRCA 10.107 970, Meeting minutes of Swiss Re's BoD, 1 January 1938–31 December 1949.

SRCA 10.107 975, Meeting minutes of Swiss Re's BoD, 5 April 1967.

SRCA 10.107 975, Meeting minutes of Swiss Re's BoD, 6 February 1968.

SRCA 10.107 977, Geschäftsverlauf und Ausgangslage, 1969–70.

SRCA 10.107 977, Enclosure 2 of the meeting minutes of Swiss Re's BoD, 17 March 1970.

SRCA 10.107 978, Enclosure 1 of the meeting minutes of Swiss Re's BoD (Meetings of the Committee of Directors), 27 June 1972.

SRCA 10.107 979, Enclosure 2 of the meeting minutes of Swiss Re's BoD, 25 June 1974.

SRCA 10.107 982, Mündliche Berichterstattung an Verwaltungsratssitzungen (Transcript of the Meetings of Swiss Re's BoD), 18 March 1980.

SRCA 10.108 184, Guggenbühl, P., Schweizerische Rückversicherungs-Gesellschaft 1863–1938, 1939.

SRCA 10.108 185, Guggenbühl, P., Schweizerische Rückversicherungs-Gesellschaft 1939–64, 1964.

SRCA 10.110 780.04 Pressekonferenz zum Jahresabschluss, 1985.

SRCA 10.116 652.02, Die Gründung einer schweizerischen Kursversicherungsgesellschaft.

SRCA 10.118 490.00.038, Swiss Re Cat Peril Team.

SRCA 10.119 090.01, R. J. Duff to the general manager of Swiss Re, 19 April 1934.

SRCA 10.121 116.04, Circulars of the Erste Allgemeine on Motor Car Insurance, 12 April 1956–2 September 1957.

SRCA 10.123 990.03, Correspondence between Swiss Re and Erste Ungarische Allgemeine Assecuranz-Gesellschaft, 7 April 1924.

SRCA 10.125 020.02, Mitteilungen des Revisionsbureaus. Die Behandlung der unechten Fremdwährungsversicherungen im Abrechnungsverkehr, 15 February 1933.

SRCA 10.125 020.02, Mitteilungen des Revisionsbureaus. Zur Frage der Autarkie in der Rückversicherung, 15 December 1933.

SRCA 10.125 590.01, A & D, 1971.

SRCA 10.143 874.02, Earthquake in Japan: Imperial Marine Fire Treaty.

SRCA 10.144 425.02, Das Erdbeben von San Francisco. Protokolle von Zusammenkünften der Vertreter der an der Katastrophe durch Rückversicherung beteiligten Gesellschaften.

SRCA 10.144 430.02, Das Erdbeben von San Francisco. Kollektivschreiben der Rückversicherer.

SRCA 10.146 212.02, Andreoli, E., Buchhaltung, Zentrales Rechnungswesen, Organisation, Revision, Statistik.

SRCA 10.146 212.02, Revisionsbureau. Seine bisherige Tätigkeit und künftige Organisation.

SRCA 10.146 212.04, Some Thoughts on Methods and Procedures in Establishing Loss Reserves in Fire & Casualty Reinsurance, 18 January 1968.

SRCA 10.146 212.04, How to Establish and Follow Excess Loss Reserves, 6 September 1968.

SRCA 10.149 770.01, Correspondence between Swiss Re and Anker, 1927–36.

SRCA 10.157 104.02, Manton, E. A. G., U.S.A. Natural Catastrophes/Naturgefahren, October 1985.

SRCA 10.158 622.01, Groupe de Travail du Risque Atomique, Meeting minutes, 16–17 January 1956, Paris.

SRCA 10.158 622.01, Commission Permanente du Risque Atomique, Meeting minutes, 11–12 May 1959, Milan.

SRCA 10.158 622.01, Comité Européen des Assurances, Commission permanente du risque atomique (memo addressed to the IAEA), 18 August 1959.

SRCA 10.158 622.02, W. E. Belser to K. Imamura, 23 April 1959.

SRCA 10.158 627.02, Special Committee for Nuclear Energy: Report of the Special Working Party Set up by the Insurance Sub-Committee to Study the Problems of Nuclear Risk Insurance, 25 June 1956.

SRCA 10.158 628.01, W. E. Belser to M. Klaas, 14 April 1956; M. Klaas to W. E. Belser, 19 April 1956.

SRCA 10.158 903.03, Frey, H., Aspekte des Rückversicherungs-Vertragsrechts. Rückversicherungskurse 1979, 6 February 1979.

SRCA 10.160 179.04, Frey, H., Rechtliche Aspekte des Rückversicherungsvertrages, February 1989.

SRCA 10.160 179.04, RV-Fachausbildung, Modul M 17 Vertragsrecht, 1991.

SRCA 10.160 179.04, PM/WT (Koordination), Modul M 17. Vertragsrecht und Schadenpraxis, April 1997.

SRCA 10.166 133.00.66, Diehl, W., Grossrisiken und Grossschäden in der modernen Versicherung und Rückversicherung, press conference, 18 April 1967.

SRCA 10.166 820.00.011, Das Risk Management-Konzept der SR.

SRCA 10.166 961.04, Ozendo, P., Information on Reinsurance Regulations.

SRCA 10.169 410.10, Froelich, E., Reisebericht Indien/Pakistan/Ceylon, 1951.

SRCA 000586, Policy Paper on Climate, 1995.

SRCA DL-04499-001 (Global Library), Froelich, E., State Insurance and Reinsurance Monopolies, 1941.

# Index

The manufacturer's authorised representative in the EU for product safety is Oxford University Press España S.A. of el Parque Empresarial San Fernando de Henares, Avenida de Castilla, 2 – 28830 Madrid (www.oup.es/en or product.safety@oup.com). OUP España S.A. also acts as importer into Spain of products made by the manufacturer.

www.ingramcontent.com/pod-product-compliance
Lightning Source LLC
LaVergne TN
LVHW081934200926
848484LV00009B/2429
* 9 7 8 0 1 9 8 7 5 4 9 1 6 *